The Realities of Work

Experiencing Work and Employment in Contemporary Society

4th Edition

Mike Noon

*Professor of Human Resource Management, School of Business and Management,
Queen Mary, University of London, UK*

Paul Blyton

*Professor of Industrial Relations and Industrial Sociology,
Cardiff Business School, Cardiff University, UK*

Kevin Morrell

*Associate Professor of Governance, Warwick Business School,
University of Warwick, UK*

palgrave
macmillan

First edition 1997
Second edition 2002
Third edition 2007
This edition published 2013 by
PALGRAVE MACMILLAN

Palgrave Macmillan in the UK is an imprint of Macmillan Publishers Limited, registered in England, company number 785998, of Houndmills, Basingstoke, Hampshire RG21 6XS.

Palgrave Macmillan in the US is a division of St Martin's Press LLC, 175 Fifth Avenue, New York, NY 10010.

Palgrave Macmillan is the global academic imprint of the above companies and has companies and representatives throughout the world.

Palgrave® and Macmillan® are registered trademarks in the United States, the United Kingdom, Europe and other countries

ISBN: 978–0–230–21304–3

This book is printed on paper suitable for recycling and made from fully managed and sustained forest sources. Logging, pulping and manufacturing processes are expected to conform to the environmental regulations of the country of origin.

A catalogue record for this book is available from the British Library.

A catalog record for this book is available from the Library of Congress.

10 9 8 7 6 5 4 3 2 1
22 21 20 19 18 17 16 15 14 13

Printed in China

The Realities of

'*The Realities of Work* is now established as a key introductory text to classical ideas and new research about work and employment in today's workplace. With a focus on the skills, routines and survival strategies used by workers to manoeuvre their way through controls, technologies and obstacles to meaningful, knowledgeable and balanced working life, Mike Noon, Paul Blyton and Kevin Morrell have updated research across all 14 Chapters to maintain the relevance of the text for understanding and explaining trends in the modern workplace.' – Professor Chris Smith, Royal Holloway University of London, UK

'This book is indispensable for students who wish to develop a detailed understanding of contemporary workplace settings. It has a comprehensive scope that is impressive and its thematic organisation systematically dissects key debates about the changing nature of working life. At the same time, its accessible prose, entertaining examples and cogent suggestions for activities and discussions make it an invaluable resource for educators who wish to convey the realities of worker experiences to their students. In short, this book should be a core text within all programmes of study that include industrial relations, HRM and work organisation as core subject areas.' – Professor Steve Vincent, Newcastle University, UK

'*The Realities of Work* is a terrific book that is part of an important project. More than a survey of concepts and theories about work, the book is designed to help the reader think through what work is in its many forms. I particularly like the accessibility of the writing, the ubiquitous examples, and the deliberate efforts to help readers think through what they read in the text with exercises, questions for reflection, and extracts that bring the material to life. In these ways, the book goes well beyond the typical textbook in making the material engaging. This is a rare text that students, particularly undergraduates but graduate students as well, will actually enjoy reading.' – Professor Jeff Lucas, Senior Lecturer in HRM, University of Maryland, USA

'*The Realities of Work* is well structured and logical with balanced style and content. It offers an explanatory, critical reading as well as the ability to think deeply about the changing world of work. It is an invaluable resource for anyone interested in work, society and organisation.' – Denis Hyams-Sekasi, University of Huddersfield, UK

'The authors are to be commended for locating their analysis of work in the current financial crisis, making their contribution relevant and applicable. Contemporary examples make the text relevant for undergraduate students, whilst the use of key concepts, exercises and extracts help complex materials become accessible and engaging. This edition will make a valuable contribution to understanding work.' – Dr. Chris Bolsmann, Senior Lecturer in Sociology, Aston University, UK

'Placing the employee at the centre of their analysis, the newest edition of *The Realities of Work*, by Mike Noon, Paul Blyton and Kevin Morrell, makes a significant and innovative contribution to our understanding of work. Combining important theoretical frameworks with a diverse range of historical and contemporary examples, *The Realities of Work* reveals how individual and collective experiences and the organisation of work are the outcome of contested social, political and economic processes and relationships. In short, this book furthers and deepens our understanding of the complexity and diversity of work, an activity which in all of its forms remains central to human experience.' – Professor Tim Marjoribanks, La Trobe Business School, Australia

DEDICATION

To our families.
MN, PB & KM

Contents

List of figures   viii

List of tables   ix

Preface   x

1   **Exploring the realities of work**   1

2   **The changing context of work**   23

3   **The meaning of work**   49

4   **Time and work**   77

5   **Work skills**   110

6   **Work routines**   138

7   **Emotion work**   169

8   **Knowledge and work**   201

9   **Survival strategies at work**   225

10 **Unfair discrimination at work**   263

11 **Representation at work**   289

12 **Hidden work**   314

13 **Work and life**   339

14 **Conclusion**   366

Bibliography   375

Author Index   411

Subject Index   417

List of figures

1.1	Exploring the realities of work	22
3.1	National comparisons in attitudes to work entitlement and obligation	61
5.1	The processes of social closure	125
6.1	Work categorisation framework and trends in skill change	165
6.2	Work categorisation framework and paradigms of work organisation	167
8.1	Spiral of knowledge creation	212
9.1	Marx's theory of the labour process and alienation	228
9.2	Acceptability of workplace fiddles	244
10.1	The process of discrimination in an organisation	286
11.1	Levels of influence on TU membership decisions	295
11.2	The vicious circle of union presence	306
11.3	The virtuous circle of union presence	310
12.1	Dimensions of hidden work	318
13.1	Proportions of working fathers and mothers working unsocial hours	348
13.2	Levels of response to work–life balance pressures	354

List of tables

1.1	Systems of classifying people according to their work	10
2.1	Changes in employment in UK manufacturing and services, 1971–2011 (thousands)	38
2.2	Number of women and men in employment in Britain, 1959–99, UK, 2011 (thousands)	39
2.3	Persons working part-time in the European Union, 2000, 2010 (percentage of total employment)	39
2.4	Unemployment rates in 25 industrial countries, selected years 2000–10 (rate as proportion of civilian labour force)	42
2.5	Temporary employment in the UK, 1996–2011	45
3.1	Summary of the SCELI findings on the reasons for working	53
3.2	Comparison of extrinsic and intrinsic work values	54
3.3	Responses to the lottery question from the *Meaning of Working* survey	55
4.1	Usual hours worked per week by full-time employees in the EU, 2003	97
4.2	Distribution of work hours of those working less than 30 hours per week, UK, 2003	99
4.3	The timing of work weeks for men and women in Britain (%)	100
5.1	Approaches to the analysis of skill	113
6.1	The key critics of Braverman's thesis	150
7.1	Some definitions of emotional labour	173
8.1	A comparison of knowledge workers and routine workers	207
8.2	Major changes suggested by Bell's post-industrial thesis	219
9.1	Blauner's four dimensions of alienation	232
9.2	Fundamental contradictions in managing the labour process	238
9.3	Interpretation of the five survival strategies	260
10.1	Categories in the 2011 Census of England and Wales	271
12.1	Time used by men and women (16 years and over) in the UK (hours and minutes per day)	330
14.1	Change and continuity in work	369

Preface

In this edition of *The Realities of Work* we continue to take a critical perspective on work. Following the global financial crisis in 2008, the need to reassert this perspective is even greater. Recession makes all the more relevant those aspects of work that are unfair or exploitative, or that depend on an imbalance of power between employer and employee, between management and worker, or between capital and labour. The crisis has had real and lasting implications for how the realities of work are experienced by tens of millions of people, making the themes we explore in many of the following chapters even more pertinent.

As in the previous editions, *The Realities of Work* puts the employee centre stage. We want to convey the importance of the employee's perspective because we believe that such an analysis is essential for understanding contemporary organisations. This was the motivation for writing the previous editions of the book, and it remains the driving force behind this fourth edition. We believe a critical analysis of the key theories, concepts and empirical evidence about the experience of work in contemporary workplaces provides students with a sound and useful knowledge base for making sense of their own work experiences (as employees or managers) both now and later in life. It also provides the basic analytical tools for understanding why the workplace is a domain of discord just as much as harmony, of paradox just as much as rationality, and of frustration just as much as satisfaction.

As we outline in the Introduction, we want students to explore the diversity of ideas and approaches to the study of work. We want them to evaluate the theories and empirical evidence and bring their own perspectives and understanding to the issues: therefore the chapter exercises have been designed with this in mind (and all of them have been tested on students). Some of the discussion in the introductory chapter is designed to help students develop their skills in critical reasoning, and should be particularly relevant to those new to social science approaches.

Readers familiar with previous editions of the book will notice that Kevin Morrell has become a co-author of the text. As well as adding new material, Kevin's input has been key to developing the arguments in the book in order to give them an up-to-date and broader appeal. In this latest edition we have retained the structure and learning features of the previous edition. The main changes have been updating to reflect some of the broader social and economic changes and to take account of recent research findings that focus on how work issues and demands affect employees. As always, some good quality articles and books may have been inadvertently overlooked, so we are happy to hear from anyone with suggestions of material to include in further editions of *The Realities of Work*.

Throughout the chapters there is a consistent set of features designed to guide learning. These are as follows.

Each chapter begins with:

- A list of 'Key concepts', which signposts the important terms that will be encountered. After reading and understanding the chapter, students should be able to define each of these terms.
- The 'Chapter aim', which specifies the purpose of the discussion.
- The 'Learning outcomes', which identify the ideas and propositions that students will gain knowledge about.

Within each chapter there are:

- 'Extracts' which provide examples of research or discuss theories that help to expand upon the points made in the text. These are designed to prompt interest, provide an illustration or act as a discussion point. The text can be read without looking at these extracts, but it is hoped that they will prove useful in support of the main narrative.
- 'Exercises' which provide the opportunity for students to reflect on the preceding material and assess their understanding. These require students to read the text and apply the theoretical ideas or make use of the concepts. Sometimes this requires them to drawn on their own experience; other times they must evaluate the research evidence presented in the text. Most of the exercises can be completed individually or discussed in small groups. They are ideally suited to tutorials/seminars.
- 'To sum up' paragraphs which bring together the key points throughout the chapters before the discussion moves on to the next set of issues.

Finally, and importantly, we wish to thank some people. First, to those who have commented on the text and therefore helped us in developing it. The list includes current work colleagues; the reviewers of the previous editions; colleagues in Universities in the UK, Australia, Canada and other parts of the world who have adopted the text for teaching purposes and have been in touch with us; and our students. The suggestions have been absorbed. Second, we want to express our appreciation for the continuing support by our commissioning editor at Palgrave Macmillan, Ursula Gavin.

As always, the biggest thank you goes to our families who make the realities of life outside work so enjoyable and fulfilling. For their love and support, Mike thanks Carolyn, Harriet and Maddie, and Paul thanks Ticky and Barley. Kevin thanks Sarah, Emily and Ruby for everything and more.

Exploring the realities of work

Chapter aim

To explain the approach this book adopts in exploring, analysing and critically evaluating the experiences of work.

Key concepts

▷ global financial crisis
▷ definitions of work
▷ classifying work
▷ socio-economic classification
▷ theories
▷ deductive and inductive approaches
▷ models
▷ typologies
▷ ideal types
▷ methods of data gathering
▷ objective and subjective
▷ theoretical and empirical
▷ qualitative data
▷ quantitative data

Learning outcomes

After reading and thinking about the material in this chapter, you will be able to:

1. Identify some causes and consequences of the Global Financial Crisis.
2. Define the term 'work'.
3. Outline a system for classifying work.
4. Explain the basic tools a social scientist uses to study work.
5. Summarise the various perspectives from which work can be analysed.
6. Identify the main themes underpinning the rest of the book.

Introduction

Up until as recently as about 30 years ago, coal miners had an unusual, but cheap and effective way of detecting poisonous gases after there had been a fire or an explosion underground. An exploratory team, sent to assess whether the conditions were safe to carry out mining, or to look for survivors, would go underground and take with them a number of canaries in a cage. Canaries are brightly coloured birds, often kept as companion animals because they are pretty to look at, but also because they are known for their singing. ('Sing like a canary' is old-fashioned slang for giving information to the police.)

The person carrying the canaries in the cage would be sent to the front of the exploratory team, and they would then move forward into the mineshaft slowly holding the canaries in front of them, almost like someone using a metal detector to look for buried treasure. There were two main reasons for taking several canaries into the mineshaft rather than just the one. One of these was because canaries regularly chirp or sing, and so a sudden silence would be more noticeable with several birds in the cage. A second was because if one of the canaries died, then there would be a spare, or two (and canaries are comparatively cheap).

What is it that would stop the canaries singing, or even kill them? The canary is particularly sensitive to toxic gases like carbon monoxide. Although people can detect some toxic or harmful gases found in mines, like methane for example, carbon monoxide is odourless, tasteless and invisible. The first clue that miners would get of its presence was if the canaries stopped singing, started to twitch or became obviously distressed. Signs of discomfort from one of the canaries, or worse still, the death of a canary would be the evidence that conditions were not safe, and the pit should be immediately evacuated.

This may sound callous or cruel on behalf of the miners, but it is certainly true that using canaries has saved many lives and the conditions for miners have historically been some of the most dangerous in any occupation: 'You never get any decent improvement in working conditions until you have a disaster in the mine. That is why they say working conditions are written in blood' (Murray and Peetz, 2010: 37).

The image of the canary and the coal mine has been used in quite a number of settings: to describe some industries' relationship to economic cycles (McKean, 2010); to argue that some locations are early warning sites in relation to climate change (Schendler, 2009); also in the discussion of investment products used in the Global Financial Crisis (GFC) (Davies, 2010). Here we want to use it as one way of looking at GFC.

Using this image as an allegory, or extended metaphor, in the case of GFC, the problems we have been collectively suffering for the last few years were caused by an at first invisible but extremely damaging and widespread problem to do with bad, or 'toxic' debt (i.e. debt that was unlikely to ever be repaid). We will come to the canary in a moment, but let us look at this part of the allegory first, the toxic debt.

Causes: toxic debt, ratings companies and subprime mortgages

Ratings companies in the US (such as Standard & Poor's and Moody's) had categorised debts based on 'subprime' mortgages as secure. Ratings companies effectively either give a bill of health, or raise concerns about investment products – in practice they use a scale. These same organisations have recently been causing widespread alarm by suggesting different governments are not as likely to pay their debts.

Although ratings companies categorised 'subprime' mortgages as secure, in fact these mortgages were very far from secure, and they were actually those that were less likely to be repaid. 'Subprime' mortgages were sold in many cases by people who were acting unethically and were offered bonuses to sell the products even if they were well aware that the people to whom they were selling were unlikely to repay or ever to be able to afford a mortgage.

The term 'subprime' actually means that the people taking out these mortgages were less than ideal (or prime) borrowers. These bad (toxic) debts were then turned into financial products that were sold to investors and used as security against other debts (i.e. to guarantee repayment). Because these toxic debts had been given secure ratings, other investors believed they were more valuable assets than they actually were.

Partly because of the interconnectedness of the global financial markets, and partly because of 'innovations' in the development of financial instruments, there was a multiplier effect. Toxic debts were used as guarantees for much larger sums of money. The crisis came about when some of these transactions began to unravel and when institutions realised the 'assets' they had were actually worth nothing. Panic followed because no one knew the extent of the problem, and it led to a collapse of trust with banks unwilling to lend to each other. This problem was not restricted to investment banks or even just to banks because some of the banks were considered 'too big to fail'. In other words, governments had to bail out these banks by taking on their debt, and in doing so they were financed by taxpayers.

The 150-year-old canary

The canary in this – the first prominent victim to the problem of toxic debt – was Lehman Brothers, one of the oldest, largest and most well-respected investment banks on Wall Street. It collapsed on the 15th of September 2008 – the largest bankruptcy in US history. When Lehman Brothers stopped singing the world went into shock – a global economic meltdown that it has still not recovered from.

Writing in *The Guardian*, Richard Wolff (2011) describes how the collapse of Lehman Brothers made the poisonous 'corruption and theft' by global banks plain for all to see. In the years before its collapse Lehman Brothers executives had earned what Wolff describes as 'stupendous' bonuses – amazingly, their Chief Executive, Richard Fuld, at one stage defended his pay over seven years by saying it had 'only' been 310 million dollars (that's $310,000,000). A report on its collapse to the US court made it clear that the bank's executives had made 'mammoth misjudgments' and used 'various legal and semi-legal mechanisms…to manipulate their accounts, and otherwise violate the spirit and letter of laws and regulations'.

Lehman Brothers had failed because of making huge investments in products based on 'subprime' mortgages. This was misjudgement, but the bank was guilty of more than just misjudgement. In order to try to make as much money on these products as possible they had committed fraud as well. Wolff describes a report in the *New York Times* showing how Lehman had 'secretly manipulated its balance sheets' by disguising its activities. The bank had channelled transactions through Hudson Castle, the name of another much smaller company that was owned by the bank. In 2010, the Attorney General of New York started legal proceedings against Lehman Brothers' accountants – Ernst and Whitney. In doing so he accused them of having 'substantially assisted…a massive accounting fraud'. Wolff summarises the death of what we call the '150-year-old canary' by saying that it:

> opened a window on strategies and tactics of many large private banks around the world. The hows and whys of their catastrophic mishandling of their 'fiduciary duties' – basically, to be fundamentally prudent and trustworthy in how they manage other people's money – stand revealed. They no longer deserve public trust.
>
> Lehman Brothers' collapse and its aftermath threatened global capitalism and not merely other big global banks. 'Too big to fail' thus became those banks' slogan in demanding and obtaining the dominant influence over governments. After Lehman's collapse, governments bailed out those banks, no matter the cost.

It is because of this that, as Wolff suggests, a – currently still unfolding – crisis directly related to the Global Financial Crisis has been levels of government debt in some 'Eurozone' countries (European countries that use the Euro). The most dramatic concerns have been in relation to Greece, but Ireland and Portugal were also unable to re-finance their debts in 2010 because investors had no confidence in their being able to pay further loans back (because they were concerned that further loans to these governments would also be toxic debts). He continues:

> Consider the irony: governments today impose austerity [cuts and financial hardship] on the rest of us because 'the markets' demand no less to keep credit flowing to those governments. Behind this dubious abstraction – 'the markets' – hide the chief lenders to governments. Those are the same global banks that received the government bailouts paid for by massive government borrowing since 2007.

In 2010, European finance ministers agreed a rescue package of 750 billion Euros – the European Financial Stability Facility (EFSF). This was increased in 2011. Although greatest concern in the Eurozone crisis has focused on the so-called PIG countries (Portugal, Ireland and Greece); Spain and Italy have had scares relating to rising levels of government debt (sometimes these five are referred to as the 'GIPSI' countries – Greece, Italy, Portugal, Spain, Ireland). This has been an even more serious concern because these countries each have a much larger Gross Domestic Product (GDP). Meanwhile, the UK, though outside the Euro, is also exposed because such a large part of the UK's economy is dependent on financial services (and because the UK government loaned money to Ireland). Even though the UK government would not directly have to bail out the Euro, most overseas trade is with the Eurozone, and the UK has very high levels of foreign debt. The interconnectedness of the world's financial systems, and the severity of the problems of toxic debt mean that, speaking dramatically but also accurately, nowhere is safe from the effects of GFC.

The consequences of GFC

Since 2008 and the collapse of Lehman Brothers, many people now feel far less secure at work. One way to describe the consequences of GFC – and we return to consider this topic in more detail in Chapter 3 – is to use the idea of the psychological contract. The psychological contract is not something that is written down anywhere (unlike the formal contract you would receive from many employers, and unlike any relevant employment legislation). The psychological contract can be thought of as a kind of loose collection of expectations, commitments, unspoken promises, understandings, or agreements between the employer and employee. Some of these are taken for granted, or taken on trust, others are learned during the course of work. No written contract can ever set down each and every aspect of the employment relationship, so the psychological contract is a shorthand we use to describe the normal, unwritten 'rules of the game'. GFC has meant that the rules of the game have changed, and as a result the realities of work are different.

In the private sector, historically the psychological contract has meant something like an expectation that an employee will be treated well if they are loyal and work hard, and (in many, though certainly not all private sector jobs) that they can expect bonuses or additional rewards – such as promotion, or perhaps shares in the company – if they perform particularly well, or if the company prospers. In the public sector, the psychological contract has included some of these aspects (though pay is often on a fixed scale that is agreed collectively, and of course there are no shares or profits to be allocated among public sector workers).

In both sectors employees have had an expectation that the terms and conditions under which they joined the job would be honoured throughout their career.

This is of particular relevance in relation to pension schemes, where a great many public sector workers have been told several years into paying for such a scheme that they will have to retire later, for a reduced pension, and that they will also have to pay more into their scheme. In other words, they have been told to work longer, for less and in the meantime to get paid less for doing so. The case for this is usually expressed in terms of people living longer, and governments often try to marginalise public sector workers by saying that private sector pensions are worse, but the GFC has been a contributory factor because governments have been hit by high levels of debt, and so need to reduce levels of spending. As Wolff says (above), 'governments today impose austerity [cuts and financial hardship] on the rest of us because "the markets" demand no less to keep credit flowing to those governments'.

The changes imposed on Greek workers (such as a later retirement age and lower pension) led to wide-scale rioting, but there have been less violent protests throughout the world, including the 'occupy Wall Street' movement, a protest that began in September 2011. Often using as their slogan the phrase, 'We are the 99%', the occupy movement suggests that the vast majority of the world's citizens are being made to pay for the mistakes of a wealthy few (the 1%) (more is available at http://occupywallst.org/). There is a great deal of anger because many people feel betrayed by their governments, who they feel are to blame for the crisis. In a sense, the psychological contract people had with their politicians has also been broken. In everyday speech we might call this a loss of trust in 'the system'. This means that what is more widespread than changes to particular workplaces is a general loss of public trust, of the kind Wolff describes above.

As well as a more general sense of insecurity and loss of trust, the crisis has had real and lasting implications for how the realities of work are experienced for tens of millions of people, and has been linked to an increase in incidences of depression and anxiety, and poorer psychological functioning (Sargent-Cox, Butterworth and Anstey, 2011). As Marmot and Bell (2009) put it, 'Global recession is likely to damage our health as well as our wealth', and because of this, 'Five billion people in low and middle income countries are at risk'.

In developing countries, though they played no part in the creation of the crisis, the consequences of GFC are devastating. Because of reductions in national income as a result of GFC, a research paper published in 2009 by the World Bank suggested that as many as 30,000 to 50,000 more infants (overwhelmingly infant females) would die in sub-Saharan Africa (Friedman and Schady, 2009). In a review of research carried out by the Overseas Development Institute (ten, country-level case studies), McCord reported that, 'The global financial crisis has had a devastating effect on poverty levels in developing countries' (McCord, 2010).

Although GFC is the clearest example in most people's lifetimes of how capitalism has harmed ordinary workers, there have been no radical attempts to reform how capitalism operates. This has prompted some to explore when the next similar crisis will be, rather than whether there will be another crisis (Ghosh, Ostry and Tamirisa, 2009). There have also been no policy reforms that would encourage the organization of labour through trade unions, 'The global financial system is not being revised or scrapped – merely reformed via changes at its margins – while reforms encouraging labor organization have languished' (Miller, 2010: 437; see also Baccaro, 2010).

One of the most remarkable accounts of GFC was given by the billionaire investor Warren Buffett, who described the complacency and fantasy before the world's financial systems crashed:

> People were having so much fun. And it's a little bit like Cinderella at the ball. People may have some feeling at midnight it's going to turn to pumpkin and mice, but it's so darn much fun, you know, when the wine is flowing and the guys get better looking all the time and the music sounds better and you think you'll leave at five of twelve [just before midnight] and all of a sudden you look up and you see there are no clocks on the wall and – bingo, you know? It does turn to pumpkins and mice. It's hard to blame the band. It's hard to blame the guy you're dancing with. There's plenty of blame to go around. There's no villain. (Quoted in Sorkin, 2010: 548)

The contradictions and complexities in global capitalism, and the sheer mess that was, and is, the GFC mean no one person is responsible, no one person is in charge, and no one institution or government can be believed in. Yet all of us will be feeling its effects for decades. One of the key ways in which GFC will affect us is through changes in how we experience the realities of work.

GFC and the realities of work

What do we mean by the 'realities of work'? Well, as in previous editions, this book examines work from the perspective of the employee. It does this using both theory and research findings. Plenty of books explain the principles and methods of management, but very few address what it is like to be managed. In other words, the employee's perspective is often overlooked or taken for granted.

So, we write about the effects of being managed: the experiences of employees in organisations as they cope with the strategies, tactics, decisions and actions of managers. This means that the main character in our discussion is 'the employee' – but of course at times other characters feature, such as managers, policy makers, trade unions, the unemployed, academic commentators, and – just as above – those organisations and individuals responsible for GFC. To explore these experiences, we draw widely from the social sciences and we have looked for empirical evidence and theoretical discussions that are not always found in mainstream texts.

We believe employees actively counteract management; in some circumstances this challenges management interests, in others it can help (for example, by creating conformity among workgroups). These counteractions take different forms, but often their focus is on managerial control. Employees can resist or undermine control in a number of ways, for example, by taking additional (unofficial) rest periods or organising work in ways that ease pressures, increase income or create a sense of autonomy. Because these counteractions are widespread, and because they are significant for those involved, it is important to understand that these aspects of work behaviour are not fleeting or frivolous departures from the one true path laid down by management. Instead, they are enduring and entirely rational responses by workers whose interests only partially coincide with those of management. These workers have their own interests, for example, to preserve their energy, maximise income, protect their family life, gain control over their work environment, and, to have fun.

We try to capture the diversity of work – the fact that workers experience both satisfaction and alienation, that they both cooperate and resist, have common interests with management and also opposing ones, and that workers see their distinct interests in both individual and collective terms. The challenge that faces us is to explore the varied experiences of work – in essence, 'the realities of work'.

Below we identify important aspects of the realities of work by mapping out the terrain this book explores. First though, it is important to make some key points about how work can be defined and classified, and about the particular approach we have taken. To do so we will look at the tools that can be used to explore the concept of work and the perspectives that can be adopted.

Defining work

Before reading this section, try Exercise 1.1 which will help you think about how we should define work.

Exercise 1.1

What do you think?

1. For each of the following situations, decide whether you would classify the task as 'work'. Justify your decision in each case.
   (a) You are a wealthy stockbroker and don't have time for household jobs, so you pay an electrician to rewire a plug in your house.
   (b) The electrician drives home and then rewires a plug in his own house.
   (c) Your friend rewires the plug in exchange for a tip on which shares to buy.
   (d) To relax after a busy day on the trading floor you rewire the plug yourself.
   (e) When the plug is rewired, you use it to play the multiplayer online game 'World of Warcraft', where you and a group of other players combine to rescue a dwarven princess from the evil Dark Iron Clan.
2. Now try to write a short definition of 'work'.

After Exercise 1.1 you may have arrived at the conclusion that the boundary between work and non-work activity is hazy. You may also have a definition of work that you are comfortable with, even though it is not perfect. If you have accomplished this, you have already developed a way of thinking about the realities of work. In short, this is the view that although complex, contradictory and sometimes frustrating, we can seek to analyse, understand and explain social phenomena.

So how does your definition of work match up to others? The *Concise Oxford Dictionary* defines work as, 'application of effort or exertion to a purpose'. Thomas (1999: xiv) more precisely identifies three components essential to work:

1. Work produces or achieves something (it is not an end in itself).
2. Work involves a degree of obligation or necessity (it is a task set either by others or by ourselves).
3. Work involves effort and persistence (it is not wholly pleasurable, although there may be pleasurable elements to it).

We can test this three-component definition by assessing it against various tasks, for instance serving a customer in a shop, fixing a broken washing machine, phoning a client, digging a hole, giving a presentation and so on. Serving in a shop achieves something (a sale and customer satisfaction), involves obligation (set by the employer) and involves effort (responding to customer needs). The definition also helps to define as work the tasks and chores expected of us in day-to-day life, like driving to work, cleaning and ironing clothes, getting the kids ready for school or engaging in small talk with clients/customers.

Generally the definition holds up to scrutiny, but there is one notable problem. Many activities that might be described as leisure also meet the three criteria. Playing sport (1) achieves something, (2) presents a self-imposed challenge and (3) requires effort and persistence. The same could be said of learning a foreign language or a musical instrument, painting (the house or on canvas), walking the dog, or rescuing a dwarven princess. Also, some activities might fit the three criteria but may be 'leisure' in one context and 'work' in another. Cooking and looking after children are examples of this. So, it is not only the activity that defines work, but also the circumstances under which the activity is undertaken.

One way of removing some of this confusion is to focus on work that is paid. In fact, most books on work restrict their attention to paid work: employment. Clearly, given the number of people involved, the time devoted to it and its importance as a source of income, this is an important component of work. It is also employment in what might be called 'visible work' – that which society views as the principal form of work. 'Real' work in these terms is seen to be that which is remunerated. But at the same time, there are huge areas of invisible or 'hidden' work which, if paid for, could equal or exceed the total value of paid work. This includes household-based work (cooking, cleaning, child-rearing, home improvement and so on) and a range of activities falling under the heading of voluntary work. Work can also be 'hidden' if it involves illegal activities, or if it is undertaken for payment that is not declared to the tax authorities.

What is needed is to strike a balance that gives greater recognition to the different activities that constitute people's work. Such a balance is necessary not only because of the scale of different spheres of work but also because of the links that exist between paid and unpaid work, visible and hidden work, and work and non-work activities. The fact that unpaid work is mainly undertaken by women, and that doing unpaid work limits access to paid work, makes the study of the different areas of work important. So, while some of the issues covered in the book pay most attention to work in the form of employment, at several specific points we draw attention to a broader definition of work. This underlines the significance of the different kinds of work in their own right, and the significance of hidden work for a fuller understanding of the nature and character of employment. In addition it is important to consider the balance between work and non-work activities – often referred to as the work–life balance – because this reveals how interrelated people's work and non-work lives are, and because change in one can have a significant impact on the other.

To sum up

Just because it is challenging to arrive at a definition or understand a concept does not prevent us from attempting to do so. Also, just because there are contradictory opinions does not mean there is no point engaging with the issues. Our immediate task – or if you like, our work – is to try to arrive at usable definitions as a basis for classifying and analysing work.

Classifying work

There are various ways of classifying work; the most common of which are listed in Table 1.1. Such classifications allow distinctions to be made between different groups of employees and so provide a basis to explain difference, such as different pay levels, gender differences, different expectations and orientations to

Table 1.1   Systems of classifying people according to their work

Criteria of classification	Examples
The way jobs are undertaken	Manual/non-manual
	Skilled/semi-skilled/unskilled
The main purpose of the work	Specific occupational groups
Job status	White-collar/blue-collar
Temporal pattern	Full-time/part-time
	Permanent/temporary
Work location	Workplace/home
	Formal economy/informal economy

Source: Based on discussion by Frenkel et al (1995).

work, differences in behaviour at work and so on. This emphasis on classifying and explaining is the purpose of much social science. (The section below explains some of the basic techniques of social science.)

Throughout the following chapters, examples are given of these various methods of classifying work. You will also be introduced to other classification schemes – for example, the distinction between types of 'knowledge workers' (Chapter 8) or different types of 'emotion work' (Chapter 7). There are also classifications within particular categories of work – for instance, we identify different types of 'hidden work' within the informal economy (Chapter 12).

Social scientists are constantly finding new ways of classifying work. One example is the system of socio-economic classification based on a person's type of employment contract, rather than his/her income. Those at the top have longer-term contracts, receive a rising income, greater opportunities and wider benefits (for a fuller explanation, see Extract 1.1, and then try Exercise 1.2).

New systems of classifying work are being developed for understandable reasons. In particular, changes in the context and nature of work – economic changes, globalisation, new customers' demands, technological developments, new management techniques and so on – mean that existing classifications can become outdated and misleading. For example, Frenkel, Korczynski, Donoghue and Shire (1995: 777) argue that:

> The manual/non-manual distinction is a less meaningful reference point as routine manual work is increasingly automated and the characteristics of skilled production workers become similar to those of technicians... The main purpose of work is also a less reliable criterion as workers undertake a wider range of tasks, for example contributing to improvements in work processes and assuming functions previously undertaken by supervisors and managers.

To sum up

Classification systems are developed to assist our understanding of the dynamic nature of work. They are a way to simplify complexity by grouping people into types, usually based on the work they do. Such systems are important tools to use when studying the realities of work.

Extract 1.1

A new class system

In 2001 the UK introduced a new way of classifying people: National Statistics Socio-economic Classification (NS-SEC). This system is designed to take into account:

- Labour market situations: a person's source of income, economic security and prospects of economic advancement.
- Work situations: a person's location in the systems of authority and control, and their extent of autonomy at work.

The result is a system of eight analytical classes:

NS-SEC categories	Examples
1. Higher managerial and professional occupations	Company directors, senior managers, police inspectors, doctors, architects,
2. Lower managerial and professional occupations	academics, lawyers
3. Intermediate occupations	Teachers, journalists, social workers, optometrists, operations managers
4. Small employers (less than 25 employees) and own-account workers (non-professional)	Police officers, secretaries, paramedics, driving instructors
5. Lower supervisory and technical occupations	Shopkeepers, farmers, publicans, self-employed electricians,
6. Semi-routine occupations	taxi-drivers
7. Routine occupations	Train drivers, landscape gardeners, railway construction workers,
8. Never worked and long-term unemployed	TV engineers Shop assistants, childcare assistants, receptionists, cooks, hairdressers Lorry/van drivers, cleaners, waiters, refuse collectors, couriers

This means the emphasis is placed on the employment contract and the way employees are regulated through these contracts in three forms:

- In a 'service relationship' the employee renders 'service' to the employer in return for 'compensation' in terms of both immediate rewards (e.g. salary) and long-term or prospective benefits (e.g. assurances of security and career opportunities). The service relationship typifies Class 1 and is present in a weaker form in Class 2.
- In a 'labour contract' employees give discrete amounts of labour in return for a wage calculated on amount of work done or by time worked. The labour contract is typical for Class 7 and in weaker forms for Classes 5 and 6.
- Intermediate forms of employment regulation that combine aspects from both forms (1) and (2) are typical in Class 3.

(Quoted from ONS, 2001a: 3–4)

The system also introduces separate classes for those people who have self-employed status or who run small businesses (Class 4) and those who are unemployed or who have never worked (Class 8). Full-time students are excluded from the classification.

Exercise 1.2

What do you think?

Read Extract 1.1 which explains the new way of classifying people according to their employment contract.

1. As a 'student' you are excluded from this classification, but in which class would you put your current part-time job (or a job you have undertaken in the past)?
2. In which class would you put:
   (a) your mother or father's occupation?
   (b) your grandfather's and grandmother's occupations?
3. What practical uses for social scientists does such a system of classification have?

Studying work

Conceptual tools of the social scientist

The ideas in the following chapters come from people doing a job of work – most are social scientists (sociologists, psychologists, economists, political scientists and so on). Like any other occupational group, social scientists have a set of 'tools' they use. Of course, people are different in terms of how they use specific tools for their jobs. Consequently, the outcome (output) of their work can differ. One characteristic of social scientists' work is that it depends on conceptual or abstract tools. In particular these include theories but also models, typologies (systems of classification like those above) and different methods of data gathering.

Theories

Theories appear in various of forms, but they often set out a cause and effect relationship, or an association, and present an explanation. An example might be, 'increasing maternity leave entitlements will allow a firm to attract better female job applicants' (a cause and effect relationship) because the firm will be at a comparative advantage in the labour market (an explanation). To illustrate this further, below is a list of theories about work. We have included one theory from each of the chapters in this book – so we will be exploring them later, along with many other theories. You will notice that they are all in the form of a proposition or statement that specifies a relationship between concepts, and that (ideally at least, and perhaps subject to more detailed definitions) these propositions are testable:

- Advanced capitalist economies have experienced a decline in manufacturing and a growing dominance of the service sector because of the effects of globalisation.
- Once basic needs are met, people work for reasons other than money.
- Employees are working harder than ever as a result of new management practices designed to address the demands of intensified competition.
- Skilled status has often been denied to women because social relations are dominated by male interests.
- There is an inevitable tendency towards the deskilling of work because of the desire of managers to control and regulate labour.
- Workers are expected to manage the emotions of customers because increasingly, organisations compete on the basis of the quality of the service encounter.
- Irrespective of their conditions of work, all employees find ways of creating time, space and enjoyment in the working day, which helps them to tolerate the oppressive and exploitative elements of work.

- People from minority ethnic groups have fewer opportunities in the workplace because they suffer direct and indirect racial discrimination.
- The knowledge of employees is increasingly being expropriated (taken) by managers to meet the challenges of an information age.
- Employees choose to belong to collective bodies such as trade unions because of a fundamental power imbalance in the employment relationship.
- The formal economy is supported by a vast amount of work that remains hidden from view because it is illegal or unrecognised.
- Changes in employment patterns and the experience of work are leading to greater proportions of people reappraising their work–life balance.

While it is easy to make theoretical statements like these, it is far more difficult to develop methods for testing them. That is the challenge the social scientist is faced with. Typically, this process will involve:

- specifying the concepts involved (defining the problem and reading up on previous similar investigations);
- deciding on a method for investigating the issue (a methodology);
- undertaking the investigation (doing the research);
- analysing and interpreting the findings;
- publishing the conclusions.

Throughout the book you will find examples of how theorists have developed propositions and then how they and others have sought to support, reject or modify theories as a result of the research.

Of course, at each of these stages different decisions and interpretations could be made by different social scientists, which affect the outcome of the investigation. So, any single study might result in acceptance of a theory by some researchers, rejection by others and modification by others. A case in point, as you will see in Chapter 6, is the theory of the deskilling of work: some researchers argue deskilling has taken place, others suggest the opposite – that there has been upskilling, while a third group suggests both effects are occurring simultaneously. Naturally, this is frustrating if you are looking for 'the answer', and some people are tempted to ignore certain types of research so as to avoid facing the problem of conflicting evidence. They might even reject the idea of theorising completely and argue that what needs to be applied is simply 'common sense' (see Extract 1.2). But explanations are usually more convincing if they weigh up different kinds of evidence.

Extract 1.2

Isn't it just common sense?

You will have heard people say, 'It's just common sense', when they are trying to justify an action or idea. However, the claim that something is 'common sense' is often used by people who do not wish to, or cannot, explain their reasoning. There are two main dangers of saying 'it's common sense':

• It is not always common. When we describe an idea, issue, theory, policy, practice or whatever as 'common sense' we often mean it fits our own understanding of the world. However, the same understanding might not be shared by people from different social backgrounds, ethnic groups, age groups, occupational groups or by people with different values and beliefs (political, cultural, religious and moral). In other words, the idea, issue or theory is not common to them. Just because something is sensible does not automatically make it common. For example, taking a siesta during the middle of working days in the summer is common sense in southern Europe – but not in northern Europe.

• It is not always sense. Albert Einstein described common sense as 'the collection of prejudices we have acquired by the age of 18'. In other words, common sense explanations often close our minds to other possibilities. Just because something is common does not automatically make it sensible. Some common sense understandings are later proven by rational, logical enquiry and experience to be misguided and ill informed. Consider, for example, the now discredited but once 'common sense' beliefs that the world is flat, that smoking does not damage your health, that women cannot be successful managers, and that brown corduroy is sexy.

Typically, therefore, social scientists rarely justify something as common sense. Instead, they try to justify their theories and ideas.

Purpose of theories

The point of theorising is to establish a line of inquiry that will raise some specific questions and hopefully lead to an answer (but see Extract 1.3). So theorising is an important stage in helping to frame the appropriate questions, rather than blundering about unsure of what you are looking for. However, sometimes it can be good to approach an issue without any preconceived theories. Some researchers, for example, prefer to go into an organisation to study a work process or work group with a set of themes, but not developed theories. This alternative approach is often described as 'grounded theory' (a term coined by Glaser and Strauss, 1967) and is designed to uncover concepts, issues and ideas gradually and progressively, from which theory can later be built.

These two approaches can be described as deductive and inductive theorising:

• Deductive theories are based on the principles of developing ideas and concepts into a framework or set of hypotheses that can then be tested by observation or experiment (in other words, by doing empirical research).

• Inductive theories are developed from observation of particular instances and patterns (empirical research) that can then be built into general propositions.

In practice, much social scientific research involves both deductive and inductive theorising.

Is there always an answer?

One of the typical responses of social scientists when asked a question is that 'It depends'. This does not necessarily mean they are failing to give a straight answer but rather that there are many factors that could influence the answer. It might be that the question has not been specified precisely enough, or else there is a range of possible answers to the same question, depending on the frame of reference for the question. It is rather like someone asking 'what one added to one makes'. 'Two' would be an adequate answer, unless they were mixing primary colours, or were referring to different volumes of a liquid, or different products, or opposing magnetic poles...and so on. In other words, frustrating though it may seem, social scientists must frame and specify questions precisely.

Throughout the chapters you will encounter attempts that social scientists have made to answer questions about working life in organisations. You will see also how different answers emerge to the same questions, and will have to make your own judgement as to which are the most convincing. The more you know and understand, the more you might be inclined to answer, 'Well, it depends' when faced with a question.

Models

Models are simplified versions of the world. They are representations of reality that allow understanding or exploration in an artificial (and safe) environment. For example, airline pilots develop their skills in a flight simulator. This models the real world of flying in two ways: first, it provides an exact copy of an airline cockpit controls and the motion of the aircraft; second, it provides a 3D representation of the approaches to different international airports.

In social science, models typically take the form of a visual representation of processes and actions; they are often flowcharts showing the links between different features (concepts, people, departments and so on). In this sense, models are often synonymous with theories, and there is a tendency in social science not to distinguish between model and theory. We have adopted this convention in the book, so, for example, Figure 9.1 in Chapter 9 is a flowchart of Marx's theory of the labour process and alienation, but it could just as easily be described as Marx's model of the labour process.

In some circumstances you might come across 'idealised' or 'normative' models, which are designed to specify how things should be, rather than represent the current situation. Such models are typically designed to guide action, so they are commonly used by those who wish to persuade others to change current processes or practices – for instance, they are often used by management consultants.

Typologies

Typologies are ways of grouping and classifying different sorts of phenomena. In the previous section we used a typology to distinguish between three different types of theory, and earlier we discussed various classifications of work (which are typologies). The point of typologies is to simplify complex social structures and processes and thereby assist attempts to understand and explain such phenomena. As an example, imagine you are with a group of friends deciding where to go and eat. You might ask, 'Shall we go Indian, Chinese or Italian?' In effect you have developed a typology of restaurants that simplifies the wide range of possible meals available.

The importance of systematically developing typologies was identified by the influential sociologist Max Weber (1949). He devised the notion of the 'ideal type' (a term often misunderstood because it is sometimes mistakenly thought to mean 'best' type). Weber used the term 'ideal type' to refer to the theoretical classification against which any observed types could be matched. For example, for the classification of restaurants above, the three mentioned are all 'ideal types'. One type is not better than another, but each one is different from the other two. It also means that if, for example, we found a restaurant that sold mostly Indian food but had a few non-Indian items on the menu we would say it approximates the Indian ideal type. In other words, it does not match it exactly. Again we are not saying it is better or worse, merely that it is closer to the 'ideal-type Indian restaurant' than any of the other types of restaurant.

Of course our three-type restaurant classification is incomplete because there are many other types of restaurant (French, Lebanese, Thai, Mexican and so on) outside these three categories. But that is also the point of developing typologies. Such systems allow us to identify exceptions, to seek to explain these, and, if appropriate, modify our typologies accordingly.

Extract 1.4

Using 'ideal types' to classify work

The following quote by Barley (1996: 407) explains how work can usefully be classified into 'ideal types'. However, it also warns how outdated ideal types can become problematic because they provide irrelevant comparisons with which to analyse current jobs:

'The-worker-on-the-assembly-line' is [an] ideal type. It invokes images of an individual, often in an automobile factory, standing beside a swiftly moving conveyor, repeatedly performing the same operation on each assembly that flows by. Boredom, fatigue, routine, lack of autonomy, and little need for thought or education are the hallmarks of such work. Although factory jobs have always been more varied than this, the ideal type nevertheless evokes a constellation of attributes that capture the family resemblance among many factory jobs. The clerk, the professional, the secretary, the farmer, and the manager are other prominent ideal-typical occupations.

Ideal-typical occupations are culturally and theoretically useful. By reducing the diversity of work to a few modal images, ideal types assist us both in comprehending how the division of labor is structured and in assigning status to individuals. They help parents shape their children's aspirations. They provide designers of technologies with images of users. They assist sociologists in developing formal models of attainment. It is not clear how we could think in general terms about worlds of work without such anchors. The problem is that ideal-typical occupations are temporally bound.

Like occupational classifications and cultural dichotomies, ideal-typical occupations lose relevance as the division of labor and the nature of work change. For example, the ideal-typical farmer is an independent businessman laboring in the fields from sunrise to sunset with the assistance of a tractor, a few hired hands, family members, and little formal education, but extensive practical knowledge of crops, weather, animals, and soils. Modern farming bears little resemblance. Today, many farmers are subcontractors for agribusiness, have a college education, understand chemical properties of soils and fertilizers, and manage their farms with the help of computers.

Typologies are extremely popular – see Extract 1.4 for a work-related example. You will encounter plenty more in the following chapters and undoubtedly you will have seen typologies on other courses and in other texts. It should always be remembered that typologies are designed to help simplify the complexity and variety of the social world. This means they are developed to group together similar phenomena. Rarely will you find an exact match between an observed phenomenon and an ideal type.

Methods of gathering data

Social science data typically comes in two basic forms:

- *Quantitative data*: data in numerical form, such as the number of people in a particular workplace, or the percentage of staff on part-time contracts.
- *Qualitative data*: data in non-numerical form, such as employee opinions about their working hours, or a description of a particular work process.

Sometimes the terms 'hard data' and 'soft data' are used to describe the two types of data described above. Our preference is not to use these labels because they have misleading connotations. 'Hard' gives the impression of being strong, fixed and robust, and 'soft' gives the impression of being weak, malleable and woolly, but in practice these descriptions can apply to both quantitative and qualitative data. For example, would you trust the supposedly hard data that 90 per cent of hospital workers are satisfied with their salary if you knew that was based on a questionnaire filled in by only ten hospital administrators? Similarly, would you label as 'soft data' the description by a heart surgeon of the work process in his/her operating room?

Throughout the subsequent chapters you will encounter both quantitative and qualitative data. In our opinion, social scientists can use both types of data to make sense of the social world. However, not all commentators agree with this view.

Some would argue that the social world, by definition, cannot be measured in the same way as the physical world (they might be called interpretivists, or constructivists). They might suggest it is futile to bring the quantitative methods and techniques used by physical science into the realm of social science, and that the emphasis should be on qualitative data (they would probably also resist the term 'data' because they would feel data can not simply be given or collected, but that research itself creates data).

In contrast, others argue the social world does lend itself to being meas-ured and explored in the same way as the physical world, and therefore the same quantitative methods and techniques can and should be used, although applied in different ways (they might be called realists). These two camps – there are many others, and we are speaking very simply here by way of basic introduction – would use different methods of gathering data. The interpretivist would recommend qualitative methods such as interviews, observation, par-ticipation and documentary analysis. A recent example of interpretivist analysis can be found in Leitch, Hills and Harrison (2010). The realist would primarily recommend quantitative methods such as computer simulations, questionnaires, controlled experiments, and statistical analysis (but they could use qualitative data too). A recent example of realist research (in the same broad subject area as Leitch et al) is Haynie, Shepherd and Patzelt (2012).

We draw on both approaches in this book because we believe both kinds of data have much to offer and that their different approaches can:

- uncover different aspects of the same social phenomenon;
- account for the same social phenomenon in different ways;
- encourage us to have open minds on different issues.

By drawing on both, we think it is possible to gain a better perspective of the diversity of the social world and the competing explanations of social action and processes. It also allows us to appreciate and comment on the contradictions and paradoxes in work that surface time and again – as you will see.

Exercise 1.3

What do you think?

Consider the following statement: 'A happy worker is a productive worker.'
1. Is this a theory? Justify your answer.
2. If someone said the statement is 'just common sense', how might you respond as a social scientist?
3. What method of inquiry would you adopt to assess the statement?

Analysing work: ways of looking

From the comments in the previous section, it should be apparent that we have chosen an approach that encourages an open-mindedness when analysing work. In particular, we are advocating that you identify how different approaches can be combined to help more complete understanding. To do this we need to combine different perspectives with a sense of history.

Given the central role of paid work to industrial capitalism, and to individuals, it is not surprising the subject has given rise to extensive theoretical consideration which, at best, offers a stimulating variety of ideas. But, no single theory successfully captures the cross-cutting nature of work experiences: the ways in which work encapsulates both conflict and cooperation, satisfaction and alienation, tension and fit. We draw on various theories to locate and interpret work experiences and worker behaviour within a broader conceptual framework. So, the book does not advocate or adopt a single theoretical perspective but is informed by a range of theories. It seeks to tread the difficult – but ultimately more rewarding – path of incorporating different theories without on the one hand becoming tied to a single orthodoxy, or on the other hand, being lost amid confusion.

We have also tried to achieve a balance between theory and empirical research. There is a rich empirical tradition in academic research that has illuminated our understanding of the experience of work. Moreover, empirical studies display a variety of research methods, all of which are legitimate and worthy attempts to explore the realities of work – although, of course, they vary in quality and rigour. Throughout we show how different research methods have been used to address a variety of questions: methods which range from ethnography to statistical analysis. Similarly, there is diversity in the levels of analysis: from detailed studies of particular workplaces to international comparative surveys. In some instances too, these different methods have been used to address the same research question, producing a range of interpretations that compete with one another for theoretical supremacy; nowhere is this better illustrated than over the issue of skill discussed in Chapter 5. As committed, active researchers ourselves, we believe theory and empirical research go hand in hand: data without theory is as inadequate as a theory without data.

We reject any idea that the essence or 'true' experience of work can be captured in a single theory or argument. The world of work, and people's experience of the realities of work, is more complex. The activities that make up work are highly diverse, and conducted in a wide variety of settings, with those taking part displaying the full range of character and biographical variation. In addition though, it is clear that people subjectively experience work in a wide variety of ways. So, as this book's title indicates, what is needed is an understanding of the realities, rather than any all-embracing reality, of work.

Analysing work: a sense of history

Throughout the discussion we draw on perspectives of both past and present. All too often management texts fail to acknowledge the historical traditions of work and working, which means that the reasons why particular practices, policies or ideas came into being are obscured. At worst, such an ahistorical approach means that each issue is dealt with as a contemporary problem that can be solved by a quick-fix solution: typically in the form of the latest buzzword or policy to come from self-styled management gurus. It is little wonder if the result is at best mixed. We feel such an approach shows a contempt for the past that is both ill-advised and anti-academic. In contrast, we have tried to instil in our analysis a respect for the past in terms of ideas, practices, theories and research. Our concern is to show that the realities of work are embedded with resonant themes, abiding struggles and unresolved problems. 'New' issues and ideas are often in practice a new expression of the dilemmas and concepts of a previous period.

However, this does not mean we overlook major changes in the world of work. Some commentators suggest that the regimes of the past are giving way to a new era where emphasis is shifting from key sectors of work being organised on the basis of large-scale, standardised, mass production operations (with all that entails in terms of the size of organisations, the nature of jobs and patterns of control) to smaller-scale, more flexible forms of organisation. These can take full advantage of more flexible technologies to service less standardised, more fragmented and more volatile product markets. It is clear that a combination of factors, including changes in levels of competition, the nature of markets and available technologies, is resulting in significant changes in the character of many work organisations.

In all industrial societies there has been a shift from an emphasis on the manufacturing sector to the service sector. The dominance of the latter as the larger source of employment is well established and increasingly researchers are exploring the impact of this on employees – most notable has been the eagerness of researchers to study call-centre workers. The expansion of service work has brought about an increased interest in how it differs from other types of work (Korczynski, 2002). Two specific examples of this are:

- The increase in activities involving direct contact with the public and the delivery of 'customer care' where an explicit part of the job is to display a particular set of emotions (Chapter 7).
- The greater emphasis on knowledge-intensive activities to underpin the information needs of service-sector organisations (Chapter 8).

In other, more immediate ways too, the character of work has been changing markedly in recent years. Nowhere is this more apparent than in the growing feminisation of the workforce, with many industrial societies approaching a point in their history where a majority of the workforce is female. With the sociology of work criticised for being unreflective of women (see, for example, Tancred, 1995), with organisation theory being condemned as frequently gender blind (e.g. Wilson, 2003) and with many individual studies criticised (rightly) as being written largely by men about men working in factories, this point in industrial history, when the balance is shifting towards a majority of the workforce being female, makes it an appropriate time to consider more closely the contemporary realities of work for both women and men.

To sum up

We are interested in:

- seeking to explore diversity and variation in the work experience;
- studying the many interests and struggles within the employment relationship;
- drawing on varied theoretical perspectives on work and methods of research and analysis;
- combining an appreciation of the history of work with contemporary issues.

Mapping the realities of work

Our objective is to convey an impression of work from the perspective of the employee and to explain this through the use of theory and research evidence. We have drawn widely from the social sciences and provide empirical evidence

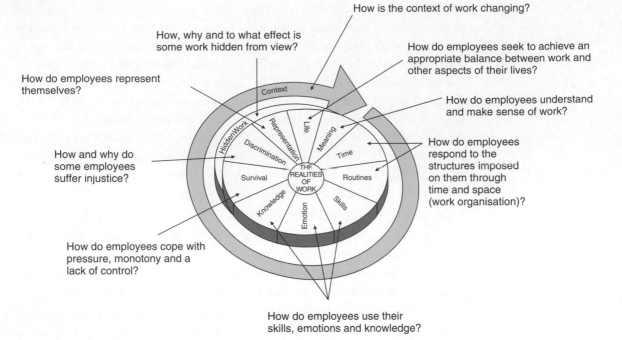

Figure 1.1   Exploring the realities of work

and theoretical discussions that are not always to be found in mainstream texts (particularly those concerned with 'how to manage'). In selecting the key issues to include we have focused on how work is experienced and on several core questions:

- How do employees understand and make sense of their work?
- How do employees respond to the structures imposed on them through time and space (work organisation)?
- How do employees use their skills, knowledge and emotions?
- How do employees cope with pressure, monotony and a lack of control?
- How and why do some employees suffer injustice?
- How do employees represent themselves?
- How, why and to what effect is some work hidden from view?
- How do employees seek to achieve balance between work and other aspects of their lives?

From these central questions we have derived ten components of the realities of work, each addressing a key theme raised by the questions. These make up the chapters of the book. This conceptual map of our terrain is shown in Figure 1.1. The chapters that follow explore each component.

2

The changing context of work

Key concepts

▷ political context
▷ deregulation
▷ privatisation
▷ economic context
▷ globalisation
▷ competitive strategies
▷ industrial structure
▷ workforce composition
▷ part-time employment
▷ self-employment
▷ location of employment
▷ job insecurity
▷ redundancy
▷ unemployment

Chapter aim

To examine how the political and economic contexts for work are changing and consider the main trends in the composition of the labour force.

Learning outcomes

After reading and thinking about the material in this chapter, you will be able to:

1. Identify the main developments in the international political environment that affect the world of work, particularly (i) the liberalisation of trade and (ii) the growth of alliances that cross national boundaries (i.e. supranational alliances).

2. Recognise the influence of change in national political contexts for the nature of work and employment.

3. Develop an understanding of the main changes in the overall economic context, particularly economic globalisation.

4. Identify the main changes in the industrial structure, particularly the shift from manufacturing to services.

5. Assess the main changes taking place in workforce composition.

6. Consider the changing experience of work in terms of changes in levels of unemployment, redundancies, temporary work and job insecurity.

Introduction

It is often said that the world of work has undergone dramatic changes over the past 20 to 30 years. Some have gone so far as to describe these changes in terms of a fundamental shift in the nature of capitalism itself: from 'Fordist' to 'post-Fordist' forms of production; in other words from mass production systems to flexible specialisation, from industrial to post-industrial society, and from modern to post-modern forms of organisation (see also the discussion in Chapters 6 and 8). Such terms usefully indicate the breadth and depth of change and also the way that many individual changes can be interpreted as part of a much broader direction of change. At the same time as recognising these trajectories, it is important to explore the specific changes themselves because shorthand terms risk disguising as much as they reveal. Not only do they encourage generalisations about the direction in which society is heading, but they also involve making sweeping assumptions about where it has been.

In this chapter, we need to cover a lot of ground fairly quickly. Our purpose is to present an overview of how the context of work has changed, and in so doing offer a backdrop against which we can locate the more specific experiences of work that are discussed in later chapters. Even an overview has to be selective however, since contexts can be defined at several levels: a worker may be based in a particular work setting, but in turn their workplace is situated within a local economy, which itself is embedded in regional, national and international economic contexts. These economic contexts are in turn interrelated with, and influenced by, political contexts that also operate at each of these levels. So, in this chapter we need to note three things. First, we need to look at some of the main changes that have been taking place in the political context of work over the past two decades. Second, we have to consider broad changes in the economic context. Third, we need to look at changing patterns of employment. Many of the issues raised in this chapter feed directly into more specific arguments covered in more detail later. For now though, the task is to capture a sense of the breadth of change at these different levels. To do this, the chapter is divided into three sections:

1. Changes in the political context of work over approximately the last two decades.
2. Changes (often related) in the economic context, together with some of the main responses to those changes.
3. Changes in the structure and patterns of employment.

Changes in the political context of work

It is impossible to analyse 'the realities of work' without considering the political context for work. Work organisations are actually embedded in a number of political contexts: the international political environment, the national political context and regional and local politics. These are considered briefly below in relation to the aspects of the political context that have impacted upon the workplace.

The international political environment

A number of international political developments have taken place over the recent period, and two are particularly notable in considering the realities of work:

- the gradual liberalisation of trade;
- the creation of supranational alliances in Europe, North America and Asia.

Trade liberalisation

Countries ('nation states') try to promote liberalisation of trade if it enhances economic growth. At the same time, national governments often try to protect more vulnerable domestic industries and markets. This tension means that in many sectors (most notably agriculture but also sometimes manufacturing) there are considerable barriers to trade (duties, charges or 'tariffs' on particular goods) which have restricted the development of international trade. Nevertheless, since the founding of the General Agreement on Tariffs and Trade (GATT) in 1946, the overall trend both through GATT negotiations and through regional agreements has been towards a more liberal trading environment.

The sector in which trading has been most liberalised is that of financial markets, through the removal of restrictions on international movements of capital (Milberg, 1998: 83). This acted as a key driver influencing the growth of economic globalisation (see below), but a lack of regulation also contributed to the Global Financial Crisis. Other sectors have also experienced a significant degree of market liberalisation. Entry into the long-distance telecommunications industry, for example, has been widely liberalised, as has access to local and mobile telecommunications in most industrial countries (OECD, 2000a: 152). Similarly, international air passenger transport has also experienced a degree of market liberalisation in recent years, though market restrictions remain in this, as in many other sectors (see Extract 2.1). Where international markets have become noticeably more liberalised is within three major regional groupings of countries in North America, South East Asia, and particularly Europe. We examine these separately below.

Market liberalisation in the aviation industry

Traditionally, the air transport market has been subject to a high degree of state regulation covering market entry, capacity and prices. State ownership was the norm for the majority of the world's major airlines. These carriers enjoyed national 'flag carrier' status and preferential access to international markets through bilateral agreements between national governments.

Pressure to relax regulation has come from a variety of sources, most notably growing political support for 'free market' capitalism within a more liberalised and privatised economic regime (many flag carriers have been privatised).

After the deregulation of the US airline industry in the late 1970s, the most significant liberalisation has been in Europe, where a single market for aviation came into being in 1997, with any EU-registered carrier gaining the right to operate services within and between any of the EU member states.

This reduction in state control, particularly over the entry of new carriers, operations, pricing and capacity, has had certain immediate effects, most notably the growth of independent low-cost carriers. Many of these operate from second-tier and regional airports. However, relaxation of state regulation over the passenger airline market remains partial. Apart from regional agreements such as those covering the European Union, the majority of international routes are operated by the two countries involved, and protected by bilateral (two party) air service agreements.

Sources: Blyton, Martinez Lucio, McGurk and Turnbull (2001); OECD (2000a).

Supranational alliances

Much of the world's trade takes place within and between the three regional areas of North America, Europe and East Asia, and the main political steps to create regional free markets have occurred in these regions. These have been through the formation of the North America Free Trade Agreement (NAFTA), the Association of South East Asian Nations (ASEAN) and the European Union (EU). NAFTA and ASEAN have remained largely economic alliances, but the EU has taken integration considerably further, with a growing number of member states that have established a widespread political and social agenda, though primarily to support the EU's economic programme.

The breadth of this integration in Europe has m ade it particularly significant in terms of its impact on work and employment. For example, EU countries (member states) are subject to a growing body of European law. This increasingly affects work organisations by obliging employers (and countries as a whole) to comply with European legislation, even if individual national governments are reluctant. For example, the European Court of Justice (ECJ) forced the British government to enact additional equal pay provisions to take into account EU legislation about work of equal value (Rubinstein, 1984).

In the mid-1990s, the UK government was required to change the law on employment protection to give part-time workers the same qualifying period as their full-time counterparts. This related to statutory employment rights concerning, for example, redundancy pay and unfair dismissal compensation (Dickens, 1995: 209). ECJ rulings in 2005 affecting employment in the UK included a decision that the hours that doctors and other healthcare workers spent 'on call' must be included as working time. This meant that they would form part of the calculation of hours specified in the Working Time Directive (Tait and Taylor, 2005).

A key development relating to EU-wide employment rights was the establishment of the European Community Charter of the Fundamental Social Rights of Workers (known as the Social Charter). In 1989 it was accepted as a political proclamation (with no formal legal status) by 11 of the then 12 member states (the UK was the exception). However, it established the direction in which social policy was to develop, and by 1992 the 11 member states began implementing the Social Charter through the EU institutions by signing a Protocol on Social Policy as part of the Maastricht Treaty (the Social Chapter). Again the then Conservative government in Britain refused to be a signatory, and it was not until the incoming 1997 Labour government that this opt-out decision was reversed.

The main vehicle for developing the work and employment aspects of the Social Charter has been through European directives. These have covered such issues as working time, part-time workers, parental leave, sex discrimination and the rights of employees in European multinationals to works councils (representative bodies of workers) (Bach and Sisson, 2000). Once such directives have been issued, they are then implemented via legislative changes at the national levels (see below).

EU-wide legislation is intended to harmonise conditions and rights of employees across national boundaries. This is seen to be particularly important by the more prosperous states such as Germany which might otherwise fall victim to 'social dumping': where companies transfer aspects of production to countries within the EU that maintain lower wages, less employment protection and fewer employment rights, thus decreasing the costs and overheads of labour. Such differences put pressure on member states with favourable employment terms and conditions to lower them in order to provide a competitive environment. The logical consequence of such differences is a spiralling down or 'race to the bottom' on employment protection.

The national political context

Despite the importance of international agreements over trade and supranational political alliances, the national political context remains a major source of influence on the world of work and employment. As an economic manager, employer and legislator, the state has a major bearing on the experience of work (Blyton and Turnbull, 2004: 170–213). Even key supranational developments such as the implementation of EU directives (above) are carried out via changes in national legislation (see Bach and Sisson, 2000: 31–3; Gennard and Judge, 2005). Similarly, a central aspect of greater market liberalisation has been the deregulation of individual nations' economic sectors. This liberalisation has been given a particular impetus by widespread privatisation of former state-owned monopolies, such as the supply of electricity and water. Indeed, in terms of the national political context affecting work and employment, privatisation is among the most prominent political developments worldwide over the past generation.

Privatisation activity

The 1980s and particularly the 1990s witnessed a substantial growth in privatisation throughout the world, and widespread privatisation activity has continued into the present century. Factors encouraging privatisation have included government desires to raise revenues and avoid new investment costs, and the widespread decline in the power of left-wing parties which in the past have been more in favour of state ownership (Toninelli, 2000).

In the 1990s, the most active countries pursuing large-scale privatisation programmes were Australia, France, Germany, Italy, Japan and Spain, and several countries in Latin America, notably Chile and Mexico. Since that time, privatisation activity has also become increasingly prominent in Russia and the former Soviet bloc countries in central and eastern Europe, and also to a growing extent in China (Megginson and Netter, 2001; Parker and Kirkpatrick, 2005). Around the world, the main sectors subject to privatisation in the recent period have been manufacturing, telecommunications, financial services, public utilities and transport.

Labour market deregulation

The UK stood in the vanguard of privatisation activity, and for Conservative governments of the 1980s and 1990s in the UK, privatisation represented a major plank in a broader project of deregulating economic activity. This was particularly marked in relation to the labour market with the objective of allowing employers greater freedom of operation. This policy of labour market deregulation was underpinned by theories of neo-classical economics which hold that economic revival and success is dependent on allowing market forces to operate free from any 'artificial' constraint or government intervention. It was argued that competitiveness had been hampered in the past by high labour costs caused by the restrictions imposed on employers by employment protection legislation, and the power and influence of trade unions. On the basis of this reasoning, successive Conservative governments after 1979 embarked on a series of incremental changes that sought to deregulate employment and restrict the influence of trade unions. Some aspects of these policies were reversed or curtailed by the New Labour government elected in 1997, for example, by the introduction of a national minimum wage and the establishment of rights for trade unions to pursue membership representation cases, as well as the implementation of European directives (see above). However, many of the broader labour market policies have remained in place, and since 2010 the coalition government under Prime Minister David Cameron has continued in the tradition of earlier Conservative administrations, for instance, by exploring ways to make it harder for employees to make claims for unfair dismissal. This has a direct comparison with earlier measures to deregulate employment such as extending the period employees need to work before qualifying for employment protection rights; abolishing wage-setting mechanisms for the least organised groups; and restricting the operations of trade unions (see Blyton and Turnbull, 2004, for details).

Deregulating employment can shift the balance away from employment protection towards employment flexibility. This greater flexibility carries a number of consequences for those in or out of work (see discussion of job insecurity below). However, in identifying the full extent and implications of labour market deregulation in the UK, we need to take care. It is something of a misnomer to talk of UK governments 'deregulating' the relations between capital and labour. Relative to many other economies, the labour market and employment relationships in the UK have never been highly regulated.

In the UK, for example, legislation on such basic employment issues as the maximum hours a worker is permitted to work, or the minimum number of days holiday a person is entitled to, has until recently been notable by its absence. The same holds for the type of employment contracts that an employer can offer. For example, unlike some other countries there is no requirement for employers in the UK to justify the offering of temporary rather than permanent contracts. In this respect, the deregulation of labour markets which took place in the UK in the 1980s and 1990s is all the more significant: it removed and reduced regulations in a context already characterised by a low degree of regulation. In a country where labour market regulation is only modest, further reforms to deregulate have considerable symbolic significance. They say something fundamental about the relations between capital and labour and suggest that an administration feels there is little need to protect the latter against the powers of the former.

One significant aspect to UK privatisation in terms of the realities of work is that in the past an important way the state regulated employment within and around the public sector was through Fair Wages resolutions. These were based on the principle that when a private sector firm was awarded a government contract, its employees should be paid at the same level as public sector workers. This was part of a broader state approach to acting as a 'good employer', and disseminating good employment practices more widely. The good employer approach also extended to its encouragement of trade union representation, leading to very high levels of union organisation throughout most of the public sector.

However, the shrinking of the public sector through privatisation and the commercialisation of those activities remaining within the public sector was accompanied by the abandonment of Fair Wages resolutions. This reduction has only partially been offset by expansion in employment in the health and education sectors in more recent years (see Hicks, 2005). Moreover, the growth in 'competitive tendering' (bidding between rival companies for contracts) across the public sector in the 1980s and 1990s resulted in most tenders being won on the basis of least cost. Of course, low wage levels are an important means of keeping costs down when tendering. Together, the increase in competitive tendering and the ending of the concept of 'fair wages' removed further perceived sources of inflexibility from the labour market. In terms of the realities of work, these had real consequences concerning wage rates for employees working on government contracts.

Regional and local political environments

As states such as the UK also move to more devolved political arrangements, political activity at regional and local levels becomes more significant. One of the most vivid examples of how sub-national (regional or local) politics can have an impact on work is the extent to which it encourages (or inhibits) capital investment in an area. This can be through programmes such as the creation of local enterprise zones to stimulate economic growth and employment (OECD, 2005b: 107–8). In terms of encouraging capital investment, a UK example relates to the location of the Nissan car company in the north-east of England. In this instance, various parts of the local state (the local authority, the county council and the local development corporation) acted to purchase land in sufficient quantity (over 900 acres) to attract the car-maker. This was with the prospect of being able to expand its operations on the site much above its originally stated plans (Crowther and Garrahan, 1988).

More recently in the UK and Europe, an important focus of regional policy and development has been the growth of regional airport facilities (and surrounding infrastructures). Much of this growth is closely linked to the rapid expansion in low-cost airline traffic over the past decade (Buyck, 2005); though this of course has its problems in terms of upsetting residents near to airports, or those who live under flight paths. The current UK coalition government has discussed contentious schemes such as the proposal of an additional runway for Heathrow, the building of a new airport for London in the Thames estuary and an underground railway linking Heathrow and Gatwick (Heathwick).

In the UK the local political context has also proved to be a site where an alternative political agenda can be orchestrated from that prevailing at national level. The elections for a Mayor of London in 2000, for example, created a rallying point for opposition to the national government's policy of privatising the London Underground. More recently London Mayor Boris Johnson came out strongly in favour of a new Thames estuary airport though this was not seen as the national government's preferred option. Such examples must be treated with caution, however, for while they illustrate the potential importance of local politics in the UK, the influence of the latter remains limited, both by the increasing power of Whitehall (Hoggett, 1996) and by the general inability of regional political mechanisms such as the Scottish and Welsh Assemblies to challenge the decisions of powerful multinationals successfully.

For example, when the Anglo-Dutch steelmaker Corus announced in early 2001 its decision to close substantial parts of its steelmaking and plating facilities in south Wales with the loss of approximately 3000 jobs in Wales (and 6000 in the UK as a whole), this decision could not be modified by the Welsh Assembly, despite the latter's efforts of persuasion and financial incentives (*Financial Times*, 17 January 2001, p. 6; see also Extract 2.3). And, the decision in 2011 to award a contract for building trains to the German company Siemens was made partly because of supranational (EU) restrictions placed on tendering and procurement. These decisions can have a devastating effect on local areas through the loss of thousands of jobs.

To sum up

The nature of work is influenced by political factors operating at various levels from the international political arena to local political contexts. Many of the political projects being pursued at different levels are interconnected, including the search for further privatisation, greater labour market deregulation and broader trade liberalisation.

Changes in the economic context

Globalisation and competition

One of the most marked economic developments over the recent period has been the progressive globalisation of economic activity. Just as earlier periods of industrial development witnessed a gradual shift in the extent to which enterprises were oriented towards national rather than local markets, the last quarter-century has seen a marked increase in the cross-national nature of goods and service production. It needs to be recognised that the term 'globalisation' is problematic. Many different meanings have been applied to it. Some have criticised the term because it implies that what is currently occurring is fundamentally different from previous patterns of development rather than an extension of those patterns (see, for example, Hirst and Thompson, 1996; Kleinknecht and ter Wengel, 1998).

Although the term 'globalisation' has often lacked precision, we agree with the view that there is now compelling evidence that global activity is continuing to grow, that national economies are becoming increasingly integrated into global trading relations, and that large companies increasingly make decisions on a global basis, not least as a result of the trade and capital liberalisation measures that political negotiations have brought about (see above). Furthermore, the term 'globalisation' usefully reflects that, in an increasingly industrialised world, a growing number of countries are important for global trade. Countries such as China, India, Korea, Taiwan, Singapore and Brazil are prominent industrial producers and major international traders.

A workable definition of economic globalisation is 'the integration of spatially separate locations into a single international market' (Blyton et al, 2001: 447). The main economic dimension to this is the reduction in costs that is realised when conducting business on an international basis. This includes, in particular, transport and transaction costs, such as travel time, freight rates and the cost, speed and ease of communication.

Nowhere is the spread of globalisation more clearly illustrated than in the accelerated growth in world trade. The consequences of the Global Financial Crisis are partly so devastating because of interconnections in trade. During the 1990s and the first decade of the present century, world trade grew at a considerably faster rate than total output of goods and services. On average, world trade grew by 4.3 per cent per annum in the first decade of the present century. This has represented a much higher rate of growth than world total output (GDP), which grew on average by 2.5 per cent (WTO, 2011).

Exercise 2.1

Over to you...

The focus of the discussion here is economic globalisation. However, globalisation has many other dimensions: for instance, the diffusion of global brands, or the influence of (Western) cultural industries such as film and music and the associated values they promote (individualism and consumerism). This even extends to political systems and values such as the ones discussed in this chapter (trade liberalisation, deregulation of employment). All these can reinforce the spread of economic globalisation.

Identify an example of social or cultural globalisation. What are the effects of that type of globalisation? (If you want to learn more about globalisation, a good starting point is Ritzer's *Globalization: The Essentials* (2011), which is an accessible summary, written with students in mind.)

Multinational firms

Within this overall expansion in trade, multinational firms play a very large and increasing role and are the principal carriers of economic globalisation. Driven by such factors as the differential cost and availability of labour, favourable exchange rates and the importance of being situated within, rather than outside, multi-country free trade areas (such as the European Single Market) the scale of multinational activity has continued to grow.

One of the main effects of globalisation (in terms of the spread of industrialism, and the increased dominance of multinationals) has been to intensify competition in many markets. A growing number of local and domestic markets have become exposed to wider competition, either as a result of international trade or through activities of multinationals producing for the 'host' country market. This leads to remarkable complexity that goes unnoticed in daily life.

For example, a worker in the UK Midlands could be employed by the (Japanese-owned) Toyota car factory. They could travel to and from work in a British-manufactured Ford (a US multinational with a base in the UK) and shop at lunchtime in the (German-owned) ALDI supermarket. They could go into Birmingham at the weekend to buy a chair from the (Swedish) IKEA superstore (IKEA is in turn owned by a Dutch corporation). Then, before watching *Neighbours* (an Australian soap) on their Sony television (made in the UK in a Japanese-owned factory) they would have to assemble the chair themselves. After *Neighbours* they might fancy a burger from the local (American-owned)

McDonald's and on the way call home on a Samsung mobile (a South Korean multinational), that was powered by a battery made in China (and finished in Vietnam), using a network owned by Orange – a French company that in 2010 merged with the German company T-Mobile!

Intensification of competition

Besides the pervasiveness of multinationals, other factors have fuelled the intensification of competition, not least an accelerated diffusion of new technologies. This generally results in companies enjoying a more restricted technological advantage for a more limited time. Related to this, technological advances in telecommunications have accelerated the speed with which companies can effectively operate in geographically dispersed markets. This undermines any advantage of proximity and exclusivity from which local producers might previously have benefited.

The effects of intensified competition on work and workers can manifest themselves in a variety of ways depending on how employers respond to competitive pressure. Decisions such as acquisitions, relocation, which markets to operate in, whether to sell parts of a company, which products to develop or abandon and which technologies to employ are all influenced by competition. At the same time, however, in the search for competitive advantage and efficiencies, labour and labour costs frequently play a central role. This can most easily be seen to be true when labour costs represent a high proportion of overall costs. But it also applies where labour costs are a much smaller proportion of overall costs and are more open to manipulation (at least in the shorter term) than other, more fixed costs. Even if the cost of labour (or cost of one part of a workforce) is only a fraction of the total cost, it can be the focus of management attention if it is the only movable cost. So in cost-cutting exercises temporary workers and part-time staff may well suffer first because they are easier to dismiss than full-time or permanent staff who enjoy greater rights.

In the international air passenger transport industry labour costs represent only 25 to 35 per cent of total operating costs (Doganis, 1994: 18); however, many other costs (e.g. aircraft and fuel prices) are less open to manipulation, thus making labour one of the few 'variable' elements of cost, at least in the short term. As a result, in the face of deregulation and growing competition in the industry, there has been strong pressure on airline managements to improve competitiveness via cuts in their overall labour costs (Blyton et al, 2001). This pressure increased because of fluctuations in the price of oil which peaked in 2008 at nearly $150 per barrel and have since stabilised but remain much higher than historical trends (Milmo, 2011).

There are essentially two contrasting strategies that employers may adopt towards labour in the search for competitive advantage. On the one hand, they can try to increase the output that labour achieves. On the other hand, they can try to reduce its cost. In practice, of course, these two strategies do not represent the only choices available and they are not mutually exclusive. Instead, they are located at each end of a continuum of responses, with employers likely to seek improvements in their competitive position by a mixture of responses designed to increase performance and/or to reduce costs. Variation in employment practices is unlikely to be between one extreme and the other. Instead it will be between the relative priorities given to performance improvement and cost reduction. Even so, it is helpful to describe the two ends of this continuum in a little more detail, because they indicate how broad economic (and political) strategies have important consequences for the realities of work:

- One end of the continuum entails seeking competitiveness through improved performance and relies on creating a highly effective workforce, capable of yielding increased levels of output. This could be associated with greater levels of training and investment or skill (working smarter), or perhaps more pessimistically with the implementation of management techniques and incentives that lead to people increasing their effort (working harder).
- The other end of the continuum, involving a labour strategy based on lowest cost, is likely to mean minimising expenditure on training, resulting in a low-skill, low-productivity, low-cost workforce.

The choice between these strategies (or the relative weight given to each within more-complex strategies) is not only an economic choice but also reflects political policies and constraints. One important reason, for example, that employers in Germany have generally pursued a 'high-skill, high-performance' strategy is because state policies on training and vocational education have resulted in an extensive training infrastructure. They have also meant a comparatively high level of skill development among the labour force.

Added to this, alternative strategies such as minimising labour costs by hiring in workers when demand is strong, then firing them when demand drops, are less readily available to German employers because of statutory restrictions governing redundancy and dismissal. This contrasts with the UK where there is little regulatory constraint on employers' ability to hire and fire. Given this, and the comparatively low development of national training and vocational education provision in the UK, it is evident how political policies in the two countries have influenced markedly different labour strategies.

It has been widely argued that the UK has been leading the way for those countries pursuing a low-cost competitive strategy. This has consequences in terms of levels of investment in skills, wage levels (including non-wage labour costs such as sick pay and pension contributions) and the (low value-added) nature of much of the productive activity taking place (for a discussion, see Blyton and Turnbull, 2004). The low wage levels and widespread availability of labour (caused partly by high unemployment at different periods; see below) have been important factors encouraging a high level of foreign direct investment into the UK compared, for example, with many other EU countries. Much of this investment has required only low or modest levels of skill development, with many activities involving assembly operations of one form or another (e.g. in the manufacture of motor components).

The paucity of the education and training structure in the UK compared, for example, with many of its western European counterparts has been well documented (see, for example, Keep and Rainbird, 2005). So too has the UK's level of productivity and performance (see Blyton and Turnbull, 2004: 49–55). The broader point for our present discussion, however, is that many of the salient aspects of work – types of jobs available, levels of income, extent of training and skill development, and degree of job security – can only be understood in the broader context of overall competitive strategies and the political and economic climate within which those strategies are developed and pursued.

Exercise 2.2

Over to you...

Assume you are a senior human resources manager in an organisation that in the past has competed on the basis of producing high-volume goods to cater for the low-cost end of a consumer market (selling fixed-focus 'point and shoot' cameras).

Because of a change in consumer behaviour to favour higher specification and better quality digital equipment, your company has taken the decision to switch its strategy. It wants to get out of the low-cost end of the market, change its brand name and compete by producing very high specification, and much more high-cost, equipment: high definition, 'bridge' and single lens reflex (SLR) cameras (bridge cameras are a step up from point and shoot, but not quite as sophisticated as SLR cameras).

1. In terms of the workforce, what are the main changes that you anticipate will need to be made? List these and rank them in order of importance.
2. Now rank these again in terms of which change you would begin with (followed by second and third in order of priority for introduction) and explain the reasons for your decisions.
3. In addition to meeting the objective of successfully switching production to higher quality cameras, what other consequences would you imagine could come about because of the changes you have listed?

Organising production

Aside from the question of overall strategies aimed at higher performance or lower cost, greater competition and the search for more efficient operations have led to significant changes in how organisations produce goods and services. For example, the twin factors of advances in technological capability and the search for greater efficiency have stimulated the development of more advanced forms of production control. This is associated with production processes being 're-engineered' or 're-configured' to improve the sequencing and integration of different stages of productive activity within organisations. This is designed to increase the efficiency with which production 'flows' through an organisation with the minimum of bottlenecks. Partly this involves the supply of materials and the timing of manufacturing processes being matched more closely to customer orders, so goods are produced 'just-in-time' to meet delivery requirements. This reduces the amount of capital tied up in stocks of raw materials, work in progress and finished goods. In terms of the possible impact on people's experience of work (discussed further in Chapter 4) one effect of just-in-time could be an increase in work intensity, or at least a reduced ability to create greater control over work pace by building up 'banks' of part-finished items, which can be drawn on to ease work pressures at a later point.

Quality

Closely associated with these changes in production processes has been an increased emphasis on output quality. Japanese manufacturers such as Toyota led the way in making the management of quality a key component in overall production and competitive strategy. The increased emphasis on quality has manifested itself in a variety of management initiatives such as quality assurance, quality circles and Total Quality Management (TQM) (Deming, 1982; Hill, 1991; Juran, 1979; Oakland, 1989; Strang and Kim, 2005). This has given rise to additional phrases in management jargon such as 'continuous improvement', 'zero defects', 'internal customers', 'world best practice' and 'right first time'. More emphasis has been given to assuring quality at the point of production rather than at final inspection, in an attempt not only to ensure a better quality product but in particular to avoid the cost of reworking defective output. As discussed in more detail in a later chapter, among the effects of these changes for the experience of work has been an increased emphasis on quality assurance. There has been a requirement for workers to take greater responsibility for inspecting their own work and that of their work colleagues.

To sum up

A major development in the economic context of work is increasing economic globalisation, driven primarily by the expansion of multinational firms. Choices between different competitive strategies impact significantly on the nature of work and employment. Other key changes influencing the experience of work include the increased emphasis on more efficient organisation of production and higher quality output.

Changes in industrial structure and employment

The structure of employment is never static but reflects and marks out patterns of change in particular industries and broader sectors of activity. The pace and some of the contours of change vary from one industrial society to another; nevertheless, a number of broad developments are evident and reflected in the changing structure of employment. Measurement of the structure and location of economic activity, the characteristics of the workforce, the nature of employment contracts and patterns of unemployment, redundancy and insecurity all indicate the aggregate nature of employment and the ways this is changing over time.

A number of measures are interconnected: the simultaneous growth in service sector, female and part-time employment, for example. Also, some of the trends that can be identified are influenced not just by structural shifts in the economy but also by cyclical factors which can accelerate or inhibit longer-term changes. At the same time, what is revealing is the robust nature of many of the structural changes. Cyclical effects such as economic recession, and even more dramatically the Global Financial Crisis, have, in many cases, only had a modest influence on several of the aspects of employment change (e.g. the growth in part-time working). They may temporarily slow some of the trends but rarely cause even a short-term reversal in longer-term developments. This is true even of those aspects of the employment experience, such as redundancy, unemployment and job insecurity, that in the past were closely associated with recession conditions, but in more recent times have seemingly become rather more loosely tied to overall economic conditions (see discussion of job insecurity, and Extract 2.4).

Employment in service and manufacturing industries

Throughout the industrial world, there has been a pronounced and progressive shift in employment from primary and secondary sectors to the tertiary, service sector. In the OECD, seven out of every ten employees work in the service sector, with a growing number of countries registering a level of four-fifths or more of their employees located in services. This contrasts with earlier decades when in 1971, for example, the corresponding proportion of employees working in the service sector in OECD countries was five out of ten, and in 1961 just over four out of ten (Blyton, 1989: 37).

Looking at the UK in more detail, in the period between 1971 and 2011, the number employed in manufacturing in the UK fell by almost 5.4 million or two-thirds (Table 2.1). In the same period, the number employed in services rose by more than 14.3 million, an increase of over 125 per cent. As a consequence, by 2011 over ten times as many people were employed in the service sector in the UK as those in manufacturing. When all industries are taken into account (agriculture, forestry and fishing, mining, electricity, gas and water supply, and construction, as well as manufacturing and services) the proportion of total employees engaged in the service sector in the UK stood at over four-fifths (84%) in 2010 (ONS, 2011), up from just over half (52.6%) of the total employees in employment who worked in services in 1971. In contrast, manufacturing employment by 2010 had fallen to less than one in ten (8.9%) of the total in employment (ibid).

Table 2.1   Changes in employment in UK manufacturing and
services, 1971–2011 (thousands)

	Manufacturing	Services
1971	7,890	11,388
1981	6,107	13,102
1990	4,756	16,643
2001	3,802	20,524
2011 (June)	2,534	25,731
Actual change: 1971–2011:	−5,356	+14,343
Percentage change: 1971–2011:	−67.9%	+125.9%

Sources: Adapted from *Employment Gazette* (Historical Supplement 4)
October 1994 and *Labour Market Trends* (various).

Male and female workers

This increasing predominance of service sector employment has also been
reflected in other changes occurring in the nature of the employed workforce,
particularly the proportions of male and female, and full and part-time workers in
the workforce. The period since the 1970s has witnessed a marked growth in the
proportion of the female workforce. Several factors are important in accounting
for this change, reflecting changes in both the demand for, and supply of, labour
(the available labour or the 'supply-side').

However, 'demand-side' factors – the kind of labour that businesses or customers want, rather than what is available – are dominated by the shift to service sector employment and the increased opportunities for employment among
women in service industries. This has been a key factor behind the increase in
women's overall share in the workforce over the past generation. As Table 2.2
indicates, in the late 1950s, women comprised just over one-third of the total
employed in the UK. By 2011, this proportion stood at over 46 per cent. As the
participation rate of women continues to rise, the reality of a feminised workforce, where a majority of the employees in employment are women, becomes
an increasing possibility. A workforce where the majority are female is already a
reality in several regions in the UK and in various industries, particularly in the
service sector.

Part-time employment

As well as an overall change in employment towards a greater proportion of
jobs being held by women (the majority in the service sector), there has been a
particular growth in the number of people working part-time. Across the EU27
as a whole, almost one in five (19.2%) employees were working part-time in 2010.
However, among the EU member states this proportion varies considerably, with
six countries reporting a part-time proportion greater than one in four of total
employees, while nine countries recorded part-time levels at below one in ten of
total employees (see Table 2.3).

Table 2.2   Number of women and men in employment in Britain, 1959–99, UK, 2011 (thousands)

	1959	1979	1999	2011*
Females	7,174	9,435	11,477	13,521
Males	13,817	13,176	10,967	15,547
Total	20,991	22,611	23,444	29,069
Proportion of females in total	34.2%	41.7%	49.0%	46.6%

*3rd quarter.

Sources: Employment Gazette and *Labour Market Trends*, various dates.

Table 2.3   Persons working part-time in the European Union, 2000, 2010 (percentage of total employment)

	2000	2010
Austria	16.3	25.2
Belgium	18.9	24.0
Bulgaria	...	2.4
Czech Rep.	5.3	5.9
Cyprus	8.4	9.3
Denmark	21.3	26.5
Estonia	8.1	11.0
Finland	12.3	14.6
France	16.7	17.8
Germany	19.4	26.2
Greece	4.5	6.4
Hungary	3.5	5.8
Ireland	16.4	22.4
Italy	8.4	15.0
Latvia	11.3	9.7
Lithuania	10.2	8.1
Luxembourg	10.4	17.9
Malta	6.8	12.4
Netherlands	41.5	48.9
Poland	10.5	8.3
Portugal	10.9	11.6
Romania	16.5	11.0
Slovakia	2.1	3.9
Slovenia	6.5	11.4
Spain	7.9	13.3
Sweden	19.5	26.4
United Kingdom	25.1	26.9
EU27	16.2	19.2

Source: Adapted from Eurostat (http://epp. eurostat.ec.europa.eu).

Exercise 2.3

Over to you…

As noted in the discussion on part-time employment, the proportion of employees who work part-time varies greatly between EU member states. What factors can you think of that might account for this variation?

Across the OECD countries as a whole, over seven out of ten part-time jobs are held by women; in the EU countries the proportion is nearer eight out of ten (in the UK in 2009, 75% of part-time jobs were held by women; ONS, 2010: 50). Overall, around nine out of ten part-time jobs are in the service sector.

Self-employment

In addition to the proportion of the labour force who are employees, there is a significant minority who are self-employed. Among industrial countries in the OECD, levels of self-employment are highest where agriculture and small family businesses remain major sectors of activity: for example, in Greece, Italy, Korea, Mexico, Portugal and Turkey.

In the UK, self-employment increased substantially (by almost half) during the 1980s, primarily because of the twin forces of: (i) high levels of unemployment and limited job vacancies and (ii) state financial support for those moving from being unemployed to self-employed. In addition, as part of their efforts to cut direct labour costs, many companies from the 1980s onwards abandoned employment contracts in favour of commercial contracts by requiring some of their workers to alter their status from being employees to being self-employed. This occurred, for example, among workers operating outside the main workplace, such as service engineers and milk deliverers and, particularly, in the construction sector (see Evans, 1990). Where self-employed individuals are simply selling their skills to an organisation they are sometimes referred to as 'labour only subcontractors', and these comprise a high proportion of the more than two million enterprises with no employees operating in the UK.

In recent years in the UK, the proportion of the total workforce who are self-employed has risen further (14.1% of the overall workforce were self-employed in 2011, compared to 11.1% in 2001). In 2011, 70 per cent (2.9 million) self-employed were men and 72 per cent of the self-employed worked full-time.

The location of employment

Size of employing organisation

It may be common to think of a 'typical' employing organisation as one that is fairly or very large. In fact the vast majority of enterprises with employees operating in the UK employ less than ten people. Only a small percentage employ more than 100 employees and only a small percentage of these are large (500 or more employees) (see Dale and Kerr, 1995). However, the largest businesses account for over one-third of total non-government employment. Large-scale enterprises predominate in the energy and water sector, mining and quarrying, chemicals and parts of the financial sector. Small firms, on the other hand, are particularly numerous in parts of the manufacturing sector (including printing and publishing, furniture and fabricated metal products) as well as in agriculture, construction and most service industries (including business services, entertainment, catering, and vehicle maintenance and repair) (ibid).

In terms of trends in firm size, there is some indication that average firm size is declining and that the proportion of total employees working for smaller firms is gradually increasing. In part, this reflects the shift from manufacturing to service activities (smaller firms being more prevalent in service industries), the closure of many formerly very large establishments (such as steel plants and shipyards) over the past 30 years, and the increase in outsourcing activity by larger firms. Smaller firms also figure prominently in statistics on employment creation. As the OECD has noted, however, 'volatility in employment levels...appears to be an intrinsic characteristic of small businesses' (OECD, 1995: 128). In other words, smaller firms figure prominently in statistics of gross job gains and gross job losses.

Location of work

As employment in production industries, particularly traditional industries such as coal, steel and shipbuilding, has declined, so too has the proportion of total employment located in the main industrial conurbations. There has been a growing tendency to establish and expand service activities and new manufacturing projects on 'greenfield' sites, often in semi-rural areas (Massey 1988; see also Sayer and Walker, 1992). For a significant minority of workers, their work is located in their own homes. One of the areas of growth in homeworking in recent years has been the expansion of teleworking – see Extract 2.2 (also, Felstead, Jewson and Walters, 2005a; Sullivan and Lewis, 2001).

Extract 2.2

Teleworking doubled in size

According to the Labour Force Survey (LFS) analysed by Ruiz and Walling (2005), by the mid-2000s, there were over 2.4 million teleworkers in the UK – that is, workers using both a telephone and a computer to carry out their work, either at home or in different places using home as a base. This total represents a doubling in the proportion of teleworkers in the UK workforce between 1997 and 2005: by 2005 over 8 per cent of the workforce in the UK were teleworkers compared with 4 per cent in 1997.

The LFS reports on two different kinds of teleworker: those working mainly in their own homes, and those working in different places (such as clients' premises, on the train, or in cars) while at the same time using home as a base. In 2005, most teleworkers (1.8 million out of the 2.4 million total) worked in different places using their homes as a base; the remainder (0.6 million) worked mainly in their own homes.

In terms of the characteristics of teleworkers, a majority (62 per cent) were self-employed in 2005. Almost two-thirds (65 per cent) were men, and it is male teleworkers who are particularly likely to telework in different places. Ruiz and Walling's analysis of the LFS also shows that teleworking is more common, and growing at a faster rate, among older workers (50 years and over) than among younger age groups (particularly 16–24 year olds).

In terms of occupation, nine out of ten teleworkers work in managerial, professional, technical and skilled trades occupations. The occupational groups that are most likely to work in their own homes as teleworkers (rather than working in different places) are administrative and secretarial occupations. The rate of teleworking is highest in skilled trades. Among skilled workers, those employed in the building trade are particularly prominent among the teleworking population. The self-employed builder using a computer and telephone to conduct his/her business is a very different picture of a 'typical' teleworker from past stereotypes of white-collar workers being remotely connected to their organisation and using the telephone and computer to undertake tasks at home.

Unemployment, redundancy, temporary work and job insecurity

Unemployment

It is difficult to compare unemployment rates between countries because of different definitions of unemployment. It is also difficult to draw an accurate comparison of present-day rates of unemployment with those of earlier periods. This is complicated by the many changes made to the basis on which unemployment statistics are calculated. In the UK since the late 1970s, for example, there have been over 30 such changes (see Blyton and Turnbull, 2004: 75).

Despite these difficulties, however, important long-term trends in the rate of unemployment in the UK and elsewhere remain evident. The principal pattern in the UK is that levels of unemployment have risen from around 2 per cent in the 1950s and 1960s to a peak of over 11 per cent in the mid-1980s. Even during periods of strong economic growth, unemployment rates have tended to remain higher than the rates during growth periods a generation ago (annual averages throughout the 1990–2011 period, for example, ranged between 5.1 and 8.7%). Table 2.4 shows a comparative picture among industrial countries for the period 2000–10, which indicates that levels of unemployment in many countries were at comparatively high levels at both dates.

Table 2.4   Unemployment rates in 25 industrial countries, selected years 2000–10 (rate as proportion of civilian labour force)

	2000	2010
Austria	3.5	4.4
Belgium	6.9	8.3
Canada	6.8	8.0
Czech Rep.	8.9	7.3
Denmark	4.3	7.3
Finland	9.8	8.4
France	8.5	9.4
Germany	7.5	6.8
Greece	11.4	12.5
Hungary	6.5	11.2
Ireland	4.3	13.5
Italy	10.1	8.4
Japan	4.7	5.1
Luxembourg	2.6	6.0
Netherlands	2.9	4.4
New Zealand	6.1	6.5
Norway	3.4	3.6
Poland	16.1	9.6
Portugal	4.0	10.8
Spain	10.8	20.1
Sweden	6.7	8.4
Switzerland	2.6	4.5
United Kingdom	5.5	7.9
United States	4.0	9.6

Source: Adapted from OECD (2011) Economic Outlook, Paris: OECD.

As well as the variation between countries, unemployment rates vary considerably between different groups. In the UK at the beginning of 2011, for example, the unemployment rate among 16 and 17 year olds was 37.5 per cent, compared to 4.6 per cent for people of 50 years and over (ONS, 2011).

Alongside this trend of gradually rising unemployment over the past four decades, the proportion of the total workforce that has experienced a period of unemployment in recent years is considerable. The prevailing level of unemployment at any particular time comprises the difference between those coming onto the unemployed register and those leaving it. These unemployment 'flows' are far greater than changes in the unemployment level might suggest. Taking the example of an unexceptional month (we have chosen May 2005 to illustrate the point), the level of registered unemployed in that month was down by 4600 compared with the previous month. This figure, however, is the product of an inflow of new unemployment registrations of almost 40 times that amount (202,300) during the month and an outflow of 206,900. In a proportion of cases, the same individuals become unemployed (and re-employed) more than once in any given year, thus figuring several times in the inflow and outflow statistics. Studies have shown that between one-third and two-fifths of new registrations are likely to have previously been unemployed during the same year (DfEE, 1995b: 355). What the magnitude of the flows also underlines, however, is the breadth of experience of unemployment within the workforce as a whole. It is also a contributor to perceptions of job insecurity (see below).

The level of unemployment does not reflect the total picture of job shortage, however. In addition to those officially counted as unable to find work, there are millions more who have become prematurely (and involuntarily) retired, or who have otherwise dropped out of the labour market because of a perceived lack of prospects of finding work. Changes in the participation rates of men in the labour market show the scale of this 'discouragement effect'. The proportion of men of working age who are active in the labour market (in work or registered unemployed) has fallen in several industrial countries over the past two decades. This is to a point where in the UK in 2009, for example, over one in six (17%) males of working age, and not in full-time education, were not active in the labour market (ONS, 2010: 55). This is a degree of inactivity which, in the past, Hutton (1995: 1) identified as having 'incalculable consequences' for overall well-being and social cohesion in the country.

While men's economic activity rate has declined, women's overall activity rate has increased. As a result, the gap in men's and women's activity rates narrowed from 16 to 9 percentage points between 1992 and 2009 (17% inactivity rate for men, 26% for women) (ONS, 2010: 55).

Two further points are worth making in regard to unemployment. First, unemployment and the extent to which people have been made unemployed impacts materially and psychologically on those directly affected. In addition, the impact is extended by a general heightening of awareness of job insecurity and the perceived difficulties that can be experienced in gaining employment once unemployed. These difficulties are clearly expressed in the scale of long-term unemployment. For example, in 2011 almost one-third (33.1%) of those unemployed in the UK had been unemployed for at least a year. Furthermore, there is a disproportionate presence of some groups (such as younger and older workers and ethnic minorities) among the long-term unemployed.

The effect on people's attitudes to work and job insecurity of high levels of unemployment was vividly summed up in the UK back in the 1980s by Ron Todd (then chief negotiator at the Ford Motor Company and later general secretary of the T&GWU), who commented that 'we've got 3 million on the dole and another 23 million scared to death' (quoted by Bratton, 1992: 70). The second point is that the rate of flow of individuals onto unemployed registers has been affected by the circumstances under which redundancies have been declared.

Redundancy

Labour Force Surveys in the UK indicate that between mid-2009 and mid-2011, over 900,000 redundancies took place. Redundancies are nothing new, of course. What is new over the past two decades, however, is the causes of redundancy. In the past, redundancies have been a consequence of economic difficulty, as Cappelli (1995: 577) comments: 'Firms clearly laid off work-ers because of cyclical downturns or other situations where their business declined, but reductions in other situations were extremely uncommon.' However, increasingly common is the tendency for employers to announce redundancies as a cost-cutting measure even at times when the business and the economic outlook are buoyant.

Quoting Cappelli (ibid) again, 'workforce reductions are increasingly "strategic or structural in nature" as opposed to a response to short-term economic condi-tions'. The experience in the UK over the past two decades is very similar: firms announce redundancies when they are doing badly and when they are doing well, with the constant shaving of workforce totals being used as a method of cost con-trol. A key reason for this, Cappelli argues, is that outside the organisation – and particularly among shareholders and investment markets – cutting workforce levels has come to be taken as a sign of restructuring, efficiency-saving and likely improvement in profitability. The upshot is that redundancy announcements can improve share prices. Cappelli (1995: 571) quotes one US study, for example (by Worrell, Davidson and Sharma, 1991), which found that stock prices rose on average by about 4 per cent in the days following layoff announcements that were part of general restructurings (see Extract 2.3). Since 2008, the Global Financial Crisis has changed this picture once again since unemployment has risen across many Western economies, but we should not forget that redundancies are not always simply an economic necessity for organisations. They are also a way of realising cost savings.

Redundancies at Corus

On Thursday 1 February 2001, the Anglo-Dutch steelmaker Corus announced 6050 redundancies in the UK – more than a fifth of its UK workforce. This followed 4500 job losses made the previous year by the company.

The job cuts announced in 2001 involved the ending of iron and steel-making at its large Llanwern plant in south Wales, the closing of two finishing plants also in south Wales, and reductions in workforce totals at several other plants elsewhere in the UK.

On the day of the job cuts announcement, the company's share price, which had been falling in the previous period, immediately jumped by almost a tenth (9.7 per cent) in its value, rising from 74.75 pence on the close of business on 31 January to 82 pence at close on 1 February.

Temporary work

There are a number of categories of work that are temporary in nature, in that they are limited in duration. These include jobs that are casual (the work available only on an ad hoc basis) or seasonal, and those which involve fixed-term contracts and temporary work acquired through agencies. This variety of forms that temporary work can take makes cross-national comparisons of trends in temporary work difficult. The general picture, however, appears to be a mixed one. While some countries (including Australia, France, the Netherlands and Spain) have recorded increases in the relative size of their temporary workforces over the past 20 years, others have been characterised by more stable levels of temporary work.

In the UK, temporary workers represented 6.1 per cent of the total employed population in mid-2011 – a decline from the levels prevailing a decade earlier (Table 2.5).

Of the 1.5 million temporary employees in the UK in 2011, slightly more than half (51.4%) were women. The temporary workforce is distributed across a range of industries, though amongst women a significant proportion of temporary workers are located in teaching, childcare and related occupations, and sales.

Job insecurity

Higher average levels of unemployment over the past two decades, the continuing level of redundancies and (in some countries at least) a higher level of temporary working have all made job insecurity a prominent concern to many contemporary workers. This differs from the realities of work experienced by their counterparts a generation ago (Burchell et al, 1999). Further, as Allen and Henry (1996: 66)

Table 2.5   Temporary employment in the UK, 1996–2011

	1996	2000	2004	2011
Temporary employees (thousands)	1,671	1,696	1,496	1,510
Proportion of total employees (%)	7.4	7.1	6.1	6.1

have pointed out, the growth of subcontracting in the private sector and the move towards contracting out of public services have led to a growth in 'precarious employment'. This is where jobs are secure only for the length of the contract. Bryson and Forth (2010), in their analysis of British Social Attitudes surveys between 1985 and 2009, identify a small but persistent increase in the average level of perceived job insecurity over the period.

Heightened levels of corporate merger and acquisition activity have also added to this feeling of job precariousness.

At the same time, it should be noted that many employees continue to spend a significant part of their career with a single employer (Doogan, 2001, 2009). Thus, overall, while a significant proportion of those in employment build up long service in one organisation, for others, work is a much more precarious affair, with insecurity, redundancy, temporary contracts and unemployment contributing to an overall experience of a fragmented, rather than a unified, working life. This is an experience which Sennett (1998) argues is highly damaging to personal integrity and individual financial solvency, as well as to the degree of societal polarisation between employment-rich and employment-poor households (see Extract 2.4).

Extract 2.4

The end of career?

In the United States at the end of the 1990s, the California Management Review (CMR) published a debate over the end of long-term jobs. One of the leading proponents of 'the end of career' thesis, Peter Cappelli (1999), argued that a number of factors have combined to bring the 'jobs for life' era to an end. These include: competitive pressures, volatile markets, more demanding shareholders, the need for flexibility, weaker trade unions, changing skill requirements and technological advances. His thesis is that a prolonged period of widespread, permanent, full-time employment with predictable advancement is over. This is being progressively replaced by shorter-term employment relationships. Richard Sennett (1998: 22) argues a similar point, commenting that the motto of contemporary capitalism is 'no long term'.

The alternative viewpoint in the CMR debate is put by Sanford Jacoby (1999), who argued that this portrayal of contemporary industrial society is not adequately supported by labour market evidence, and is thus inaccurate. Jacoby argues that measures such as average job tenure, and more generally the continuing experience of work in many public and private sector industries, indicate that long-term employment relationships remain widespread. Jacoby suggests the notion of long-term careers is far from over. This counter-argument agrees that there are changes occurring, both in the overall labour market and within individual organisations, but that these do not amount to support for an 'end of career' thesis.

Exercise 2.4

Over to you...

1. Which of the arguments described in Extract 2.4 do you find the more convincing? Give reasons for your answer based on your own career plans or experiences.
2. If Cappelli's argument is at least partially correct, what do you think are the main implications for
   (i) employees and (ii) those managing employees?

To sum up

Developments in the structure of work and employment have significantly changed workforce composition. This is notable in terms of the size and location of workforces, the distribution of employment between service and manufacturing sectors, the proportion of male and female workers, the proportion of those working part and full-time and the proportion of those working as employees or self-employed. Unemployment, redundancy and the use of non-permanent contracts have created a heightened sense of insecurity for many employees.

Conclusion

This chapter has illustrated some of the ways in which broader influences and developments impact upon the everyday realities of work. Political policies, from local planning decisions to national strategies on deregulation, to the harmonisation of employment conditions across countries, have significantly influenced the context for work. With the growing integration of many national economies into multinational associations such as the EU, the transnational political influences on work are likely to be increasingly evident. This may be at the expense of both national and local political mechanisms.

This increasing economic and political association between different blocs of countries has also been one of the influences on levels and patterns of competition within individual sectors and markets. The growth in competition in general can be seen to have affected the experience of work in various ways. In particular, this may have been experienced through a more intensive managerial search for both performance improvement and labour cost reduction.

The consequences of these objectives are visible in a variety of managerial strategies concerning the workforce. They also reflect broader political conditions, such as the degree of statutory regulation of employment and the national provision of education and training. Competitive pressures from rising industrial nations have also led to fundamental restructuring of developed industrial societies. These have experienced a decline in many of the sectors on which their industrialism was initially built (such as coal, steel, textiles and shipbuilding), as well as a growth in other, primarily service sector, industries. This shift has been reflected not only in a decrease in manual and rise in non-manual jobs but also in major changes in workforce composition. The prominence of male production workers has given way to an increasingly feminised workforce, and one in which a significant proportion of employees work part-time.

In addition, an important change in the overall context of work over the past generation has been the degree to which work has become a more precarious activity. Indefinite employment and long service with a single employer have, for many, given way to a more fragmented job history. Higher levels of unemployment, coupled with high redundancy rates and job insecurity, have resulted in a growing proportion of the workforce experiencing paid employment as an intermittent, rather than a regular, activity. One issue this raises is whether, as work becomes more fragmented and as the experience of non-work becomes more common, the values associated with work also show signs of being in decline. In the following chapter we examine the concept of work values more closely.

3

The meaning of work

Key concepts

▷ economic necessity to work

▷ moral necessity to work

▷ extrinsic rewards

▷ intrinsic rewards

▷ consumption

▷ post-materialism

▷ the work ethic

▷ disciplined compliance

▷ conscientious endeavour

▷ work centrality

▷ work obligation/duty

▷ post-industrial society

▷ leisure society

▷ the psychological contract

Chapter aim

To assess why people work, with particular emphasis on the economic and moral dimensions of work.

Learning outcomes

After reading and thinking about the material in this chapter, you will be able to:

1. Evaluate the importance of the economic need to work.
2. Assess the economic commitment to employment drawing on survey evidence.
3. Explain the meaning of the work ethic.
4. Analyse four key themes of the work ethic:

    a. work as an obligation;

    b. work as a central life activity;

    c. work as conscientious endeavour;

    d. work as disciplined compliance.

5. Outline and evaluate theoretical perspectives that explain the change in the work ethic.
6. Explain how changes in the work ethic might be linked to changes in the psychological contract.

Introduction

Paid work is one of the principal means by which we evaluate others. In this chapter we explore the concept of work, and assess why so much emphasis is placed upon what a person does for a living. Our main concern is to analyse the reasons why people work (see Extract 3.1).

We assess the meaning of work in terms of two features: the economic necessity to work and the moral necessity to work. In relation to the economic necessity, we explore the material reasons for working, and ask whether people would carry on some form of work even if they had no financial need to do so. In terms of the moral necessity we introduce the concept of a 'work ethic', which supposedly encourages people to work irrespective of any economic necessity. In the remaining sections of the chapter, we reflect on how contemporary changes might be affecting the work ethic, in particular the issues of the development of the post-industrial society, of greater leisure and of changes in the psychological contract.

Reasons for working

The following are all direct quotes from people about their work. They illustrate how the meaning of work differs between individuals and they highlight some of the key issues this chapter explores. Read the quotes and then try Exercise 3.1.

I enjoy being in work to a certain extent. I don't enjoy the work. But I actually enjoy being here. There are a lot of friends in work…. It's merely a means to an end to get the money at the end of the month and that's all it is. My home life is far more important than my work life. I know I have to have the job. I have to do the work. But I value the home life far more than I do the work life. (Male)

I'm happy working, it does quite a lot for my, sort of self-confidence I think. It's probably very important, you know…. I can't see me being the type of person who would be just happy being at home…. I don't think I'm that type of person. (Female)

It's my duty isn't it as, like, a father to actually go to work and provide for my kids. (Male)

I enjoy being with people you know, I do enjoy working with people like. I don't think I would if I had to – I don't think I would give up work…. I used to think when I had my first daughter I'd love to give up but no. I don't think I could be in the house all day. (Female)

I've never, ever not worked because I've never taken any time off for maternity or anything like that. So I've always worked and it is important to me…. Work, the job I'm actually doing now is a big part of my life […] I take a lot of it home even if it's not carring it home, it's in my mind. I don't switch off. (Female)

If I didn't work, I'd probably end up going sort of stupid…. I think working is one of the most important things in the world, if you want to survive and better yourself you've got to have money. And it means working. (Male)

I don't enjoy being home. I get the buzz. I enjoy working with people. I enjoy the customers. And now I enjoy the authority…sad but there I am. But I do enjoy the job. (Female)

I like working. It gets you out of the house. You socialise, you've got friends…. I'd hate to be unemployed. I like to be active. I just love, well I don't love work, nobody loves work, that's a stupid thing to say. But it's what makes the world go round at the end of the day. (Male)

I am enjoying my life so much because…I'm enjoying my work. Even Saturday or Sunday, all right, I would read work related stuff. I'm not a nerd, I also go out to watch movies and that sort of thing, but I enjoy it so much that I don't really take it as a job. I take it as part of my life and I do that anyway. Like if I'm not getting paid I would still study that sort of thing. I would read it in my leisure time anyway and making it a part of my job I make money from it. So it is a paradise. Heaven. (Male)

Sources: The final quote is from Barrett (2004: 789); the other quotes are from Charles and James (2003: 247–51).

What do you think?

1. Identify the key reasons for working that emerge from the quotes in Extract 3.1.
2. What factors might you expect to influence the attitudes to work shown in the quotes?
3. Compare the quotes from the men with those from the women. What did you find?

The economic necessity to work

Working to live

Intuitively, we know people work in order to earn money to live; it is through paid work that basic needs are satisfied because it provides money for subsistence (food, housing, clothes and so on). However, there is a major problem with accepting this argument as it stands. Can we really talk about the need to work for the purpose of subsistence when most societies provide a welfare system that (in theory at least) prevents people from falling below a basic level of subsistence? Social welfare provision in the form of unemployment benefit, housing allowances and free medical care were specifically designed to act as a safety net, preventing people from becoming destitute. It is the prime example of the state's intervention to stop its citizens being left totally at the mercy of market forces.

Both right-wing and left-wing politicians have argued that the state benefit/welfare system can act as a deterrent to work because it provides a supposedly satisfactory standard of living. The issue arises because in some situations someone could undertake a week's work in a low-paid job and receive comparable income to someone claiming welfare benefits. Moreover, when people take a low-paid job after being on unemployment benefit, they often lose their entitlement to other allowances (such as housing). As a consequence they find themselves financially worse off. This is the classic poverty trap – where the welfare system can act as a financial disincentive to work, even though the person may be keen to be employed.

Some governments have recognised this problem of financial disincentives and have introduced a range of 'in work' benefits: means-tested allowances that can be claimed while in employment. Critics of this policy argue that it exacerbates the problem by effectively subsidising employers who pay low wages. Indeed, it actively discourages them from increasing wages as the employee would lose benefit, and the employer would have to take up the supplement currently funded by the taxpayer. There are two alternative policy solutions which both focus on increasing the differentials between paid work and benefit, although they differ dramatically in their approach:

1. Lower state benefits: this approach considers that benefits are the problem, suggesting the need to lower unemployment allowances and other welfare payments to increase the incentive to work for low wages, thus making unemployment seem 'less attractive'.
2. Raise low wages: this approach is aimed at increasing low wages, typically through setting a national minimum wage, which would similarly increase the differential between those who were in work and out of work, but which would be aimed at making low-paid work 'more attractive'.

Working to consume

As this discussion suggests, in developed capitalist economies it is not just that people need to work to subsist; rather, people work to earn money to acquire consumer power. Money is the means to the goal of consumption, whether that is commodity consumption (smart phones, designer clothes, cars and so forth) or service consumption (drinking, gambling, eating out, using the gym and holidaying). The central, distinguishing feature between those people in work and those who are unemployed is that the former have much higher (although varied) levels of consumer power, and consequently more choice about their lifestyles. This rise of consumption has been one of the fundamental developments of the twentieth century (Ransome, 2005), and some commentators suggest that the nature of consumption has changed in recent years, from mass to niche markets (Piore and Sabel, 1984). This has helped to sustain consumption as one of the defining features of our identity. Moreover, others argue that consumption has become so important that the experience of shopping can be seen as a leisure activity in its own right (Featherstone, 1990).

Given the importance of the link between work and spending power, it is hardly surprising that when asked, most people will say that earning money is the prime reason they go to work (or want to work in the case of the unemployed). This unremarkable observation was verified in the UK by researchers working on a major project entitled the Social Change and Economic Life Initiative (SCELI). We refer to this several times in this book. The researchers questioned people about their reasons for wanting a job, and from analysis of over 5000 responses they found that the majority (68%) worked for the money, either to provide for basic essentials, or in the case of 27 per cent to buy extra things and enjoy some economic independence from the primary earner in the household.

Perhaps the most surprising aspect of this finding is that the figure is not higher than 68 per cent. To uphold the (intuitive) assumption that people work simply for extrinsic reward (money), we might have predicted the figure to be 95 per cent or more. However, an astonishing 26 per cent said that they did not work for the money, but for 'expressive' reasons, in other words for the intrinsic rewards work can bring, such as enjoyment, satisfaction and a sense of achievement. Moreover the percentage of people indicating these expressive reasons remained very similar irrespective of the gender or employment status of the respondent. (See Table 3.1 for a summary, and Rose, 1994, for a comprehensive analysis of the SCELI data.)

Table 3.1   Summary of the SCELI findings on the reasons for working

	Full-time		Part-time		Self-employed		Unemployed		Housewife returners	Totals
	Men	Women	Men	Women	Men	Women	Men	Women		
Sample size	1786	1026	21	802	248	118	457	272	480	5210
Monetary reasons	75%	69%	77%	66%	69%	60%	69%	65%	65%	68%
Expressive reasons	26%	27%	28%	21%	29%	34%	25%	25%	21%	26%
Other reasons	1%	7%	3%	14%	2%	7%	4%	10%	14%	6%

Source: Adapted from Rose (1994: 294).

Post-materialism

The fact that a significant minority of people say they work for intrinsic reward leads some commentators to argue that materialist values in advanced capitalist societies are waning. Inglehart (1997) suggests people are increasingly opting for interesting and meaningful work, rather than high salaries. This reflects a 'post-materialist' orientation to work, emphasising quality of life. The term 'downshifting' is sometimes used to describe people who have given up high-flying careers and large salaries for a less work-focused, less-materialist way of living (see also Hamilton, 2003). While this post-materialist lifestyle is undoubtedly adopted by some people, the key question is, how widespread has it become? Is it the start of a new trend, or merely the response of a small minority of people to the increasingly stressful nature of work?

An analysis of this hypothesised increase in post-materialism was undertaken by Russell (1998) using data from the International Social Survey Programme. Her analysis focused on a comparison between three European countries (Britain, West Germany and Italy) in two periods of time, 1989 and 1997. The survey measured a range of attitudes to work which generated an overall score for extrinsic and intrinsic work attitudes in each country. The post-materialist thesis predicts that, compared with 1989, the score in 1997 for the extrinsic value of work will have decreased while the score for the intrinsic value will have increased. The results (see Table 3.2) reveal a mixed picture, which led Russell to conclude that while there is some evidence of post-materialist values, the overall thesis is not borne out by the data. To explore how this conclusion might have been reached, try Exercise 3.2. We return to the issue of downshifting, and other responses that individuals can make to achieve a better 'work–life balance', in Chapter 13.

Table 3.2   Comparison of extrinsic and intrinsic work values

	Britain		Western Germany		Italy	
	1989	1997	1989	1997	1989	1997
Overall extrinsic value score	3.2	3.1	3.2	3.1	3.2	3.2
Overall intrinsic value score	3.3	3.2	3.4	3.4	3.3	3.2
No. of respondents	750	604	703	722	611	530

Notes: Respondents were asked 'How important do you personally think the following items are in a job?': high income; job security; good opportunities for advancement; an interesting job; a job that allows someone to work independently. Their responses were scored on a scale of 0 to 4 – the higher the score, the higher adherence to the particular item being considered. An extrinsic value score for each respondent was calculated by averaging the first three items. An intrinsic value score was based on the last two items. The overall score for extrinsic and intrinsic value is the average across all respondents.

Source: Adapted from Russell (1998: 92).

The commitment to employment

International evidence

One of the most comprehensive international comparative studies is the *Meaning of Working* survey (MOW, 1987) which analyses evidence from eight countries. Respondents from these countries were asked what they would do about work if they acquired a large sum of money and could live comfortably for the rest of their lives without working. This is known as the 'lottery question', and it is frequently used by social researchers in order to get a general view about a person's commitment to employment.

The responses to the lottery question are presented in Table 3.3, ranked according to country. Although the majority of people in each country would continue to work, the table suggests that it is in Britain and Germany where the greatest proportion of people indicated they would stop working. These proportions are noticeably higher than the next ranked country, Belgium (around 30% for Britain and Germany, compared with 16% for Belgium). When looking at proportions of people who would continue in the same job or who would want to work under different conditions are examined, the ranking is almost reversed. Respondents from Japan and Yugoslavia (and to a lesser degree, Israel) demonstrate the highest commitment to their existing employment. In contrast, respondents from Britain are the least inclined to want to remain in their existing job. Similarly, for the United States, Belgium, Germany and the Netherlands a greater proportion of people would want to continue to work under different conditions than remain in the same job, although the differences between the proportions are much smaller than those in Britain. Taken overall, the MOW data suggests people generally have a commitment to employment (although not necessarily to their current job), and that this is affected by national setting as well as age, occupation, individual differences and life experiences.

Table 3.3 Responses to the lottery question from the *Meaning of Working* survey

Percentage of respondents who, if they were financially secure, said they would:					
Stop working		Continue working in the same job		Continue working but under different conditions	
Ranking					
1	Britain	31	Japan	66	Britain	53
2	Germany	30	Yugoslavia	62	USA	49
3	Belgium	16	Israel	50	Belgium	47
4	Netherlands	14	Netherlands	42	Netherlands	44
5	USA	12	USA	39	Germany	39
6	Israel	12	Belgium	37	Israel	37
7	Japan	7	Germany	31	Yugoslavia	34
8	Yugoslavia	4	Britain	16	Japan	27

Source: Adapted from MOW International Research Team (1987).

British evidence

A survey of employment in Britain (Gallie and White, 1993) assessed the attitudes of 3855 people in 1992 regarding a wide range of issues concerned with work. When asked the lottery question, 67 per cent of people indicated they would continue to work, and there was very little difference in the replies of men and women (68% compared with 67%). Assuming this sample is representative, it suggests the majority of people derive more from work than their salary.

It could be argued that intrinsic satisfaction depends on the nature of the job being done, and that professional workers might be more inclined to stay at work than semi-skilled manual workers, regardless of financial security. Gallie and White (1993) took this into consideration in their analysis and found that the majority of people in all job categories would continue to work even if there was no financial need, although the proportions increased, the higher the job levels of the respondents. In addition, the survey revealed that employment commitment was highest among people in their early 20s and declined with age.

The general picture is that most survey respondents were committed to the principle of being employed, but it is important to note the following points:

- They were not necessarily committed to their particular jobs.
- They were not committed to working full-time, but rather stated a preference for a working week of between 16 and 30 hours.
- They did not necessarily want to maintain their existing conditions of employment, such as work environment and location.

A further point to think about is that the respondents may have been reflecting the socially desirable norm of being 'in work' rather than demonstrating an individual commitment to employment. We return to this issue later in the chapter when we consider the moral necessity to work, but for now let us assume that the respondents are committed to employment. This prompts an additional question: 'What causes individual commitment to work?'

From their analysis of further questions asked in the survey, Gallie and White (1993: 67–9) isolate seven influences on employment commitment. To summarise their argument, we can say that employment commitment will be stronger:

- the more qualifications the person has;
- the greater their feeling of having been successful in their career;
- the higher they value 'hard work';
- the more they feel they have personal control over their destiny;
- the higher their preference for their current job;
- the lower their preference for 'an easy life';
- the higher their attachment to their current organisation.

Of course, this does not mean all these influences have to be present before a person feels committed to employment, but it indicates the possible range of influential factors.

To sum up

The evidence suggests it is not enough simply to argue that people work for extrinsic rewards. Clearly, income beyond the subsistence level is an important reason for working, but surveys reveal that a substantial minority of people work for reasons other than money (the expressive needs, noted above), and that a majority of people say they would continue to work even if there was no financial need to do so. It seems that other factors influence attitudes to work; factors which, some have argued, include a moral necessity to work.

Exercise 3.2

What do you think?

If you currently have a job (part-time or full-time), try this next time you are at work.

- Ask your co-workers the lottery question.
- Encourage them to explain their answers.

Write down a few notes to remind yourself of their opinions, then later on answer the following questions:

1. How similar or different are their responses from each other?
2. How might you explain any differences of response?
3. How do their responses compare with those from the research reported in this chapter?

The moral necessity to work

Implicit in much of the discussion in the previous section is the idea that work is 'good': a virtuous, dignified and worthy activity for people to engage in. In other words, there is a moral dimension to work, commonly accepted by society, which values endeavour and enterprise through employment above leisure. Being 'in work' becomes morally desirable irrespective of any financial or social benefit to the individual. This moral dimension to work is usually called 'the work ethic', and it has traditionally been associated with characteristics such as diligence, punctuality, obedience, honesty and sobriety. So, where does this moral dimension to work come from? And what relevance does it have for understanding contemporary orientations to employment?

One of the best accounts of the development of the work ethic in the UK is provided by Anthony (1977). Drawing on Weber (1930), he traces the work ethic from the roots of Protestantism in the seventeenth century, which defined work as a religious calling, through either the Lutheran belief that a state of grace could be achieved through endeavour, or the Calvinist doctrine of predestination whereby work became part of a lifestyle demonstrating one's salvation. The

Protestant work ethic became the foundation upon which the ideology of work associated with industrialisation and capitalism was built. As Anthony (1977: 44) argues:

> Work had every advantage. It was good in itself. It satisfied the selfish economic interest of the growing number of small employers or self-employed. It was a social duty, it contributed to social order in society and to moral worth in the individual. It contributed to a good reputation among one's fellows and to an assured position in the eyes of God.

Similarly, in his consideration of the work ethic in the United States, Rodgers (1978: 14) argues:

> The central premise of the work ethic was that work was the core of moral life. Work made men useful in a world of economic scarcity. It staved off the doubts and temptations that preyed on idleness, it opened the way to deserved wealth and status, it allowed one to put the impress of mind and skill on the material world.

Other commentators have noted how the work ethic seems to be a feature of a wide range of societies and have suggested that it seems to be a universal human value (see Extract 3.2).

Extract 3.2

The work ethic: a universal concept?

The work ethic is often referred to as the Protestant work ethic in the UK and Australia, and in the United States as the Judeo-Christian ethic. These religious labels have sometimes been used to imply there are distinct features to the work ethic that make it prevalent only in Protestant-dominated countries. As we note in the main text, these usually emphasise the value and importance of duty, commitment, effort and obedience. However, commentators have suggested that these features of the work ethic can be found in many cultures and among many nationalities, so it is not uniquely Protestant. To illustrate this point, consider the quotes below.

The Islamic work ethic

The concept of the Islamic work ethic (IWE) has its origin in the Quran, the sayings and practice of Prophet Mohammed, who preached that hard work caused sins to be absolved and that 'no one eats better food than that which he eats out of his work'. For instance, the Quran often speaks about honesty and justice in trade, and it calls for an equitable and fair distribution of wealth in the society. The Quran encourages humans to acquire skills and technology, and highly praises those who strive in order to earn a living. The Quran is against laziness and waste of time by either remaining idle or engaging oneself in unproductive activity .... The Islamic work ethic views dedication to work as a virtue. Sufficient effort should go into one's work, which is seen as obligatory for a capable individual.

In addition, work is considered to be a source of independence and a means of fostering personal growth, self-respect, satisfaction and self-fulfilment. The IWE stresses creative work as a source of happiness and accomplishment.

Hard work is seen as a virtue, and those who work hard are more likely to get ahead in life. Conversely, not working hard is seen to cause failure in life.

(Ali, 1988)

In brief, the Islamic work ethic argues that life without work has no meaning and engagement in economic activities is an obligation.

(Yousef, 2001: 153)

The Buddhist work ethic

Reading from interpretations of Buddha's teaching on the ethics of material progress (Nanayakkara, 1992)…Buddha encouraged the proper utilization of human resources to develop the economy. Therefore he presented a very effective work ethic to motivate the workforce. But this work ethic encouraged teamwork and in its widest connotation meant an appropriate attitude toward work. Religion seems to play a major role in this and it is argued that contrary to popular belief that Buddhism is pessimistic in outlook, there is abundant textual evidence that Buddha formulated a work ethic that encouraged workers to put forth their best effort. Buddha singled out laziness as a cause of the downfall of men and nations and urged that everyone should put forth effort. He stressed that one should be one's own master. He encouraged qualities such as initiative, striving, persistence, etc.

(Niles, 1999: 858)

The Catholic work ethic

Roman Catholic bishops will instruct their flocks that manual work can be a remedy for self-indulgence, dishonesty and individualism. A paper, 'The Spirituality of Work', by a committee set up by the bishops of England and Wales, states that going out to work does not guarantee salvation, but it helps. However, the paper also issues a warning of one danger of work: 'It is a prime way of creating wealth, and so presents the risk of serving only to fill the human horizon with a lust for wealth and possessions.' The committee of Catholic laity and workers sets out a list of prayers, hymns and meditation for use in the workplace. They should be used while giving 'proper attention to safety at work', the paper advises. The concept of the 'work ethic' as promoted by St Paul, traditionally thought of as a Protestant ideal, is embraced. 'Mother Teresa of Calcutta understood that all people were called to holiness – even journalists' the paper states. The committee cites the suggestion in St Paul's letter to the Ephesians 'that manual work, or labour, is a suitable remedy for individualist, self-indulgent and dishonest styles of life'.

(*The Times*, 16 January 2001)

Although the notion of the work ethic is appealing, it presents us with an analytical problem: how do we disentangle the notion of a moral commitment to work from that of an economic need to work? Can we really argue that there was a general acceptance of a work ethic in industrialising nations before the birth of social welfare systems? And even after the emergence of decent wages, is the moral dimension to work any easier to pin down?

To answer these questions, four key themes associated with the work ethic need to be examined:

1. Work as an obligation (emphasising duty).
2. Work as the central life activity (emphasising commitment).
3. Work as conscientious endeavour (emphasising effort).
4. Work as disciplined compliance (emphasising obedience).

Each of these will be considered in turn, although as the discussion reveals, in practice there is an overlap and merging of the themes.

Work as an obligation

This theme reflects the importance of doing your utmost to seek paid employment rather than remaining 'idle'. Studies of the attitudes of the unemployed reveal there is a widespread desire not to be perceived as 'lazy'. This might encourage work even if levels of pay are only marginally higher than unemployment benefit (see, for example, Turner, Bostyn and Wight, 1985). To a large extent this may be the result of the desire to be a 'good provider' for one's family. A study of basic life values conducted in the mid-1960s (Yankelovich, 1973) revealed that 80 per cent of US adults linked the importance of being the breadwinner to masculinity. So, being 'in work' not only conferred economic power on the individual, but it also helped to forge a masculine identity – a man who was unemployed was not only unable to provide for his family, he was also less of a man. Other studies have echoed the association between employment and male identify. For instance, McKee and Bell (1986: 141) comment:

> The loss of the male economic provider struck deep chords among both wives and husbands and a passionate defence of men's right to provide was invariably raised…. Fundamental emotions concerning self-esteem, self-image, pride, views of masculinity, respectability and authority resounded in the expressions of both men and women.

Alternatively, it could be argued that the growth of unemployment in Western capitalist societies means the perception that work is the way to becoming a 'breadwinner' is being eroded. It is a forceful argument, particularly when there has been an abandonment of the political commitment to achieving full employment. This means some of the responsibility for this chance lies with the government for failing to provide enough jobs. In other words, as Offe (1985: 142–3) puts it:

> [As] the experience (or the anticipation) of unemployment, or involuntary retirement from working life increases, the more the effect of moral stigmatisation and self-stigmatisation generated by unemployment probably wears off because, beyond a certain threshold (and especially if unemployment is concentrated in certain regions or in certain industries), it can no longer be accounted for plausibly in terms of individual failure or guilt.

But the opposite might also be the case. When work is in short supply, the value placed on it (its scarcity value) rises. This can help to explain why most of the unemployed continue to search for work even when economic conditions offer little hope of secure, long-term, full-time employment. In a further twist to the argument, it may be suggested that when people are faced with unemployment, they are likely to cope much better (in terms of their mental health) if they do not see work as a duty (Warr, 1987). In other words, a strong work ethic might help motivate some people to hunt for work, but it might have a detrimental effect on their ability to cope if they are unable to find a suitable job. On the other hand, a weak work ethic may help some people accept being unemployed, but in so doing it could also inhibit their motivation to gain employment.

Figure 3.1   National comparisons in attitudes to work entitlement and obligation

An attempt to assess the pervasiveness of 'work as a duty' was undertaken in the international survey on the *Meaning of Working* (MOW, 1987). The researchers examined two issues:

* *obligation to work*: the view that everyone must work to the best of their ability and thereby contribute to society;
* *entitlement to work*: the view that everyone should have the right to a meaningful and interesting job with proper training.

These are two separate dimensions, and so an individual's orientation to both can be measured. The MOW researchers were able to plot the responses from each country to demonstrate how the orientation to (1) obligation to work (duties) and (2) entitlement to work (rights) can vary in different national settings. The important aspect to consider from these findings is the overall balance exhibited by respondents from each country – these differences are illustrated in Figure 3.1.

Work as a central life activity

This theme stresses that paid work is the most important part of life, coming before all non-work activities. Some of the most revealing empirical evidence can again be found in the *Meaning of Working* survey (ibid: 79–93). The researchers defined work centrality as 'the degree of general importance that working has in the life of an individual at any given point in time' (ibid: 81). They developed a method of measuring work centrality that involved asking people to assess working against four other important aspects of their lives: family, community, religion and leisure. Overall, the analysis revealed that in terms of importance and significance, respondents judged work second only to family. In the combined national samples, 40 per cent placed family as most important, while 27 per cent placed working as most important among these five key life roles (ibid: 252). Of additional interest are the effects of three variables: age, nationality and gender. The first two we shall deal with briefly, but the third warrants more detailed comment.

Effect of age

A person's work centrality tends to increase with age. The finding is perhaps not surprising given that people may be promoted or take on more responsibility within an organisation the older they get. This is coupled with the tendency for a person's social life to 'slow down' with age (though family is likely to take a more central role).

Effect of nationality

Work centrality varies according to national differences. The MOW survey data suggested that respondents from Japan were considerably more work-centred than other countries; in Britain, respondents displayed the lowest degree of work centrality.

Effect of gender

Men typically have higher work centrality than women. Caution should be exercised in interpreting this finding, however, because it does not necessarily mean that women are innately less interested in work; rather it might reflect the different roles widely expected of men and women. It is still the case that domestic obligations (particularly cleaning, cooking and childcare) are disproportionately undertaken by women (see Chapter 12). This not only requires them to be less work-centred (more time and thought must be devoted to the family) but also provides an alternative focus to their lives from which they might derive a sense of fulfilment. As Hakim points out, there has been a failure to recognise how the female labour force is composed of at least two distinct groups that differ dramatically in work orientations: those who choose full-time work, and those who choose the homemaker role. She states:

> [The first] group has work commitment similar to that of men, leading to long-term workplans and almost continuous full-time work, often in jobs with higher status and earnings than are typical for women. The second group has little or no commitment to paid work and a clear preference for the homemaker role; paid employment is a secondary activity, usually undertaken to earn a supplementary wage rather than as primary breadwinner, and is in low-skilled, low-paid, part-time, casual and temporary jobs more often than in skilled, permanent full-time jobs.

> (Hakim, 1991: 113)

Of course, it is debatable whether women are really as free to choose their roles as Hakim suggests. As we argue in other chapters, patriarchy (rule by a male elite) constrains these 'choices' (for analysis of the key debates see Crompton, 2002; McRae, 2003; Walby, 1986, 1990, 1997). Nevertheless, for men, the choice of being homemaker is still not widely accepted by society. In that sense, the moral obligation to be work-centred is more imposed on men than women. The general expectation by employers is that a man will want a full-time job, whereas a woman may settle for part-time work.

In addition to domestic obligations, there may be structural reasons for the lower work centrality reported by women. As we note throughout the book, women more frequently have jobs with lower pay and benefits, lower status, less autonomy, less responsibility and less job security. Also, these poor-quality terms and conditions are frequently a feature of part-time jobs, the majority of which are undertaken by women (see Chapter 2). This is perpetuated because of a widely held assumption that women (in general) have low work centrality. This means a woman in a full-time job is frequently faced with male managers and co-workers who assume she is less committed to a career in the organisation because she may leave to start a family (supposedly deferring to her family-centred values):

> Managers' perceptions of job requirements and procedures for assessing merit have been shown to be saturated with gendered assumptions. ... Feminists can argue (as they have for years) that not all women get pregnant, but it seems unlikely that this will stop managers thinking 'yes, but no men will'.
>
> (Liff and Wajcman, 1996: 89)

Finally, it is worth noting how these possible reasons for lower work centrality can link together. The imbalance of domestic responsibilities means that many women find part-time work more convenient, and consequently find themselves in jobs which are both intrinsically and extrinsically poorly rewarded. In this instance, employment becomes de-centred, yet is endured to provide either an adequate income for the family or an independent income for the women. So among women working part-time, or women not in paid employment, it would not be surprising to find lower work centrality. The proper way to assess whether gender affects work orientation would be to compare like with like: men and women in full-time jobs with similar status and terms and conditions. In practice, this is an extremely difficult comparison to make given the horizontal (in terms of occupation) and vertical (in terms of seniority) segregation of labour by gender. Many occupations are horizontally segregated – occupations such as nursing and hairdressing are predominantly female, while engineering and the building trades are dominated by men. Occupations are also often vertically segregated – most senior positions are held by men. An analysis comparing men and women with similar qualifications suggests gender differences have changed. Evaluating the findings from UK surveys carried out between the mid-1980s and the early 2000s, Rose (2005) argues there has been a convergence between male and female attitudes. More women say they look on work to provide necessities, independence and money rewards over the long term. Also, fewer men say they see themselves as the natural breadwinner.

Irrespective of gender, Moorhouse (1984) challenges the view that for most people work is a central life activity in any sense other than occupying the majority of their waking hours. He argues there is a need to distinguish between what people find important (qualitatively central) from what occupies large amounts of their time (quantitatively central). It is only the former, he argues, that offers any sociological insight into working lives. The MOW (1987) research revealed a high work centrality on both measures: people found work important and it occupied large amounts of their time. But, like all the surveys of this type, it still leaves us with the conundrum of whether people find work important because it occupies large amounts of their time – in other words, to use Moorhouse's terms, whether its quantitative centrality determines its qualitative centrality. In addition, such an approach fails to broach an arguably more interesting question: whether people think work ought to be so central (both qualitatively and quantitatively). In part we can address this issue by examining the third theme of the work ethic: conscientious endeavour.

Work as conscientious endeavour

This theme of the work ethic emphasises the importance of doing a job diligently. No matter how menial the task, the individual is encouraged to put effort and care into it in order to produce the best outcome. It is summed up in the maxim: 'If a job's worth doing, it's worth doing well.'

A contemporary expression of this can be seen in the management rhetoric of 'customer care'. Typically, these are initiatives requiring employees not only to show great respect but also to make customers feel as though they are being individually looked after. This increasingly requires employees to manage their own emotions to elicit a good feeling in the minds of the customers. This 'emotion work' is being recognised as so important for the competitiveness of contemporary organisations that even people in low-paid, low-status jobs such as shop work are required to be increasingly diligent in this aspect of their work. This issue is explored in detail in Chapter 7.

The theme of conscientious endeavour also implies activity, whether this is physical or mental. The extent of activity of course varies from job to job and task to task. People may place different value on different forms of activity – in particular the difference between manual and non-manual work. Those who value the former tend to invoke the idea of dignity in physical labour, and sometimes suggest that a person has not really done 'a fair day's work' unless they have 'got their hands dirty'. The stress on the virtue of practical rather than knowledge- or emotion-based activity has often been used to differentiate work supposedly suited to men from that supposedly suited to women. In effect this has supported gender divisions at work by creating an artificial, gendered notion of what constitutes skilled work (see Chapter 5). It has increasingly defined customer contact jobs as emotion based, and therefore more suited to women (see Chapter 7). The importance of the physicality of work for men is neatly summed up in the following quotes from male printer workers in Cockburn's study of technological change in the printing industry:

> I like to do a man's job. And this means physical labour and getting dirty, you understand ... working brings dignity to people I think, they are doing something useful, they are working with these [he demonstrated his hands] that have been provided for that. That's what it is all about. Craftsmanship.
>
> (Quoted in Cockburn, 1983: 52)

> People have to work and get their hands dirty, you get more satisfaction out of it than those people that sit there, you know, like a tailor's dummy at an office desk.
>
> (Ibid: 108)

The roots of this notion of work lie deep and are particularly evident in working-class culture, especially among men (see, for example, Collinson, 1992). This is vividly illustrated by Willis's classic study of a group of working-class 'lads' which reveals how a counter-school culture constructs and reinforces the value of physical labour over mental work:

> Manual labour is outside the domain of school and carries with it ... the aura of the real adult world. Mental work demands too much, and encroaches – just as the school does – too far upon those areas which are increasingly adopted as their own, as private and independent .... Thus physical labouring comes to stand for and express, most importantly, a kind of masculinity and also an opposition to authority .... It expresses aggressiveness; a degree of sharpness and wit; an irreverence that cannot be found in words; an obvious kind of solidarity. It provides the wherewithal for adult tastes, and demonstrates a potential mastery over, as well as an immediate attractiveness to women: a kind of machismo.
>
> (Willis, 1977: 103–4)

A further element of conscientious endeavour is the idea that work has some purpose. In other words it is a productive activity that is valued by others. This is important because considerable effort may go into activities for which people do not get paid. Indeed, Moorhouse (1987) has argued that people are as productively active (if not more so) in leisure pursuits as they are in their work. The effort that goes into activities as varied as gardening, DIY, creating your own website, sport, gaming and amateur dramatics confirms this point. Similarly, a huge proportion of highly productive activity is unpaid – notably domestic and voluntary work. Also the informal economy (from e-bay to drug dealing) is a sizable part of productive (and paid) activity that is rarely acknowledged by wider society (discussed in Chapter 12).

Although productive activity is possible in a variety of spheres, it is key to work centrality – the theme above of the work ethic – and as a consequence is identified with employment. As Jahoda (1979: 313) argues, people might contribute to the community in a variety of ways, but work roles 'are the most central roles and consequently people deprived of the opportunity to work often feel useless and report that they lack a sense of purpose'. This is conveyed by the comments of an unemployed miner in a study by Parry (2003: 240):

> I was unemployed, on the dole, first time for a lot more years than I care to remember ... where you had targets before and you're working and had goals to go for, once you're on the dole you stay up late at night, why bother getting up in the morning? Nothing to aim for, to go for. It certainly shook me up, definitely, definitely. I found out how easy it was to get into that position.

The unemployed are not only deprived of the economic rewards derived through work, but they are also denied the moral approval of their conscientious endeavour if they use their initiative to find paid work unofficially (e.g. cash-in-hand jobs) or fill their spare time with non-paid productive (and self-rewarding) activities like voluntary work, gardening, writing poetry and so on.

Work as disciplined compliance

This fourth theme of the work ethic is particularly important *because* it underlines two components essential to capitalist production: (i) the acceptance of the management prerogative and (ii) obedience to time structures.

The management prerogative

The 'management prerogative' refers to the right of managers to direct the workforce as they deem fit, based on their 'expertise'. It can be associated with a style of management that stresses the unitary nature of the employment relationship: that is, the absence of any major conflict of interest and the position of management as the sole legitimate authority. This concept of unitarism, originally defined by Fox (1966), received particular attention during the 1980s with the emergence of a new rhetoric of human resource management (HRM). This emphasises the common goals of employees and managers in organisations. HRM ignores any plurality of interests and imbalance of power in organisations and invokes the idea of organisational commitment and cooperation to secure efficient and effective performance directed towards strategically designed corporate goals. These are often expressed in a waffle-filled mission statement. The employees' disciplined compliance with the values and goals of the organisation is perpetuated by management through the development of employment policies and a corporate culture that stresses individualism. This either marginalises or completely removes any collective representation through trade unions. (For a full discussion of the multifaceted nature of HRM, see Legge, 2005.)

Obedience to time structures

The second element is disciplined compliance with the time structures imposed by management. The working day provides a time structure which clearly differentiates periods of work and leisure. Traditionally, the Monday to Friday '9 to 5' pattern of working hours provided structure not only to the working day but also to the whole of working (and waking) lives. As discussed in Chapter 4, however, these time patterns are undergoing substantial change in contemporary society. Nevertheless, the majority of people still have a structure imposed by the time routines of their paid work. The importance of this structure is often not evident until people are faced with its removal, particularly through the loss of their jobs. One of the foremost researchers on the effects of unemployment sums it up succinctly:

> Everybody living in an industrialised society is used to firm time structures – and to complaining about them. But when this structure is removed, as it is in unemployment, its absence presents a major psychological burden. Days stretch long when there is nothing that has to be done; boredom and waste of time become the rule.
>
> (Jahoda, 1982: 22)

For people out of work, the problem becomes how to fill the unstructured days, and how to create new structures to take the place of the one they have lost. It is well illustrated by the following quotes from two different studies of unemployment – one in Scotland, the other in England. The first quote is by an unemployed woman in her mid-30s, and the second by an unemployed male steelworker of the same age:

> I used to think it'd be great not to work…when I was working…I'd 'imagine having a day off' – it was a treat. Now, I've got every day, and every week, and every month…and maybe every year to do *nothing*. There never used to be enough hours in the day for me when I was working…now, I know what an hour is…it just drags round.
>
> (Quoted in Turner, Bostyn and Wight, 1985: 485, emphasis in original)

> When you're employed you make use of all your time. You come home from work, have a quick bite to eat, a cup of tea, and get stuck into some job you've got to do. You know you've only got a set time. But when you're unemployed you've got all the time in the world and you think, ah, I won't do that today, I'll do that tomorrow. You take a slap-dash attitude, which is wrong.
>
> (Quoted in Wallace and Pahl, 1986: 121)

To sum up

If all four themes are put together, the work ethic can be described as the belief that it is the duty of everyone to treat productive work as their central life activity and to perform it with diligence and punctuality under the direction and control of managers. It is rare that complete submission to the work ethic would be expressed by an individual, but elements of the four themes are reflected in attitudes to work, as has been illustrated by the research quoted above. The general point emerging from the discussion so far is that work is seen by many people as a worthy activity in its own right, over and above the economic rewards it brings. This leads us to the question whether the moral dimension to work is changing; more specifically, whether as a result of changes in the structure and nature of paid employment the work ethic is in terminal decline and is ceasing to have any contemporary relevance.

Extract 3.3

Polish workers have a terrific attitude to work

Nick Warner, who runs a business supplying workers to pack boxes for supermarkets, said that 95 per cent of the 400 people on his books were Polish or Portuguese.

Poles were the most reliable and displayed a 'terrific attitude', he added…. 'You can ask them to work tomorrow and they will be waiting for you to pick them up in the morning.'

'The average English guy we are looking for has given up on the work ethic, there is just no incentive to find employment.' Mr Warner, group general manager of Central London-based Good People Recruitment, added: 'We work very closely with job centres to get people off Jobseekers Allowance and into fulltime employment.'

'But we have found that, with the other benefits they are often on, such as housing benefit and child support payments, they can earn more sitting on their backsides doing nothing than they can working 40 hours a week for us.'

'We have a great problem motivating these people.'

Quote from *Daily Mail*, 'Workshy British force boss to recruit Poles', 9 February 2005.

Exercise 3.3

What do you think?

Read Extract 3.3 and then answer the following questions:

1. Aside from the 'terrific attitudes', why else might it be advantageous for UK companies to employ non-nationals, particularly from Eastern Europe or outside the European Union?
2. Do you share Mr Warner's view about the unemployed in countries such as Britain? If not, why not? If you share his view, what would you do about it?

The demise of the work ethic?

As already noted, survey evidence about why people work is inconclusive. On the one hand, it suggests that most people say economic need urges them to work. Yet, on the other hand, most say they would continue to work even if there was no economic necessity for them to do so. Despite this ambiguous evidence, some politicians and academics argue that people are increasingly instrumental in their attitudes to work and suggest that there has been a steady deterioration in the work ethic. Within this perspective, it is possible to identify two explanations that account for the demise of the work ethic. They each suggest a fundamental shift has occurred in the economic context: either to (1) a post-industrial society, or to (2) a leisure society.

A shift towards a post-industrial society?

This explanation stresses the impact of economic developments and argues that the work ethic is in decline because of structural changes in society, which has meant that we have moved from an era of industrialisation to a 'post-industrial' age. The argument contends that while the work ethic was an appropriate basis upon which to build industries, it no longer has relevance in a post-industrial society. This approach is most closely associated with Bell (1973, 1976), who argues that advanced industrial economies are undergoing a shift to become post-industrial societies. This is occurring through changes in the social structure including a transformation in the economic base from manufacturing to services, which leads not only to increasing numbers of people being involved in the delivery of services but also increasing demand for, and consumption of, services: from tourism to participative sports; from psychotherapy to massage parlours. Concomitant with this structural change is an increasing importance on information-handling activities which means more white-collar jobs requiring higher levels of education and training, and the emergence of professionals as the dominant group, deriving influence through specialist theoretical knowledge. We examine these ideas in more detail in Chapters 6 and 8.

If we apply Bell's thesis, it challenges the notion of the work ethic in two ways:

- First, it means that a work ethic developed for an age of industrial production is no longer relevant for a structurally different society: one based on the increasing consumption of services.
- Second, it suggests that the work ethic will cease to have any moral influence. There will no longer be a moral necessity to work because the post-industrial society is shaped by technological advances, increased efficiency and greater theoretical knowledge, so the cultural realm will have diminishing influence compared with the economic realm.

Critics of Bell (e.g. Webster, 1995: 30–51) would argue his whole notion of a post-industrial society is mistaken because it creates a false dichotomy (an either-or) between manufacturing and services. This is a false dichotomy because in practice the two are interdependent (Gershuny and Miles, 1983). The service sector is helping to sustain the manufacturing sector through 'producer services' (Browning and Singelmann, 1978) such as banking, insurance, marketing and distribution. What is more, there is an increasing expansion not only of service work but also of service products, so the move may be towards a 'self-service' economy (Gershuny, 1978). For example, people drive cars rather than use public transport, and buy washing machines and vacuum cleaners rather than use laundry and cleaning services. This more complex picture of social and sectoral change suggests there is a continuity of economic development rather than a dramatic structural shift. So it follows that the work ethic might similarly adapt to reflect these changes in patterns of production and consumption. It also brings into question Bell's assumption that the social structure can be separated from the realm of culture – if there is no structural shift, then similarly there is a question mark over the supposed break with culture (even if one accepts such a separation as feasible in the first place).

A shift towards a leisure society?

Gorz (1982, 1985) argues the work ethic has ceased to have relevance because of the emergence of increased leisure time, which is 'liberating' people from work. He suggests technological change has led to labour-saving work processes and the creation of a post-industrial age in which leisure and productive activity outside work are increasingly important. Work ceases to be central in people's lives in terms of hours spent working. Gorz (1985: 40–1) projects a future scenario where people will be engaged in work sharing, with the equivalent of no more than ten years of full-time work during their life.

Similarly, it is envisaged that income would not be based on having a job or the amount of work performed; instead, everyone would be guaranteed a minimum income in exchange for a right to work (and an obligation to perform socially necessary work). Demand for goods and services would be stimulated by the guaranteed minimum income for all, but consumption would only be one side of the equation, because the liberating factor for Gorz is the contraction of economic and market activity, and the 'expansion of activities performed for their own sake – for love, pleasure or satisfaction, following personal passions, preferences and vocations' (1985: 53). This 'autonomous activity' could take any form, providing it stemmed from individual choice, and so, for some, this would involve competitive, free enterprise for financial gain. In other words, the purpose of life is self-fulfilment, which will differ from person to person, so with less work time and more free time people can be allowed to pursue fulfilment in whatever manner they choose.

To summarise two volumes of work into a single paragraph does Gorz an injustice. His vision of the future is so at odds with capitalism that it may seem a dream. Certainly there are many aspects of Gorz's thesis that can be criticised, but the discussion here will be confined to three main problems with the notion of leisure replacing work, and hence representing evidence of the demise of the work ethic.

First, there is the difficulty of what 'leisure' means. There is a range of activities, from housework to volunteering, for which people do not get paid yet which fills up their time. It is questionable whether they all could be described as leisure, since most involve (unpaid) effort and many are obligations (especially to the family) rather than free choice (see Chapter 12 for a full discussion). Indeed, perhaps these activities equally demonstrate a work ethic. If a type of work ethic is evident in leisure activities, the move to a leisure society will not dilute the work ethic so much as refocus it.

Second, there is a problem with the location of the work ethic. Even if it is assumed that more leisure time will encourage the majority of people to relinquish any commitment to the moral necessity of work, this does not automatically lead to the demise of the work ethic. As Veal argues, and as expressed in our criticism of Bell's thesis, the work ethic is a cultural phenomenon and as such will not be dislocated easily. On the contrary, the resilience of the work ethic might act as a barrier to the type of leisure society that Gorz envisages:

> The possibility remains…that the work ethic exists within the culture – not necessarily in the hearts and minds of the workers, but among the media, educationalists, the ruling classes, and so on. Thus it has an official existence, rather like an established religion, without being embraced by the population as a whole. In that case, it could be hindering progress towards a more 'leisured' society.
>
> (Veal, 1989: 268)

Third, theories of a leisure society fail to stand up against empirical evidence. Many people in work are working longer and more intensely (as we explore in Chapters 2 and 4). This means it is false to suggest that the work ethic is under threat because of people having more leisure time and shifting the balance of their lives away from work towards leisure activities.

To sum up

The conclusion to be drawn from Bell and Gorz is that the traditional work ethic must be abandoned because it is dysfunctional in contemporary society: it is not suited to the changing patterns of employment which emphasise the service sector and force a redefinition of the roles of work and leisure. While there is evidence to support each writer's analysis of the structural change (much of which was assessed in Chapter 2), it does not necessarily signal the demise of the work ethic. Instead, what may be occurring is a realignment of the components of the work ethic to match contemporary economic circumstances. Before reading the next section, read Extract 3.4 and then attempt Exercise 3.4.

Extract 3.4

Overwork – the new work ethic?

In a book entitled *Willing Slaves*, journalist Madeleine Bunting laments the effects of the overwork culture on contemporary society. Far from there being a demise of the work ethic, she argues that it is a strong force, particularly among white-collar professionals, and that it is driven by both consumption and a search for status. She argues as follows:

If someone complains about having to work too hard, sooner or later they'll say that they have 'no choice'. Probe a little further and what becomes clear is that, for much of the workforce living well above the poverty line, the connection between pay and overwork is about aspiration to particular patterns of consumption. This is murky territory, where one person's 'needs' are another's 'desires'.

But money, and the consumer goods we can buy with it, don't tell the whole story of why some people in the high-skill, high-income bracket are working harder. Once the upper-middle-class desired leisure and scorned anything that looked like trying too hard; now they are rarely parted from their mobiles or Blackberry handhelds. They look exhausted, complain of too much work, yet do nothing about reducing their burden.

Part of this is the hangover of a period of high unemployment, when predictions of 'the end of work' made having lots of work a status symbol. But more important is the emergence of a new form of elitism

3.4 cont.

in the labour market: work as vocation and work as pleasure. In a society that places a high premium on self-expression and fulfilment, to have a lot of interesting work is a status symbol.

The new work ethic has been astonishingly successful at exploiting the insecurities of employees and disciplining them to work harder than their parents or grandparents probably ever did – and with zero job security. The feat has been remarkable, particularly in corporate America, where hundreds of thousands of white-collar workers throughout the early to mid-1990s were made redundant, yet managed no collective protest. Instead, they redoubled their efforts – hours of work lengthened significantly over the same period – to devote most of their waking hours to those same corporations. The new work ethic tantalises the white-collar worker with the possibility of satisfactions that are just out of reach, thus heading off potential challenges to the way work is organised, and continually throwing the problem back on to the individual to resolve.

As far back as the 1950s, the great US sociologist, C. Wright Mills, worried that white-collar workers sold not just their time and energy, but also their personalities to their employer. He believed that work took up too much of people's time, and shaped them in such a way as to destroy meaningful life outside work. The overwork culture makes his fears as real as ever.

Source: Extracts from Bunting (2004).

Exercise 3.4

What do you think?

Compare the views of Bunting (see Extract 3.4) with those of three theses that you have already encountered.

1. The post-materialism thesis (from the section on the economic necessity to work).
2. The post-industrial society thesis (Bell).
3. The leisure society thesis (Gorz).

The work ethic and the psychological contract

It can be argued that the work ethic is being challenged because of changes in workplace employment practices that put different demands and obligations on employees – changes that have occurred because of the greater intensity and dynamism of the competitive environment. Much of this change has been described in Chapter 2, where, in particular, we noted the impact of globalisation. One of the concepts used by some commentators to assess the impact of these broad structural and economic changes is the 'psychological contract' between employees and employers (for a recent review see Conway and Briner, 2009; for earlier influential work see Grant, 1999; Herriot, Manning and Kidd, 1997; Rousseau, 1995; Sparrow, 1996). It is necessary to define this concept before looking at how it is supposedly changing workplace values and thereby affecting the work ethic.

There are various definitions of the psychological contract from different authors, but it can be described as:

> The beliefs of each of the parties involved in the employment relationship about what the individual offers and what the organization offers. For example, an individual employee might be willing to offer loyalty to the organization and in return expects to get security of employment. Unlike the employment contract, the psychological contract is not written down and changes over time as new expectations emerge about what the employee should offer and what they can expect to get back in return.
>
> (Heery and Noon, 2001: 288)

In reviewing the research that has been undertaken into changes in the psychological contract, Martin, Staines and Pate (1998) suggest that two contrasting views exist about the effect on employees: the pessimistic view and the optimistic view.

The pessimistic view concludes that competitive market pressures have led to changes in the structure and processes of organisations (such as delayering, lean production, flexibility and team working) and an obsessive focus on the customer. This results in:

- work intensification,
- reduced job security,
- neglect of employee welfare and satisfaction,
- fewer career opportunities,
- less training and development.

The consequence is that employees feel let down by employers as their expectations of 'the deal on offer' are no longer being met. The psychological contract has been broken.

The optimistic view concludes that despite these competitive pressures, 'the traditional psychological contract built around job security and a career is still alive and surprisingly well' (Guest, Conway, Briner and Dickman, 1996: 1). There is:

- greater employability,
- more demand by employees for training and development,
- greater functional flexibility among employees,
- more mobility between organisations.

Consequently the psychological contract is intact in some organisations and being 'redrafted' in others to accommodate the new competitive conditions.

Both the pessimistic and optimistic perspectives might be valid. For some employees the psychological contract has been breached and they resent this, while for others a change in the psychological contract might be welcomed. Indeed, Herriot (1998: 107) questions the notion of the psychological contract and argues that 'different individuals will have different perceptions of their psychological contract; there will be no universal notion of what "the deal" is in any one organisation'. This is an important point for two reasons. First, it reminds us there is diversity in any workforce regarding their values and orientations to work (thereby emphasising the importance of a pluralist perspective). Second, it alerts us to the possibility that the idea of 'the psychological contract' is a misconception – so perhaps the same can be said about 'the work ethic'.

It is possible to argue that a supposed 'demise in the work ethic' is without foundation because it is based on the false assumption that a work ethic was generally held by people in the first place. There can be no overall demise, if there was never any general acceptance of a work ethic. As Rose (1985: 16) states:

> A possibility is that some sections of the working population did in the past hold work values approximating to a work ethic … while many others were affected in lesser degree by public doctrines about work deriving from it.

Essentially this is an argument for diversity; it suggests that there are, and always have been, numerous orientations to work and that the notion of a monolithic work ethic misrepresents this diversity. This does not preclude the possibility of changes in work values, but it rejects the view that a general shift has occurred. This emphasis on diversity is argued by Moorhouse, who stresses the importance of gender, class and ethnicity upon work values:

> The meanings of work are not likely to be neat and simple, or form some uncomplicated 'ethic', but are rather likely to be jumbled and variegated, so that any individual has a whole range of types and levels of meanings on which to draw, and with which to understand or appreciate the labour they are doing at any particular moment.
>
> (Moorhouse, 1987: 241)

We have considerable sympathy with this view, especially since one of our starting points (as outlined in Chapter 1) is to demonstrate the plurality and subjectivity of work experiences. Often, people use 'work ethic' to mean a positive attitude to work, even though, as has been shown above, it reflects a number of things. Not all of these will be adhered to by those claiming to have a strong work ethic. Our analysis suggests it is probably a gross oversimplification to write and talk about a single work ethic because the term has a variety of meanings which can easily lead to confusion or ambiguity in interpretation – a type of problem we will also encounter in dealing with other concepts in the study of work, such as skill (Chapter 5). However, when any of the themes associated with the 'traditional work ethic' are in evidence in contemporary society, we can use the plural 'work ethics' to show the importance of a moral dimension to employment beyond economic need.

Conclusion

Throughout, this chapter has been addressing a fundamental question: why work? The evidence indicates that economic need remains an important feature of work, but this does not explain the entire picture. The majority of people say that they would continue to work even if there was no economic compulsion to do so, which suggests that work may also be fulfilling other needs. Aside from earning money (an extrinsic need), people are likely to cite a variety of intrinsic needs that work helps to satisfy. Many of these reflect the moral dimension to work: for example, the search for achievement, creativity and fulfilment, or a sense of worth, purpose or duty. In other words, work is perceived as the proper sort of activity in which to be engaged, a message that is powerfully reinforced through a shared culture in capitalist societies, and most typically expressed as a work ethic. As has been noted, the work ethic concept has a variety of meanings, but in so far as it characterises a moral dimension to work, it remains an important feature of work orientations, and talk of its demise is premature.

Clearly, work provides an opportunity to socialise with people outside of the family and virtually all work involves interaction with other people – co-workers, managers, subordinates, customers, clients and/or the public. We can speculate, therefore, that work fulfils an important social need in people. As Jahoda (1982: 24) argues:

> Outside the nuclear family it is employment that provides for most people this social context and demonstrates in daily experience that 'no man is an island, entire of itself': that the purposes of a collectivity transcend the purposes of an individual. Deprived of this daily demonstration, the unemployed suffer from lack of purpose, exclusion from the larger society and relative isolation.

This reality of work playing an important role in social identity continues to be evidence in studies where workers are interviewed. For example, Doherty (2009: 97) concludes from his case study evidence from the private and public sectors 'that work does still fulfil for people important personal and social needs and that the workplace remains an important locus of social relations'.

The research evidence suggests that people rarely express social factors as a reason for working, yet throughout the subsequent chapters numerous examples are evident of the importance of the social dimension of work:

- how time (Chapter 4) and skills (Chapter 5) can be socially constructed;
- how social interaction helps people to get through the working day (Chapter 9);
- the social phenomenon of discrimination (Chapter 10);
- the social dependency that drives some employees to seek collective representation (Chapter 11);
- the social isolation that characterises some aspects of hidden work (Chapter 12).

For most people work is a place to socialise, and complex social systems develop within the workplace which often spill over into leisure time. Moreover, whole communities may be socially linked through the workplace where there is a single major employer within a locality – for example, a manufacturing plant, a hospital, a large retail store or a call centre.

Similarly, organisations are often seeking to establish and reinforce their own corporate culture which encourages identity with the organisation through social interaction. In short, work is an important source of social interaction, but for the majority of people the meaning of work lies more in its economic and moral contribution to the human condition.

4

Time and work

Key concepts

▷ time and capitalist development

▷ time consciousness

▷ time discipline

▷ controlling working time

▷ work absence

▷ duration of working time

▷ part-time work

▷ presenteeism

▷ overtime

▷ arrangement of working time

▷ shift working

▷ annual hours

▷ zero hours

▷ variable hours

▷ flexitime

▷ utilisation of working time

▷ intensity of work

Chapter aim

To identify the importance of time in the overall experience of work and assess the approaches of managers and workers to working time issues.

Learning outcomes

After reading and thinking about the material in this chapter, you will be able to:

1. Understand the importance of time consciousness in the development of industrial capitalism.

2. Recognise how attendance and absence behaviour sheds light on the degree of employees' time consciousness.

3. Distinguish different employee coping strategies towards aspects of working time.

4. Assess current issues in the duration of working time, including the prevalence of long hours working or 'presenteeism'.

5. Identify patterns of change in the arrangement of working time.

6. Assess developments in the utilisation of working time and the debate over work intensity.

Time in the workplace – an overview

Time is a key component in work, as it is in all aspects of human activity. The way time is experienced is fundamental to an individual's overall experience of work. Having too much time to complete a task can slip easily into feelings of boredom. The sense of having too little time can be a major contributor to work-related stress. Even where tasks can be finished comfortably within a given time, dissatisfaction can still arise if the tempo of work remains unchanging. Indeed, introducing variety into the pace of work is an important means of reducing the monotony inherent in many jobs. Where variation in the tempo of work does not occur naturally, many employees will seek to create it, at times by speeding up their work pace and at other times by working more slowly. This breaking up of the working period into distinctive segments, each with its own temporal characteristics, is one strategy that many work people employ to 'get through' a monotonous working day (see Chapter 8).

All workplaces function on the basis of an array of overlapping time schedules. These vary enormously, ranging from a few seconds for specific and repetitive tasks, such as work on many assembly lines or making up orders in a fast food outlet (see Chapter 6) to many years for the planning, construction and commissioning of major plant, such as a new steelworks or the siting of a new office headquarters. The clock is critical in every contemporary work organisation, allowing the coordination of multiple, simultaneous and complex activities in ways that could not be achieved without the close synchronisation made possible by accurate time measurement.

This ability to synchronise individual activities within an overall production process has been a key feature of industrial development. The ability to measure time in finely divided units has allowed greatly improved levels of coordination, and thereby a growth in the scale and complexity of operations. This has brought with it an unleashing of productive capacity through a much-increased division of labour. Indeed, for writers such as Mumford (1934: 14), 'the clock, not the steam engine [was] the key machine of the industrial age', the critical innovation which set the industrial revolution firmly in motion. So too for Hassard, who comments that:

> As the machine became the focal point of work, so time schedules became the central feature of planning. During industrialism the clock was *the* instrument of co-ordination and control. The time period replaced the task as the focal unit of production.
>
> (Hassard, 1989: 18, emphasis in original)

Just as organisations as a whole function by utilising many different timescales, individual workers operate on the basis of a diverse set of time schedules. These may range from the short cycle times of a machine-paced task, to the length of their working day, working week and working year, and ultimately their working life. Working time is experienced in both an objective and a subjective way. For example, for many workers, particularly those working in factories, the working day is punctuated by bells or buzzers that objectively signal the start and finish of defined working periods, meal times and rest breaks. In addition, however, the clock dominates many workers' subjective thoughts about work; its hands or digits may seem to be move especially slowly for those who feel chained to jobs they despise and dream of being somewhere else.

As we discuss later in the chapter, three aspects of working time, in particular, shape the overall experience of work:

- *Duration*. How long people work shapes their overall experience of time at work. Since the early nineteenth century, the issue of the length of the working period has been a major focus for employment relations, with campaigns by workers and social reform groups to reduce working time regularly confronting employers opposed to any reduction in the length of productive activity.

- *Organisation*. To many workers, just as important as the amount of time they spend at work is when those hours are worked – that is, how the agreed working time is scheduled or arranged across the 24 hours of the day and the seven days of the week. Longer opening times and economic pressures to work more intensively are two factors that contribute to employers' demands to extend the working period.

- *Utilisation*. Besides questions of duration and organisation, the relationship between work time and overall work experience is influenced by the extent to which working time is actually spent in productive activity – that is, the degree to which working time is utilised. The utilisation of working time may be changed either by altering the pace of work or by changes in the length and frequency of non-productive periods. Key to this issue of work time utilisation is the question of whether or not work is becoming more intensified over time. Evidence on this is reviewed later in the chapter.

These three interrelated elements – the duration, organisation and utilisation of working time, or what Adam (1990) calls the time, timing and tempo of work – combine to shape workers' overall experience of their working time. In turn, these temporal aspects form a key element in the broader experience of work, and in the way that work impacts upon non-work life (an issue we examine separately in Chapter 13). Yet issues of time have in fact been the focus of comparatively little research enquiry. Time is in a sense unnoticed, because it is ever present and this has probably acted against it being addressed directly as a research topic. The subjective nature of working time has been particularly under-recognised, with too common a tendency to view work time in terms of 'clock time' – regular, mechanical and one-dimensional – rather than an aspect of social existence, which is experienced in a variety of ways.

Although we have suggested that time should be considered simultaneously in terms of different dimensions (the interplay between elements of duration, organisation and utilisation), there has been a tendency for those campaigning for change to address themselves to only one of these aspects. For instance, people have campaigned about the length of the working day, the hazards of night work or the need in certain activities for greater rest periods. At times, the result of this has been that changes introduced to one aspect of working time have been accompanied by unforeseen (and from the worker's point of view, potentially disadvantageous) changes in another aspect. Reductions in the working period may have only been secured by agreeing to an increased tempo of work or a greater spread of working time across the week.

While the complexity of working time has generally suffered from insufficient attention, leading writers on the world of work, such as Marx and Taylor, did recognise the centrality of work time to capitalism and to efficient work organisation. While Marx (1976) analysed the particular relationship between the working period and the creation of surplus value, Taylor (1911) was concerned with the most efficient ways in which an individual's work time could be utilised. This concern subsequently gave rise to generations of 'time and motion' studies (detailed observation of an activity through analysis and timing of every stage to improve efficiency).

The remaining sections of this chapter are concerned with the two views of time in the workplace:

- the main developments in management's approach to working time, and their implications;
- the ways workers subjectively experience working time and try to alleviate perceived negative aspects of managerially defined time patterns, through the development of alternative time-reckoning systems.

The chapter begins with a discussion of workers' internalised attitudes towards working time. The development of more closely controlled and coordinated time schedules may be a particular feature of industrial capitalism, but employers' efforts to control workers' time have also been assisted by employees bringing to their job:

- a growing sense of time consciousness – an increased awareness of time;
- a sense of time discipline – a growing self-control over the organisation of one's time.

We argue that the result of this has been a developing sense among the labour force of the importance of punctuality, regularity and what constitutes a 'fair day's work'.

To sum up

Time is a critical component of work and organisation; employees' experiences of work are heavily influenced by their experience of working time. The organisation and utilisation of time, as well as its overall duration, combine to shape employee experiences of time at work.

The (partial) growth of time discipline

The making of a capitalist time consciousness

E. P. Thompson (1967) argued that the creation of a greater time consciousness and time discipline among the workforce represented a key feature in the development of an urbanised, industrialised economy. For Thompson, developments such as the spread of the school system, with its emphasis on punctuality and its daily diet of bells and whistles, helped to embed a stronger time consciousness and time discipline into the working classes (see also Lazonick, 1978). The importance of time-keeping as taught in schools was reinforced by moral instruction from church and chapel about the sin of idleness, the duty to view time as a scarce resource and the importance of exercising time thrift by employing all time, including working time, to greatest effect. (See also discussion of the work ethic in Chapter 3.)

Other significant factors for Thompson include the spread of clocks and other timepieces which heightened general awareness of the time, and probably more importantly, the emergence of an acquisitiveness among the working classes. Prior to industrial capitalism, the lack of available goods for purchase and a lack of opportunity for workers to progress beyond their existing material position meant many people saw work as something necessary for subsistence. Once a subsistence level had been attained, any desire to continue working, rather than spend time in other activities, diminished. Weavers, for example, might 'play frequently all day on Monday, and the greater part of Tuesday, and work very late on Thursday night and frequently all night on Friday' in order to make a sufficient wage (Pollard, 1965: 214). In this way, while the weavers could not avoid the necessity of earning an income, they had some control over the timing of their work.

The importance of control over working time was not restricted to the textile districts. For example, a widespread unofficial practice was honouring 'Saint' Monday. Sunday was the rest day from work each week; large numbers of workers also habitually took many Mondays off as unofficial holidays to extend the weekend (Reid, 1976). As some Saint's days were holidays (holy days), Monday was given the nickname 'Saint Monday'. With the growth of capitalism and larger-scale production, however, Thompson (1967) argues that there was more for workers to spend their wages on. As a result, bourgeois (i.e. capitalist) values relating to ambition, hard work and thrift became increasingly common among the working classes. Aspirations towards greater material comfort were no longer restricted to the middle and upper classes but also became common among poorer workers. According to Thompson, the overall effect of these various influences was to create a different attitude among workers towards time, leisure and income. It increased their willingness to keep regular time in order to maximise wages and thus their purchasing power.

Pollard (1963, 1965) similarly emphasises the importance of time discipline and regular attendance for the development of the nineteenth-century factory system. However, unlike Thompson, who focuses particularly on the development of self-discipline in time-keeping, Pollard places more emphasis on external factors, especially the actions taken by employers to impose greater time discipline. For Pollard (1965: 213), the developing factory system required 'regularity and steady intensity in place of irregular spurts of work'. This did not come easily to the new factory operatives and had to be reinforced by systems of rules, backed by punishments. For example, many nineteenth-century employers sought to control lateness by imposing fines or by locking the factory gates after the start of the work period, thereby forcing anyone arriving late to lose a whole day's pay (Pollard, 1965: 215).

These attempts to establish regular attendance and punctuality were part of a broader employer effort to enforce a strict factory discipline towards work habits, standards of cleanliness and drinking. Enforcement took the forms of elaborate rules, close supervision, fines, corporal punishment and summary dismissals for even minor transgressions. Despite their different emphases on internal and external influences on the development of time discipline, Thompson and Pollard reach the same conclusion: that gradually the industrial workforce demonstrated greater time discipline.

One reading of Thompson and Pollard is that the question of workers' time discipline was settled sometime in the nineteenth century, with workers abandoning their previous carefree approach in the face of overwhelming opposition from school, church and employer. However, on closer inspection it is clear the employers' victory was never complete, and that in several important respects workers' time discipline has remained partial and problematic (Whipp, 1987).

To sum up

Industrialisation has been accompanied by important developments in time consciousness and time discipline. Nevertheless, working time remains a contested 'frontier of control' between management and labour. Each tries to exert greater influence over different aspects of the working period. We can gain insight into workers' attitudes towards time discipline by examining attendance and absence patterns, as well as by looking at what time-related practices they engage in while at work.

Exercise 4.1

What do you think?

Thompson identifies time discipline as critical to the development of industrial capitalism.

1. Do you think it is correct to give time discipline such an important place in the development of industrial capitalism? What reasons do you have for saying this?
2. Think about your own sense of time discipline. Would you say that you have strong or weak time discipline? How might someone be able to observe your personal sense of time discipline?
3. What have been the most important influences on the development of your time discipline: your family, school, peer group or other influences? Rank the influences in order of importance.

Attendance at work

'Most workers', as Edwards and Scullion (1982: 107) point out, 'attend work for most of the time.' Nicholson (1977: 242) makes a similar point: 'Most people, most of the time, are on "automatic pilot" to attend [work] regularly.' Whether the driving force is personal values, or habit, or economic necessity, or fear of an employer, employees' attendance at work is characterised far more by regularity than by absence. Yet, while workers' time discipline towards attendance is high, it is rarely complete: many workers occasionally absent themselves even when they are able to go to work. In a study of attendance and absence in Britain, for example, Edwards and Whitston (1993) found that, on average, workers had been absent from work on over 16 days during the previous year. More recent estimates in the UK have indicated a lower average absence level. A 2005 survey by the Chartered Institute of Personnel and Development (CIPD), for example, found an average absence level of 8.4 days per employee per annum (CIPD, 2005). Barham and Begum (2005), in their analysis of absence in the UK, estimated the cost of absence to the UK economy at over £11 billion in 2003.

Voluntary absence

Absence from work can, of course, be the result of genuine illness and thus be involuntary and unavoidable. However, it is also clear that a proportion of total absence is voluntary and avoidable (and comparable to related time-keeping aspects such as lateness and leaving work early). The CIPD survey reports that employers believe around one-seventh of absence is not genuine (CIPD, 2005: 42); others would put that proportion higher. Voluntary absence goes by different names at different times and in different regions – 'skiving', 'having a duvet day', 'bunking off', 'pulling/throwing/taking a sicky', 'swinging the lead', 'on the hop' and 'wagging' are some. For obvious reasons, it is difficult to get precise data on voluntary absence (admitting to being voluntarily absent could cost workers their jobs). However, evidence from different periods indicates a persistent tendency for some workers to 'skive off' occasionally. McClelland (1987), for example, identifies the continued practice of Saint Monday throughout the latter half of the nineteenth century in the north-east engineering industry, even though it was under attack from employers. Pollitt (1940: 59) gives a graphic description of how some boilermakers would extend their holidays before the First World War:

> It was at Tinker's boiler-shop in Hyde that I first learnt the custom of the brick in the air. The first day after a holiday we would all ... make a ring in the yard, and the oldest boilermaker ... would pick up a brick, advance to the centre of the ring, and announce 'Now lads. If t' brick stops i' th' air, we start; if t' brick cooms down, we go whoam (home).' I do not remember any occasion on which we did not 'go whoam'.

Likewise, in the 1920s, an estimate for the dock-working industry indicates that on average over nine million man-hours a year were lost through voluntary absence (Wilson, 1972: 77). Some industries, such as coal mining, were characterised by comparatively high levels of absence, with unauthorised absence frequently higher around holidays, particularly among younger age work groups (McCormick, 1979: 146–7). More generally, absence levels in some industries and organisations have shown a considerable resistance to decline (indeed many have risen) despite increased managerial attention. There is no indication that attendance patterns of white-collar workers are any better (from a managerial perspective) than those of manual workers.

Many organisations seek to control lateness and absenteeism by different means of time-recording and by a variety of punishments and incentives, including disciplinary action (ultimately ending in dismissal) for those persistently absent. Less frequently, some employers give bonuses for those attending punctually every day in a given period. Nevertheless, for some employees, going absent from work clearly represents a way of fulfilling family or other responsibilities, or gaining a respite from excessive work pressures. For others, taking occasional days off acts as a way of coping with 'the routine frustrations of going to work' (Edwards and Scullion, 1982: 110). It can be an escape from the continuous repetition of work, eat and sleep. As one woman in Edwards and Scullion's study put it, 'It's not really boredom with the job. It's just that things get too much for you and you need a rest; you feel generally fed up' (ibid).

In this way, workers occasionally relax the moral pressure of time discipline. Of course, temporary absence will rarely resolve the source of work pressure for individuals, but it might help them cope better with those pressures. In their study of nurses in two North American hospitals, for example, Hacket and Bycio (1996) found that occasionally going absent did not generally mean that things got better for employees, such as in relation to their stress levels or their physical health. Nevertheless, these authors suggest that the occasional absences taken by the nurses may have acted to keep these work pressures at manageable levels and prevent the stress levels and other effects from getting any worse.

The gap between 'complete' and 'actual' time discipline of workers is also reflected in attitudes towards the legitimacy of voluntary absence. In their study of attendance in four organisations, Edwards and Whitston (1993) sought opinions on three hypothetical situations: a worker taking an extra day off having recovered from an illness, a working parent taking time off to look after a child who is ill, and a worker staying at home to get away from work pressures. Over four-fifths (84%) of the male and female workers interviewed accepted the legitimacy of going absent in at least one of these hypothetical cases – a pattern of response which the authors concluded reflected 'a widespread acceptance of the need for workers to go absent in situations which management might see as voluntary or illegitimate absence' (ibid: 45; see also Exercise 4.2).

What do you think?

You work in an organisation where some employees are regularly absent and their behaviour seems to receive little attention from management. The absences make the jobs of those attending work harder because of the extra work that needs to be covered. The resulting extra fatigue and the annoyance at those regularly absenting themselves builds up and you begin to take occasional days off yourself, but far fewer than some of your colleagues.

1. Do you think that your behaviour is justified? Why or why not?
2. What does your behaviour signal with regard to your time discipline?
3. If you were a manager in the organisation, what steps would you take to manage the absence problem differently?
4. What do you think would be the different consequences of your way of managing absence?

Organised absence

While much voluntary absence is unorganised, in the sense that it is an action taken by an individual without the involvement of others in a work group, by no means all absence is unorganised. Heyes (1997: 70), for example, describes the organisation of 'knocking' in a chemicals plant, where pairs of employees collaborated so that the voluntary absence of one of the pair would result in over-time working by the other (paid at a premium rate). These roles were reversed later in order to share the financial gains from the joint 'knocking' activity.

In other situations, work groups have been able to arrange their work in similar fashion. In the dock-working industry, for example, dockers employed a system known as 'welting' (also known in some areas as 'spelling'), where half a gang left work for an hour or more, and the other half then swapped places with them when they returned. The development of this informal arrangement appears to have been widespread; Wilson (1972: 215), for example, identifies a similar arrangement operating in dock work in many different parts of the world. Such a practice not only provides an easier work regime for those involved but may also extend jobs over a longer period of time and could even result in increased earnings if, as a result of 'welting', work was carried over into (premium-paid) overtime.

Just as dockers engaged in welting would be highly unlikely to be recorded by management as absent, Edwards and Scullion (1982: 102) identified a similar pattern operating in a metals factory. There, workers with a relatively high degree of control over their work organisation had developed a working pattern which enabled individuals to take it in turns to leave the factory for up to half a day, without being recorded as absent. It is important to note that such time-keeping arrangements stem not only from the way that workers have organised their work but also from managerial tolerance of the behaviour – or to put it differently, management's unwillingness (or inability) to enforce their control over the organisation of work. As will be discussed below, this issue of work time utilisation is one which, in recent years, has been the subject of increased managerial scrutiny.

It is also important to note that, just as work group norms may encourage absence as an informal element in the effort–reward bargain, work group norms and peer pressure can also act in the opposite direction. For example, where there are high workloads and tight staffing levels, voluntary absence might be viewed very negatively by the group, since one person's absence is likely to put significantly greater pressure on those attending (Nicholson and Johns, 1985). Similarly, in some work settings, there is a norm of very high levels of attendance, possibly reflecting a high degree of job commitment among the group (Savery, Travaglione and Firns, 1998). Someone taking more absence than the rest of the group in such a setting might incur peer pressure to conform to the group attendance norm.

As well as acting to encourage or suppress voluntary absence, attitudes held by the work group may also influence perceptions of what constitutes 'legitimate' reasons for voluntary absence. For instance, a work group may acknowledge the 'legitimacy' of voluntary absence to care for a sick child, irrespective of the work pressure implications for the remainder of the group attending work.

Controlling absence

Accounts of work organisation in general, and studies of absence behaviour in particular, suggest that there exists a widespread tendency for managers to tolerate a degree of voluntary absence. In part, this probably reflects the difficulties management typically face in trying to establish whether individual short-term absences are voluntary or involuntary. Absences are likely to attract greater management attention, however, where they exceed a level judged to be 'acceptable', or where production systems are so highly interdependent and/ or where staffing levels contain so little spare capacity that covering for absent individuals is difficult.

As mentioned earlier, managerial efforts to control absence can range from giving bonus payments for unblemished attendance records to holding interviews with those whose absence or lateness exceeds a certain level. Ultimately management may invoke disciplinary procedures ending in dismissal for those persistently absent or late. Clearly, the existence of such sanctions and the ultimate threat of dismissal will affect many people's decisions over whether or not to go absent voluntarily, and how frequently. Besides this threat of sanctions, an additional discouragement to go absent frequently (particularly those engaged in manual work) is that being absent may result in a significant loss of income.

These instrumental reasons (fear of job loss and desire to maintain income) are important factors in controlling levels of voluntary absence. Yet, at the same time, the persistence of voluntary absence underlines the fact that employers have so far failed to instil into their workforce a complete time discipline. Many workers still have some discretion over their attendance. Management's continued need to monitor attendance, and their lack of success in totally suppressing voluntary absence, indicates a continuing tension between two temporal rationalities:

- On the one hand, is a managerial logic based on control and definition of the working period, and the requirement for workers to utilise the whole of that period.
- On the other hand, is an employee's logic emphasising the need to break up the monotony of work, or to reduce work pressures by occasionally being absent or arriving late.

To sum up

The tension between these two logics represents a continuing source of conflict and bargaining in the employment relationship. While management seeks to maximise utilisation of the working period, employees seek to limit the physical and/or psychological harm of a demanding or unchanging work period. The resulting tension is, as we shall see, relevant in assessing recent efforts by management to impose greater control over employees' time. It is also relevant for considering in what ways (and how effectively) workers are able to resist these efforts and maintain a different logic in relation to their working time.

Employees' temporal coping strategies

Exercising control over working time

One of the ways employees can cope with routine in their work is by being able to change that routine, at least to some degree. The ability of employees to control time in this way has been found to have a considerable impact on their overall experience of work. Macan (1994), in a study of US public sector employees, found that employees who perceived themselves as having control over their work time were significantly more satisfied. They also reported lower work-stress levels than their counterparts who did not perceive themselves as having much control over their work time.

Routines can be changed in a number of ways. One of these is through flexible working hours, or 'flexitime' arrangements. With flexitime, employees are able to vary start and finish times, provided they are present during a core period (e.g. between 10 am and 3.30 pm) and provided a contractual hours total is worked over an agreed period. As well as formal flexitime systems, less formal arrangements are widespread. Studies of flexitime show that they are generally very positively regarded by employees, and can also yield various benefits for the employing organisation. Indeed, an analysis of 27 studies of flexitime concluded that 'flexible work schedules favourably influenced productivity, job satisfaction, absenteeism and satisfaction with work schedule' (Baltes et al, 1999: 505; see also further discussion of flexible working hours below). A far-reaching form of flexitime is the initiative taken in some German firms to introduce 'trust-based working hours' (*Vertrauensarbeitzeit*). In this system, employees are given full control over their working time pattern, provided agreed work is completed and contractually agreed hours are fulfilled (Trinczek, 2006). (See also Extract 13.5 for a discussion of one study of this flexitime system.)

This importance of being able to exercise some control over working time is well illustrated in a study by Berg (1999). In a study of steel workers in 13 steel plants in the United States, Berg found a significant positive relationship between (i) the extent to which a company was perceived as helping its workers balance work and family responsibilities and (ii) workers' overall job satisfaction. This balance was achieved by informal procedures such as supervisors allowing workers to come in late or leave early to take care of family responsibilities, or more formal procedures involving time away from work to deal with family issues (Berg, 1999: 130).

Extract 4.1 can usefully be compared (or contrasted) with Berg's findings, as it also involves a study of steel workers (in this case, in the UK). This case highlights the effects of removing employee discretion over working time.

Extract 4.1

Employee response to work time restrictions

As part of a study of employee attitudes to the introduction of teamworking, employees from two steel finishing plants were surveyed, with responses from over 800 workers. In these plants the introduction of teamworking had been accompanied by two other changes in working time. These entailed first the introduction of a new shift system which fixed the rotas for both rest days and holidays for individual employees for the following five years. Second, management at the plants had introduced a much tighter control over the previous practice of employees informally changing shifts with co-workers to accommodate non-work activities (e.g. sporting events and children's activities). Management's espoused aim in banning these informal swap arrangements was to build up team coherence by keeping the teams working together more closely than had been the case with previous work crews.

However, the restrictions imposed on both the timing of holidays and the informal shift swaps were poorly received by many employees, not only because of the way they constrained employees' flexibility over working time, but also because these constraints were seen to be unfairly distributed, with only those on shifts being subject to the restrictions, whilst those working only the day shift – including the majority of managers – retained the freedom to take holidays when they wished. The following comments are typical of many:

The most contentious issue with teamworking is the five-shift working rotas which no shift worker in the works wanted. It is a totally inflexible system with no provision for social events, family needs or sickness. It is the most demoralising aspect of the new regime e.g. it will now be three years until I can take my child on holiday during the school's summer break.

Whoever thought of the five-shift system obviously did not have any family to think of.

Holidays: we are told when to take them. This is very annoying when it appears that management can take a day off when it suits them.

I find it impossible to book any time off for a social event or family occasions as all holidays and rest days are pre-arranged for us by management.

The main reason for the apathy and rock bottom morale among shift workers in my plant is the new work rota...whereby [the company] tell us when to have all our holidays as well as our normal days off. There is no flexibility. We feel we are automatons owned by [the company]. All the hardship is put on shift workers...while day workers and managers are unaffected and probably don't know the resentment that we shift workers feel.... We don't like having our leisure time dictated to us.

These negatively perceived working time changes contributed to a lowering of morale at the plants. Overall, over four in five (83 per cent at one plant and 84 per cent at the other) thought that morale had declined since the introduction of teamworking, despite perceived positive effects of teamworking such as greater job variety, more opportunities to use their abilities and greater freedom to choose their method of working.

Such was the negative reaction to the working time changes that when the researchers returned to the plants one and a half years later, they found that while the new working time rota remained in operation, the ban on informal shift changes had been relaxed as a result of the employee reaction.

Source: Bacon and Blyton (2001).

'Making' time and 'fiddling' time

If one frontier of control over working time is whether or not workers attend work, another involves control over the working period itself: the extent to which the work period, as defined by management, is actually spent working. Production problems, such as shortage of materials and production bottlenecks, are among several possible causes of non-productive periods (White, 1987). In addition, however, non-productive time can be created by workers themselves to achieve an easier work regime (and as a result, a more favourable effort–reward bargain). As Ditton (1979) and others have pointed out, workers can achieve time manipulation in a number of ways. Two of these are 'making' time and 'fiddling' time.

Making time

Making time involves arranging work to produce breaks that would not occur otherwise. Traditionally, a common means of achieving this is by what Blauner (1964: 100) terms 'working up the line'. This is a pattern of accelerated working which results in workers building up a 'bank' or 'kitty' of finished output, which can then be drawn upon to create a break or an easier work period (see also Burawoy, 1979 and Ditton, 1979). As Blauner's reference to a 'line' suggests, this practice has been particularly associated with assembly-line operations, but in other situations too, in both manual and non-manual settings, workers can alter the tempo of work by building up banks of finished output in this way. In Edwards and Whitston's (1993: 301) study, this practice was known in one plant as 'using the back of the book', referring to workers completing tasks but not immediately recording them (see also Webb and Palmer, 1998).

Fiddling time

In addition to making time, managerially defined work time structures can also be 'fiddled'. At their simplest, fiddles can take the form of employees delaying the start of work, covertly extending the length of breaks or stopping work before the official end of the working period. Where work time is recorded by clocking equipment, time fiddles may also involve manipulating the clocking procedures, so time officially recorded as spent working is actually greater than the time actually spent at work. This might involve, for example, workers being clocked out by others, after they have already left (see Ditton, 1979 and Scott, 1994). Other ways that time might be fiddled include sabotaging equipment or causing a machine breakdown, resulting in a pause in work while repairs are carried out (see also the discussion of sabotage in Chapter 8).

Mars (1982) argues that in jobs which are dominated by repetitive, short-cycle activities, workers' ability to control time is likely to be seen in actions that slow a job down. An example of this might be employees trying to manipulate the way jobs are timed by work-study engineers. If employees can convince those timing the jobs that they actually take longer to perform than is the case, any resulting 'standard' or 'official' times will actually have slack built in. This will give employees more control as to the time they take to do the required work (i.e. they can work with a reduced tempo).

Where jobs are not so repetitive but involve completing one task Mars argues that the source of workers' time control is more likely to lie in speeding up the work process. Examples of this might be to refuse collecting or bus driving, which involve travelling along a route (Mars calls these kinds of activity 'linear', rather than 'short-cycle'). By speeding things up, this potentially creates unofficial free time mid-way or at the end of the task. As an example of this working time strategy, Mars quotes Blackpool tram crews who, if they succeeded in making the journey along the designated route in a faster time than was timetabled, secured an additional unofficial break period:

> The main aim of being a tram conductor is to control the job and to stop it controlling you. This is why tram crews will go to all sorts of extremes to get a tram from A to B ten minutes earlier than it should get there so that they can get a ten-minute break the other end. The times are so worked out that if you follow the route properly you'll never get any tea-break at all and you'll be working your guts out for the whole shift. So the main aim of the job as I see it is to fiddle time.
>
> (Blackpool tram conductor quoted by Mars, 1982: 82)

This conductor gives importance to gaining some control of time away from the managerially defined timetable. We return to this issue again later.

Fiddling time on the factory floor

The following are extracts from an account of participant observation in a British-based subsidiary of a Japanese manufacturing company, given the pseudonym 'Telco'. The company is a supplier of products to motor vehicle manufacturers, with a workforce of 400. The authors identify various ways that employees made additional time for themselves during the working day.

Making time represented action to gain pockets of space away from the drudgery and physical demands that were a consequence of the routine, continuous and fast-paced nature of work at Telco.

[One] task was to perform a series of checks on the finished units as they came to the end of the line. First, they would be put on a machine for a specified time which simulated hot conditions, to ensure that they responded appropriately. Then they went to the 'lumo' (illumination) booth, where a complete electronic functional test was performed. Finally, they went to inspection and packing. The women had worked together on this section for several years, and familiarity with the operations also meant that they had found a number of shortcuts which they exploited. For example, with the heating process, rather than leave the units on the machines for the specified length of time demanded by the work standard, when the unit had indicated that it responded appropriately to the temperature, it was removed and replaced with another, irrespective of whether the full time cycle had been completed.

The ability of this work-group to manipulate standard operating procedures allowed them to collude to gain some control over the pace of work. The use of the 'lumo' booth provides an example of this collusion. The 'lumo' booth is completely enclosed with a full-length black curtain, thus preventing anyone from seeing in. Only one operator was supposed to work in the 'lumo' booth, but it provided an ideal meeting place for the workers in this group to chat, knowing that even if the work became backed up they could clear the backlog quickly by shortcutting official operating procedures.

Source: Webb and Palmer (1998).

What do you think?

Think about a job you have worked at in the past.

1. What ways of gaining some time for yourself can you recall? If there were several, rank them in order of importance.
2a. Using Mars's distinction, did your job involve mainly short-cycle or linear activity?
2b. To what extent were the ways that you adopted to gain some control over time consistent with Mars's argument about the different opportunities that jobs provide for controlling time?
3. If there were few or no ways for you to gain any control over your work time, why was this? If there were several reasons, what were the most important?

Coping with monotony

In accounts of workers seeking to manipulate time, an often-mentioned objective is to counter the effects of monotony. Altering the otherwise unchanging tempo of repetitive tasks represents an attempt to introduce greater variety and help workers 'get through' their working day (see Chapter 8). One way of achieving this is by breaking up the day into different segments. A particularly vivid account of workers breaking up a monotonous working day is Roy's description of 'banana time'. Observing a work group in a US clothing factory, Roy was particularly interested in how workers dealt with the 'beast of monotony' without 'going nuts' (Roy, 1960: 156). Workers had to repeat very simple operations over a long (12-hour) day.

Central to the workers' coping strategies was the division of the day into different elements (over and above the formally recognised meal times and coffee breaks). These additional interruptions occurred almost hourly and were very short. The breaks were designated as different 'times' and normally featured the consumption of some food or drink. Also, and importantly, they were a focus for banter (informal joking and chat) between the members of the work group. 'Peach time', for example, happened when one member of the work group offered some peaches to share, invariably accompanied by verbal banter from the others about the (poor) quality of the fruit. An hour later came 'banana time', which routinely involved one member of the group stealing (and eating) a banana from another's lunch box, again to the accompaniment of much verbal banter. 'Window time' came next, followed by 'pick up time' and later 'fish time' and 'Coke time'. These different times punctuated the day, acting as a focus of jokes and other social interaction, and capturing the attention of members of the group, giving them something to think about as they resumed work. The combined effect was to make an otherwise monotonous work day pass more easily:

> The major significance of the interactional interruptions lay in … a carryover of interest. The physical interplay which momentarily halted work activity would initiate verbal exchanges and thought processes to occupy group members until the next interruption. The group interactions thus not only marked off the time; they gave it content and hurried it along.
>
> (Roy, 1960: 161)

To sum up

Some workers may try to modify an unchanging work period by voluntary absence, modifying their work time pattern or by fiddling or making time. Roy's portrayal of 'banana time' highlights another way in which a work group introduced greater temporal variation into an otherwise uniform work period. In all cases the effect has been to introduce temporal variety, and also to introduce an alternative logic, or degree of counter-rationality into the workplace.

This interplay between managers' and workers' logics in relation to working time is far from static. There have been significant developments in the organisation and utilisation of working time in recent years. Many of these have important implications for workers' experience of time, and the extent to which they are able to influence and modify managerial logic. As the next section examines, changes are also evident in relation to the duration of work time. In some important areas there has been an absence of change.

Recent developments in the duration of working time

The total amount of time people spend at work is determined by many variables including:

- their age of entry into, and exit from, the labour market;
- whether work is full or part-time;
- whether work involves overtime and/or short-time working;
- the amount of absence from work;
- length of paid holidays;
- experience of unemployment;
- extent to which maternity, paternity or unpaid leave is taken;
- whether individuals are involved in single, dual or multiple job-holding.

So, many different factors influence overall work time. Historically two aspects of working time duration – the length of the working day and working week – have periodically been a major focus of dispute between employers and employees. Just as workers have sought improvements in pay, they have periodically campaigned for reductions in working hours too. These calls for shorter hours have often met with opposition from employers, who have claimed that cuts in working time would damage their competitiveness. Even so, the length of the basic working week has fallen considerably over the past century and a half, typically from over 60 hours to less than 40 hours per week (Blyton, 1985, 2008). This has been a result of several factors – not least, continued increases in labour productivity, but also employers' preference over time for reducing working hours rather than agreeing to increased pay.

Despite this reduction in basic weekly hours, in practice, many workers continue to work far longer as a result of high levels of paid and unpaid overtime working (and in some cases, multiple job-holding). In the UK in 2009, for example, one in six full-time employees usually worked in excess of 48 hours per week (ONS, 2010: 50). Indeed, so significant is the amount of hours worked in excess of basic hours that the average working time of many full-time employees has increased over the past two decades. As well as in the UK, this has also been the subject of much discussion in Australia (Bittman and Rice, 2001; Campbell, 2002) and the United States, notably Schor's (1991) account of 'the overworked American'. Jacobs and Gerson (2001) identify that the increase in work time is particularly evident if family rather than individual work patterns are considered. In Canada too, a similar picture is evident: a large-scale study by Duxbury and Higgins (2006) found that the proportion of people reporting they usually worked in excess of 50 hours per week more than doubled between 1991 and 2001 (from 11 to 26%).

The long hours worked among some groups and in some organisations have given rise to a debate over 'presenteeism'; we consider this below, before examining paid overtime working in more detail.

Presenteeism

In 2009 in the UK, the longest average working week (45 hours) was reported by those who were managers or senior officials, with professionals not far behind (44 hours per week, on average) (ONS, 2010: 50). This tendency for many managerial and professional groups to work long hours of unpaid overtime has attracted increased research interest. Some of this is focused on the pressures that employees feel under to demonstrate their commitment to the job by being at their desk for long hours each day. The term that has been coined for this is 'presenteeism' (the opposite of 'absenteeism') (Cooper, 1996; Simpson, 2000). There are many reasons presenteeism might exist, among them workload pressures, fears over job insecurity and a desire for promotion. It is also clear that some organisations operate a 'long hours' culture in which there are pressures to conform to the work time norm in order to succeed. Perlow (1999: 68–9), for example, comments on this in her study of software engineers in the United States:

> Simply being physically present was thought to be critical to one's success… . Engineers perceived that the longer they worked, the more they were given credit for contributing and, therefore, the more highly they were regarded by their managers.

One of the key variables influencing long hours working is the work time pattern of those in senior positions in a workplace. Such individuals may not only expect similar time commitment from their subordinates, but may also act as role models for how to achieve a senior level job within the organisation (see Extract 4.3).

Extract 4.3

Having a workaholic for a boss

Tim Delaney's typical working day begins at 8.15 in the morning and ends at 9 pm. As head of the London advertising agency Leagas Delaney, he frequently expects to put in extra hours on Sunday morning if there is work to be done.

Delaney is, by most people's definition, a 'workaholic'…. He says that his long hours are driven by a desire 'to get the work done, to do the right thing, and not to let people down', as well as perfectionism. 'When you are writing an ad,' he points out, 'you can always make it better.'

He also expects the people who work for him to put in long hours. 'If someone left the office at 5.30 each day and the results were fabulous, then I'd say OK,' he says. 'But in this business there are so many opportunities to be seized that it's unlikely that anybody would be justified in doing that.'

He feels no compunction about asking his staff to work weekends, and says that although they might feel occasional resentment, they respect him. 'Everyone wants their general to be leading them by example. What they don't want is somebody who tells them: you do this, I'm going out to dinner.'

Delaney may be an exceptional taskmaster, and advertising a demanding business, but the evidence in recent years indicates that people in the UK are working increasingly long hours. Ten per cent of the population or more could be regarded as 'workaholics' by virtue of the hours they put in.

But what is it like to work for someone like that? Is it inspiring, or is it just stressful?

The Chartered Institute of Personnel and Development (CIPD) has carried out some research into the subject which appears to show that, for most people, having a workaholic boss is regarded far more positively than might be expected, although there is a clear danger that you will feel under pressure to work longer hours yourself.

The CIPD's report, Married to the Job?, looked at how other workers perceived workaholics. Some 38 per cent surveyed said their bosses worked more than 48 hours a week; 28 per cent described that person as a 'workaholic'. But 70 per cent of this latter group regarded the boss in question as a 'good example' and only 3 per cent said they resented the long hours he/she worked.

Melissa Compton-Edwards, the report's author, says the research showed that many people are inspired by a boss who works long hours, but it also demonstrated a downside: nearly a third said their workaholic boss would sometimes pressurise or bully them when he or she couldn't cope, and a quarter of those who had a workaholic colleague said they ended up working longer hours themselves in order to avoid looking lazy.

Source: Alexander Garrett; 'Business: work. My name is Tim…I'm a workaholic. Is the "lunch is for wimps" culture healthy?' *Observer,* 4 February 2001.

A long-hours culture may not only be an organisational characteristic: whole societies, such as Japan, have also been characterised as operating a long-hours culture, with employees demonstrating their commitment to the group through their long work hours and their tendency to work at least a part of their holiday entitlement (Shimonitsu and Levi, 1992). Technological developments, such as smartphones and laptops, mean an increasing proportion of individuals remain in touch with, and contactable by, their employing organisation even when they are away from work. This extends their potential work period (Fuchs, Epstein and Kalleberg, 2001: 13; see also Chapter 13).

Presenteeism has a number of potentially detrimental aspects. Simpson (2000: 164) highlights how it can act unfairly against women in organisations, because men are often in a better position than women with children to stay much later than the official end of the working day. Second, long work hours are frequently linked to the inefficient organisation of work time. Perlow's (1999) study referred to above highlights the way in which improved scheduling of work allowed shorter work days to be achieved.

Paid overtime

It is clear even from the information available on weekly work hours that among some groups, paid overtime working is the norm. Machine operatives, for example, recorded an average working week of 44 hours in 2009 (ONS, 2010: 50), a figure significantly heightened by overtime working. Later, there is a discussion of whether or not work has become more intensive over time. However, levels of overtime working indicate that, for many, work is also characterised by its extensiveness. For many people work occupies a large part of their total waking hours.

Cross-national variation in work patterns

In a separate cross-cultural study, Perlow demonstrates that there is nothing inherent in software engineering that required a particular or long hours pattern. After spending time with engineers performing similar software activities in organisations in China, India and Hungary (each part of a larger joint venture with a US-based multinational corporation), the author found quite distinct attitudes in the three countries to the working day and working at weekends.

For example, engineers in China worked a relatively short, intensive eight-hour day from 8 am to 5 pm with a one-hour lunch break. These engineers rarely worked weekends. The engineers in India in contrast worked a longer day (most working 9 am to 7 pm, but often staying later) with regular weekend working, especially on Saturdays.

The engineers in Hungary fell somewhere in between these two extremes, working longer hours when work pressure required, but also enjoying the greatest flexibility of the three in determining their work hours. Perlow comments that in Hungary, the engineers typically worked from 9 am until 6 pm, sometimes 7 pm, but it was not unusual for someone to come in later, leave early or work from home. These engineers however, put in longer hours (including weekends) when work required it, such as the final day before installing a new system.

Source: Perlow (2001).

What do you think?

Perlow's research shows that the same activity being carried out in three different countries is associated with three distinct work patterns.

What do you think are likely to be the main factors giving rise to this variation? Identify the possible factors operating at (a) work group (b) company and (c) societal levels.

Studies over several decades have demonstrated a link between long hours, fatigue, declining productivity and increased accidents and injuries (see, for example, Rosa, 1995). In terms of the effects of long hours on individual health, an analysis by Sparks and colleagues (1997) of 21 studies concluded that there is a small but significant relationship between poorer physical and psychological health and longer work hours. Ferrie and Smith (1996: 47), in their study of several thousand adults, found that those working very long hours (60 hours a week or more) were twice as likely to report a depressed mood, compared with those working fewer hours (see also Spurgeon, 2003).

Studies in this area have largely concentrated on the people working the long hours, but account also needs to be taken of the physical and psychological impact of long work hours on other family members. It influences the way child-rearing and other domestic responsibilities are shared, for instance (see Ferrie and Smith, 1996; Jacobs and Gerson, 2001). We take up the more general issue of how long hours working impacts upon non-work life in Chapter 13 (see also the discussion of domestic work in Chapter 12).

Within Europe, average weekly hours of full-time employees in the UK are particularly high. Among male workers, usual hours worked by UK males are among the longest of the EU member states, while among female full-time workers only Latvia, Slovenia and the Czech Republic exhibit longer weekly working hours (see Table 4.1).

Table 4.1   Usual hours worked per week by full-time employees in the EU, 2003

	Males	Females	All
Latvia	44.3	42.2	43.3
United Kingdom	44.6	40.4	43.1
Poland	43.2	39.6	41.5
Czech Rep.	42.2	40.5	41.4
Slovenia	41.9	40.9	41.4
Estonia	41.8	40.4	41.1
Greece	41.9	39.6	41.0
Hungary	41.6	40.2	41.0
Malta	41.7	38.8	40.8
Slovakia	40.9	40.0	40.5
Spain	40.9	39.4	40.3
Portugal	40.9	39.2	40.1
Austria	40.1	39.9	40.0
Cyprus	40.5	39.6	40.0
Sweden	40.1	39.6	39.9
Luxembourg	40.3	38.6	39.8
Germany	40.0	39.0	39.6
Ireland	40.6	37.7	39.5
Lithuania	40.1	38.6	39.4
Denmark	40.1	37.7	39.2
Finland	40.1	38.2	39.2
Belgium	39.6	37.7	39.0
France	39.6	37.7	38.8
Netherlands	39.0	38.0	38.8
Italy	39.9	36.6	38.7
EU25 average	41.0	38.9	40.2

Source: Adapted from Eurostat Labour Force Survey.

These long work hours in the UK reflect a high level of overtime working. Several factors may account for this level of overtime working in the UK, including (prior to the introduction of the EU Directive on Working Time) the past absence of statutory controls on the maximum number of work hours an individual is permitted to work. Also significant for many workers is the importance of overtime earnings for supplementing (low) basic wage levels. Industries where long hours working involving paid overtime is especially common for men are parts of manufacturing, construction, the motor trade, hotels, transport and security. For female employees, bar work is an activity particularly associated with long hours working.

Though overtime is often paid at a premium rate (e.g. time and a half, or double time) it represents a preferable option for many employers, compared with introducing shift working and hiring additional staff. Overtime potentially offers a more flexible means of extending the working period, but it can also reduce pressure on employers to raise basic wage levels, since the availability of overtime work is offered as an incentive to attract and retain staff in otherwise low-paying jobs. For employees, however, it means the overall experience of work is strongly tainted by long hours. There is also less opportunity to pursue other, non-work activities (see also Chapter 13).

In a number of (mainly manual) occupations, the requirement to undertake overtime is a contractual obligation. As noted above, in others (among many white-collar, managerial and professional occupations) there is a widespread expectation that additional hours (paid or unpaid) should be worked to complete tasks that are outstanding, and more generally that working long hours is a sign of commitment (and an unwillingness to work extra hours indicates a lack of commitment).

The pattern of working time is characterised not only by some experiencing very long hours of work, but also by a growing diversity of working time schedules. A significant proportion of the work force is employed for only a very few hours each week. In practice, the pattern of hours in paid work is both gendered and polarised. A large number of men work long weekly hours, and large numbers of women (as discussed further below) work comparatively few hours.

Hours of part-time workers

The overall growth of part-time working, and the fact that most part-time jobs are held by women, has already been noted (see Chapter 2). An important aspect of part-time working is that many part-time jobs involve very few hours. This is particularly pronounced in Britain compared with other EU countries (Rubery, Fagan and Smith, 1995), and it is also evident in the United States (Jacobs and Gerson, 2001: 41).

In the UK almost half of part-time male workers and approaching two-fifths of female part-time workers work 16 hours per week or less, while around one in five of the men and one in eight of the women normally work fewer than eight hours per week (see Table 4.2). Occupations that are disproportionately reflected among those working short weekly hours include certain health service

Table 4.2   Distribution of work hours of those working less than 30 hours per week, UK, 2003

Percentage with normal basic hours in the range	Males (%)	Females (%)
8 or less	18.5	12.4
8–16	29.9	25.5
16–21	19.1	25.4
21–30	32.4	36.8

Source: Adapted from *New Earnings Survey*, 2003, Part F, Table 45.1.

occupations, teaching, sports and fitness occupations, together with restaurant and bar staff. For employers, part-time working in general, and the use of short schedules in particular, allows the concentration of workers at times when work pressures are at their highest. For many employees, however, jobs comprising only a few hours per week yield only very limited income, often leading to the necessity for multiple job-holding.

Zero hours contracts

If some jobs are characterised by their short duration, others operate on the basis of no guaranteed duration at all. 'Zero hours' contracts (also known as 'reservism' and 'on call' arrangements) involve employers guaranteeing no definite hours to employees, but simply calling on workers as and when required. In some sectors, such as education, similar arrangements have long existed in the form of teachers being 'on supply', with work being offered, usually at very short notice, to cover absence or other reasons for teachers being away from the classroom. More recently zero hours contracts have developed, initially in the retail sector, again primarily as a means for employers to cover absence.

Such contracts provide employers with a very high degree of temporal flexibility, but workers hired on such contracts are typically afforded no job security, and no guarantee of earnings or hours. At the same time these contracts are restrictive in that employees need to keep themselves available ('on call'). This limits their opportunities to pursue other activities. Despite their limitations, zero hours contracts are not accepted by employees just because nothing more secure or predictable is on offer. There are groups, such as students and those recently retired, for whom the occasional work entailed in zero hours contracts may fit very well with their other commitments and lifestyle.

There has been little aggregate information on the development of zero hours working. The Workplace Employment Relations Survey (WERS) found zero hours contracts to be operating for some employees in 5 per cent of British workplaces in 2004 (Kersley et al, 2005: 29). However, other estimates of the actual numbers of employees with zero hours contracts put the total at less than 1 per cent of the total workforce (see, for example, Arrowsmith and Sisson, 2000: 302; Equal Opportunities Commission, 1998: 34). This indicates that many organisations reporting the use of zero hours contracts were operating these for only small numbers of staff.

To sum up

Working time patterns are increasingly characterised by diversity, with very long weeks worked by some and very short weeks worked by others. Despite a downward trend in basic weekly hours of full-time employees, many continue to work far longer than the basic week by undertaking a large amount of paid or unpaid overtime.

Changes in the organisation of working time

Growing diversity in working time patterns

Several factors in recent years have encouraged employers to increase their total operating hours. In the service sector, this reflects partly the general increase in opening hours and is a result, for example, of the liberalisation of Sunday trading, changes in licensing hours, extension of banking hours and late evening or 24-hour opening of retail and other service activities. In manufacturing, increased investment in technology, coupled with a faster rate of technological obsolescence – electronic equipment becomes quickly outdated – has forced employers to consider more ways to be competitive.

A gradually declining basic work week combined with pressures to maintain or increase operating times has meant there is less of a match between individual work hours and operating hours. Instead of an organisation's operating time being the same as the employees' work period (e.g. 9 am to 5.30 pm) the operating time has expanded (e.g. to 10 pm) with the additional time being covered, by shift work, such as a part-time evening shift. These kinds of patterns are not new of course. Hospitals, hotels, continuous process operations, transport, postal services and parts of the engineering sector have long been used to a distinction between the length of the operating period and individual work hours. What is new in recent years is the spread of shift working into areas where it has traditionally been rare, such as in retailing and financial services. This pressure to extend hours impacts not only on weekdays but also on weekends.

When viewed in combination with the greater use of part-time schedules, the extension of operating hours has created an overall working time pattern which is diverse, not only in terms of the number of hours that people work, but also in terms of when they work those hours. There is a popular belief that a majority of people still work Monday to Friday, from 9 am to 5 pm or thereabouts. In practice, however, this is far from the actual experience of the majority of employees. In Britain, only around a third of employed men and women operate such a working time pattern (Table 4.3; see also Hill, 2000).

Table 4.3   The timing of work weeks for men and women in Britain (%)

Full-time, Monday to Friday, starting between 8–10 am, finishing between 4–6 pm	34
Full-time, Monday to Friday, other hours	7
Part-time, Monday to Friday	11
6 or 7-day week	23
1 to 5 days, some weekend work	11
1 to 4 days, no weekend work	14

Source: Hewitt (1993: 23).

What do you think?

A growing amount of work is undertaken in the evenings, at night and during the weekend. If you were
to undertake work at any of these times (or if you were asked to), what do you think are (or would be)
(a) the main advantages and (b) the main disadvantages of working during these periods? List up to four
advantages and four disadvantages.

Shift working

There are various ways in which an employer can schedule working hours to
create a longer working period. The use of overtime for this purpose has already
been noted. In addition, a long-established means of lengthening the working period is by operating a shift system; a simple definition of shift work is 'a
situation in which one worker replaces another on the same job within a 24-hour
period' (Ingram and Sloane, 1984: 168). Various shift-work patterns exist:

• Some extend across the whole day and week – for example, continuous
  three-shift working, with shifts starting for example, at 6 am, 2 pm and 10 pm.
• Others extend the productive period but not across the entire day or week –
  such as 'double day' shifts, for example 6 am–2 pm and 2 pm–10 pm.

Around 3.6 million people in the UK (14% of the UK working population) do
shift work. Shift working is most common among male manual workers, with
shift work particularly evident in such sectors as metal manufacturing, chemicals,
vehicle production, health and transport.

Just as working very long hours can have a negative effect on health (see above),
so too can certain shift-work patterns, such as night working. For many, night
shifts (and in particular the requirement to be active at a time when the body
is normally resting) are associated with poor sleep quality, digestive problems
and other consequences of the disruption to physiological rhythms (Blyton,
1985: 67–70; for a detailed review of issues surrounding working time patterns
and health, see Spurgeon, 2003). Working at night and sleeping during the day
can also create social problems for individuals and families, disrupting the practical organisation of domestic life, the quality of relations within the family and the
satisfactory performance of parental roles (Mott et al, 1965; see also Chapter 13).

Compressed work weeks

One reason that the proportion of employees working shifts has not risen even
higher is the replacement of formal shift-work systems with alternative working time arrangements which extend the productive period, but do not incur
the wage premiums usually paid to workers on shifts. One example of these
arrangements is 'compressed' work weeks, where employees work their total
weekly hours in longer work periods but for fewer than the normal number of

days (e.g. working for longer hours on nine days every two weeks rather than working the hours over ten days). Spurgeon (2003: 56) notes that one of the most common forms of compressed working time in recent years has been the introduction of 12-hour shift working (see also Baltes et al, 1999). For an example of the introduction of a 12-hour working pattern, see Extract 4.5.

Extract 4.5

More time with the family

In a follow-up study of work reorganisation in the iron and steel industry to that described in Extract 4.1, two further UK steel plants were studied to see how they negotiated the introduction of the changes. One of the most interesting findings to emerge was the importance of working time changes simultaneously negotiated at one of the plants. While at the Scunthorpe works (a large integrated steel plant in the north of England) the introduction of major work changes was accompanied by the retention of an eight-hour work pattern, at the Teesside works (a similar large integrated plant about 70 miles further north), the work changes were accompanied by a move from eight to 12-hour working in all but one of the nine main production departments.

Both plants operate on a continuous 24-hour, seven-day basis, and the working time system at Teesside typically involves employees working four 12-hour shifts, followed by four days off, this pattern being concluded by an 18-day break after working 40 shifts. (All employees have an annual hours contract based on an agreed 36.5-hour working week.) For many employees at Teesside this working time pattern involves working a basic year of 147 shifts, far fewer than under the previous eight-hour system.

From interview and survey comments, it was clear that the majority of the Teesside workers welcomed the compressed working time represented by the 12-hour working, and that this in turn influenced views on the acceptability of other changes occurring at the plant. In the main, comments referred to the value of the additional non-work days that the new shift pattern generated. Comments such as 'more time off with the family' were frequently made, and as one employee put it, 'If you are at work you get your hours in while you're here and then benefit by the extra time off.' Indeed, some employees commented on their ability to compress their work time even further by switching shifts with colleagues at the start and/or finish of the 18-day break. As one recounted, 'I swap regularly; I swap my four days on so I have [a] 26 [day break].'

At the Scunthorpe plant, on the other hand, workers felt they had gained little in compensation for the job losses and more intensive work regime following the work changes introduced.

Source: Bacon, Blyton and Dastmalchian (2005).

Seasonal, annual and variable hours

Attempts by employers to extend the length of the productive work period have also been accompanied, in a growing number of cases, by attempts to redefine what constitutes normal work hours. This has been in order to reduce the amount of time attracting (premium-paid) overtime rates. Examples of negotiations over the redefinition of normal and overtime periods are longstanding, occurring, for example, in Australia (see discussion in Deery and Mahony, 1994: 333–5) and Germany. In Germany, extensive negotiations over working time during the 1990s included discussions on payments for Saturday working, and temporary increases in weekly hours without incurring overtime payments (Blyton and Trinczek, 1995).

In the UK and elsewhere, an example of managerial efforts to reduce reliance on overtime during busy periods has been the introduction of 'seasonal hours' working, where the normal work week is lengthened during busy periods and reduced during slacker times. A number of consumer electronics firms in the UK operate under this pattern, with longer work weeks (up to 44 hours) in the months prior to the busy Christmas period, and shorter hours in the following months to bring the average work week back to the contractually agreed level. For the employer this arrangement reduces overtime payments during the busy months and limits excess labour capacity in the quieter periods (Blyton, 1994: 517–18). For employees, however, this seasonality of the working period can be more problematic, since it is likely to entail both a loss of overtime earnings and eliminate any discretion workers may have enjoyed over whether or not to work overtime.

An extension of seasonal hours arrangements are 'annual hours' contracts, under which employees work an agreed number of hours per year, with working time schedules (including holidays) determined at the beginning of 12-month cycles. Such arrangements usually build in flexibility for employers either by establishing a schedule where more hours are worked during busy periods, or by leaving some of the agreed total hours as non-rostered work time. For these employees are effectively 'on call' and can be brought into work to cover unforeseen circumstances (Arrowsmith and Sisson, 2000: 299–302; Blyton, 2008). In 2009 in the UK, 5 per cent of full-time employees and 4 per cent of part-time employees were covered by annual hours contracts (ONS, 2010: 51).

Seasonal and annual hours arrangements not only create the potential for reducing overtime costs but also enable a closer matching of available labour with levels of output demand. Together with arranging hours to cover longer operating periods, this desire for a closer matching of work schedules with output demand has become a major focus for employers. In some sectors, demand fluctuates considerably over the working day and week. In parts of the retailing industry, for example, demand rises significantly during lunchtime periods and towards the end of the week. One of the ways working time schedules have been arranged to reflect this is via the introduction of various part-time schedules which increase the volume of available labour during busy periods. So, it has become common practice in retailing to schedule part-time workers to work during lunch periods and/or at weekends.

A growing practice is also the use of variable hours contracts, with workers contracted for a minimum number of hours per week (typically 16 hours) but can be assigned work for 30 hours or more in a week, depending on demand. Jobs with variable hours have become common in sectors such as retailing (Backett-Milburn et al, 2008; Lambert, 2008) and care (Blyton and Jenkins, 2012).

Flexible working hours

Employees can exert some influence over how work hours are arranged in flexible working hours systems and via informal working time arrangements.

According to Labour Force Survey statistics, one in eight (12.6%) full-time employees in the UK (11% of men and 15% of women) and approaching one in ten part-time employees work flexible working hours or 'flexitime' (ONS, 2010: 51). However, when the WERS researchers asked employees if they could have access to flexitime if they needed to because of domestic circumstances, approaching two-fifths (38%) of employees said they could work flexitime if it was needed (Kersley et al, 2005: 29).

Other arrangements that provide some flexibility to employees include term-time working and job sharing. In 2009 in the UK, one in nine female part-time employees (and just over one in fifteen full-time female employees) worked on a term-time only basis. A much smaller proportion (2.1% of female part-time employees) worked on job-sharing contracts (ONS, 2010: 51).

Flexitime working remains far more common among non-manual workers, particularly in larger public (and recently privatised) service sector organisations, than among their manual counterparts and others located in manufacturing and smaller establishments in the private sector (Kersley et al, 2005: 28; Wareing, 1992). Beyond formal flexitime systems, a proportion of employees operate less formalised systems which provide an element of choice over start and finish times. Those in higher-level jobs typically enjoy greater access to this informal flexibility. For example, in Wareing's (1992) study, half the employees in professional occupations had a measure of flexibility over their start and finish times, compared with less than one in ten of those in semi-skilled occupations. Many employees gain some flexibility over working hours by reaching informal 'understandings' with other workers and with management in relation, for example, to start and finish times. Such informal agreements are also reflected in much of the overtime that is worked. For a proportion of workers, overtime working is a contractual obligation. However, in a large-scale (though now somewhat dated) study in Britain, Marsh (1991) found that in the period immediately prior to her survey, more than three male full-time workers in every ten and over a quarter of full-time female workers had agreed to work extra time at short notice. This is a far higher proportion than the 6 per cent who indicated they were required by their contracts to work overtime (see also Horrell and Rubery, 1991).

To sum up

Much paid work takes place outside what has traditionally been thought of as the normal working period. Employers increasingly use different contractual arrangements and shift-work patterns to arrange working time to maximise labour coverage and flexibility and minimise labour cost. Formal and informal flexitime arrangements are ways employees can exercise a degree of choice over the scheduling of their work hours.

The utilisation of working time

Just as increased attention has been given to organising working time to cover longer opening/operating periods, and to concentrating labour time at periods of highest work pressure, greater attention has also been paid to increasing the extent to which labour time is effectively utilised. In the 1980s, White (1987: 51) estimated that in engineering, between 20 and 40 per cent of paid time was non-productive. As noted earlier, part of the explanation for this lies in scheduling and production problems such as shortages of materials, equipment breakdown and a lack of orders, together with poor management.

As we have seen, however, non-productive time (from a managerial perspective) can also be created by workers to establish an easier or more varied work tempo. Three recent developments relating to work time utilisation: (i) redefinition of the working period, (ii) 'lean' systems and (iii) flexible working are relevant here:

- *Redefinition of the working period.* There has been an increase in management initiatives designed to define the working period. These tend to exclude, rather than include, preparatory activities such as changing into and out of work clothes and walking to and from the actual work area. Efforts to tighten the definition of the working period have centred on practices such as 'bell to bell' working, which refers to the bells or buzzers announcing the start and finish of working periods, with employees required to be in position to commence working when the bell for the start of the shift sounds, and only terminating work after the bell that signals the end of the shift (Blyton, 2008: 517).

- *'Lean' systems.* The development of just-in-time (JIT), kanban and similar process systems which form a major element in 'lean' manufacturing systems also has potentially important implications for working time utilisation. This has been facilitated by advances in information technology. Under a JIT regime, for example, emphasis is placed on work 'flowing' steadily and continuously through the different stages of production, with components arriving just in time to be incorporated into the manufacturing process, and only minimum stocks held of materials, work in progress and finished articles. Among other implications, this method of organising production undermines any ability workers have to build up 'banks' of finished or part-finished work which, as discussed earlier, could be used to create an additional break or an easier work pace later in the working period.

- *Flexible working.* The growth of task flexibility during the past two decades represents a third area of workplace change with potentially important implications for time utilisation. Since the early 1980s, developments in work organisation based on broader job definitions, reduced skill demarcations and enlarged jobs have led to significant changes in the way individual tasks and work groups are organised. By 2004 in the UK, two-thirds of workplaces had trained at least some of their staff to be functionally flexible (capable of doing different jobs), and over four out of five employees trained in this way were undertaking jobs other than their own at least once a week (Kersley et al, 2005: 11). This blurring of skill boundaries and widespread development of greater flexibility among less skilled workers has had the effect of increasing the mobility of labour between tasks within workplaces. It has also represented part of a broader shift towards more jobs being covered by fewer workers, as organisations seek cost cutting through staff reductions.

Such managerial attempts to impose a time-reckoning system, together with responses by workers to operate a counter system which creates or extends additional rest periods, have been an ever-present feature of industrial capitalism. Marx, for example, remarked on employers' continual efforts to maximise 'surplus labour time' by seeking to extend the working period and by efforts to minimise the 'porosity' of the working day: the number of holes or 'pores' in the working day when workers are not actually working. Marx (1976: 352) characterised employers as continually 'nibbling and cribbling' at workers' meal times and other breaks in an attempt to maximise the quantity of labour effort in the working day. As contemporary managerial interest in bell-to-bell working and similar practices illustrates, this issue of productive work time continues to be as significant an issue for twenty-first century managers as it was for their nineteenth-century counterparts.

Related to this growth of flexibility in many work contexts has been the introduction of teamworking (Procter and Mueller, 2000). The WERS found that approaching three-quarters (72%) of workplaces indicated that they had at least some core employees organised into formally designated teams, though the extent of autonomy of these teams varied considerably (Kersley et al, 2005: 10–11). As management attempts not only to locate more responsibility for performance within work groups, but also to increase flexibility through greater worker interchangeability, and reduce costs by cutting the number of supervisory posts, it may be expected that interest in teamworking will continue to be strong in coming years.

In some contexts, working in teams has proved only marginally different from prior systems of work organisation based around less formal (but nonetheless important) work group arrangements. However, the circumstances under which teamworking has been adopted (often in the context of job reductions, lower staffing levels and increased emphasis on quality assurance) means that, for many, teamworking is part of a significant change from what has gone before. This is not least in terms of the additional responsibilities held by the team over such areas as task allocation and quality.

Harder work?

The above aspects of workplace change, and evidence of rises in productivity in the 1980s, prompted writers such as Elger (1990, 1991) to consider the extent to which increased productivity was the result of work becoming more intensive (see also Guest, 1990; Metcalf, 1989; Nolan, 1989). More recently Green (2001, 2004; Green and McIntosh, 2001) has undertaken detailed analysis of evidence on changing work pressures and work effort.

Whether or not workers are working harder is, in practice, difficult to say with accuracy, because it is complicated by various factors, not least the lack of any systematic objective study of effort. Other factors complicate comparisons of effort: for example, the experience of working harder can be the result of a faster work pace, a longer work period and/or reductions in the extent of non-work time (Elger, 1990). Effort may comprise the expenditure of either (or both) manual and mental energy. This means that, identifying a decline (or increase) in one may not give an accurate picture of what has happened to levels of effort overall. So, it is often argued that automation and other technological changes have reduced the degree of physical effort required to perform many jobs. There has been a decline in employment in manufacturing in general, and in heavy industries such as iron and steel-making, shipbuilding and coal mining in particular. This has been taken as evidence that the number of jobs in the labour force as a whole requiring high expenditure of (physical) effort is likely to have declined.

Yet various attitude studies show that despite the decline of heavy industry, many workers report having experienced an increase in effort (in terms of both physical and mental effort). Clearly there are potential bias problems if these studies rely on self-reports (asking workers whether or not they feel they are working harder than they used to). Nonetheless, the strength and consistency of worker opinions on questions of effort suggest support for the argument that effort levels have indeed risen. Green (2001, 2004; Green and McIntosh, 2001) shows that in national and cross-national surveys since the 1980s, an increased proportion of employees have consistently reported that they are working under greater pressure. This is reflected, for example, in the growing proportion of people reporting that they 'mostly' or 'always' work 'under a great deal of pressure', that their job involves 'working at high speed' or 'working to tight deadlines'. For Green (2001: 68), the evidence creates 'a picture of continually rising work effort' over the 1980s and 1990s. Green also points out that surveys undertaken at different time periods point to the growing importance of 'fellow workers or colleagues' as a key source of work pressure by the late 1990s. As Green (2001: 70) remarks, 'It seems that peer pressure has come into its own as a source of labour intensification.' This is relevant given increases in the use of team working (above).

Other factors associated with increased work intensity include working with technology – those working with computers are more likely to report growing intensity – and those experiencing major work reorganisation (Green, 2004). Elger (1991) argued that the drive for greater flexibility contributed to labour intensification because reorganisation and reductions in workforce numbers, with the fewer remaining workers covering more tasks, resulted in more intensified work regimes. This is echoed in the study by Edwards and Whitston (1991: 597), where, for example, one of the factors affecting the perceived increase in effort levels among railway platform staff was that the standard labour allocation had been cut from three workers per railway platform to two. Similarly, in the steel study cited in Extract 4.5, a prominent characteristic of the plant under investigation was continued cuts in workforce numbers, with those remaining required to cover a broader range of tasks. Competitive pressures in the private sector have fuelled a search for lower labour costs, and as a result potentially stimulated labour intensification. Also, funding shortages and political demands for more efficient public services have led to a corresponding search for reductions in labour costs in the public sector, and in-house groups have been forced to be as competitive as external providers of similar services.

To sum up

Management is ever concerned with increasing the productive use of working time. One of the outcomes of this has been employees consistently reporting that they are working harder. Developments such as flexibility and teamworking are among the factors contributing to this experience of labour intensification.

Conclusion

Time is a central factor shaping the experience of work. What this chapter has underlined is the growing diversity of time schedules: a diversity reflected in the different lengths of working hours, the ways those hours are variously organised across the day and week and the degree to which working hours are actually utilised in productive activity. We also stressed the different ways that management and workers perceive working time. On the one hand, a managerial logic emphasises the linear quality of time, the importance of regularity for the coordination of different time schedules and the importance of maximising the productive use of contracted working time. On the other hand, however, a workers' logic is also evident, seeking in part to limit the harmful aspects of an intense or unchanging work tempo. These two logics exist side by side and influence each other. This means that the formal time regime defined by management typically bears only a partial resemblance to actual working time patterns performed by their employees.

These two logics also reflect a tension between the objective and subjective nature of time. The managerial logic is essentially based on a view of time as 'clock time': time as a scarce resource, and a commodity capable of being 'spent', 'wasted' or 'lost'. The objective character of time in this sense is summed up in the classic cliché of capitalism, 'time is money'. On the other hand, however, workers experience time at work subjectively: it can pass quickly or slowly, can be varied or monotonous and, for many, will be experienced as cyclical rather than linear. One day more or less repeats the cycle of the previous day, or even one hour repeating the pattern of the previous one. Workers can try to improve the way time is experienced in different ways, ranging from occasional absence to escape the routines of work to the creation of different 'times' within the working day, when the tempo of work is altered and the regularity of time is suppressed.

The relationship between the objective and subjective character of time, and between a managerial temporal logic and a workers' temporal logic, represents an ongoing tension in the employment relationship. On the one hand, for example, continuing levels of voluntary absence indicate workers are able to show some control over the most basic issue of whether they are at work. On the other hand, management's introduction of tighter staffing levels and practices such as bell-to-bell working signal their pursuit of higher levels of working time utilisation.

The tension between the two logics may be expected to continue for the foreseeable future and manifest itself within particular aspects of working time. For example, management's efforts to cut labour costs by restricting the periods defined as overtime (via arrangements such as variable, seasonal and annual hours contracts, and different part-time schedules) are likely to be countered, to a degree at least, by workers seeking to establish an easier pace of work which allows, among other things, unfinished work to be carried over into (premium-paid) overtime hours. Such a carry over of work into overtime remains particularly important in those low-paying jobs where workers rely heavily on overtime earnings. Of course, an obvious cost to those working long hours is the reduced time available for non-work activities and responsibilities. In broader societal terms, the cost is also that while many are working very long hours to earn an acceptable wage, others remain unemployed and underemployed for want of available or sufficient work. Overall, it is a situation satisfactory to neither group. However, despite an ongoing debate over work-sharing and the reorganisation of working time, to date this has remained an issue lacking the political will to bring about any significant change.

5

Work skills

Key concepts

D skill in the person

D skill in the job

D skill in the setting

D complexity and discretion

D tacit skill

D social closure

D ideological, political and material processes of social closure

D social regulation

D social construction of skill

D gender and skill

Chapter aim

To explore the concept of skill and critically evaluate three different approaches to its definition and measurement.

Learning outcomes

After reading and thinking about the material in this chapter, you will be able to:

1. Identify three approaches to evaluating skill.
2. Explain how to assess skill in the person and identify the limitations of this approach.
3. Explain how to assess skill in the job using:
   a. the concept of complexity,
   b. the concept of discretion.
4. Explain how to assess skill in the setting using the concept of social closure.
5. Explain how skill can be seen as (i) a socially constructed phenomenon that has (ii) disadvantaged women through ideological, political and material processes.

Exploring the concept of skill

Of all the concepts we encounter when studying the realities of work, 'skill' stands out as the most difficult to pin down. Yet, strangely enough, it is perhaps one of the few topics that most people might claim to have an understanding about. If you ask someone about a job, they would more than likely be able to tell you whether it is skilled or not, and they would probably be able to give a reasonable explanation as to why they considered it skilled. The problem, however, is that we all stress different aspects of a job in evaluating whether it is skilled or not. In extreme cases, the lack of consensus over what constitutes a skilled job is less important because the job attributes are diverse enough for people to reach general, if not specific, agreement. For example, most people would probably agree that the surgeon's job is more skilled than the hospital porter's job, or that the teacher is more skilled than the school caretaker – but some comparisons are far more problematic. To illustrate this, complete Exercise 5.1.

Exercise 5.1

What do you think?

For each of the pairs of jobs listed below, decide which is the most skilled and justify your decision. In other words, explain the criteria you are using to decide how skill should be evaluated.

1. The hotel receptionist compared with the security guard.
2. The computer games software programmer and the paramedic.
3. The cleaner and the car-park attendant.
4. The insurance broker and the travel agent.
5. The police officer and the social worker.

To reach an agreement on comparisons such as those in Exercise 5.1, it is necessary to achieve consensus on what is meant by the term 'skill'. This is not an easy task because skill is a definitional minefield. However, in the rest of the chapter we will enter this dangerous territory!

First we must ask, why worry about defining skill at all? This is a reasonable question, and the answer, as explained below, is that skill is fundamental to the status that people attach to different occupations, and it is frequently linked to pay. Moreover, skill is a key factor in determining the structure of employment, most notably in the way it acts to reinforce gender divisions relating to labour in society.

Locating skill

The first puzzle that needs to be solved is the problem of where skill resides. Is it part of:

- the person?
- the job?
- the setting?

Cockburn (1983: 113) suggests all three aspects need to be taken into account. In her study of (male) print workers she argues that:

> There is the skill that resides in the man himself, accumulated over time, each new experience adding something to a total ability. There is the skill demanded by the job – which may or may not match the skill in the worker. And there is the political definition of skill: that which a group of workers or a trade union can successfully defend against the challenge of employers and other groups of workers.

A closer consideration of Cockburn's research will be undertaken later in the chapter, but it is worth pausing to give some thought to her three categories because each suggests a different approach to examining skill:

1. *Skill in the person.* Any analysis that concentrates on the person is likely to attempt to identify individual attributes and qualities and seek to measure these through, for example, an aptitude test under experimental conditions. Typically, this approach has been informed by the work of psychologists. Similarly, a questionnaire might be administered to assess a person's education, training and experience, which could then be used as a proxy for (i.e. an indicator of) skill – a method frequently adopted by economists.
2. *Skill in the job.* If the analytical focus is the job, then the concern is less with the person performing the task than with the requirements embedded in the task itself. In this case, attention would be turned towards the complexity of the tasks required to perform the job competently – an approach typically taken by management theorists. It would also include the extent of discretion over the work – an issue of particular interest to industrial–employment relations theorists.
3. *Skill in the setting.* If the focus is on the political and historical setting, an analysis would be assessing the way skill has developed over time and has been 'constructed' by different interest groups, rather than being a feature of the person or the job. This way of looking at skill is an approach pursued by some sociologists (particularly gender theorists) and social historians.

These differences in approach to analysing skill are summarised in Table 5.1. It illustrates how the focus tends to be associated with different methods of analysis and shows how academic disciplines have tended to address different aspects of skill.

Table 5.1   Approaches to the analysis of skill

Focus	Principal area of concern	Typical approach taken	Typically adopted by
Person	Individual attributes acquired through: ■ education ■ training ■ experience	Questionnaire surveys Use of proxy measures (e.g. qualifications, number of years of training) Aptitude tests/experiments	Economists Psychologists
Job	Task requirements ■ complexity ■ discretion	Job analysis Job evaluation	Occupational psychologists Management theorists Industrial/employment relations theorists
Setting	Social relations	Case studies of industries and occupations Ethnographic studies of workplaces	Social historians Sociologists Gender theorists

To sum up

It is possible for several theorists to arrive at contrasting conclusions about skilled work because they are focusing on different features and are using different methods of analysis.

Now we have charted the terrain, it is necessary to explore each of these areas in closer detail. To do this the rest of the chapter has been divided into three sections, each analysing a different aspect of skill: the person, the job and the setting. Each section draws out the strengths and weaknesses of the particular approaches, thereby demonstrating that there is no simple way of assessing skill. Following this, a final section illustrates the contemporary importance of the concept of skill by examining how it can perpetuate gender divisions in relation to labour.

Skill in the person

In this first approach, skill is generally considered a quality possessed by the individual. It can take numerous forms – for example, knowledge, dexterity, judgement and linguistic ability – but the assumption is that it is gained by a person during education, training and experience. At first sight, this is an attractive conception of skill because it is relatively easy to measure and produces quantifiable data that can be incorporated into statistical analyses. For example, people can be asked to complete a questionnaire listing their years in formal education, their number of qualifications, the amount of training they have undertaken and their on-the-job experience.

It is not surprising, therefore, that many labour economists are satisfied with these measures as a proxy for skill. This is typified by the approach of human capital theorists (e.g. Becker, 1964), who argue that in a market economy, a person's human capital will determine his or her value as an employee. From this perspective it is argued that people can choose, as individuals, to increase their human capital through taking advantage of educational opportunities and training. Conversely, they can choose to ignore these opportunities, with the consequence of lowering their relative value in the labour market. For human capital theorists, responsibility for success in work clearly lies with the individual; they call on the notion of a meritocratic society, where individual endeavour is rewarded.

Problems with the human capital approach

Inequality of opportunity

This approach is simplistic if it assumes that everyone has the same opportunity of access to the activities that improve human capital. This is clearly not the case. For example, private education generally provides children with better facilities, smaller class sizes and a more intense learning environment, but such education is available only to the minority of children whose parents can afford it, together with a small number who are awarded scholarships. Similarly, take the example of experience: in order to gain work experience, a person has to be offered a job, but when there are high rates of unemployment allowing employers to pick and choose, a person with no work experience is less likely to be offered a job and hence is unable to gain work experience. Opportunities to get work experience as an intern may also depend on family contacts, for example. These examples illustrate the fundamental problem that people do not compete on equal terms because there is not a level playing field.

Validity of the skill measures

A more general problem is whether the variables of education, training and experience are valid measures of skill. The number of years a person spends in formal education is linked to qualifications attained, but even then it does not necessarily mean that the skills learned will be appropriate or transferable to work. Similarly, while the measurement of training may be a better indicator of industry-specific knowledge and aptitude, it does not take into account the applicability of the training to a specific context.

Use value of the skill

Should measurement include only those attributes that have a current value – in other words, the measurement of 'skills in use' rather than skills possessed? For example, if a person learns to speak Welsh and gains a qualification proving his/her competence, does this constitute a skill? If it has some market value, human capital theorists would say 'yes', but if few employers require Welsh speakers, its value is severely reduced. In other words, a particular skill can be seen as an asset based on its market value. In this sense, all knowledge and abilities can be seen as potential skills, but it is the demand for them and their supply that give them value. Therefore, measuring the skills possessed by the person can be misleading without exploring the labour market context (see Extract 5.1).

Extract 5.1

The supply of and demand for skills – measuring qualifications

In an analysis of the United States and Canada, Livingstone (1998) found considerable discrepancies between the skills people possess and the skills they are expected to use at work. He describes this as the education–jobs gap, and argues that the rise in educational qualifications and work-related knowledge has outpaced the development of jobs where people can put this knowledge to use.

Similarly, in the UK, an analysis of qualifications by Felstead, Gallie and Green (2002) revealed that the proportion of over-qualified workers has increased from 30 per cent in 1986 to 37 per cent in 2001 ('over-qualified' means that the person doing the job has higher qualifications than are required by the job). In particular, at the bottom of the skills hierarchy, the demand for workers with no qualifications greatly outstrips supply: an estimated 6.4 million jobs required no qualifications but there were only 2.8 million people in the labour force with no qualifications. In other words, speaking somewhat simplistically, for every unqualified person there were more than two potential jobs). This contrasts with 1986, when the estimates of numbers of jobs requiring no qualifications and people without qualifications were broadly matched at around just under 8 million (Felstead et al, 2004: 154–8). Of course cynics might question whether the marked increase in those with qualifications between 1986 and 2001 represents a real skills increase. Instead it could reflect an increasing tendency to give formal accreditation to attributes that were once not considered skills. This means it could actually be a sign of declining standards.

The evidence from both studies suggests there is 'underemployment' of the skills available in the labour market. One problem that this raises is so-called 'credentialism'. This is the tendency for employers to ask for higher qualifications for a job without changing the job content, to make use of the improved skills of job holders. The likely consequence for employees is that they feel dissatisfied because they are not using their skills and may consider the job insufficiently challenging.

A broader definition of 'skill in the person'

The limitations noted above mean that the skills a person has may be wider than those captured in measures such as formal qualifications. As a consequence we may need a broader definition of individual skills. This need not simply look at formally recognised achievements. Indeed, it has been argued by some commentators that there is a growing tendency to broaden the definition of skill in the person by labelling certain personal characteristics as skills. For example, Grugulis, Warhurst and Keep (2004) note that attitudes, character traits and predispositions (tendencies to certain moods) are being described by employers as required skills (and also as typically lacking in the labour market). Some commentators use the term 'soft skills' to mean a range of these behavioural and attitudinal qualities that workers can (or should) be able to offer (e.g. Moss and Tilly, 1996).

This broadening of the definition might be explained to some extent by the changing demands of work. Chapter 2 described the growth of the service sector and outlined how the requirements of customer-facing roles have changed. (We explore the demands of many such jobs in Chapter 7 as we evaluate emotion work.) It is also the case that internal restructuring can lead to new forms of work organisation and therefore different qualities are demanded – for instance, the ability to work in teams. This being the case, it would seem appropriate that additional qualities need to be assessed, hence broader definitions of skill need to be considered. However, there are at least three objections to such an approach:

- The first objection is that these new qualities should not be considered skills at all. Lafer (2004) argues that a skill is a quality learned or developed by individuals that will secure them a living. Many of the new 'skills' (punctuality, appearance, manners, and so forth) are not skills in this sense because, alone, they cannot secure a living wage, although they might be a prerequisite for getting a job in the first instance, and they are often also qualities required to remain in employment. In Lafer's (2004: 117) words, 'Traits such as discipline, loyalty and punctuality are not "skills" that one either possesses or lacks; they are measures of commitment that one chooses to give or withhold based on the conditions of work offered'. The consequence of broadening the definition of skill in such a way means that the concept of skill in the person becomes increasingly meaningless, and therefore useless (Grugulis, 2007; Lloyd and Payne, 2009; Payne, 2009).

- The second objection comes from commentators who see the broadening definition as being a move by employers to shift responsibility to others for developing qualities such as punctuality, conscientiousness, teamworking, respect for authority and so forth. The objection is not with the meaningfulness of the concept of skill – indeed, a broader definition is considered useful, particularly if this involves recognising previously undervalued skills and especially those associated with jobs in which women predominate (see the discussion later in this chapter). Instead, the objection is with the implications of incorporating the 'new skills'. As Grugulis, Warhurst and Keep (2004: 12) state:

  > By changing the meaning of skill to embrace attitudes and behavioural traits or by increasing the emphasis placed upon the possession of such characteristics, employers have been able to shift responsibility for the creation or reinforcement of some of these attitudes and traits away from their roles as managers and motivators of their employees and onto the education and training system.

- A third objection is that there might be a political motivation behind accrediting a greater range of abilities and attributes as skills. Through the process of redefining skill and issuing certificates to prove the attainment of skills, a government can more easily claim that the skill base of the workforce is increasing – even though many of the now certified skills may have been possessed and used by the workforce in previous periods without formal recognition. This does not detract from the importance of recognising lower-level skills, but caution must be taken in assuming either that this represents a step increase in the skills base for the workforce, or that employers will pay the individual any premium for these certified skills when they are so widely held.

To sum up

The approach of assessing skill in the person tends to view skill as an attribute possessed by an individual, and sometimes described as a person's human capital. While this appears to be a relatively simple way of assessing skill, the problems lie in the methods of measurement and then putting these into practice.

Exercise 5.2

What do you think?

Below is a list of individual qualities that might be required by an employee who deals with customers face-to-face. Which of them would you describe as skills? Explain your reasoning:

- punctuality,
- a friendly manner,
- ability to calm down an irate customer,
- a positive attitude to work,
- a sound knowledge of the company products/services,
- good standard of numeracy,
- good verbal communication.

Skill in the job

In this section the analysis focuses on assessing the skill required by the job, rather than the skills possessed by the person doing the job. Of course, in an ideal situation the two would match, but the reality is that some people are more skilled than their job requires, while others are insufficiently skilled. By focusing on the job rather than the person, this potential mismatch is removed from the analysis, thereby allowing us to explore skill by looking at the complexity of the job and the extent of discretion in the job.

Assessing the complexity of jobs

It seems reasonable to suppose there is an association between the complexity of the tasks required by the job and the overall level of skill: the more complex the tasks, the more skilled the job can be said to be. This also suggests that if the extent of complexity in a particular job is measured it should be possible to arrive at a skill level. For instance, in their skills survey, Felstead, Gallie and Green (2004) ask questions about the qualifications required to get the job; the length of training required for the type of work; the time it takes to learn to do the work well; and the importance of 36 different activities that the work might involve (such as caring for others, working with computers, dealing with people, physical stamina, writing reports). The assumption behind such an approach is that it is possible to derive an objective measure of complexity. This is an appealing idea because it means that different jobs could be compared and ranked according to their complexity. This ranking could be reflected in systems of status and remuneration (typically taking the form of job evaluation schemes). Although it seems a feasible and logical exercise, in practice it is notoriously difficult to do because evaluating job content has a subjective element. Two main difficulties are encountered.

The difficulty of observing

Imagine being in the position of observing a job and assessing its complexity. The job might appear complex if it is unfamiliar. For example, to the observer who cannot drive, driving is likely to seem a very complex activity involving physical coordination, spatial awareness, concentration and quick decision making. Yet for the seasoned driver it might not be viewed as a complex skill at all, not least because it is a widely shared ability. This presents a paradox: a fair evaluation would mean the observer having familiarity with the task, but this familiarity may lead the observer to undervalue the task. In other words, there are problems with relying on observation because of the subjectivity of the observer.

The difficulty of asking

A possible alternative approach is to ask the person doing the job to identify its complexity. But this also poses problems for similar reasons: familiarity and adeptness may lead a person to undervalue a task. As Attewell (1990: 430) argues:

> [Mundane activities] become socially invisible to both the actors performing them and to observers familiar with them.... They become buried within their practitioners – either psychologically in the form of habits and non-conscious information-processing or somatically [in the body] in muscles and neurons (knack, deftness and cunning).

This suggests that both observation and self-assessment would lead to a general conclusion that much of human activity in work (as well as outside) is not complex and, by implication, requires little skill. As Attewell points out, this is particularly ironic because when a person achieves a high level of competence, they internal-ise procedures and routines so the task can be accomplished 'without thinking'. For the novice, each situation and each problem is unique and uncertain and so they must apply conscious thought, but 'the maestro has been there before and has more (nonconscious) routines to apply' (Attewell, 1990: 433). To put this in another way, beginners rely on abstract rules which have been derived by others, and they use these to guide their progress and accumulate experience; experts rely on context-bound knowledge that they have developed through experience and are therefore less conscious of the decision-rules they are using.

Similarly, Manwaring and Wood (1985) identify the importance of considering 'tacit skills' (based upon the analysis of Polanyi and Prosch, 1975; Koestler, 1976; Kusterer, 1978) to suggest that work necessarily involves the internalisation of learning. This means tasks can be performed successfully by drawing on unconscious thought, and that different degrees of awareness are required both within and between jobs. The more frequent unfamiliar situations are, the less likely it is that existing routines are effective, and so this requires greater awareness. From this perspective, it might be argued that skill is embedded in all jobs but tacit skills are taken for granted rather than being formally recognised.

Some of the most undervalued tacit skills are the social skills required in many jobs. Such skills are central to many jobs where customer interaction is key. Research into the work of customer service representatives (CSRs) in the financial services sector in Australia and Japan has revealed the increasing importance and recognition of social skills. Korczynski, Shire, Frenkel and Tam (1996) explored the everyday work of front-line staff dealing with telephone queries from customers. They found that the social skills played a vital role in:

- establishing a rapport with the customer;
- assessing the attitude of the customer;
- persuading the customer to purchase a product.

In fact at two of the three organisations studied, management recognised that social skills were so vital that they changed their recruitment policy – no longer selecting graduates but instead employing a range of people with social skills. Similarly, a study by Darr (2004) of technical salespeople selling cutting-edge technologies (part of the workforce sometimes labelled 'knowledge workers' – see Chapter 9) revealed that technical skills are most valuable to employers only when accompanied by social skills. The 'geek' with a huge amount of technical knowledge but no social skills is not an asset when it comes to sales or after-sales service.

In addition to the social skills required in service sector work, Hampson and Junor (2010) have identified further hidden skills that employees use. Their analysis of the day-to-day activities of public service, education and health employees in New Zealand leads them to identify the importance of the process skills of 'awareness shaping' and 'co-ordinating'. Awareness shaping takes the form of employees being able to sense contexts or situations, monitor and guide the reactions of others and make judgements about the impact of their actions. Co-ordinating involves employees sequencing and combining their activities, interweaving them with the work of others and maintaining the workflow. The complexity of these activities even for low-level personal service jobs is well illustrated by the comments of an Occupational Therapy Assistant that Hampson and Junor interviewed:

> Time management [is] ... something I've been working on with the team leader ... because I cover different areas, I'm learning to say no, and work in with the other therapists. [They] ask you to do different things, because there's only a certain amount of time that you have in the day and being able

to say 'No, I can't do that now, but I can do it at such and such a time'. So you're planning all the time and then being able to adjust your day – because there're little emergencies and things that pop up all the time, so you've got to fit those in.

(Hampson and Junor, 2010: 537)

The increasing requirement for customer service work has led some researchers to argue that many of the service sector jobs require the skilled control and manipulation of emotions (e.g. Bolton, 2004, 2005; Bolton and Houlihan, 2007; Korczynski, 2005) – we explore this in detail in Chapter 7. In complete contrast, Lloyd and Payne (2009) point out that some of the skill claims are overstated. They argue that broadening the definition of skill considerably reduces its conceptual value. It can lead, they argue, to the assumption that all routinised service work is skilled even though, as they show through their interviews of call centre employees, the workers themselves do not consider their jobs as skilled. In particular, comments from their interviewees reveal the lack of complexity in the job, the mundanity of the tasks and the lack of challenge in the work. The comments of the call centre workers also show they have relatively little influence over the way they do their tasks; this is an aspect that traditionally has been considered an important indicator of skill, as the next section explains.

Assessing the extent of discretion in jobs

Another way of assessing skill is to examine it in relation to the discretion that employees can exercise when undertaking their jobs and hence the amount of control they have over their work.

The amount of discretion

Discretion is the ability to choose between alternative courses of action. Other things being equal, the greater the number of decisions required by an activity, the greater the level of skill required in exercising discretion. So the more an employee is able to exercise his/her judgement, the more skilled a task may be said to be. In this way skill levels might be assessed by examining the amount of rules employees are obliged to follow. Assuming the rules are comprehensive and clear then the more rules, the less scope there is for discretion and the lower their skill will be judged to be. This distinction between prescribed (rule-dominated) and discretionary (choice-dominated) work was first conceptualised by Jaques (1956, 1967). While it is a useful schema, it must be treated with caution, as Fox (1974: 19–20) points out:

> It is easy to accept…that no work role can be totally discretionary. The occupant of the most elevated post has to operate within prescribed limits, usually a great many. It may be more difficult, however, to accept that all jobs contain discretionary as well as prescriptive elements. Surely many jobs in our kind of industrial society are totally prescribed; totally without

discretion? Such a view cannot be sustained. However elaborate the external controlling structure of mechanical, administrative, technical or policy prescriptions, some residual element of discretion always remains.

This resonates with our earlier discussion about tacit skills, which argued that all jobs require discretion, even though such discretion may not be identified by the job description or acknowledged in the reward system. The problem of using discretion as an indicator of skill is that we are focusing on the visible when many of the choices and judgements exercised in the work process remain invisible.

The time-span of discretion

A second concept identified by Jaques (1967) is the 'time-span of discretion'. This is the length of time that a person is allowed to exercise discretion free from surveillance by superiors: the longer a person's period of autonomy, the higher their skill level. Again, however, this is somewhat limited in its usefulness as far as defining skill is concerned. A major problem with the concept of time-span of discretion is that it fails to take into account the significance of the task and the consequences of making a mistake. For example, a gardener may be allocated a patch of land to tend and be left completely alone for long periods. He has few rules to follow and could work incompetently for weeks before it came to anyone's notice. Conversely, the anaesthetist exercises her judgement within a strict framework of rules, and even a slight error of judgement will come to the attention of her work colleagues within minutes.

Discretion is also a misleading indicator because it fails to take into account the interdependence of many modern jobs. The notion of discretion tends to suggest an image of a romanticised past associated with the craft worker, which is really inappropriate when thinking about current jobs. As Attewell (1990: 443) argues:

> The ideal of the artisan conceiving an object, choosing tools and procedures unconstrained by external rules or routines, and fabricating the object from first to last step is so at odds with the reality of modern work that everyone today, from managers down, appears deskilled.

To sum up

The common theme that links the two notions of 'skill as complexity' and 'skill as discretion' is that both approaches emphasise skill as being principally about the requirements of the job. From this perspective, skill is seen as an objective feature of work and therefore can be measured through an analysis of job content in terms of both technical complexity and discretionary requirements. Consequently, researchers tend to view skill as consisting of sub-components, each of which can be measured. A good example of this approach can be seen in Extract 5.2 – read it and then attempt Exercise 5.3 to test your understanding of this section.

Extract 5.2

Measuring skill in the job – perception mismatches

One of the problems of measuring the skill required by the job is that there can be different perceptions depending upon who is doing the evaluating. Most notably, there might be stark differences between the views of employees – who might wish to overstate the skills they need in order to argue for higher remuneration or status, and managers – who might be inclined to understate the skills required to hold down wages and increase status differentials.

This potential perceptual mismatch has been explored by Green and James (2003), who designed a research experiment that allowed them to get the opinions of 110 job holders and their line managers about the skills involved in performing their jobs. The technique of matching pairs of employees and line managers means that it is possible to look at the differences in ratings between each employee and his or her manager, and then draw conclusions about the extent and cause of any differences. To do this they used a statistical analysis that took account of differences in gender, age and job tenure (time employed in a job). To measure the skills involved, the job-holders and their line managers were asked to rate various aspects of the jobs using the same answer scales (allowing overall scores and means to be calculated and compared).

The complexity of the job was assessed by asking about:
- four specific groups of job skills (verbal, physical, problem solving, planning);
- the qualifications needed to undertake the job.

The extent of discretion was assessed by asking about:
- the choice over how the job is done;
- the closeness of supervision;
- the freedom to decide how hard to work.

Green and James arrive at three main conclusions from their analysis:

- There is a good match between the perceptions of the job-holder and the line manager concerning the specific skills (verbal, physical, problem solving and planning) and the level of qualifications needed. However, there is a marked difference of opinion in terms of the discretion element: the job-holder generally judges the job to entail more discretion than the manager believes.
- Employees tend to rate the skills needed to undertake their job slightly higher on average than their line managers.
- Gender differences between the employee and line manager have an effect. When the manager is male and the employee is female there is a tendency for the difference between their estimates of the skill level of the job to be greater than with other gender combinations.

In respect of the third finding, Green and James are careful to point out that their data alone do not allow them to conclude that male managers are understating the value of female employees (since there is no independent measure of skill in their research). However, such a finding would not be surprising to those who argue that the skills of women have traditionally been undervalued by male managers – an issue explored in the section on the social construction of skill.

Source: Based on Green and James (2003).

Exercise 5.3

What do you think?

Apply the measures of complexity and discretion used by Green and James (Extract 5.2) to analyse the jobs that you were asked to compare in Exercise 5.1 at the beginning of the chapter. They are listed again

5.3 cont.

below. Of course, you might have to make an informed guess about some of the measures because you will not possess detailed information about the jobs:

- the hotel receptionist compared with the security guard;
- the computer games software writer and the paramedic;
- the cleaner and the car-park attendant;
- the insurance broker and the travel agent;
- the police officer and the social worker.

Now consider these questions:

1. Have you arrived at different conclusions than your previous assessment of these jobs?
2. Were the measures of complexity and discretion helpful? Explain why or why not.
3. Were there any problems in applying them?
4. Do you have a systematic and defensible set of conclusions about the comparative skill levels of the jobs? Explain why or why not.

Skill in the setting

An assumption underpinning both the 'skill in the job' and the 'skill in the person' approach is that the concept of skill can be objectively defined. But both approaches can be criticised for being overly rational because they often ignore the historical development of skill. Conceptions of skill are not dispassionately developed on blank pieces of paper; they are negotiated socially and politically over time, and they reflect the power and influence of diverse interest groups. This has been the case because skill is considered a measure of worth (both social and economic). As Sadler (1970: 23) has observed, skill is:

> to a considerable extent determined by social factors present in the work situation and in the occupational culture at large … [so includes] the evaluations placed on particular kinds of activity and on particular classes of individual and the actions of organised pressure groups directed at safeguarding the earnings and job security of particular trades and professions.

Consequently, to understand skill it is important to examine the setting in which the valuation of skill is negotiated.

As a starting point of the analysis, it is vital to consider one of the fundamental concepts of sociology as defined by Weber (1947) and elaborated by Parkin (1979) and Kreckel (1980). This is the notion of 'social closure', whereby people with a shared interest protect themselves by acting collectively to form a group that is in some way demarcated. Entry to the group is regulated by the existing members, thus they may choose to exclude or include outsiders depending on whether it serves their interests. Weber argues as follows:

> Whether a relationship is open or closed may be determined traditionally, affectually or rationally in terms of values or expediency. It is especially likely to be closed, for rational reasons, in the following type of situation.

> A social relationship may provide the parties to it with opportunities for the satisfaction of various interests, whether the satisfactions be spiritual or material, whether the interest be in the end of the relationship as such or in some ulterior consequence of participation, or whether it is achieved through cooperative action or by a compromise of interests. If the participants expect that the admission of others will lead to an improvement of their situation, and improvement in degree, in kind, in the security or the value of the satisfaction, their interest will be in keeping the relationship open. If, on the other hand, their expectations are of improving their position by monopolistic tactics, their interest will be in a closed relationship.
>
> (Weber, 1947: 127–8)

In the case of an occupational group, social closure provides the means of establishing a position at least partially autonomous of labour market competition. Instead of being exposed to the vagaries of the free market, the group is united by a 'consciousness of difference' (ibid: 127), and a willingness to act to regulate itself and influence market forces. This process of achieving occupational social closure is vital in establishing skilled status, and the next section explores it in more detail.

Social closure and skilled status

The overall process of occupational social closure is composed of three interacting sub-processes:

- *An ideological process*: where individuals recognise a shared set of values and beliefs, and reinforce these symbolically.
- *A political process*: where group members act collectively, combining their resources in pursuit of common goals. There will remain a plurality of interests within the group, but they have a mutual interest in combining and institutionalising their relationship (e.g. in the membership of a trade union).
- *A material process*: where members of the group seek to take ownership of the tools and technology of the work process and to control, or at least to influence, the organisation of work.

These three processes are represented by a diagram (see Figure 5.1), and each is described in more detail below.

The ideological process

A key component of social closure is the shared beliefs and values of the occupational group. In this respect the group can be characterised as a subculture seeking to establish and ring-fence its separate identity (Turner, 1971). One of the most important ways the group maintains this distinct identity is through the manipulation of occupational language and symbols. For a group wishing to lay claim to skilled status, it allows opportunity to mystify the work by obscuring the mundane activities and portraying an image of complexity. Language acts as a

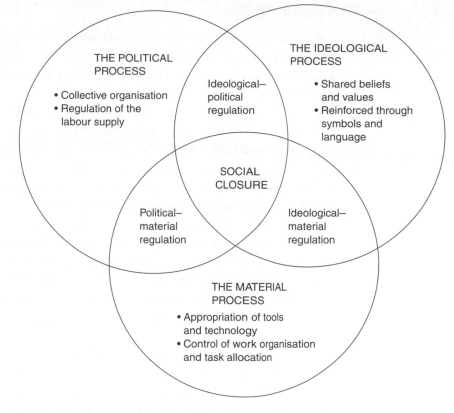

Figure 5.1   The processes of social closure

particularly important regulatory device because it can be used to both exclude and include. In this sense it demarcates the in-group from the out-group – it draws a line between 'us' and 'them'. Being able to use occupation specific jargon or highly technical language symbolises membership of the group. It identifies those who have gained enough experience and familiarity with the occupation to speak and understand the exclusive language. For example, many people have heard the technospeak of computer technicians – an impenetrable jargon that is meaningful to them but bemuses others. Perhaps the clearest examples of this are in medicine – for instance, the title of this recent editorial in the *Annals of Neurology*, 'Systemic inflammation, oligodendroglial maturation, and the encephalopathy of prematurity' (Volpe, 2011).

New entrants to an occupation are quickly reminded by the language that surrounds them that they are on the edge of things. For example, newcomers in an engineering plant might – as a practical joke – be sent for the 'long stand', the 'long weight' (wait), the left-handed screwdriver or the 'glass hammer' – thereby exposing their naivety and lack of familiarity with the setting. Symbolic regulation is also established by rituals, rites of passage, initiation ceremonies, humour and other forms of social control. Examples of these are explored in Chapter 9 (see also Extract 5.3).

The political process

As well as the shared values and beliefs leading to a collective identity, a group can reinforce this through its own representative body that allows members to organise and act collectively. Typically, it has been trade unions and professional associations that have performed this role (see Chapter 11 on representation at work for a full discussion). Such organisations demonstrate that the occupational group has a collective interest that is different from, and separate to, the interests of the organisation where members of the occupation are employed. In other words, it suggests that in some instances employees have a dual commitment: to the employing organisation and to the body that represents their occupation (the trade union or professional association). There are occasions when this poses particular dilemmas. For example, a hospital doctor may wish to prescribe a particular drug or treatment because it is in the best interests of the patient, but might also be conscious of the high financial cost to the hospital of doing so, with the resultant loss of treatment for other patients. The doctor's professional commitment (to provide the best care for the particular patient) conflicts with his/her organisational commitment (to use hospital resources effectively to care for patients in general).

An occupation's representative body also plays a key role in regulating the supply of labour. This is important if the members of an occupational group wish to establish and maintain a premium price for their work. In normal circumstances the scarcity of appropriately 'skilled' employees will push up the wage that an employer is willing to pay. Restricting the availability of labour is therefore in the interest of an occupational group. The control of supply has traditionally occurred through the regulation of entry into the occupation. To regulate entry, for example, a trade union typically sought in the past to establish a 'closed shop' (also known as a 'union shop' in the United States), which obliged employers to offer work only to workers who held union cards and were therefore deemed appropriately skilled to be able to accomplish the work safely and with competence. By limiting membership to those who were appropriately qualified, the union could influence the labour supply. It could also impose sanctions on members who broke union rules or acted against the interests of co-workers, by suspending their membership and consequently preventing their continued employment. Similarly, professional groups such as lawyers, doctors and accountants also operate a type of 'closed shop' (although they do not use this term), because to work in these professions one has to have passed the exams regulated by the professional body and be a member of the relevant professional association.

Overall, control over the supply of labour helps to build skilled status by restricting the size of the occupation and thereby implying that only those with special ability can do the job. Coupled with this is the increased price of labour which suggests work of special value, thus further reinforcing the status of the job.

The material process

In addition to controlling entry, occupational groups also need to control or exert influence over the way the work is accomplished. This can be achieved through two means. The first involves influencing the organisation of the work and the allocation of tasks. This requires regulating which person is allowed to undertake particular jobs, and traditionally this has encouraged demarcation where specific employees are limited to certain tasks according to their level of training and seniority. The second means of controlling the material process requires taking control of the tools and technology associated with the work. The workgroup seeks to control how the technology is put to use and to prevent access to it by other groups. Penn (1985: 121) expresses it as follows:

> Skilled manual workers in mechanised factory milieux [environments] are defined by their high degree of social control over the operation and utilisation of machinery. These exclusive controls involve a double exclusion, both of the management from the direct or complete control over the labour process and of other workers who offer a potential threat to such controls.

In other instances appropriation involves redefining the tools or technology (see Extract 5.3 for a good example). However, where organisations require employees to undertake a wider variety of tasks (functional flexibility) then the material process of social closure is potentially undermined because such flexibility broadens the access to particular tasks among the existing workforce. Nevertheless, as we shall see in Chapter 9, employees find creative ways to reassert their influence over work processes, so control of the material process continues to be a relevant tactic.

To sum up

In order for an occupational group to lay claim to skilled status it must establish its separateness and distinctiveness. It can achieve this through engaging in the three processes of social closure outlined above: ideological, political and material. These three processes operate at the same time and are mutually reinforcing, but social closure is achieved only when all three processes are carried out.

Extract 5.3

The symbols of skill in everyday occupations

There is symbolism embedded in the 'tools of the trade' which helps to differentiate an occupational group and allows its members to claim skilled status. This is particularly well illustrated by the case of construction workers discussed by Steiger (1993). Combining his findings with the work of Riemer (1977) and Applebaum (1981), he argues that owning the 'tools of the trade', and being able to use them properly is an important feature of defining skill. This is not least because the tools – and by definition the skills one possesses – are in full view. Common tools, such as the shovel used by the labourer, are looked down upon, whereas more specialised tools carry skill status. 'Rarity is important because ... only "rare" specialised tools are emblematic of skill. That rarity is important should be of no surprise in a capitalist economy' (Steiger, 1993: 555).

Interestingly, Steiger also cites the example of plumbers, for whom technological advances (such as the advent of plastic piping) have reduced the need for specialist tools. The plumbers' response has been to shift the emphasis away from the tools on to their ingenuity and ability to improvise. In this sense, their occupational closure has become symbolised not through the visibility of tools (which are readily available to anyone) but through the invisible 'know-how' which only the 'skilled' plumber has acquired. This is particularly noteworthy because it takes us back to our earlier discussion of tacit skills. The plumbers are elevating the importance of their embedded knowledge that cannot be appropriated by others, or replaced by new technologies.

In the past few years, plumbers in the UK have consolidated their position further because apprenticeships have declined and fewer young people have entered the trade. The consequent shortfall in the supply of plumbers means that the price of their labour has increased. One particular consequence of the sorts of shortfalls in trades such as plumbing is that workers from overseas (particularly Eastern European countries such as Poland) are increasingly being brought in by construction firms to work on their projects. In part this is the result of skill shortages, but it is also because of the price of labour – the overseas workers may be just as skilled as UK workers, but are often willing to work for less money. In response, UK tradespeople such as plumbers and electricians may claim that overseas workers do not possess the correct knowledge about health and safety regulations – again illustrating how skill is very much a social construction.

Social closure or social regulation?

An important point to note is that social closure is an ongoing process that changes over time. Just as groups can build upon the ideological, political and material processes to create closure, they can also lose closure by neglecting or undermining one or more of the processes. Groups may display forms of social regulation which fall short of social closure. We suggest this can be illustrated by the intersections in Figure 5.1, and they constitute three different types:

- *Political-material regulation*: a group has a representative body that influences the labour supply, the organisation of work and the use of technology in the workplace but does not share a collective identity through a common set of values.
- *Ideological-material regulation*: a group shares an identity through a common set of values, influences the organisation of work and the use of technology in the workplace, but has no representative body and cannot control the supply of labour.
- *Ideological-political regulation*: a group shares an identity, and has a representative body that influences the labour supply, but cannot influence the organisation of work and the use of technology within the workplace.

The introduction of new technology is typically seen as a development that can affect all three of the processes. It can challenge the ideological process by breaking down traditional lines of demarcation between tasks: blurring the boundaries between occupational groups and their separate identities. It can influence the political process by forcing a reappraisal of the qualifications and training needed to undertake the work (thereby affecting the labour supply). And it can reconfigure the material process by redesigning the jobs and requiring the use of different equipment and tools.

A group has the strongest claim to skilled status if it has full social closure. However social regulation provides opportunities for creating differences on which claims to a skilled identity can be built.

Exercise 5.4

What do you think?

Choose an occupation from the list below and assess the extent to which it has achieved social closure. Use Figure 5.1 as a guide.

If the occupation has not achieved full social closure, which type of social regulation has it achieved?

- accountant,
- school teacher,
- fruit picker,
- journalist,
- firefighter,
- hotel receptionist,
- heart surgeon,
- website designer,
- personnel/human resource manager,
- refuse collector,
- minister of religion,
- nanny,
- taxi driver,
- actor.

You might want to repeat this exercise to see differences between occupational groups. You could also try it out on any other occupation or job with which you are familiar.

So far, the discussion has focused on how skill definitions are constructed by occupational groups. However, there is a far more widespread impact of social construction and it raises some serious issues concerning fairness and equality.

Gender and skill – the social construction of disadvantage

It is possible to argue that a form of social closure exists which centres not on occupational group, but on gender. The evidence suggests that just as an occupational group may seek to construct a notion of skill in its own interest, so too, men have acted as a social group. They have constructed skill in such a way as to benefit their own gender and to disadvantage women. To illustrate how this occurs, consider this example of a law firm.

Suchman (1996) describes the use of image-processing technology for the document management systems of a large law firm. The definitions of skill and work there were gendered. Most lawyers in the firm were males, but the support staff were not, and the latter's work, although vital, was devalued. The process, called 'litigation support', entailed the creation of a database index that guided access to a very large number of documents. Orderly access to and structured retrieval from files was vital to assembling arguments for cases. The males described the document coding as 'mindless' labour, potentially a target for auto-mation or offshore placement. In fact, document coding was a highly knowledge-intensive activity, involving considerable discretion and independent judgement, so that documents that were separated from each other were cross-referenced and 'linked' (articulated) for later structured retrieval (Suchman, 1996: 415–17). This articulation work, a form of knowledge work, had been rendered invisible by the gendered definitions of skill employed by the males who dominated the workplace (Hampson and Junor, 2005: 170).

A considerable amount of evidence like this explores how jobs come to be 'gendered' and how this disadvantages women (Bradley, 1989; Walby, 1986). As a framework for discussion about this, we can use the three interlinking proc-esses discussed above: the ideological, political and material processes of social closure.

Gender and the ideological process

Underpinning the concept of skill is an ideology of gender which labels some attitudes and forms of behaviour as masculine and others as feminine. These identities are not just found in the workplace, but throughout society – they may vary slightly from culture to culture. They result in stereotypes about what being a man or woman means. As Matthaei (1982: 194) found, 'a basic force behind sex-typing of jobs was the workers' desires to assert and reaffirm their manhood or womanhood and hence their difference from the opposite sex'.

Jobs can be associated with gender stereotypes which reflect (and reinforce) dominant cultural beliefs about male and female. For example, jobs requiring physical strength, stamina or logical thought have traditionally been considered masculine, because these are attributes supposedly possessed more by men. On the other hand, women, allegedly being innately sensitive, patient and dextrous, have been associated with caring, repetitive and intricate work.

The source of this belief is the view that a work role is a reflection of a 'natural' ability: in other words, determined by and constrained by biology. For example, in Cockburn's study of print workers (1983: 171–90), the men argued that their job was not suitable for a woman and offered a number of commonly held views why women could not and should not do their work:

- women lacked the strength;
- there was too much standing involved;
- they lacked the mental ability;
- they did not have the right temperament (aversion to technical work);
- they were too temperamental (emotional, bursting into tears);
- they were unreliable (because they had periods);

- they would be exposed to bad moral influences (such as swearing, practical jokes, vulgarity);
- they would force men to behave differently.

For the print workers, women represented a threat because their entry into the occupation challenged the ideology of what constituted male work:

> It's man's work. If you hear of a man secretary, a lot of people raise a few eyebrows. Well, it's the same with a woman working alongside a man doing *his* job ... if I said to my mates I was working with a woman, they would feel, say, oh, he's doing a woman's job – because they can see that a woman *can* do it.
>
> (A print worker quoted by Cockburn, 1983: 180, emphasis in original)

Similarly, a Transport and General Workers Union shop steward at an electrical components factory is quoted by Charles (1986: 163):

> There's been a great increase in humdrum jobs like the jobs here, that you wouldn't get a man doing.... But the women can sit at a bench eight hours and pick up little fiddly screws and put them in. I think it's fantastic, and they can go for week in week out, you know – but you'll never get a man doing it, so that's why you need...women working.

Such opinions are not exclusive to men. Consider, for example, the views of these women quoted by Pollert (1981: 99) in her study of a tobacco factory:

> Kate (stripping room):   I can't imagine a man doing my work. It's too boring for a man. Women have much more patience.
>
> Gale: Men'd go mad. It'd kill them with boredom! Girls are expected to do that kind of thing. Girls are thought to be the weaker sex.

In white-collar work, there is similar evidence of sex stereotyping of skill. A vivid example of this is provided by Collinson and Knights (1986), whose case study of an insurance company reveals how the male managers manipulated the setting (the work organisation), the recruitment process, selection criteria and rationale for promotion to segregate the office according to gender, and to justify this in terms of business rationale. The effect is to relegate women to a position of inferiority. This subordination is then used against women and explained as being a product of their gender. To illustrate this, consider the quotes below (taken from Collinson and Knights, 1986: 155, 158, 162, 165):

> *Branch manager*:   Women aren't taken seriously in the insurance world. It can be a soul-destroying job. Inspectors have to advise our professional clients who recommend insurance and pensions to their clients, and we want them to recommend us. Yes, it can be a soul-destroying job, and women are either not hard-bitten enough to ride off insults or those that can are pretty unpleasant people.
>
> *Office manager*:   My job is to keep them [the female clerical staff] as busy as possible ... . You can't keep all six happy at the same time. With some you can tell their monthly changes, even the other girls

say so. Sometimes when they're having a good chunner [moan] about the inspectors I have to impress on the girls that if it was not for the men, there'd be no jobs for them, if the blokes don't go out and sell insurance.

Personnel officer, Head Office: The door is always open to move into the career structure, but we've found by and large, they're girls who are not particularly ambitious, looking forward to getting married, leaving and having a family and that's about the measure of it.

Senior pensions clerk: I'm very temperamental, you see. This is another thing Mr Brown [the branch manager] drew to my attention. I can get annoyed very easily and I also get strong moods. He said, 'There's no way you could go out to a broker with some of the moods you have.'

The assumption frequently made is that work is not a central life interest for women. Research discussed in Chapter 3 suggests this is a false assumption when comparing work orientations of men and women in full-time work. However, the view persists that the central life interest for all women is the family (either their existing one or the prospect of one), and so they are considered more willing to tolerate boring, repetitive jobs with low career prospects and little responsibility. But this argument may be circular. Are women given boring work because they are perceived to have a lower work orientation, or might it be they have a lower work orientation because they only have access to boring, repetitive, low-paid, undervalued jobs? It could also be that stereotyping men's and women's work limits the type of jobs available to either gender; but in addition it also disadvantages women because it fixes an idea of what is 'women's work'. The argument is summed up by Jenson (1989), who identifies the way work performed by women tends to be seen as involving some natural female 'talent', whereas work done by men is viewed as involving a learned skill.

Extract 5.4

Gender and skill

The critical importance of gender in defining skill was first explored in a keynote article by Phillips and Taylor (1986). They conclude, 'it is the sex of those who do the work, rather than its content, which leads to its identification as skilled or unskilled' (1986: 63). In arriving at this position they bring out two important issues which help to identify the importance of the ideological process of social closure:

• Where men and women work in similar processes, doing jobs of similar content, men are more likely to achieve skilled status. The research of Rubery and Wilkinson (1979) into box and carton manufacture is used to illustrate this point. The production of cartons and paper boxes involves a similar process except that while box production involves exclusively female labour, carton manufacture is undertaken by men and women. The latter is recognised as semi-skilled; the former as unskilled. Similarly, Spradley and Mann (1975) reveal that the work of waitresses is equally as demanding of a range of abilities as the work of bartenders, yet unlike the (male) bartenders, the waitresses do not enjoy skilled status.

• Where new work processes were introduced allowing employers to deem some jobs 'female' from the outset, the work tended to be classified as low-skilled, 'not simply by virtue of the skills required for it but by virtue of the "inferior" status of the women who came to perform it' (Phillips and Taylor, 1986: 61).

In an excellent analysis of women's work in a range of industries, Bradley (1989) argues that the hosiery industry (mainly making tights) provides the best example of the feminisation of an occupation. Feminisation can mean women are brought in not directly to take over the work of men, but to work on newly reorganised and degraded work processes. Thus, women are at a disadvantage from the outset: 'The work of women is often deemed inferior simply because it is women who do it. Women workers carry into the workplace their status as subordinate individuals, and this status comes to define the value of the work they do' (Phillips and Taylor, 1986: 55).

The picture then is of a general undervaluation of jobs where women predominate. This disadvantage is frequently institutionalised and consolidated by job evaluation schemes that either fail to recognise all the attributes of jobs mainly performed by women, or value these attributes lower than comparable work mainly performed by men (Horrell, Rubery and Burchell, 1994; Neathey, 1992; Steinberg, 1990). The overall effect is a relatively lower pay rate for jobs where women predominate. For example, job evaluation schemes typically rate fiscal responsibility (such as devising budgets or counting cash) more highly than social responsibility (such as caring for the sick or minding young children). Indeed, we will explore later (Chapter 7) how social skills are often taken for granted and frequently undervalued by employers. Another example is that physical strength (a supposed male natural ability) is often rated higher than dexterity (a supposed female natural ability). The danger is that the evaluation process is widely considered fair because it is seen as an objective measure of skill – but, as noted earlier in this chapter, such an assumption is naive. In Steinberg's words:

> job evaluation systems…have been constructed to embed cultural assumptions about what constitutes skilled and responsible work in a way that significantly benefits men through the work they have historically performed.
>
> (Steinberg, 1990: 454)

They institutionalise and perpetuate the ideology of masculine and feminine work, and in this way assist in the ideological process of social closure.

Gender and the political process

In many settings men have been proactive in seeking to protect and differentiate their skills from those of women. The situation is summed up well by Steinberg (1990: 476):

> Skill determinations are socially constructed in highly political contexts, in which males – whether employers or employees – exert considerably more power to maintain their definitions of skill…. Struggles over the meaning of skill between employers and (primarily male) employees have been frequent, bitter, and hard fought. When employees have won, males have

maintained their skill designations and wage rates, even in the face of the deterioration of job content. When employees have lost … skill designations are lowered, wage rates deteriorate, and male employees exit to be replaced by women.

As work processes have changed, men have sought to hold on to their skilled status. Often this has been to the detriment of women (as we explain in more detail below) so that 'skill has been increasingly defined against women – skilled work is work that women don't do' (Phillips and Taylor, 1986: 63).

Trade unions have played an important role in this political process, providing the means by which male workers can organise and exclude women from their trades (Hartmann, 1979). The historical analysis of gender relations in employment by Walby (1986: 244) leads her to conclude that:

> from the last quarter of the nineteenth century an increasing proportion of trade unions used grading and segregation as their response to women's employment, rather than the exclusionary strategy …. It is almost never the case that a union which included men did not follow one of these two patriarchal strategies.

According to this, the political process of organising through trade unions has disadvantaged women in terms of both (i) access to 'skilled' work, and (ii) the attainment of skilled status for jobs where women predominate. In addition, research shows that the domination of the male agenda persists within trade unions, and that 'a wide gap exists between what the unions claim for women and what they deliver, but more to the point, between what they claim and what they *attempt* to deliver' (Cunnison and Stageman, 1995: 237–8).

Gender and the material process

Cockburn (1983, 1985, 1986) explores the importance of material aspects of male domination. Through this she is able to identify the way that men take control and ownership of tools and technology. This gives them an advantage in developing notions of what counts as skilled work. Her argument is based on the importance of two related concepts: physical effectivity and technical effectivity.

Physical effectivity

The first part of Cockburn's argument is that the physical differences between men and women are often exaggerated to the benefit of men. Obviously, there are biological differences between men and women, but these limit each gender in only a very small range of tasks – most of which are not work based. Similarly, there are physical differences in average height and body weight, but again these are not necessarily relevant in most jobs. Gender differences are encouraged through childhood and socialisation – with men being more expected to participate in physical activities. As a consequence, men, on average, attain physical effectivity to a greater extent than women.

Technical effectivity

The second part of Cockburn's argument concerns technical effectivity: familiarity with and control over machinery and tools. As noted above, such control is important in constructing a skill identity. Cockburn argues that men have historically acquired control over the design of technology and work processes, and as a consequence this perpetuates existing patterns of dominance. As Wajcman (1991: 41) puts it, 'men selectively design tools and machinery to match their technical skills. Machinery is designed by men with men in mind. Industrial technology thus reflects male power as well as capitalist domination'. This does not necessarily imply an organised conspiracy by men against women, but it certainly reflects a gender-centricity resulting in some machinery and tools being too bulky or heavy for the 'average' woman. There are exceptions to this which prove that alternative approaches are available. Clarke (1989), for example, shows how the increased availability of female labour in Sweden prompted Volvo to invest in the design of tools ergonomically suited for the 'average' woman. For instance, they developed hydraulic lifting devices to lessen the physical requirements of vehicle assembly. But such examples remain rare.

Generally, technical effectivity is sustained through an ideology that perpetuates the notion that men are technically more competent than women. Nowhere is this more evident than the division of labour in the home (see, for example, Oakley, 1974, 1982; Pahl, 1984). Cockburn vividly portrays this in a chapter entitled 'The kitchen, the tool shed' (1985: 198–224). She illustrates how men not only acquire technical effectivity through work but can use this to improve their social standing in the community, through, for example, being the person who can fix cars or do some rewiring. Women, on the other hand, are discouraged from transporting any technical skills into the home. A woman may use pliers, screwdrivers, Allen keys and a soldering iron at work, but at home these are almost invariably kept for the exclusive use of men and are locked in the tool shed. Acutely aware of how technical effectivity can construct advantage, men jealously guard their knowledge:

> Men's know-how is seldom passed by men to women as a cost-free gift, taught in a serious, generous and genuine way. Often it is hoarded behind a cachet of professional knowledge or craft skill and handed out sparingly, reluctantly. Sometimes it is dispensed from a great height and purposefully used to put women down.
>
> (Cockburn, 1985: 202–3)

The two components of physical and technical effectivity support of the exercise of male power. As Cockburn (1986: 97–8) argues, 'the process … involves several converging practices: accumulation of bodily capabilities, the definition of tasks to match them and the selective design of tools and machines'. This shows how the material power base, constructed historically, is maintained for the benefit of men.

To sum up

Through exploring ideological, political and material processes, it is possible to see how skill has been constructed in a way that advantages men. In particular, the work of Cockburn demonstrates the way men have, in some occupations, taken control of technology through ideological, political and material means and used it to define their own work as skilled and women's work as unskilled. In this sense, there is an ongoing process of gendered social closure. This is embedded in the power of occupational groups and their institutions and the patriarchal structures of management.

Exercise 5.5

What do you think?

1. Consider each of the jobs listed below and note down whether the image that comes into your mind is of a man or a woman:
   • nursery care worker,
   • nightclub bouncer,
   • midwife,
   • beauty therapist,
   • electrician,
   • librarian,
   • financial advisor,
   • train driver.

2. The likelihood is that your gender assignment to these jobs reflects whether they are currently more likely to be undertaken by men or women. Now consider why this gendered image is dominant. To do this, take two jobs that you have 'assigned' to a gender and explore why they seem to be male or female. You will need to reflect on the points made in the previous section about the gendered nature of the ideological, political and material processes.

3. Now reflect on your own point of view: do you think the jobs ought to be gendered in this way? Explain and justify your reasoning.

Conclusion

The controversy surrounding skill is likely to continue as long as there remain different theoretical perspectives from which to look at what skill is, and how (or if) it can be measured. Once again, it demonstrates the importance of acknowledging the plurality of approaches to a particular problem. By exploring the diversity of meanings, this chapter has been able to explain the principal competing interpretations of skill. Instead of suggesting there is one way of looking, the analysis has explored different angles and produced a more complex picture with greater depth. As the different viewpoints have been brought into focus, so new aspects of the notion of skill have come into sharp relief.

As has been shown, the social construction of skill can be used to integrate the different approaches because it provides a framework for understanding both technical (objective) measures and social (subjective) meanings of skill. In other words, 'skill' is constructed by drawing on meanings that incorporate all three elements explored above: the person, the job and the setting. These provide the resources that allow the claim to skilled status to be made. However, making this claim depends on successful social closure, in terms of political, ideological and material processes.

The concept of skill is important because it has important consequences. It can be used by different interest groups to lay claim to status, special treatment and higher rewards. This has impacted on the gender division of labour with a dramatic undervaluing of the work of women.

A further issue remains unanswered: to what extent might there be a general historical shift in the nature of skill? Might skill be hard to define because work is continually changing and demanding different abilities? And if such a change can be detected, in which direction is it heading? Are people becoming less skilled or more skilled? These questions lie at the heart of the next chapter.

6

Work routines

Chapter aim

To explain the dominant forms of work organisation and explore competing theories of skill change.

Key concepts

▷ Taylorism

▷ Fordism

▷ deskilling

▷ labour process

▷ upskilling

▷ human capital

▷ offshoring

▷ flexible specialisation

▷ polarisation of skills

▷ compensatory theory of skill

▷ automating and informating

▷ range of work

▷ discretion in work

▷ work organisation paradigms

Learning outcomes

After reading and understanding the material in this chapter you will be able to:

1. Describe the main features of Taylorism and assess their relevance to contemporary work.
2. Describe the methods and application of Fordism.
3. Explain the theory behind the deskilling thesis.
4. Outline and evaluate the main criticisms of the deskilling thesis.
5. Explain the theory behind the upskilling thesis.
6. Outline and evaluate the main criticisms of the upskilling thesis.
7. Describe alternative approaches to examining skill change.
8. Use the work categorisation framework to analyse jobs.
9. Explain the relationship between skill change and work organisation paradigms.

Introduction

This chapter addresses a puzzle that has occupied the minds of researchers and theorists for decades: whether the fundamental shifts that have been occurring in the nature of work are causing people to experience either deskilling and degrading, or upskilling and enrichment, in their working lives. We have previously noted (in Chapter 2) some of the structural changes occurring in patterns of employment, but here we assess the impact of these broader employment dynamics by focusing on the nature of work tasks.

To explore these issues, the chapter is divided into five sections. The first examines two dominant traditions in work organisation – Taylorism and Fordism – using contemporary examples to illustrate the central principles of each. This provides the basis for the next three sections, each of which examines a different perspective on how work is changing: the deskilling thesis, the upskilling antithesis and the attempts to synthesise these contrasting approaches. The fifth section of the chapter develops a conceptual framework to integrate the analysis.

Dominant traditions of work organisation – Taylorism and Fordism

Routine work in the service sector – burgers and Taylor

Imagine the scene: you are visiting a city for the first time. It is lunchtime and you are feeling hungry, you do not have much money to spend on food, and you only have 30 minutes before your train leaves. As you look along the busy, unfamiliar street you recognise a sign in the distance: a large yellow letter 'M'. A sense of relief overwhelms you as you head for the home of American pulp cuisine, McDonald's. Any uncertainty and anxiety has been replaced by the predictability of the McDonald's experience: no matter where you are, you will get the standard-tasting burger, covered with the same relish, lodged in the same bun, served in the same packaging for consumption in the familiar decor of the restaurant.

Consistency is McDonald's strong selling point – if you are one of the company's 50 million daily customers, you will know exactly what you are going to get when you order your Big Mac and large fries, in any one of McDonald's 31,000 outlets in 119 countries. Of course, to guarantee such a standardised product, the work processes as well as the food have all been standardised. So leaving aside the issue of the product itself, how can we characterise and understand work at organisations such as McDonald's?

If we use a metaphor, we can describe McDonald's as a well-maintained machine in almost every aspect of its operations, from the customer interface to the centralised planning and financial control (Morgan, 1986). Employees at McDonald's (or 'crew members' as they are called) are treated as components of this machine. Each receives simple training to perform a number of tasks, which require little judgement and leave limited room for discretion. Crew members are given precise instructions on what to say, what to do and how to do it. They are the necessary 'living' labour joining the precisely timed computer-controlled equipment that cooks the burgers, fries the potatoes, dispenses the drinks, heats the pies, records the order and calculates the customer's change:

> Much of the food prepared at McDonald's arrives at the restaurant pre-formed, pre-cut, pre-sliced and pre-prepared, often by non-human technologies. This serves to drastically limit what employees need to do…. McDonald's has developed a variety of machines to control its employees. When a worker must decide when a glass is full and the soft-drink dispenser needs to be shut off, there is always the risk that the worker may be distracted and allow the glass to overflow. Thus a sensor has been developed that automatically shuts off the soft-drink dispenser when the glass is full.
>
> (Ritzer, 1993: 105–6)

This logic of automation is extended to all the processes, with the consequence that the employees push buttons, respond to beeps and buzzers and repeat stock phrases to customers like subjects in a bizarre Pavlovian experiment. The dehumanising effects can often be seen in the glazed expressions of the young people who serve you. But the most poignant, if not ironic, aspect of all this is that one of the world's most successful multinational corporations at the beginning of the twenty-first century relies on labour management techniques that were developed at the beginning of the twentieth century. Indeed, the pioneer of 'scientific management', F. W. Taylor, would have certainly recognised and endorsed the principles upon which McDonald's is organised.

Exercise 6.1

McJobs are good for some people

Some young people are well suited to boring jobs. That was one of the conclusions reached by Gould (2010) in a study of McDonald's restaurants across Australia. In an interesting piece of research, Gould distributed a questionnaire to managers and crew members in 50 restaurants with the approval of the McDonald's corporation. Responses were received from 812 crew members and 102 managers (the total Australian McDonald's workforce is about 55,000, based in 733 outlets). The findings confirmed that the work is organised around Tayloristic principles: 'crew overwhelmingly perceive their duties as comprised of a limited range of non-complex tasks which, by implication, should be done in a prescribed way' (Gould, 2010: 799). However, Gould argues that this has less of a negative effect on employees than often assumed by McDonald's critics (e.g. Leidner 1993, Royle 2000 and Schlosser 2002). The benefits of working at McDonald's include job security, the possibility of a career and flexible working hours.

Most notable, Gould's survey data leads him to conclude that it is important to take a person-specific perspective on fast food work – so looking at individual differences to explain attitudes to the work. In particular, there seems to be an age-related effect:

Compared with their older peers, crew work may be more suitable and offer greater benefits to younger teenagers who mostly appear relatively content. As they get older, crew indicate that they find the work easier and more repetitive and, in these respects, less attractive. Such trends are statistically significant. Older crew are also more inclined to assert their rights at work, a tendency which may be less compatible with a fast-food work environment. (Gould, 2010: 797)

Gould concludes that those who are satisfied with working at McDonald's are not in the minority and have not been indoctrinated. They work there because they are not looking for a complex job and the flexibility suits their lifestyles.

1. What issues do Gould's findings raise about how we should consider routine jobs?
2. What else would you need to know in order to evaluate these findings thoroughly?

F. W. Taylor's guiding principles

The ideas of Taylor have been well documented elsewhere (see, for example, Kelly, 1982; Littler, 1982; Rose, 1988), so it is only necessary here to restate the central principles to see how closely aligned the contemporary work processes at McDonald's are to concepts that were originally published in 1911. Efficiency was Taylor's guiding obsession. His own work experience as an engineer led him to believe there was an optimum way of performing any job: the 'one best way'. It was the task of management to discover this through the application of rigorous scientific testing, which involved breaking all activities down into their smallest components and systematically analysing each step. No activity was too complex or too mundane to be subjected to this scientific analysis, argued Taylor (see Extract 6.1).

Applying scientific management

Taylor illustrates his theory with the example of managing pig-iron handling and shovelling.

Probably the most important element in the science of shoveling is this: There must be some shovel load at which a first-class shoveler will do his biggest day's work. What is that load? ... Under scientific management the answer to this question is not a matter of anyone's opinion; it is a question for accurate, careful, scientific investigation. Under the old system you would call in a first-rate shoveler and say, 'See here, Pat, how much ought you to take on at one shovel load?' And if a couple of fellows agreed, you would say that's about the right load and let it go at that. But under scientific management absolutely every element in the work of every man in your establishment, sooner or later, becomes the subject of exact, precise, scientific investigation and knowledge to replace the old, 'I believe so,' and 'I guess so.' Every motion, every small fact becomes the subject of careful, scientific investigation.

(ibid: 51–2)

Now one of the very first requirements for a man who is fit to handle pig iron as a regular occupation is that he shall be so stupid and so phlegmatic that he more nearly resembles in his mental make-up the ox than any other type. The man who is mentally alert and intelligent is for this reason entirely unsuited to what would, for him, be the grinding monotony of work of this character. Therefore the workman who is best suited to handling pig iron is unable to understand the real science of doing this class of work. He is so stupid that the word 'percentage' has no meaning to him, and he must consequently be trained by a man more intelligent than himself into the habit of working in accordance with the laws of this science before he can be successful.

(Taylor, ibid: 59)

Having discovered the 'one best way' of performing a task, management's responsibility was to allocate tasks to employees, attempting to fit the right person to each job. The employee should have the requisite skills, acquired through systematic training, to complete the task at hand, and no more than those required by the job.

Emerging from Taylor's principles of organising the work process is a distinctive managerial ideology in which four themes dominate:

- *Division of labour*: this involves the separation of manual work (the doing) from mental work (the thinking). By removing from the employee any discretion over the organisation and execution of work, managers are able to secure control over the method and pace of working. As we shall see, this can have important consequences for determining the skill definition of a work activity.

- *Planning*: managers play an important role in planning each activity to ensure that it is in line with business objectives. In pursuit of these objectives, employees are to be used dispassionately, along with capital equipment and raw materials, in the search for greater efficiency, productivity and profitability. As a consequence, rigorous selection and training of people (to instil required behaviours) become a critical management function.

- *Surveillance*: based on the assumption that people cannot be trusted to perform their jobs diligently, there needs to be control through close supervision and monitoring of all work activities. Hierarchies of authority are constructed giving legitimacy to surveillance and simultaneously constructing a 'division of management' (Littler, 1982: 53).

- *Performance-related pay*: Taylor's deeply entrenched belief was that people were essentially instrumental, and so money could be used as a powerful motivator providing it was linked directly to the productivity of the individual: a linkage achieved by piece-rate payment systems.

While the logic of Taylorism is impeccable, the conditions of work it produces are often dehumanising and bleak: a set of highly segmented work activities, with no opportunity for employees to use their discretion and a system of close supervision to monitor their work performance. However, the practice of Taylorism has not necessarily followed the theory as closely as its original protagonist would have wished, leading some commentators (notably Edwards, 1979; Palmer, 1975) to argue that Taylor's influence has been overstated because the practical impact of his ideas was limited – not least because of the collective resistance exerted by employees through trade unions.

Certainly, in Taylor's own lifetime the diffusion of the principles of scientific management was modest. Many managers remained unconvinced about the possibility of planning and measuring activities sufficiently accurately to enable the 'science' to work. There were also competing ideas about the nature of job design from the human relations movement (starting with the famous Hawthorne experiments in the 1920s) which brought out the importance of the social factors at work and challenged the economic assumptions underlying Taylor's theory of work design (Schein, 1965).

Notwithstanding these reservations, Taylor's ideas have made (and continue to make) a crucial impact on the thinking about job design and the division of labour. Indeed, as Littler (1982) argues, we must be cautious of assuming a linear progression of management theory where each set of ideas neatly supersedes the previous ones. The persistence of Taylorist principles in contemporary organisations is testimony to the resilience of Taylorism (e.g. see the discussions by Bain, Watson, Mulvey, Taylor and Gall, 2002; Jones, 2000; Nyland, 1995). Of particular importance is the way that service sector organisations such as McDonald's can use features of 'classic' Taylorism in a similar way to the manufacturing industry. Indeed, we might ask whether shovelling chips into a cardboard carton is the twenty-first century equivalent of shovelling pig iron into a furnace, which Taylor studied a century earlier.

The widespread effects of Tayloristic division of labour in the expanding service sector was noted by Ritzer (1993). He contends that McDonald's represents the archetypal rational organisation in search of four goals: efficiency, calculability, predictability and control. McDonald's is a contemporary symbol of a relentless process of rationalisation, where the employee is simply treated as a factor of production. Ritzer's thesis (rather pessimistically) is that both theoretically and empirically this constitutes a general process of 'McDonaldisation' which extends beyond work into the culture of society (Ritzer, 1998). His conclusion suggests there is an inevitable tendency towards a dehumanisation of work – a theme that echoes the work of the deskilling theorists, whose ideas are explored after considering a second key actor in the design of jobs in the twentieth century.

What do you think?

Taylor was obsessed with finding the ultimate solution to the problem of organising work. He believed that by analysing and measuring work activities it was possible to find the optimum method of performing every task. In effect, he was suggesting that by careful, scientific, logical analysis, using his guiding principles, managers can find the best way of managing.

1. What is your opinion about Taylor's theory? What are your reasons for agreeing or disagreeing with him?
2. Why do some organisations follow his methods, whilst others reject them?
3. Consider your own work experiences. Would you describe the work as Tayloristic? If not, does it have elements that reflect Taylor's principles of work organisation?
4. Are some jobs impossible to Taylorise? Use examples to explain why/why not.

Routine work on the assembly line – chickens and Ford

If asked to visualise an assembly line, many people would probably have an image of a car plant, with a steady procession of partly finished vehicles passing groups of workers (or robots) who are rapidly attaching windscreens, wheels, spraying paint and so on. This has been the stereotypical image of assembly line work, not least because its innovative form was originally developed and exploited by the Ford Motor Company – an issue that we return to below.

Let us imagine a different contemporary work setting. You are in a massive room dominated by the sound of humming and churning machinery, though you can occasionally hear the voices of an all-women workforce. The room is cool and the air heavy with the smell of blood. Overhead, weaving around the factory is a conveyor from which hooks are suspended; hanging from each hook is the carcass of a dead bird. It is a chicken factory, made up of a variety of 'assembly lines' that convert live birds into the packets of meat displayed in supermarkets.

The work is Tayloristic in the sense it is segmented into simple, repetitive operations. For example, 'packing' involves four distinct tasks each performed by different employees: inserting the giblets (internal organs) and tucking the legs in, bagging the chicken, weighing it and securing the top of the bag. Not only are these and similar tasks around the factory simple and repetitive, but the pace of the work is also relentless. This is vividly portrayed by an employee carrying out 'inspection' in such a chicken factory, interviewed for a television programme, 'Dangerous Lives':

> *Employee*:   The line was coming round with about four and a half thousand birds an hour and you used to have to check the chickens for livers, hearts or anything, by putting your hand in the backside of a chicken,

> feeling around and then bringing anything out, dropping it in the bin, and then going on to the next. Used to be, sort of, every other chicken.
>
> *Interviewer*: You were doing two chickens at a time?
>
> *Employee*: Yes, both hands in chickens together. You hadn't got time to wipe your nose or do anything really.
>
> *Interviewer*: Did that line ever stop?
>
> *Employee*: Only if they had a breakdown, you know, a pin went in the line, or there was a breakdown or anything.
>
> *Interviewer*: So you were doing over 2000 chickens an hour?
>
> *Employee*: Yes.
>
> *Interviewer*: 14,000 chickens a day?
>
> *Employee*: Yes.
>
> *Interviewer*: What did you think about that?
>
> *Employee*: Hard work. Real hard work!

Similar experiences of unremitting 'hard work' have been found by researchers studying the harsh realities of factory life in different industries: for example, Pollert (1981) in the tobacco industry, Westwood (1984) in hosiery (legwear), Cavendish (1982) in motor components, Beynon (1973) and Linhart (1981) in cars and Delbridge (1998) in auto components and consumer electronics. In Chapter 9, the experiences of employees are explored in closer detail, but for now, the emphasis is on the work organisation principles which give rise to the assembly line.

Henry Ford's methods

The name most commonly associated with the development of the assembly line is Henry Ford. His unique contribution was in adapting Taylorist principles to a factory setting geared to the mass production of standardised products. Ford established a production method benchmark against which assembly line work has since been assessed, and the term 'Fordist' has come to be used to describe the combination of linear work sequencing, the interdependence of tasks, a moving assembly line, the use and refinement of dedicated machinery and specialised machine tools (for a detailed discussion, see Meyer, 1981). It has been argued that Fordism is distinguishable from Taylorism because it is a form of work organisation specifically designed for efficient mass production (Wood, 1989).

The success of Ford as mass *production* can only be fully appreciated if seen as part of a system of industrial organisation that also sought to create, perpetuate and satisfy mass *consumption*. The development of mass markets provided the demand for large numbers of rapidly produced standardised products. This was shown best by the output at the Highland Park factory which rose from 13,941 Model-T Fords in 1909 to 585,400 by 1916 (Williams, Haslam and Williams, 1992: 550). This volume of mass production was only possible because of the development of capital equipment capable of producing on a large scale, and the creation of an efficient electricity supply to drive the machinery. In other words, mass production, mass consumption, technological innovation and segmented work organisation were ingredients in Ford's recipe for success. Consequently, as Littler (1985) has argued, Fordism came to be the preferred form of organising work for mass production. It was adopted by Ford's main competitor in the United States, General Motors, and then by Ford's European rivals – Austin, Morris and Citroen. Fordism also transferred to other, newer industries such as electrical engineering and chemicals.

A widely accepted view is that Fordism is synonymous with mass production, rigidity and standardisation, and that the impact of the ideas pioneered by Ford has been widespread. However, there are some voices of dissent. Williams and colleagues (1987, 1992) argue that Fordism has become a stereotype, distorted over time by British and US academics who are keen to attribute failing industrial performance to the persistence of an outdated form of production. In a detailed analysis of Ford's production operations at Highland Park (1909–19), Williams et al (1992) reveal a picture of greater flexibility and less standardisation of the product than most texts on the subject would suggest. Overall, however, such findings do little to dispel the picture of an authoritarian work regime with closely monitored, machine-paced, short-cycle and unremitting tasks.

As the chicken factory example illustrates, Fordist principles persist in contemporary work settings, and these are not restricted to factory work. One can argue that his assembly line can be found in other work settings (see Extract 6.2). McDonald's shows Fordist elements in terms of its mass production of standardised products for mass consumption. Similarly, the supermarket in general, and checkout operations in particular, embody a Fordist approach to retailing: the customer's items pass along the conveyor and are swept across the barcode reader by an operator who carries out a series of repetitive actions. The flow-line, the dedicated machinery and the segmented work tasks are evidence of Fordist principles of work organisation. Similarly the chicken, as an object for consumption, is typically reared through (Ford-like) battery farming, slaughtered and processed in a Fordist factory, and sold through a Fordist retail outlet (the supermarket) or even consumed as chicken pieces in a Fordist restaurant.

Extract 6.2

The white-collar assembly line?

Researchers undertaking an extensive study of call centres in Scotland have come to the conclusion that although not all call centres are identical, the majority of them can justifiably be seen as 'white-collar factories' because employees are subjected to Tayloristic management techniques and the type of routinised, repetitive work normally associated with the assembly line (Taylor and Bain, 1999; Taylor, Hyman, Mulvey and Bain, 2002). The following is a quote from their study:

The typical call centre operator is young, female and works in a large, open plan office or fabricated building.... Although, probably full-time, she is increasingly likely to be a part-time permanent employee, working complex shift patterns which correspond to the peaks of customer demand. Promotion prospects and career advancement are limited so that the attraction of better pay and conditions in another call centre may prove irresistible. In all probability, work consists of an uninterrupted and endless sequence of similar conversations with customers she never meets. She has to concentrate hard on what is being said, jump from page to page on a screen, making sure that the details entered are accurate and that she has said the right things in a pleasant manner. The conversation ends and as she tidies up the loose ends there is another voice in her headset. The pressure is intense because she knows her work is being measured, her speech monitored, and it often leaves her mentally, physically and emotionally exhausted.... There is no question that the integration of telephone and computer technologies, which defines the call centre, has produced new developments in the Taylorisation of white-collar work.

(Taylor and Bain, 1999: 115)

An alternative perspective is taken by Korczynski, Shire, Frenkel and Tam (1996) in their detailed analysis of three call centres (two in Australia and one in Japan). They argue that while the customer service representatives have routine aspects to their work, it is misleading to equate their jobs with the sort of routine work typically found in factories. This is because service work relies on the extensive use of social skills when dealing with customers, which can provide a source of creativity for employees. In short, they are cautious not to equate service work with routinisation or deskilling, yet also suggest that there is little evidence of substantial upskilling taking place, even though there were some opportunities for it to occur in their case study companies.

To sum up

The significance of Taylor, Ford and mass production for the way work has been organised is profound. These principles and methods changed the work process by introducing greater amounts of rigidity and regulation, which in turn had important consequences for the skill content of jobs. In particular, this raises the question of whether work, in general, is becoming less or more skilled. The evaluation of the different attempts to answer this question begins with the deskilling thesis.

Thesis – the deskilling of work

The year 1974 saw the publication of one of the most influential books concerned with the study of work: Braverman's *Labor and Monopoly Capital*. Braverman's thesis is that there is an inevitable tendency towards degradation and deskilling of work as capitalists search for profits in increasingly competitive economic environments. His contribution to the study of work must not be underestimated. Although his thesis has since been subjected to a great deal of criticism, in the 1970s, it injected adrenaline into the tired discipline of industrial sociology, and it continues to have an impact on how work is analysed. Indeed the book was republished in 1998. The discussion below explains the central argument of this 'deskilling thesis' and identifies the main criticisms.

Braverman's argument

At the risk of oversimplifying, Braverman's argument is this. Managers perpetually seek to control the process by which a workforce's labour power (its ability

to work) is directed towards the production of commodities (goods and services) that can be sold for a profit. The control of this labour process is essential
because profit is accumulated through two stages: first, through the extraction
of the surplus value of labour (the price of a commodity has to be greater than
the costs incurred in its production); and second, through the realisation of that
value when the commodities are actually sold. These two stages are frequently
referred to as 'valorisation' (a process where value is realised). In other words,
managers seek to control the way work is organised, the pace of work and the
duration of work, because these affect profitability. Control of labour is the link
between the purchase of labour power and valorisation. In Braverman's analysis
the managerial obsession with labour control is the key to understanding capitalism, and it leads managers to seek ways of reducing the discretion exercised by
the workforce in performing their jobs. In order to exert their own control over
the workforce and limit the control and influence of employees, managers pursue
a general strategy of deskilling which, according to Braverman, can be identified
in two forms: organisational and technological.

Organisational deskilling

Organisational deskilling is embedded in the Tayloristic principle of the separation of the conception and execution of work. The conceptual tasks (the more
challenging and interesting parts of the job, such as planning, diagnosing
problems and developing new working methods) are transferred to technical
and managerial staff, while the execution of the work (often the mundane,
less-challenging part of the job) remains in the hands of shopfloor workers.
Theoretically, this process allows managers to limit the discretion of the shopfloor workers and to secure a monopoly over technical knowledge about the
work. This can be used to exercise greater direct control over the activities of
the workforce:

> A necessary consequence of the separation of conception and execution is
> that the labor process is now divided between separate sites and separate
> bodies of workers. In one location, the physical processes of production
> are executed. In another are concentrated the design, planning, calculation
> and record-keeping.... The physical processes of production are now car-
> ried out more or less blindly, not only by the workers who perform them,
> but often by lower ranks of supervisory employees as well. The production
> units operate like a hand, watched, corrected, and controlled by a distant
> brain.
>
> (Braverman, 1974: 124–5)

Technological deskilling

Technological deskilling occurs when automation is used to transfer discretion
and autonomy from the shopfloor to the office (from blue-collar to white-collar

workers) and to eliminate the need for some direct labour. Braverman focuses on the example of the operation of machines by numerical control (NC) – the latest technology at the time he was writing and before the invention of the microchip – which allowed the planning and programming of the machines to be undertaken away from the shopfloor by technical staff, who prepared punched paper tapes that contained the information for the machine to run automatically. Prior to NC, the machinists would use their own judgement and discretion to set and operate the machines, but they were subsequently left only with the relatively simple tasks of loading and switching the machines. In other words, a technological development (NC – and then later on computer numerical control) allowed the separation of task conception from task execution. This sort of new technology does not inevitably lead to a deskilling of work, but Braverman argues that managers selectively use automation to this end, in order to secure their central objective of exerting control over labour. He writes:

> In reality, machinery embraces a host of possibilities, many of which are systematically thwarted, rather than developed, by capital. An automatic system of machinery opens up the possibility of the true control over a highly productive factory by a relatively small corps of workers, providing these workers attain the level of mastery over the machinery offered by engineering knowledge, and providing they then share out among themselves the routines of the operation, from the most technically advanced to the most routine…. [But such a possibility] is frustrated by the capitalist effort to reconstitute and even deepen the division of labor in all its worst aspects, despite the fact that this division of labor becomes more archaic with every passing day…. The 'progress' of capitalism seems only to deepen the gulf between workers and machine and to subordinate the worker ever more decisively to the yoke of the machine…. The chief advantage of the industrial assembly-line is the control it affords over the pace of labor, and as such it is supremely useful to owners and managers whose interests are at loggerheads with those of their workers.

(Braverman, 1974: 230–2)

There have been plenty of writers willing to comment on Braverman's work. McLoughlin and Clark (1994) divide these into 'sympathisers' and 'agnostics' (see Table 6.1). If you want to explore the issues in more detail, a good starting point is Thompson (1989) followed by the chapters in the edited collection by Knights and Willmott (1990). There is also a thorough and persuasive defence of the value of Braverman's thesis by Tinker (2002), who particularly takes to task the more recent postmodern criticisms of Braverman's analysis of the labour process (e.g. O'Doherty and Willmott, 2001). The main criticisms of and revisions to Braverman's thesis are summarised in the next section, but before reading this, attempt Exercise 6.3.

Table 6.1   The key critics of Braverman's thesis

Sympathisers Accept the general approach but offer some refinement	Agnostics Acknowledge some value in the approach, but consider it inadequate
Friedman, 1977a,b, 1990	Littler, 1982
Burawoy, 1979	Wood, 1982
Edwards, 1979	Littler and Salaman, 1982
Zimbalist, 1979	Knights, Willmott and Collinson, 1985
Armstrong, 1988	Knights and Willmott, 1986, 1990
Rose, 1988	Watson, 1986
Thompson, 1989	

Source: Based on McLoughlin and Clark (1994).

Exercise 6.3

What do you think?

Interview someone who has been employed in the same organisation for about ten years and ask them about the changes they have experienced. The interview need not be long, but you should structure it in such a way to ensure that you find out about the type of changes introduced and the effect they have had on work.

You must then use this information to assess whether this helps to substantiate or refute Braverman's deskilling thesis and produce a written or verbal report. Remember there were two components to Braverman's argument, organisational deskilling and technological deskilling, so your interview should be designed in such a way as to elicit information on both these aspects of change. Your report should make explicit reference to these.

Six common criticisms of the deskilling thesis

Criticism 1: the deskilling thesis ignores alternative management strategies

Friedman (1977a, 1977b, 1990) argues that it is false to assume a single trend towards deskilling, since this fails to acknowledge the occasions when it is in the interest of managers to leave some discretion in the hands of employees. He calls this a strategy of 'responsible autonomy' and contrasts it with the 'direct control' which Braverman described. Friedman had in mind job enrichment and quality circles, but a contemporary expression of responsible autonomy is the notion of 'empowerment', whereby individual employees are expected to take responsibility for their own actions and initiate improvements in the way they work for the benefit of the organisation as a whole. Under responsible autonomy, employees are not deskilled but management continue to control the labour process. Thus, the argument here is that there is a wider choice in the mechanisms employed by management for the accumulation of capital than Braverman suggests.

Criticism 2: the deskilling thesis overstates management's objective of controlling labour

The control of the labour process is not an end in itself, but a means to achieve profit. To concentrate solely on labour control objectives ignores the importance of valorisation:

> It is not simply the *extraction* of surplus value in the labour process which is problematic for capital, but the *realisation* of that surplus through the sale of commodities in markets…. In other words we need to consider the *full circuit* of industrial capital as the starting point for analyses of changes in the division of labour: purchase of labour power; extraction of surplus value within the labour process; realisation of surplus value within product markets. There is no sound theoretical reason for privileging one moment in this circuit – the labour-capital relation within the labour process – if our objective is to account for changes (or variations) in the division of labour.
>
> (Kelly, 1985: 32, emphasis in original)

Moreover, the assumption that labour issues (rather than, for example, product development, marketing or investment) are the central concern of management during strategy formation is highly questionable (Purcell, 1989, 1995). Thus, as Littler and Salaman (1982: 257) contend, the process of capital accumulation acts beyond the labour process:

> The firm is primarily a capital fund with a legal corporate personality, linked to a production process…. While the production process results in a flow of income to the firm, this does not preclude alternative sources playing a major role or even a predominant one e.g. currency speculation, cumulative acquisition and asset stripping, commodity speculation, and credit manipulation of various kinds.

Child (1972, 1984, 1985) has highlighted the importance of political manoeuvring by managers in an organisation who, as key decision makers, are making 'strategic choices' that reflect their own values and vested interests. The argument here is that internal politics have a greater impact on deciding how work is organised, and on skill requirements, than Braverman implies. The logic of capitalist accumulation may remain the overarching tendency, but this can be mitigated by managers at all levels who are defending their vested interests.

As a consequence, the criticism is that Braverman's thesis underestimates the diversity and complexity of management objectives. The assumption that there is a single shared objective by management – that of labour control – ignores the plurality of interests within management and the diverse, and sometimes competing, objectives (Batstone, Gourlay, Levie and Moore, 1987; Buchanan, 1986; Buchanan and Boddy, 1983; Child, 1985). For example, in research into technological change in the UK provincial newspaper industry undertaken by one of the authors (Noon, 1994), it was found that when managers were questioned about the objectives for introducing new technology, they stressed different reasons which seemed to reflect their own functional responsibilities. In other words, the objective of increased control over labour was not the primary focus for most managers. Instead, they said technological change provided new opportunities in terms of product quality, product development, production control, efficiency and flexibility, together with a reduction in labour cost. This suggests that while labour control objectives may be relevant, they must be placed within the context of broader business objectives. As Armstrong (1989, 1995) argues, the pervasive influence of management accountants at board level in UK companies tends to lead to more strategic thinking based on financial concerns rather than human resource matters.

Criticism 3: the deskilling thesis treats labour as passive

Employees have not been very compliant and have resisted change towards deskilling through both trade union collective action and individual action. Indeed, Edwards (1979) argues that management has sought more sophisticated forms of control as a direct response to (and as a way to suppress) worker resistance. He argues there has been a shifting reliance from the 'simple control' typified by the methods of direct supervision that Taylor advocated, to the 'technical control' of the mechanised assembly line (and more recent developments in computer technology) and the 'bureaucratic control' of workplace rules, procedures and a regulated internal labour market.

Criticism 4: the deskilling thesis understates the degree of consent and accommodation by employees

The work of Burawoy (1979) stands as an important counterpoint to Braverman in that it explores the extent to which the workforce consents to its own subordination. In part, this contrasts also with the previous criticism because it suggests that, rather than challenging management control of the labour process, the workforce may develop an informal culture that offers alternative definitions of the work situation and provides the opportunity for meaningful activity. The labour process is thereby redefined as a type of game through which the employees can derive satisfaction (e.g. by beating the clock, outwitting the supervisor or manipulating the rules). These games act as powerful means of social regulation (self-control) among the work groups and obscure the exploitative nature of the labour process. In so doing, they unwittingly provide alternative additional sources of control for management. Such a brief summary hardly does justice to the subtleties of Burawoy's work, but these issues will be analysed in more detail in Chapter 9.

Criticism 5: the deskilling thesis ignores gender

Beechey (1982) has argued that several problems emerge from the gender-blind nature of Braverman's argument. First, he fails to appreciate the importance of women's distinct role as domestic labourers because of his 'conceptual isolation of the family from the labour process and of both the family and the labour process from an analysis of the capitalist mode of production as a whole' (Beechey, 1982: 71). Second, his discussion of the pre-industrial family can be criticised for romanticising the past and ignoring the existence of patriarchal structures. Third, his concept of skill fails to explore gender dimensions; an issue already analysed in detail in Chapter 5, where it was noted that the social construction of skill is particularly important in creating 'gendered jobs', resulting in the undervaluation of women's labour power and skills.

Criticism 6: the deskilling thesis overlooks skill transfer possibilities

The failure of Braverman to recognise that deskilling in one area of work may be compensated by upskilling in another is most forcefully argued by Penn (1983, 1990), whose ideas are examined in some detail later. However, it might be argued that this constitutes one of the most unfair criticisms of Braverman. As Armstrong (1988) points out, Braverman explicitly recognised that change would occur unevenly across industries, and that in some instances new skills and technical specialities might be temporarily created within the workforce.

A defence of Braverman's thesis

A persuasive defence of Braverman comes from Armstrong, who argues that:

> any sensitive reading of his work should reveal that Braverman actually regarded the deskilling tendencies of technical change as a system-wide dynamic or 'law of motion' in capitalist economies which could, temporarily and locally, be interrupted or reversed by a variety of factors, many of which have been rediscovered by his critics as supposed refutations.
>
> (Armstrong, 1988: 157)

This is an important point because, like all meta-theory (i.e. theory about theory), Braverman's thesis will never be able to explain all contingencies, yet this does not necessarily mean its analytical insight is worthless. Indeed, as Armstrong suggests, many of the 'critics' are in practice offering revisions and amendments to the theory, rather than rejecting it.

Another defender of Braverman, Spencer (2000), suggests that the constant revisions and modifications to Braverman's original ideas by subsequent labour process theorists (academic commentators and researchers) show they have lost sight of the subversive intent of Braverman's original text and have become obsessed with the social relations of the workplace, rather than the broader critique of capitalism. In short, Spencer laments the way that Braverman's ideas have been brought into the mainstream, and now run the risk of aiding rather than tormenting capitalism.

Braverman has also been defended against the attacks from academics of a postmodern leaning by Tinker (2002), who suggests that such attacks are deficient for a host of reasons, which he elaborates in detail. One of his main arguments is that the political aims and impact of Braverman's work are under-appreciated (not least the wide reading of the text by non-academics), and that postmodernist analysis:

> is blind to the social and historical specificity of Braverman's political task; exposing 'skill upgrading via education' as an ideology that obfuscates economic decline, recession and deindustrialization.
>
> (Tinker, 2002: 251)

He is also scathing about the philosophical position of postmodernists, which leaves them resorting to philosophies of indecision and able to offer only frivolous, condescending and politically timorous advice to working people (ibid: 273). In contrast, for Tinker, the abiding value of Braverman's analysis is that 'It debunks academic dogmas of management, popular nostrums about skill upgrading via education, and the tacit promises to restore a "golden past" (ibid: 274).

While some commentators (e.g. Lewis, 1995) remain unconvinced by defenders of Braverman, a re-reading of the original text reveals that Braverman had a less deterministic approach than is frequently attributed to him. Therefore, the deskilling thesis needs to be seen as an overall tendency, rather than a universal law applying in all cases:

> Braverman does *not* propound a universal law of deskilling. What he *does* claim is that there exists a general tendency for deskilling to occur in capitalist economies which will become actual where products and processes make this possible and where its effects are not masked by initiatives aimed at changing technology for other reasons.
>
> (Armstrong, 1988: 147, emphasis in original)

If Braverman's thesis is to be countered, it should be challenged on comparable terms: rather than a tendency towards deskilling, there is an opposite trend towards upskilling occurring within capitalist economies. It is to this antithesis that the discussion now turns.

Antithesis – the upskilling of work

Whereas the deskilling thesis drew from Marxist economic theory and the crisis of capitalism in industrial societies, the upskilling thesis tends to be based on the economics of human capital theory concerning a supposedly new stage of capitalism: the post-industrial society. Human capital theorists (Becker, 1964; Fuchs, 1968) suggest that, increasingly, firms are investing in their workforces through greater training provision, thus shifting the emphasis to 'human capital' as a central means of accumulating profit. One argument for this is that rapid advances in technology require a more educated, better-trained workforce in order to cope with the increasing complexity of work tasks (Blauner, 1964; Kerr, Dunlop, Harbison and Myers, 1960). In turn, this is linked to an ever-reducing demand for manual/physical labour as Western capitalist economies undergo a structural shift away from manufacturing towards service sector activities (Fuchs, 1968).

This shift in the economic base of advanced industrial societies is considered by commentators such as Daniel Bell (whose ideas are summarised in Chapter 3) to signal a fundamental transformation to the post-industrial society, in which theoretical knowledge becomes 'the axis around which new technology, economic growth and the stratification of society will be organized' (Bell, 1973: 112). In other words, the upskilling thesis suggests that the general tendency is towards more complex work requiring higher levels of skill. As a consequence, the shift in the pattern of work organisation will not be towards degradation (as Braverman suggested) but to an enrichment of work. Extract 6.3 provides survey evidence about upskilling patterns in Europe.

The upskilling thesis found expression in Piore and Sabel's (1984) concept of 'flexible specialisation'. They argue that the crisis of accumulation under capitalism is leading to an important shift away from Fordism towards more craft-based, flexible, innovation-led and customer-focused work organisation. So, just as the move from traditional craft production to mass production was 'the first industrial divide', the move from mass production to flexible specialisation is described by Piore and Sabel as 'the second industrial divide'.

The new emphasis is on flexible production systems, which can meet the demands for customised products in increasingly diversified markets. In particular, developments in microelectronic technology allow for more flexibility in the use of capital equipment: machinery no longer needs to be dedicated to specific tasks but can be reprogrammed to perform a variety of tasks. Traditional production methods typically involve long set-up times for the machinery, which mean large production runs are necessary to recover the cost; short production runs for small batches are an inefficient use of the equipment. In contrast, computerised machinery requires shorter set-up times, enabling greater diversity of (small batch) production without incurring the inefficiencies. In other words, economies of scale now have to be considered alongside economies of scope. This is important because customers are supposed to be increasingly discerning and wanting a greater variety of goods which allow them to express their individual identity (Sabel, 1982). Economies of scope become a necessity in a dynamic, competitive market where customers want variety and choice. Computerised production and information-processing capabilities provide the technological infrastructure and (according to the upskilling thesis) bring a demand for highly qualified rather than deskilled labour.

Coupled with this are changes in work organisation that mean employees are expected to work in different ways. Principal among these is teamworking, which is seen as a move away from the individualised, segmented work processes to flexible teams of employees who are multiskilled and take greater responsibility for their work through increased task discretion (control over the work methods, time and quality). It is argued that working in this fashion requires employees to develop and use a wide range of skills. In particular this has been associated with various supposedly post-Fordist production techniques in manufacturing, such as lean production (Womack, Jones and Roos, 1990) and business process re-engineering (Hammer and Champy, 1993).

Extract 6.3

Skill change in Europe

Gallie (2005) assessed the impact of skill change in 15 EU countries by analysing the results of two surveys of employees – one conducted in 1996, the other in 2001. Skill change was measured by asking people whether or not their jobs have become more skilled, evaluating the amount of training received, and assessing the extent to which employees considered they had control over their work (the first two are measures of complexity, the third is a measure of discretion).

Among Gallie's findings are the following:
- The dominant trend is upskilling.
- The pace of upskilling slowed down after the mid-1990s.
- Women are less likely than men to have experienced increases in skill.
- The decline in the pace of upskilling has affected women and men in similar ways.
- The reduction in the pace of upskilling is evident in 12 of the 15 countries in Europe surveyed.
- The decline in the pace of upskilling is statistically significant only in Finland, Germany, Great Britain, Greece, Ireland, the Netherlands and Spain.

One particular aspect of skill that showed clear evidence of decline was job control (the measure of discretion). Employees were asked questions about whether they have a say in what happens in their jobs. Gallie found the following:
- There is a significant decline in job control between the two periods.
- Women were typically in jobs with lower opportunities for control than men in both 1996 and 2001, but the decline in job control was similar for both sexes.
- Job control scores declined in nine of the 15 countries, although the trend reached statistical significance in only seven countries: Belgium, France, Great Britain, Italy, the Netherlands, Spain and Sweden.
- Only in Denmark was there evidence of an increase in control over jobs.

Source: Summarised from Gallie (2005).

Five criticisms of the upskilling thesis

Criticism 1: the upskilling thesis falsely assumes that the growth of the service sector will create skilled jobs

The growth of the service sector and the increasing importance of considering the customer can give the impression that all white-collar workers are now engaged with handling customer interactions, and that the traditional routinised factory work associated with manufacturing has given way to more varied, expressive forms of work involving customer interaction. It is certainly the case that customer-facing work involves the use of skills that require the management of emotions (see Chapter 7 for a full discussion), but much of the new service work is as monotonous and dull as work on an assembly line.

Korczynski (2004) analysed the work of back-office staff in an insurance company and two banks in Australia. He found that work tended to be routinised with little scope for discretion in how the tasks were performed (particularly in the case of the insurance company). This was reinforced through performance-monitoring systems which set targets (e.g. processing a set number of applications per day) and measured work quality. There was no customer interaction, staff were not required to have (or learn) customer-oriented skills, and on a day-to-day basis they referred to customers in an impersonal way. Echoing the findings of earlier case studies (Crompton and Jones, 1984; Sturdy, 1992), the conclusion Korczynski drew is that back-office work in financial services resembles the formalised, routinised and regulated processes consistent with traditional bureaucratic forms of work organisation. This makes back-office, service work very similar to Fordist production work.

Front-line service work – where the majority of the working day involves dealing with customers either face to face or over the phone – tends to be organised in ways that are slightly less rigid, because of the variation in customer interaction requiring social skills and elements of emotional labour. Even so, front-line service employees are typically faced with a huge amount of routine and repetitive activity. (See Extract 6.2 for two perspectives on call centre workers.) Korczynski (2002) uses the term 'customer-oriented bureaucracy' to suggest that the essential features of bureaucracy are present (e.g. hierarchies, rules and procedures) but that the customer is cared for in the process:

> The concept of the customer-oriented bureaucracy captures the requirement for the organisation to be both formally rational, to respond to competitive pressures to appeal to customers' wishes for efficiency, and to be formally irrational, to enchant, responding to the customers' desire for pleasure, particularly through the perpetuation of the enchanting myth of customer sovereignty [the myth that the customer is 'King' or always right].
>
> (Korczynski, 2002: 64)

This means employees have to work within clearly defined rules and follow procedures and protocols, while ensuring that customers feel satisfied about the service they are receiving and gain the impression that they are in control (the myth of customer sovereignty). As we shall see in Chapter 7, this may require employees to use a range of skills to manage their own emotions and those of the customers.

Criticism 2: the upskilling thesis overstates the extent to which advanced technology requires higher skill levels

The upskilling thesis is as vulnerable as the deskilling thesis to the criticism that there are numerous managerial objectives which reflect vested interests and politics – so the design of work will be based on these just as much as 'technical' decisions about skill requirements. In the 1980s, research revealed that managers could choose to implement technology in different ways that have variable skill consequences for employees. In their study of United Biscuits, Buchanan and Boddy (1983) show that even within one company there can be a mixture of skill changes associated with the introduction of advanced technology which makes any generalisation about upskilling or deskilling difficult to substantiate. Similarly, Sorge, Hartman, Warner and Nicholas (1983) reveal how computer numerical control (CNC) technology was used by British managers to deskill shopfloor workers and turn them into mere machine minders. In contrast, in Germany, the same technology was implemented in such a way as to integrate the (skilled) programming into the work of the operators, and in doing so enhancing their skill (also relevant here is Zuboff's (1988) dual impact theory of technology, which is discussed later in this chapter).

Criticism 3: the upskilling thesis overstates the extent of change

Generally, theorists who support the upskilling thesis, and those who support flexible specialisation in particular, assume a radical break with Fordism is taking place. However, this understates the resilience of mass production for mass markets. For example, the almost insatiable demand for consumer electronics has typically been met by the supply of goods manufactured using production systems that are labour intensive and low skilled (see, for example, Delbridge, Turnbull and Wilkinson, 1992; Sewell and Wilkinson, 1992a). Similarly, the flexible specialisation thesis overstates the extent to which small batch production will create upskilled and multiskilled workers. As Pollert (1991) and Smith (1989) point out, small batch production can and has adopted low-skilled, short-cycle assembly line techniques. So the criticism here is that the upskilling thesis relies on a false dichotomy between mass and craft production (see, for example, Hyman, 1991; Williams, Cutler, Williams and Haslam, 1987; Wood, 1989).

Criticism 4: the upskilling thesis overstates the skill-enhancing impact of new working methods

Employees have not experienced an enhancement of their skills through teamworking to the extent that the upskilling thesis suggests. In an analysis of survey data covering the period from 1996 to 2001, Gallie, Felstead and Green (2004) found that teamworking in the UK was on the increase, but this was accompanied by a decline in task discretion (measured by asking people how much influence they had over how hard they worked, what tasks they did, how they did the tasks and quality standards). This means that although an increasing proportion of the workforce is working in teams, these are not the semi-autonomous teams envisaged by the upskilling thesis.

A survey of ten European countries (Benders, Huijen and Pekruhl, 2001) revealed that forms of team or group working existed in 24 per cent of the workplaces. However, in the majority of these only a minority of core employees were covered, or else the groups had a very restricted range of decision-making rights (mainly concerning the regulation of day-to-day tasks, such as scheduling the work and improving the work processes). Issues such as controlling absence or organising job rotation were least likely to be delegated, and in only 4 per cent of organisations were the majority of core workers in what might be described as semi-autonomous teams. There was also notable variation between countries, with organisations in Sweden and the Netherlands being the most likely to have work groups and also the most likely to have groups who possessed real decision-making authority. Italy and Ireland were the countries with organisations least likely to have adopted group working. The authors of this European survey purposely used the term 'group working' rather than 'teamworking', because they argue it more accurately captures the range of forms or working arrangements – only some of which require upskilling.

Other studies confirm that the term 'teamworking' can mean a variety of things (Procter and Mueller, 2000). In the case of service sector work, it has been shown that 'team' often signifies nothing more than a group of workers who share one supervisor (Frenkel, Korczynski, Shire and Tam, 1999); as such, teamworking cannot be equated with upskilling.

Case studies can be useful in revealing how changes, such as increased flexibility and teamworking, do not result in enhancing skills so much as increase the volume of work at the same skill level. For example, commenting on the impact of multiskilling in a case study of a bank, Grimshaw, Beynon, Rubery and Ward (2002: 105) note that 'multi-skilling was introduced with limited employee discretion over how to vary and control and the timing and division of tasks…. Expansion in the range of job content was associated with increased pressure and a strong loss of autonomy'. Equally, in their case study of a telecommunications call centre these authors found that teamworking did not involve multiskilling or job rotation but was a form of teambuilding based on social activities during work time, representing an attempt by managers to break the monotony of the routinised work of employees.

Criticism 5: the upskilling thesis needs to be put into a global perspective

With the rise of the multinational organisation, it is no longer sufficient to consider change simply in a national context. The reduction in demand for low-skilled work in one country might be accompanied by increased demand in another country. As a result, it becomes problematic to try to interpret a fall in the demand for low-skilled labour in one national context as a sign of general upskilling. It may indicate a global redistribution of demand for skills, reflecting the mobility of capital in the search for lower labour costs and the pursuit of greater profitability.

A good illustration of this point is the tendency for large organisations in advanced capitalist economies to outsource parts of their customer services and back-office data processing to countries where labour is considerably cheaper. Typically, Australian companies are outsourcing to India and Indonesia, UK companies to India, US companies to the Philippines and Costa Rica and French companies to Morocco. This process, known as 'offshoring', means that when customers make an inquiry to their bank, insurance company, phone company or rail network they are likely to find themselves talking to an employee in a call centre in another country. Service sector organisations can now use information and communication technology (allowing real-time interaction with customers) to relocate parts of their operation anywhere that can provide an equivalent but cheaper service. In addition to voice services, paper-based operations (e.g. customer complaints, application forms, financial transactions) can take place in remote locations without it affecting the quality of service. This global shift in the location of customer service work means that skill increase in one location may be matched with a decline in other locations, as organisations find new means of sustaining and accumulating profit – and, of course, this is not at all surprising to supporters of the deskilling thesis.

Extract 6.4

Cyber coolies in India?

A research institute funded by the Indian government has produced a damning report on the working conditions inside call centres. It has labelled the educated, intelligent graduates who work there as 'cyber coolies', and claims that they are wasting their talents on undertaking mindless, repetitive work for Western organisations.

According to *The Observer* newspaper, the study claims that the call centre workers are employed under constant surveillance, in an atmosphere similar to that in 'nineteenth century prisons or Roman slave ships'. Despite the relatively high salaries, and modern working environments, the study concludes that 'most of these youngsters are in fact burning out their formative years as cyber coolies' doing low-end jobs.

The true monotony of the work is disguised by 'camouflaging work as fun' – introducing cafes, popcorn booths and ping-pong tables into the offices. Meanwhile, quotas for calls or emails successfully attended to are often fixed at such a high level 'that the agent has to burn out to fulfil it', the report claims.

With employees working through the night to cater for clients in different time zones, the work requires staff 'to live as Indian by day and Westerner after sundown' and takes a 'heavy toll' on agents' physical and mental health, the study states. But more importantly, call centre work 'leads to a wastage of human resources and de-skilling of workers' which will have a high impact on Indian industry in the long-term.

Source: *The Observer* (2005) 'Painful truth of the call centre cyber coolies', 30 October.

Exercise 6.4

What do you think?

Consider criticism number 5 of the upskilling thesis and read Extract 6.5.

1. What limitations might there be to offshoring that could mean some skilled jobs in the service sector could not be transferred to places such as India?
2. To what extent is technology playing a role in the offshoring process?
3. Have the so-called cyber coolies been upskilled or deskilled by the offshoring? Explain your reasoning.
4. Who are the winners and losers in the case of offshoring to India?

To sum up

The upskilling thesis is as ambitious as the deskilling thesis in attempting to arrive at a theoretical framework that reflects a general tendency of skill change. However, in both cases the unidirectional argument needs to be qualified, as the various criticisms have shown. It is highly problematic to answer whether the dynamics of skill change can be simplified in such a way. A more robust theoretical approach might be to hypothesise multidirectional change within different sectors, industries, occupations and tasks. Three approaches which address such a synthesis are examined in the next section.

Syntheses – polarisation, compensation and the dual impact of automating and informating

There have been various attempts to synthesise the perspectives of deskilling and upskilling by arguing that both are occurring, with some people being upskilled while others are deskilled. This section reviews three different approaches to explain how and why this might occur: polarisation, compensation and the dual impact of technology. There is some common ground between the three approaches, and they should not be seen as competing theories but rather as complementary explanations of the effects of upskilling and deskilling.

The polarisation of skills

The polarisation of skills perspective argues that different segments of the workforce will be affected in different ways. For instance, higher occupational groups such as professionals and managers might see their skill levels increase, while those lower in the occupational hierarchy, such as operatives, might experience a diminution in skill. Similarly, those workers on permanent, full-time contracts might be upskilled while their co-workers on part-time or fixed-term contracts (and other non-standard arrangements) might find they are given fewer opportunities to increase their skill levels. Polarisation approaches might also argue that the differences could be linked to structural features, such as the sector or industry, or argue that other contingencies, such as whether or not employees can exert influence through trade unions, will affect the likelihood of being upskilled or deskilled.

Research in the Netherlands (see Extract 6.5) and the United States reveals the differential impact of technological and organisational change on the work of different employees. Milkman's (1997) case study of the General Motors' plant in Linden, New Jersey, depicts a complex picture of work transformation, but it reveals how skilled workers were given opportunities to acquire new skills and retrain, while their semi-skilled counterparts on the production line were denied such opportunities. Similarly, in an entirely different industry (case studies of software and data processing) in a different country (the UK), the same pattern was found whereby changes in skill requirements had the effect of advantaging those already highly skilled 'depriving others of not only the few skills they have but also any hope of a route out of a low skills, low income trap' (Grugulis and Vincent, 2009). The common feature across these case studies is the consequence of upskilling for one group and deskilling for the other: a polarisation effect.

Extract 6.5

Skill polarisation in the Netherlands

As part of a research programme examining the effects of automation on job content, de Witte and Steijn (2000) analysed the responses of 1022 Dutch employees to a questionnaire. The respondents were asked about:

- the amount of autonomy (freedom or control) they had in their work;
- the complexity of their jobs;
- the extent of automation in their work.

From analysis of the responses to these and other background questions, de Witte and Steijn, conclude:

- There is a general trend in upskilling associated with increasing automation.
- Professionals and white-collar workers experience the most upskilling.
- Blue-collar workers are least likely to experience upskilling.
- Some blue-collar workers experience substantial deskilling.

To explain deskilling amongst blue-collar workers, de Witte and Steijn suggest that 'internal differentiation' is occurring. This term means that automation leads to an *increase* in the complexity of the job *but not* the autonomy of the job. However, this internal differentiation is less likely to occur amongst the professional and white-collar workers; for them automation brings an increase in both complexity *and* autonomy.

The compensatory theory of skill

The argument put forward by proponents of the compensatory theory (Penn, 1990; Penn, Gasteen, Scattergood and Sewel, 1994; Penn and Scattergood, 1985) is that the general theories of both upskilling and deskilling are inadequate to explain the complexity of skill change. Instead, 'middle-range' explanations based on actual data offer a better way forward. This is because technological change generates both deskilling and upskilling, and in different forms. First, the effects are international: 'the shift of routine manufacturing from advanced, core economies to less developed, peripheral economies, and the increasing internationalisation of the capital goods (machinery) industry' (Penn, 1990: 25). Second, the effects differ between and within occupations: some groups are advantaged by having a more skilled and central role, while others find themselves deskilled and marginalised. More specifically:

> technological changes tend to deskill *direct productive roles* but put an increased premium on a range of *ancillary skilled tasks* that are associated with the installation, maintenance and programming of automated machinery. This is because modern machinery incorporating micro-electronics tends to simplify many production skills but renders maintenance work far more complex…. [However] within maintenance work itself…there is a far

greater need for new electronic based maintenance skills than for traditional mechanical maintenance skills.

(Ibid, emphasis in original)

This position highlights the importance of a broader picture of skill change across occupational groups, industries and national contexts.

Automating and informating – the dual impact on skill change

The important role of advanced technology in reconfiguring skills is explored in detail by Zuboff (1988). She argues that a distinction must be drawn between the processes of automating and informating, since they have impacted upon skills in different ways. Automating work operations involves replacing people with technology and so it is characterised by a deskilling of work and a reassertion of management control over the work process. However, technological developments also provide opportunities to generate detailed information about work operations. These could, if systematically gathered and analysed, increase the visibility of the productive and administrative work undertaken in an organisation. In other words, technology is informating the work process, and that data requires interpretation using cognitive ability. This constitutes an upskilling of work and provides 'a deeper level of transparency to activities that had been either partially or completely opaque' (Zuboff, 1988: 9).

Taken together, the processes of automating and informating lead to a reduction in action-centred skills (doing), but an increase in intellective skills (analysing). At the same time:

> these dual capacities of information technology are not opposites; they are hierarchically integrated. Informating derives from and builds upon automation. Automation is a necessary but not sufficient condition for informating.

(Ibid: 11)

Zuboff also argues that although automating displaces people, it is not yet clear what the full effects of informating are. While managers can choose either to exploit or to ignore the informating process, her own case study evidence suggests that the tendency has been for managers to stress the automating process and ignore the informating potential. This is not surprising because the informating capacities of advanced technology force managers to rethink traditional structures, work organisation and forms of control:

> The shifting grounds of knowledge invite managers to recognize the emergent demands for intellective skills and develop a learning environment in which such skills can develop. That very recognition contains a threat to managerial authority, which depends in part upon control over the organization's knowledge base…. Managers who must prove and defend their own legitimacy do not easily share knowledge or engage in inquiry. Workers who feel the requirements of subordination are not enthusiastic learners…. Techniques of control that are meant to safeguard authority

create suspicion and animosity, which is particularly dysfunctional when an organization needs to apply its human energies to inventing an alternative form of work organization better suited to the new technological context.

(Ibid: 391–2)

The analysis presented by Zuboff is detailed, so this summary cannot really do justice to the subtlety of her argument. Still, it illustrates how both the deskilling and upskilling theses are inadequate as single explanations of skill change. While the former concentrates on the process of automating, the latter is focused on the process of informating. As a result, both approaches overlook the dual impact of advanced technology.

To sum up

The syntheses above are more firmly based on empirical research than either the deskilling or the upskilling thesis. All three syntheses identify the possibility of deskilling and upskilling occurring simultaneously, and therefore they reject the notion of an overall general tendency in one direction only. In moving away from general theorising to context-specific understanding of skill change, they can more easily take account of the diversity of empirical evidence. These syntheses also converge in concluding that the overall picture is one of differing experiences of skill change.

Discussion

Possible trends in work transformation, as represented by the various approaches above, can be depicted using a simple framework. As with any model that seeks to simplify the complexities embedded in work organisation, this is limited, but it does allow us to make some important analytical distinctions. The framework draws on Fox (1974), Friedmann (1961) and Littler (1982) by proposing that work can be described as varying along two dimensions:

- *The range of work.* Work can vary according to the range of tasks that the employee performs. At one extreme, an employee will perform a very narrow range of tasks, while at the other extreme the employee will be expected to perform a wide range of different tasks.
- *The discretion in work.* This refers to the extent to which employees have the ability to exercise choice over how the work is performed, deciding such aspects as the pace, quality, quantity and scheduling of work. At one extreme there will be very little opportunity for employees to use their discretion in this way, while at the other extreme work will require employees to use discretion constantly.

By combining these two dimensions as in Figure 6.1, it is possible to visualise the way jobs may vary and to plot four ideal-type (abstract) cases:

1. *Specialist work*: high discretion over a narrow range of work.
2. *Specialised work*: a narrow range of prescribed tasks.

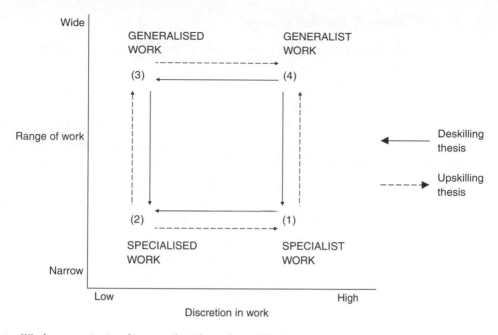

Figure 6.1   Work categorisation framework and trends in skill change

3. *Generalised work*: a wide range of prescribed tasks.
4. *Generalist work*: high discretion over a wide range of work.

A good way to illustrate this typology is to look at a single work setting and assess how different jobs within that setting can be placed in one of these four categories. In a hospital, the paramedics and nurses are undertaking generalised work, the doctors perform generalist work, the porters do specialised work and the surgeons are responsible for specialist work. To take another example, in a nightclub the manager is doing generalist work, the DJ is doing specialist work, the bar staff are doing generalised work and the bouncers are doing specialised work. This type of categorisation can be undertaken for any workplace. Of course not all jobs will fit neatly into one category (some nurses are specialists and have a great deal of discretion, for instance), but that is always a limitation of such frameworks. However, if a job does not fit neatly into a category it may indicate that the work is undergoing a transition – the sort of skill change that we discussed above and elaborate below.

Exercise 6.5

What do you think?

Think of a workplace with which you are familiar, list the main jobs and attempt to categorise them using the work categorisation framework. Remember, this framework cannot tell us about the importance of the work. It does not indicate the value of the work, but it helps us to classify the nature of the work.

Now take several of these jobs and speculate how they could change along the two dimensions (range and discretion) in line with the two theses. You will need to think about the specific tasks required by the jobs.

Mapping the skill changes

In addition to classifying the nature of jobs, the work categorisation framework can be used to show the trends proposed by the skill change theses:

- The deskilling thesis is based on the idea that there is a general trend towards low-discretion jobs comprising a narrow range of tasks. This reveals itself in the form of a degradation of work along the 'discretion' dimension. In other words, discretion is removed from generalist work (making it more generalised) or from specialist work (making it more specialised). Similarly the deskilling thesis suggests a simplification of work along the 'range' dimension, so the work would entail a narrower range of tasks. This would turn generalised work into specialised work, and generalist work initially into specialist work, and then into specialised work through the degradation process. These trends are represented by the solid arrows in Figure 6.1.

- The upskilling thesis identifies an opposite trend towards high-discretion jobs comprising a wide range of tasks. There is an enrichment of work along the 'discretion' dimension: by increasing the extent of discretion, specialised work becomes increasingly specialist and generalised work becomes increasingly generalist. In addition, the upskilling thesis suggests that multi-tasking is becoming a feature of all work, so there are changes along the 'range' dimension. Specialised work is becoming more generalised and specialist work is becoming more generalist. The broken arrows in Figure 6.1 show these trends.

- Those researchers who reject a general tendency of either deskilling or upskilling would argue that a mixed pattern emerges. This means that change could occur along any of the paths represented by the arrows, and such changes are likely to vary greatly both between and within countries, sectors, industries, occupations, workplaces and workgroups.

Conclusion – mapping skill change onto work organisation paradigms

Finally, we can return to the issue of work organisation with which we began the chapter. We argued that Taylorist and Fordist methods have had a dominant influence on work organisation, so how do these relate to the different theories of skill change? In Figure 6.2, the work categorisation framework is drawn again, but this time we have mapped onto it the dominant forms of work organisation that can be associated with each work category. The term 'paradigm' – which here means a distinctive pattern or approach – can describe these forms of work organisation. So we can refer to the Fordist paradigm (a pattern of work similar to that developed by Ford). What do these paradigm terms mean, and how do they relate to the theories of skill change?

The word 'Fordism' appears in all the paradigms. This is no accident because the Fordist paradigm had a massive impact on how work was organised during the twentieth century. That is why we discussed it so much at the beginning of

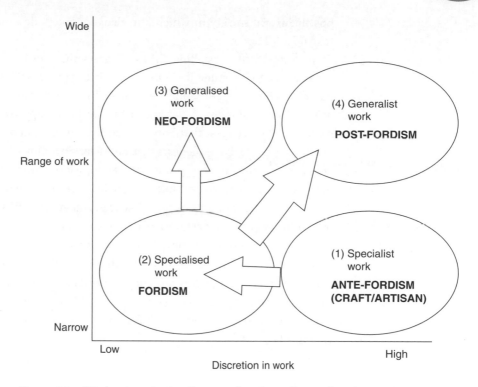

Figure 6.2 Work categorisation framework and paradigms of work organisation

this chapter. Because of its impact, other paradigms of work organisation can be defined in relation to Fordism. So:

- Post-Fordism: means 'after Fordism' and refers to types of work organisation that do not rely on the principles of Taylor or the methods of Ford.
- Neo-Fordism: means 'new Fordism' and refers to types of work organisation that have adopted many of the basic methods of Ford but have adapted them – particularly through more flexible working practices – to fit contemporary circumstances.
- Ante-Fordism: means 'before Fordism' and refers to types of work organisation that rely on craft-based skills, often associated with the independent, self-employed artisan (craft worker).

The deskilling and upskilling theses both accept that (in general terms) craft/artisan production in the nineteenth century gave way to Fordism, which dominated the majority of the twentieth century. However, they offer contrasting interpretations of how work organisation is now changing. The upskilling thesis suggests a dramatic change has taken place in advanced capitalist economies in recent decades. This 'paradigm shift' to post-Fordism is based on new concepts of work organisation (incorporating multiskilled workers, self-managed teams, networked organisations and teleworking), an increasingly dominant service-based economy (which we explore in Chapter 7), and frequently characterised as the post-industrial society in which knowledge workers dominate (an issue we will take up in Chapter 8).

In contrast, the deskilling thesis suggests that Fordism is continually being renewed as the dominant mode of work organisation, so there has been no paradigm shift. The consequence is specialised work comprising a narrow range of low-discretion tasks. A variant of this deskilling approach comes from commentators who suggest that Fordism has evolved into neo-Fordism (e.g. Harvey, 1989). This perspective suggests that multi-tasking, new management techniques (such as just-in-time, lean production and business process re-engineering) and increasingly automated and internationalised production processes have revitalised Fordism. Proponents of this view (e.g. Aglietta, 1979) stress the importance of continuity with the past, rather than characterising change as a quantum leap into a new dimension of capitalism. From this perspective, new forms of work organisation continue to reproduce traditional divisions of labour and essentially dispiriting and alienating experiences for employees. Employees cope with these in the best way they can (as we evaluate in Chapters 9 and 10), and sometimes join for collective support to make their voices heard (which we discuss in Chapter 11).

7

Emotion work

Chapter aim

To explore the growth of 'emotional labour' in contemporary work organisations and assess its significance for the employees involved.

Key concepts

▷ emotion

▷ emotional labour

▷ feelings

▷ emotional dissonance

▷ emotional display

▷ surface acting

▷ deep acting

▷ customer service

▷ coping strategies

▷ employee well-being

▷ alienation

▷ emotional exhaustion

▷ gender and emotional labour

Learning outcomes

After reading and thinking about the material in this chapter, you will be able to:

1. Define what is meant by emotional labour.
2. Identify factors that have brought about the expansion of emotional labour.
3. Explain the increased importance attributed to it by management.
4. Explain how employees learn and experience emotional labour.
5. Assess employee reactions to emotional labour.
6. Identify how managers seek to manage this aspect of employee behaviour.
7. Evaluate research on the consequences of emotional labour for health and well-being.
8. Point to wider implications of the growth of emotional labour, in particular for the position of women in the labour force.

Introduction

In an economy where more and more people are involved in service work, an increasing number of jobs involve carrying out what can be called 'emotional labour' (Grandey and Diamond, 2010; Kim, 2008; Liu et al, 2008). Bolton and Boyd (2003) emphasise that emotional labour is not a uniform activity but varies in both type and intensity, yet we can quite readily point to occupations that involve this kind of work. Typical examples include airline cabin crew (who may be expected to smile under almost any circumstances and for long periods) and call-centre staff (who may have to remain polite with difficult customers perhaps knowing that their calls are recorded 'for training purposes'). But there are a host of other occupations that involve emotional labour: tour guides, checkout operators, emergency service workers, waiting staff, bank staff, beauty therapists, healthcare employees, and even jobs we might not think of as 'emotional', for instance bouncers, debt collectors or lecturers. In all these, and many other jobs, emotional labour is a key aspect of the job.

In most service occupations involving direct contact with the public (either face-to-face or voice-to-voice), the way employees deliver a service has itself become an increasingly important part of the service. In some settings of course, the significance of 'good service' has always been appreciated. In a restaurant, for instance, a diner's experience depends not only on the quality of the food but also on the atmosphere, or ambience. This depends to a large extent on the way waiting staff treat customers. So, as well as performing essential tasks (giving advice about the menu, taking down orders accurately, serving and clearing away the meals), they are expected to behave in a manner which contributes to a positive and welcoming ambience. They may well be expected to do this even with very difficult customers. As one said, 'I always smile at them…that's part of my uniform' (quoted in Hall, 1993: 460).

In situations like this, the 'service and its mode of delivery are inextricably combined' (Filby, 1992: 37); or, put differently, 'the emotional style of offering the service is part of the service itself' (Hochschild, 2003: 5). In recent years, the range of activities involving emotion work has expanded. For most supermarket checkout staff, for example, it is no longer enough to charge up the goods speedily and handle cash, cheques and credit cards accurately; this also has to be service 'with a smile', a friendly greeting, eye contact and a cheery farewell. These requirements apply whatever the circumstances:

> The worst thing is that you are on the till trying to go as fast as you can and you can hear them [the customers] moaning that you are slow…there are times that I just want to look up and say shut up but you have to be busy and keep smiling.
>
> (Supermarket checkout operator, quoted in Ogbonna and Wilkinson, 1990: 12)

Similarly, on an aircraft, cabin crew are expected to display an air of confidence, even if they do not feel it themselves:

> Even though I'm a very honest person, I have learned not to allow my face to mirror my alarm or my fright. I feel very protective of my passengers. Above all, I don't want them to be frightened. If we were going down, if we were going to make a ditching in the water, the chances of our surviving are slim, even though we [the flight attendants] know exactly what to do. But I think I would probably – and I think I can say this for most of my fellow flight attendants – be able to keep them from being too worried about it.
>
> (Delta Airlines flight attendant quoted in Hochschild, 2003: 107)

Similarly, in High Street banks, management now attach greater importance to the warmth and friendliness of the cashier. Extract 7.1, which relates to a customer service questionnaire distributed by a leading UK bank, shows these aspects of employee behaviour are increasingly monitored by employers.

We all learn through processes of socialisation in families, schools and elsewhere how to control (or perhaps even 'manage') emotions in different contexts. Many children, for example, are taught not to be overwhelmed by adversity, but to persevere by 'putting on a brave face' or 'grinning and bearing it'. In a sense, this is to create an emotional 'mask', or persona, behind which real feelings can be hidden. Indeed in many work situations, individuals are required to suppress some emotions and often to display others (Austin, Dore and O'Donovan, 2008). Doctors are taught to control their emotions towards pain and death, to remain neutral and detached.

Similarly, people in authority may regard it as appropriate to maintain an emotional distance between themselves and their subordinates, so as to avoid compromising their ability to exercise discipline over those under them. Likewise, those at lower levels within organisations may continue to 'show respect' for those higher up the hierarchy, even if they regard those at more senior levels as incompetent. So, in many situations in both work and non-work life, gaps occur between expressed and felt emotions. This is what Snyder (1987: 1) refers to as 'the public appearances and private realities of the self'. Some have identified how this can lead to 'burnout' (Kim, 2008) or 'emotional exhaustion' (Martinez-Inigo et al, 2007).

When serving you today

Barclays bank is one of many companies that use customer surveys to monitor response not only to banking services, but also to the nature and style of service delivery. The Barclays surveys are distributed twice a year and comprise ten questions relating to a service interaction just completed.

The survey is headed 'When serving you today, how was I at …'. Each of the ten questions has an 11-point response scale, the ends of which are anchored by the words 'Poor' and 'Exceptional'.

Three questions seek responses to the employee's competence in relation to banking services: 'demonstrating knowledge of our products and services', 'sorting out any problems or concerns' and 'offering advice'. Four questions seek customer judgements on the efficiency of the employee during the interaction: 'making an effort to serve you quickly', 'carrying out everything competently', 'explaining things clearly' and 'listening attentively'. Three questions are designed to monitor the emotional style of the interaction, ratings being sought for the quality of 'acknowledging/greeting you', 'appearing pleased to see you' and 'making you feel I treated you as an individual'.

Each survey form is individually numbered and is therefore traceable back to individual bank branches and employees.

Our main interest in this chapter is in jobs where employees are explicitly required to adopt particular sets of 'emotion rules'. These define – often in considerable detail – which emotions they must publicly display, or suppress, in the performance of their job. Although, implicitly or explicitly, such rules have long represented important elements in many occupations; three developments in more recent years make this aspect of work worthy of closer attention:

- It is only in the last three decades that researchers have paid specific and detailed attention to emotional aspects of work performance and their wider significance: most of the studies in this area have been published since 1980.
- There has been a substantial increase during that time in the proportion of jobs that are 'customer facing', that is, where employees are in direct contact with customers of different kinds. In large part, this growth reflects the expansion of the service sector (see Chapter 2). In addition, a significant proportion of manufacturing jobs (such as in sales and purchasing) rely heavily on contact with customers and outside suppliers.
- There has been greatly increased recognition given to 'customer service' as a vital aspect of competitiveness; this in turn has increased the importance attached to the emotional performance of employees in direct contact with customers.

The meanings attached by management to customer relations (so-called customer care) are examined later in the chapter. So too are the experiences of, and implications for, those delivering that 'care'. Before this, however, it is necessary first to briefly consider what different writers on this subject mean by the terms emotion and emotional labour.

Emotion and emotional labour

Defining emotional labour

The question 'what is an emotion' is a long-standing one. As Rafaeli and Sutton (1989: 4) comment, though it was more than a century ago that writers such as Charles Darwin and William James wrote on the subject of emotion, those currently seeking to define and interpret human emotions remain baffled by a number of unanswered and seemingly intractable questions. The subject of human emotion, like the range of emotions a person can express, is very broad. We don't have the space (or expertise) to explore the social, psychological, anthropological or biological accounts of emotion. It is enough to note that many agree that emotions in the workplace centrally concern an individual's feelings. *Emotion in Organizations*, for example, described itself as 'a book about feelings' (Fineman, 1993: 1; see also Fineman, 2000), others similarly refer in their titles and subtitles to 'feelings' (James, 1989) 'human feeling' (Hochschild, 2003) and 'real feelings' (Van Maanen and Kunda, 1989).

Even when we narrow the focus on emotions to feelings expressed in the workplace, it is clear the topic is still enormous. Work represents an important part of social existence and encompasses the range of human feelings that develop over time wherever any social group interacts – love, hatred, fear, compassion, frustration, joy, guilt, depression, elation, envy and so on. Also, a great deal of research is concerned with exploring the feelings people have about work, for instance, in relation to job satisfaction, commitment and motivation. So, here the focus is narrowed even further to address those increasingly common situations where service workers are required, as part of their job contract, to display specific sets of emotions (verbally or nonverbally) with the aim of inducing particular feelings and responses among customers. This can be summed up as 'emotional labour'. Hochschild (2003: 7) coined this term to refer to 'the management of feeling to create a publicly observable facial and bodily display' (see Table 7.1). This form

Table 7.1   Some definitions of emotional labour

Author	Definition
Hochschild (1983)	'the management of feeling to create a publicly observable facial and bodily display'
Ashforth and Humphrey (1993)	'the display of expected emotions'
Morris and Feldman (1996)	'the act of expressing organizationally desired emotions during service transactions'
Mann (1999)	[the discrepancy between] 'the emotional demeanor that an individual displays because it is considered appropriate, and the emotions that are genuinely felt but that would be inappropriate to display'
James (1989)	'labour involved in dealing with other people's feelings'
Pugliesi (1999)	distinguishes between 'self-focused' emotional labour (centred on the management of one's own feelings) and 'other-focused' emotional labour (directed towards the management of the feelings of others)

of labour, like physical or mental labour, is purchased by employers for a wage. Also, just like the principles underpinning Taylor's scientific management, the performance of emotional labour can be specified in sets of rules, and its adherence monitored by different forms of supervision and control.

Exercise 7.1

What do you think?

Look at the list of definitions of emotional labour in Table 7.1 and, for each one, give an example of a job where the definition might apply. Try to think of examples other than those already mentioned in the chapter so far.

A number of writers such as Mann (1999: 353) and Lewig and Dollard (2003) see the dissonance, or conflict, between real and displayed emotions as the core characteristic of emotional labour. James (1989), on the other hand, defines emotional labour slightly differently, in terms of the work involved in dealing with other people's emotions – the sort of labour, for example, widely performed in hospitals and hospices (where Nicky James conducted her research).

This emotional labour task of managing other people's emotions is also well illustrated in Lively's (2002) study of legal assistants in the United States. In her interviews, the assistants make many references to the difficult task of dealing with emotionally distraught clients, particularly those dealing with issues of divorce or bankruptcy. As two of her respondents comment:

> You're dealing with people in their most emotional state of all times – only death, in an individual's life, is probably equally as emotional as divorce.
>
> (Lively, 2002: 208)

> Bankruptcy…is a very emotional procedure for the people involved…. Generally, by the time a client comes to see us to file a bankruptcy, they probably should have come to see us 6 months or a year ago. They probably have waited too long [and] they are just completely blown away with people collecting from them and threats of repossessions…it's a very emotional situation.
>
> (Ibid: 209)

Looking at them alongside one another, the definitions in Table 7.1 are in practice closely related. In Hochschild's approach, for example, the employee's emotional display is designed to induce a particular set of feelings, or state in the recipient of the labour (e.g. the 'satisfied customer'). Similarly, for the nurses in James's study, and the legal workers Lively studied, one important way in which patients'/clients' grief, anger or anxiety is dealt with is by the nurses and the legal assistants regulating their own emotions.

To sum up

By placing different emphases on the performer and recipient of emotional labour, the various definitions underline the essentially interactive nature of this form of labour. It is work performed by employees in direct contact with others (customers, patients, clients); but the response of those 'others' directly affects the experience of employees performing emotional labour, and it also affects the attitudes of employers and their assessments about how that labour should be performed.

Real versus displayed emotions

This discussion raises a key issue: what lies at the heart of emotional labour is not necessarily the expression of real emotions, but displayed emotions, which may or may not be truly felt. As the examples of the supermarket employee and the waiter show, people in service industry often have to smile – and the smile must look authentic – whether or not they feel positively disposed towards the customer. Where employees are required, as part of their job, to demonstrate feelings they might not really have, they are performing emotional labour. Their work role involves aspects not unlike those of an actor – for example, adopting the role and the 'script' of the 'happy worker' who is pleased to be of service (no matter how the customer responds). This language of performance (script, actor, role) is nicely used by a Cathay Pacific flight attendant: 'We say we are all entertainers now because everyone is on stage' (quoted by Linstead, 1995: 198).

Indeed, a number of sociologists and psychologists have considered social life, including life within work organisations, from a performance or 'dramaturgical' perspective (see, for example, Goffman, 1969, 1971; Höpfl, 2002; Mangham and Overington, 1987). This perspective sees social life as a series of scripted performances in which people act out parts that are consistent with the 'selves' they wish to present. Individuals act out, or perform, different scripts in different social situations. Goffman (1969: 183) refers to 'the arts of impression management' in terms of how individuals present themselves to the outside world, how different circumstances elicit different performances from the 'actors' involved, and how people 'self-monitor' their performances and adjust these as conditions alter. (See also Snyder, 1987, for a discussion of self-monitoring.)

The allegory of the theatre and associated terms – actor, performance, role, script, being 'on' and 'off' stage – can be applied to an analysis of emotional labour, and the rules for emotional display (Höpfl, 2002). At the same time, from a dramaturgical perspective, emotional labour can be seen as a variant of what already happens in most other social contexts. So, in jobs requiring emotional labour, employees perform a particular emotion script, just as in other settings individuals perform other emotional displays, some of which are likely to be as inauthentic as those indicated by the checkout operator quoted earlier, who is required to smile even at rude customers.

The key difference between these work settings and other settings, however, lies in the fact that those employees performing emotional labour are required to follow what Ekman (1973) and Ashforth and Humphrey (1993: 89) term the 'display rules', as part of their job. Discretion and choice over the nature of displayed feelings are removed or reduced, and the emotional performance becomes part of the effort–wage bargain in the same way that physical performance does. So, emotions become codified and then become a commodity that can be bought, sold and managed. As discussed later, for some critics of emotional labour (such as Hochschild, 2003) one problem is that some jobs require employees to undertake 'unacceptable' levels of emotional display, with potentially detrimental effects on the individuals involved. Underlying this is a more basic problem, or question perhaps: to what extent should emotions, the things that make us most human, be subject to 'management' (to control, and processes of commodification). Before examining these issues, it is useful to consider the factors behind the increase in emotional labour in a little more detail.

To sum up

Emotional labour involves acting out (performing, displaying) certain emotions in line with rules established by management.

The expansion of emotional labour

The growth in service activities

Chapter 2 highlighted the degree to which advanced industrial economies have experienced a shift in industrial structure. This has meant a diminishing proportion of the total workforce engaged in the primary and secondary sectors, and a growing proportion located in the tertiary, service sector. While an important aspect of service activity involves organisations providing services for one another (e.g. consultancy), the growth in the service sector has been particularly notable in the area of personal services. Many of these services are in established industries. However, there has been a growth in consumer choice.

The growth of services to individuals can be categorised in various ways. Lynch (1992), for example, identifies an expansion in:

- financial services (including banks, building societies and insurance companies);
- travel services (e.g. coach, rail and air services, together with related activities such as car hire);
- leisure services (e.g. hotels, restaurants, cinemas, theatres, pubs, clubs, sporting facilities);
- provisioning services (different types of retail outlets);
- communication services (e.g. telephone, media);
- convenience services (e.g. hairdressing, travel agents).

In addition, in the public (and increasingly, the privatised) sector there has been a growth in competition in, for example:

- educational services,
- health and welfare services,
- environmental services.

Increased emphasis on customer service

This expansion in service activities alone would be enough to raise awareness of the significance of how employees interact with customers. However, a major reason why attention has come to focus so strongly on the nature of that interaction reflects not only the fact that such interactions have become more numerous, but that they are also occurring in an increasingly competitive environment. This means that the significance of those interactions on the customer's overall judgement of the service is increasingly recognised by management and, as a result, given greater emphasis. Increased competitiveness reflects a general growth in service choices (e.g. should we go to a theme park, a zoo, swimming pool, bowling alley, go paint-balling or the cinema?) and also the multiplication of very similar services within a particular locality (shall we take the kids to eat at McDonald's, KFC, Pizza Hut or Burger King?), as well as the extension of existing services, perhaps as a result of advances in technology (travel agents are equipped with computer reservation systems enabling them to provide a much extended service, and public libraries offer access to much greater sources of information – and, both these facilities compete with the Internet).

One effect of this growth of very similar services (which is as obvious in financial services as it is in air travel providers, supermarkets, the fast food industry and elsewhere) is a tendency to even out many of the differences in price and elements of the service 'product'. Overall, burgers are very similar, as are the guest rooms in the different hotel chains, the airline seats and the various products offered by different estate agents, banks, travel agents and supermarkets.

In such an environment, where the actual services being offered for sale are not particularly differentiated, increased significance becomes attached not to the physical nature of the service being offered, but to its psychological nature. The facilities at different banks, for example, may be almost identical, but in which one do the customers feel that they have been 'treated' the best? In this situation, the aim of any particular service provider comes to centre on making customers feel more positively disposed to that service, so they return to that particular service provider (be it a shop, restaurant, airline, or hotel) when a repeat service is sought. This psychological element is of particular significance in the recent expansion of emotional labour.

The goal of securing a favourable psychological response from the customer has given rise to a much greater emphasis on customer service or 'customer care'. Notions of customer care have long existed, of course, embodied in such maxims as 'service with a smile' and 'the customer is always right'. But the growth of a more detailed and extensive customer care philosophy can be traced to the growing importance attributed to customer relations within the 'excellence' movement (Peters and Austin, 1985; Peters and Waterman, 1982), and the spread into the service sector of ideas such as Total Quality Management and 'continuous improvement', originally formulated within manufacturing contexts (Deming 1982; Juran, 1979).

In part, customer care involves simply the efficient delivery of a service – a high-quality product, delivered on time and to specification. However, with the duplication of very similar services, customer care manuals have also come to emphasise additional means of securing customer satisfaction. For example, the following comment by a management writer on the psychology of customer care (Lynch, 1992: 29) is implicit in much of the thinking behind customer care:

> Any action which increases the self-esteem of the customer will raise the level of satisfaction … . Conveying in a sincere manner the message 'You are better than you think you are' is a powerful tool for any service provider.

Thus, boosting the customer's self-esteem is seen to be an important aspect of customer care. There are various ways of achieving this esteem or status enhancement; Lynch (1992), for example, cites the importance of using the customer's name. Indeed, the whole manner in which an employee may be required to deliver a service (smiling, gaining eye contact, giving a friendly greeting) can contribute to putting customers at their ease, showing deference to them, making them feel special, even sexually attractive (Hall, 1993; Linstead, 1995; Wood, 2000).

In some situations, attributing status to the customers, and thereby potentially raising their self-esteem, is expressed in ways other than establishing 'friendly' relations. The undertaker's staff, for example, demonstrate a sensitivity to (and thus acknowledge the status of) the feelings of the bereaved by performing their duties in a solemn way (at least while in sight of the bereaved). The waiter at a very high-class restaurant may also acknowledge a customer's status by being unobtrusive (though remaining attentive and efficient) thereby acknowledging the customer's right to privacy and his/her status as someone with the ability to eat at such an expensive restaurant (Hall, 1993). In a family-friendly restaurant (such as T.G.I. Friday's), on the other hand, status is still attributed to the customer, but in the form of the waiting staff creating a more openly friendly relationship (see Extract 7.2).

Extract 7.2

Performing service at T.G.I. Friday's

In an analysis of empowerment at T.G.I. Friday's, Lashley (1999) reveals how the waiting staff are required to manage their behaviour to reflect the variation in the customers throughout the day. For example, at lunchtime, business customers predominate, in the afternoon there are more families and in the early evening there are mainly couples. Each group will require a different approach, and in this way the staff are performing emotion work.

As Lashley (1999: 797) explains,

'Dub-Dubs', as the waiting staff are called, have to advise customers on the menu and how best to structure their meal. They also have to identify the customer's service requirements and deliver what is needed. In some case, 'having a good laugh with the customers is needed', in others, they need to leave the guests to their own devices, or create the necessary celebratory atmosphere to match with a birthday or other party occasion. At other times they have to entertain restless children. So, employee performance requires more than the traditional acts of greeting, seating and serving customers. Employees have to be able to provide both the behaviours and the emotional displays, to match with customer wants and feelings.

Exercise 7.2

What do you think?

This part of the discussion argues that customers are increasingly influenced by the quality of the emotional labour. Given that we are all customers, it is useful to ask ourselves how important emotional labour is to us. And, more specifically, how much it influences our patterns of purchasing goods and services.

1. How aware are you of the emotional labour that customer-contact staff are performing on you? (Provide specific examples.)
2. Do you think the amount of emotional labour you experience is increasing? In what ways?
3. How important is it to you that people who are delivering a service to you perform emotional labour as part of that service – is it more important to you in some settings (e.g. a restaurant) than others (such as a supermarket)?
4. If it is more important to you in some settings than others, why?

What these various aspects of customer care underline is that in a context of intensifying competition, how a service is delivered has come to be defined as central to organisational success. As a result, those staff in direct contact with the customer, either face-to-face or voice-to-voice, have become increasingly recognised as key representatives of the organisation. Customer-facing staff are in crucial 'boundary-spanning' positions – linking the organisation to external individuals or groups. One chief executive of a major airline summed up these interactions between organisational members and customers as key 'moments of truth', on which the latter form lasting judgements about the organisation as a whole (Carlzon, 1987).

To sum up

Management have come to pay much greater attention to how employees perform their interactions with customers. In some settings, highly detailed rules and 'scripts' have been established, specifying which emotions must be displayed, and which suppressed; these display rules are monitored and backed up by sanctions (and less frequently, rewards) in an attempt to secure full compliance. This codification is a step to commodification. However, the fact that systems of punishment and reward exist at all indicates that compliance with the rules of emotional display remains problematic in many organisations. As the next section examines, in practice, many employees experience difficulties (as well as satisfaction) in performing this aspect of their job, and they resort to various strategies to cope with the exacting demands of emotional labour.

Experiencing emotional labour

Selection and training for emotional labour

While various situations exist where employees are required to present feelings that are solemn (undertakers), disapproving (debt collectors) or even hostile (nightclub bouncers or police interrogators), most consideration has been given to the more common contexts where employees' emotional performance is designed to induce or reinforce positive feelings within the customer. In each of these contexts, the required emotional performance typically involves 'a complex combination of facial expression, body language, spoken words and tone of voice' (Rafaeli and Sutton, 1987: 33). This combination is secured primarily through the processes of selection, training and monitoring of employee behaviour.

Nonverbal elements form an important part of many jobs involving emotional labour and can be prominent criteria in selection decisions. At Disneyland, for example, the (mainly young) people recruited to work in the park are chosen partly on the basis of their ability to exhibit a fresh, clean-cut, honest appearance – the nonverbal embodiment of the values traditionally espoused in Walt Disney films (Van Maanen and Kunda, 1989). Airline companies also emphasise nonverbal aspects of the work of customer-contact staff, including the importance of a high standard of personal grooming, covering such aspects as weight regulation, uniform, and even colour of eyeshadow (Hochschild, 2003; Williams, 1988).

Similarly, at most supermarkets, checkout operators are expected to conform to particular patterns of nonverbal behaviour even when not serving. For example, one checkout operator, Denise (name changed), commented in an interview with the authors that at her store not only were the checkouts constantly monitored by closed-circuit television equipment, but that supervisors regularly patrolled behind the checkouts, preventing any of the operators from turning round to talk to fellow operators by whispering the command 'FF', which meant 'Face the front'. Denise and her colleagues were required not only to 'FF' but also to sit straight at all times; they were strictly forbidden, for example, from putting their elbows on the counter in front of them to relax their backs.

Nonverbal rules of emotional display play an important part in many service organisations, but it is the verbal rules that have increasingly been emphasised in a growing number of settings involving direct contact with customers. In some contexts, employees receive little or no guidance on the 'correct' verbal behaviour. Seymour and Sandiford (2005), for example, show how in small workplaces such as pubs emotion skills tend to be picked up through experience. In other settings, however, the prescribed verbal repertoire is passed on through detailed training and instruction. At her supermarket, for example, Denise has been instructed to greet the customer, smile and make eye contact, and when the customer paid by cheque or credit card, read the customer's name and return the card using his or her name ('Thank you, Mrs Smith/Mr Jones').

This verbal display of friendliness and deference represents an increasingly common feature not only in supermarkets (Ogbonna and Wilkinson, 1990) but also in other areas of retailing and service activities involving the public. At McDonald's, counter and window crews are trained in highly routinised scripts, which include a number of verbal and nonverbal emotional labour elements (smiling, being cheerful, polite at all times and so on) (Leidner, 1991).

These scripts are not only designed to create a particular 'tone' for the interaction and a particular 'end' (a sale and customer satisfaction), but their high level of routinisation also allows for dealing with a high volume of customers with a minimum of delay.

Exercise 7.3

What do you think?

Think about any job you have had that involved a degree of emotional labour. This might have been working, for example, in a bar, a restaurant, a supermarket, a shop, in a crèche or as a holiday rep.

1. Overall, did you find the emotional labour part of the job enjoyable or not enjoyable?
2. What were the enjoyable aspects of the emotional labour?
3. What were the aspects that were not enjoyable?

Both verbal and nonverbal emotional labour is prominent in the work of waiting staff (see, for example, Hall, 1993; Mars and Nicod, 1984; Spradley and Mann, 1975). They are expected to perform a number of physical tasks, but in addition, a warm, friendly and deferential manner is widely seen by employers as a key element in creating a positive ambience. For the staff, there is an additional, instrumental reason for performing their emotional labour effectively: a significant part of their income derives from tips. Studies have shown that those who smile more do better at attracting larger tips than those who do not (Tidd and Lockard, 1978, cited in Rafaeli and Sutton, 1987). Also, one study found that tips to waitresses were higher where the waitress had made physical contact with the (male) customers by, for example, a fleeting touch of the hand when returning change, or touching the customer's shoulder (Crusco and Wetzel, 1984). Such studies appear to underline further the significance of the service provider boosting the customer's self-esteem by making them feel attractive. This boosting of self-esteem and the financial implications of doing so effectively are even more pronounced in parts of the nightclub industry, as the case in Extract 7.3 illustrates.

It is the airline industry, however, that gave rise to one of the groundbreaking studies of emotional labour (Hochschild, 2003), and this has since been followed by further studies of emotional labour among airline cabin crew (Bolton and Boyd, 2003). In her study of Delta Airlines flight attendants (cabin crew), Hochschild explored the development, performance and consequences of emotional labour. Selection and training are shown to play particularly important roles in inculcating particular 'feeling rules' into the recruits. Selection criteria, for example, included both nonverbal and verbal aspects. Not only were physical attributes and overall appearance taken into account in the selection process for flight attendants, so too was the ability to 'project a warm personality' and display enthusiasm, friendliness and sociability (Hochschild, 2003: 97).

Fantasy labour in the fantasy factory – strippers and lap dancers

Several researchers in the United States have studied the labour of dancers working in strip clubs – a setting Wood (2000) referred to as the 'Fantasy factory'. These studies provide insights into particularly charged venues where emotional labour is undertaken. They also reinforce a number of the points made elsewhere in the chapter, particularly relating to the requirement of the dancers to display some emotions and suppress others, and the financial inducements attaching to the 'counterfeiting of intimacy' (Boles and Garbin, 1974; Foote, 1954). Also, this is a setting where – overwhelmingly – women perform emotional labour for consumption by men, with potential consequences for the status of each.

In some clubs studied, the strippers performed their stage act for tips, these being secured in important part by the women making frequent eye contact with individuals which 'made a customer feel as if a dancer were specially interested in him' (Ronai and Ellis, 1989: 277). In addition, following the staged routines in some of the clubs, the women offered personal dances ('table' or 'lap' dances) to individuals for additional payment. These table dances represent a key source of income for the women, and in efforts to secure them, a variety of emotional labour activities are undertaken.

The essence of these is to make the (usually male) customer feel particularly important, sexy and desirable, which in turn leads the man to buy additional dances. Many of the dancers interviewed by Ronai and Ellis (1989) and Wood (2000) comment that the sexually charged looks, actions and phrases which make up this 'seduction rhetoric' need to appear genuine – to buy dancers, many individual customers had to feel that the women had 'dropped the routine' and were genuinely interested in, and attracted by, the customer. 'The smile must be convincing. The eye contact must be engaging ... to make believable their attention and interest in the customers' (ibid: 24, 28). This is especially the case for regular customers, who can represent an important source of income (and presents, etc.) for individual dancers, but who are also very well placed to judge whether the verbal and nonverbal behaviour of 'their' dancer is repetitive or phoney (Ronai and Ellis, 1989: 287).

As well as expressing 'genuine' emotions, at the same time in conversations with the customers the dancers were required to suppress other emotions (like being bored or unattracted to the individual) as well as other aspects of their life. This was particularly the case if they were married and had children – attributes which potentially 'jeopardised his [the customer's] ability to see her as a sexy, sensual, and most important, available, woman' (Wood, 2000: 10–11).

'If I tell him I'm married and have a child, he's not going to think I'm sexy anymore. Men come in to see sexy, erotic, women who they think are party girls. Motherhood they can get at home' (dancer quoted in Wood, 2000: 16).

Emotional labour plays an important part in regulating customer emotions and controlling the interaction, making sure that customers know (and remain within) the limits of the interaction in what is, potentially, a risky situation for the worker.

Of course these encounters include an economic exchange (money paid in return for a dance provided). But, in common with several other arenas of emotional labour, the exchange is also a psychological one, and more to the benefit of the male customer. 'Strippers increase the status of men through labor aimed at creating a designated impression for the men themselves – the impression of being interesting, sexy and desirable' (Wood, 2000: 15). The emotional costs of stripping, in terms of stigmatisation, rejection by customers, offensive behaviour as well as physical assaults, can be considerable. As Ronai and Ellis (1989: 296) sum it up, 'Stripping, as a service occupation, pays well, but costs dearly.'

However, while the selection process is used to identify those who have the predisposition to perform emotional labour effectively, Hochschild emphasises the training sessions as the place where the flight attendants are given more precise instruction on how to perform their role. As well as training in the technical aspects of their job (such as what procedures to follow in an emergency), instruction is also given on the emotional aspects of the work. At its simplest, the training affirms the importance of smiling:

> Now girls, I want you to go out there and really *smile*. Your smile is your biggest *asset*. I want you to go out there and use it. Smile. *Really* smile. Really *lay it on*.

> (Pilot speaking at a Delta Airlines Training Centre, quoted in Hochschild, 2003: 4, emphasis in original)

Considerable emphasis is given to the employee's smile and accompanying pleasant and helpful manner. Flight attendants are encouraged to think of passengers as 'guests in their own home', for whom no request is too much trouble (ibid: 105). The cabin crew member's smile is designed not only to convey a welcome (in the way the supermarket operator's smile and restaurant worker's smile endeavours to do) but also to project a confidence and a reassurance that the company in general, and the plane in particular, can be trusted with the customer's life (ibid: 4). The emphasis in the training is on fully identifying with the role, in order to generate a more 'sincere' or 'genuine' smile – 'smiling from the inside' – rather than a false-looking smile (see also Bolton and Boyd, 2003: 301).

It is one thing to be able to smile at friendly, considerate and appreciative customers, but another to smile under pressure, such as the bar worker, waitress or checkout operator faced with large numbers of customers, or service workers in general faced with offensive individuals. It is in these problematic circumstances that management also require compliance with display rules. It seeks to achieve this partly by encouraging employees to interpret the situation differently, to suppress any feelings of anger or frustration and respond in the manner prescribed by management, perhaps through trying to encourage employees to take the perspective of the customer (Rupp et al, 2008).

The problem of dealing with difficult customers arises particularly in studies of call-centre staff (see, for example, Callaghan and Thompson, 2002; Korczynski, 2003; Taylor and Tyler, 2000). In their study of telephone sales agents, for example, Taylor and Tyler (2000: 84) describe how the (mainly female) agents are trained not to get angry with offensive (often male) customers. As one trainer commented:

> If a man's having a go at you ... he might even be embarrassing you ... don't get ruffled, you've got to keep your cool. Remember that you are trying to offer him something and get him to pay for the privilege. He can really talk to you how he wants. Your job is to deal with it ... *just take a few deep breaths and let your irritation cool down* ... think to yourself he's not worth it.

> (Emphasis in original)

This example matches closely with aspects of the emotion training of the Delta flight attendants described by Hochschild (2003), in particular the instructions on how to respond positively to awkward, angry or offensive customers – 'irates' as they are known in Delta. A key training device for dealing with such passengers was to reconceptualise them as people with a problem, who needed sympathy and understanding. Thus, employees were encouraged to think that perhaps the passenger who was drinking too much and being offensive was doing so to mask a fear of flying (or a stressful job, sadness at being away from home or whatever). Underlying this training is the requirement for attendants to respond positively to such passengers, reflecting the fact that they may be frequent flyers and thus important sources of revenue to the company. Thus, the attendants are required to 'think sales' (ibid: 108), no matter how irksome or rude the passenger is being.

Different ways of doing emotional labour

It is clear from these studies that workers perform a variety of forms of emotional labour and do so in different ways. Hochschild (2003), for example, distinguishes between 'surface' acting and 'deep' acting (Wharton, 2009). Surface acting involves a behavioural compliance with the display rules (facial expression, verbal comments and so on) without any attempt being made to internalise these rules: the emotions are feigned or faked. Deep acting, on the other hand, involves employees internalising their role more thoroughly in an attempt to 'experience' the required emotions and deliver a more authentic display (Groth, Hennig-Thurau and Walsh, 2009). Selection procedures and training programmes such as the ones described by Hochschild are designed to elicit deep acting – so that by developing a set of inner feelings (towards the company, the customer and the attendant's work role), the outward behaviour follows automatically.

Exercise 7.4

What do you think?

Surface and deep acting are two ways of performing emotional labour and have different implications for how employees approach and perform their work role.

1. What are the advantages and disadvantages of each approach?
2. Overall, if you had to recommend to someone how they should handle their emotional labour, would you advocate a surface acting or a deep-acting approach? Why do you say this?

Extract 7.4

Acting natural

Deep acting of the type described by Hochschild has also been encouraged in more recent years by managers encouraging employees to behave 'naturally' rather than simply stick to a rigid prescribed script. In efforts to create a more 'genuine' interaction, an increasing number of organisations are giving employees the freedom to 'be themselves', to be 'more natural' and 'more authentic' in their interactions with customers.

Rosenthal, Hill and Peccei (1997), studied a major UK food retailer which in the mid-1990s moved away from highly scripted forms of service as part of a 'Service excellence' initiative. These researchers found many employees preferred being able to be more 'natural' in their dealings with customers, compared with the previous need to adhere to pre-set company scripts (ibid: 493).

However, as Taylor (1998: 92) points out in a study of telephone sales staff, in practice the degree of empowerment within this 'emotional autonomy' can be very limited. Management at the telephone sales organisation sought a 'naturalness' from employees only in so far as the expression of positive dispositions by staff helped build up a rapport with customers. To put it another way, acting natural was fine in the eyes of management as long as it served the organisation's objectives – to increase sales and improve customer service. The emotional autonomy did not extend to empowering employees to tell rude customers just where to get off.

Ashforth and Humphrey (1993: 94) point out that these two 'routes' to emotional labour should be supplemented by a third, which takes into account the situation where the expected emotional display is fully consistent with an individual's own inner feelings (see also Ashforth and Tomiuk, 2000). In such cases, there is no need for the worker to 'act' at all, since the emotion is in harmony with what the individual would have naturally displayed as part of his/her own identity. In such situations there is no emotional dissonance – that is, no incongruence or gap between felt emotions and displayed emotions (or put differently, between feeling and action) (Lewig and Dollard, 2003). An example is a nurse who has entered that occupation to fulfil a strong desire to care for people who are ill. Other examples in the emotional labour literature include youth shelter workers who identify very closely with the plight of the young people seeking refuge in the shelter (Karabanow, 1999), highly enthusiastic employees attached to 'high-commitment' organisations (Martin, Knopoff and Beckman, 1998), and certain types of call-centre worker whose values are highly congruent with those sought by the employer (Jenkins, Delbridge and Roberts, 2010).

To sum up

Emotional labour involves extensive verbal and nonverbal behaviour. Both of these form important elements in the selection and training programmes for various occupations. Emotional labour may be performed through surface or deep acting or in circumstances where the employee so fully identifies with the job that no 'acting' is involved at all.

However, even those who identify fully with their job will have their off-days and occasional bad moods. At those times they – like their counterparts who identify with their job less strongly – will be required to manage their emotions to hide their true feelings.

Reactions to emotional labour

Problematic circumstances for performing emotional labour

For many employees, for much of the time, performing emotional labour is unproblematic. Smiling at customers often elicits a smile in return, and the creation of a friendly interaction. As the flight attendant in Extract 7.5 comments, 'It's great to come off a flight on a high, you've made the passengers happy and receptive to you. As you're saying Goodbye you're getting a response, eye contact, thank you's' (Williams, 2003: 532 and Extract 7.5). As Korczynski (2003: 57) comments, customers can be 'a key source of meaning and pleasure in service jobs', representing an important source of job satisfaction (see, for example, Lewig and Dollard, 2003: 328–9). Likewise, among services such as hairdressing and beauty therapy, researchers have noted the presence of 'genuine feeling' between worker and clients, and a 'reciprocity' in the relationships between employees and customers (Furman, 1997; Sharma and Black, 2001; Sheane, 2011).

Extract 7.5

Emotional labour over Australia

In a study of almost 3000 flight attendants in Australia, Claire Williams (2003) highlights both the pleasurable and the problematic aspects of emotional labour among this occupational group.

Overall, a higher proportion of the flight attendants found the emotional labour aspects of their job stressful (44 per cent) than a source of satisfaction (34 per cent) (the remainder seeing this aspect of their job as neither stressful nor satisfying). However, further analysis of the comments that the flight attendants made indicated that, for many, emotional labour was a source of both satisfaction and stress. As one put it:

It's great to come off a flight on a high, you've made the passengers happy and receptive to you. As you're saying Goodbye, you're getting a response, eye contact, thank you's, hope to see you next flight! Then there are days when you're happy and friendly and they just don't want to acknowledge your presence or nothing you can do will help solve their problem. You are verbally abused and left standing red faced with a plastic smile crumbling on your face.

Interestingly, a common explanation among those who found emotional labour a great source of satisfaction was the way that encouraging and forcing themselves to look more cheerful actually made them feel better. They also noted a sense of achievement derived from overcoming difficulties at work.

Williams also reports several examples of sexual harassment among her sample, particularly from members of sports teams and businessmen (though also from flight crew and other members of the cabin crew). Overall, almost four out of five (79 per cent) of women flight attendants (and 61 per cent of male flight attendants) reported that they had to deal with verbal sexual harassment in their jobs, with other instances of physical sexual harassment.

An important factor in the impact of harassment on the attendants was how management dealt with harassment: whether they were supportive towards the flight attendants or whether they maintained a bias in favour of the customer. Emotional labour was much more likely to be reported as satisfying where the flight attendants felt valued by the airline companies – not only in relation to support over sexual harassment instances, but also other employee issues such as health and safety concerns.

Williams concludes that the organisational context – in particular the nature of management attitudes and behaviour towards their employees – influences how emotional labour is experienced at work.

Source: Williams (2003).

Also, as just noted, there will be service employees who are very positively disposed to their work. For them, to smile while doing it is wholly consistent with their general feelings towards the job and the customer. In these latter cases, there is little or no dissonance or 'gap' between the individual's felt and expressed emotions at work: expectation and actuality are closely aligned. In Sharpe's (2005) study of adventure guides, the emotional labour performed, despite the lengthy time periods involved, was also found to be largely unproblematic (see Extract 7.6 for a more detailed account of this study). For Sharpe, a key factor in this is her perception of all individuals incorporating many versions of the 'self' (rather than as Hochschild tended to emphasise, the existence of 'one true self'). Because of this, the employees of the trekking firm are seen as capable of performing the emotional labour of the guide role – in ways that involved acting differently (more outgoing, extrovert and so on) to when they were away from the job – without this causing any particular difficulties. We return to this point again later.

Extract 7.6

The emotional labour of adventure guides

As Erin Sharpe (2005) points out, emotional labour figures prominently in the work of adventure guides. Though far removed from the work contexts of most groups discussed in the literature on emotional labour, the emotional labour component of the guide's job is considerable. It is also an interaction between employee and customer that goes on for days, and in close proximity.

The author reports a study of 'Wanderlust', an outdoor adventure company specialising in canoe and kayak trips in North and Central America and Australia. Data were collected from participation on eight Wanderlust trips.

The company emphasised the importance of guides handling their emotions in three particular aspects of the job. First, the company put particular emphasis on safety, and as part of this, guides adopted an emotional demeanour that underlined their status as a safe and competent guide, remaining calm in dangerous or risky conditions. As one guide told the author of the study: 'An emotion I don't want to manifest is fear … it can lead to chaos and loss of control …. I don't want people to lose confidence in my ability when I'm scared. So you have to develop a certain amount of control of your fear and your emotions' (Sharpe, 2005: 37–8).

The second area of emotional labour for the guides was in generating fun among the groups they were leading. Guides were responsible for making the trips enjoyable, and this entailed telling jokes, smiling and laughing a lot, being energetic, upbeat, outgoing and 'generally working to maintain a fun-loving attitude'. This was clearly much easier for the extrovert than the more introvert guides. As one guide put it:

For me, doing a trip is almost like putting on a show, and keeping that attitude is tough …. It's like I step on a stage and a different persona comes over me. Most of the people who have seen me on trail consider me a huge extrovert, when I'm actually a borderline introvert. It takes an extra effort for me to be that person.

(Ibid: 39)

The third aspect of the guides' emotional labour was seen to be encouraging a sense of community. For the guides this meant that socialising and getting to know the participants was part of their job responsibilities, including befriending those who had difficulties mixing with the rest of the group.

The guides noted various ways of coping with the emotional demands, including finding ways to remove themselves physically for periods of time (using pretexts such as organising equipment and checking the weather radio).

Overall, the study shows that maintaining the required persona could be emotionally exhausting. However, unlike Hochschild's (2003) discussion of emotional labour among flight attendants, Sharpe found no sense of the guides being estranged from their 'real' selves. The author interprets and discusses this in terms of a picture of the self as made up of multiple selves rather than 'one true self'. So while guides were required to act differently than they would do at home, they did not consider these actions as fake, but rather that their 'guide persona' was one of many versions of their self. So, Sharpe argues that while emotional labour may be demanding and exhausting, and involves the use of various coping strategies, nevertheless it does not necessarily involve any alienation from a true self.

Source: Sharpe (2005).

Other circumstances can arise, however, where the performance of emotional labour becomes much more problematic for the individual. One relates to the overall amount of emotional labour demanded by the job, especially where the emotional display is required over long periods of time. Cabin crew members aboard intercontinental flights, for example, not only work long duty times but also suffer from additional fatigue as a result of jet lag and interrupted sleep patterns. The strain of prolonged emotional display, particularly where customers are being difficult or offensive (see below), is illustrated in the following extract from Hochschild (2003: 127):

> A young businessman said to a flight attendant, 'Why aren't you smiling?' She put her tray back on the food cart, looked him in the eye and said, 'I'll tell you what. You smile first, then I'll smile.' The businessman smiled at her. 'Good', she replied. 'Now freeze and hold that for fifteen hours.'

A second problematic circumstance is where the dissonance between felt and displayed emotions is particularly acute. As Lewig and Dollard (2003: 379) demonstrate in their study of call-centre workers in South Australia, emotional dissonance exacerbates the level of emotional exhaustion that employees experience (see also Grandey, 2003). High levels of dissonance may arise if the required emotional display is considered inappropriate by the worker performing the task. The supermarket employee Denise quoted earlier, for example, expressed considerable difficulty with using the customer's name when handling cheques or credit cards. To Denise, a shy, self-effacing woman, this seemed 'too forward, too familiar' in a situation where she was not acquainted with the individual whose name she was required to use; the result was a continuing unease and embarrassment.

A commonly reported situation of emotional dissonance is where employees are required to maintain a particular emotional display towards customers who are being rude or offensive (Sliter et al, 2010). Examples of objectionable behaviour are evidenced in many studies of emotional labour, and they occur in all settings from the supermarket checkout, the hospital and the restaurant to the aircraft cabin, the call centre and the nightclub. Instances range from verbal abuse to physical assault. In Lewig and Dollard's (2003) call-centre study, the aspect of work that employees considered to be the most stressful (e.g. more than meeting performance targets) was having to deal with angry and abusive customers. The impact of such abuse can be very considerable. Korczynski (2003: 64), for example, quotes a manager at a banking call centre in Australia as saying 'staff will feel dejected for the rest of the day after one abusive phone call'.

To handle these sort of problematic situations, and generally to reduce the stresses of the emotional aspects of the job, it is clear that performers of this kind of labour adopt a variety of coping strategies. Before turning to these, however, we briefly examine the monitoring of emotional labour by management.

Monitoring emotional labour

It is one thing for management to issue sets of guidelines and instructions and run training programmes and refresher courses to perfect and sustain various forms of emotional labour; it is another, however, to be confident that once trained, employees will carry out the emotional labour as specified at all times. What managers seek is that the prescribed emotional labour is conducted 'authentically'. In this, they are reflecting the findings of studies, such as Grandey and colleagues (2005), that have demonstrated the contribution to customer satisfaction of 'display authenticity' – the latter resulting either from genuinely authentic behaviour or from an apparent authenticity that is the outcome of skilled impression management.

That managers recognise the tendency for employees to lapse in their emotional display is reflected in the practices adopted to monitor and modify employee behaviour: disciplining those falling short of the prescribed standards and (less frequently) rewarding unusually high performers. Many of the studies of emotional labour highlight particular supervisory practices, often covertly conducted, to check employee behaviour. Airlines, for example, regularly use 'ghost riders' to check on how employees perform their roles; similarly, supermarkets employ 'mystery shoppers' (people hired by the company and disguised as customers) to monitor performance of checkout operators. At Disneyland, supervisors hide themselves around the park to check on the behaviour of workers while remaining unobserved themselves (Van Maanen and Kunda, 1989).

Telephone call-centre supervisors routinely listen into calls, and these may be taped for use in appraisal meetings with employees (Taylor, 1998: 93; Taylor and Tyler, 2000: 83; see also Callaghan and Thompson, 2002). In their survey of 55 call centres in Scotland, Taylor and Bain (1999: 106) identified nine measures used by management in a majority of centres to monitor employee performance. These included quantitative measures such as length of calls and time between calls. However, the most common measure of all – present in more than four out of five call centres – was the monitoring of employee 'politeness towards customer'.

In addition to these various monitoring methods, a growing number of services regularly issue 'customer service' questionnaires (like the banking illustration given earlier) to gain information about the demeanour and emotional style of the employee. Extract 7.7 gives another example of such a questionnaire used in the UK – this time involving the performance of postal delivery workers.

Extract 7.7

Assessing performance in Royal Mail

Royal Mail distributes questionnaires to customers to measure the service provided by local delivery offices. Various questions ask about time of deliveries, condition of mail received, extent to which letters are delivered to the wrong address, and so on.

In addition, several questions seek information about the postal worker's attitude, appearance and emotional style. Not only the questions, but also the response scales used provide insight into employer expectations of postal employees. These questions and response choices include:

1. Does your postman/postwoman show respect for your property and the neighbourhood?
   - shows very little respect;
   - shows some respect but could be more careful;
   - always shows respect.

2. Which best describes your postman/postwoman's appearance?
   - often looks a bit scruffy;
   - usually reasonably tidy;
   - always neat and smart.

3. How friendly is your postman/postwoman?
   - never seems cheerful or acknowledges me;
   - acknowledges me, but only if I greet him/her;
   - acknowledges me, but doesn't always seem cheerful;
   - always seems cheerful and acknowledges me.

The questionnaire includes the address and postcode of the household completing it, thus allowing identification of individual delivery offices, postal delivery rounds – and specific postal employees.

Emotional labour coping strategies

Despite this level of surveillance it is clear that those required to perform very frequent repetitions of an emotional display and/or perform emotional labour over long periods adopt various coping strategies, both in response to the general pressures and to handle particular situations such as angry or offensive customers. At their simplest these strategies involve employees retiring to places, such as a rest room or canteen ('off-stage' areas where customers are not present) where they can 'let off steam'. Here, employees can express their anger or frustration in ways which are denied to them when performing their job:

> We do get some very difficult customers…when you get too angry you just go into the [back] office and have a good swear at them and you come out smiling.
>
> (Supermarket employee, quoted by Ogbonna and Wilkinson, 1990: 12)

This 'off-stage' area may be as simple as the space created by employees turning their back on the customer – and the opportunity this provides for gestures such as face-pulling or eye-rolling that indicate to other employees a dropping of the emotional mask. In studies of emotional labour, such strategies are reported in a wide variety of contexts from High Street retail stores (Martin, Knopoff and Beckman, 1998: 450) to strip clubs (Wood, 2000: 25) and guided treks (Sharpe, 2005 and Extract 7.6). As well as 'letting off steam', one of the additional benefits of these off-stage behaviours is that they may reinforce the degree of co-worker solidarity: a solidarity or collective response which both Karabanow (1999) and Korczynski (2003) identify as an important factor in coping with jobs with high emotional labour demands.

Other strategies for coping with rude customers include engaging in covert activity which at the same time maintains the mask of emotional display: for example, the waiter who tampers with the offensive customer's food in some way, or the sales assistant who manages to look in all directions except at the loud customer who is demanding his or her attention. Vincent (2011: 1374) terms this 'emotional misbehaviour'. Disneyland ride operators deploy a number of covert activities in response to their situation, and particularly when confronted by offensive customers. These can include the 'break-up-the-party' ploy of separating pairs into different rides (despite there being room for both on the same ride), the 'seat-belt squeeze' in which customers are over-tightened into their seats, and other variants of inflicting physical discomfort (Van Maanen and Kunda, 1989: 67).

Call-centre employees also report a variety of covert methods for dealing with rude or offensive customers. These include limiting the amount of information provided and responding in a tone of voice which, while officially conforming to the rules, in practice allows employees to restrict their required emotional display. One operator in a telecommunications centre described this in the following way:

> Some customers are just a pain in the arse and they treat you like dirt. But I've worked out a way of saying things that puts them in their place. If you choose your words carefully, there's no way they can pull you in and dig you up for what you've said.

> (Quoted in Taylor and Bain, 1999: 113)

A telephone sales agent in the study by Taylor and Tyler (2000: 89) makes a similar point:

> If I don't like someone…it's difficult to explain but I will be efficient with them, giving them what they want and no more, but I will not be really friendly…. I sometimes have a really monotone voice, sounding a bit cold…. I will not laugh at their jokes, for example.

Resistance in call centres is also facilitated by experienced employees being able to tell when their calls are being monitored by supervisors (ibid: 89). This allows for more overt coping strategies such as disconnecting offensive calls (see also Wang et al, 2011, for a recent study of employee sabotage in response to customer mistreatment of employees).

A more general defence mechanism for coping with the demands of emotional labour is referred to in several studies by phrases such as 'switching off', 'switching to automatic' or 'going robot'. Filby (1992: 39), for example, refers to emotional labourers' ability to 'switch onto autopilot'. These various expressions refer to behaviour involving a continued outward adherence to the basic emotional performance, but an inward escape from the pressures of the job: a 'surface' rather than 'deep' acting out of emotional labour. Many performers of emotional labour, for example, are expected to smile as though they mean it ('smile from the inside') so that customers believe in its authenticity or sincerity and do not see it as simply part of an act. To switch into automatic may involve limiting this expression of 'sincerity'. Employees may have only limited scope for adopting this strategy, however, if 'sincerity' is also monitored. British Airways passengers arriving at London Heathrow, for example, are regularly canvassed about the service they have just received: did the check-in staff at the departure airport use the passenger's name; did they look them in the eye and smile; and did the smile seem genuine or forced – on a scale of one to four (Blyton and Turnbull, 1998: 69)?

There are also other coping strategies and ways individual employees protest against the pressure of display rules. Hochschild (2003), for example, notes the use of 'slow-downs' among flight attendants and the way some employees enact minor infringements of uniform and appearance codes as a way of not being fully submissive to management instruction. Likewise, Hampson and Junor (2005) note examples of customer service workers siding with customers in ways that may run contrary to management instruction. Overall, what such actions, protests and coping strategies indicate is that, in some cases at least, employees experience difficulties in continually performing their role as laid down in training manuals and management instruction.

To sum up

Emotional labour becomes problematic under certain circumstances. Reflecting this, management have established extensive means to monitor employee compliance with particular sets of display rules. Despite this surveillance, employees adopt various strategies to cope with excessive emotional labour.

Some critical commentators argue that in extreme cases, the demands for emotional labour have consequences for the workers involved that go significantly beyond the (relatively) minor irritations of the rude customer. In particular the demands of emotional labour can have physical and psychological health implications. Also, emotional labour has particular implications for women in the workplace.

Some wider implications of emotional labour

Emotional labour and employee well-being

In principle, just as emotional labour may be a source of job satisfaction for those who gain fulfilment from the work they perform, it is also potentially a source of job dissatisfaction and alienation (see discussion of alienation in Chapter 9). Indeed, some writers suggest alienation arising from emotional labour could be particularly acute, since the nature of the task carries the potential for individuals to become self-estranged – detached from their own 'real' feelings – which in turn might threaten their sense of identity (Shupe and Bradley, 2010). This is seen to be particularly the case with 'surface' acting. Judge, Woolf and Hurst (2009), for example, found surface acting much more likely to be associated with negative mood, emotional exhaustion and decreased job satisfaction, compared to 'deep' acting (see also Scott and Barnes, 2011 for a similar pattern of findings). Where expressed emotions are not felt, this gap between real and displayed feelings may cause feelings of falseness. Various writers have drawn attention to this 'falseness' potentially leading to poor self-esteem, depression, cynicism and alienation from work (Ashforth and Humphrey, 1993: 97).

Prolonged requirement to conform to emotional display rules, or where these rules require an intensive display of an emotion script, could also contribute to 'emotion overload' or emotional exhaustion. This is perhaps particularly harmful if, after their regular shift of emotional labour, women have to perform a 'second shift' of emotion work at home (looking after a child/children, their spouse or elderly relatives) (Hochschild, 1989; Wharton and Erickson, 1993).

However, while there is a potential for emotional labour to be dissatisfying or alienating, how much is this the case in practice? Overall, the evidence on this question remains somewhat mixed.

In her initial study of flight attendants, Hochschild highlighted a number of negative aspects of the job, leading to 'an estrangement between self and feeling and between self and display' (2003: 131). Hochschild identifies such problems as 'feeling phony' (ibid: 181), with the flight attendants being unable to express genuine feelings or identify their own needs – inabilities which, for some, resulted in problems of establishing and maintaining close relationships in their private lives (ibid: 183).

Wouters (1989), however, argues that the costs of emotional labour should not obscure more positive aspects. For Wouters, the distinction between true and displayed feelings is not as hard and fast as Hochschild implies, for individuals perform all sorts of emotional scripts, outside as well as inside the workplace – a multiplicity which undermines any distinction between the 'displayed' feelings in emotional labour and 'true' feelings expressed elsewhere (see also discussion in Extract 7.6). Wouters (1989: 116) also argues that the costs of emotional labour must be offset against the positive side of such jobs, including the pleasure that many derive from serving customers and receiving from them a positive response in return.

This argument reiterates the point made earlier: that there are individuals who strongly identify with their work role, and for whom their job and the emotional display rules entailed in that job are fully consistent with their personal values and identity. Indeed, for some employees it is this 'fit' between personal values and job demands that has attracted them into the job in the first place. For such individuals, the performance of the tasks is likely to enhance, rather than reduce, psychological well-being (Ashforth and Humphrey, 1993: 100–1; see also Jenkins, Delbridge and Roberts, 2010).

What do you think?

Hochschild and Wouters disagree on how we should view emotional labour. For Hochschild, emotional labour is a potentially major problem, while for Wouters, any difficulties entailed in this type of labour are more than offset by the positive aspects of jobs such as those of flight attendants.

Which of these arguments do you think is the more convincing, and why?

A number of more quantitative studies have been conducted to measure the effects of emotional labour on employees' health and well-being (e.g. Judge et al, 2009; Scott and Barnes, 2011). These often examine impact on job satisfaction, stress levels, degree of 'emotional exhaustion' (or 'burnout') and various physical symptoms. Again, however, these studies do not all point in the same direction, though certain general patterns are identifiable. Among the factors which may militate against a more consistent picture are:

- A lack of a standard measure of emotional labour (some studies, for example, simply measure the presence of emotional labour, while others concentrate on the gap between real and displayed emotions as the core measure of emotional labour).
- The diverse range of occupations studied. Among others, these include debt collectors, military recruiting staff, nurses, hairdressers, chauffeurs, travel guides, university employees, shop assistants, waiters, banking staff, bus drivers and survey research workers: a range which incorporates a wide variety in the type and extent of emotional labour demands.
- The potential importance of organisational and managerial context; for example, the extent to which managers enforce particular emotion rules and support (or fail to support) staff who are being subjected to abuse of one form or another from customers.

Several studies identify possible health problems related to emotional labour. In her study of university employees in the United States, for example, Pugliesi (1999) found emotional labour was associated with increased perceptions of job stress, decreased job satisfaction and lower levels of overall worker well-being. Morris and Feldman (1997) similarly found an association between one aspect of emotional labour – the degree of emotional dissonance – and the extent of 'emotional exhaustion' among over 500 respondents drawn from nursing, recruiting and debt-collecting organisations in the United States. Mann (1999) too found a relationship between reported degree of emotional dissonance and higher stress levels among respondents in 12 UK companies, while Lewig and Dollard (2003) report a similar correlation between emotional dissonance and emotional exhaustion.

While Pugliesi found emotional labour to be associated with higher stress and lower well-being regardless of other job factors, a number of other studies have highlighted the importance of certain conditions under which emotional labour has a more marked effect for the people involved. For example, in their study of workers involved in a survey research organisation in the United States, Schaubroeck and Jones (2000) found that overall, emotional labour was associated with the presence of a number of health symptoms. However, this association was mainly present among individuals who reported low levels of job involvement and a low level of identification with the organisation. As the authors conclude (Schaubroeck and Jones, 2000: 179), this finding suggests that 'emotional labour is most unhealthful when one's emotional expressions on the job are not an authentic representation of one's personal beliefs'.

In an earlier study, Wharton (1993) also identified the importance of particular job factors in moderating any effects of emotional labour on employees. In a study of over 600 banking and health service employees (almost two-thirds of whom were judged to hold jobs which required emotional labour), Wharton found no simple relationship between emotional labour and variables such as the degree of 'emotional exhaustion': as a whole, workers performing emotional labour were no more likely to suffer from emotional exhaustion than others. There was also no evidence of the expected relationship between emotional labour and job satisfaction (indeed, those performing jobs involving emotional labour were slightly more satisfied overall than those performing other jobs). What the study found, however, was that people performing emotional labour were less likely to experience emotional exhaustion if they had greater autonomy over how they carried out their work.

To sum up

Despite the variation in results between individual studies, available evidence indicates that, in certain circumstances at least, emotional labour is associated with stress, emotional exhaustion and a lower level of general well-being. This is more likely to be the case where demands for emotional labour are high and/or where emotional dissonance is marked. The latter is likely to be greater among those who identify least with their job or with the organisation they work for. Those with very restricted degrees of control over how they perform their jobs may also find performing emotional labour to be a more negative experience than those with higher levels of job autonomy.

The gender implications of emotional labour

As well as its potential for creating feelings of alienation and emotional exhaustion, several commentators have pointed to possible negative implications of emotional labour for women's position in the labour force. In particular, it may reinforce certain gender stereotypes which in the past have been detrimental to women (see, for example, Hochschild, 2003; James, 1989; Mumby and Putnam, 1992). Three aspects of emotional labour are central to this argument:

• The distribution of emotional labour reflects a gender imbalance: the majority of those doing emotional labour for a living are women. Hochschild

(2003), for example, estimates that twice as many women as men occupy jobs that require emotional labour. Moreover, even in single occupations employing both men and women, a number of studies have identified an expectation that the women employees will perform more emotional labour than their male counterparts (Morris and Feldman, 1996: 997; Taylor and Tyler, 2000).

- Most people performing emotional labour occupy relatively low positions within work hierarchies, with emotional labour rarely being ascribed the status of a skill (see Payne, 2009 for a discussion of emotional labour and skill; also Jenkins, Delbridge and Roberts, 2010). Thus, just as women in general are located disproportionately within lower levels of occupational hierarchies, they are similarly disproportionately represented among those lower-status jobs requiring emotional labour. For some (see, for example, Ashforth and Humphrey, 1995; Domagalski, 1999; James, 1989) this reflects the status of 'rationalism' within contemporary capitalism, and also the customary association of rationality and masculinity (Pringle, 1989). In combination, these create a contrast between jobs that are seen to be highly 'rational' and as a result are afforded high status (and are disproportionately occupied by men), and jobs that are more 'emotional' and are accorded much lower status (and are filled disproportionately by women).

In hospitals, for example, it is the rational skills of the (mainly male) doctors and hospital managers that are accredited the highest status and rewards, while the emotional well-being of the patient – a key ingredient in their return to full health – is borne largely by the (mainly female) nurses and auxiliaries and tends to be unrecognised and much more poorly rewarded (James, 1989). This tendency to attribute status to some jobs rather than others is related to the issue of the social construction of skill, discussed in Chapter 5.

The main emotions displayed in emotional labour – in particular those involving a display of caring – act to reinforce gender stereotypes, and in particular that 'caring' is an emotion that is more 'natural' in women. Women are widely seen to be not only naturally more caring than men but also more emotional than men, and more used to dealing with other people's feelings, as part of their domestic caring role. Various studies, for example, have indicated that women are the primary providers of emotional support for their partners and children (see discussion in Wharton and Erickson, 1993: 469).

Critics of emotional labour argue that, as a result of this greater responsibility for emotion management in the domestic sphere, this comes to be viewed as a 'natural' ability in women, or a 'talent' which they have, rather than a skill which has to be acquired (see Chapter 5 for a discussion of gender and skill). The effect is for management to treat emotional labour as an extension of this natural talent, not a learned skill – with the effect that it is not accorded the status of a skill. It leads management to select women rather than men for many jobs involving emotional labour: see, for example, Leidner (1991) on the distribution of work tasks in McDonald's, and Taylor and Tyler (2000) on the selection of candidates for telephone sales positions.

So, just as the skills employed (disproportionately by women) in the domestic sphere tend to be under-recognised (see Chapter 10), so too the performance of emotional labour skills in the paid work sphere tends to go under-recognised and under-rewarded. Filby (1992) correctly points out that it would be misleading to argue that all emotional labour deserves 'skilled' status: indeed, 'much emotion work...is untutored and probably poor' (Filby, 1992: 39; also Payne, 2009). Nevertheless, as the foregoing discussion has illustrated, in a number of different contexts, emotional labour is learned through considerable training and is performed in far from straightforward circumstances.

An extension of this argument of reinforcing stereotypes is that many front-line service jobs involve the performance of tasks as deferential servants – on aircraft, in hotels and in restaurants and nightclubs, for example. It may be argued that, since the majority of emotional labour jobs are performed by women, this potentially reinforces an image of women as servants – an image already emphasised by the unpaid and problematic status of domestic activities. This is particularly pertinent to those settings comprising mainly women performing emotional labour for a largely male customer group; it is mostly men, for example, who fly business class on airlines, eat business lunches, stay at hotels on sales conferences and visit certain types of nightclub. As well as the nurturing and servant roles, some emotional labour jobs also involve women workers emphasising other aspects of their 'feminine' qualities, in particular applying their sexuality as a way of 'keeping the customers happy'.

As Hochschild (2003: 182) describes, flight attendants are required to play these different roles simultaneously: 'those of the supportive mother and those of the sexually desirable mate', manifesting themselves in 'both "motherly" behavior and a "sexy" look'. Similarly, Linstead (1995: 196) argues that through the nature of their advertising, airlines 'make no secret of their wish to entice a predominantly male clientele on board in the lucrative first and business sectors with gently erotic evocations'. In general, this message may be more subtle now than in the 1970s – when airlines used such advertising slogans as 'I'm Cheryl, fly me' (quoted in Lessor, 1984: 42) and 'We really move our tails for you to make your every wish come true' (quoted in Hochschild, 2003: 93) – but the message remains, nevertheless.

Sexuality is similarly present in other settings of emotional labour. Filby (1992), for example, in his study of women working in betting shops, noted the sexual banter between cashiers and (mostly male) customers, which forms part of the employees' task of building customer relations and customer loyalty to that branch. Likewise, Hall (1993) indicated the existence of the 'obligatory job flirt' which occurs in many restaurants, again as part of a broader management requirement to 'keep the customer happy'. This mix of emotional labour and sexuality is most extreme in the strip clubs described by Wood (2000) and others, where much of the income-generating activity for the women dancers depends on their ability to flirt and raise the sexual self-esteem of their (overwhelmingly male) customers.

However, the arguments about women and emotional labour are not as clear-cut as some of these critics have suggested. As noted above, it is not necessarily the case that women performing emotional labour experience a negative reaction. Indeed, Wharton (1993) in her study found that women performing emotional labour were significantly more satisfied than their male counterparts engaged in similar types of work. As a result of patterns of socialisation, for example, 'women may be better equipped than men for the interpersonal demands of frontline service work and thus experience those jobs more positively than their male counterparts' (Wharton, 1993: 225).

Also, in the longer term, other factors may act in favour of changing the position of women performing emotional labour. The growth of jobs requiring emotional labour results in more men needing to manage their emotions as part of the job. As the number of both women and men performing emotional labour rises, this may affect the way emotional labour is delivered, particularly where the clientele is becoming less male-dominated. Linstead (1995: 196) notes, for example, the acknowledged need among airline companies to shift the nature of emotional labour in business and first class to attract the growing market in female business travellers.

As the emphasis on effective service increases, employees and groups such as trade unions will also potentially be able to use this recognised importance as a lever for improving the status and rewards pertaining to those performing these types of jobs. Indeed, at least one writer (Foegen, 1988) has called for workers performing emotional labour to receive separate 'hypocrisy pay' as a recognition of the task involved. More generally, trade unions in Britain have made significant inroads into areas such as call centres: in the survey of call centres by Taylor and Bain (1999: 113–14), more than half had a union or staff association, with unions not only negotiating standard items such as pay, holidays, hours and overtime payments but also raising such concerns as job stress and levels of employee monitoring and surveillance.

Taking this point further, emotional display does not render women powerless. Indeed, in certain circumstances, the 'emotion' could be used as a source of power. Linstead (1995), for example, writing about a strike among Cathay Pacific (CP) flight attendants points to the attendants' explicit use of emotional display as a means of attracting media attention and public support. The 'perfumed picket line', as it was dubbed by one of the Hong Kong newspapers, gained much more coverage than the CP 'managers in suits'. While the attendants did not win the strike (not least because management was successful in hiring outside crews to operate a reduced service), the flight attendants nevertheless indicated their potential power to 'turn the seductive skills which company training had developed into an effective weapon to mobilize public opinion' (Linstead, 1995: 190).

To sum up

Several writers have highlighted gender implications of emotional labour, and particularly the way that emotional labour can act to reinforce gender stereotypes in the workplace. The overall picture is quite complex, however, indicating the need for more insight into the particular contexts in which emotional labour acts to the detriment of women's status in the labour market.

Conclusion

Analysing the growth and implications of emotional labour underscores a number of broader developments and issues in contemporary industrial society. The demand for emotional labour has grown not simply because of the expansion of the services available to the general public, but also because of the competition between those services and the identification of customer relations as a key to business success in a competitive environment. Though long established in various areas of employment, a required emotional display and self-management of feelings have become part of an increasing number of jobs. There is every indication too that this aspect of work will grow further in coming years, as a public increasingly used to a high level of 'customer care' raises its baseline expectation of what constitutes an appropriate level of that 'care' in an ever-widening range of services.

As well as reflecting a growth of, and increased competition between, service providers and the greater significance attached to customers, the topic of emotional labour touches on other issues raised elsewhere in this book. Most notably, emotional labour is an aspect of work that to date has been performed predominantly by women, often while occupying comparatively low positions within their work organisations. It is an aspect of women's work which has also typically been accorded relatively little status. So, just as women in general have not typically benefited from how the concept of 'skill' has been understood (see Chapter 5), emotional labour itself has not been accorded prestige or skilled status. Instead, the performing of emotional labour has tended to be seen as something that women are 'naturally' good at – an innate talent rather than an acquired skill.

At the same time, as has been noted, it is important not to adopt too simplistic a view of emotional labour. It is an aspect of work that varies considerably in its nature and degree. Its impact on employees will depend on the character of the individuals involved, and some will be far more predisposed to the requirements of emotional labour than others. For many, emotional labour represents a relatively minor part of their job; it may not be unpleasant and can often help to create a more friendly working environment. For instance, smiling at others often elicits a smile in return. It is in cases where the demands of emotional labour are excessive that it becomes problematic, potentially giving rise to feelings of alienation, loss of sense of identity and emotional exhaustion. Still, even in these situations workers employ a number of coping strategies to minimise the harmful effects of emotional labour.

8

Knowledge and work

Chapter aim

To examine knowledge as a defining feature of contemporary work and society.

Key concepts

▷ knowledge work

▷ types of knowledge: embrained, embodied, embedded, encultured and encoded

▷ explicit and tacit knowledge

▷ knowledge workers

▷ professionals

▷ the entrepreneurial professional

▷ knowledge creation

▷ continuous improvement (kaizen)

▷ knowledge capture

▷ expropriation of knowledge

▷ information society

▷ information age

▷ network society

Learning outcomes

After reading and thinking about the material in this chapter, you will be able to:

1. Define 'knowledge work' using different types of knowledge.

2. Specify the distinctive characteristics of knowledge work by:

   a. comparing knowledge workers with routine workers;

   b. comparing knowledge workers with professionals.

3. Explain knowledge creation and the transformation of tacit into explicit knowledge.

4. Recognise the importance of knowledge capture and evaluate how this is achieved through techniques such as continuous improvement.

5. Assess whether the need for managers to acquire knowledge benefits knowledge workers.

6. Explain and evaluate:

   a. Bell's idea of the information society.

   b. Castells's description of the information age and the network society.

Introduction

Knowledge and information are becoming the strategic resource and transforming agent of the post-industrial society...just as the combination of energy, resources and machine technology were the transformational agencies of industrial society.

(Bell, 1980: 531)

In an economy where the only certainty is uncertainty, the one sure source of lasting competitive advantage is knowledge. When markets shift, technologies proliferate, competitors multiply, and products become obsolete almost over-night, successful companies are those that consistently create new knowledge, disseminate it widely throughout the organization, and quickly embody it in new technologies and products.

(Nonaka, 1991: 96)

The productivity of knowledge and knowledge workers will not be the only competitive factor in the world economy. It is, however, likely to become the decisive factor, at least for most industries in the developed countries.

(Drucker, 1998: 17)

These three quotes have one theme in common: the belief that knowledge is becoming central to organisations and the economies of advanced capitalism. Though each of them is from the last century, they remain relevant today. If knowledge and knowledge work become increasingly important, it suggests that those people in such knowledge-intensive roles ('knowledge workers') will have a central and influential position in the occupational structure of society. This is supported by some people's description of our era as the information age.

In many respects the idea is appealing – not least for those who, as knowledge workers, are supposedly becoming more influential. But does the idea really stand up to scrutiny? Who are these so-called 'knowledge workers'? What role and influence do they have? Is this influence significantly greater than in earlier times? Does it mean that we are now living in an information society?

The importance of these issues has led to a sizable amount of work on 'knowledge management' (Amalia and Nugroho, 2011; Easterby-Smith and Lyles, 2003; Newell, Robertson, Scarbrough and Swan, 2009; Robertson and Swan, 2004) as well as related work in organisational strategy on dynamic capabilities (Dixon, Meyer and Day, 2010; Teece, 2007). Our specific concern – because it reflects the topic of the realities of work – is with the knowledge workers themselves, rather than these more strategic or organisation-level issues of managing knowledge. The chapter is divided into five sections. First, we examine the concept of knowledge work. Second, we define knowledge workers using two different approaches. Third, we assess knowledge within the workforce, concentrating on the processes of knowledge creation and knowledge capture. Fourth, we discuss whether knowledge workers can be considered a special group precisely because their expertise cannot be expropriated (taken over and owned) by management. Fifth, we look at the concept of the information society using two theorists, Daniel Bell and Manuel Castells.

Knowledge work

One central problem when defining 'knowledge work' is establishing whether the term refers to the inputs of that work, the outputs, or the work process. For example, the work of a travel agent is based on the input of knowledge (information about the availability of holidays, hotels and flights) which the agent processes to produce a service outcome – your holiday. As writers, we are processing information (from other writers and researchers) to produce more information (this book) – so both the input and output might be described as knowledge, or knowledge building (LeCroy, 2010). These distinctions seem straightforward, but the problem is almost all jobs involve using knowledge in some form. Take the example of taxi drivers: neither the inputs (the driving) nor the outputs (delivering passengers to their destinations) would be described as knowledge work, but the work process involves drivers applying knowledge (of the location, the best route, the local traffic and so on). Indeed London cabbies traditionally referred to their training to get a licence (where they effectively have to memorise a road map of London) as 'doing the Knowledge'.

So the problem with a broad definition of knowledge work is that it is too inclusive to be of any use – everyone is a knowledge worker because everyone's work involves knowledge in some form. Consequently, researchers have sought to find a tighter definition. For example, Winslow and Bramer (1994) suggest that knowledge work is concerned with (i) interpreting and applying information; in order to (ii) add value to the organisation; through (iii) creating solutions to problems and making informed recommendations to management. By locating this definition within an organisation and having the test of whether it 'adds value', they are limiting the number of occupations which would count as knowledge worker. An alternative approach is to think about the type of knowledge being used.

Types of knowledge

Although it is probably accurate to say that almost all jobs entail some aspect of 'knowledge', the type of knowledge required differs considerably. The work of Blackler (1995) is particularly useful here because, from an extensive review of previous writers, he distinguishes five forms of knowledge (a recent extension and application is in Chiang, Han and Chuang, 2011). The descriptions below are based on his categories:

- *Embrained knowledge.* The abstract, conceptual and theoretical information that we have in our heads. It can be applied to solve problems and 'think around' issues in a creative way.
- *Embodied knowledge.* Practical and applied ways of doing things learned from experience. Problems are solved by drawing upon previous experience and a wealth of information about the specific context.

- *Encultured knowledge.* Shared understandings about 'how things are done around here'. An essential part of the organisational culture or the workgroup's culture (see Chapter 9).
- *Embedded knowledge.* Systematic routines that mean a person can perform a task or activity 'without thinking'. The task becomes 'second nature' to the person, to such an extent that the knowledge, learning and skill behind it are submerged from view. This idea has already been encountered (Chapter 5) when discussing tacit skills.
- *Encoded knowledge.* Information conveyed by signs and symbols. This book is a form of encoded knowledge. Information technology has increased the potential for encoding, manipulating and transmitting knowledge.

Blackler observes that these five forms indicate that 'all individuals and all organisations, not just the so-called knowledge workers or knowledge organisations are knowledgeable' (1995: 1026). He also suggests that it is not so much that knowledge work is becoming important per se, but that the emphasis is shifting within the forms of knowledge: from embodied and embedded to embrained, encultured and encoded knowledge.

Extract 8.1 provides an example of how these concepts can be applied. Read it and then test your understanding by trying Exercise 8.1.

Extract 8.1

Forms of knowledge at Xerox

Brown's (1991) account of efforts to develop Xerox as a learning organisation provides an example of how the development of each of these different forms of knowledge may contribute to organisational learning. Brown pointed to the advantages for a company like Xerox of undertaking new product development in close association with potential customers (i.e. he identified the relevance of the embedded knowledge of Xerox's customers for an understanding of their reactions to new office machinery). He illustrated how design engineers at Xerox learned from ethnographic studies of how people interact with machines (i.e. from studies of the ways in which encoded knowledge interacts with, and may disrupt, embodied knowledge), and he emphasised too how studies of communications between engineers in Xerox have revealed how essential dialogue is between them (i.e. encultured knowledge) to increase their effectiveness in solving problems. Finally, Brown emphasised the importance of encouraging senior managers to develop new appreciations of their company's established practices (i.e. he pointed to the importance of developing embrained and encultured knowledge at senior management levels).

Source: Blackler, 1995 (1025–6).

Exercise 8.1

What do you think?

Read the paragraphs below and identify the five types of knowledge.

Maria inserts the photocopy card into the machine but it flashes up a message saying 'P15 error'. However, she removes the card, rubs it on her sleeve, reinserts it and the photocopy machine hums into action.

The photocopy technician had previously told her that when such an error message occurred it meant that the card had been magnetised and the only thing to do was to throw it away (even though this cost the company money because of the lost credit on the card). Although Maria believed the technician, the next time it occurred she thought she'd try to clean it on her sleeve. She tried this because sometimes it worked when her cashpoint card was rejected by the cash machine at the bank, and the two cards looked similar. Sure enough it had solved the problem with the photocopier.

The other secretaries in the office have seen Maria doing this, and they all now use 'Maria's magic method'. They encouraged Maria to email the technician about it. He replied that it was due to the effect of static electricity, and that he would pass the tip on to others who had the same problem and get it added to the 'users troubleshooting guide' on the company website.

Criticisms of knowledge work

There are critics of the concept of knowledge work (e.g. Collins, 1997; Kumar, 1995; Thompson, Warhurst and Callaghan, 2001; Warhurst and Thompson, 1998, 2006). Rather than worry about the different meanings of the term, such critics tend to argue, more fundamentally, that the term is meaningless, or a smoke screen for familiar forms of domination and exploitation at work. In particular they raise two objections:

- Much supposed 'knowledge work' is routine and involves undertaking tasks that require very little training and offer employees very little discretion. For instance, when Fleming, Harley and Sewell (2004) analysed occupational data covering 1986–2000 from the Australian Bureau of Statistics, they found that the white-collar jobs that accounted for the largest growth were characterised by similar types of lower-level knowledge work. They state, 'these occupations tend to be associated with knowledge handling and servicing provision (e.g. customer relations representatives) with low levels of discretion and analytical skill, rather than those that are often considered to be autonomous and empowered knowledge productive jobs (e.g. higher education researchers)' (Fleming, Harley and Sewell, 2004: 735).
- *Knowledge work is not a new phenomenon.* Employees have always used their knowledge to do their work, and managers have always attempted to make use of their knowledge to improve the effectiveness and efficiency of work. In other words managers have consistently sought to appropriate the employees' knowledge, while employees have often tried to protect it (particularly through trade union regulation, see Chapter 11, and informal work practices, see Chapter 9).

Extract 8.2 provides an illustration of the arguments that some of the fiercest critics use to challenge the usefulness of the concept. However, other commentators have suggested that while the term 'knowledge work' can be ambiguous, there is no reason that a precise definition cannot be developed and used to analyse different types of 'knowledge worker'.

Knowledge work sceptics

Proponents of the knowledge economy fail to appreciate that most tertiary [service] sector growth has occurred not in knowledge work but in the low-paid 'donkey work' of serving, guarding, cleaning, waiting and helping in the private health and care services, as well as hospitality industries.

We find that much of the 'knowledge' work, for example in financial services, requires little more of workers than information transfer.... Much of the growth in service work has been in the more explicitly 'interactive' categories such as telesales or call-centres. This type of work has its own routine in that the process is likely to be governed by scripted interactions, and monitored for deviance by supervisors.

All workers are, of course, knowledgeable about their work – and always have been.... It has long been management's job to make capital out of the originality of what labour knows and does.... The knowledgeable worker is therefore not a post-industrial phenomenon but rather an integral part of the development of industrial capitalism.

It might be useful to jettison the overly-broad notion of *knowledge* workers in favour of a more realistic appreciation of the growth of *knowledgeability* in work. The managerial instruments to register and if possible capture employee knowledge have some innovative forms in teamworking and off-line problem-solving groups. But we should not lose sight of the role played by the development of traditional Tayloristic techniques.

Source: Warhurst and Thompson (1998: 5, 7) (emphasis in original).

Knowledge workers

The 'knowledge worker'

Frenkel, Korczynski, Donoghue and Shire (1995) come to a similar conclusion to Blackler and argue that there has been a change in the nature of work so that different kinds of knowledge are increasingly being used at work: theoretical or abstract knowledge, rather than contextual knowledge. If we put this into the same terms as Blackler's (outlined above), it means an increased emphasis on embrained knowledge rather than embodied and embedded knowledge.

However, Frenkel et al are also aware of the dangers (raised by the critics) of using the term 'knowledge worker', and have developed a clearer definition based on identifying features in the act of work. They suggest that as well as the type of knowledge required, it is important to look at the extent of creativity involved in the work, and the type and level of skills being used. This leads Frenkel et al (1995: 780) to the following definition:

> Knowledge workers rely predominantly on theoretical knowledge, and their work requires a high level of creativity for which they mainly use intellective skills.

Table 8.1 shows how these characteristics of knowledge workers can be contrasted with those of workers undertaking the type of work described in Chapter 6 (on routine work). These two types can be seen as the far extremes – many employees will lie somewhere between these two types if the various aspects of their work are analysed according to the dimensions suggested here. It is important

Table 8.1   A comparison of knowledge workers and routine workers

Dimension	Knowledge worker	Routine worker
Form of knowledge	Theoretical (embrained)	Contextual (embodied and embedded)
Extent of creativity(generating an original output – response, idea, solution, product, etc.)	High (open-ended, unusual)	Low (rule-based, mundane)
Type of skill	Intellective (reasoning based on abstract cues, inference, synthesis and systematic thinking)	Action-centred (physical sensing and dexterity)

Source: Based on Frenkel, Korczynski, Donoghue and Shire (1995).

to recognise that a particular job can vary between the dimensions: for instance, a landscape gardener could be considered to rely on contextual knowledge and action-centred skill (so could be closer to a routine worker in these respects) yet they may also be highly creative (more like a knowledge worker along this dimension). To get a feel for this method of comparing jobs, try Exercise 8.2.

Exercise 8.2

What do you think?

Using Frenkel et al's three dimensions (see Table 8.1), evaluate the jobs listed below. You are unlikely to have detailed knowledge of the jobs, but you should have enough general awareness of what each job involves to give reasons for your evaluation. Remember, the 'knowledge worker' and 'routine worker' are the extremes, so the jobs you are evaluating are likely to fall somewhere between these on one or more of the dimensions.

- registered nurse,
- customer service representative (in a call centre),
- architect,
- laboratory technician,
- skilled production worker.

The entrepreneurial professional

An alternative definition of 'knowledge worker' has been provided by Reed (1996). He rejects the notion of knowledge work being concerned solely with the act of work – in particular information processing and manipulation – which he views as far too inclusive and lacking in theoretical precision. Instead Reed suggests that it is preferable to characterise such work as a form of 'expert work' performed by specialists. In devising this definition he is also keen to distinguish 'knowledge workers' from other types of experts – in particular, professionals. (See Extract 8.3 for an explanation of the meaning of profession.)

Whereas Frenkel, Korczynski, Shire and Tam (1999) argue that knowledge workers can be distinguished from professional workers, Reed prefers to describe 'knowledge workers' as a particular type of professional. He labels this type of worker the 'entrepreneurial professional' and provides the examples of financial and business consultants, project engineers, computer analysts and media consultants (a recent analysis of consultants that develops some of Reed's ideas is in Muzio, Kirkpatrick and Kipping, 2011). Drawing on this description, we can distinguish this kind of knowledge worker by three characteristics:

- They have task-specific, highly specialised cognitive (thinking) and technical skills.
- They rely on a combination of embrained, embodied and embedded knowledge.
- They aggressively market themselves as people with specialist expertise that can solve complex organisational problems.

To underline their distinctiveness, a contrast can also be drawn between knowledge workers and two other professional groups: liberal/independent professionals, and organisational professionals (Blackler, Reed and Whitaker, 1993).

1. *Liberal/independent professionals* – for example, doctors, architects and lawyers:
   - have an occupational-specific knowledge/skill base;
   - rely on embrained and encoded knowledge;
   - have traditionally operated comparatively free from the jurisdiction of particular organisations by controlling the access to the education and training required to qualify and practise. By carrying this out – it is sometimes referred to as occupational closure (through the social closure processes described in Chapter 5) – they have been able to establish a monopoly and gained public recognition of their expertise.

2. Organisational professionals – for example, managers, administrators and technicians:
   - have an organisation-specific (localised) knowledge base;
   - rely on embedded and encultured knowledge;
   - have at best built partial occupational closure, through establishing educational and bureaucratic credentials within the organisation. This produces organisational recognition and gives them powerful positions within technical and status hierarchies.

Importantly, Reed suggests that knowledge workers are well suited to the context of global capitalism and the increasing commercialisation of public sector organisations. In this sense, they are the new face of the professions. It is a view consistent with other commentators who have argued that the liberal/independent professions have, since the 1980s, faced radical challenges as a result of political, economic and technological change (Abbott, 1988; Burris, 1993; Crompton, 1990; Freidson, 1994). In the words of Reed (1996: 589):

> The predominantly private sector, entrepreneurial professions/knowledge workers have been the real 'winners' in the economic, technological, political and cultural restructuring generated by the shift to a more globalized and flexible regime of capital accumulation. Research suggests that the 'occupationally-owned' assets of the liberal/independent professions and the

'organizationally-controlled' resources of the organizational/managerial professions are both under threat, if not terminal decline. If this is the case, then it offers a golden opportunity to the entrepreneurial professions/knowledge workers to exploit the potential for cognitive expansion, material advancement and socio-political enhancement that these developments present.

Although he does not use Reed's terminology, a similar distinction between 'knowledge workers' and traditional professionals is made by Scarborough (1999: 7):

> Lacking the demarcations and controls of conventional professional groups, knowledge workers are defined primarily by the work that they do – work which is relatively unstructured and organizationally contingent, and which thus reflects the changing demands of organizations more than occupationally-defined norms and practices.

To develop this definition, Scarbrough highlights three ways that knowledge workers can be distinguished:

1. Unlike traditional professionals, they cannot monopolise specialist knowledge and so cannot derive power from closure. However, this does not mean they are powerless. Instead their power derives from their scarcity within a liberal market environment.
2. Knowledge workers are more dependent on employers because 'knowledge work is less a matter of the application of predefined expertise [as with professional work] and more a joint product of human interactions with informational and intellectual assets delivered through information and communication technologies' (ibid: 7).
3. Knowledge workers are more instrumental than professionals. They consider the knowledge in terms of its value rather than whether it is good in its own right.

Points 1 and 3 (above) echo Reed's view that knowledge workers are well adapted to the market forces of advanced capitalism. Point 2 underlines the way that knowledge workers depend on a particular organisational context, rather than being independent professionals. This differs from Reed because it suggests a potential means of organisational control that he does not consider appropriate for knowledge workers.

To sum up

'Knowledge worker' means different things for our two sets of commentators. For Frenkel et al, it denotes work that requires theoretical knowledge, high creativity and intellective skill. For Reed and Scarbrough it denotes a specific type of expertise and professional influence. These two examples demonstrate the importance of clarifying how the concept is being used. As with other concepts explored in the book, it illustrates how a variety of views and approaches can be adopted when exploring aspects of work.

Although they use different definitions of the concept, it is interesting to see that the commentators arrive at the same conclusion, in the sense that they see knowledge work as an increasingly important phenomenon. Frenkel et al point out that changes in the content of jobs mean more people are becoming knowledge workers, while Reed argues that the expert power of the knowledge workers means they are becoming influential and dominant among the professional groups. If this is the general trend, it is clear that managers are going to turn their attention to ways of acquiring this knowledge from the workforce. This is the subject of the next section.

Extract 8.3

Defining and analysing professions

The question of how to define and analyse a profession has been a long-standing concern in the analysis of work. Here we provide a brief overview of the main approaches – although there are numerous variations within each of these broad approaches.

Trait approach

Theoretical perspective: Functionalist

Definition of profession: An occupational group with certain unique characteristics. In particular:

- high proportion of theoretical knowledge;
- lengthy period of education and training;
- peer evaluation of competence;
- professional association;
- code of conduct;
- altruistic service.

Main research concern: How an occupational group attains these features in order to achieve professional status.

Occupational closure approach

Theoretical perspective: Neo-Weberian

Definition of profession: An occupational group with monopolistic control over knowledge.

Main research concern: How an occupational group achieves and protects this monopoly through the process of social closure (see Chapter 5). In particular, the way professionals build power and influence by controlling entry into the occupation, regulating the work processes within the occupation and developing a distinct occupational identity/culture.

Dynamic meaning approach

Theoretical perspective: Relativist/interpretivist

Definition of profession: No general definition is accurate because 'profession' is not a fixed concept. All occupations change and develop, so the term 'profession' means different things in different circumstances.

Main research concern: How occupations change and how the concept of 'profession' is used in specific contexts at different times.

In some empirically based accounts of professionals (e.g. Broadbent, Dietrich and Roberts, 1997) there seems to be:

- a complete rejection of the trait approach as being static and theoretically sterile;

8.3 cont.

- a recognition of the value of the processual features of the occupational closure approach (e.g. Fitzgerald and Ferlie, 2000);
- a preference for the dynamic meaning approach (e.g. Hanlon, 1998; Randle, 1996).

Other terms

'Professionalisation' is the process through which an occupational group achieves professional recognition and status. Likewise deprofessionalisation means the loss of this recognition and an associated reduction in status and influence.

'Semi-profession' is a term sometimes used to describe an occupation that has some but not all the trapping of a 'true' profession. In particular it is used to describe groups that have a professional body, code of conduct and regulated training, but have not achieved autonomy in relation to the client or the employing organisation. Recent changes in the status and autonomy of professional groups have made the term 'semi-profession' somewhat meaningless, and most contemporary commentators have abandoned it.

Other texts

A thorough analysis of all these concepts and the current approaches to the analysis of the professions can be found in texts such as Abbott (1988), Freidson (1994), Macdonald (1995) and Witz (1992). Good starting points are the articles by Saks (1983) and Crompton (1990), or for a more recent review Muzio et al (2011).

Knowledge within the workforce

So far we have looked at knowledge as a way of distinguishing between groups of employees. Now we turn to the idea that knowledge is present in all forms of work and is a potentially exploitable commodity, which makes it susceptible to management control. In particular this section explores the importance of knowledge creation and knowledge capture.

Knowledge creation

The term 'knowledge-creating company' was coined by Ikujiro Nonaka to characterise the way that some Japanese organisations differed from their Western counterparts. He was identifying the way that organisations such as Honda and Canon help their workers to create knowledge by providing an environment in which everyone is encouraged (and even expected) to think and behave creatively and imaginatively in constant pursuit of new ideas, new methods of working and new ways of looking at common problems. In the words of Nonaka (1991: 97):

> To create new knowledge means quite literally to re-create the company and everyone in it in a nonstop process of personal and organizational self-renewal. In the knowledge-creating company, inventing new knowledge is not a specialized activity – the province of the R&D department or marketing or strategic planning. It is a way of behaving, indeed a way of being, in which everyone is a knowledge worker – that is to say, an entrepreneur.

Most important is knowledge that can provide a competitive advantage for an organisation (i.e. knowledge that can allow it to outperform competitors in the same industry):

> New knowledge always begins with the individual. A brilliant researcher has an insight that leads to a new patent. A middle manager's intuitive sense of market trends becomes the catalyst for an important new product concept. A shop-floor worker draws on years of experience to come up with a new process innovation. In each case, an individual's personal knowledge is transformed into organizational knowledge valuable to the company as a whole. Making personal knowledge available to others is the central activity of the knowledge-creating company. It takes place continuously and at all levels of the organization.

(Nonaka, 1991: 97–8)

Nonaka is concerned with the way new knowledge surfaces and gets passed throughout the organisation. In other words how knowledge can be transformed from being tacit (hidden, or not visible) to explicit. We discussed tacit knowledge or skill earlier in Chapter 5 when we pointed out that skill is often embedded in employees. Skill can become embedded in a way of working without employees recognising its significance or importance. According to Nonaka, the importance of recognising tacit knowledge is the first stage in knowledge creation. Rather than leaving this embedded knowledge in its tacit form, it has to be transformed into explicit knowledge (something that is visible and able to be captured).

Nonaka suggests that the interrelationship between tacit and explicit knowledge can produce a sort of knowledge spiral (see Figure 8.1). An organisation should encourage individuals to pass on their tacit knowledge to others who then standardise this as explicit knowledge, in the form of procedures, manuals and so on. This experience in turn enriches the tacit knowledge of the individuals involved and the cycle repeats itself, so you have a virtuous spiral of knowledge creation.

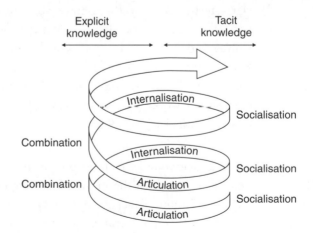

Figure 8.1   Spiral of knowledge creation

Source: Based on description by Nonaka (1991).

To illustrate this we can recall the simple example of the photocopier incident from Exercise 8.1. To describe this using Nonaka's spiral, Maria's method of reactivating the photocopy card is based on tacit knowledge, which has been picked up by her work colleagues (the socialisation stage). She then makes the knowledge explicit by communicating it to the photocopier technician in an email (what is called the articulation stage – or sometimes also referred to as externalisation). The technician then formalises it as an official solution that anyone who uses the machine can try out (the combination stage). Other users take the new knowledge on board and build it into their understanding of how to use the photocopy machine (the internalisation stage) – in other words it becomes part of their tacit knowledge. This example illustrates how the knowledge creation spiral transforms tacit knowledge into explicit forms.

While Nonaka's analysis is helpful and the term 'knowledge creation' is useful, it very much depends on the individual employee's willingness to share knowledge. This, Nonaka argues, requires an appropriate organisational culture where both knowledge creation and knowledge sharing are valued by all managers and employees. However, Nonaka's spiral does not show what might be called the dark side of knowledge management. This is the various ways in which an organisation's managers try to acquire the knowledge in their workforce, irrespective of whether the employees wish to share that knowledge, and often in the absence of a knowledge-based organisational culture. In other words, it does not fully address knowledge capture.

Knowledge capture

Knowledge capture describes processes through which managers try to acquire the ideas, judgement and creativity of those intimately involved in their work so that they can develop this as explicit knowledge. The assumption that lies behind this process is that all employees have some knowledge about their job that could be passed on to others, which might help improve the effectiveness and efficiency of the organisation. Even an employee doing a fairly low-skilled task will possess knowledge about how to accomplish it. For example, a trolley collector in a supermarket car park knows the best and safest way to push the trolleys, the easiest routes back to the store, most common places for trolleys to be abandoned and so on. This is not rocket science, but it is knowledge that would be useful for the store manager to capture, make explicit (by writing it down) and pass on to new trolley collectors. This might prove valuable because the turnover of trolley collectors is very high, so if this information can be formalised and passed on quickly there are reduced costs in inducting someone new into that job.

An example of how knowledge can be captured is provided in Extract 8.4. It shows an attempt to make explicit the knowledge in the heads of employees. After reading it, try Exercise 8.3 which raises some issues about the effects on employees of such attempts to capture knowledge.

Knowledge pooling in a law firm

Law firm McGrigor Donald, which has offices in London and Glasgow employing 52 partners and 150 fee-earning staff with support workers, has shown the courage of its convictions by removing one of its fee-earning partners from the front line and placing her in a backroom role with the 21st-century title of Director of Knowledge Management.... Christine McLintock, a former specialist in corporate banking law, says that much of the company's information is stored in the minds of the individuals it employs. That information, in most cases gathered by long experience, is a prime asset but not one that all in the company can draw on.

Her first priority is to release as much of the simpler information as possible and get it on an accessible computer system. In addition she is striving to get more complex ideas exchanged on a face-to-face training level.

The main basis of McLintock's strategy is to effect a change of culture by concentrating on the more junior employees, but backed by the cooperation of the senior ones. 'It's a two-pronged thing. We are trying to change attitudes and culture: to try to encourage knowledge-sharing and to increase the value of it in people's minds,' says McLintock.

[One] innovation has been the streamlining of the more simple aspects of the company's work, pooling knowledge to produce a comprehensive document management system and using the company intranet to access previous work that can help prepare documents for current clients.

This is partly the result of client pressure. With the de-mystification of the law in recent years, a process aided by access to information systems such as the Internet, the company recognises that clients' expectations have increased.

'Clients don't want to pay a lot of money for what they perceive as mundane tasks. We are trying to keep our edge on competitors,' says McLintock. Furthermore she predicts a time when clients will be able to access the company databases directly on some sort of pay-per-use basis. The knowledge pooling work is laying the foundations of this.

She says that by convincing staff to share information, they are freed to do the more complex work which will give a chance for more creativity.

Source: Sunday Times, 'Power from the knowledge pool', 31 January 1999.

What do you think?

Read Extract 8.4
1. If the knowledge-pooling exercise is successful, what are the advantages and disadvantages for:
   a. the junior employees?
   b. the senior employees?
2. If all law firms adopted this approach, how might it affect the professional status of the lawyers? To justify your answer, you may need to refer to Extract 8.3 that dealt with defining and analysing professions.

Why try to capture knowledge?

Organisations try to capture knowledge to compete more effectively. In an increasingly globalised, dynamic and intense competitive environment, companies constantly need to search for a competitive edge. Customers expect quality, variety, value for money and innovation of products and services. This means an organisation's managers must constantly look for improvement in products, processes and service delivery. As well as copying ideas from competitors (to survive) they must look to creativity from within (to gain a competitive advantage). Employees are a valuable source of such creativity. We are not concerned with those people whose job it is to be 'creative' in this way, such as those involved in research and development, members of a marketing department or senior management. Instead because of our focus on the realities of work, we are concerned with how tacit knowledge is made explicit.

Knowledge capture is of long-standing interest. Chapter 6 outlined Braverman's concern about deskilling through a form of knowledge capture. This centred on the way Tayloristic work organisation and new technology offered opportunities to separate the conception and the execution of work. Essentially this is separating the theoretical knowledge of the work (the thinking) from the practical action (the doing). Chapter 9 suggests that this capture of knowledge can never be fully complete because employees who undertake the work will always learn from experience. This allows them to find new ways of working that they might use to the benefit of themselves or their work colleagues. However, for decades, managers have tried systematically to acquire this knowledge. This approach is vividly expressed by Dohse, Jurgens and Malsch (1985: 128) as 'mining the gold in the worker's head'. In particular these techniques have been associated with an increased emphasis on managing quality, and especially important in achieving this is the concept of continuous improvement.

Capturing employee knowledge through continuous improvement

Continuous improvement (also known as *kaizen* in Japanese-owned companies) encourages employees and managers to look constantly for ways to change any system or process that will improve performance. The concept stems from Japanese production systems, in particular motor giants such as Toyota. Once an improvement has been suggested, it is evaluated and if found to be of benefit, it is standardised across the operation. Advocates such as Womack, Jones and Roos (1990) argue that this helps to humanise the workplace, and that employees experience the intrinsic reward of seeing their ideas put into practice and getting recognition from management – which in some cases might lead to more favourable appraisals or one-off bonuses.

In contrast, critics argue that such a system is exploitative because it captures the ideas of shopfloor (low-level) employees and adopts them across the organisation to realise performance improvement, but it does not reward those who came up with the idea in the first place. Researchers argue that continuous improvement can have a damaging effect on employees because it means an environment where individuals and teams are expected to put forward ideas that lead to an intensification of work (Garrahan and Stewart, 1992; Graham, 1995; Lewchuck and Robertson, 1996; Rinehart, Huxley and Robertson, 1997). For example, finding an innovative way of cutting down time in a production process might lead to improved efficiency or output, but for the employee it might also remove a period of rest from the production process. In many situations it might not be in the employee's own interest to find 'improvements'.

There are more concerns about which groups benefit most from any improvements. Chapter 4 shows that employees can be very inventive and creative in order to find ways of freeing up time or making informal breaks in the working day (other ways such creativity can be expressed are explored in Chapter 9). However, in those instances it is the employee who benefits directly from his/her creativity – and sometimes this benefit is shared with work colleagues. Under the *kaizen* system, research suggests that the main beneficiaries of creative improvements are managers. For example, Danford's investigation of Japanese firms in south Wales leads him to argue that:

> Under the cloak of a benign 'one team' ideology, workers become involved in securing for their employer higher levels of capital and labour utilisation, reductions in idle time, an intensification of their labour and a more sophisticated form of worker subordination. They do this by apparently offering to management knowledge of those facets of individual tacit skills and customary practice which provide workers with the means to exert some control over the labour process.
>
> (Danford, 1998: 58; Gallie, Zhou, Felstead and Green, 2012,
> offer a recent review of the relationship between teams,
> skill development and employee welfare)

That management gains more from continuous improvement than employees is hardly astonishing. As we show throughout the book, commentators frequently refer to the imbalance of the employment relationship – or more forcefully, the exploitative nature of labour process. An example of this is Braverman's work (Chapter 6). In other words, the possibility that managers will seek to expropriate the knowledge of employees, through techniques such as *kaizen*, is consistent with traditional Taylorist and Fordist management practice. Collins (1997: 47) comments:

> All the lessons of history tell us that when management becomes interested in appropriating the knowledge which workers have with regard to work skills and processes, the conditions under which we work tend to deteriorate.

While this is the preferred interpretation of commentators with a labour process orientation (e.g. Delbridge and Turnbull, 1992; Dohse, Jurgens and Malsch, 1985; Garrahan and Stewart, 1992) and those of a Foucauldian persuasion (e.g. Sewell and Wilkinson, 1992b), others have suggested a far more complex picture. In particular, some note that context plays an important part in influencing the employee experience of quality improvement initiatives (e.g. Edwards, Collinson and Rees, 1998). In some organisations employees are not resistant to quality initiatives and techniques such as continuous improvement. Not only do these initiatives increase variety in work, they also provide a feeling of involvement, even though the employees realise they are working harder than they used to. Moreover, research also reveals that even continuous improvement regimes are never totally complete – the employees will still find ways of getting around the system in order to gain individually or collectively (Webb and Palmer, 1998; see also the survival strategies discussed in Chapter 9).

To sum up

Knowledge creation and capture are important aspects of work that managers seek to control. Knowledge creation describes the importance of nurturing and developing new ideas, while knowledge capture is the process of transforming the tacit knowledge of individuals into explicit knowledge that can be shared throughout the organisation. In both senses, the management strategy is expropriation – the acquisition and control of knowledge from within the workforce.

However, some commentators suggest that knowledge workers are distinct because, in general, their knowledge cannot be expropriated. We look at this idea next.

Knowledge as something that cannot be expropriated

Potentially, workers whose knowledge cannot be made explicit are in a strong bargaining position. This is summed up by the well-known management commentator, Peter Drucker:

> Knowledge workers, unlike manual workers in manufacturing, own the means of production. They carry that knowledge in their heads and can therefore take it with them. At the same time, the knowledge needs of organizations are likely to change continually. As a result, in developed countries more and more of the critical work force – and the most highly paid part of it – will increasingly consist of people who cannot be 'managed' in the traditional sense of the word. In many cases, they will not even be employees of the organizations for which they work, but rather contractors, experts, consultants, part-timers, joint-venture partners, and so on. An increasing number of these people will identify themselves by their own knowledge rather than by the organization that pays them.

(Drucker, 1998: 18)

In this quote, Drucker is assuming that knowledge does not lend itself to expropriation and is mobile. We saw in the previous section that many expropriation techniques are available to managers. On the issue of employees 'carrying knowledge in their heads', we only need to think back to the discussion in Chapter 5 on skill to realise that such knowledge is mobile only if it is valued by other organisations – in other words, as long as it is not firm-specific. In practice, much tacit knowledge is likely to be task-specific (embedded knowledge) or firm-specific (encultured knowledge). This means that even though knowledge may not be something that can be expropriated, it is not necessarily mobile, so the range of workers to whom this quote applies is likely to be relatively narrow – perhaps Reed's 'entrepreneurial professionals' we describe earlier.

In the second part of the quote, Drucker raises an important issue about management control of the 'knowledge workers'. He suggests their relationship with the organisation is indirect. In other words, rather than being full-time employees, knowledge workers are more likely to be external specialists and experts on temporary and part-time contracts. Ironically this means that the value-creating, highly paid, knowledge workers will be part of an organisation's contingent workforce, in the same way that some low-skilled, low-paid workers in various support roles are (e.g. cleaners and security guards). This type of numerical flexibility delivers performance, but not necessarily organisational commitment or loyalty.

Exercise 8.4

What do you think?

Assuming Drucker is correct, would you want to be a knowledge worker? Explain your reasoning, taking into account the risks and opportunities.

Bringing 'knowledge workers' in on a contingent basis poses a dilemma. On the one hand it allows new and specialist knowledge to be brought into the organisation, but on the other hand it allows firm-specific knowledge to leak out of the organisation (Matusik and Hill, 1998). So if, as Drucker argues, knowledge is increasingly the source of a firm's competitive edge, the knowledge workers who are responsible for creating this edge may make any competitive advantage short-lived because they can transfer it to other organisations. If so, then it would not be the contingent (external) knowledge workers who are likely to provide the competitive edge, but the permanent (internal) employees of an organisation. This is a perspective consistent with the 'resource-based view of the firm' (Barney, 1991), the concept of 'the knowledge-creating company' (Nonaka and Takeuchi, 1995), as well as the 'dynamic capabilities' approach to the firm (Dixon et al, 2010). But it also suggests that more fundamental change might be occurring within society, in which knowledge workers become central because of their control of information. This change has been described by some in terms of the information society.

The information society

The concept of the information society has occupied sociologists for several decades; Webster (1995) offers an analysis of the main themes and key theorists, and May (2002) or Som, Hilty and Köhler, A. (2009) are examples of discussions of more recent developments. We focus on two commentators who remain central to the debate: Daniel Bell and Manuel Castells.

Daniel Bell and the information society

Earlier in the book (Chapter 6), you encountered some of Daniel Bell's ideas (1973, 1976) in relation to the changing nature of skill. Bell assumed society had undergone a transformation from industrial to post-industrial, and as a consequence there was a general trend of upskilling work. Bell's work is relevant here because he was one of the first to suggest that this change meant an increasingly important role for information.

Bell suggests pre-industrial society was based on agricultural work, industrial society was based on factory work and post-industrial society (PIS) is based on service work. Growth in the service sector that we discuss in several chapters is taken by observers such as Bell as evidence that we are now in the post-industrial stage.

Information is also important in Bell's analysis. He argues that information-based activities are the core to the PIS, and that therefore white-collar workers and professionals have become the dominant employee groups. So, he is emphasising the importance of knowledge workers (above), and this explains how he is able to argue a trend towards upskilling (see Chapter 6). He also argues that theoretical, scientific knowledge will drive innovation and policy making at organisational and governmental levels, giving rise to a new technical, professional elite – like the entrepreneurial professionals described by Reed (see above). Table 8.2 illustrates the main changes seen in Bell's account.

In his original work published in 1973, Bell was unable to predict the significance of the microprocessor hence underplays the role of information and communication technologies. He later addressed this (Bell, 1980), and notes the importance of computers, the pricing and the power of information (which gives it the same status as any commodity – it can be bought and sold), and the significance of advances in telecommunications (see also Lyon, 1986). Consequently, Bell adopts the term 'information society' to represent the social structure of the supposedly post-industrial era.

It would be fair to describe Bell's analysis as an optimistic one. He assumes work will increasingly become information-intensive (and therefore skilled) and as a result more satisfying. This can be questioned on at least two fronts:

1. It exaggerates the extent of information-based work – much service sector work is mundane, repetitive and requiring no information processing.
2. Even if service sector work is information-intensive, it is not necessarily satisfying or rewarding (many people have prejudices about working in a call centre, or in telesales, for example).

There are detailed criticisms of Bell's work (e.g. Webster, 1995; Kumar, 1995; Rose, 1991), but this should not detract from the importance of his observations.

Table 8.2   Major changes suggested by Bell's post-industrial thesis

Pre-industrial society	Industrial society	Post-industrial society
Agricultural work	Factory work	Service work
Domination of raw muscle power	Domination of machines	Domination of knowledge
Dependency on extractive activities	Dependency on fabrication activities	Dependency on information activities

His contribution is acknowledged by our second theorist, Manuel Castells, who takes a very different perspective.

Manuel Castells, the information age and the network society

In the opinion of Manuel Castells (1998, 2000), the information society is not simply a service society – so the growth of the service sector cannot be taken as significant in its own right. Instead, Castells introduces us to the idea that it is the network which is the social structure uniquely characteristic of the current 'information age'. He chooses his term 'network society' carefully so as to distinguish his analysis from those who describe an 'information society'. He agrees with Bell that knowledge and information have a critical role to play in the development of society. However, Castells argues that knowledge and information are not unique to contemporary society. Rather it is the particular form that they take (constituted around microelectronics-based information/communication technologies and genetic engineering) that distinguishes them as the basis of a network society (see Extract 8.5).

Extract 8.5

Castells – The network society

In the last two decades of the twentieth century a related set of social transformations has taken place around the world. While cultures, institutions, and historical trajectories introduce a great deal of diversity in the actual manifestations of each one of these transformations, it can be shown that, overall, the vast majority of societies are affected in a fundamental way by these transformations. All together they constitute a new type of social structure that I call the network society.

We have entered a new technological paradigm, centred around microelectronics-based, information/communication technologies, and genetic engineering. In this sense what is characteristic of the network society is not the critical role of knowledge and information, because knowledge and information were central in all societies. Thus, we should abandon the notion of 'Information Society', which I have myself used some times, as unspecific and misleading. What is new in our age is a new set of information technologies. I contend they represent a greater change in the history of technology than the technologies associated with the Industrial Revolution, or with the previous Information Revolution (printing). Furthermore, we are only at the beginning of this technological revolution, as the Internet becomes a universal tool of interactive communication, as we shift from computer-centred technologies to network-diffused technologies, as we make progress in nanotechnology (and thus in the diffusion capacity of information devices), and, even more importantly, as we unleash the biology revolution, making possible for the first time, the design and manipulation of living organisms, including human parts. What is also characteristic of this technological paradigm is the use of knowledge-based, information technologies to enhance and accelerate the production of knowledge and information, in a self-expanding, virtuous circle. Because information processing is at the source of life, and of social action, every domain of our eco-social system is thereby transformed.

Source: Castells (2000: 9–10).

To justify his argument, Castells (1998) undertakes an extensive analysis of social, economic and cultural change around the world – which he elaborates in three volumes covering 1488 pages of text. All we need do here, however, is note some of the key theoretical points he makes that are most relevant for our purposes.

One central concern is with the way economic activity can increasingly be characterised as informational, global and networked:

- *Informational*: the productivity and competitiveness of all economic units (firms, regions, countries) are determined by their capacity to generate knowledge and manage/process information. Elsewhere, this has been described as the informational mode of development, and it is important to recognise that Castells is not suggesting this replaces capitalism, but that information becomes an essential feature of capitalist development and accumulation.

Extract 8.6

Inequality in the information age

Long before Francis Bacon coined the phrase 'Knowledge is power', quick access to information endowed the recipient with a comparative advantage. The arrival of an information society turns it from an advantage into a necessity. Speed of access to information – whether share prices, new scientific research or news – is more vital than ever.

And in the information age you need not only knowledge of facts but also knowledge of the skills that produce the knowledge industry, because most new jobs require them.

Within these trends, subtler changes are taking place. For instance, circles of those with privileged knowledge are widening at the expense of those outside them. In pre-web days, for instance, only an elite circle of people had access to insider knowledge and analysis in the City. Now, thanks to the proliferation of financial web sites with instant (and usually free) access to share prices, charts, analysis and instant gossip, the insider circle has greatly increased.

But the gap between those in the loop and those outside it is widening, especially as knowledge itself becomes the source of competitive advantage. The digital revolution has opened up a new divide within existing workforces. Older workers (over 40s these days) find that, suddenly, youth is preferred over experience, and stored knowledge is devalued, counting for nothing because of the cultural revolution within the new companies. Suddenly, twenty-somethings are running their own companies instead of being corporate cogs in a bigger machine.

No one is more outside the loop than developing countries. When you read of the amazing electronic markets that are being constructed to harness the deflationary powers of the web and bring down the prices of raw materials and commodities, remember who is at the other end of the chain. Almost certainly it will be a developing country which was already suffering from the decline of its main source of income (commodities), even before the success of the internet.

The fruits of the information revolution are going disproportionately to those who are already in the loop. A new underclass is being created in developing countries – and within developed ones – from which it will be even more difficult to escape.

Source: V. Keegan, 'If knowledge is power', *Guardian*, 7 September 2000.

- *Global*: the core and strategic activities of capitalism (finance, trade, science and technology, services, production, communication and labour) can function anywhere and at any moment – they are not constrained by place or time:

    Globalization is highly selective. It proceeds by linking up all that, according to dominant interests, has value anywhere in the planet, and discarding anything (people, firms, territories, resources) which has no value or becomes devalued, in a variable geometry of creative destruction and destructive creation of value.

(Castells, 2000: 10)

- *Networked*: the central mode of organising is the network, in which firms or segments of firms (departments and functions) are temporarily connected for the purposes of achieving specific business projects, and then are allowed to disintegrate:

> Major corporations work in a strategy of changing alliances and partner-ships, specific to a given product, process, time, and space. Furthermore, these co-operations are based increasingly on sharing of information. These are information networks, which, in the limit, link up suppliers and customers through one firm, with this firm being essentially an inter-mediary of supply and demand, collecting a fee for its ability to process information.

(Ibid: 11)

In contrast to Bell's optimism, Castells stresses the potential polarising effects of the information age. In particular, he distinguishes between those people who become a strategic and integral part of the networks of capitalism and those who remain outside the network – although still needed by capital (see also Extract 8.6). The distinction hinges on the informational capacity of labour – hence he uses two terms for these primary and secondary groups:

1. *self-programmable labour*: those who are retrainable and adaptive;
2. *generic labour*: those who are exchangeable and disposable.

In some respects this echoes models of labour flexibility – in particular the distinction between the core workforce and the periphery. However, it differs in one important respect: Castells is not concerned with the relationship between employees and organisations, but with the relationship between labour and value chains. This is a key distinction because it means that the position of the employee in the workplace is of less importance than the location of labour in the network. And the essential factor that influences the centrality of that labour is its informational capacity: its ability to add value through information processing.

To sum up

There are two messages in Castells's analysis. The first is that the network society gives rise to connected, valued individuals who are more in control of their destinies. Yet this is accompanied by a second, bleak message that warns that the network society also discards people, leaving them devalued and dispossessed. While this has always happened under capitalism, Castells identifies this downside to the information age – a continuation of the discarding of human potential that has always occurred under capitalism. This contrasts with Bell's vision of the information society, which tends to ignore the possibility that the fate of individuals is not necessarily within their control.

Exercise 8.5

What do you think?

1. Consider the accounts of Bell and Castells. Which one are you more convinced by? Justify your answer.
2. Castells arrives at the (for some) controversial conclusion that 'the networking of relationships of production leads to the blurring of class relationships. This does not preclude exploitation, social differentiation and social resistance. But production-based, social classes, as constituted and enacted in the Industrial Age, cease to exist in the network society' (Castells, 2000: 18).
   a. What does Castells mean by this?
   b. What evidence is there to support or reject this conclusion?
3. Bell and Castells (in different ways) are arguing the case for there being 'a paradigm shift in society'.
   a. Explain what this statement means. Hint: look back to the end of Chapter 6 to refresh your memory about paradigms.
   b. What is the basis of the supposed paradigm shift?
   c. How would you go about arguing an alternative viewpoint: the case for continuity, rather than a paradigm shift?

Conclusion

Three key themes have surfaced in this chapter. The first is that knowledge work is increasingly important. Contemporary organisations rely on knowledge and information to sustain and to enhance their competitive position. This means that the knowledge present in all types of work is increasingly being identified by managers as a potential commodity. In other words, the knowledgeability of employees is a valuable resource to be exploited. One view is that this denotes very little change – it is merely a continuation of the long-standing exploitative relations between employers and employees within capitalism. An alternative view is that the nature of the expropriation has changed, with more emphasis being put on theoretical concepts and shared understanding, rather than on practice and experience. This is shown by the way that tacit knowledge is encoded into explicit knowledge (knowledge creation), and the way techniques such as continuous improvement and quality management establish organisation-wide norms and values (knowledge capture).

A second theme is that 'knowledge workers' are a distinct group who can be distinguished from other types of workers. The main commentators in this chapter – Frenkel et al, Reed, Drucker, Bell and Castells – share this view although they do not exactly agree on which occupations fall into the category. They do agree though that 'knowledge workers' are increasingly influential in contemporary workplaces. Knowledge is more important to organisations, but 'knowledge workers' also occupy an increasingly central and privileged position.

This links into the third theme: there has been a fundamental shift in the nature of contemporary society. The control and manipulation of information has become a central organising principle, captured in the phrases information society and information age. This shift has positive connotations for Bell and Drucker, while Castells is more cautious, pointing to the positive effects for some people and the negative impact on others.

9

Survival strategies at work

Chapter aim

To explore how employees survive at work by developing coping strategies.

Key concepts

▷ alienation

▷ forced labour

▷ voluntary labour

▷ false consciousness

▷ powerlessness

▷ meaninglessness

▷ isolation

▷ self-estrangement

▷ making out

▷ control versus consent

▷ workplace fiddles

▷ joking at work

▷ sabotage

▷ whistleblowing

▷ escaping

▷ consent and resistance

▷ interpreting workplace behaviour

Learning outcomes

After reading and understanding the material in this chapter you will be able to:

1. Describe four types of alienation identified by Marx.
2. Explain and assess Blauner's version of alienation.
3. Describe the concept of 'making out' and evaluate its role in creating consent within the workplace.
4. Classify various types of workplace fiddles and suggest why they occur within the workplace.
5. Explain four functions of joking at work.
6. Describe and interpret the importance of workplace sabotage.
7. Explain the concept of escaping within a workplace context.
8. Assess whether the five survival strategies should be interpreted as forms of consent or resistance.

Introduction

This chapter, perhaps more than any other in the book, illustrates the importance of viewing work as a rich and varied human activity. It is concerned with the ways in which employees get through their working day: how they survive the boredom, tedium, monotony, drudgery and powerlessness that are a feature of many jobs. In examining this issue, we need to cover a wide range of concepts and research evidence. At the same time, we focus on one central principle: that in order to 'survive' work, people need to be resourceful and creative in developing strategies that allow them to cope. They do this in two main ways (i) by asserting some control over their work, and (ii) by creating some meaning for their work.

In this chapter we try to examine informal activities at work – that is, those things that are normally hidden from the gaze of the outsider. It is in informal activities where the subjective experiences of workers create shared understandings and norms (ways of behaving, moral rules or codes of conduct). These guide behaviour and embed routines. At the same time, these informal activities take place in a world that is much regulated. The constraints imposed by power holders (especially managers) limit the actions of both individuals and workgroups. The result of the tension between these is a curious mixture of consent and resistance to work.

The chapter begins with a discussion of alienation. We then look at how alienating tendencies can be countered through various creative strategies by employees. After looking at the empirical research on informal work behaviour, five survival strategies are explored: 'making out', fiddling, joking, sabotaging and escaping. We conclude by exploring whether these strategies are forms of workplace consent or resistance, or both.

Alienation – an objective state or a subjective experience?

Alienation is one of the most difficult terms to define in the academic study of work. In fact, if we were trying to define and explain 'alienation' fully it would be possible to write a whole chapter on the concept. We think of it as describing a process where a harmony or a unity is somehow upset: perhaps where something natural is made to seem artificial or strange, or where things that should ordinarily always be considered together are somehow separated and pulled apart from one another (alienated from each other). Rather than spending a long time discussing alienation, we outline two different perspectives. The first treats alienation as an objective state, and builds on concepts from Karl Marx; the second introduces elements of subjectivity into the analysis of alienation, and is based on a study by Robert Blauner.

Alienation as an objective state

Marx argues that alienation is an intrinsic part of the capitalist labour process (see Chapter 6). Therefore it is an unavoidable, objective state in which all workers find themselves. Alienation occurs because workers give up the right to control their own labour when they sell their labour power (i.e. when they agree to be paid to work in a system where money is exchanged for their work – capitalism). This means that discretion over how and when work should be undertaken becomes a matter for employers (rather than being something the worker can control). So there is a subordination of employees to their employer (or to managers who act on behalf of the employer, and are sometimes called 'agents of capital'). Because of this subordination, work becomes a degrading and dehumanising activity:

> [Under capitalism] all the means for developing production are transformed into means of domination over and exploitation of the producer; that they mutilate the worker into a fragment of a human being, degrade him to become a mere appurtenance, make his work such a torment that its essential meaning is destroyed.
>
> (Marx, 1930: 713, quoted in Fox, 1974: 224)

As a result of this system, according to Marx, employees experience four types of alienation:

- from the self,
- from the product of their labour,
- from their 'species being' (explained below),
- from others.

Each of these is described in more detail below, and you can see how they are linked together by looking at the top half of the flowchart in Figure 9.1:

- *Alienation from the self.* Marx believed that work ought to be a source of satisfaction in its own right (intrinsic satisfaction). However, under capitalism work is simply the means for people to acquire money to satisfy their needs outside

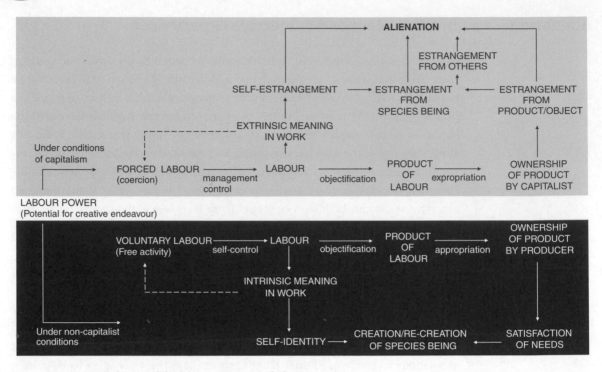

Figure 9.1   Marx's theory of the labour process and alienation

working hours. In other words, people only find extrinsic meaning in work (they enjoy what the work can get them, rather than the work in itself). As a consequence, employees experience 'self-alienation' because while they work under the instruction of their managers, they cannot be themselves. They are separated (alienated) from their true selves. To get a better idea of how vividly Marx expressed this, see Extract 9.1. Also see Cox (1998).

- *Alienation from the product of their labour.* The output (the product or object) of someone's labour is the physical expression of the effort that has been undertaken and the skills that have been used. Marx labels this process 'objectification'. Under capitalism, this output is not owned by the employee; it becomes the property of the capitalist (the process of expropriation). As a consequence, employees see this output as distant and separated from themselves. They become alienated from the product of their labour – in other words, the product becomes an alien object. Or, as Marx expresses it:

> The *alienation* of the worker in his product means not only that his labour becomes an object, an *external* existence, but that it exists *outside him*, independently, as something alien to him, and that it becomes a power on its own confronting him; it means that the life which he has conferred on the object confronts him as something hostile and alien.
>
> (Marx, 1969: 97, emphasis in original)

Alienation from one's labour is quite a difficult concept to grasp, but it may help to consider an example. If you think about the relationship that a painter or sculptor has with their work (a work of art), you can imagine that in a sense it will express their 'soul'. They will have put something of themselves into that work and will have an intimate relationship with the materials they have used. They will have seen it through all the stages from their first imagining of it through to the final work of art. If, however, they then sell that artwork on, it becomes the property of someone else. It is no longer theirs in a literal or contractual sense, but also, because it has been sold, their work is in a sense reduced from something spiritual or human to a commodity with a specific value expressed in terms of price. This price only makes sense in relation to other objects with prices and so their 'output' is no longer a unique artwork, but a good that can be traded, and that is worth more or less than quantities of goods like copper, wood or gold. In different ways, through sale, they become alienated from their work. Of course in many jobs in capitalism workers do not have control of the total labour process from imagining, to design, to execution. This means there is much greater potential for them to be alienated, or distanced/separated from their work (because they are, in a sense, just one part of a machine):

• *Alienation from the 'species being'.* Alienation from the self, and from the product, has wider implications on humanity as a species. Marx argues that it is through work that people express their creativity and produce the means of their own existence and in so doing realise what it is to be human. This free, creative endeavour is the very purpose of life, but under capitalism work becomes coercion: forced labour. This means that people become divorced or estranged from their very nature; they are left alienated from their 'species being'.

• *Alienation from others.* Because they are alienated from their true, essential nature, people are also alienated from each other. Marx's argument here stems from a belief that human beings are distinct from animals because of their self-awareness – this is effectively an argument Marx developed from the ancient Greek philosopher Aristotle (Morrell, 2012). Unlike an animal, a person can understand the world through his/her own actions, speech and behaviour, and the actions, speech and behaviour of others. However, the three previous forms of alienation combine to create conditions in which the unique qualities of humankind are diminished. Under forced labour, people are owned and controlled. They experience this directly and also recognise this state of alienation in other people. Consequently, they are alienated from their own humanity and also alienated from others.

Figure 9.1 summarises this discussion by mapping the relationships between the various concepts in Marx's theory of the labour process and alienation. The top half of the flowchart shows how each of the concepts is linked and leads to alienation at work.

Self-estrangement under the capitalist labour process

[The worker] does not affirm himself but denies himself, does not feel content but unhappy, does not develop freely his physical and mental energy but mortifies his body and ruins his mind. The worker therefore only feels himself outside his work, and in his work feels outside himself. He is at home when he is not working, and when he is working he is not at home. His labour is therefore not voluntary, but coerced; it is forced labour. It is therefore not the satisfaction of a need; it is merely a means to satisfy needs external to it. Its alien character emerges clearly in the fact that as soon as no physical or other compulsion exists, labour is shunned like the plague. External labour, labour in which man alienates himself, is a labour of self-sacrifice, of mortification. Lastly, the external character of labour for the worker appears in the fact that it is not his own, but someone else's that it does not belong to him, that in it he belongs, not to himself, but to another. Just as in religion the spontaneous activity of the human imagination, of the human brain and the human heart, operates independently of the individual – that is, operates on him as an alien, divine or diabolical activity – in the same way the worker's activity is not his spontaneous activity. It belongs to another; it is the loss of his self.

Source: Marx (1969: 99–100)

Non-alienating conditions

The bottom half of the flowchart in Figure 9.1 suggests how under non-capitalist conditions the problem of alienation might be avoided. If each of the components is compared with its equivalents in the top half of the diagram, it is clear that while there are similarities, the difference is that the person undertaking the work remains in control of both his/her labour and the product of his/her labour. The consequence of self-control over one's labour is that a person is more likely to derive intrinsic meaning from the work being undertaken, rather than only seeing it as a means of getting money. In turn, this might mean that people's self-esteem and feelings of worth are enhanced – therefore it contributes to their self-identity. Similarly, control over the product of their labour (appropriation, or ownership rather than expropriation, or loss of ownership) means that the outcome of people's effort remains in their possession. They can choose how to use this to satisfy their needs. Overall, there is no alienation because the four features of estrangement do not occur.

The concept of false consciousness

For Marx, alienation was an objective state under which all employees within capitalist relations suffered. In a sense, this makes it impossible to study alienation empirically, because it does not matter whether people feel or say they are alienated. Marx asserts that capitalism leads inevitably to alienation. In other words, subjectivity (people's interpretations) is not part of the analysis. Marxists are likely to argue that people who claim to be satisfied and fulfilled at work are merely expressing a 'false consciousness': they fail to appreciate the objective reality of their position as people who are subordinated and exploited under capitalism.

What do you think?

The bottom half of the flowchart in Figure 9.1 is idealistic. Indeed, you might argue that it is unrealistic given that capitalism is the dominant form of work organisation. However, there might be workers around the world who, although often operating within conditions of capitalism, experience some of the elements illustrated by the bottom half of the flow chart.

1. To explore this idea, take each of the occupations below and assess its work using the concepts provided in the flow chart:
   - a farmer in a small community in a developing country;
   - a freelance photographer;
   - a full-time housewife/househusband;
   - an Internet entrepreneur;
   - a prostitute;
   - a shopkeeper (self-employed);
   - employees in a workers' cooperative (where every employee owns an equal share of their organisation and has an equal say in all decisions as to how it is run);
   - a drug dealer;
   - an artist (painter, sculptor etc.).

2. You have probably found evidence of non-alienation in some of these occupations. How might a Marxist use the concept of 'false consciousness' to suggest your analysis is inadequate?

Alienation as a subjective experience

An alternative way of looking at alienation is to start from two assumptions that differ from those suggested by Marx:

Assumption 1: alienation is not inevitable under capitalism.

Assumption 2: work has different meanings for different people.

Both of these assumptions suggest that it is inadequate to view alienation as an objective condition (the same for all employees under capitalism). Instead, alienation should be considered a subjective experience (differing from situation to situation, and person to person). One of the most notable attempts to explore alienation in this way is by Blauner (1964) (Oldham and Hackman, 2010 offer a more recent, relevant review). Blauner begins from the proposition that 'alienation is a general syndrome made up of a number of different *objective conditions and subjective feelings-states* which emerge from certain relationships between workers and the sociotechnical settings of employment' (Blauner, 1964: 15, emphasis added). He argues that alienation should be divided into four dimensions, each of which can be investigated for different workers to enable a profile of alienation to be drawn up.

Blauner's four dimensions are summarised in Table 9.1. To illustrate how these dimensions can be used to assess work, we have selected two jobs to compare, nursery assistants and car-park attendants. To carry out such an analysis in detail would mean assessing the views of people who actually do these jobs, but for illustrative purposes we will have to rely on some general assumptions. In terms

Table 9.1 Blauner's four dimensions of alienation

Conditions of alienation	Definition	Possible indicators/ measures of alienation	Corresponding conditions of freedom non-alienation
1 Powerlessness	Employees are controlled and manipulated by others or by an impersonal system (such as technology) and cannot change or modify this domination	▪ Extent of control over the conditions of employment ▪ Extent of control over the immediate work process: – pace of work – method of work	Autonomy (empowerment)
2 Meaninglessness	Employees lack understanding of the whole work process and lack a sense of how their own work contributes to the whole	▪ Length of work cycle ▪ Range and variety of tasks ▪ Completeness of task	Purposefulness
3 Isolation	Employees experience no sense of belonging in the work situation and are unable or unwilling to identify with the organisation and its goals	▪ Type and extent of social interaction – formal – informal	Belonging
4 Self-estrangement	Employees gain no sense of identity or personal fulfilment from work, and this detachment means that work is not considered a worthwhile activity in its own right	▪ Instrumental attitudes ▪ 'Clock-watching' ▪ Expressions of boredom	Self-expression

Source: Summarised from Blauner (1964: 15–35).

of the dimension of powerlessness, both nursery assistants and car-park attendants are likely to have little control over their conditions of employment, but they might differ in terms of their experiences of control over the work process.

The car-park attendant's work (assuming they are based in a kiosk at the entrance/exit of a car park) will be paced by the arrival and departure of customers, and they are likely to be doing the same repetitive tasks. The nursery assistant's pace of work will fluctuate with the demands of the children, their age, busy periods (meal times) or quiet times (afternoon sleeps), staffing levels, the requirements to keep paperwork. They will have some influence over this, for example, by distracting children onto different tasks, or occupying a group at once so a co-worker can take a break. They will also have some control over the approach they take to the work (albeit within prescribed guidelines) – exercising considerable creativity and freedom in how they relate to the children. In terms of the second dimension of meaninglessness, the short-cycle, repetitive tasks of car-park attendants may give a sense of achievement, although the lack of range and variety ultimately suggest the work would be dull. Nursery assistants have a greater range and variety of tasks, with longer work cycles and far less predictability in the work. Potentially this makes the work not only more meaningful but also vulnerable to more frustrating experiences. Caring for children needs considerable reserves of patience.

In terms of isolation, both jobs involve contact with others, but whereas the interactions between car-park attendants and their customers are brief and formal, nursery assistants will experience extended periods of highly informal interaction with children, as well as interaction with other members of the nursery staff (both formal and informal) and parents (mainly formal). Finally, in terms of self-alienation, nursery assistants are likely to experience a greater sense of fulfilment than car-park attendants. Of course there will be boring aspects to the job, and sometimes the time will drag, but the variety and unpredictability might compensate for this. Car-park attendants are likely to find activities to distract themselves from the work – reading the newspaper, listening to the radio – because it is not usually considered to be fulfilling in its own right (though if one were also responsible for security, which could be fulfilling an important and meaningful function).

Overall, it is likely a nursery assistant will feel alienation less than the car-park attendant, although this assessment depends on the subjective experiences of particular individuals in these roles. It would be possible to find some nursery assistants who express attitudes that reflect a sense of powerlessness, meaninglessness, isolation and self-estrangement, and car-park attendants whose work gives them a sense of autonomy, purposefulness, belonging and self-expression. The subjective aspect to Blauner's theory distinguishes it from that of Marx.

Even though Blauner acknowledges the subjectivity of alienation, like Marx, he also considers that there are objective conditions which tend to produce alienation. Rather than generalise about the capitalist system as a whole, Blauner differentiates *between* capitalist enterprises (organisations) according to their technology, and generalises from this:

> There is … no simple answer to the question: Is the factory worker of today an alienated worker? Inherent in the techniques of modern manufacturing and the principles of bureaucratic industrial organization are general alienating tendencies. But in some cases the distinctive technology, division of labor, economic structure, and social organization – in other words, the factors that differentiate individual industries – intensify these general tendencies, producing a high degree of alienation; in other cases they minimize and counteract them, resulting instead in control, meaning, and integration.
>
> (Blauner, 1964: 166–7)

Ultimately, this leads Blauner to a position of 'technological determinism': he suggests that greater automation will free workers from the drudgery of assembly lines and machine minding and will result in decreasing alienation for employees (ibid: 182–3). This is an optimistic projection that suggests the problem of alienation will be resolved within capitalism – a position which, as we have seen in Chapter 6, was vehemently challenged by Braverman (1974) and subsequent labour process theorists.

Criticisms of Blauner's work

Blauner has been criticised for trivialising Marx's notion of alienation 'by conceptualising it in subjective terms' (Watson, 1987: 107). However, while numerous criticisms can be levelled at Blauner's work (e.g. in relation to the data upon which he based his conclusions; see Eldridge, 1971), the problem of being 'overly subjective' is not one of them. Certainly Blauner is accepting the importance of subjectivity because the implication of his thesis is that different employees will have different alienation profiles. But Blauner seems far more interested in using this to generalise about occupational groups, and in particular to assess whether certain types of production technologies led to greater alienation than others. In fact, as his analysis progresses, subjectivity disappears from the discussion. If his thesis were only examining subjective experience, then his focus would be on individual employees, rather than occupational groups. In addition, he would probably be more concerned with exploring whether employees doing similar jobs experience alienation differently, and the extent to which this leads to individual, rather than collective profiles of alienation.

Yet in spite of these criticisms, Blauner's biggest contribution is to reclaim the concept of alienation from Marxist theorists. By reinterpreting the concept and breaking it down into the four separate dimensions, he provides components of alienation which vary in intensity and are also measurable (or more accurately, comparable). This turns alienation from an absolute concept (with fixed, objective measures), to a relative concept (where measures take account of context). It makes it possible to see how objective conditions of alienation might not always result in subjective feelings of alienation.

So, for instance, considering the case of the nursery worker versus the car-park attendant, both of them might lack of control over the labour process, and both might be managed, and work for pay (all of which are objective conditions of alienation). However, it might be that they do not similarly experience subjective feelings of alienation if there are compensating factors in their work (if the nursery assistant gets more intrinsic pleasure from her – and it is likely to be her because this occupation is heavily gendered – work, for example). Allowing subjectivity into the discussion of alienation helps to interpret the complexities and dynamics of employee behaviour and orientations to work. It also means that as observers of the realities of work, we need to recognise there can be multiple meanings and interpretations of behaviour, even where there may be common structural constraints. In the extreme, this attitude is summed up in a famous phrase by one of the greatest English writers, John Milton. In the epic poem *Paradise Lost* he has Satan say (after being banished from Heaven), 'The mind is its own place, and in itself can make a heaven of hell, a hell of heaven.'

Exercise 9.2

What do you think?

1. Use Blauner's four dimensions of alienation described in Table 9.1 to analyse each of the jobs listed below:
- supermarket checkout operator,
- barrister specialising in criminal law,
- assembly line worker in a factory wiring together road safety signs;
- secondary school teacher.

(If you prefer, you could use examples of jobs you have done yourself or that you are familiar with.)

2. What are the difficulties or drawbacks in applying Blauner's four dimensions to particular jobs?

So far we have considered two approaches to alienation. The first, based on Marx, views alienation as an objective condition of all work under capitalism. The second, illustrated through the work of Blauner, suggests that alienation varies between occupations, and is experienced subjectively by employees. Although these approaches differ, they both recognise that employees can experience alienation at work. In the rest of this chapter we explore how (if at all) employees try to survive alienation at work.

Surviving alienation

Our main claim here is that employees develop coping strategies which combat alienation through processes and actions that are informal. In other words, employees try to take some control over their own destinies by inventing methods of coping that are outside the formal influence of management. These methods also offer opportunities for employees to challenge the dominant values and beliefs of managers – in other words to counter managerialist logic. Employees do this by devising their own interpretations of tasks, rules and social interactions at work. Sometimes these counter-strategies are developed collectively and carried out by groups of employees; in other instances, they represent individual attempts to survive. As we shall see, these employee-owned initiatives are dynamic rather than fixed, creative rather than mundane, and pluralist (they acknowledge different sources of authority and power) rather than unitarist (only acknowledging one source of – managerial – authority).

The five main survival strategies of employees are listed below, and in the sections that follow, each is explored in more detail:

- making out,
- fiddling,
- joking,
- sabotage,
- escaping.

Making out

The term 'making out' is usually associated with the research undertaken by Michael Burawoy (1979). Like many of the empirical studies discussed in this chapter, Burawoy's method of data collection was based on getting close to the subject of interest – that is, employees at work. It involved participating in the work process in order to experience directly the workplace dynamics and develop an understanding of the meaning and significance of social interaction at work.

With the permission of management, Burawoy began work as an employee in the machine shop of an engine plant which was a division of a multinational company in the United States. From this position as what would technically be called 'participant–observer', Burawoy witnessed an elaborate system of informal behaviour by employees. This served to regulate the work process and ensure that targets were met, but at the same time provided the opportunity for the workers to reassert some control over their working day. He argues that these unofficial shopfloor activities can be seen as a series of games employees play. These are games concerned with beating the system, finding the angles, working out dodges or discovering loopholes – in other words, 'making out':

> The game of making out provides a framework for evaluating the productive activities and the social relations that arise out of the organization of work. We can look upon making out, therefore, as comprising a sequence of stages – of encounters between machine operators and the social or non-social objects that regulate the conditions of work. The rules of the game are experienced as a set of externally imposed relationships. The art of making out is to manipulate those relationships with the purpose of advancing as quickly as possible from one stage to the next.
>
> (Burawoy, 1979: 51)

Burawoy builds on the pioneering work of Roy (1952, 1953, 1955) to explore how making out is essentially concerned with ways that employees get around the formal rules and regulations laid down by management. At its simplest, making out is to do with how employees secure higher earnings by creatively manipulating incentive systems (mainly piece-rate payment schemes – where someone is paid for each item they produce). However, Burawoy's research led him to argue that economic gain is not the sole motivator for making out. Instead, he suggests (1979: 85) a range of interlinking motives:

- to reduce fatigue;
- to pass the time;
- to relieve boredom;
- to enjoy social and psychological rewards of making out on a tough job;
- to avoid social stigma and frustration of failing to 'make out' on an easy job.

Burawoy describes informal rules and practices that he and his co-workers followed as they joined the game of making out. It is important to recognise that although they were adapting to the alienating tendencies in the work, and manipulating management's rules for their own ends, they were not fundamentally *challenging* the rules or undermining management's prerogative (right) to set the rules. In fact, by playing the game of making out they were actually *consenting* to the formal rules and structures imposed by management. They were trying to work with, or perhaps around these rules, rather than trying to replace or overturn them. Burawoy (1979: 81–2) describes this important point by asking the following:

> The issue is: which is logically and empirically prior, playing the game or the legitimacy of the rules? Here I am not arguing that playing the games rests on a broad consensus; on the contrary, consent rests upon – is constructed

through – playing the game. The game does not reflect an underlying harmony of interests; on the contrary, it is responsible for and generates that harmony.... The game becomes an end in itself, overshadowing, masking, and even inverting the conditions out of which it emerges.

Extract 9.2

Making out among refuse collectors

McIntosh and Broderick (1996) evaluate the impact of compulsory competitive tendering (CCT) on the work of a local authority cleansing department. In addition to identifying changes in the organisation of work, they note the impact on the ability of the refuse collectors to 'make out' through a system of 'totting':

> Totting involved sifting through bags and bins in search of 'valuables' or 'sellables' which were then either kept or sold – many refuse collectors regularly took part in car boot sales. The pooling of lead and copper and returned bottles was also an important source of extra income.... Management were often willing to turn a blind eye and saw much of these activities as rewards for doing such a low-status job.... Such activities have not gone completely but the opportunity to tear open bags (a number of households were often identified as being sources of 'tot') has been drastically circumscribed due to the pressures of the workload.
>
> (McIntosh and Broderick, 1996: 424)

In addition, some of the social aspects of the work that made the job bearable have been affected by work intensification, as these quotes from drivers illustrate:

> We had regular people who gave us tea and biscuits, butchers would give us sausages and a bit of meat for doing little jobs for them. Most of that is gone now, we don't have time to stop and do odd jobs. (p. 424)

> We used to have time to chat to the old folks and stop a couple of times a day for tea round people's houses. We used to have customer care. Now you are lucky if you see anyone, let alone talk to them. (p. 425)

Manufacturing consent

Writers such as Crozier (1964), Mayo (1933), and Roethlisberger and Dickson (1966) have argued that games undermine management objectives because they express a counter-control by the shopfloor. But Burawoy concludes that far from representing any kind of threat to capitalism, games 'manufacture consent'. They support a kind of agreement or concession to existing social relations of production. Because they do this, games actually help to secure the creation of surplus value (i.e. they enable exploitation of labour under capitalism). By challenging the periphery (margins) of the rules, the core of those rules – to produce for the employer – goes uncontested. By this argument, Burawoy shifts the focus of analysis away from control towards consent. He argues that the labour process under advanced capitalism should not just be seen in terms of management's control over employees. It should also be seen as a way in which employees are persuaded to consent to their own subordination. By consenting to be subordinate, they are effectively cooperating with management's overall objectives (Burawoy, 1985: 126). In other words, while Braverman (1974) emphasises management *control* (see Chapter 6), Burawoy describes employee *consent*.

Control vs consent

The tensions between control and consent have been brought into sharp focus by Hyman (1987, especially pp. 39–43). In a summary of Hyman, Table 9.2 illustrates contradictions in the labour process. We can see the source of these contradictions if we begin by acknowledging that management faces two competing pressures. One is a need to control and direct employees to ensure that production and performance targets are met. The second pressure is the need to enlist the skill and cooperation of employees in meeting those targets. So the first is about control, the second about consent. These competing pressures lead to four contradictions:

- *Contradiction 1.* Management has to limit and at the same time make maximum use of employee discretion. Managers need to limit discretion because employees might use it against management's interests (perhaps by making out). Managers also need to make best use of it because their employees can use it to generate surplus value (profit). Putting this in Marxist terms, Cressey and MacInnes (1980: 14) explain this paradox:

  > For even though capital owns (and therefore has the right to 'control'), both means of production and the worker, in practice capital must surrender the means of production to the 'control' of the workers for their actual use in the production process. All adequate analysis of the contradictory relationship of labour to capital in the workplace depends on grasping this point.

- *Contradiction 2.* Management has to impose systems of close supervision to ensure that objectives are complied with, and at the same time provide the space and freedom for employees to work creatively. Friedman (1977b) argues that managers face a choice between two broad supervision strategies of trying to establish either 'direct control' (which means the simplification of work and close supervision) or 'responsible autonomy' (wider discretion over how work is

Table 9.2   Fundamental contradictions in managing the labour process

	Control		Consent
Management aim:	To secure employee compliance	vs	To enlist employee cooperation
Contradiction 1:	Limiting discretion	vs	Harnessing discretion
Contradiction 2:	Close supervision (direct control) (low trust)	vs	Employee autonomy (responsible autonomy) (high trust)
Contradiction 3:	Disposable labour (numerical flexibility)	vs	Dependable labour (commitment)
Contradiction 4:	Cohesive workforce	vs	Collective solidarity

Source: Based on Hyman (1987: 39–43).

completed, with less supervision). These strategies do not resolve the contradiction; they just express it in a different way (you could not pursue both strategies at once). Direct control might be the best way to guarantee compliance, but it comes at the cost of commitment; responsible autonomy may lead to greater commitment, but it does not guarantee compliance with management wishes. Some managers might vary the emphasis on control or consent depending on the group of employees: responsible autonomy for highly skilled, core employees in scarce supply but direct control over low-skilled, peripheral workers who are easily replaced. But even responsible autonomy might need to be moderated with some direct control given that, 'there are few (if any) workers whose voluntary commitment requires no external reinforcement' (Hyman, 1987: 42).

More cynically, it could be argued that responsible autonomy is a ploy by managers to disguise their dependency on the workforce. By emphasising autonomy, empowerment, discretion and an absence of close supervision, they can engage in more subtle attempts to exploit labour:

- *Contradiction 3.* Management requires labour to be disposable and, at the same time, dependable. If labour power is a commodity, employees can be hired or fired according to the changing requirements of the business (reflecting seasonal, weekly, or even daily fluctuations in demand). Managers can therefore seek to maximise the disposability of labour. However, a so-called hire-and-fire policy (where workers are treated just like any asset that can be bought, sold and replaced) would undermine the commitment of employees to the organisation. It would also make those whose skills were scarce or valuable very aware of their market value (and possibly in a position to bargain for far higher wages). On the other hand, to have policies that emphasised nothing but dependability (such as guaranteed employment security, or a rule of only promoting from within the organisation rather than hiring from outside) would reduce the ability of managers to change the labour force to match fluctuations in demand. This trade-off between commitment and flexibility has become one of the central problems for contemporary human resource management (for fuller discussion see Noon, 1992: 23–4).

- *Contradiction 4.* Managers need to create a cooperative, cohesive workforce, but – precisely because they are cohesive and cooperate with one another – a workforce may develop a collective solidarity that could be used against management's interests. Similarly, policies aimed at individualising the workforce and controlling the individual worker (e.g. pay based on individual performance, individual appraisal and promotion) could undermine the basis of cooperation between employees that management needs to benefit from collective working.

Burawoy suggests, 'coercion must be supplemented by the organisation of consent' (1979: 27). This helps to think about the above contradictions embedded in the labour process under capitalism. Essentially, contradictions reflect fundamental differences of interest between employers and employees. It is in the employers' interest to secure as much surplus value as possible from the labour of their employees. It is in the employees' interests to limit exploitation and to get maximum payment for their effort. Because of this, employers and managers try to disguise the appropriation of surplus value, and it is because the game of making out aids this process (of obscuring exploitation) that managers are generally content to go along with it. It is only when making out becomes counterproductive that managers seek to suppress it:

> The participation [of workers] in games has the effect of concealing relations of production while co-ordinating the interests of workers and management…. It is through their common interest in the preservation of work games that the interests of workers and shop management are co-ordinated. The workers are interested in the relative satisfactions games can offer while management, from supervisors to departmental superintendents, is concerned with securing co-operation and surplus…. The *day-to-day adaptations of workers create their own ideological effects that become focal elements in the operation of capitalist control.*
>
> (Burawoy, 1985: 38–9, emphasis in original)

Criticisms of Burawoy

Burawoy's analysis is persuasive. It helps to explain why work that is alienating can be endured rather than challenged. However, his work has faced two important criticisms:

- *Burawoy's analysis ignores gender.* The workplace he studied was entirely male, so he had no opportunity to explore the importance and effect of gender on the social organisation of production. Gender might have an important effect on several of the features that Burawoy characterised as being critical to the manufacture of consent: the shopfloor culture encouraging competition, game playing as an end in itself, the structure of work, the social hierarchy and workgroup dynamics (for a fuller discussion, see Davies, 1990). A similar point could be made about other sociological variables (race, ethnicity, age, educational level).
- *Burawoy overstates the role of consent.* Burawoy's focus on consent may mean he misses a genuinely subversive element in some of the making out he describes. Although it is incorporated into the system, the employees could still be said to be challenging the system rather than going along with it. After all, they are constantly subverting control of the labour process by continually inventing new ways of making out. As Clawson and Fantasia (1983: 676) comment:

> Over and over again, Burawoy takes some feature of the workplace which had generally been identified as evidence of workers' progressive potential, and argues that it actually serves to reinforce the system. He does not seem to understand that a phenomenon can do both things at the same time, that something can be itself and its opposite. In other words, Burawoy's Marxist argument lacks a dialectical analysis.

To sum up

Burawoy argues that employees creatively find time and space to pursue their own objectives within the broad rules set by managers. This process of making out provides them with both extrinsic and intrinsic rewards and so ultimately amounts to consent to the regime established by management. Managers tolerate making out because such activities help obscure the ultimately exploitative nature of the labour process under capitalism. However, critics suggest Burawoy is too quick to interpret behaviour as consent and that he disregards the extent to which making out is a form of resistance, by informal actions that subvert management's intentions.

This last point needs emphasis because it has important implications for the rest of the chapter. What seems to have happened is that in concentrating on the importance of consent on the shopfloor, Burawoy has lost sight of the role of resistance. Making out is not just about consent: it may also represent a form of resistance. In other words, in considering making out as a survival strategy, we should be aware of its dual impact. This is important to keep in mind as we look at the next survival strategy: workplace fiddling.

Fiddling

In one way or another, everyone is on the fiddle. It might take a direct form, such as stealing supplies from the workplace (paper, pens, printer ink, building materials, produce) or artificially inflating expense claims. Fiddling can also be indirect, such as doing repairs to personal items using the company's equipment and materials or making personal phone calls. Perhaps the most common fiddle now is 'cyberloafing': using the Internet for personal reasons, such as for emails, or sites and services like Facebook, Twitter, YouTube, eBay, or even engaging in cybersex (Lim, 2002). Employees also fiddle time from the organisation (Chapter 3). Even in highly regulated environments with tight monitoring there are opportunities to fiddle the system. For example, Townsend (2005) describes how employees in an Australian call centre learned how to manipulate the call monitoring system to provide extra rest breaks. A call centre operator explains:

> We can take a call, and if they [customers] need to pay a bill then we transfer them into the computer interactive system 'cardgate'. What we can do is hit transfer but we don't release the button. So then we are on mute while the customer does the interactive computer processes. And that really gives you three or four minutes. Sometimes I go and have a cup of tea or maybe go to the toilet, every now and then I go out for a cigarette. The best part is that the cardgate system does not hang up when the caller is finished if we remain on transfer. I can sit there for 20 minutes if I want to but I don't push my luck, 10 minutes for a cigarette is plenty. And a call of that length isn't unusual so it won't stick out in your stats. You have to think these things through, the last thing I want to do is get caught by being greedy.
>
> (Townsend, 2005: 56)

The list of fiddles at work is as extensive and varied as human ingenuity, and for many it represents an important additional (covert) element in their total rewards, and an important way of altering the balance of the effort–reward bargain.

Researchers have identified fiddles that are endemic (widespread) in particular occupations (see, for example, Ditton, 1977), but Mars (1982) perhaps went furthest in analysing the practice and significance of workplace fiddles. It is useful to summarise his work briefly here, because it reveals not only the relationship between forms of fiddling and the occupational structure, but also illustrates how for many, the motive for fiddling goes far beyond any anticipated financial benefit. Indeed the frequently small financial gain would not seem to justify the risks involved unless other factors influence the decision to fiddle.

Mars (1982) developed a typology of fiddling and linked this to distinctive characteristics of different occupations. He uses two dimensions to categorise jobs: (i) whether jobs are subject to extensive rules and close supervision; (ii) whether jobs involve group activity and are characterised by strong workgroup controls. The presence or absence of these dimensions lead to four different occupational categories, each of which provides different opportunities for fiddling. He labels people who choose to exploit the opportunity to fiddle as 'hawks', 'donkeys', 'wolves' and 'vultures' – each label describes characteristics of how they fiddle, as explained below:

- *Hawks:* People who work as individuals rather than as part of a group and also are not subject to close supervision; examples include journalists, entrepreneurial managers, waiters and taxi drivers. Someone owning and operating a small business would also fit into this category.
- *Donkeys:* People in jobs that are highly constrained by rules and who work in relative isolation, such as shop assistants and many assembly line workers.
- *Wolves:* People who 'work – and steal – in packs' (Mars, 1982: 2), with groups operating according to clearly defined rules, controls and hierarchies that govern their fiddling activity. Examples here might include airport baggage handlers and dock gangs.
- *Vultures:* People who need the support of a group to fiddle, but who act alone. Mars includes in this category occupations such as travelling salespeople and hotel worker, where group support may be needed to collude with a fiddle. For example, delivery drivers could share knowledge about which places they can deliver 'short' to (where they can steal some of a load), where checks are unlikely to be carried out, and where to sell the extra goods afterwards.

In drawing such distinctions, Mars usefully points to the different opportunities and constraints for fiddling that characterise different jobs. It reveals that fiddling of one form or another is possible in (and endemic to) almost all occupations. Thus, for a large part of the workforce, the rewards from their job comprise not only the visible element (their wage or salary, paid holidays, pension and so on) but also an invisible element, reflecting fiddled goods and/or fiddled time. Even in jobs which at first sight appear very highly constrained by close supervision and/or detailed rules governing behaviour, fiddling still takes place. Moreover, it occurs even when penalties are severe and where the possible amounts to be fiddled are small in comparison to the gravity of the sanctions applicable if the person is caught.

This suggests that financial benefit from fiddling is only one motive and, for many people, not the most important one. For some, fiddling provides the only interest in an otherwise monotonous workday – a survival strategy. The risk element of being caught may add a sense of excitement. For others, fiddling may be an expression of frustration or resentment, 'a way of hitting out at the boss, the company, the system or the state' (Mars, 1982: 23). This seems to be an important factor in the case of the hotel cleaners in Extract 9.3.

Extract 9.3

Theft in the hotel

The following is an account by an employee who worked as a cleaner in a hotel in Finland.

We have two trolleys at each floor which we have to share with one another. We can fill them with, for example, soaps to last us for the day, but after only a few hours we have to fill it up again. Nobody talks about this or lets on that it is strange, but we are all well aware of what is going on. Apart from hygiene supplies and other small things like tea bags, shower caps, sewing and tooth brush kits, which seem to disappear at a rapid pace, thefts of a bit bigger type occur. It happens that hotel guests forget private things in the rooms and we cleaners are supposed to hand them in at the office, but that does not always happen. Also products from the minibar, not only chocolate and crisps but also spirits, tend to disappear quickly. When it comes to alcohol I only dare to steal two mini-bottles of vodka during my whole time at the hotel – and I go to another floor, pretending to fetch more tea bags, in order to do so.

Kim [another cleaner] steals more than I do. On one occasion in her apartment she shows me two crammed drawers with the results of her raids, which include working clothes and toilet paper. Apart from useful goods she steals things like 'Do not disturb' signs and 'Pillow menu' signs. The main point, she says, is not to get hold of the things as such but the *action* in itself. She takes something home every day and thinks it is rewarding that she can get away with it. The thefts become a positive trait of our working day as we get something else than the boring work tasks to think about. Stealing has become a game and through it we have found some meaning in work. Not once do Kim or I feel that we are doing something morally wrong – rather our bitterness at our working conditions justifies more thefts. Considering all the stress and hard work we think we actually deserve some free soap.

Source: Lundberg and Karlsson (2011: 146)

Why managers tolerate fiddling

Although the types, motives and outcomes of worker-initiated fiddles vary, the picture is even more complex when management's approach to fiddling is taken into account. It is sometimes assumed workers engage in fiddling in spite of the best endeavours by management to prevent it, but managers frequently 'turn a blind eye' to fiddling activity, provided that it does not rise above a certain level, or does not involve fiddling a third party (e.g. the customer). A survey of 813 UK

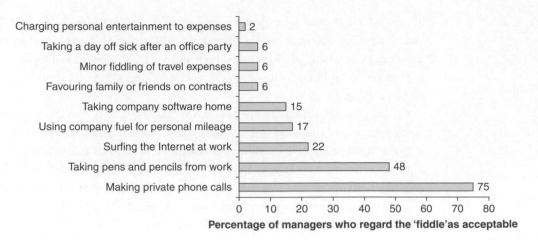

Figure 9.2   Acceptability of workplace fiddles

managers by *Management Today* (2000) revealed that 50 per cent were aware of fiddling in their workplace, but only four in ten would be prepared to take action to stop it occurring. This toleration varies according to the type of fiddle involved, as Figure 9.2 illustrates.

There are several possible motives for managers to tolerate fiddling:

- It might reflect awareness of the near-impossibility of stamping out fiddling entirely. If one form of fiddling is suppressed, another is likely to develop to take its place.
- It might help management to maintain a cooperative workforce – if all fiddling was heavily policed this might increase dissatisfaction and reduce the degree of consent to other management objectives.
- It might enable management to pay lower wages. For those working in hotels and restaurants, fiddles (not declaring taxable income from tips, or diluting drink, for instance) help subsidise low wages. In Ditton's (1977: 17) study of bread salespeople (who are generally low-paid and who work long hours), supervisors agreed to overcharge customers to subsidise low wages.
- It might be because managers themselves are also involved in fiddling, either for their own monetary gain or to protect their position. Mars (1982: 68), details the case of a supermarket where, to balance stocks against stock records, checkout operators were asked by managers to fiddle customers. More recently, a study by D'Abate (2005) based on interviews with 30 middle managers across a variety of industries in North America revealed that a large amount of company time and resource was spent on conducting their personal affairs in business hours. The list includes making personal appointments, organising personal time, paying bills, participating in betting syndicates, reading, daydreaming and even watching television. The most widely reported behaviours were personal phone calls, having conversations about non-work issues and surfing the Internet.

To sum up

Although a covert activity, fiddling of one form or another appears to be an integral element of most occupations. In terms of a 'survival strategy', fiddling normally involves breaking the rules, whereas making out involves working within the rules. But the distinction is not always clear cut. However, for most people involved in some form of fiddling at work, the monetary value of the fiddling is likely to be small – so much so that the efforts required to prevent it are often not seen to be worthwhile. Fiddling can yield additional income but also represents a source of social and psychological gain to individuals responding to aspects of their job, those in authority over them, their co-workers and/or their customers.

Exercise 9.3

What do you think?

Read Extract 9.3 about 'theft in the hotel', then answer the following questions.

1. Using Mars's typology, into which category would you put the cleaners?
2. Put yourself in the position of the cleaners. Might you do the same thing? Explain your reasoning.
3. Should the other cleaner 'blow the whistle' on Kim? Why or why not?

Joking

This section explores the significance of humour at work. Recent studies of humour can be found in Korczynski (2011) and Westwood and Rhodes (2007), but it is important to begin the analysis by acknowledging the pioneering work of the anthropologist Radcliffe-Brown, who identified the significance of the 'joking relationship' between people:

> What is meant by the term 'joking relationship' is a relationship between two persons in which one is by custom permitted, and in some instances, required to tease or to make fun of the other, who, in turn, is required to take no offence…. The joking relationship is a peculiar combination of friendliness and antagonism. The behaviour is such that in any other social context it would express and arouse hostility, but it is not meant seriously and must not be taken seriously. There is a pretence of hostility and real friendliness. To put it another way, the relation is one of permitted disrespect.
>
> (Radcliffe-Brown, 1952: 90–1)

Subsequent studies of joking and humour have argued that these activities are a natural part of work organisations and also perform four important functions:

* Joking maintains social order and releases tension.
* Joking challenges authority.
* Joking forges group identities.
* Joking alleviates monotony and makes work tolerable.

Each of these is explained in the following sections.

Joking maintains social order and releases tension

A primary function of joking is the prevention or reduction of antagonism; typically it develops between people who are required to be in close contact for long periods of time, yet who have some divergence of interests. Not surprisingly, therefore, the concept can be applied to work settings where teasing and banter are part of the daily routine of organisational life. For example, Bradney used the concept of the joking relationship to explain how sales staff in a large department store regulated their interpersonal relations. She argued that joking helped to mitigate the intrinsic antagonisms caused by the formal work roles and structures:

> There is clearly a divergence of interests among sales assistants … as a result of their formal relationship. Each wants to increase her own sales – to earn both a better living and the approval of her employer – and is in competition with the others to do this. There is also every likelihood of hostility and conflict between them when they interrupt and hinder each other just at a time when this interferes most with selling.
>
> (Bradney, 1957: 183)

The 'joking relationship' provides the employees with an informal structure through which differences of interest and status are negotiated through playful insults and teasing ('permitted disrespect') rather than with open hostility. Bradney concludes:

> By means of a tradition of joking behaviour between its members, which is quite unknown to the management, this store is able to avoid considerable tension and disagreement that would be likely to occur as a result of the difficulties inherent in its formal structure. In so doing it gives the employees a source of positive enjoyment in carrying out their routine activities and incidentally, by means of this, renews their energy to cope even more adequately with their routine problems.
>
> (Ibid: 186–7)

To take another example, Spradley and Mann (1975) used participant observation to explore the working lives of cocktail waitresses, and showed how humour reinforces the gender division of labour. Waitresses worked closely with the male bartenders, and strong bonds developed between them. Yet there was a clear status differential, with the waitresses in a subordinate position. Waitresses quickly learned that the needs of the bartenders came first because they had the power to make the waitresses' work comfortable or difficult. The joking relationship between the barmen and the waitresses was one way that conflict caused by this power imbalance was mediated. The bartenders would use humour to assert their status, cover their own mistakes and to reprimand a waitress. On the other hand, the waitresses employed humour to assert themselves, particularly as a response to feelings of unfairness and power-lessness. Spradley and Mann conclude:

> Anger and frustration are dissipated and feelings of inequality felt by the waitresses are deflected…. It creates a buffer between the waitress and bartender in potential conflict situations and provides a means for handling inadequate role performances that occur in full public view…. But the joking relationship also maintains the status inequality of female waitresses and reinforces masculine values. By providing a kind of 'safety valve' for the frustrations created for women in this small society, joking behaviour insures that the role of female waitresses remains unchanged.
>
> (Spradley and Mann, 1975: 100)

To take a more extreme example, Sanders reports how humour helped prostitutes to cope with the negative emotions that surface in their work; in particular it provided a means of dealing with the disgust they might feel towards a client. In the words of one of the prostitutes:

> There are some men who are so smelly and not nice to be round. So we have to laugh to get through the whole thing. I could tell you so many situations where we have laughed and laughed our way through a service, not with the clients but at the clients. When you are laughing it doesn't feel like such a daunting job when we have a giggle about the clients.
>
> (Sanders, 2004: 283)

This suggests that humour plays an important role in enabling an employee to cope with the inevitable frustrations, tensions and even degradations of working life. As a safety valve, it allows an individual to let off steam, without challenging the power structures and inequalities that have led to the frustration in the first instance (Wilson, 1979). Spradley and Mann's (1975) waitresses enjoyed moments where they asserted themselves through humour, but the gendered power structure remained intact. Similarly Boland and Hoffman (1983), in a study of a small machine shop, noted how the machinists would often put cartoon-like drawings into the steel drums containing the finished pieces for the quality inspectors at the customer's plant. The jokes poked fun at the competence of the inspectors and management, compared with the skill and judgement of employees in the machine shop.

Joking challenges authority

Joking at work is a way of challenging authority structures. In other words, jokes are an expression of the informal triumphing over the formal (Douglas, 1975). This raises the question whether humour may be construed as a subversive activity at work. Korczynski (2011) in his study of a blinds factory (which he describes as a Taylorised factory) suggests the importance of context in humour is under-researched and that workplace humour there was primarily 'resistive'.

The routinisation that was a central feature of the factory provided a context within which routine itself became satirised or made absurd through humour – for instance, someone pretending to be a cuckoo clock by 'cuckooing' every 15 minutes.

Humour also offers a way in which routine is overturned, for instance workers joke with each other by rearranging each other's tools when they are away on a break. Humour is how employees resist the labour process and the product of the work itself – someone is given as one of her presents on the day of leaving a blind made in the factory. She then cuts a hole in the middle of the blind and has photos taken with her face in the hole. Korczynski describes satire, and mockery (of supervisors and a workplace participation meeting), and a profound sense of humour, and a 'sense of resistance', but it is hard to see direct evidence in his study of how humour fundamentally challenges the labour process. One explanation for his insistence that humour is 'resistive' may come in the role that it has in building collective identity. A supervisor at the factory describes how the workers generally have a smile on their face, which Korczynski (2011: 1436) describes as:

> a smile that was embedded in an autonomous shopfloor culture in which the meaning of humour was primarily resistive.

Indeed his co-workers/research subjects had a strong collective ethos, and as well as agreeing to informal production limits had walked out collectively in protest at conditions being too cold in the factory the year before his research.

Other empirical studies of humour reveal few examples where humour is used in a subversive manner. One example can be found in Westwood's study of a clothing factory. As participant–observer, she cites a 'prank' that resulted in the end-of-day buzzer being set off ten minutes early and the women fleeing the building with glee, fully aware that it was not the official leaving time:

> The next day management instituted an investigation into what was termed 'the incident'. The shopfloor was absolutely delighted that their speedy exodus had caused such obvious pain to management. Everyone who was asked about it shook their heads wisely, at once 'agreeing' with management's view that this was a very serious matter, while keeping quiet about the identity of the buzzer-pusher.
>
> (Westwood, 1984: 91)

The use of humour to undermine authority by ridiculing managers or organisational processes is considered by some as clear evidence of humour being a strategy of resistance (Ackroyd and Thompson, 1999; Collinson, 2002). It certainly has such potential, but incidents of clear resistance tend to be less strategic than opportunistic. There are some exceptions: for example, Rodrigues and Collinson's (1995) study of a Brazilian newspaper and Taylor and Bain's (2003) studies of Scottish call centres show how humour can be used to coordinate an oppositional culture among employees and provide a forceful weapon in collective organisation. To illustrate the collective acts of resistance, consider the quotes below from two employees interviewed by Taylor and Bain (2003: 1502–3):

> When you were nominally following the rules, you would do so in such a way as to be subversive. The dress code changed and we were told, 'You have to wear a shirt and tie.' So we got word round, 'Tomorrow, wear shirts and ties that make us look as unprofessional as possible.' I wore a tie about four or five inches wide, illustrating the history and future of the motor car in glorious Technicolor, along with a purple-checked shirt. Everybody dressed like this and there was nothing managers could do.
>
> One night a manager ... was showing new starts round, and he passed the mission statement, which was prominently displayed on a wall. Suddenly, he remembered he had ten people in tow and he hadn't pointed it out to them. So he led them back and started reading it when, spontaneously, about ten of us stood up and saluted him, singing 'The Star Spangled Banner'. And, of course, these new starts got the message that there was no respect for either management or company.

Taylor and Bain (2003: 1506) conclude that in this organisation:

> The [trade union] activists were instrumental in their use of humour, clear in the knowledge that it helped make them and the union popular and served to weaken managerial authority and legitimacy. Subversive satire was allied to a wider collective purpose.

Although there are instances such as these, where humour acts as a rallying point for collective organisation against management authority, what is striking from broader case evidence is the extent to which humour is highly regulated and ritualised by the workgroups. Far from subverting authority, humour tends merely to issue mild challenges (this is true of the extracts in Korczynski, 2011). These seem more about preserving the status quo than overturning it. Indeed, it could be argued that jokes provide an outlet for the expression of frustration and discontent which might otherwise build up unchecked, and eventually become channelled into activities that have more serious consequences for the organisation (see the discussion on sabotage below).

Joking forges group identities

Humour plays a part in establishing a group identity. Humour is one of a number of cultural devices to establish group norms and perpetuate the group's values. Humour reinforces the existing social structure and performs a boundary function (Linstead, 1985b: 744): protecting the group from outsiders and separating insiders (perhaps co-workers) from outsiders (perhaps supervisors). For example, in a vivid description of humour among engineering workers in a vehicle plant, Collinson (1988) reveals how supervisors and white-collar staff became the butt of jokes for the engineers: jokes which explicitly put them down as being stupid, manipulative and effeminate, and in that way different from the hard-working, proudly masculine 'fellas' on the shopfloor.

Newcomers and deviants were also controlled by humour. For example, apprentices were subjected to initiations which range from embarrassing, like being sent for a 'long stand' (a joke which the person they were sent to for a long stand was in on – and where they were left waiting for a long time – i.e. a long stand), to humiliating: 'Pancake Tuesday is always celebrated by "greasing the bollocks" of the apprentices with emulsion then "locking them in the shithouse, bollock naked"' (Collinson, 1988: 189). These practical jokes 'not only instructed new members on how to act and react, but also constituted a test of the willingness of initiates to be part of the male group and to accept its rules' (ibid: 188). It was all about bringing people into line; for example, Collinson was told in reference to a lad who entered the company with 'diplomas galore':

> They had a French letter [a condom] on his back by ten o'clock. They had him singing and dancing in the loo with the pretext of practising for a panto-mime ... we soon brought him round to our way of thinking.
>
> (Ibid: 189)

In some instances this can have a pernicious (damaging, corrosive) effect, with employees feeling excluded or victimised. In particular it can become a form of harassment, creating severe difficulties for women in male-dominated environments (see, for example, Jenkins, Martinez Lucio and Noon, 2002) or ethnic minorities (see Chapter 10 and Extract 9.4).

In Collinson's study, humour was also used by the engineers to control colleagues who were considered not to be working hard enough under the collective bonus scheme. Humour was a way of bringing co-workers into line in order to maximise earnings. The effect of all this was eloquently summed up by the engineer who commented that:

> The men are the gaffers now. They watch each other like hawks. The nature of the blokes is such that they turn on each other.... You're more worried about what the men think than the gaffers.... I'm just as bad if there's someone not working.
>
> (Collinson, 1988: 197)

Joking alleviates monotony and makes work tolerable

Conformity and compliance at work can also be encouraged by humour in another way: by obscuring the monotony of the work process. This is vividly demonstrated by Roy's (1960) participant observation as a machine operator in a factory (examined in more detail in Chapter 4). When Roy first joined the factory he became acutely aware of how tedious the work was, but as he became embroiled in the jokes and pranks on the shopfloor, he found himself distracted from the boredom. Many of the jokes became predictable daily events – 'banana time', 'peach time', 'window time' and so on – and these rituals suppressed some of the drudgery of the 12-hour working day by punctuating it with moments of humour. Indeed, it was only after a serious argument had broken out, causing the social cohesion of the workgroup to break up and all interaction to be 'strictly business', that Roy was reminded of the tedium of the work process and began to experience fatigue. In other words, humour provided a means of coping with the boredom and the hard work.

Humour allows people to distance themselves from the unpleasant and boring aspects of work (Cohen and Taylor, 1976: 34), as exemplified by the engineering worker from Collinson's study (1988: 185) who commented that, 'Some days it feels like a fortnight…. I had to stop myself getting bored so I increased the number of pranks at work.' Or the women in Westwood's study who used jokes, often related to sex, to spice up the drudgery of the day. A favourite joke of some of the women in the factory she studied was to:

> Draw lewd pictures of penises and naked men and women, give them captions and send them around the units hoping that they would embarrass some of the other women and provoke a response…. Written jokes were passed around and sniggered at through the working day. It all added excitement and 'a bit of a laff' to the factory days. Sex, of course, was a crucial ingredient and always managed to spice up the end of the day.

(Westwood, 1984: 91)

From this point of view, the practical joking and the repartee revealed by the studies cited above are merely examples of employees taking a break from work by indulging in a pleasurable activity. To think about this and the other functions of joking, try Exercise 9.4.

Extract 9.4

Where joking is very much beyond a joke

A broker at a London firm sued his former employers for racial discrimination and unfair dismissal. He claimed that he was subjected to anti-Semitic abuse, including the names 'Yiddo' and 'Jew boy'. He also objected to the way a Jewish skull-cap was placed on top of the office television whenever a Jewish person was giving the financial bulletins. On one occasion he was told to put on a Nazi uniform (hired by the company) as punishment for turning up late. He refused to put on the costume, not least because his grandmother had died in Auschwitz.

The company claims that the culture of the office meant that 'banter' was a way of relieving stress in such a high-pressured job. They said that it was applied to everyone, and that the broker himself had engaged in it, calling his manager a 'big-nosed tosser', his colleague a 'fat Jock' and non-Jewish people in the office 'Yoks' (Yiddish slang for gentiles). Furthermore they said there was a 'bad taste costume' ritual whereby brokers who arrived late had to dress up in humiliating outfits hired by the company: for example, a Welsh broker had to wear a Bo Peep costume.

Source: Based on reports in *The Guardian*, 'Skull cap used by "race jokers" ', 1 February 2001, and *The Times*, 'Brokers "used racial abuse to relieve stress" ', 1 February 2001.

Exercise 9.4

What do you think?

Using your knowledge of the four functions of joking, interpret the events described in Extract 9.4.

Now choose an example of the use of humour from your own work experience (past or present). Which of the four functions most adequately explains the motivations of those involved?

To sum up

It is difficult to generalise about the significance of humour in work organisations because of the importance of context, and the impact of subjectivity. The meaning of 'a joke' is negotiated by the participants of a setting, but its significance may vary from individual to individual. The same humorous incident can be perceived in various ways, and may have different meanings for different participants. However, irrespective of the specific interpretation an individual puts on a humorous event, the empirical evidence suggests a common theme: joking at work plays an important regulatory function by providing a means of expression that assists group cohesion and deflects attention from the dehumanising aspects of work. On occasion it is used to challenge authority, but rarely does it undermine the existing power hierarchy. In this way joking is a vital factor in obscuring the social relations of production, and suppressing the alienating tendencies of work.

Sabotage

'Sabotage' usually makes one think of people engaged in wilful acts of destruction, as retribution for some felt injustice, such as the Luddites in the 1820s (who destroyed new machinery that was progressively replacing their jobs). More contemporary examples might be the software engineer who writes a malicious line of code into a programme, or the disgruntled sacked, military official who leaks classified documents to the media. However, this popular image of sabotage fails to account for the complexity and subtlety of motivation and method (e.g. Dubois, 1979; Edwards and Scullion, 1982; Taylor and Walton, 1971).

In particular, Linstead (1985a) identifies two key problems in the analysis of sabotage. First, there is the difficulty of trying to interpret the action, especially whether it represents an intentional, malicious attempt to destroy or disrupt the work process or the product. Second, there is the problem of whether or not to designate the action as rational behaviour. Should all acts of sabotage be explained in terms of a logical cause or thought process, even if we have no explanation from the saboteur? Both these problems highlight the need for contextual information before trying to understand the meanings and motives of sabotage behaviour.

These problems make it difficult to make too many general statements about sabotage. For instance, there is a need to take account of the subjective experience of the alleged saboteur. Even so, it is useful to classify acts of sabotage into two broad categories (loosely based on Taylor and Walton, 1971):

- A temporary expression of frustration with the work process, rules, managers, co-workers or indeed any aspect of the organisation. In such circumstances sabotage is likely to be the wilful, malicious act of a frustrated individual. Their anger is placated and tension dissipated by, for example, kicking the photocopier, or being intentionally rude to a customer. Although undesirable in the eyes of management, the consequences of such sabotage are transient and generally offer no serious threat to the functioning of the organisation. Such incidents may even be seen as tolerable and necessary expressions of dissent, which act as a kind of safety valve.

- The second more dramatic category is where sabotage is an attempt to assert control over the work process. This presents a direct challenge to authority, and has far more serious implications for management. In some cases, such sabotage may be expressed as individual action (e.g. stopping a machine by, literally, 'putting a spanner in the works'); in other cases, a challenge can only be brought about through collective action (e.g. customs officers at an airport 'working to rule' by checking every passenger, thus causing enormous disruptions).

As with the case of humour, acts of sabotage can have different meanings for different people involved, so in practice there is far more complexity than these simple categories might suggest.

Another problem is that many acts of sabotage do not easily fit into either of these categories but are located in a grey area between the two. Consider the following example cited by two of the first academics to consider the significance of sabotage at work, Taylor and Walton (1971: 228):

> When 600 shipyard workers employed on the new Cunarder Q.E.2 finished on schedule they were promptly sacked by John Brown's, the contractors involved. With what looked like a conciliatory gesture they were invited to a party in the ship's luxurious new bar, which was specially opened for the occasion. The men became drunk, damaged several cabins, and smashed the Royal Suite to pieces.

One interpretation might be that this was a rational act of reasserting control by a group of workers reflecting their alienation from the product of their labour. Another interpretation is that the frustration of the sacking, linked to the indignity of being invited to 'celebrate' this, unleashed a temporary destructive, irrational urge. Then again, perhaps the men were just so drunk that they would have gone on the rampage irrespective of where they were drinking. All three interpretations might have some truth. Indeed, each might be applicable to different workers: the behaviour may have been the same, but the reasons behind it may have differed. If questioned, the workers might have attributed different meanings and significance to their behaviour – provided, of course, they could remember the incident once they had sobered up.

Virtuous sabotage? The case of whistleblowing

Some instances of what (from a managerial perspective) could be considered sabotage are carried out by someone who feels they have a duty to make public wrongdoing in their organisation. This is usually called 'whistle-blowing'. The bad publicity that follows is clearly disadvantageous for the organisation, but are whistleblowers really saboteurs? If they believe they are performing a public service, they have virtuous rather than malicious motives. For example:

> Joy Cawthorne resigned as an instructor at an outdoor activity centre in protest over its safety standards. Subsequently, she gave evidence against her former employer after four children died in a canoeing accident in Lyme Bay. The managing director was convicted of manslaughter and sentenced to three years' imprisonment.
>
> (Lewis, 1997: 6)

An alternative interpretation is that a whistleblower is an aggrieved or disgruntled employee seeking revenge. This means they are acting with malicious intent, so whistleblowing constitutes a form of sabotage. While this might be the case in some instances, it is also clear that whistleblowing is costly for an individual's career. Whistleblowers often face harassment or retaliation (Micelli and Near, 1992), are sidelined in career terms, lose their job or find it difficult to get alternative employment (Alford, 2001). Glazer and Glazer (1989) found that over two-thirds of the 64 whistleblowers they interviewed had become unemployed as a result. So according to Perry (1998: 240–1), 'whistle blowing might well be classified as a form of occupational suicide – or perhaps accidental career death'.

Unintentional sabotage?

Analysing sabotage becomes even more confusing because actions may have destructive or damaging results even if there are no ill intentions behind the actions. Indeed, there are numerous instances when attempts to adjust the work process to achieve productivity targets, and thus 'make out', carry the risk of potential negative long-term consequences. For example, Taylor and Walton (1971: 232) describe the practice in aircraft assembly of using an instrument called a 'tap' which allows wing bolts to be more easily inserted but potentially weakens the overall structure. Using the tap is strictly prohibited by factory rules, yet its use continues covertly because without it production cannot function effectively. So should the workers who use 'taps' be described as saboteurs? Or are they merely irresponsible workers?

In the following example there is little evidence of malicious intent behind the worker's actions; he is easing the work, making out as best he can within the rules set by management:

> The engines passed the [worker] rapidly on a conveyor. His instructions were to test all the nuts and if he found one or two loose to tighten them, but if three or more were loose he was not expected to have time to tighten that many. In such cases he marked the engine with chalk and it was later set aside from the conveyor and given special attention. The superintendent found that the number of engines so set aside reached an annoying total in the day's work. He made several unsuccessful attempts

to locate the trouble. Finally, by carefully watching all the men on the conveyor line, he discovered that the [worker] was unscrewing a *third* nut whenever he found two already loose. It was easier to loosen *one* nut than to tighten two.

(Mathewson, 1931: 238, emphasis in original, cited in Hodson, 1991: 281)

In the next two examples, the employee's behaviour in each case reflects a frustration with the conditions of work imposed by management. The first incident takes place in a brewery, and the second in a wire manufacturing company. Read them and then try Exercise 9.5:

One of the young male workers [in the brewery] took a bottle in his hand and made a throwing motion with it. Later, on break, I asked him what he was throwing at. He replied that he was not throwing at anything in particular…. He said that he didn't want to do any damage, that he was just bored and that it would be fun to lob bottles out like grenades and watch them crash and blow up…. He added, 'It's so dull out there I'd just like to make something happen, to have something interesting to do or see.'

(Molstad, 1986: 231)

[Bobby] was originally called to make a small adjustment on the depth of the machine's applicator. It was a simple adjustment accomplished by loosening a single screw. In a normally equipped shop it would have been a five-minute job, but Bobby could not find the proper screwdriver. We searched all the toolboxes, but the screwdrivers were either too large or had been ground at the ends. Bobby asked Carroll [the boss] if he could buy a screwdriver at the hardware store down the street. Carroll refused and told him to grind one of the ones we had. Bobby tried, but ended up stripping the screwhead so badly that nothing could get it out. Then Carroll came to the floor and in typical fashion chewed Bobby out in front of everybody. After Carroll left, Bobby brought the applicator over to the bench and used a ten-pound copper mallet to smash a machine part that cost hundreds of dollars to replace.

(Juravich, 1985: 135–6)

Exercise 9.5

What do you think?

Using your knowledge of sabotage, interpret the incidents in the brewery and the wire manufacturer.

There are occasions where the consequence of an act of sabotage is separated in time and space from the saboteur. For example, some hackers design and spread computer viruses in what are intentionally malicious acts of sabotage. At the same time, they may have no specific organisational target for these viruses. Their motives seem to be the challenge of creating something that destroys the work of others, or is self-advertising, or is ingenious enough to survive detection, but the consequences of their actions may never be known to the perpetrators. They remain unaware of how extensively and to whom these viruses spread.

To sum up

With sabotage, as in the case of joking, it is difficult to interpret the behaviour of individuals and understand the meaning they give that behaviour. Not all acts that have destructive consequences are planned, or rational, or done with malicious intent. Stupidity, thoughtlessness, arrogance and irrationality may better explain sabotage behaviour in some circumstances. However, while making out, joking, and – to some extent – fiddling are widely tolerated by management, sabotage is not. It is viewed as a negative activity, perhaps because it presents a direct challenge to authority, and carries a more easily quantifiable cost: physical or reputational damage, and loss of production, customers and so on. Nevertheless, just as with the other forms of informal behaviour, sabotage can also be interpreted as a way in which employees (individually and collectively) respond to alienating tendencies at work.

Escaping

The term 'escape' can be applied in two ways that are relevant here:

- *Physical escape:* by quitting the job (temporarily – through absence, or permanently – by leaving the organisation). This is relatively easy to identify as it can be represented in job turnover figures and levels of absence. High labour turnover may indicate dissatisfaction with the job, although sources of this dissatisfaction may be diverse and difficult to pinpoint: pay, conditions, job content, promotion opportunities, superordinates, co-workers, recognition, equity or some combination of these. As noted in Chapter 4, voluntary absence (taking a day off) is used by a significant proportion of people as a temporary respite from work pressures and frustrations.

- *Mental escape:* by withdrawing into one's own thoughts. This is more complex to analyse because it is harder to detect and can take a variety of forms. One way of coping with boredom, for example, is to retreat from conscious activity into daydreams. The work is performed in an automaton-like fashion, relying on internalised routines (as discussed in Chapter 5) which free the person to concentrate on thoughts outside of work. In this sense, the person can 'escape' into a world of their own. Indeed, this may be the only way of coping for some service sector workers (such as flight attendants) who have to put on a cheerful face for hours on end (discussed further in Chapter 7).

Physical and mental withdrawals are not mutually exclusive. For example, Deery, Iverson and Walsh's (2002) analysis of call centre work reveals how the combined effects of monotonous, low-discretion work, close monitoring by management and intense interpersonal interaction (sometimes with abusive customers) damages well-being. The coping strategy of emotionally exhausted employees combined absence (physical withdrawal) and a less helpful, depersonalised approach to customers (mental withdrawal).

More generally, employees might combine the two forms of escape by mentally distancing themselves from their work tasks and daydreaming about how to escape from their particular job: perhaps by gaining qualifications at night school, securing a small-business grant or playing the lottery. For instance, in her analysis of the monotonous work on the shopfloor of a manufacturer of healthcare products, where the layout of machinery inhibited conversation and radios were banned by management, Pass (2005: 14) comments:

> One male worker explained that the only way to get through the day was to become 'robotic', allowing your mind to escape whilst your body continued maintaining the speed of the line. After 5 years of working in the Blow-Moulding department, checking bottles all day, he said he frequently spent his time mentally winning the lottery.

Employees might realise that dreaming of their own escape was pointless, and instead tolerate work in the hope it will secure a better future for daughters and sons. As Westwood (1984: 235) observes from her study of hosiery workers:

> [The] women wanted their daughters to have the opportunity to pursue education and training as a means to a life which would be more autonomous. There was a strong sense from the women that they did not want their daughters to be undervalued or wasted in the way they had been.

A similar attitude is evident among male workers, particularly for their sons. To take an example from Collinson's (1992: 185) study of engineering workers:

> [Alf, 30 years old] feels imprisoned on the shopfloor with little possibility of promotion.... Investing in the self-sacrificing role of parental breadwinner, Alf holds on to a belief in 'personal success' and dignity.... He insists, 'I've not done too bad, I keep me family. But it's too late for me. I've been telling the lad I want him to do better than I've done. He'll have every opportunity I didn't have. I'm probably more ambitious for the kids than I am for me. If I could give them my ambition, I'd consider myself a success then. Some, if they got a lad in here [the factory] would think it were a success, me, I'd consider it a failure.'

These views represent a type of deferred gratification or success by proxy (by someone else), and unite two parts of escaping: the mental escape that comes about through dreaming, but where the dreams are about the physical escape of one's children (from similar conditions of boredom and oppression).

The instances of withdrawal in these examples reflect a coping strategy based on resigned acceptance of the status quo. While it is likely that such employees would not display very high commitment to the organisation or enthusiasm for their work, it does not mean they would perform their tasks badly (i.e. inefficiently or carelessly). Indeed it may be a means of coping with the repetitive and boring work that characterises low-skilled, routine jobs (see Chapter 6).

A related form of mental escape is cynicism, where employees distance themselves from the values of the organisation, and express this disbelief, but continue to remain in the organisation and do the job effectively. Fleming and Spicer (2003) argue that this 'disidentification' with the values of their employer allows workers to distance themselves from the organisation and thereby prevents them from directly challenging the norms and values. In other words the employees engage physically with the tasks and conform with the rules, but are not engaged with the values and beliefs represented in the organisational culture – so they are working at a 'cynical distance'. To illustrate their point, Fleming and Spicer (2003: 166) give the following hypothetical example:

> Instead of a McDonald's worker identifying with the values enshrined in the training programmes (quality, team work, cleanliness, efficiency and so on), she may be extremely cynical toward the company and see through to more base managerial motives (perhaps wearing a 'McShit' tee-shirt under her uniform in a clandestine fashion). Crucially, however, she performs as an efficient member of the team nevertheless.... Even though our cynical McDonald's employee has transgressive tastes in clothing that dis-identify with her employer, she acts as if she believes in the prescribed values of the organization and it is at this level that cultural power is operating in its most potent form.

The cynicism might also be a collective act, where employees share their disbelief in the values of the organisation, mock it and yet remain loyal. For instance, Fleming's account of working in a call centre in Australia reveals how employees felt patronised by the management culture. Fleming (2005: 1481) describes the exchange among a group of employees who were discussing some of the training material they were meant to take home to work on:

> Jane: Yeah, you get a handbook and it says [*in a childish American tone*] 'What are the 3Fs?' and you think [*in the same sarcastic tone*] 'Oh, gee, would they be the 3Fs I saw on the other page?' It's very much an adult/child relationship they are trying to instigate here.
>
> Mark: [*in a sarcastically immature voice*] I keep mine with me on my desk all the time. I might just forget the 3Fs so I can never be without it.
>
> Jane: [*in a fatherly voice*] What about your recognition certificate, son – have you got that?
>
> Mark: Of course!
>
> Jane: [*back to her own voice*] I don't. I lost mine [*laughs*].

Fleming and Spicer (2003) see cynicism as a form of resistance to management, because it reveals that employees have not internalised the values. Also, it might form the basis of a counter-culture within the workplace (Fleming, 2005) – a counter to managerialist logic. At the same time, cynicism allows employees to distance themselves from the values of the company, and therefore it does not mean directly challenging management or leaving the organisation. In our typology this can be described as a form of mental escape.

To sum up

Physical escape by employees can be a serious problem for management because they need either to address absence or to revise recruitment and retention policies. Mental escape does not necessarily present a problem for management: unlike making out, fiddling, joking, sabotage and physical escape, the mental escape from work does not raise a direct challenge to managerial logic. It is the most passive of the informal behaviours we have explored, but it also suggests perhaps the greatest defeat by managerial logic: a surrender to work as alienation.

Extract 9.5

Work blogging

In January 2005, Joe Gordon was sacked from the Edinburgh branch of Waterstone's bookstore for his satirical blog, The Woolamaloo Gazette, becoming the UK's first highly publicised fired blogger case. Gordon, a senior bookseller in the store, had called the company 'Bastardstone's' on his blog, nicknaming his 'sandal-wearing' boss as 'Evil Boss' and calling him a 'cheeky smegger' for asking him to work on a bank holiday. [...] The firing incident generated energetic discussion on Gordon's blog, in which he highlighted the help he was getting from his union in defending himself. The word 'Bastardstone's' quickly proliferated around the Internet, attracting mainstream media attention. Over the following weeks, Gordon broadcast details of his successful appeal, which had resulted in an offer of reinstatement from Waterstone's, and announced that he had accepted a position at Forbidden Planet International (FPI), running their corporate blog.

Source: Schoneboom (2011: 17)

Incidents such as the one above have led to the phenomenon of work-blogging being studied by researchers (e.g. Richards, 2008; Schoneboom, 2007, 2011) in order to explore the extent, content and significance of work-blogs.

So far, research findings reveal that work blogs tend to be concerned with:
• venting frustrations about work, customers and managers;
• conveying humorous anecdotes;
• sharing experiences with other people in similar jobs;
• trying to portraying the realities of their work to outsiders.

The question therefore arises as to whether work blogs should be seen as a survival strategy used by some employees. Richards (2008) suggests that they are much more than simply a way of coping with work. He argues they are a new form of resistance because all work blogs express disagreement with management and the work processes at some time, are aimed at sharing information with other like-minded people, and constitute a new means of revealing conflict at work. In addition, Schoneboom (2011) suggests that the individualised acts of employee resistance have the ability to galvanise support and in some circumstances can generate collective action against an employer.

Conclusion – surviving by consent and resistance

We discussed five strategies that employees can adopt to deal with the alienating tendencies of work: making out, fiddling, joking, sabotage and escaping. These represent 'unofficial' or 'informal' behaviours at work: they demonstrate the importance of looking below the surface into the depths of the workplace where other, complex patterns of action and meaning can be found. To explore this domain, it is necessary to use research methods and designs that get close to the subject. This can be either through direct involvement (participant observation – sometimes done covertly) or detailed case-study analysis (semi-structured interviews and close observation). One or more of these methods or designs was employed by all the researchers we discussed in this chapter. Their work has helped shed light on a side of work that was previously in the shadow of managerialist rhetoric. Such informal behaviours are being carried out on a daily basis by employees in a bid to survive the worst aspects of their work.

However, it is appropriate to sound a note of caution. To explain work as 'a struggle for survival' may be melodramatic. Also, it is too simplistic to characterise the five survival strategies as always problematic for management not defensible. Each of the strategies can represent (and be interpreted as) consent or resistance to management. This requires explanation, and so Table 9.3 summarises the different behaviours that could be interpreted as representing consent or resistance for each of the five survival strategies.

The problem of different interpretations

Table 9.3 is designed to show how each of the survival strategies could be interpreted in different ways:

- There can be different interpretations of *different* survival strategies. For example, some people might consider making out, joking and escaping as forms of consent, while viewing fiddling and sabotage as forms of resistance.

Table 9.3   Interpretation of the five survival strategies

Survival strategy	Interpreted as a form of consent	Interpreted as a form of resistance
Making out	Acts of 'game playing' within the organisation's rules, which result in mutual benefit for employees and managers	Acts that undermine management control by bending the rules to satisfy the self-interest of employees
Fiddling	'Deserved' perks that help subsidise wages and confer status on employees	Theft that affects profitability and undermines the integrity of everyone in the organisation
Joking	Forms of group self-regulation that preserve the status quo and provide a way of letting off steam	Challenges to management authority that undermine the status and policies of managers and make them appear foolish
Sabotage	(a) Expressions of frustration or irresponsible behaviour (letting off steam) (b) Well-meaning actions that have unintended negative consequences	(a) Malicious acts against property and people, intended to 'get even' with the organisation (b) Well-meaning actions intended to 'expose' the organisation (whistleblowing)
Escaping	Acts of withdrawal that result in employees accepting the status quo, even though they disagree with management policy or objectives	Acts that result in withdrawal of goodwill or mental and physical effort, thereby reducing organisational performance and undermining management objectives

- There can be different interpretations of the *same* survival strategy. For example, some people might see making out as a form of consent, while others would view it as a form of resistance.
- There can be different interpretations from context to context. In other words, behaviour associated with a survival strategy might be considered consent in one context but resistance in another.

To illustrate this, consider the following example. A builder employed on a new housing development has taken a few bags of cement. The builder might consider this an allowable 'perk', but the site manager might interpret it as theft (a sackable offence). On the other hand, the builder might be stealing to 'get back at' the employer, and perhaps the site manager turns a blind eye to occasional theft, because the builder is a reliable worker. So the same fiddling behaviour might be an expression of either consent or resistance (by the builder); equally, it may be interpreted (by the site manager) either as resistance (therefore a problem) or consent (no problem). In addition, the interpretations by the builder and site manager might be the same or different, which adds another layer of complexity to the situation.

Exercise 9.6

What do you think?

If you currently have a part-time job (or have taken a vacation job in the past), think about the various strategies you and your colleagues used to get through the working day:

1. Try to provide examples for each of the five strategies: making out, fiddling, joking, sabotage and escaping.
2. Take each example in turn and decide whether it should be viewed as a form of consent or resistance. Justify your decision.

Interpretation is complex

Even if a particular behaviour seems clearly to fall into one category, there are often alternative interpretations. Take, for example, the escape strategy of absence from work. Regularly taking days off is generally seen as unacceptable by management and is often viewed with disdain by fellow employees (especially those with a strong work ethic). However, suppose a secretary was absent from the office the first Monday in every month in order to take an elderly parent to the hospital for a regular check-up. Should these extra 12 days unofficial paid leave be taken as acts of resistance? Or, might such regular absences enhance the secretary's consent to managerial authority when in work? Similarly, are all jokes innocuous ways of coping by letting off steam? Or, might the pointed humorous comments aimed at the supervisor slowly erode the latter's status and authority? Even sabotage poses problems of interpretation. Does the photocopier fail to work because it has been kicked by an employee, or does an employee kick the photocopier because it fails to work?

Once again, as in previous chapters, a complex picture of the realities of work emerges. This requires the analysis of work to incorporate a number of interpretations, experiences and behaviours. It forces us to question unreflective, supposedly 'common sense' understandings that frequently litter management textbooks and the popular press. Such questioning and analysis puts us in a position to challenge the dogmatic viewpoints of those who state that all rule-bending is problematic, all fiddling is costly, all sabotage is destructive, all joking is fun or all absence is simply laziness.

10

Unfair discrimination at work

Key concepts

▷ fair and unfair discrimination
▷ criteria of discrimination
▷ stereotypes
▷ race and ethnicity
▷ exclusion from employment
▷ harassment
▷ everyday racism
▷ institutional racism
▷ sameness and difference
▷ equal treatment and special treatment

Chapter aim

To analyse discrimination and consider its impact on employees.

Learning outcomes

After reading and understanding the material in this chapter you will be able to:

1. Define and apply the concept of discrimination.
2. Assess how discrimination disadvantages some people's search for employment, with particular reference to race and ethnicity.
3. Assess how discrimination occurs within the workplace, with particular reference to race and ethnicity.
4. Explain how perceptions of fairness depend on assumptions made about the principles of sameness and difference.
5. Map out the process of discrimination and explain why perceptions of fairness vary between different individuals, and between different social groups.

Defining discrimination

Imagine you saw the following job advert. As you read it, ask yourself this question: what aspects of the advert are discriminatory?

> Sales executive required for a medium-sized electronics firm wanting to expand its customer base into Japan. Applicants must have at least five years previous experience of international sales and be aged between 28 and 35. Fluency in Japanese is essential. The job requires energy, dedication and adaptability, as considerable periods of time will be spent working abroad. Starting salary will be commensurate with age and experience, and a mixed benefits package will be offered in line with personal requirements.

So, which parts of this advert are discriminatory? Well, the correct answer is: all of it! Almost any job advert will be discriminatory. Discrimination is simply the act of identifying differences between things, as a step to choosing one thing in preference over another. This employer wants to discriminate between people on the basis of whether or not they have the appropriate attributes to carry out the job (experience, fluency in Japanese, energy, dedication and so on). The important thing to remember is not whether discrimination is occurring but whether the discrimination is based on fair criteria. For example, the requirement of fluency in Japanese discriminates in favour of people who can speak the language: if you cannot speak Japanese, you will not get the job and therefore you have been discriminated against. The employer would argue that this is fair because it is an essential requirement for the job. However, if you believe 'fluency in Japanese' is not a necessary requirement to do the job, you could argue this is an unfair criterion on which to discriminate. One can imagine that fluency could well be a necessary requirement, but this (fictional) advert also states that the applicants must be aged between 28 and 35, therefore people are being discriminated against on the basis of age – which is far more open to question, and would be unlawful in many countries. Again, there is discrimination in terms of 'previous experience', and then less tangible qualities such as 'energy' and 'adaptability'. If we doubt whether any of these are fair criteria on which to discriminate, this will influence opinions about the overall fairness of the recruitment.

The issue then is not the question of discrimination itself (differentiating between applicants, and then selecting on the basis of that difference), but the *fairness* of the discrimination (whether the grounds for discriminating are legitimate and justifiable). In everyday speech, when people talk of 'discrimination' they invariably mean unfair discrimination and it is typically used as a criticism, but it is important to remember that processes such as recruitment and selection have to involve some kind of discrimination. This is because, like many other aspects of work under capitalism, the recruitment process does not simply identify difference; it creates differences between people: some people are selected and employed and others are not. Because of this, work can marginalise, or preferentially treat some instead of others – not just those within an organisation, but those left standing outside, who perhaps never get the chance to work because of the cards life dealt them.

Try Exercise 10.1 to assess your own opinions about fairness of discrimination.

Exercise 10.1

What do you think?

For each of the situations described below, decide whether you consider the discrimination justifiable or unjustifiable. In each case explain your reasoning.

1. A Sikh bricklayer is denied a job on a building site because the hard hat would not fit over his turban.
2. He is also denied a job as a security guard because all staff are required to wear a uniform that includes a peaked cap.
3. A Muslim office worker is sacked for taking long lunch breaks every Friday. Instead of taking lunch he has a five-mile journey to the mosque for prayers.
4. An office worker with strong body odour is dismissed after numerous complaints by co-workers in the open-plan office.
5. A woman with a facial disfigurement (as a result of a house fire) is taken off the customer service desk at her supermarket when she returns to work after the accident, and given a less visible, back-office role.
6. A shelf stacker in the same supermarket applies for her job, but his application is rejected because he has visible tattoos on his neck and hands.
7. You are not allowed into a nightclub because the doorman says you 'look like a troublemaker'.

Victims of discrimination

The main kinds of difference, often taken as the main drivers of unfair discrimination, are as follows:

- sex/gender (these are not the same as we explain below),
- race/ethnicity (again, these are not the same as explained below),
- disability,
- sexual orientation,
- religion/belief,
- age,
- class.

When considering this list of differences there are two important points to bear in mind.

1. The list is not exhaustive.

Indeed there are a vast range of characteristics on which people differ and that might influence how they are treated; for example accent, educational background, personality and a host of aspects associated with appearance and norms of attractiveness, such as weight, height, hair style, piercings, tattoos and choice of clothing. However, with the exception of class, many countries have legislation that aims to give some protection to employees and job applicants in order to prevent managers making decisions about appointments, promotions, training, pay and so forth based only on these differences in the bullet list.

2. The list is also not mutually exclusive.

Some people experience unfair discrimination for multiple reasons: a position poignantly summed up by these quotes from two women in a study by Moore (2009: 664):

> I'm just a nursing auxiliary…actually there's a lot of discrimination when you're at the bottom of the ladder, there's a lot of discrimination against you especially when you're black…and as I said, if you're learned [well educated] maybe you don't get the same discrimination, but if you're at the bottom of the scale or the ladder, you do get it…ageism, racism, everything you get it.

Another interviewee, a 52-year-old Pakistani woman trying to get back into work comments:

> I personally think from what I'm experiencing is that it's very difficult when you're old to find a job. Everybody it seems to me is looking for a younger person. I think that people of 50 plus face discrimination…being a woman you are always…always…do you know what I mean? You get these feelings; do you know what I mean? But sometimes the people on the street are more racist to you; from my background, the way I dress, perhaps the way I talk, perhaps even the way I look. So yes, you are discriminated all the time. It's just that sometimes it's hurtful, sometimes it's scary and sometimes you don't care…like for the certain jobs that I've put applications in, I feel like an older woman. I have asked for a job in a shop as a sales assistant, I've asked for a job on the stalls and things like that. They look at you and 'Oh, I don't think you can do that job'…being an older woman, maybe a woman and also physical appearances like, you know, they want a younger person who shows more cleavage – I don't cover fully and all that, but I do wear a scarf.
>
> (Moore, 2009: 662)

Not only are these differences varied, they also overlap so that a person might be treated differently because, for example, she is both a woman and disabled. It means that researching how people experience discrimination can be complex and problematic (for a discussion see Healy, Kirton and Noon, 2011).

Extract 10.1

A definition of stereotyping

Stereotyping is the act of judging people according to your assumptions about the group to which they belong. It is based on the belief that people from a specific group share similar traits and behave in a similar manner. Rather than looking at a person's individual qualities, stereotyping leads us to jump to conclusions about what someone is like. This might act against the person concerned (negative stereotype) or in their favour (positive stereotype). For example, the negative stereotype of an accountant is someone who is dull, uninteresting and shy – which of course, is a slur on all the exciting, adventurous accountants in the world. A positive stereotype is that accountants are intelligent, conscientious and trustworthy – which is equally an inaccurate description of some of the accountants you are likely to encounter.

10.1 cont.

The problem with stereotypes is that they are generalisations (so there are always exceptions) and can be based on ignorance and prejudice (so are often inaccurate). It is vital for managers to resist resorting to stereotyping when managing people, otherwise they run the risk of treating employees unfairly and making poor-quality decisions that are detrimental to the organization.

Source: Heery and Noon (2001: 347).

Negative stereotypes

Underlying most discrimination is a stereotype about a particular group of people, which means individuals are not judged according to their own qualities (see Extract 10.1). This is a two-way process in the sense that stereotyping does not just mean the stereotype one group gives to others (the object group). Stereotyping also occurs where people think of themselves as being in a group (the subject group). The object group tend to be attributed a negative stereotype, while the subject group tend to give themselves a positive stereotype. Subject groups may be comparatively powerless, or economically disadvantaged, which in our society would include, for instance, women, the working class, people from minority ethnic groups, people with disabilities, children, the elderly, the mentally ill; as well as tabloid hate figures such as travellers, asylum seekers and lately perhaps even bankers and politicians. In contrast, those more often in the position of judging others, the powerful, would tend to be male, white and middle class. To illustrate the effects of such stereotypes, look at the quotes below made by Partners in different law firms in a study by Ashley (2010). They reveal first the stereotypes that these senior lawyers have, and second how they assume their clients will share their stereotyped assumptions and how this might impact on their business:

> There was one guy who came to interviews who was a real Essex barrow boy, and he had a very good CV, he was a clever chap, but we just felt that there's no way we could employ him … I just thought, putting him in front of a client…. You just couldn't do it. [Partner ,Law firm]
>
> There are limits to what we can do and what we can be because ultimately we have clients…. I'm not saying that people from certain ethnic backgrounds are not … but there is a question of, inevitably, there is a question of does the face fit … that's the world we live in and compete in … that does have … a restraining impact. [Partner, Law firm]
>
> (Source for both quotes: Ashley, 2010: 720)

People with disabilities are particularly prone to negative stereotyping. A study by Reynolds, Nicholls and Alferoff (2001) reveals a stereotypical image of 'the disabled employee' as having lower productivity, higher absence and greater dependency on others. This leads to a general perception of disabled people as being 'hard to employ'. Not only does this reduce access to jobs, but it also perpetuates a general tendency to marginalise disabled people: 'a process by which disabled people find themselves, in various ways, on the edges of social life, only being considered as a "side" issue, or as a necessary "extra" problem' (Reynolds, Nicholls and Alferoff, 2001: 193). Further effects of the stereotyping and exclusion of people with disabilities can be found in Oliver (1996) and Foster (2007). A recent study by Foster and Fosh (2010) suggests that it is only through trade unions that disability concerns genuinely feature as part of an organisational agenda (and of course not all workplaces are unionised).

The problem of age-typing of jobs is revealed in a study by Oswick and Rosenthal (2001). Their survey of managers shows how certain jobs are thought of as best suited to specific age groups, and that age discrimination is then justified by managers on these grounds. According to the respondents it was legitimate to discriminate in favour of older workers when the job demanded stability, loyalty and maturity, and against them when fitness, energy and innovation were required. Other studies have found this age discrimination by managers is influenced by stereotypes and social norms (e.g. Riach 2007, 2009). Research has also revealed that older employees themselves can sometimes adopt the negative stereotypes projected by employers, and thereby reducing further their employment prospects by undermining their self-esteem and confidence (Loretto and White 2006; Porcellato et al, 2010).

Just as there are ageism stereotypes and assumptions about older workers, there can also be problems of being too young, particularly where this intersects with gender as illustrated by these comments of employees in a study by Jyrkinen and McKie (2012: 68, 69):

> You are not necessarily taken seriously, because you are a young woman. Sometimes it is just because you are young, sometimes it is because you are not a man, and sometimes it is both. (Alice, Scotland, 35)
>
> In the [previous company] there were men in the executive group who were 57 years of age, who were then moved under my supervision, and were left out of the executive group then. And of course, there was some kind of friction there, when there is a so called 'young woman' in her 40s as their boss, such as 'this is not the way it should be'. Well, there then was this kind of undermining because of sex and age. (Tina, Finland, 45)

Overall the result is a pernicious (wide-spread and corrosive or harmful) process involving:

> the stereotyping of a person according to their social group and irrespective of their individual attributes; the association of a particular job with the need for certain attributes; and the matching of the stereotype to the job rather than the individual. As well as being morally questionable, it is also bad personnel practice, assuming the objective is to get the best person for the job.
>
> (Noon and Ogbonna, 2001: 11)

To sum up

Discrimination means applying criteria to choose between people. The key issue is the fairness of the criteria upon which the discrimination is based. Fair criteria lead to discrimination that is justifiable (fair discrimination), whereas unfair criteria lead to unfair discrimination (in everyday speech we usually just call this 'discrimination'). Unfair discrimination is unjustifiable and needs to be addressed. At the heart of discrimination is the stereotyping of a person according to assumptions about the group to which they belong.

Experiencing discrimination

This section explores the key features of how discrimination is experienced by drawing on examples of race and ethnicity. This is not to imply that this category of discrimination is more important than the others – later in the chapter we look at sex/gender discrimination – but focusing on one criterion of discrimination allows the key concepts and sites of discrimination to be illustrated.

Defining race and ethnicity

It is important to clarify what is meant by 'race' and 'ethnicity'. As we have seen in other chapters, many of the concepts we come across when studying work are socially constructed. That is, they are not the kinds of things we can have objective, neutral and scientific measurements or descriptions for – in the way that we could agree what the height or weight of something was. Whereas physical objects have a fixed height or weight, we actually 'make' (construct) social objects/phenomena when we talk about or measure them. Chapter 5 gave an example of this in relation to how 'skill' is socially constructed rather than an objective measurement.

To recap quickly, here is a simple example of 'social construction' in effect. You are at a party, about to be introduced to Dave. Your friend who knows Dave tells you before meeting him that he is 'really laid back'. So you spend some time chatting to Dave. He doesn't say much but you leave him standing by the fridge in the kitchen and walk off thinking 'yes that Dave he really is laid back'. Now imagine that before you met Dave, your friend had said, 'Oh, Dave's here, I better introduce you to him because he will see us, but be warned he is a bit weird.' In that situation, the same things would feel very different. Even something that was factually nothing – a long silence – would feel different. You might end up having a 'weird' conversation with Dave because you would be analysing his behaviour far more carefully. As a result you could end up proving your friend's unscientific assessment of him as 'a bit weird' to be true.

That is a very simple example of how descriptions of social phenomena construct those phenomena, but far more complex phenomena are socially constructed. Race and ethnicity are in many ways socially constructed: they are concepts that can be used by a particular group – for instance, a minority ethnic group – to define themselves and thereby identify their difference from 'the other'. Alternatively, and at the same time, they can be concepts imposed by one group on another, and then given some particular meaning or significance through stereotyping. In the second case, social construction is one way to describe unfair discrimination, where a person from a majority or dominant group focuses on elements of a person's behaviour, appearance, attitude, belief or biography (life story) which they believe identify that person as being in some important way different.

This is social construction because discriminating on the basis of those characteristics is not simply describing a difference, it is 'making' (constructing) a difference. Of course, people differ from each other in many ways but in terms of establishing group identity, it is usually only certain differences that are perceived to be relevant – these 'relevant' differences are often traditional or historical, and are reinforced by a group's values, beliefs and norms. We discuss race and ethnicity as examples here:

- *Racial* differences are related to physical features, the most obvious example being skin colour.
- *Ethnic* differences are related to cultural features such as language, customs and religion.

A group (whether it is a Nation or a small team of workers) arrives at some common understanding as to what racial and/or ethnic differences are relevant in distinguishing themselves from others. From context to context, and group to group, racial and ethnic boundaries are drawn differently and have varying relevance.

There is considerable debate about the concept of 'race' because it has been discredited by biological science: everyone is of mixed 'race'. Geneticists now argue that there is more genetic variation *within* supposed racial groups than *between* racial groups. Politically, however, it remains important because, as Mason (1994) points out, some people behave as though clearly identifiable groups do exist, hence the continued relevance of the concept of racism. (For a fuller review of this detailed debate see Anthias, 1992; Anthias and Yuval-Davis, 1992; Miles, 1993.)

The controversy over race has led to an increasing focus by social scientists on using 'ethnicity' as a way of defining difference. But the concept of ethnicity is not without problems (e.g. see the debate between Smith, 2002 and Modood, Berthoud and Nazroo, 2002).

The widely agreed legal definition of an ethnic group is that it has a long, shared history and a cultural tradition of its own, and that this can be identified through characteristics such as a common geographical origin, a common language, a common literature, a common religion and the characteristic of being a minority in a larger community (Forbes and Mead, 1992: 23). However, much of the categorisation of 'ethnicity' tends to rely on a mixture of physical differences (primarily skin colour) and geographical origin. For example, Table 10.1 shows the categories used in the 2011 Census of England and Wales.

Table 10. 1   Categories in the 2011 Census of England and Wales

---

What is your ethnic group?

A. White
    English/Welsh/Scottish/Northern Irish/British
    Irish
    Gypsy or Irish Traveller
    Any other white background
B. Mixed/multiple ethnic groups
    White and Black Caribbean
    White and Black African
    White and Asian
    Any other mixed/multiple ethnic background
C. Asian/Asian British
    Indian
    Pakistani
    Bangladeshi
    Chinese
    Any other Asian background
D. Black/African/Caribbean/Black British
    African
    Caribbean
    Any other Black/African/Caribbean background
E. Other ethnic group
    Arab
    Any other ethnic group

In addition, it is important to recognise that race and ethnicity, like gender, are central to understanding work in organisations (Nkomo, 1992). However, this has been limited by ethnocentric bias in much academic research (ethnocentric means focusing on the concerns of one ethnic group – usually the one in a position of power and privilege). Even so, there is research we can draw upon to explore the disadvantages faced by many people from minority ethnic groups.

Disadvantage in finding employment

People from minority ethnic groups often experience discrimination in getting jobs through a lack of equal opportunity (Heath and Cheung, 2007). In the UK, the rate of unemployment for the ethnic minority population is consistently higher than the white population, although there are important differences between and within ethnic groups – particularly disadvantaged when it comes to securing employment are Pakistani and Bangladeshi men and women (Berthoud and Blekesaune, 2007; Modood et al, 1997; Pilkington, 2001).

In terms of the effects of the Global Financial Crisis, it has also been observed that in times of recession, when competition for jobs intensifies, people from minority ethnic groups tend to be more disadvantaged. This population experiences a faster rising rate of unemployment and it reaches a higher peak than the white population, although in periods of recovery, the rate falls more quickly than among the white population. Therefore, when comparing rates of unemployment between people from minority ethnic groups and whites, the overall pattern of unemployment has to be taken into account: the difference will vary according to economic peaks and troughs (Brah, 1986; Dex, 1983; Jones, 1993; Modood et al, 1997; Rhodes and Braham, 1986; Smith, 1981).

Training opportunities

Exclusion from employment is also a reflection of the relevance of an individual's skills. So, access into jobs is likely to be related to the training and retraining undertaken. Access to training schemes is particularly important for people from ethnic minority backgrounds because it provides a vital means of improving employment prospects (particularly if the labour market is already biased against them through unfair discrimination). Research reveals that just as there are barriers to employment, there are also barriers for people from minority ethnic groups within government training schemes designed to improve employment prospects. For example, an analysis of the provision of training schemes for unemployed adults revealed that people from minority ethnic groups were joining the scheme in representative proportions, but they did not enjoy the positive outcomes (jobs and qualifications) to the same extent as their white counterparts (Ogbonna and Noon, 1995; Noon and Ogbonna, 1998). Interviews with the providers of the training and the trainees themselves revealed two types of disadvantage:

1. *Discrimination among the training providers* (these were private firms providing off-the-job instruction). Unfair discrimination was experienced in terms of the time spent with each trainee (people from minority ethnic groups received less attention), the stereotyping of ability, and in a few cases, verbal abuse.

2. *Discrimination among the placement providers* (these were local organisations that provided hands-on experience). First, placements were generally difficult to secure for all trainees, and faced with direct competition from white trainees, people from minority ethnic groups were less successful (the providers could pick and choose, and some were found to be using overtly racist criteria) (Ogbonna and Noon, 1995: 551–6). Second, when placements were secured, trainees from minority ethnic groups were less likely to be placed in major institutions such as banks, insurance companies and department stores. Instead, there was a tendency for them to be sent to (or only be accepted by) small companies (many of whom saw this as useful 'free labour') and voluntary organisations. While at least providing some work experience, neither of these types of organisation had the resources to provide adequate on-the-job training to back up the skills learned in the classroom. They also did not have the vacancies to offer employment following the completion of the placement period.

These findings echo earlier studies that have similarly revealed unfair discrimination in training (see, for example, Cross, 1987; Cross, Wrench and Barnett, 1990; Lee and Wrench, 1987).

Recruitment and selection

Another key area where disadvantage is experienced by people from minority ethnic groups is in the process of recruitment and selection. Studies in the UK have revealed discriminatory practices in both the private and public sectors (Brown and Gay, 1985; Jenkins, 1986; Jewson, Mason, Waters and Harvey, 1990), in white-collar and professional occupations (Firth, 1981; Hubbuck and Carter, 1980; Noon et al 2012), and among graduate recruiters (Brennan and McGeevor, 1987; Noon, 1993). The problem for researchers, however, is how to identify discrimination in recruitment and selection, particularly if, as Jenkins (1986: 240) argues, the majority of discrimination among employers 'is neither strikingly visible nor necessarily self-consciously prejudiced'. One way of tackling this problem is with research using covert methods. See an example of this approach in Extract 10.2 and then try Exercise 10.2.

Extract 10.2

A covert experiment on racial discrimination

An experiment was conducted by one of the authors (Noon, 1993) and then repeated six years later (Hoque and Noon, 1999), in which speculative letters of application were sent to personnel managers in the UK's top 100 companies from two fictitious MBA students – one whose name identified him as Asian, and the other as most likely white. The purpose of the research was to test how effective the equal opportunity practices were in the companies. In theory, the applicants should have been treated the same because the factual content of the letters was identical and the 'candidates' were equally qualified. The experiment also controlled for other factors that might affect the results, such as the time the letters were sent and the person replying.

Through a statistical analysis of the responses to the letters it was possible to examine three issues:

- whether the applicants were equally likely to receive a reply;
- whether the quality of the replies was the same for both candidates;
- whether there were differences in the quality of response from companies with and without equal opportunity statements in their annual reports.

The findings for the two studies are summarised overleaf.

Issue	Main findings of 1992 study	Main findings of 1998 study
1. Likelihood of response	Both applicants were equally likely to receive a reply	Both applicants were equally likely to receive a reply.
2. Quality of response	Better quality (more encouraging) replies were sent to the white applicant	No statistically significant evidence of unequal treatment in terms of quality of reply. The disappearance of unequal treatment is explained by those companies moving into the top 100 rather than by improvement from those companies remaining within the top 100.
3. Effects of equal opportunity statement	Companies with equal opportunity statements were more likely to treat both applicants the same. When discrimination occurred in companies with equal opportunity statements, it was against the ethnic minority applicant.	Having an equal opportunity statement made no difference to the treatment of the applicants. Companies with specific mention of equal opportunities for ethnic minorities were more likely to discriminate against the ethnic minority applicant.

Source: Hoque and Noon (1999).

What do you think?

Read Extract 10.2 and then answer the following questions.

1. What do the findings suggest about the state of equal opportunities in the top 100 companies in 1998 compared with 1992?
2. How might you explain the findings relating to the equal opportunity statements?
3. This research is based on the use of covert methods. Those answering the letters did not know they were subjects of research.
   a. What might be the ethical objections to this type of research method?
   b. How might the researchers in this case justify their choice of methods?
   c. What alternative methods could have been used?

The realities of potential discrimination are fully acknowledged by job seekers who are from minority ethnic groups. In a fascinating study of new graduates, Kirton (2009) finds that her interviewees had high aspirations and youthful optimism but their ethnicity and gender identities meant they were acutely aware of the potential labour market discrimination, as the following quotes illustrate.

> I feel that there are a lot of stereotypical views about Asians, especially if you are wearing the hijab; they [employers] feel you're being oppressed, that you are someone who doesn't speak for yourself. I guess they think that you won't fit into their type of organization because they see us differently. (Female, Bangladeshi)
>
> Being a Muslim and trying to get a job is probably much harder than it was before. I know that, everyone knows that; maybe I'm a pessimist, but I believe that. If you have an Asian girl competing with a white girl with exactly the same qualifications, well they'll go 'She's Muslim and she might blow up my company one day, so let's go with the white girl.' (Female, Pakistani)
>
> Well if I was to go into accounting, I'd have no problem [laughs] coz I'm Chinese and that would probably get me in the door. (Female, Chinese)
>
> The thing that bothers me about the place where I work at the moment [one of the top four supermarkets] is that about 95 percent of the workers are Bengali and the highest position with a Bengali is checkout supervisor. There's no department manager from a Bangladeshi background – no store manager, no duty manager. I find that astonishing that with 95 percent of your workforce Bengali, you can't find anyone suitable for a senior position. (Male, Bangladeshi)
>
> As soon as you go out of the city you realize that yeah you are a minority. But living in London, you don't always think about it like that. I know that if I decided to work outside of London or outside a major city in the UK, then I think that it [racism] might become more of an issue. (Female, Bangladeshi)

(Kirton 2009: 22, 23, 24)

Kirton (2009) argues that because of the mix of awareness and aspiration among the graduates she interviewed, they should not be seen as passive victims of discriminatory processes. This mix of attitudes places them in a strong position to confront the challenges of discrimination.

Other case study research has also found evidence of racial and ethnic discrimination in recruitment. Frequently this appears to be the result of negative stereotypes held by managers in charge of the selection process (see, for example, Hubbuck and Carter, 1980; Jenkins, 1986; Jewson et al, 1990). Indeed, Ram (1992) found that in order to access the white-dominated business society, even some Asian employers discriminated against people from minority ethnic groups in favour of whites.

Disadvantage in the workplace

Having secured a job, people from ethnic minority backgrounds can experience further unfair discrimination in terms of full recognition of achievement and promotion. Using the nationally representative UK Workplace Employment Relations Survey data from almost 24,000 respondents in 1880 workplaces, Noon and Hoque (2001) compared the work experiences of white and ethnic minority employees. They found that men and women from minority ethnic groups received poorer treatment on a range of measures related to current job performance, promotion opportunities and pay. Jones's (1993) analysis of occupational structure revealed that people from minority ethnic groups were disproportionately clustered in jobs that were held to be lower skilled. People from minority ethnic groups were also notably under-represented in senior management grades in large organisations – a situation experienced by women too. The pattern remained broadly the same in a later survey (Modood et al, 1997), although the authors make important distinctions between ethnic groups – in particular the notable disadvantaged position of Caribbean and Bangladeshi respondents compared with the more favourable position of Chinese respondents. It is important to recognise that there are different experiences between ethnic groups, so although minorities might have in common the general experiences of discrimination, the impact or effect for some minorities is worse than for others:

> 52 per cent of male Bangladeshi workers in Britain are in the restaurant industry (compared with only 1 per cent of White males), while one in eight male Pakistani workers is a taxi driver or chauffeur (compared with a national average of one in 100). By contrast, approximately one in 20 working Indian men is a medical practitioner – almost ten times the national average. While the first two occupations offer little or no opportunities for progression, quite the reverse is true for the medical profession. This fact will influence, in very different ways, the career trajectories of Bangladeshi and Pakistani men on the one hand, and Indians on the other.
>
> (Cabinet Office, 2003: 24)

This clustering into certain occupations, coupled with gender segregation into types of jobs, is a consistent finding in analyses of employment data (e.g. Blackwell, 2003). Not only does this limit opportunities for some, but it also perpetuates stereotypes. The frustration of not being able to break out of certain occupational clusters is well illustrated by the women in the following quote:

> I have an African surname, so it takes me longer to get a job in the first place. When I do, I'm often the first black person who has been employed there. I worked in an ad agency in Soho of 400 people and I was the only black employee. Four hundred people!
>
> I've been in meetings where co-workers have been visibly disturbed because I had something intelligent to say. I've watched white colleagues with fewer qualifications get paid more. I've been promoted to senior positions but never quite made it into management. Many of my friends have experienced the same: intelligent, articulate women bullied or pushed into accepting jobs for which they're overqualified. We're fine as carers or cleaners. We're not supposed to be executives.
>
> (Quoted in 'Neither seen nor heard', *Guardian*, 2005: 5).

Extract 10.3

Legal harassment?

The following quotes are from an Asian woman employed as a policy adviser at the Law Society, the governing body for solicitors in England and Wales. Her remarks were made at an employment tribunal hearing where she alleged she had been subjected to bullying and harassment:

> There appears to be a culture of fear against minority groups at the Law Society.... Racist stereotypes appear to flourish.

> [At a leaving party, a female senior manager] made reference to Asians being reliable little workers and said I was lucky I was not Afro-Caribbean because everyone knows they are lazy and have attitude problems.

> She subjected me to bullying and harassment, this often took the form of being ostracised.... I felt belittled by her all the time.

> Once I had complained of bullying and discrimination not only was my health and welfare called into question but rumours were circulated that I was mad and weird. No wonder then that there is a culture of fear.

The case was settled out of court for an undisclosed sum.

Source: The quotes are from *Daily Express*, 15 April 2005: 23.

Harassment

Irrespective of the type of work being undertaken, many people from minority ethnic groups experience regular discrimination from co-workers and customers. This can take the form of verbal abuse and racist jokes, being ignored or talked over, being excluded from work-based activities and also social events, having their authority or ability undermined, and being constantly criticised over petty issues. In an analysis of nurses in the UK National Health Service, Shields and

Price (2002) found that 39 per cent of nurses from minority ethnic groups had been victims of racial harassment from work colleagues compared with 4 per cent of white nurses. Sixty-four per cent of nurses from minority ethnic groups had experienced racial harassment from patients or the patients' families, compared with 17 per cent of white nurses. The authors go on to state:

> Black African nurses are by far the most likely to experience racial harassment from work colleagues. Interestingly, Black Caribbean and South Asian nurses are also significantly more likely to suffer such abuse than their South-east Asian colleagues, while foreign-born nurses are also more vulnerable to racial harassment attacks. Clearly, it is not just the attribute of a particular skin colour that lies behind this abuse from work colleagues. It may be the case that linguistic accent or other cultural factors are important factors in determining whether work colleagues racially harass a particular individual.
>
> (Shields and Price, 2002: 14)

A particularly vivid example of harassment is the case of the UK fire service, where a confidential Home Office report in 1994 revealed an alarming amount of racial and sexual harassment. This ranged from verbal abuse and being ostracised (socially excluded) to physical attacks. For instance, it highlighted the experience of an Afro-Caribbean firefighter: 'The first day, the blokes tricked us…. They threw a bucket of water over us. We laughed our heads off and I thought "I've been accepted"' (*The Observer*, 1994). Clearly this could be construed as an initiation ritual (the sort of event explored when analysing humour in Chapter 9), but whereas the 'ragging' continued for this particular firefighter, it stopped for his white colleague. He goes on to explain how the attacks increased in severity:

> They dragged me out of my bed, put me under the shower. They tied me up, they put me under the water tower and filled it with water. I nearly drowned. They grabbed me and set me head-first in a fire bin. They set my shoes on fire, whacked me in the head. They'd tell me to do things to test my strength, and then while I was exercising try and trip me up, knock my hands away.
>
> (*The Observer*, 10 April 1994)

Instances such as these led to an investigation of the fire service, and a further Home Office report 'Equality and fairness in the fire service' (published in 1999) labelled the service racist, sexist and homophobic (discriminating against people who are gay):

> In one of the most damning indictments of a public sector body, the report found the fire service to be one of the last bastions of white, male, laddish culture. Stronger leadership and cultural changes were needed to improve equality and fairness for staff, said the report, which found prejudice was rife among the overwhelmingly white male officers in the service. Women regularly suffered sexual harassment from colleagues, while gay and lesbian

firefighters risked vilification if they were open about their sexuality, the report concluded. Firefighters from ethnic minorities faced routine name calling, were forced to fit in with the prevailing white culture, and often felt they were passed over for promotion because of their skin colour.

(*Guardian*, 1999)

In 2005 the fire service in one UK region banned firefighters from belonging to far-right political organisations on the basis that they would be a danger to the public and work colleagues.

Dramatic cases of racial harassment can also be found in the private sector. For instance, in October 1999, 800 workers at Ford UK's Dagenham factory staged a walk-out in protest against alleged 'entrenched racism', which included harassment by foremen and racial taunts (*Financial Times*, 7 October 1999). This followed an earlier industrial tribunal case against the company (which admitted liability) where it was revealed that an Asian employee had experienced persistent abuse:

> Mr Parma suffered years of routine abuse by his foreman and his team leader. Once, he opened his sealed pay packet to find the word 'Paki' scrawled inside. In another incident, he saw graffiti threatening to throw him to his death. On one occasion he was ordered into the 'punishment cell', a small booth in which oil is sprayed over engines, but he was not allowed to wear protective clothing. He became ill and needed medical attention. On another occasion Mr Parma had his lunch kicked out of his hands and was told: 'We're not having any of that Indian shit in here.' He was also warned that he would have his legs broken if he ever named any of his tormentors. The police were called in at one stage, but the Crown Prosecution Service decided to drop charges.
>
> (*Independent*, 24 September 1999)

Much racial harassment remains hidden and erodes the morale and self-worth of its victims, in a similar way that persistent bullying can break the spirit of a child. Sometimes it is brought to public attention because of a tragedy, such as the disturbing case of the UK postal worker whose suicide note explained that he had been racially harassed at work (*Guardian*, 9 January 2001). Mostly it requires the victim to speak out against the organisation and co-workers (e.g. Extract 10.3), which requires a considerable amount of courage because this frequently results in retaliation, thereby adding to the stress of the victim (Lee, Heilmann and Near, 2004). Examples such as those above illustrate the way certain groups are exposed through work to hostile social environments. For many people, the harsh reality is that work is a place where they experience unpleasant social interaction: harassment, in its various guises and manifestations, is entrenched as part of everyday life.

Everyday racism

The examples so far have tended to illustrate how unfair treatment can be visible and dramatic. For many employees from minority ethnic groups though, the daily experience of more subtle acts of racism makes work unpleasant (Essed, 1991). For example, studies reveal how actions such as not being given eye contact, being excluded from lunchtime socialising or not having the lift doors held open can undermine self-confidence and self-worth. These forms of social isolation are problematic for two reasons:

- The victim does not know whether the actions are racially motivated – it might just be bad manners – so some or all of these acts might go 'unacknowledged' as racist behaviour.
- The victim might sometimes (or always) attribute the acts to racist motivation, when they are not motivated by racism at all.

This attributional ambiguity identified by research into prejudice (e.g. Barrett and Swim, 1998) means that victims suffer the double anxiety of (i) negative treatment and (ii) not knowing if this was racially motivated (Miller and Kaiser, 2001). For example, look at this quote from the first black receptionist at an exclusive London hotel and ask yourself whether there is a discernible racial motivation in the behaviour of the customer, or whether he would have acted this way simply because of the status differential: that is, he is looking down on the receptionist because she is doing what he considers a menial task:

> A guest who had been coming to the hotel for several years and who was known to the managing director [came in]. His attitude towards me was hostile: I knew it and he knew it. There was nothing overt about his behaviour; he simply ignored me and spoke over my head to one of the managers as if I did not exist, had not spoken, and had not presented him with a registration card.

(Adib and Guerrier, 2003: 426)

Even if you conclude there was no racial motivation in this encounter (i.e. it was just because the receptionist was looked down on because she was doing a menial task), there is still an important racial implication. If a disproportionate number of people from minority ethnic groups find themselves in low-status roles (because of unfair discrimination), then (in comparison to whites) a greater proportion of them will experience these types of negative encounters. In other words, such negative experiences may not be directly associated with ethnicity, but they are indirectly associated – because for some people, their ethnicity confines them to certain types of work.

The combination of unfair employment processes, overt harassment and the more subtle acts of everyday racism produces conditions where unfairness has become part of the fabric of organisational life. In some settings it has become institutionalised and has a profoundly detrimental effect.

Institutionalised disadvantage

When discrimination is deeply embedded in an organisation, it is described as 'institutional' – hence institutional racism (or institutional sexism, homophobia etc.). This phrase suggests that the institution itself embodies values, structures and processes that deny equal opportunities to certain groups of employees. Rather than discrimination being seen as the attitude and actions of one person towards another, it becomes seen as pervasive across the whole organisation. This excuses individuals but blames the entire (impersonal) system. It is therefore a devastating indictment of an organisation, suggesting something rotten at its core. Within the UK, 'institutional racism' has been used to explain racist attitudes and behaviour following investigation into public sector organisations such as the Metropolitan Police, the fire service and the prison service (see Extract 10.4).

Extract 10.4

'Malicious racism' in youth prison

A confidential prison service report following the murder of an Asian inmate by a white prisoner at Feltham [youth prison] west London, has concluded that the youth jail is guilty of institutional racism, with ethnic minority staff and inmates enduring overt racist abuse by warders and failures by senior management.

The report...brands Feltham as 'institutionally racist', and found a 'damning indictment of how staff are failing in their duty of care towards prisoners'.

It concludes: 'There is evidence that racism exists at Feltham, both overtly and by more subtle methods. Minority ethnic staff should not have to tolerate the level of harassment that exists in order to feel accepted as part of the team. Similarly, prisoners should be able to live free from racist abuse by staff.'

The report says: 'Evidence found by the team suggests that a small number of staff sustained and promoted overtly racist behaviour as well as more subtle methods and that there are issues surrounding both staff and prisoners.'

'Staff from all ethnic groups told of an underlying culture that suggests the only way minority ethnic group staff can be accepted as part of the team of Feltham is by enduring racist comments and racist banter/ jokes. Senior managers know what they should be doing but have not done it. This leads the inquiry team to form the conclusion that Feltham is institutionally racist.'

The report, stamped as confidential on each of its 30 pages, found a 'failure by staff at all levels to take complaints of racist incidents seriously'. It said some of those responsible for race training believed racist jokes could be acceptable.

Half of Feltham's 717 inmates are from Asian or Afro-Caribbean backgrounds, as are 11 per cent of its 654 staff. The senior management is entirely white.

Source: Abridged from Dodd (2001).

As noted in the previous section, the culture of an organisation may perpetuate values and attitudes that exclude certain ethnic groups. In addition, however, institutional racism implies that processes within the organisation are deficient:

> The strength of [the concept of] institutional racism is in capturing the manner in which whole societies, or sections of society, are affected by racism, or perhaps racist legacies, long after racist individuals have disappeared. The racism that remains may be unrecognised and unintentional, but, if never disclosed, it continues uninterrupted.

(Cashmore, 1996: 170)

This means that processes within organisations may be embedded within structures, policies and practices that disadvantage employees, even though individual managers may not be making overtly racist decisions. There can be legislative attempts to prevent this, but disadvantage persists within organisational processes, such as:

- word-of-mouth methods for internal recruitment;
- dress codes that prevent people practising their religious beliefs;
- promotions based on informal recommendations, rather than open competition;
- informal assessments rather than formal appraisals;
- assumptions about training capabilities;
- assumptions about language difficulties and attitudes.

This structural, institutionalised disadvantage perpetuates unfairness because those who are most likely to want to change equal opportunities policies are denied access to decision-making processes. Modood et al (1997: 104–5) conclude from their survey that:

> Both men and women in nearly all the minority groups shared one fundamental difference from white men and women. They were much less likely to be in the top occupational category [managers and employers] and when they were, they were much less likely to work in large establishments. The explanations for this are likely to be complex. There may be some direct discrimination, but part of the explanation could lie in the continued importance of social-educational networks.

A prime example of this comes from a hospital in the UK which was taken to an industrial tribunal. It was found to have a macho culture which tolerated and encouraged racist and sexist language among the senior medical staff and managers. Strong social networks meant that women and ethnic minorities were excluded from important groups and decisions, most notably the payment of merit awards (financial bonuses) (*Guardian*, 4 December 2000). Such instances illustrate the important point that many of those who control policy – predominantly white, able-bodied men – have little incentive to change a system from which they benefit.

Exercise 10.3

What do you think?

1. 'The concept of "institutional racism" rather than individual racism absolves those within the organisation of any responsibility for the unfair discrimination.'
   a. What is meant by this statement?
   b. Do you agree or disagree with it? Explain your viewpoint.

2. Is it legitimate to describe an institution as racist? (Think about whether the institution can take action or whether it is the people within the institution.)

3. What action would you recommend to tackle the problems of the youth prison in Extract 10.4?

To sum up

Ethnic minorities suffer disadvantage in (i) access to work and (ii) within the workplace. The former can occur through procedures that deny impartial treatment in training opportunities or the processes of recruitment and selection. The latter typically shows itself in harassment, or subtle forms of everyday racism, or institutional racism.

Theorising discrimination

The key concepts of sameness and difference

Fairness is, as discussed at the start of this chapter, a subjective concept. At its root are moral assumptions about how people ought to be treated so that equal opportunity prevails. Two key questions present themselves:

- To ensure equality of opportunity, should people be treated the same, or should they be treated differently?
- On which aspects should they be treated the same or differently?

The answers are not straightforward. A person can be the victim of unfair discrimination either by receiving the same treatment or different treatment, depending on the circumstances. Extract 10.5 illustrates this.

Extract 10.5

Sameness and difference

A woman applies for a job as an adviser selling financial products in a company that is dominated by men.

Scenario 1: she has the same qualifications and experience as male applicants, but the all-male selection panel reject her because they consider that she would not 'fit in' with the competitive, aggressive culture of the organisation.

Scenario 2: she has the same qualifications as male applicants but has taken a career break for childcare purposes. The selection panel reject her because compared with men of the same age she has less work experience.

If we apply the concepts of difference and sameness, it is clear that:
- In scenario 1 the panel reject her by using the criterion of difference (recognising gender).
- In scenario 2 the panel reject her by using the criterion of sameness (ignoring gender).

But imagine if the panel took the opposite approach to difference and sameness. They would most likely arrive at completely different decisions.
- In scenario 1: if the panel ignored gender, they would arrive at the conclusion that she was appointable.
- In scenario 2: if they recognised that, because of her gender, she has had extra domestic commitments so cannot be compared with men of the same age then again they might conclude she is appointable.

(Adapted from Noon, 2010a)

The issue of recognising how unfair discrimination can emerge from the concepts of 'sameness' and 'difference' is addressed by Liff and Wajcman in an analysis of equal opportunity policy and gender. They reach the conclusion that attention must be paid to both because they reflect different forms of disadvantage:

> Sometimes women are disadvantaged by being treated differently when in fact they are the same (e.g. denied a job for which they are perfectly well qualified) and at other times by being treated the same when their difference needs to be taken into account (e.g. having their absence to look after a sick child treated the same way as a man who is absent with a hangover).
>
> (Liff and Wajcman, 1996: 86)

The dominant group (in this case, male employers) selectively uses the concepts of sameness and difference to construct disadvantage against women. Liff and Wajcman (following Bacchi, 1990 and Cockburn, 1991) suggest that the arguments can be turned back on the dominant group using a similar logic of selectivity, but with the purpose of eliminating disadvantage for women:

> [Equal treatment] is entirely appropriate for tackling some types of dis-crimination and can be expected to have brought benefits. Here the best way forward is for women to be treated the same as men, for example by ensuring that selection and appraisal methods are free from bias. In other cases, where women have been excluded from certain types of experience or qualification, or where they have specific demands placed on them from the home which impinge on their work, this difference should be acknowledged. Appropriate equality initiatives [special treatment] in this context would include targeted training courses, childcare or the opportunity for men and women to work different hours.
>
> (Liff and Wajcman, 1996: 86)

To summarise the problem: unfair discrimination can occur by ignoring differ-ences and giving people equal treatment, or by identifying differences and giving (some) people special treatment. The next section develops this to look at the differential impact for women and men when they attempt to break with gender stereotypes and enter jobs where they are in the minority.

Sameness and difference – the example of crossing job boundaries

There is considerable horizontal and vertical segregation of work. Men and women tend to work in different types of jobs (horizontal segregation) and at different levels within organisational hierarchies (vertical segregation). Yet there are fundamental differences in the experiences of women and men who cross gender segregation barriers (e.g. Cockburn 1991; Konrad, Winter and Gutek, 1992; Williams 1993). When women attempt to pursue a career in traditionally male occupations, they frequently experience resistance and hostility from men, and hit the 'glass ceiling' (they can see the opportunities for progression to higher levels, but are prevented from doing so). However, in a recent study of transport and construction, Wright (2011) argues that while gender and sexuality remain at the fore, the changing social attitudes of men which can make the workplaces slightly more accommodating for women compared with 20 years ago.

The situation for men who step into typically female-typed roles is far more positive. In such instances, men are more likely to find quicker progression up the hierarchy and considerable institutional support from managers. This has been described using the notion of the 'glass escalator' (Williams, 1992), conjuring up the image of a fast and assisted progression through the organisational hierarchy.

Women often have to take on 'male behaviour traits' (competitiveness, assertion, aggression, self-aggrandisement) in order to progress in male-dominated occupations because there are established norms which are fiercely protected by men. In this sense, successful women in male-dominated occupations often become 'honorary men' in the process of gaining acceptance, and downplay their difference (see Extract 10.5).

In contrast, men working in female-dominated occupations tend to be able to emphasise their different 'male behavioural traits' and are more successful in having these recognised by both co-workers and managers as bringing a fresh approach to the job. For instance, in her study of male librarians, cabin crew, primary school teachers and nurses, Simpson (2004) concluded that men benefit from their minority status in three ways:

- through assumptions of enhanced leadership abilities (the assumed authority effect);
- by being given differential treatment (the special consideration effect);
- by being associated with a more careerist attitude to work (the career effect).

In addition, men actively reinforce their difference from women (in the way they work) and emphasise masculine aspects of the role to ensure they are not stigmatised as effeminate (Lupton, 2000).

In summary, to progress in sex-atypical occupations, there is more need for a woman to be like a man than there is for a man to be like a woman. It might even be suggested that in promotion terms there is a positive advantage for a man in choosing a female-dominated occupation – although this needs to be moderated by the consideration that jobs traditionally designated as women's work tend to be undervalued in terms of skill content and consequently underpaid (as was discussed in Chapter 5).

Extract 10.6

Act like a man

Research on women in male-dominated occupations reveals how success is often dependent on the women complying with and adopting the dominant, masculine culture. This assimilation strategy can take a variety of forms and can be illustrated by the following quotes from successful professional women working in the male-dominated Canadian oil industry (Miller, 2004):

Geologist: How I perceived the men dealing with management was they would just say: 'this is the way things are'. They wouldn't say, 'these are the things we know, these are the things we don't know' which is what I tended to do. That didn't go over as well as far as getting money. So I

10.6 cont.

consciously decided that the way to approach management was to be like a man, to just come in and, whether you believed it or not, say, 'this is the way it is and we should drill here'. And the first time I did it, I was stupefied that it worked! (p. 64)

Engineer: They asked me if I knew any woman engineers, and I was a bit snarky and said, 'well, I know lots of mechanical engineers, and civil engineers, and chemical engineers, every kind of engineer, but I don't know a single, solitary person who has a degree in woman engineering' – I'm not a woman engineer, I'm an engineer – I'm an engineer first that just happens to have the body of a woman. (p. 65)

Manager: Never, ever, do I highlight that I'm a female. Never do I identify the fact that I'm a female, or different. There are a lot of power and politics at my level, and if you're male, you'd probably use that, but I don't use female power ploys. This is something else I've always done – I've got 13 people working directly for me, nearly all of them males, and if you asked me which ones are attractive, I'd have no idea – none. I think that really helps in that so many men work for me and none of them have a problem with it – it's never an issue. (p. 66)

Information systems specialist: You worked in a man's world, you really did – and you just sort of played that game, that's just the way it was. I mean it's not like you swore in meetings but you just kept the emotional side down. That's changed a lot in the last five years or so, you're allowed now to be emotional, well, not emotional, but you're allowed to have a personality, because of things like the Myers–Briggs Type Indicator (a widely used personality test).

Exercise 10.4

What do you think?

1. Identify and compare the different tactics of assimilation used by the four women in Extract 10.6.
2. Clearly these women have been successful, but what are the problems with adopting an assimilation strategy to cope with dominant male cultures?
3. Rather than assimilation, can you suggest an alternative strategy that might be used by women trying to break the glass ceiling?

Mapping the process

As can be seen, discrimination becomes more complex when it is applied to organisations. It can also be confusing because similar and different treatment can both ensure and deny fairness. To help clarify this, we can map the theoretical process behind discrimination decisions in organisations. The flowchart in Figure 10.1 shows the relationships between the concepts discussed in this section so far.

The critical group are the decision makers – typically managers at all levels. They have the power to exercise choices in line with their own beliefs and their own political agenda, although within constraints set by external pressures (e.g. legislation, public opinion and labour supply) and internal pressures (e.g. other managers, employees, trade unions, and key individuals such as the manager's own boss). This is similar to the strategic choice thesis suggested by Child

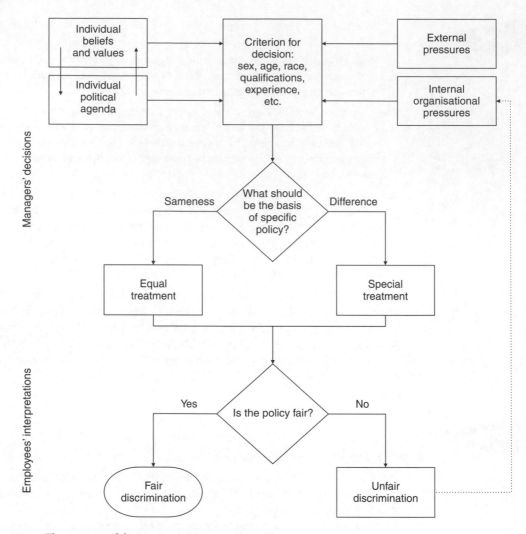

Figure 10.1   The process of discrimination in an organisation

(1972, 1997), which emphasises the political and ideological aspects of decision making by managers.

Figure 10.1 is only concerned with management decisions that directly affect other people (usually subordinates): for example, deciding whom to appoint, whom to allocate to a particular work task or team, whom to promote, whether to give someone a pay rise, whom to train, whom to make redundant and so on. In decisions such as these, important choices are made about which criteria to use to select and reject people.

As the earlier discussion highlighted, managers tend to identify a particular criterion and decide whether there should be equal treatment or special treatment; in other words, whether their policy is to be based on the principle of sameness or difference. To illustrate: in deciding upon whom to promote, senior managers might conclude that work experience with the firm is important whereas educational qualifications are not. In this case employees who have given many years of service to the firm will be looked on more favourably than newcomers (a policy based on difference leading to 'special treatment' with regard to work experience). Conversely, employees with a university degree will not be looked on more favourably than those without a degree (a policy based on sameness leading to 'equal treatment' with regard to educational qualification). A policy based on sameness or difference can be applied to any criterion, and the decision makers are the key actors in both identifying the criteria and relating a policy of sameness or difference to each criterion.

These choices made over criteria and policy are judged by other members of the organisation: people will be assessing whether discrimination is fair or unfair. If people feel there were justifiable criteria with an appropriate policy, they are likely to consider the practice fair (whether it is equal treatment or special treatment). Alternatively, if people consider unjustifiable criteria were used, or that a justifiable criterion had been distorted through an inappropriate policy, a perception of unfairness is likely to prevail. Such interpretations can be made by individuals or may be discussed by groups (e.g. work teams, trade unions, professionals, informal social cliques). For any policy or action associated with any criterion of discrimination there are likely to be different responses: some individuals and groups may interpret it as fair and others as unfair.

The extent to which people concern themselves with issues of fairness will vary according to the circumstances, and is likely to reflect whether they are directly involved with, or affected by, the outcome. The diagram does not reflect the power or the will of individuals and groups to take action, but when unfairness is perceived, this might lead to greater internal or external pressure to influence future decisions (represented by the feedback loop in Figure 10.1).

The flowchart indicates the relationships between various concepts that have been explored in this chapter so far and tries to capture the importance of structural constraints, agency (the choices of decision makers) and subjectivity (especially through the interpretation of discrimination). It is descriptive rather than normative. That is to say, it tries to show what *does* happen in the process of discrimination, rather than what *ought* to happen. It does not show *how* choice or action can affect the direction of interpretation (i.e. whether a policy is fair or unfair). Because discrimination is socially constructed it could not do this. This is an important point because it suggests that policy initiatives aimed at eliminating interpretations of unfair discrimination need to address the structural, political and moral issues.

From this analysis comes a clear message, but with a fuzzy response. The clear message is that where discrimination is perceived as unfair, it will lead to dissatisfaction. But the response to this has to be a fuzzy one because perception of unfairness depends on several factors, most notably:

- individual perspective;
- perceived appropriateness of the criterion of discrimination;
- individual and social acceptability of the type of treatment (special or equal).

To sum up

'Fairness' can sometimes mean equal treatment for everyone. In some circumstances though equal treatment undermines fairness (perhaps where people are disadvantaged through disability), and treating some people differently, or giving special treatment, might ensure fairness. This can lead to perceptions of unfairness or privilege though. The interpretation of fairness depends on whether the criterion is considered justifiable by individuals and social groups within the organisation.

Conclusion

This chapter has explored unfair discrimination and its consequences. It has highlighted the importance of understanding the meaning of discrimination and identifying the impact of stereotypes in constructing disadvantage for particular groups. In turn this means the realities of work (and access to work) differ considerably as a result of characteristics such as gender, ethnicity, disability and so forth. To view the workplace as being equally accommodating to all employees is naïve. In reviewing some of the research evidence concerning race and ethnicity, we have seen how disadvantage occurs within organisational processes resulting in an uneven and unfair distribution of social rewards such as a well-paid job, good promotion prospects and a work environment free from hostility or oppression. The wider policy questions of how to tackle the challenges of discrimination are beyond the remit of this particular chapter (although if you are interested in the more radical interventions suggested by one of the authors, see Noon 2010b and 2012). However we have explored how any intervention must rest upon an approach that accepts and combines the principles of sameness and difference.

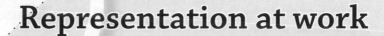

11

Representation at work

Chapter aim

To explore the nature of workers' collective representation and assess its significance for the employees involved.

Key concepts

▷ collective representation
▷ employee interests
▷ asymmetry of power
▷ frontier of control
▷ contested terrain
▷ trade unions
▷ union membership
▷ dual allegiance
▷ instrumentality
▷ solidarity
▷ union strategies

Learning outcomes

After reading and thinking about the material in this chapter, you will be able to:

1. Understand the logic behind employees seeking collective representation.
2. Identify the main factors accounting for union membership patterns, and how these operate at societal, organisational, workplace and individual levels.
3. Recognise the primary influence of instrumentality (self-interest) on employees' decision to become union members.
4. Identify the different priorities that union members have in relation to their representative organisation.
5. Assess whether union members can hold dual commitment to work organisation and union.
6. Evaluate the extent to which members think trade unions are effective on behalf of their members.

Introduction

Up to now we have considered the realities of work for employees either as individuals or as members of work groups. But in addition to being members of work teams, sections, departments and establishments in large or small organisations, workers combine into other collectives as part of their everyday work experience. The most common form this collectivism takes is membership of a trade union. Other collectives include professional associations, staff associations and various work-based clubs and societies. In this chapter, we focus particularly on trade union membership. This reflects the greater prominence of these organisations in industrial society, compared with other employee collective organisations, and also (reflecting this prominence) that there has been a great deal written about trade unions. The purpose of this chapter is to examine the nature of trade union membership more closely, to see how it casts further light on the different ways in which employees experience their working lives.

To do this, we begin by examining the rationale for trade unions, and in particular the reasoning underpinning employees' decisions to become or remain union members – and also their reasons for terminating union membership. Of particular concern are the main factors that encourage or inhibit people to join unions, and which help to explain patterns of union membership. We can point to several different levels of explanation because patterns of union membership can be understood in terms of individual, workgroup, organisation and societal factors.

Once we have identified the main factors influencing an employee's decision to join a trade union, we look at the related question of what priorities union members have in relation to their representative body, and how (and why) these priorities can change over time. An associated question here is whether workers think trade unions deliver on these priority areas, and whether overall they effectively represent their members' interests at work. One potential explanation for the decline in union membership and union influence in many (though not all) industrial countries since the early 1980s is a perceived failure by trade unions to deliver on member priorities.

In addition to issues relating to member views on their trade union, another question that has periodically been raised in studies of union membership is whether or not commitment to a union can coexist alongside commitment to the work organisation. The evidence on this is mixed, and we review the different arguments and findings.

Following examination of these issues surrounding patterns of membership and representation, we then consider the question of the future of employee representation: what the future may hold for individuals and their representative organisations, what trade unions are currently doing to try to shape a future that includes a more secure and influential union presence, and to what extent this mirrors employee views on representation. To conclude, we reflect on what this analysis of representation contributes to our overall assessment of the realities of work – and in particular how it further underlines the inadequacy of the portrayal of a single reality of work.

Joining a collective

Why should an employee consider joining a collective organisation? The answer to this in part depends on the nature of that collective group:

- Individual employees may join and remain members of a professional association because it is only through membership that they retain their professional registration. For example, all practising clinical psychologists must be members of the British Psychological Association.
- Employees may become members of a staff association automatically if their employing organisation supports such an association. So, on appointment, new employees also become members of the staff association. The staff association may represent employee opinion on joint committees with management, as well as organising social and other events for employees.
- Joining a trade union – our main focus in this chapter – more explicitly reflects a decision to become part of a body that provides collective and independent representation of employee interests.

The decision to seek collective representation by joining a trade union can be seen to reflect three key features about employees' identification of their interests at work:

1. *A recognition that the interests of employer and employees are not identical.* If the interests of the two were seen by the employee as identical, there would be no need for separate representation to that offered by the employing organisation. Employees would rest comfortably in the knowledge that because their interests were commonly shared with the employer, the latter would always and inevitably act in the interests of the employee – there could be no possibility of any alternative.

   In practice, however, while employer and employee can be seen to share various interests (such as, in most circumstances, the survival of the organisation), they also hold a number of distinct interests. This separation of interests can be identified, for example, in relation to the distribution of rewards. Management and the workforce are likely to differ in terms of their views on how any profit should be distributed among shareholders, managers and non-managerial grades. A similar separation of interests can be identified in relation to the expenditure of effort, or attitudes to designated work-time periods. From an employer's point of view, their interest lies in employees expending effort consistently over the whole of the working period, and defining that working period as the entire time that the individual is contracted to work.

   As we discussed in Chapters 4 and 9, however, employees may pursue a separate interest by covertly creating spells of reduced effort or unofficial rest periods, in order to survive a monotonous or arduous work regime – or even in some cases to protect the very job itself, where greater effort might lead to the work being divided between fewer staff. Part of the rationale for joining a trade union springs from a desire among employees to challenge the management rationality and give expression to aspects of a workers' counter-rationality (see Extract 11.1 for employee views on whether they share interests with management; and Exercise 11.1 which also relates to this question of the extent of shared interests).

In aspects of work such as work pace, work allocation and the way in which work tasks are performed, we can use the idea of a 'frontier of control' between management and employee rationalities/logics. Like other frontiers or borders throughout history, this frontier in the workplace is periodically subject to challenge by management or unions. Ground is gained and conceded, and the two parties use power, strategy and tactics to seek territorial advantage. The fact this frontier exists, and that it represents what Edwards (1979) terms a 'contested terrain' between management and workforce symbolises both the existence and importance of distinct interests in the workplace. The idea of a frontier of control also links to issues we have discussed in previous chapters relating to the realities of work. If we study the various meanings given to work, or issues of fairness and disadvantage, or constructions of skill, and other topics to do with control of the labour process, it is not long before we see differences between the interests of management and employees.

Extract 11.1

Shared interests?

In a study of workers in four sites manufacturing tinplate, two in the UK (at Ebbw Vale and Trostre, both in south Wales), one in the Netherlands (at Ijmuiden, west of Amsterdam) and a smaller plant in Norway (in Bergen on the Norwegian west coast), a representative sample of employees (a 20 per cent sample at each plant) were asked whether they agreed or disagreed with the statement that managers and workers in their organisation shared the same interests. As the table below shows, in each case only a minority of workers thought that the interests of the two groups were shared. Less than one in four of the Dutch sample thought so, compared with just over a third of the Welsh respondents and two in five of the Norwegian employees.

Identification of shared interests with management

Respondents who agreed that 'Management have the same interests as workers in the business'

UK (n = 154)	Netherlands (n = 150)	Norway (n = 38)
36%	24%	42%

Source: P. Blyton and N. Bacon, Unpublished report of findings of *Corus Packaging Plus Values Survey* (2001).

What do you think?

1. Score the issues listed below using the following scale ranging from (1) if you think managers and workers share identical interests through to (5) if you think they have partial or wholly separate interests. Give each issue a score from 1 to 5.

1	2	3	4	5
Share identical interests				Have completely separate interests

- health and safety standards
- basic pay
- introducing new technology
- levels of overtime working
- bonus payments
- flexible working hours
- equal opportunities
- company share price
- developing new products/services
- redundancy

2. Briefly explain the score you give to each issue.

2. We said earlier that the case for collective representation reflects three features relating to employees' identification of their interests. The first of these (above) is fairly straightforward: employee and employer interests sometimes diverge. The second is related to this, but is slightly more theoretical. *Trade unions exist because there is an asymmetry (imbalance or inequality) of power between employer and employee.*

   This lack of symmetry in the eyes of the employee is enough justification to seek to redress this power imbalance (to 'even things up') by combining with other employees. We said this was related to the first point (that employee and employer interests sometimes diverge), but it is crucial to emphasise that divergent interests alone are not enough to explain the case for, or rationale for, trade unions. There also has to be an imbalance in power.

   If employees saw their interests as distinct from those of the employer, but felt that power in the employment relationship was equal, then there would be less of a case for collective representation. If we imagine that there was no power imbalance (i.e. that employees were as powerful in the employment relationship as employers) then trade unions would not be needed because employees would feel able to represent themselves effectively in negotiations with management (over pay, time, working conditions, etc.). Even if we imagine trade unions still existed, their role would most likely be very different in that union membership would become a strategy of gaining dominant power over the employer (rather than an equality of power) and creating considerable advantage in determining the distribution of rewards.

In practice though, in the vast majority of workplaces, there is no prospect of equal distribution of power in the employment relationship. Almost universally, an asymmetry of power exists in favour of the employer – and is expressed in their ultimate power to hire and fire.

3. The third feature relating to the case for collective representation and employees' identification of their interests can be expressed more simply. *Joining together in a trade union shows that employees hold sufficient interests in common as to make membership of a common organisation both possible and desirable.* Employees are unlikely to believe that all their interests are shared with the interests of all of the rest of the union membership. Even so, they may join and remain part of a union because they believe their interests overlap sufficiently to allow common membership and a joint pursuit of objectives. Membership is a voluntary alliance of employees who recognise the benefits of having their interests represented collectively.

To sum up

Becoming a member of a trade union is (i) a recognition that employee and employer interests can diverge, (ii) a desire to redress a power imbalance in the employment relationship and (iii) expression of a common belief held alongside other employees – that the trade union is an appropriate vehicle to pursue their shared interests.

Reasons for membership

Explaining why employees become and remain trade union members has long been an area of interest for economists, industrial relations researchers, sociologists and social psychologists. Typically, economists have dealt with more macro, economy-level factors (e.g. overall levels of unemployment, political and legal frameworks for employee relations); industrial relations researchers have considered organisational and workplace-level contexts (e.g. whether work is particularly dangerous or demanding, the attitudes of management to trade unions); and sociologists and social psychologists have looked at work group and individual-level reasons for joining (e.g. levels of pay or job dissatisfaction, the psychological contract) (see Figure 11.1).

Societal-level factors

Our main concern in this chapter is with employees and their immediate work context because we believe these levels are the most informative about the individual's own experience of work. Before considering these, however, it is useful to note broader, macro-level influences on union membership patterns. These point, for example, to the influence of business cycles, levels of unemployment and longer-term economic 'waves' on levels of union membership (Bain and Elsheikh, 1976; Booth, 1983; Carruth and Disney, 1988; Kelly and Waddington,

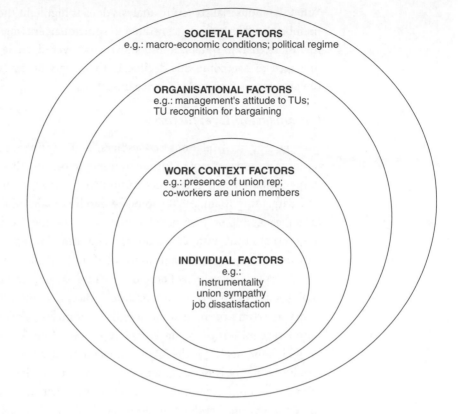

Figure 11.1   Levels of influence on TU membership decisions

1995). Also significant are the effects of government policies and laws favourable or unfavourable to trade unions (Freeman and Pelletier, 1990; Turner and D'Art, 2012); as well as broad changes in industrial and occupational structures (Green, 1992).

Much discussion has been focused on the last of these, and in particular on the impact of a decline in employment in industries where trade unionism has traditionally been strong (coal, steel, shipbuilding and other parts of manufacturing, for example). Alongside this decline has been a rise in other industries, notably private sector, service activities. Here trade unionism has not become well established. This explanation for the decline in union membership has been called the 'mountain gorilla hypothesis'. This is that the reduction in the 'natural habitat' of trade unions (traditional manufacturing industries) has led to a decline in the species (trade union members) – in the same way that the decline in the natural habitat of the mountain gorilla has meant a reduction in its population (Blyton and Turnbull, 2004: 141).

At the same time, as various writers have pointed out, this argument about changes in industrial structure does more to *describe* what has happened to union membership than to *explain* it. There is no inevitable reason that union membership will automatically decline with the growth of service employment and the decline in manufacturing jobs (Kelly, 1990; Blyton and Turnbull, 2004: 142).

What the industrial structure analysis does is highlight the extent to which union membership has been concentrated in some quarters (manufacturing, public sector) more than in others. It also shows that overall, trade unions have not as yet managed to overcome this decline in their 'habitat' by large-scale expansion in the growing private sector service industries.

Organisation-level factors

Among industrial relations researchers, a key influence on union membership patterns is management's attitude to trade unionism. This is reflected particularly in their willingness to grant 'recognition' to a union for purposes of representation and bargaining (Bain, 1970); some research has also examined the influence of union leadership on member attitudes (see Hammer Bayazit and Wazeter, 2009). In granting a trade union (or unions) recognition for representation and collective bargaining, employing organisations agree to treat the union as the representative voice of specified groups of employees. They then negotiate with that union over changes in overall terms and conditions of employment (e.g. pay rates, working hours, overtime payments and length of holidays). For Metcalf (1991: 19), this union recognition by management represents 'the fulcrum [point of leverage] on which the health of the labour movement turns'. This is because it signals to employees not only management's willingness to work with trade unions, but also the access to representation and involvement that the trade union enjoys within the organisation. Bryson and Gomez's (2005) study indicates the importance of union recognition in explaining patterns of 'never-membership' – that is, those workers who have never joined a trade union.

In the past, public sector organisations have been particularly noted for recognising trade unions and for developing extensive joint union–management machinery for consultation and negotiation. This acceptance of the role of trade unions has been a key variable in bringing about high levels of union membership in public sector organisations in many countries (Blyton and Turnbull, 2004). Turner and D'Art (2012) in their analysis of European-wide survey data also show the positive effect that a union-friendly regime has on citizens' support for trade unions (see also Scheuer, 2011 for a cross-Europe review of union membership, and Visser, 2006, for a review of union membership across 24 countries).

Exercise 11.2

What do you think?

1. What advantages may there be for employers in granting a trade union recognition?
2. What disadvantages for the employing organisation could there be in taking this step?

These societal and organisation-level analyses are useful when discussing overall trends in union membership and union density ('union density' is the proportion of potential members who are actual union members). However, they are less useful in explaining the decisions of individual employees to join (or not join), and to remain in (or leave) a trade union. For those concerned with these aspects of individual behaviour, their analysis concentrates on the immediate work context, and on individual attitudes towards trade unions.

Local work context factors

Within the immediate work context, the two key factors that appear to influence decisions to join a union are: (i) whether there is a trade union representative present, and (ii) whether or not other work colleagues are union members. The finding on the first of these is that one of the main reasons employees do not join unions is that they have not been asked to join. If asked, many join. Contact by a trade union representative appears crucial to many employees' decision to join. In those workplaces where union representatives are both present and devote more time to union activities (and thus are presumably more visible in their union role), they are more likely to recruit new members than representatives who spend less time performing their union duties (Cully et al, 2000: 204; see also Prowse and Prowse, 2006). Waddington and Whitston (1997: 529), in a wide-ranging membership survey of 12 UK unions, similarly identify the important role of local union representatives in recruitment (see also Waddington and Kerr, 2009). Likewise, Peetz (1998: 36) cites a number of Australian and other studies where lack of contact by the union was found to be a factor in low union recruitment.

In the last Workplace Employment Relations Survey (WERS) investigation in the UK, just over two-thirds (68%) of workplaces had recognised unions in which union members had access to a representative (Kersley et al, 2005). Among these union representatives, 43 per cent spent five hours or more per week on representative duties. Over three-quarters (77%) of representatives indicated they had spent time seeking to recruit new members during the previous year (ibid: 14, 15).

In relation to the second work context factor – whether or not work colleagues are union members – earlier British Social Attitudes Survey data discussed by Millward (1990) shows that the reason of 'most of my colleagues are members' was expressed by over half of the sample as an important factor in joining a union (see Prowse and Prowse, 2006, for a more recent study that underlines the importance of whether colleagues are union members in an individual's decision to join). In practice, this relationship between work colleagues' membership and the employee's own decision to join may have two aspects to it:

- Employees in unionised environments may feel uncomfortable being 'free riders' – that is, someone who enjoys many of the benefits of trade unionism such as negotiated pay increases without actually joining the union. In these circumstances, the non-members may feel under some pressure to join the union themselves. Peetz (1998: 34), in his analysis of factors accounting for why people join unions in Australia, for example, notes 'peer pressure' acting in some settings as an influence on why people join.

- Individuals may wish to become a union member like the others as a way of expressing solidarity and a common interest with their fellow workers.

Individual factors

In terms of individual factors, more attention has been given to explaining why people join unions rather than why they remain members or terminate their membership. Somewhat paradoxically, rather than look explicitly at joining behaviour, many of the studies in this area have studied people already belonging to trade unions and attempt to establish what factors led them to join. Summarising Klandermans (1986), Guest and Dewe (1988), Charlwood (2002) and others, the most common sets of individual factors associated with joining can be grouped in three categories. We outline these below and then consider their relative importance:

1. *Job dissatisfaction.* Various studies have identified a relationship between job dissatisfaction and union membership (see, for example, the discussion in Wheeler and McClendon, 1991, and Charlwood, 2002). Overall, most emphasis has tended to be placed on dissatisfaction with pay and benefits as associated with a decision to join a union (Wheeler and McClendon, 1991: 61). In addition, however, some studies have pointed to a broader range of areas of dissatisfaction which may be associated with union membership: for example, Guest and Dewe (1988) found an association between membership and dissatisfaction with opportunities for involvement in decision making.

2. *Instrumentality.* To describe someone as being instrumental, we mean they act in their self-interest, according to a kind of calculation about what brings them the most personal benefit. Clearly, some people will be motivated to join a trade union because they believe the benefits of union membership to them personally will outweigh any costs associated with that membership. Benefits centre on aspects such as improved job protection as a result of union membership, negotiated improvements in pay and conditions, and access to union representation and advice if disciplinary cases or threat of redundancy arises. There are also other benefits relating to different union services, which may range from financial advice to discounts on a variety of goods and services. Anticipated benefits tend to be of two kinds: actual benefits such as the access to union services, and potential or 'insurance' benefits for which the union can be called upon if needed, such as advice or representation. These actual and potential benefits must be weighed against the costs of membership: most directly the costs of subscriptions, but also potentially other, indirect costs that might be incurred if an employer is hostile or unsympathetic to trade union activity, or if the union is also campaigning on issues that the individual member does not favour (perhaps calling for strike action that results in a loss of pay).

3. *Solidarity or union sympathy.* These reasons for joining reflect that an individual is becoming a trade union member because of, 'a belief that joining a union is...a natural thing to do' (Guest and Dewe, 1988: 180). This positive orientation to trade unionism may be the result of socialisation (becoming

inducted into a group), such as growing up in a household where union membership was valued. Alternatively it could be a subsequent ideological orientation (an ideology is a value-based way of looking at the world). This latter orientation may derive from the experience of work itself – for example, recognising the value of trade unions by witnessing their activities at first hand within the workplace.

The significance of different individual factors

Given these three different categories of individual reasons why employees might join a union, what does the evidence show to be the most important of these reasons? We have the benefit of data on this question from the UK, Australia and the United States, and most of this data points to the primacy of instrumental reasons. Looking at the UK first, Millward (1990: 34), for example, reports British Social Attitudes Survey data showing that in a list of reasons given for joining a union, instrumental reasons – 'protection' and 'negotiating better pay and conditions' – held first and second positions. These were followed by union sympathy reasons, such as belief in unions in principle and support for colleagues. A study in the UK which explicitly examined the relative importance of the three categories (job dissatisfaction, instrumentality and belief in unions) also found that instrumental reasons were the most influential in employees' decision to belong to a union (Guest and Dewe, 1988).

Job dissatisfaction was identified as a secondary influence, while solidarity with unionism accounted for only a very small element in employees' decisions. In their study of new members in 12 UK trade unions, Waddington and Whitston (1997: 521) also found instrumental reasons for joining to be the most prominent, much ahead of union sympathy reasons.

Of the minority who did identify union sympathy reasons, these were more likely to be older rather than younger workers and full-time rather than part-time workers (ibid: 527–8). Charlwood (2002), in a later analysis of British Social Attitudes Survey data, finds support for instrumentality as the primary reason for union membership, with job dissatisfaction and left-leaning political views representing secondary influences.

This general pattern of findings is also evident in Australian survey data reported by Peetz (1998: 32–5), which similarly identifies instrumental reasons (in the form of protection and advice offered by unions) as the most commonly stated reasons for belonging to a union. Ideological reasons were expressed by only a small proportion (less than one in ten) of the Australian sample (job dissatisfaction reasons were not measured in the survey). A further significant reason for belonging to a union in Australia was given as union membership being compulsory at the employee's workplace (Peetz, 1998: 32). This used also to be a factor significant in a proportion of UK organisations until a series of legislative changes, and in particular the 1990 Employment Act, removed any compulsory requirement for union membership.

Reviewing studies undertaken both in the United States and elsewhere on this question of union membership decisions, Wheeler and McClendon (1991) also identify instrumentality as a key factor. This was particularly evident in studies outside the United States, while inside the United States instrumentality appears to represent one of several influential variables (with others including job dissatisfaction, belief in unions and nature of the job). Summarising their review by quoting Adams (1974), the authors conclude that outside the United States in particular, 'self interest is more in evidence than is solidarity' and if anything 'this tendency would appear to be on the rise' (Wheeler and McClendon, 1991: 73).

Exercise 11.3

What do you think?

1. The evidence from different countries indicates the dominance of instrumental reasons in union joining decisions. Why do you think this is?
2. Research suggests that self-interested, instrumental reasons for joining a trade union may be on the rise. Why do you think this may be the case?
3. Why do you think only minorities of people appear to join trade unions for solidaristic reasons?

We can gain insight into this topic by asking why people join a union, but we can also do this by asking employees why they have not joined a union. Here, both individual and workplace factors again feature. In the Australian data discussed by Peetz (1998: 35–8), for example, the most frequent reason given for not joining a union was an instrumental one: specifically, a perceived lack of gain from becoming a member, because of the absence of union influence or effectiveness. Likewise, in the British Social Attitudes Survey data, while many of those asked were unable to identify any strong reason for not having joined a union, of those who could state a reason, the instrumental response of 'I can't see any advantage in joining' was the most prominent (cited by 28% of non-members as a 'fairly important' or 'very important' reason for not having joined) (Millward, 1990; see also Bryson and Gomez, 2005).

To sum up

Factors influencing union membership patterns can be identified at societal, organisational, workgroup and individual levels. For individuals, the decision to join appears particularly affected by whether their work colleagues are members, whether they have been asked to join by a union representative, and whether they recognise a personal benefit from being a union member.

What do employees want from their union membership?

If union members predominantly hold an instrumental orientation towards union membership, this raises the question of what instrumental priorities they have in relation to their representative organisation. One source of information on member priorities in the UK has been the British Social Attitudes Survey. Questions in this survey provide not only an indication of the main priorities, but also how these indicate a pattern of continuity and change over time. For example, in the later 1980s, trade union members were emphasising the primacy of economic concerns in their priorities for unions – in particular, improving pay and conditions and protecting jobs – with a secondary priority being given to areas such as equity issues and having a greater 'voice' in decision making within the work organisation (Millward, 1990: 37).

However, by the 1990s, the relative weight attached to these priorities had shifted somewhat because of changes in the economic context and increased threats of redundancy. We might expect similar changes in the wake of the 2008 (ongoing) Global Financial Crisis. In the 1990s, union members were placing much greater emphasis on the need for unions to protect jobs, as a result pushing other issues such as improving pay and conditions down the list of priorities (Bryson and McKay, 1997: 37). Prior to the GFC, issues of pay and particularly pensions became increasingly prominent concerns for union members, as employers both proposed and implemented changes to pension and retirement terms as a means to reduce the cost of pension schemes.

We can gain more insight into members' beliefs about priorities for unions by considering their views on which issues they feel unions should be involved in, compared with those they feel are better left to employees to deal with. In an earlier WERS (1998) survey, for example, employees were asked about who they thought should deal with a series of different issues (Cully et al 2000: 211). Members were most strongly in favour of their union being involved with pay issues, together with disciplinary issues. When it came to 'dealing with complaints about work' however, union members were equally split between viewing the union as the best means of pursuing the issue, and dealing with it themselves. Union members appeared to see pay and disciplinary questions as ones where collective representation was appropriate, but many perceived specific work-related complaints as more of an individual issue.

Exercise 11.4

What do you think?

If you have been a member of a trade union in the past (or are currently a member), answer question 1. If you have not, answer question 2.

1. **a.** What were the main things that you wanted from your union membership? List up to three in their order of priority.
   b. Overall, how well did (does) your union satisfy these priorities? If the union has not fully satisfied your priorities, what do you think are the main reasons for this?

2. **a.** Have you ever had the opportunity to join a trade union? If so, why did you not join?
   b. What would you want from union membership that would encourage you to join a trade union in the future?
   c. Do you think you would join a union if there were one recognised at your workplace? Why/why not?

Dual commitment to employer and union

One recurring question in relation to union membership is whether or not union members can have 'dual allegiance' to their employer and their union. Can they be committed and loyal to both organisations simultaneously? Or, will their commitment be 'zero-sum' (with commitment to one only possible at the expense of commitment to the other)? This question was the subject of a number of studies in the 1950s (e.g. Dean, 1954; Kerr, 1954; Purcell, 1954) when unionism was expanding in the United States. It was returned to in the UK in the late 1970s, a period of considerable increase in white-collar unionism (Blyton, Nicholson and Ursell, 1981; Nicholson, Ursell and Blyton, 1981). Subsequently, this question attracted further interest in North America in the 1980s (e.g. Angle and Perry, 1986); and elsewhere in the 1990s (Deery, Iverson and Erwin, 1994; Guest and Dewe, 1991); and 2000s (Redman and Snape, 2005). Interest in this question during the 2000s was partly because of a continuing debate about whether trade unionism and 'human resource management (HRM)' are compatible (Guest, 1989).

The early studies indicated dual allegiance was indeed possible, with workers clearly able to express commitment to both union and company. This was found to be particularly the case where industrial relations were pursued in an atmosphere of cooperation (Rosen, 1954). Similarly in UK studies of white-collar workers, dual allegiance was also evident, with employees who had senior positions in local authorities appearing to experience little difficulty in simultaneously undertaking active union roles (Blyton et al 1981).

Subsequently, however, the findings have been more mixed. Studies in the United States continued to show evidence of dual commitment (e.g. Angle and Perry, 1986; Beauvais, Scholl and Cooper, 1990; Magenau, Martin and Peterson, 1988). Similarly, a study of unionised workers in a food-processing plant and a civil service department in the UK found a positive relationship between commitment to the work organisation and commitment to the union (Redman and Snape, 2005: 309, 319).

However, other researches in Australia and the UK have found different results. In a study of white-collar public service workers in Australia, Deery, Iverson and Erwin (1994) found no evidence of dual commitment. While they identified commitment to the work organisation as being associated with such factors as job satisfaction and feelings of autonomy, these factors were unrelated to union commitment. In Guest and Dewe's (1991) study of UK electronic engineering workers, a majority appeared to identify with *neither* company nor union – a finding the authors explain partly in terms of employee dissatisfaction with both organisations. A more contemporary study by Robinson et al (2012) applies the concept of dual allegiance in a study of 2,568 unionised South Korean electronics employees. They conclude that employees who express dual allegiance (rather than just allegiance to the union) also say they are more likely to remain working for an organisation. Robinson et al's study can be taken as evidence that for some employees dual allegiance (to employer and union) is possible, and even beneficial to the employer. For other employees though, it seems commitment may be closer to zero-sum (i.e. they are committed either to the employer or to union).

Other evidence lends support to Guest and Dewe's finding – that most employees identify with neither employer nor union, suggesting that some writers may make too much of the issue of dual allegiance, or at least that dual allegiance may not be an issue in some contexts. There is evidence to indicate that, overall, members' commitment to their union is generally weak. This is reflected, for example, in the low average attendance at union branch meetings, and the difficulty that unions frequently have in securing enough candidates to hold elections for union representative posts. In general, union members do not demonstrate a high level of union consciousness, or what Blackburn and Prandy (1965) call 'unionateness' (see also Prandy, Blackburn and Stewart, 1974).

Levels of commitment to a union may vary in relation to different activities – for instance, members may be willing to express loyalty and general belief in unions, but be less willing to challenge fundamentally employer power – for instance, by taking strike action or organising a decrease in productivity. Monnot, Wagner and Beehr (2011) describe this in terms of differences between 'militant and nonmilitant union participation', and in a very wide-ranging review of 126 studies and 70,000 participants, identify different factors that may make members more or less militant. Interestingly, they suggest that participation in more militant activity is more likely where workers are 'blue-collar' rather than 'white-collar'. This supports the idea that trade unions exist to address imbalances of power in the employment relationship, and that trade unions are likely to be needed where employee and employer interests diverge. In other words, it links to our discussion of three features of employee interests (above). Monnot et al (2011: 1139) explain the lower incidence or likelihood of militant behaviour among white-collar workers in this way:

> White collar employees have more resources to leverage and also a greater stake in the success of the organization...which may explain the stronger relationship between commitment and nonmilitant participation and the weaker relationship between commitment and militant participation. They are already receiving more resources from the organization than many blue collar workers, and they therefore might feel they have more to lose by striking. They also may feel that they do not need to take such militant action to achieve their goals if they have more influence within the organization than blue collar workers do. Just having a union may make them feel they are protected, and therefore they might view serving the union by nonmilitant participation as adequate.

To sum up

Many union members appear to experience little difficulty in simultaneously maintaining their roles of union member and employee. In the past this has been identified as evidence of employees' ability to maintain a dual allegiance to union and employer. However, it may also reflect a low level of commitment to one or both of these organisations. Commitment, and the extent of participation in union activities, can also depend on the extent to which the interests of different groups of employees diverge from those of their employer, and the relative power of groups of employees.

Do members think trade unions deliver?

The finding that other things being equal, terms and conditions of employment are better in unionised than non-unionised establishments suggests that trade unions deliver in terms of effectively representing members' interests on key elements of the employment contract (Freeman and Medoff, 1984). Many employees remain members of a trade union throughout their working lives which also suggests a widespread perception of the net benefit of union membership. However, other evidence reveals a more varied picture of employees' assessment of trade union representation.

Most notably, there is the stark evidence of the widespread decline in trade union membership in many industrial societies since the 1980s. Traxler, Blaschke and Kittel (2001: 82), for example, note marked falls in membership density between 1980 and 1995 in countries such as New Zealand, Australia, the UK, Ireland, Italy and Portugal, with smaller falls in density levels in many other countries including Belgium, France, Germany, Japan, the Netherlands, Switzerland and the United States (see also Visser, 2006; and Scheuer, 2011). Various reasons account for the decline, but whatever the contributory factors, a diminishing proportion of employees are union members. It is not that trade unions have failed to recruit over this period; it is simply that they have not recruited at a rate sufficient to overcome members' leaving (referred to as membership turnover). In the UK this has been estimated to be around 12 per cent per annum, though in some sectors such as retail, membership turnover rates are much higher; see Cully and Woodland, 1998; also Metcalf, 1991: 22).

From a variety of sources, we can piece together a picture of whether the unions are seen to be doing a good job, on what issues, and overall, whether their presence in the workplace makes a difference. In general (not surprisingly, perhaps), members of trade unions are more positive about the overall effect of trade unions than non-members, or those who formerly were members but have given up their membership. But union members are not overwhelmingly positive about the effect of unions. In the WERS 1998 sample, for example, approaching half (46%) of union members thought trade unions made a difference to what it is like at work, compared with three out of ten (30%) of non-union members and just over one-quarter (26%) of ex-union members (Cully et al 2000: 212–13). Significantly, those working in establishments where union density was highest (where a higher proportion of the workforce was unionised) were more likely to believe unions made a difference (we return to this below).

A generally similar picture is revealed by British Social Attitudes Survey data, in which employees in unionised (and non-unionised) workplaces were asked whether their workplace would be better or worse if the union ceased to exist (or if a union was introduced) (Bryson, 1999). In the unionised workplaces, while almost half (49%) of employees thought that removal of the union would make the workplace worse, a substantial minority (40%) thought the union's removal would make no difference. In non-unionised workplaces, a clear majority (65%) thought the introduction of a union would make no difference. Findings such as these would not surprise those who argue that trade unions have traditionally not had policies that serve the interests of women (Colling and Dickens, 2001), part-time workers (Walker, 2002) and ethnic minorities (Noon and Hoque, 2001; Wrench, 1987) – see Extract 11.2.

Extract 11.2

Are trade unions failing ethnic minorities?

Noon and Hoque (2001) examined whether unions were delivering effective interest representation for ethnic minority employees in an analysis of the UK 1998 Workplace Employee Relations Survey. Responses from 23,853 employees covering 1,880 workplaces were compared to assess whether there were significant differences between white and ethnic minority employees in terms of training, promotion, job performance and pay. The results show some notable differences which suggest inequality was occurring. Of particular concern is the apparent ineffectiveness of trade unions. Their analysis suggested:

- evidence of inequality between white employees and employees from minority ethnic groups in unionised workplaces.
- less evidence of inequality between white employees and employees from minority ethnic groups in non-unionised workplaces.
- employees from minority ethnic groups in unionised workplaces did not appear to receive better treatment than employees from minority ethnic groups in non-unionised workplaces.
- white employees in unionised workplaces appeared to receive better treatment than white employees in non-unionised workplaces.

The analysis also includes a comparison of men and women, and suggests that women from minority ethnic groups suffer the greatest inequality. Not only do they appear to receive less favourable treatment than white men and women, in some instances they also receive poorer treatment than men from minority ethnic groups.

The authors conclude that the results, 'add to the criticisms sometimes made of trade unions that equal opportunities for ethnic minorities are not high on their list of priorities. For union policy-makers [such findings] should raise questions about the appropriateness and inclusiveness of their current representation of ethnic minorities. The implication must be that the relevance of trade unionism to ethnic minorities diminishes if unions cannot ensure equal treatment' (Noon and Hoque, 2001: 114).

One factor that might explain why union members (and even more, non-members) fail to identify the union as making a difference in the workplace could be their perception that unions lack power in their dealings with management. In the WERS 1998 sample, only just over half (52%) of union members thought that unions were taken seriously by management, and smaller proportions of non-members and ex-members thought so (Cully et al, 2000: 213). This perception of a lack of influence increased following the decline in membership levels in the 1980s and 1990s. In the British Social Attitudes Survey, for example, the proportion indicating that 'unions have too little power' more than doubled between the mid-1980s (when one in ten thought unions had too little power) and the mid-1990s (when one in four held this view) (Bryson and McKay, 1997: 35). By the 2000s, a clear majority (72%) in a Europe-wide survey identified a need for strong trade unions to protect their pay and working conditions (Turner and D'Art, 2012).

Also relevant here is the related question of the extent to which members think that the union effectively represents their interests. In their study of employees in the electronics industry, for example, Guest and Dewe (1991) found that union members were clear that the union was the best representative of their interests on wage-related matters. Yet on other traditional issues for unions (such as job security and working conditions), a higher proportion of union members thought that senior management or their immediate boss better represented their interests than the union (ibid: 82). This tendency was even more pronounced in relation to areas such as staffing levels, overtime, introduction of new equipment, work transfer and work organisation. In these areas, only small proportions of union members saw their union representatives as best representing their interests, compared with their immediate boss or senior management.

Overall, the assessment of representation by trade unions is a mixed one. While those in unions are more likely to view union presence as making a difference, even among this group there is a substantial proportion who disagree. If one of the factors influencing these attitudes is a perceived weakness of unions in their dealings with management, then a 'vicious circle' of union presence is possible (see Figure 11.2). Among the WERS respondents, for example, where there were

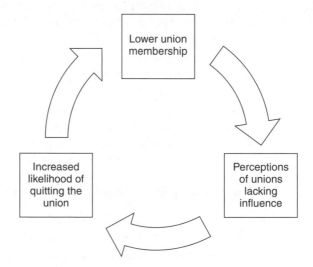

Figure 11.2 The vicious circle of union presence

fewer union members, these members were also less likely to view the union as influential (Cully et al 2000: 212). Individual decisions to quit the union because of a perceived lack of influence are likely to drive down perceived union influence even more, potentially leading to further membership losses. And, a trade union, as a collective body, is only strong because of its members.

To sum up

The picture of whether members think their union effectively represents their interests is mixed. Members are more likely than not to think that unions effectively represent them on issues such as pay and job security, but substantial minorities of members (and a majority of non-members) think the union is not effective in representing them on a wide variety of issues. Partly this reflects a perceived weakness of trade unions in relation to management, resulting in many seeing the union as making little difference in the workplace.

The future of union representation

The question of what the future holds for trade unions has been the focus of much conjecture, as recent research on trade union renewal suggests (Dibben, 2010; Hickey, Kuruvilla and Lakhani, 2010). Widespread decline in union membership, changes in the nature of workforce composition, changes in management's approach to dealing with its 'human resources' directly rather than through union representatives, and even the question of whether society is becoming more individualistic and less communal or collective in character, have all led researchers to ask whether unions are 'withering away' – past their 'sell-by' date and in terminal decline.

At the same time, other evidence suggests that pronouncements on the death of trade unions may be premature. Three issues are particularly worth noting:

- Trade unions have been in difficult positions before in terms of membership losses (such as the 1930s) and subsequently have revived. Overall, unions have shown themselves to be more capable of adapting to changed circumstances than their critics would acknowledge. This past experience has been seen by some as part of a cyclical experience among trade unions and illustrating their evolutionary character: unions periodically adapt to new environments created by changes such as those noted above (for a relevant discussion, see Hyman, 1999). The question remains, however, whether the changes currently being experienced are of a scale and diversity that make them qualitatively different from what has gone before. Is it possible, for example, that changes as a result of the Global Financial Crisis mean previous successful evolutionary changes by unions are no guarantee of being able to survive now.

- Recent declines in union membership notwithstanding, many millions of employees in industrial economies (as well as industrialising countries) continue to be members of unions (Monnot et al, 2011). What is more, the decline that has taken place has not occurred uniformly across all countries and sectors. Indeed, not only have some countries not recorded a decline in union membership, but some have also actually registered a counter-trend, with increases in union membership levels. Denmark, Finland and Sweden all recorded increases in union density levels between 1980 and 2003 (Visser, 2006).

- As well as these counter-trends, there is evidence that membership density levels may be somewhat stabilising in recent years; increased union organising and membership campaigns have played a significant part in this (Heery, Healy and Taylor, 2004; Healy, Heery, Taylor and Brown, 2004). In the UK, patterns may change if proposals suggested by the coalition government in terms of deregulation, reforms to the tribunal system, and legislation on unfair dismissal tilt the balance of power further towards the employer (Hodgkins, 2010). This could encourage more people to unionise, though the context is one where unemployment is high, and where wages are not increasing at the same rate as the cost of living meaning many people are getting poorer and at the same time are afraid of losing their jobs.

Union strategies

The academic debate on trade union revival has broadly taken place along two dimensions, relating separately to questions of union strategy towards employers and towards actual and potential members.

In relation to employers, a central issue has revolved around whether unions should (a) develop their influence by entering more partnership relations with employers, giving up adversarial relations in favour of more consensual relations designed to produce 'mutual gains' (Kochan and Osterman, 1994); or (b) adopt a more adversarial, militant approach to employers – protecting member interests by a more explicit recognition of the separation of those interests from those of the employer (Kelly, 1996).

Exercise 11.5

What do you think?

Those favouring closer social partnership for unions in their dealings with management argue that this is a way for trade unions to recover their position and gain greater involvement in the workplace. This involvement is seen, in turn, as a way of demonstrating to members and potential members the relevance of the union within the work organisation – and thus the value of joining or retaining union membership.

Those favouring a more militant approach by unions argue in contrast that the social partnership route is likely to create weak and ineffective unions by eroding their capacity to resist management and adopt an independent position. As a result of this weakness, members may become apathetic (disinterested), reducing the capacity of unions to mobilise the membership for any form of concerted action.

1. Overall, which strategy do you think trade unions should follow to expand their influence and membership appeal: partnership or militancy? Explain your reasoning.

2. Are there circumstances where one strategy would be more appropriate than the other? What circumstances, for example, might be more appropriate for pursuing (a) a partnership approach, and (b) a more militant approach.

3. Which strategy, if any, is more suitable following the Global Financial Crisis?

For actual and potential members, the debate is whether unions would be more appealing if they offered a more individualistic service, perhaps stressing the benefits of membership in terms of individual services, advice and so on; or whether they should emphasise more explicitly the collective aspects of trade unionism and the benefits deriving to members from being part of a collective body.

Extract 11.3

Organising the unorganised

The contrast between an organising and a servicing model of trade unionism has become an established feature of debate on trade union strategy in the USA, Britain and other countries.... At its most basic the distinction refers to the difference between a form of unionism in which the union as an institution acts on behalf of its members who are conceived of as clients or customers, and one in which members actively participate and 'become' the union through their collective organisation and activity.

The distinction is important...because it has been used to launch a programme for the revitalization of organised labour that is deemed equally applicable to all national cases and for all types of union. This programme originated in the United States – the term 'organising model' was first coined in 1988 in a manual for US labour organisers... – and has attracted adherents elsewhere.

Among the broad principles, the most basic is that unions must commit themselves to organising the unorganised as their first priority. Applying the organising model, in the first instance, means committing greater effort and resource to the task of recruiting workers into membership.

Membership is to be created and sustained, however, through the development of self-sustaining collective organisation among workers. In the US organisers speak of identifying workplace leaders, while in the UK they refer to activists and the need to attract and retain membership around an activist core.

A feature of this emphasis on mobilization is the use of a particular moral discourse to frame union activity, which uses the language of 'dignity, justice and respect' at work. This framing language not only legitimates union joining and activity, it also presents the union as a counter to the employer. Organising unionism is generally adversarial or militant in its assumptions and seeks to organise workers against the employer. Indeed the emphasis on collective representation arises from a conviction that workers must generate their own power resources if they are to secure concessions from employers.

Source: Heery et al (2001).

Both these aspects of union strategy – in their relations with employers and members – are concerned with increasing union influence and their appeal to prospective members. However, what tends to be missing from a lot of this discussion is an explicit reference back to what encourages employees to join a union, and what employees see as the central purposes of membership.

As we noted earlier, employees may be encouraged to join particularly if a union representative is present or whether their co-workers are already members. In deciding to join, many members have a predominantly instrumental attitude to their representative body. These two factors indicate the importance of a local presence and local activists, and the need to emphasise the union's role in advancing member interests, both by collective means and by dealing with individual concerns. The protective function offered by the union, and the ability of unions to improve pay, security and other terms and conditions of employment, influence individual member-joining decisions, and their decision to retain their membership once having joined.

As new members join, several things happen:

- Others also join, because their peers have.
- Where union density is higher (i.e. a greater proportion of potential members have become actual members), it is more likely that unions will be seen by members and potential members as influential and making a difference.
- Where potential members see the union as making a difference, they in turn are more likely to join – potentially reinforcing a 'virtuous circle' (see Figure 11.3).

Waddington and Whitston (1997: 518) describe studies showing that only around one in seven non-members objects in principle to trade unions. Charlwood's (2002: 464) analysis of British Social Attitudes Survey data suggests that two in five non-members are potential union members (this proportion indicates that they would be 'very likely' or 'fairly likely' to join if there were a trade union at their workplace). The suggestion of these studies is that the growth of unionism is being prevented by other factors: non-availability of a recognised union in the workplace (perhaps also reflecting management hostility), and a perceived lack of influence. Successfully addressing these aspects in the coming years could result

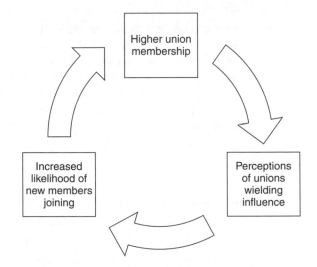

Figure 11.3   The virtuous circle of union presence

in a cycle of growth, restoring some of the position lost by the past 30-year cycle of decline.

At the same time, we should not underestimate the scale of the task facing trade unions in seeking membership in new areas. Many companies, for example, remain extremely reluctant to grant recognition to trade unions. This is particularly the case in the fast-food sector among companies such as McDonald's, Burger King and KFC/Pizza Hut. Royle writes:

> In the quick-service food industries of the USA, Canada and the UK, multinational chains are predominantly non-union. In most cases, unions have been unable to gain recognition at all; in the remainder, they have established collective agreements only for one restaurant at a time and for short periods.
>
> (Royle, 2004: 53)

In another study, Royle (2005) highlights the difficulties facing trade unions who seek recognition in countries such as Russia, which have no labour law supporting union recognition, or countries that have failed to impose any such laws.

Among many employee groups, particularly in small- and medium-sized enterprises in private sector services, the idea of joining a trade union is a long way from their immediate priorities. Extract 11.4 shows an analysis of one such group – software employees.

Extract 11.4

Software employees – their attitudes to work and trade unions

One of the challenges facing trade unions is to increase membership among groups and occupations where membership levels are currently very low. To examine this, Hyman et al (2004) examined the attitudes of software employees (systems managers, analysts, programmers and software engineers) in Scotland. In the private sector in software occupations, trade union density fell from 13 to just 8 per cent between 1996 and 2000, while among their public sector counterparts density levels diminished only slightly over this period, from 42 to 40 per cent.

Hyman and his colleagues interviewed and surveyed employees in five companies, and their results highlight five factors hindering union growth:

- *An expressed adherence to individualist values.* As one of their respondents put it, 'I wouldn't trust a union to represent my views to [the company]. I'd rather represent my views myself'; and as others commented, if a problem arises 'I sort it out', or 'I'd do something about it'.

- *Satisfaction with work.* Overall, satisfied workers appear to join a union less than unsatisfied ones (see text). The majority of the software employees studied (between 64 and 80 per cent) were satisfied with intrinsic aspects of their job (variety and sense of achievement, for example), and also with extrinsic aspects such as work conditions and career prospects. The freedom and autonomy offered by the job was particularly noted; as one employee put it, 'what's particularly important is the working environment and we are allowed to get on with our job without any real interference'.

- *Pay satisfaction.* At least three out of five respondents were satisfied with their pay. There was a slight tendency for younger workers to be less satisfied, but as the authors point out, this was also the most mobile group. The strong market position for software employees at the time of the study meant that people could contemplate leaving if they had a problem or grievance over their pay. As one put it, 'the way to make salary increases is to move job', while another commented 'if you don't like the conditions you've got, go somewhere else where the conditions are better'.

- *Awareness of union.* This awareness was generally low, and even among those more aware of trade unions, for the majority union membership held few attractions. Unions were recognised by management in one of the companies studied, and in that company the vast majority of employees were aware of its presence, and rated it effective in dealing with certain issues such as health and safety questions. Elsewhere, however, there was widespread ignorance of unions and a perception that the nature of software jobs and the software working environment made unions less important than in other contexts. As one commented, 'I don't really reckon they [trade unions] are as important...where you have predominantly professional people working in good, clean working conditions. So there is less for trade unions to actually campaign for and do anything about.'

- *The organisational context.* Four out of the five firms studied were small or medium-sized, working owners were present and active, trade unions not recognised, and a unitarist orientation was 'clearly evident' (p. 57).

The authors concluded that 'the prognosis for unions in the software sector is not promising' (p. 59). Generally satisfied employees, the value placed on autonomy, a preparedness for dealing with issues themselves and the difficulty of persuading owner–managers to recognise trade unions all limit the opportunities for unions to expand. A potential role for trade unions is discussed in terms of offering more professional services to employees (to assist career development through advice on employment contracts and other employment matters, and provide information on regional labour markets), but overall the study points to the difficulties facing trade unions in seeking to recruit among this expanding group of knowledge workers.

Source: Hyman et al (2004).

To sum up

Though the future of union representation is far from certain, it is likely that local activity will be important in any future influence wielded by trade unions within the workplace. It is hard to say whether this activity, and any resulting increase in union membership, is better encouraged by partnership relations with employers, or by emphasising the differences in interests between employees and employers. This is likely to vary depending on particular circumstances within individual work organisations and individual trade unions, and also, as Monnot and colleagues (2011) argue, on the nature of the employees.

Conclusion

This discussion of collective representation underlines one of the main themes running through the book: that the interests of employees and management are not identical. Because these interests diverge, this results in competing rationalities or logics at the workplace. Despite the decline in membership, that many unions have experienced during the past 30 years, this distinction between management and worker interests remains. So too does the asymmetry of power between employer and individual employee. This suggests that whatever the recent experience of union movements in many countries around the world, the essential case, or rationale, for the collective representation of workers remains. Employees' interests sometimes diverge from employers' interests, and employees also have less power in the employment relationship.

What this suggests is that the basis for trade union recovery remains. What is required by unions is to appeal successfully to a labour force that has changed significantly over the past generation. Evidence on what employees want from collective representation indicates that unions must stress the instrumental value in being part of the collective. This value translates not only into improved terms and conditions of employment, but also into protection and representation in dealings with management over issues such as threats of redundancy. At present, many existing union members have a mixed view on whether the union satisfies their priorities. However, most agree that where unions are stronger, they are more likely to make a positive difference, management are more likely to listen to them, and non-members are more likely to join.

It is this experience that lies behind union organising campaigns currently taking place. If successful in these campaigns, one outcome will be the need for management to rethink many current human resource management approaches. These have tended to marginalise trade unions and collective forms of representation in favour of direct communication with individual employees. The logic of HRM highlights the difficulties that much contemporary management has in accepting difference. In the terms of our book, this is a difficulty in accepting that there are multiple realities of work, and so any single (managerial) perspective on the workplace is problematic.

12

Hidden work

Chapter aim

This chapter explores the size and character of the 'hidden work' sector, and examines the different ways in which hidden work relates to work in the formal or visible work sector.

Key concepts

▷ hidden work
▷ concealed work
▷ unrecognised work
▷ deviant work
▷ nondeclared work
▷ domestic work
▷ foregone expense
▷ foregone wage
▷ voluntary work

Learning outcomes

After reading and thinking about this chapter, you will be able to:

1. Understand how work that lies outside the formal work sector may be considered 'hidden' work.
2. Distinguish between different categories of hidden work and recognise the reasons for the different categories.
3. Assess the problems with measuring the size of the hidden work sector.
4. Assess the problems associated with predicting future trends in hidden work.
5. Distinguish between different forms of concealed work and how these relate to the patterns of work in the formal work sector.
6. Distinguish between different types of unrecognised work and how these relate to patterns of work in the formal work sector.

Introduction

Up to now, our examination of the realities of work has concentrated on those activities taking place within what might be called the 'formal' or 'visible' work sector. This is where the goods and services produced are included in official statistics, such as the calculation of a country's Gross National Product (GNP), and where workers involved in the production of those goods and services receive a wage, which in turn is subject to tax. Yet to focus all our attention here would be to misrepresent the totality of work and work experience. As well as productive activity taking place within the formal economy, there are other contexts in which productive activity also occurs, but which do not figure in national accounts of production or earnings.

For example, if a joiner (a kind of carpenter) works for a firm producing windows, they will create some kind of output and earn a wage. Both of these are 'visible' in terms of production and earnings accounts. If the same joiner repairs a window in their own home or voluntarily assists in making a new door for a local youth club, none of this work will be 'visible' in terms of it being included in any national accounts. Similarly, if someone looks after a friend's child for a day and receives cash in return which is not declared to the tax authorities, this income and the work for which the payment was received will not figure in national accounts. The same might apply for people selling things on eBay, or at car boot sales. Each of these aspects of work – in the domestic and voluntary spheres, and receiving payment for work that is not declared for tax – are hidden, but they are unquestionably work, nonetheless.

Work that occurs outside the formal work sector can be 'hidden' from public gaze in one of two ways:

▷ It might be explicitly *concealed* from the authorities because it involves illegal activity. The activity itself could be a crime (such as drug dealing), or income from a legal activity may not be declared for tax, and so the overall activity is illegal because it involves tax evasion. Also in the general category of concealed work is that which involves some activities that are illegal but which is hidden because of its widespread social status as stigmatised work (such as prostitution).

▷ Work may be 'hidden' in another less explicit sense, if it is *unrecognised* as 'real' work, and so because of this those performing the tasks do not receive payment. The clearest example here is housework.

Each of these two general categories, work that is either explicitly hidden (concealed) or implicitly hidden (unrecognised), is made up of a range of individual activities. Yet at the same time, these various activities hold certain key elements in common. For example, as well as each being 'hidden' for one reason or another, they all have aspects in common with the formal or visible work sector. To explore these different aspects and implications of hidden work, this chapter is divided into three sections. The first examines the main dimensions of hidden work and considers some of the attempts to measure its size/scale, as well as trying to look at trends within the hidden work sector. The next two sections then consider the two main areas of hidden work in more detail: concealed work and unrecognised work. This is so as to establish the basis for an overall assessment of the significance of hidden work in the totality of work experience.

Defining and measuring hidden work

Consider the following imaginary case and as you read it, think about the different aspects of hidden work involved.

Jeremy, an employee at a firm of estate agents, has decided to build an extension to his house. The additional space will provide an extra bedroom for his elderly mother, Doris, who has suffered a stroke and is no longer able to look after herself in her own home. Faced with this situation, Jeremy and his wife Joanne have decided that the best thing would be for Doris to live with them so they can be on hand to give her the care she needs.

Given the urgency of the situation and the inevitable delays of 'red tape', Jeremy decided to try to get the plans for the extension through the local authority planning committee more quickly than was usual. Fortunately, his membership of the local golf club had helped him to develop a number of useful contacts, one of which was the local government officer in the planning department whose job it was to draw up the lists of property development for consideration by the planning committee. After an informal chat and a gift of a couple of bottles of whisky, the plans were put forward for consideration (and passed) very speedily.

Because he could not afford to pay a firm of builders to do the extension, Jeremy started on the work himself at weekends. However, he soon fell behind schedule, not least because every other weekend he had custody of the two children by his first marriage, which occupied most of his time. To free up some of these weekends, Joanne (a nursery nurse by training) would spend a good part of her time amusing the children. She also kept Jeremy supplied with numerous cups of tea and a cooked lunch, as well as completing various other domestic chores (such as the ironing and cleaning) that were usually left until the weekend.

Even though Jeremy was freed from the childcare and domestic chores, he still found himself making little headway with the work at weekends, and soon began to put in an hour or two on the building work during the week, by pretending to his boss that he was leaving the office early to do a house evaluation, or to have a meeting with a prospective vendor (seller). However, after a few weeks it was clear that not even this extra time was progressing the work fast enough, so one evening Jeremy called up various contacts in the building trade to try to find someone to help. He was put in touch with a building labourer, Ron, who agreed to give him a hand, working at weekends. Ron made it clear that he would want to be paid in cash, with no receipts, and that in return he would 'borrow' the equipment they would need from his employer, provided that any equipment was back on his firm's premises before Monday morning.

With the added help of Ron, the extension was soon finished and Doris duly moved in. However, while the arrangement of having Doris under the same roof meant that there was now less travelling involved in visiting her, Joanne soon found that the combination of tasks of keeping her own household going, looking after her mother-in-law and doing her job at a local nursery school was getting too much for her. As a result, she gave up her job at the nursery, although to keep some interest outside the home, she carried on doing some voluntary work in the evenings which involved organising fundraising activities for a local hospital.

This is quite a complicated case study, but even so we have simplified things for the sake of illustration. For example, we would not mean to imply that corruption and bribery of local government planning officers is in any way normal or typical. Perhaps the most remarkable aspect of this account is that although there is a large amount of 'work' being done, only two of the activities figure as part of the formal economy: Jeremy's job at the estate agents, and Joanne's job at the nursery school. The remaining work all takes place within the domains of hidden work. For example, as well as Jeremy's DIY building activities, there is the care dispensed by Joanne to her mother-in-law and to her husband's children, together with the work involved in her keeping the men supplied with food and drink as well as undertaking other domestic tasks of cleaning and ironing, not to mention the voluntary work.

In addition, the work done by Ron is also hidden (deliberately concealed). His requirement for cash-in-hand payments with no receipts suggests an intention not to declare this income to the tax authorities. The account also contains examples of some of fiddles which are often associated with hidden work: for example (and to repeat, it is only a simplified, imaginary example), the planning officer taking a bribe or 'backhander' to push Jeremy's application up the queue, Jeremy's use of office hours to work on the extension, and Ron's unauthorised 'borrowing' of his employer's equipment (see Chapter 9 for a more detailed discussion of workplace fiddling). Given these complexities and different kinds of hidden work, this case suggests the need for some means of categorising the diverse activities that fall under the general heading of hidden work.

Categorising hidden work

There are various ways in which hidden work might be categorised. Here we prefer to continue to develop the distinction made earlier between:

- Activities that are explicitly 'concealed' because they are illegal, because they contain illegal aspects and attract social stigma, or because the income deriving from legal activities is not declared to the tax authorities.
- A variety of activities or work that is 'unrecognised'. This is not explicitly or intentionally hidden, but as a result of not generally being performed for payment, it takes place outside market relations (that is to say it is not like the typical labour process under capitalism, where people sell their time and effort for payment). Because of this, it lies outside the range of activity generally considered as 'real' work.

As Figure 12.1 indicates, different individual work activities can be located under each of the two main categories. The examples given do not represent a complete, exhaustive list, but indicate the sorts of activity to be found in each of the general areas of hidden work. The distinction between different activities and categories

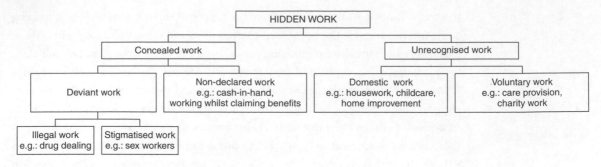

Figure 12.1   Dimensions of hidden work

will, in practice, often be blurred by individuals simultaneously pursuing more than one aspect of hidden work. However, such overlaps do not invalidate the main distinction between concealed and unrecognised work, since this distinction is based on the fundamentally different causes of their hiddenness.

Other commentators have drawn broadly similar distinctions between the main categories of hidden work. However, there is some variation in the labels used and the degree to which some categories (e.g. domestic and voluntary work) are treated as separate or as elements of a single category. For example, Gershuny (1983) distinguishes between 'household', 'communal' and 'underground' economies, and Handy (1984) refers to the 'household', 'voluntary' and 'black' economies, Smith and Wied-Nebbeling (1986) only distinguish between the 'black' (illegal) and 'self-service' economies. Rose (1985) only distinguishes between 'unofficial' and 'domestic' economies. In common with Felt and Sinclair (1992: 45), here we prefer to write about concealed and unrecognised *sectors* rather than 'economies'. This is an important difference because it emphasises that these areas are not completely separate from the formal, visible economy. Indeed, in many ways (discussed below) hidden work is inextricably tied to formal work, and many people are, to a greater or lesser extent, active in both visible and hidden sectors.

Problems in measuring the scale of hidden work

As most researchers in this area have acknowledged, it is difficult to measure hidden work, so much so that anything approaching an accurate measurement of the overall scale of hidden work is virtually impossible.

There are three immediate measurement problems in relation to hidden work:

• *What should be included or counted as hidden work?* Most attempts to measure hidden work are concerned with estimating the revenue lost to the state because of concealed market activities. This misses out activities which make up the unrecognised work sector (because they are not part of a market system). There have been far fewer attempts to quantify and measure the value of unrecognised work (such as domestic work and unpaid care work).

- *How can nonmarket activities be quantified (given a market value)?* In the few attempts that have been made to measure both the concealed and the unrecognised work sectors, a key problem has been how to put a monetary value on activities that are not paid for.
- *How can work activities that are concealed because they are illegal be measured accurately?* The very fact that these have to be concealed creates major obstacles for the quantification and measurement of those activities.

An important point to stress about the problems with measuring unrecognised work is that this is not just a concern about scientific accuracy. Most unrecognised work is carried out by women, and so if we do not take account of this, we are reinforcing gender inequality. By not giving these things a market value, this reinforces the view that such activities are not as valuable in our society. But in fact these activities underpin our society. Paid work is only prioritised over other kinds of work as a consequence of capitalism. Looking after children, the ill and the elderly is part of what makes us most human, but under capitalism this is somehow not counted as 'real' work (because it cannot be quantified and exchanged for money). In Marx's terms, this is an example of how the labour process under capitalism leads to alienation from our species-being (discussed in Chapter 9).

There is a similar issue when we consider the problems with measuring concealed work. Again these are not just questions of scientific accuracy or fact – they involve questions of value. There are parallels in how illegal and legal activities are organised as work, and between how illegal and legal organisations are managed. Some activities that are legal (selling alcohol, or tobacco) seem indistinguishable from, or potentially worse than, activities that are illegal (selling cannabis). Legal organisations can subsidise or be responsible for illegal activities such as tax evasion, discrimination and bullying, and also things like perjury, phone hacking and unlawful surveillance. The Global Financial Crisis will have caused more widespread damage through greed and recklessness by many people acting lawfully, than any criminal organisation could.

Measuring the concealed sector

The links that there are between measurement and values, and what this tells us about capitalism are more important than the debate about what should be counted where. We do not examine these measurement issues in great detail, but summarise some of the main activities and issues (for a lengthier discussion, see, for example, Feige, 1989; Smith and Wied-Nebbeling, 1986: 27–42; Thomas, 1992). As regards estimating the value of the concealed sector, attempts have included the following:

- Undertaking small-scale, ethnographic (looking at culture) studies of concealed work activities and scaling up the results.
- Generalising from investigations of single cases by the national tax office where discrepancies are revealed between declared and actual income.

- Seeking to establish differences between levels of income and expenditure in the economy as a whole, or among samples of households (using data sources such as Family Expenditure Surveys). The assumption here is that if total expenditure is greater than declared income, the additional income required for this expenditure will have been acquired through concealed activities.
- Attempting to measure the concealed sector by the amount of cash in circulation. This is based on an assumption that transactions in the concealed sector are conducted in cash. Particular attention has been given to the amount of large-denomination bank notes in circulation, on an assumption that these figure disproportionately in concealed transactions.

Exercise 12.1

What do you think?

1. Outline the strengths and weaknesses of each of the four methods of estimating the value of the concealed sector.
2. On the basis of your assessment, which do you think is likely to be the most accurate and why?
3. Are there any other methods you can suggest to obtain a better measure of concealed work?

Despite the variety and ingenuity of these attempts to measure concealed work, 'a considerable margin of error surrounds all estimates of the scale of concealed transactions' (Smith and Wied-Nebbeling, 1986: 40). This is probably putting it mildly: none of the measurement instruments applied to concealed work is precise, making estimation highly unreliable. What is more, the level of concealed or undeclared work appears to vary considerably from country to country. For example, while a European Commission report in the late 1990s estimated the level of undeclared work in the EU as somewhere between 7 and 16 per cent of GDP (EC, 1998), subsequent reports have highlighted significant variation between European countries.

In 2007, for example, a large EU-wide survey found between 1 and 18 per cent of the surveyed populations in different countries reporting that they had conducted undeclared work in the previous 12 months (Williams, 2008: 51). On average those performing undeclared work spent almost 19 hours per week on this kind of work (ibid.) In developing countries, which lack the infrastructure associated with regulation and taxation, and have different traditions associated with work, these proportions are likely to be much higher. As well as work that is wholly undeclared, Williams (2009) also reports 5 per cent of the respondents to the 2007 EU survey (and as many as 23% in Romania) reporting receiving 'envelope wages' – an (illegal) practice whereby employers pay their employees two wages: an official wage and an unofficial 'envelope' wage that is not declared, and therefore avoids social insurance and tax liabilities.

Measuring unrecognised work

The core problem of measuring concealed work is the reluctance of those taking part to have their activities made visible. The main difficulty in measuring unrecognised work is one of establishing an accurate valuation. Since those performing household and voluntary work do not normally receive payment, these activities do not have a readily calculable monetary value. There are, of course, ways to put a monetary value on these tasks. In relation to household-based work activities, for example, these fall into two general approaches: measuring the foregone expense or the foregone wage (Chadeau, 1985: 242):

- *The foregone expense* involves calculating the cost of purchasing the various tasks from the formal or visible work sector. In terms of domestic work activities, for example, this may be calculated either on the basis of the cost of employing a general housekeeper to carry out all types of domestic tasks, or the cost of hiring the specialist services of a cook, cleaner, gardener and so on.
- *The foregone wage* involves estimating the lost income incurred by the person who is undertaking the domestic work, who could otherwise devote an equivalent amount of time to paid work.

Both these methods of calculation produce a monetary value for household domestic work, but both suffer from measurement problems. Alternative methods of calculation are likely to yield quite different valuations. In general, the foregone expense is likely to produce a higher valuation of household tasks than the foregone wage. In addition, within the foregone expense method, the estimate for specialist providers of individual services will produce a significantly higher value than the estimate derived from a general provider of services (Beneria, 1999: 297).

Yet while such problems signal the need to treat any calculations with caution, it remains equally clear that *irrespective of the method of calculation, the monetary value of work activities in the unrecognised work sector is very high*. Beneria (1999: 299) estimates that unpaid work represents between a quarter and a half of total economic activity, depending on the country. Similarly, Chadeau (1985: 245–6), following a review of over 30 studies in various countries, reports that the combined average estimate from these studies indicated the value of domestic work to be equivalent to over one-third (34.7%) of Gross National Product (a nation's income).

Exercise 12.2

What do you think?

1. Why should measuring the foregone expense result in a higher estimate for the value of domestic work than measuring the foregone wage?
2. What does this tell us about the nature of employment experience and opportunities for many women?

Other writers in this field agree with these estimates. Handy (1984: 19), for example, comments that over half the country's total labour time is devoted to productive activity in or around the household, and that if this work were charged, it could amount to 40 per cent of the formal economy (see also Rose, 1985: 133). As Handy (1984) also points out, when combined with the extent of voluntary work that is undertaken this would make the size of the unrecognised work sector as much as one half of the total economy.

To sum up

Whatever the measurement problems and the range of estimates that these generate, the value of unrecognised work is vast. Given the number of people involved, and the time spent on domestic and other nonmarket activities, the monetary value of unrecognised work dwarfs the value of activities in the concealed sector. Systems of measurement and monetary valuation also reinforce gender inequalities. Unpaid care for the sick or elderly is not counted as 'real' work under capitalism; this can be understood in terms of alienation.

Problems of predicting trends in hidden work

Just as it is almost impossible to establish an accurate valuation of hidden work, it is also difficult to draw definitive conclusions about likely overall trends:

- Is the size of the hidden work sphere changing over time?
- Are some aspects changing more or less rapidly?
- What are the effects of the Global Financial Crisis on the extent of (i) unrecognised, and (ii) concealed work?

The problem here is not just to establish reliable benchmarks from which to estimate change. Other problems include the diversity of the hidden work sector, the range of potential influencing factors, and the possibility that single factors, such as the GFC, can have different effects on different aspects of hidden work.

Hidden work and the economic cycle

Consider the relationship between the amount of hidden work and the state of the economy. During periods of strong economic growth, one could argue that the scope for concealed work activity will rise as people have more money to purchase goods and services, and the formal economy is less able to keep up with the total level of demand. Correspondingly, economic recession will tend to dampen concealed work activities, as the amount of money to spend on goods and services diminishes (O'Higgins, 1989: 175).

Now consider the opposite argument, which would seem to be equally plausible. In periods of economic recession, such as brought about by the GFC, when levels of disposable income are depressed, people could try to obtain the goods and services they require more cheaply by entering into more 'cash-in-hand' transactions. Also, if unemployment rises as a result of recession, this could increase the amount of time spent on domestic and voluntary activities – unrecognised work (MacDonald, 1996).

It may also be the case that while some aspects of concealed work decline during recessions, others increase – such as 'earning while claiming' (claiming welfare payments while concealing additional income from cash-in-hand activity). As writers such as Thomas (1992) have pointed out, if one of the outcomes of recession and a lack of employment opportunities is to stimulate a growth in self-employment, this might stimulate an increase in concealed work. The self-employed sector accounts for a significant amount of concealed work by people failing to declare all the income earned (Williams, Nadin and Baric, 2011).

Similarly, a growth in formal, paid employment could limit the amount of time available for unrecognised work (e.g. voluntary work). At the same time many aspects of concealed work depend on income, contacts, opportunities and skills deriving from paid employment (Pahl, 1984, 1988; Williams, 2004: 245). The problem of identifying a relationship between the economic cycle and hidden work is not just one concerning the overall relationship between the two. This is also compounded by the fact that some elements of hidden work may increase (or decrease) in response to different economic conditions.

Trends in hidden work

Another example of the difficulties in projecting possible trends in hidden work is that while some long-term factors may have stimulated a *growth* in hidden work during the last century, others may have acted in favour of a *decline*:

- In terms of growth, an overall rise in levels of taxation over a long period potentially increases the incentive to undertake nondeclared work. The long-term decline in the basic working week in the visible work sector has also potentially increased opportunities for workers to devote more time to hidden work. And, as Gershuny (1983) argues, the decline in the total number of domestic servants in the early twentieth century was accompanied by a growth in the proportion of households performing their own domestic tasks.
- In terms of decline, a rise in women's labour market participation and the growth of the welfare state (which led to greater provision of care for the elderly, sick and disabled) potentially reduce the total time devoted to domestic and voluntary activities.

The effect of factors influencing hidden work is complicated if we take different time horizons into account. Over shorter time horizons, the development of the welfare state in the UK over the last 70 years may have altered the balance between care that is (i) unpaid, informal (unrecognised work), and (ii) paid and formal. However, legislation and policy in the UK over the past two decades (beginning with the National Health Service and Community Care Act 1990) have shifted emphasis back towards more care being provided informally.

At the other extreme, in terms of very long time horizons, economic development may be associated with a gradual decline of hidden work, as more activity shifts from the informal to the formal economic sphere (this is called the 'formalisation of work' thesis). However, as Williams and Windebank (1999) point out, higher levels of economic development may also be associated with a 'post-formalisation' stage, as households increasingly rely on informal work to get tasks completed.

To sum up

There are a variety of possible influences on the scale and development of hidden work, and it is difficult to measure. Although overall trends cannot clearly be defined, the amount of hidden work performed remains very substantial and it is unlikely to be declining significantly (or to do so in the foreseeable future). The effects of GFC could mean this sector of work could grow further.

Exploring hidden work – concealed work

'Concealed' work is one of many labels that have been applied to that aspect of hidden work which directly or indirectly involves illegal activities. Other terms that have been used include the 'black', 'shadow', 'submerged', 'irregular', 'underground', 'unobserved', 'unofficial', 'illicit', 'subterranean' and 'informal' sector or economy (Feige, 1989; Gershuny, 1983; Rose, 1985; Smith and Wied-Nebbeling, 1986; Thomas, 1992).

We choose to use 'concealed' because we think the most important aspect of this kind of work is that it involves market transactions that are deliberately hidden. This may be either because they are illegal in themselves, or because they contain illegal aspects and are subject to a social stigma, or because they are associated with fraudulent behaviour – such as the evasion of taxes or working while claiming social security benefits (Smith and Wied-Nebbeling, 1986: 2). Though relatively simple, even this categorisation is not problem-free, however, partly because it covers such a wide scale of activities (e.g. from small-scale cash-in-hand transactions to multimillion-pound drug trafficking). Also though, by gathering all these different activities and applying a label to them, this might suggest it is possible to draw a distinction between the 'concealed' and the 'visible' sectors. In reality, however, as we say above, this distinction is more blurred and problematic because there are crossovers between illegal and legal activities, and between illegal and legal organisations.

Deviant work

One of the main reasons people conceal the work they are engaged in is because it is illegal. Yet some of the categories more commonly used to describe aspects of visible work also apply to deviant work. For example, for some people, criminal activity is a part-time pursuit, a supplement to other income acquired through legal channels. For others, however, crime is their full-time 'occupation'. Indeed, references are commonly made to individuals who are 'professional' criminals, pursuing a criminal 'career' (for a discussion of crime as alternative work behaviour, see Ferman, 1983: 217).

Not all deviant work is illegal. The very large (see Extract 12.1) but mainly hidden sex industry comprises different forms of work (e.g. prostitution and the production of pornography), some aspects of which are legal, others not. In terms of prostitution, for example, in the UK it is legal to work as a prostitute in a private place; however, it is illegal to live off the immoral earnings of someone else (to profit from prostitutes), and soliciting payment for sex is also illegal in that it is unlawful, 'to loiter or solicit in a street or public place for the purpose of prostitution' (Street Offences Act 1959, quoted in Lacey, Wells and Meure, 1990: 362).

Again here we face a problem not just of measurement but of ethics and values if we try to assess the activities of the sex industry. Legislation in the UK which prevents soliciting but allows prostitution has been criticised for criminalising prostitutes, rather than those who wish to pay them in return for sex. In Sweden, Norway and Iceland, prostitution is treated as a crime by the person paying for sex on the basis that sex in return for payment cannot be consensual and is therefore an act of rape (the prostitute in this case is not committing a crime).

In the sex industry, the label of deviant work reflects the degree to which sex workers are stigmatised by the rest of society (Goffman, 1963; Woollacott, 1980). This may change as collectives of sex workers continue to campaign for greater legal protection and employment rights, and as police and other authorities (in some countries and localities) move in the direction of exercising greater control of the sex industry through registration and licensing procedures, rather than prohibition (O'Connell Davidson, 1998; West, 2000).

However, the stigmatisation of sex workers remains widespread. Despite any gains stemming from collective representation and any changes in approach by police authorities and judiciaries, social stigma and legal pressures continue to combine to cast prostitutes (and other sex workers) as 'outsiders' in the world of work (Becker, 1963). This shared experience as outsiders can help to generate a supportive work culture among many of the workers themselves (Sanders, 2004; Woollacott, 1980: 198), but these workers – overwhelmingly women – face constant dangers of abuse, disease and injury, as well as psychological damage (see also Adkins, 1995; Brewis and Linstead, 2000a, 2000b).

Extract 12.1

A growth industry

The sex industry (e.g. pornography, lap-dancing, chatlines, websites, prostitution) is huge. One estimate, by the European parliament's women's rights committee, is that the sex industry turns over more money annually than the total of all military budgets in the world (Bindel, 2004). In Thailand alone, the sex industry has been estimated to involve between 150,000 and 200,000 girls and women at any one time (plus a tiny proportion of male prostitutes) (Kazmin, 2004). In the UK the sex industry has accounts for billions of pounds per year (Devi, 2000). The industry has grown substantially as a result of the Internet. Sex sites are by far the most common sites visited, and account for most of the sales and profits in the industry. As far back as 1998, for example, over 70 per cent of Playboy's $318 million sales were accounted for by the Internet.

As well as the rise of the sex industry on the Internet, the 'live' sex industry is also growing. One study has estimated that 80,000 men in London visit prostitutes each week (quoted in Devi, 2000: 16). Of the 33 London boroughs, ten have established red light areas; Westminster alone has more than 130 identified brothels. There are now upwards of 40 table or lap-dancing clubs across London, and in the United States, the Inland Revenue Service estimates that the table-dancing club sector is worth $8 billion per annum.

What do you think?

1. Can you think of other work sectors that are hidden because the work conducted is stigmatised by society in some way?
2. What aspects of this work have brought about the stigmatisation?

Nondeclared work

For many people, their main experience of concealed work will be work undertaken for payment but hidden from the tax authorities. It is widely believed that the biggest source of untaxed income is the self-employed, whose income is not subject to tax collection through pay-as-you-earn (PAYE) arrangements. Individual investigations by the Inland Revenue in the UK show that a significant proportion of the self-employed fail to declare all their income to the tax authorities. (See Chapter 2 for discussion of the growth of self-employment.)

Aside from the self-employed population, particularly in periods of high unemployment, undeclared income from 'working and claiming' has regularly been targeted by governments. Different political administrations have made much of their determination to clampdown on 'benefit cheats' – those claiming social security while also acquiring income from work that is not declared to the authorities. This governmental selective attention means pursuing small-scale frauds by social security claimants but with an enthusiasm that is not shown towards richer counterparts who engage in large-scale tax evasion. This may reflect class bias and the political appeal of lowering the social security bill by removing 'benefit cheats'. The reality is though that catching benefit fiddlers is much easier than targeting multi-nationals who have more sophisticated ways of tax-dodging and can always ultimately threaten to relocate to more favourable tax regimes.

In targeting benefit fraud governments are usually assisted by sections of the press (such as, in the UK, the *Sun* newspaper's 'Split on a scrounger' campaign, with a telephone hotline for anonymous callers), and by a willingness among some to 'shop' neighbours whom they suspect of benefit offences to the local social security office (see also Pahl, 1984: 95). What these government and press campaigns reflect is a perception that unemployed people are particularly involved in cash-in-hand activities. This would seem common sense in that they are available for such work by virtue of not having a formal job, and can afford to take jobs at a lower payment than would be offered in the visible work sector, because any wage is supplemented by the welfare benefits also being claimed.

Clearly, a proportion of the total cash-in-hand work is undertaken by the unemployed, though often for very small payment (see Extract 12.2; also MacDonald, 1994, 1997). The growth of small subcontracting firms in both manufacturing and services has probably extended the availability of cash-in-hand work into a wider range of sectors over the past three decades. What Pahl (1984) and others have shown, however, is that it is wrong to portray most cash-in-hand work activities as being undertaken by the unemployed.

On the contrary, much of this work is carried out by people who are already in employment and are undertaking additional work in their spare time (like Ron in our earlier example). The extra resources available to those in employment increase their access to additional work. Employment provides contacts as well as sufficient financial resources to acquire the equipment and materials necessary for undertaking other work (garden machinery, power tools, transport and so on), together with the skills necessary for conducting other activity.

On the other hand, unemployment is for many an intensely isolating experience (whatever contacts were made while in employment are soon lost), but also the (low) level of unemployment income restricts the unemployed in extending their own concealed activity. They may only be able to work in areas requiring little or no capital expenditure, such as labouring for others or cleaning windows (Pahl, 1984: 97). The distinction between employed and unemployed means income and status for the former rather than the latter. In the same way, employment – and the benefits stemming from employment – provides access to more highly rewarded areas of concealed work. The unemployed are largely restricted to lower-paying activities.

Extract 12.2

Fiddly jobs

'Fiddly jobs' is one expression given to work for payment that is undertaken while claiming social security or unemployment benefits. Estimates differ on the extent of fiddly jobs. MacDonald (1994: 509) quotes studies which found variation in undeclared working ranging from one in seven families having had fiddly jobs, to up to two-thirds of poor households. In MacDonald's own sample of over 200 people in the north-east of England, just under one-third had done fiddly jobs.

Most of the jobs MacDonald investigated were short term (typically a day or two), irregular, infrequent and poorly rewarded. The most common were as subcontracted labour in the nearby steelworks (particularly doing cleaning or maintenance jobs), construction work, car mechanics, taxi driving, window cleaning, and bar work. The people engaging in fiddly work were disproportionately white, working-class males in their 20s and 30s who had skills and/or a reputation for reliability, and who moved in the social circles through which fiddly work was distributed.

The people undertaking fiddly work viewed it as an accepted survival strategy, reflecting the low level of state benefit they received. It was also seen as risky (because of the possibility of being caught by the benefit authorities), hard work, unsociable (often involving long and irregular hours), and low paid.

Fiddly jobs, despite their irregularity and infrequency, nevertheless provided some beneficial work routine for the individuals. As MacDonald comments (1997: 119), 'For this sample of poor and long-term unemployed people fiddly work became a necessary way of maintaining individual self respect and household incomes.'

If work options are restricted by being unemployed, the restrictions are even greater for some other groups such as asylum seekers who are awaiting the outcome of Home Office decisions – and hence with no legal right to work – and illegal immigrants with no visas and work permits (either because they have been denied them, or they have expired). Individuals in these categories cannot earn wages (and illegal immigrants cannot claim benefits legally); therefore many will face little choice but to work illegally (Forshaw and Pilgerstorfer, 2005).

In turn, this exposes these groups to employment conditions where employment legislation is ignored, low wages are paid, long hours demanded, and in some cases work is carried out under very hazardous, even life-threatening, conditions (see Extract 12.3). In the UK, the growth of 'gangmasters' who organise illegal immigrants and others as casual labour (particularly in the agricultural sector), and their failure either to adhere to employment legislation or to declare their activities to the tax authorities, led to the Gangmasters (Licensing) Act 2004. This requires gangmasters to join a register, and gives powers to officials to increase the transparency of gangmasters' activities (Forshaw and Pilgerstorfer, 2005: 159).

Extract 12.3

A tragic outcome of unregulated working

In February 2004, 23 Chinese cockle pickers were drowned in Lancashire's Morecambe Bay as rising tides cut them off more than two miles from the shore. The workers – most or all of whom were illegal immigrants, mainly from the coastal Fujian province in China – were working for a Chinese gangmaster. The cockling industry in Morecambe Bay is a lucrative one. The shellfish lying on the sands have an estimated value of £6 million. However, as the easier sands near the shore have become exhausted, cocklers have been forced to venture further out, despite the dangers of tide and quicksand.

The tragedy highlighted several issues regarding this aspect of concealed work. First, the reliance of the agricultural and food processing sector on seasonal work has in turn created a reliance on gangmasters who organise groups of casual workers. Second, the illegal immigrant status of some of these workers leaves them open to exploitation. Not able to work legally, these individuals become submerged into an unregulated labour market, and are sometimes required – as vividly demonstrated by the fate of the Chinese cockle pickers – to work in highly dangerous conditions.

This cockle-pickers case is not an isolated one, though no others have so far reached such a tragic conclusion. However, the presence of gangmasters in the agricultural sector is widespread, associated with a largely submerged economy. Gangmasters are frequently accused of exploiting migrant (and illegal immigrant) labour, demanding high fees for arranging work, and then using the debts incurred to extract long working hours for low pay. For a graphic account of life in this largely hidden world of gangmasters and casual work, see Pai (2004). Recent legislation in the UK (the Gangmasters (Licensing) Act 2004) has sought to bring a higher degree of regulation into this area of activity.

To sum up

Work may be concealed because it is illegal, or undeclared, or stigmatised in some way. The total volume of concealed work is very large and probably growing. A lot of attention has been given to concealed work undertaken by the unemployed. In practice, this probably accounts for only a small proportion of the total monetary value of concealed work activities.

Exploring hidden work – unrecognised work

Domestic work

The hidden work sector is dominated by domestic labour within the household. This is the case however its magnitude is measured – in volume of activity, number of people involved, total time spent or overall value of activities. It is domestic work too, and the way that it is organised and performed, that has particularly significant implications for the pattern and experience of work in the visible work sector. Here there is only space to explore certain aspects of domestic work, but even a brief examination shows the various points at which this work touches upon and shapes the broader realities and experiences of paid work. More generally, this underlines the continued prominence of domestic work in overall work experience. A number of the issues raised in the following discussion are also taken up again in Chapter 13 (Work and Life).

Domestic work and paid employment

A number of these points of contact between domestic work and paid employment have already been highlighted in earlier chapters:

- In the discussion of attitudes towards time-discipline in Chapter 4, for example, we noted how the household, together with schools and other institutions, has played an important part in the development and internalisation of values of regularity, punctuality and time thrift.
- More broadly, the home is a key location for childhood socialisation, including socialisation relating to work values (see Chapter 3).
- Home also represents an important source of material support for those in paid employment. The household delivers labour to the workplace in a condition fit for work: clothed, fed, rested.
- Over and above these physical contributions, home also provides an important source of psychological support for those in paid work. It can be a context in which they can relax, 'wind down', and 'switch off' from the pressures of their job. Alternatively of course, work can be an escape for some from unhappy home lives.
- The desire for comfort and well-being at home also acts as a motivation to continue paid work.

In addition to these different support roles in relation to the formal work sector, the home also exerts a major influence on the overall pattern of labour market participation. The large amount of time expended on housework and childcare limits the time available for other activities, including paid employment. But the main point here is that domestic work has not simply limited the labour market participation of people in general: it has especially limited the participation of women in paid work.

In almost every country in the world women disproportionately shoulder the responsibilities of domestic work, particularly in those countries that exhibit greater societal-level gender inequality (Fuwa, 2004). As industrialism developed in the twentieth century, the increased prominence of the male 'breadwinner' left women with the larger part of domestic responsibilities. Even though the participation rates of women in the labour market have risen considerably since the post-1945 period, and especially since the 1960s (see Chapter 2), this has not been matched by a corresponding sharing of the burden of household work between men and women. Neither has there been an equalising of the overall responsibility for work at home.

Table 12.1 highlights the distribution of activities among males and females in the UK. In some aspects there is comparatively little difference between the sexes: for example, men and women spend roughly the same amount of time each day sleeping, travelling and undertaking personal care activities. However, what is clear is that women spend much more time than men on domestic work, while men on average spend more time than women in paid employment. Indeed, if time spent on paid work, unpaid housework and childcare are combined, the differences between men and women are relatively small. Sullivan (2000) notes that in surveys since the mid-1980s, this approximate parity (equality) in overall work time between men and women has continued. But at the same time the significance of the distribution of paid and unpaid work remains: men are dispro-portionately engaged in paid activities; women are disproportionately engaged in unpaid domestic work. In addition, as writers such as Duncombe and Marsden (1995) point out, this division relates not only to the distribution of physical work

Table 12.1 Time used by men and women (16 years and over) in the UK (hours and minutes per day)

	Males	Females
Sleep	8.23	8.33
Leisure[a]	5.17	4.52
Employment[b]	4.17	2.42
Housework and childcare	2.17	4.03
Personal care[c]	2.07	2.19
Travel	1.28	1.21
Other	0.09	0.10

Notes:
Figures for 2000–01.

(a) includes watching TV, video, DVD; social life; hobbies, sport and entertainment.
(b) includes study and voluntary work.
(c) includes eating, drinking, washing, dressing.
Source: Adapted from *Social Trends 2005* (ONS, 2005).

tasks, but also the emotional work that takes place in the household. Women continue to shoulder a disproportionate amount of the emotional caring work, with their male partners giving priority to their paid work roles (see also the discussion of emotional labour in Chapter 7).

Exercise 12.4

What do you think?

1. Why do you think that the relative proportions of domestic work undertaken by men and women changed only marginally as women's participation in paid employment began to expand in the 1970s? (See Chapter 2.)
2. If, as the evidence suggests, the pace of change in the distribution of domestic work quickened in the 1980s and 1990s, why do you think this might have been so?
3. What is your own experience of the gender division of domestic work in your family? Explain whether you think this division is fair and justifiable.

For many women entering or re-entering paid employment, doing so has added to the total amount of work they have to do, rather than led to an equalising of overall (paid and unpaid) work responsibilities with their male partners. Gershuny, Godwin and Jones (1994: 152) argue that, 'Married women in employment bear a disproportionate "dual burden" of paid and unpaid work', with women disproportionately undertaking a 'second shift' of domestic work when their paid work shift is over (Hochschild, 1989). Indeed, early analyses of the growth of paid work among women detected only very slow change in the distribution of unpaid work roles (and especially the overall responsibility for those activities). However, subsequent survey evidence and comparisons over time point to a somewhat greater pace of change in later years. This suggests that there may have been a 'lagged adaptation' (Gershuny et al, 1994: 179) relating to the distribution of work tasks. Change in the sharing of domestic work has occurred, but more slowly and later than changes in female labour market participation.

In a 20-year comparison of how people spend their time, Sullivan (2000) found a 'significant' increase in male participation in domestic tasks. However, an unequal distribution of those tasks persisted. Even where both adults worked full-time, by the late 1990s, women still accounted for 60 per cent of total time spent on domestic work (though this was down from 68% in the mid-1970s) (ibid: 443). Also, a cross-national survey conducted in Britain, Norway and the Czech Republic suggests that any growth in male participation in domestic work may have stalled in more recent years (Crompton, Broackmann and Lyonette, 2005). The authors suggest this reflects pressures of work intensification and longer working hours, which disproportionately affect those in 'career' jobs – and the people in those positions remain disproportionately male.

Extract 12.4

Grateful slaves?

An Australian study by Baxter and Western (1998) has explored an apparent paradox in domestic work: that despite shouldering responsibility for most household tasks, a large percentage of women are satisfied with the division of household labour. Possible reasons that the authors identify for this include women accepting that there is little alternative to the prevailing situation; women holding a traditional attitude towards the role of men and women which encourages them to accept the bulk of household tasks; women working fewer hours in paid work, creating a feeling of having primary responsibility for household tasks; and the possibility that women enjoy doing housework tasks more than men.

Drawing on a national survey of over 1700 men and women, Baxter and Western found that women in Australia spent far longer on domestic labour than men: an overall average of 43 hours per week for women, compared with 16 hours for men.

However, only around one in seven women reported any dissatisfaction with the way they and their partners divided childcare or household tasks. Perhaps not surprisingly given the distribution of hours, very few of the men (only around one in 30) indicated any dissatisfaction with the way the tasks were divided.

Looking further at the attitudes to housework, the authors found that if husbands participated in certain household chores that were conventionally the responsibility of women – such as preparing meals, cleaning the house, doing the washing or ironing – women were more satisfied, even if in practice the men did not spend long on any of the activities, compared with their partners. The authors comment that 'This finding implies that for most women the key issue is having "help" with some specific activities rather than an equal division of time on housework' (p. 117).

Other factors positively correlated with women's satisfaction with housework included whether they held more traditional gender role attitudes, and whether they were satisfied with their paid employment. In addition, more educated and younger women tended to be less satisfied than their less educated and older counterparts.

Note: the term 'grateful slaves' is taken from Hakim (1991).

Women, household work and labour market participation

Because women shoulder a disproportionate share of responsibilities for household tasks and childcare, this has various implications for their position in the labour market:

- Women are more likely to exhibit a greater discontinuity in labour market activity, with periods of employment interspersed with periods of childcare. This in turn contributes both towards a lower rate of progression within internal career hierarchies and a resulting disproportionate occupancy by women of lower level and more poorly paid jobs (see also, Chapter 10).

- With women more likely to be occupying less well-paid jobs than their male partners, this tends to lead to any mobility among many couples being male driven: couples relocate on the basis of the labour market for the male's job. These mobility patterns heighten any negative effects on women's position in the labour market, because women may be forced to seek employment in labour markets that have been chosen to suit the job requirements of their male partners rather than themselves.

- The nature and growth of part-time working can be used to illustrate how women's domestic work responsibilities influence their participation in the labour market. Four-fifths of part-time workers are women, and more than two-thirds of female employees work part-time (see Chapter 2). One of the reasons that employers seeking to expand part-time working have been able to secure an adequate supply of available labour has been because many women look to combine paid employment with their domestic responsibilities. For many, this combination can only be achieved by engaging in part-time rather than full-time employment.

Several factors make women's disproportionate involvement in household work problematic. For example, much of the activity that comprises household work is both highly repetitive (e.g. cooking, cleaning, washing and ironing) and immensely time-consuming. Also, for much of the time, housework activities are performed in isolation, and at times under considerable time pressures. The combined effect of these factors is that many find housework a source of frustration, dissatisfaction and low self-esteem. The strength of these negative feelings can, for many, outweigh any positive aspects of domestic work deriving from, for example, a degree of autonomy, or involvement with child development.

Another key factor though is that domestic work is work that is unpaid. The absence of payment is what makes this aspect of work 'hidden'. In addition, most domestic work remains practically as well as metaphorically hidden (it takes place 'behind closed doors'). This adds to the 'invisible' nature of this aspect of work.

To sum up

Domestic work is hidden not only in terms of its status and social recognition, but also in terms of national accounts of total work output – because it is unpaid, as well as by the private nature of much of household life. It remains predominantly undertaken by women.

Voluntary work

Like unpaid domestic labour, voluntary work – which has also been called 'communal' work (Gershuny, 1983) and 'gift work' (Handy, 1984) – is generally (though not exclusively) unpaid. It is also, normally, work undertaken outside the family, and as the name implies, is voluntary rather than 'forced' in any way. A typical definition of voluntary work is 'work undertaken with benefit to others outside the immediate family, not directly in return for wages, undertaken by free choice, not required by the state or its agencies' (Davis Smith, 1992: xi). For Gershuny (1983), one of the long-term factors stimulating the growth of voluntary work has been the rising cost of buying in services from the formal economy. This has led to an increased self-provisioning from within the community. However, it is important not to overlook that unpaid work has always been a basis on which communities, particularly rural communities, have functioned (see, for example, Felt and Sinclair, 1992).

The scale of voluntary work

Like other aspects of hidden work, voluntary work is characterised by its large-scale and broad diversity. A recent national survey found that almost three out of five (59%) of the population in the UK had taken part in at least one type of formal volunteering in the previous 12 months, while almost two-fifths (39%) had done so at least once a month (Low et al, 2008). On average, these regular volunteers had spent 11 hours volunteering over the past four weeks.

Those active in voluntary work tend to be people in paid employment (particularly in managerial and professional occupations), and in middle age rather than younger or older age groups. Men and women tend to volunteer for different types of work: women are more likely to undertake voluntary work in schools, with social welfare groups and to engage in fundraising activities; men are disproportionately active in voluntary work involving sports groups and committee work (ONS, 2010; for corresponding findings on the nature and scale of volunteering in the USA, see Boraas White, 2006).

The range of activities that constitute voluntary work is vast, and incorporates informal activities (such as doing an elderly neighbour's shopping) and various social exchange or mutual self-help activities (such as participating in a babysitting circle) as well as work in the more 'formal' voluntary work sector. This is itself composed of an almost endless range of activities: from the St John's Ambulance to prison visiting, from voluntary fire services to charity shops, from trade union activity to environmental work, and from canvassing during elections to serving on the local Neighbourhood Watch committee (see Extract 12.5 for one such example).

As Harding and Jenkins (1989: 119) point out, voluntary work is also diversified in terms of the levels at which activities take place: while some voluntary activities are local in character, others are part of national or even multinational voluntary organisations. Studies of voluntary activity in the UK have found that the most common activities include organising events, raising money, leading a group, being a member of a committee, providing transport, undertaking administrative work and giving advice or information. The most common areas for voluntary activity relate to sports, social clubs, children's education, religion, health and social welfare (ONS, 2010; Low et al, 2008).

Extract 12.5

Volunteer firefighters

An area of voluntary activity that is particularly important in Australia and New Zealand is voluntary firefighting. In Australia, fire services are organised on a state-wide basis, and the New South Wales Rural Fire Service claims to be the world's largest fire service with 69,000 volunteer members. In the neighbouring state of Victoria, the County Fire Authority (CFA) has around 58,000 volunteer members, supported by just over a thousand career firefighters, officers and support staff. The fire service in Victoria is divided into over 1200 CFA brigades, and collectively these are responsible for 2.5 million people and

12.5 cont.

over 150,000 square kilometres of land. Severe droughts in recent years and the prevalence of bush fires close to centres of population have brought into greater prominence the importance of this voluntary community activity.

Similarly in New Zealand, volunteers play a key role in the country's firefighting capability. Of the 359 fire districts in New Zealand, only a handful (19) are served mainly by paid firefighters; the vast majority are staffed wholly or largely by volunteer firefighters. Overall, there are just over 1500 paid firefighters in New Zealand and 11,000 volunteer firefighters (plus 400 support staff). While in some areas, professional and volunteer firefighters coexist happily alongside one another, it is evident that in other areas there is a greater degree of animosity between the two groups, with on the one hand, professional firefighters accusing the volunteers of being undertrained and ill-equipped for firefighting, while on the other hand, volunteers can show resentment towards professionals for being paid for doing the same job that they do for nothing (Welham, 2004).

Source: K. Welham, 'In the news: Summer volunteer firefighters', *The Press* (Christchurch, NZ), 10 January 2004, pp. 11–12.

Voluntary work and paid work

Voluntary work has numerous connecting points with the paid work sector. The two are in fact often undertaken side by side (as in aspects of health, education and social service provision; see below and also Extract 12.5). MacDonald (1997: 113) notes that working in the voluntary sector can also be a source of experience, skills, contacts and references necessary for voluntary workers to pursue paid employment. While some studies have shown that overall, working voluntarily does not speed up unemployed people's move out of unemployment (Hirst, 2002), at the very least it may improve an individual's sense of confidence about their ability to perform a job, or may help a change in direction into the work area of the voluntary activity.

In addition, many voluntary jobs give rise to very similar feelings to those experienced in paid work. Voluntary jobs can provide structure to people's lives just as paid work does, and are sources of job satisfaction and individual fulfilment. At the same time, working voluntarily frequently leads to a time commitment that creates fatigue and stress among the volunteer workgroup just as is felt among groups of workers in the paid work sector. Likewise, many voluntary jobs (like working as a volunteer for the Samaritans, for example) entail a great deal of emotion work, with the various outcomes that this can give rise to (see Chapter 7).

Rather than try to consider all possible intersections between voluntary work and paid work, we will take one example to illustrate the relevance of this aspect of hidden work for understanding visible work. Given its growing prominence in public debate in recent years, a useful example is the voluntary provision of care for someone who is elderly, sick or disabled. Historically, caring for the sick and elderly has represented a major aspect of voluntary activity. Prior to the introduction of a welfare state, much of this care took place within the household and the community. The rise of state-funded care reduced reliance on care within the community, but by no means did it totally eliminate the need for such care.

More recently, various factors have once again increased the significance being placed on care provided within the community rather than by the state. One of these factors is the general increase in life expectancy, resulting in a larger proportion of the population living into very old age. Estimates in Britain suggest that the proportion of the population over 85 may be 50 per cent higher by 2031 than it was in the early 1990s (Corti and Dex, 1995: 101). Second, as mentioned earlier, at the same time as the proportion of elderly people in the population is rising, the state (through legislation such as the NHS Community Care Act) has increased the emphasis placed on the self-provision of care. This reasserts the role of families and others close to those requiring care, and of voluntary organisations, rather than care being dispensed directly by state-funded professional care facilities (Means and Smith, 1994: 118–20). A Department of Health report summed up its view on the importance of voluntary work in this area:

> The Department of Health believes that volunteers working alongside social service departments bring vital added value to the implementation of community care policies, supporting people to live independently in their own homes and participate in their local communities.
>
> (Department of Health, 1996: 1)

Clearly, caring for someone who is old, disabled or ill could be categorised, depending on the circumstances, as either domestic work or voluntary work. Caring for a spouse in one's own home is part of many people's everyday domestic routine. On the other hand, many people provide care in someone else's home, for example, by paying regular visits to an elderly neighbour. This overlap of categories is not overly important. As we stated earlier, in practice, many activities relating to hidden work cross conventional boundaries. What is more important is not the issue of precise measurement, but the relevance of caring for a broader understanding of work as a whole.

Several issues arise from the relationship between the voluntary dispensing of care and the formal work sector. These include, for example, whether or not voluntary care undermines the role and status of those who perform a care function as part of their paid employment. It also involves considering whether a willingness among the public to perform some tasks voluntarily has restricted the growth of occupations that otherwise would have expanded to meet a greater demand for care provision.

However, probably the most important aspect of the interaction between caring and employment is the impact that providing care has on the carer's access to the labour market and on their employment experience. Looking after a sick or elderly person is very time-consuming and significantly influences a carer's activity and career in the formal work sector.

According to data from the British Household Panel Study (a survey of over 5000 households in Britain), by the 1990s, almost one in seven adults were providing informal care for someone sick, disabled or elderly (Corti, Laurie and Dex, 1994; Corti and Dex, 1995: 101). Just under one-third of the carers were looking after someone in their own home, while two-thirds provided care for someone living elsewhere. While a higher proportion of carers were women (17% of the female adult population), the proportion of men (12% of the male adult population) providing care was nevertheless significant. Over a third (35%) of all co-resident carers (those looking after someone in their own home) spent at least 50 hours per week on caring. Women spent more time on care than men, both inside and outside the household.

Given the amount of time devoted to providing care, it is only to be expected that this will impact significantly on carers' patterns of paid employment. This is indeed what Corti and her colleagues found (Corti et al 1994). Overall participation rates of women and men carers in the formal work sector were significantly lower than for those not involved in caring. Among those carers in employment, the likelihood of working part-time rather than full-time was significantly higher. Carers were also more likely to occupy lower-level jobs than those not involved in caring. Many involved in co-resident care in particular indicated that family responsibilities had prevented them from either looking for a job, or accepting a full-time job or changing jobs. Caring responsibilities had also required many to work fewer hours or leave paid employment altogether (ibid: 28, 38). Such effects are not surprising given the time spent on caring. In the study by Corti and colleagues (1994: 37), for example, two-fifths of the male and female co-resident carers who held full-time jobs also spent 20 hours or more a week on caring.

To sum up

Studies of carers (see also, for example, Arber and Ginn, 1995) show the extent to which they are forced to forego employment opportunities, or change their working patterns to fit in with their caring responsibilities. Caring activity provides another illustration of how hidden work impacts upon the nature and experience of work in the visible work sector.

Exercise 12.5

What do you think?

This chapter has highlighted a number of types of hidden work. From your own experience, of jobs you either have undertaken yourself or have personal knowledge of, give some examples of (i) concealed work and (ii) unrecognised work. Try to think of examples that have not already been discussed in the chapter.

Conclusion

Overall hidden work accounts for as much, if not more, work activity as the formal work sector. This chapter's analysis of hidden work indicates how, for many, the realities of work are shaped by experiences away from 'visible' employment. What is more, these hidden work realities are clearly highly diverse, for example:

- the woman at home caring for a young family;
- the unemployed person working voluntarily to maintain some routine and a sense of purpose;
- the older individual discouraged from seeking paid employment, using time available for house repairs and DIY;
- the daughter or son working part-time while at the same time caring for an elderly parent;
- the individual who secures an income through illegal activity of one sort or another.

The range of activities is as great as, if not greater than, the diversity of work experiences in the visible work sector.

Each of these areas of hidden work deserves greater recognition and more careful analysis to reflect their significance in many people's lives. In this chapter, it has been possible only to touch upon the diverse realities of hidden work. What is clear even from this brief examination, however, is not only the scale and importance of hidden work, but also the degree to which hidden and visible work are interrelated.

The degree of interrelatedness is such that analysis of one kind of work cannot be satisfactorily undertaken without due recognition being given to the other. Last, the diversity of hidden work adds considerably to the overall diversity in work experiences and in the realities of work. This theme of diversity is found throughout the book, and we comment more on it in the next chapter.

13

Work and life

Key concepts

- ▷ work–life balance
- ▷ time-based conflict
- ▷ strain-based conflict
- ▷ behaviour-based conflict
- ▷ 'breadwinner'
- ▷ 'homemaker'
- ▷ dual-earner households
- ▷ role conflict
- ▷ downshifting

Chapter aim

To explore the relationship between paid work and non-work life, particularly through the concept of 'work–life balance'.

Learning outcomes

After reading and thinking about the material in this chapter, you will be able to:

1. Explain the concept of work–life balance and distinguish between three sources of conflict between work and non-work spheres: time-based conflict, strain-based conflict and behaviour-based conflict.

2. Identify various factors that have led to a greater emphasis on work–life balance (in the labour market, in working hours, and in work and non-work experiences).

3. Assess responses to developing greater work–life balance: at the individual, community, organisational and societal levels.

4. Speculate about the future of work–life balance.

Introduction

At various points throughout the book, we have argued the case for a broader approach to the study of work than is typical. For example, in the previous chapter, we considered undeclared, stigmatised and unrecognised work as well as work in the visible, formal sector. More generally, our approach, as outlined in Chapter 1, has been to focus particularly on how employees experience work – the everyday lived reality of jobs and working life for different groups of people.

One of the themes (developed particularly in Chapters 3 and 9) is that for many workers, for some or all of their time, work is not their central life activity or a source of great fulfilment. Instead, it is something to 'survive' and 'get through', something to be endured in order to 'bring in the money', and on which the rest of their life depends. In this chapter we take this discussion further by more explicitly locating work, and people's attitudes to work, within the bigger picture of adult life. The idea behind this is that we will understand the experience of work more fully if we recognise how work fits into the rest of people's lives. We have gone part of the way towards this already – for example, by examining people's motivation to work and their work values, and exploring developments in working time patterns. This chapter brings these and other issues together, using the discussion and debate over work–life balance as a way to explore the changing relationship between work and non-work life.

'Work–life balance' is a regular issue in the popular and academic press, as well as in political debates and discussions between employers and employees (see Extract 13.1). It is an issue that is attracting growing attention in various countries around the world (see, for example, contributions to Blyton, Blunsdon, Reed and Dastmalchian, 2006, 2010). The interest in the topic is such that the expression itself has jumped the normal linguistic barriers: the exact phrase 'Work–life Balance' is widespread in Germany where it has become a frequent subject for discussion in the media, politics and the workplace (Trinczek, 2006: 113). In Japan, the Japanese pronunciation of the English term, *waaku raifu baransu,* is also increasingly in common usage (Craig, 2010: 129).

Career choke

'Women Like Us' is a social enterprise and a recruitment company that specialises in part-time work. Their mission is, 'to give everyone the choice to fit work around the needs of their family' (http://www. womenlikeus.org.uk). In 2011 they carried out telephone interviews with 1,000 employers and monitored 4,000 job vacancies from 1,000 employers. They reported on their findings in March 2012 and this work was featured across the national press. It has implications for work-life balance, and also for thinking about unfair discrimination on the basis of gender. They found many working mothers faced 'career choke'. They define this as:

the dead end choice between trading down on their skills and experiences to accept a role beneath their level of worth, and not working at all.

One of the key findings underpinning their analysis of career choke was that only 3% of available part-time jobs were for a full-time equivalent salary of £20,000 or more. Also, in terms of all advertised jobs, only 1 in 19 jobs that pay £20,000 or more are for part-time workers.

Because there is a lack of well-paid part time jobs, this does not just disadvantage highly skilled or highly qualified women. It means that even in lower paid and lower skilled jobs, because there is such competition, mothers with lower skills can find it difficult to compete. Highly qualified working mothers may 'trade down' and accept jobs for which they are over qualified because they have no choice – their careers have been choked.

In response to the report, Theresa May, the Home Secretary and Minister for Women and Equality, said:

We need to help women balance work and family life. To do this, the government is extending the right to request flexible working and introducing a new system of flexible parental leave. If we fully used the skills and qualifications of women who are currently out of work, it could deliver economic benefits of £15–20 billion per year.

Additional legislation could be helpful, and there may be benefits to the national economy, but at the same time, increasing the amount of regulation associated with recruiting working mothers could mean employers discriminate more against them. Although legislation might refer to 'parental' leave or rights for 'parents', the burden of caring for children falls disproportionately on women.

We begin with a brief discussion of some of the definitional issues surrounding work–life balance, partly because the term itself contains a confusion. For the majority of people, 'work' is a major part of their 'life', rather than something that can be separated out and presented as being somehow distinct from life (implied in the phrase 'work–life'). It is also important to recognise at the outset that work–life balance means different things to different people, depending on their work and their non-work circumstances. The causes of any 'imbalance' will also vary, and we distinguish different forms of imbalance.

We follow this discussion by considering some of the main factors behind the growth of attention being paid to work–life balance: what is making it such a prominent issue in the contemporary world of work? We focus on four areas of change:

- labour market participation
- patterns of working hours
- the experience of work
- the non-work world.

From this discussion, we move on to consider different patterns of response to perceived work–life imbalance. We consider responses by individuals, communities, organisations and national policy makers to identify the breadth and significance of the developments taking place, and also to recognise limitations in the current range of response options, as well as the need for a broader view of possible alternatives. We conclude this section by using role conflict theory to think about what types of response may be available to those experiencing imbalance or conflict between their various social roles (worker, spouse, parent, community member and so on). Finally in the chapter, we consider the prospects for work–life balance, in the light of current developments and possible future trends.

To sum up

Work does not take place in isolation, but forms one important component of most adults' lived reality. Potentially, these different components will come into conflict if demands from one sphere impact on others.

What do we mean by work–life balance?

'Work–life balance' refers to the ability of individuals to pursue their work and non-work lives successfully, without undue pressures from one undermining the satisfactory experience of the other. What makes for a satisfactory work–life balance will vary from person to person, reflecting a wide range of individual circumstances and preferences.

Much attention has been given to the effects of work time squeezing other aspects of non-work life. This is important for all sorts of people, and we shall look at the issues in more detail below. But we should also recognise that a time squeeze is not the only issue on the work–life balance agenda. For those under or unemployed, for example, work–life balance may primarily present itself as a problem of too much time on their hands and too little structure to the day (Jahoda, 1982; Warr, 1987). For those earning very low wages or with debts and little or no savings, work–life balance may be a dual problem: perhaps they will have to work long hours or take an additional job to make ends meet, and at the same time experience difficulty in making the most of any free time because of insufficient financial resources (Blyton and Jenkins, 2012; Warren, 2004).

Although most attention has been grabbed by issues of time – working parents juggling paid work and child-rearing, for example, or managers and others working long hours simply to get through their workload, or long-term carers trying to fit a paid job around their caring responsibilities – for some, work–life imbalance can come from a different set of constraints. Overall, a key factor in understanding work–life balance is identifying the degree of choice that individuals experience in their work and non-work lives. This in turn influences their ability to create and maintain their desired form of balance.

This search for understanding is further complicated, however, by the fact that the term 'work–life balance' itself is problematic. The term juxtaposes (separates and puts next to one another) 'work' and 'life'. In reality, 'work' is clearly a part of, rather than something distinct from, 'life' (Taylor, 2001). Yet, despite such problems (and in the absence of a more satisfactory term), the idea of work–life balance represents for many a sense that the demands in one sphere of life should not negatively impact on other spheres. And, for those studying work and the way in which work is experienced, the significance that people appear to attribute to work–life balance (on which, more below) underlines that it is not sufficient just to look inwards at the characteristics of work itself. Work also needs to be viewed more broadly in terms of how well it allows individuals to fulfil their other social roles.

In principle, any 'imbalance' between work and non-work could take one of two main forms:

• pressures of work making it harder to fulfil responsibilities in non-work spheres, such as the family
• family or other pressures making it more difficult to fulfil work obligations.

As we shall see, both directions of pressure or imbalance are important, but much discussion has focused on the pressures that work exerts on non-work life (for a discussion of the impact of domestic work on paid work, see Chapter 12).

Greenhaus and Beutell (1985) identify three main sources or signals of conflict between the different spheres of work and non-work activity:

• *time-based conflict:* time spent in one sphere results in less time than needed being available for other spheres
• *strain-based conflict:* strain experienced in one sphere makes it difficult to fulfil obligations in other spheres
• *behaviour-based conflict:* role behaviours required in one sphere are inappropriate for role behaviours needed in other spheres.

So, for example, 'time-based conflict' can result from pressures to spend long hours at work, or take work home to complete, thereby creating problems for fulfilling domestic obligations at home. In Hyman, Baldry, Scholarios and Bunzel's (2003) study of call centre and software workers the potential for work to spill over into domestic life was obvious. One software engineer, for example, commented on how being on call resulted in work problems severely impacting on home life:

> It can be quite disrupting…. I mean if I have nights like I had last night, where I was actually paged six times in the course of the night, although I had only to respond to two of those but it still disrupts your sleep. I mean I was paged at midnight and again at 3 and that really wakes you up.

Similarly, in the same study (p. 235), a team leader at a call centre commented on how the expectations associated with supervisory jobs affected life outside work:

> We have got to take some work with us and do extra work at home.... It's not a 9–5 – you have to take work home and finish it off.

An example of 'strain-based conflict' on the other hand could be that pressures at home – for instance, stemming from family illness or personal problems – create difficulties in attempting to concentrate on, and fulfil, work obligations. Likewise, work strain can spill over into the non-work sphere. In the Hyman et al's (2003) study, both call centre and software workers reported work strains intruding on home life; as a call-centre worker and a software technician commented:

> Sometimes if you have had a really bad day with constant calls or...had 40 calls in the queue it is very tiring. I've been exhausted and grumpy when I've went home.
>
> It's got more difficult as the years in [the company] have gone on. It reached a point about a year ago where there wasn't really a life; the mobile was left on the whole time.

An example of behaviour-based conflict may be when people transfer work-related behaviours (such as issuing instructions to subordinates) into other spheres such as the home where they are inappropriate. This can cause conflict between members in the household.

Exercise 12.1

What do you think?

1. Think of a job that you are familiar with that has a spillover effect into non-work time. Consider the form that the spillover takes: is it time-based, strain-based, behaviour-based or some combination of these? What are the main reasons for this spillover occurring?
2. Think of another job that has or had no spillover effect into non-work life. What are the main reasons for this lack of spillover?
3. Would you want a job with potential spillover? Explain your reasoning.

To sum up

Work–life balance refers to people's ability to pursue their work and non-work lives successfully, without one making excess demands on the other. What constitutes 'balance' will vary from person to person, depending on their circumstances.

Factors contributing to the work–life question

A long-running concern

Recent discussion of work–life balance is not the first time this issue has surfaced in society, though the term itself is fairly new. A key source of work–life imbalance in earlier periods of industrial development, for example, was that of very long normal work hours (around 12 hours a day or even longer in the early stages of industrial development). With all family members working, the imbalance was clear, with entire families 'living to work' rather than 'working to live'. A central argument in the political movements for shorter hours for young people (including the Factory Acts of 1833 and 1847 in the UK), and subsequently in the trade union campaigns for a shorter working day, was that without such reductions, young people would have no time for education, and both they and adults no time for any non-work activities other than sleep (Blyton, 1985). When the eight-hour day was achieved in Australia (Australian trade unions led the world in securing a shorter working day), the slogan of those campaigning for shorter hours was 'eight hours of work, eight hours of rest and eight hours of recreation'. This slogan had been associated with the earlier, enlightened British entrepreneur Robert Owen; it aptly sums up the need for greater temporal balance in the lives of working people.

The twentieth century witnessed further falls in the length of basic weekly hours, coupled with the gradual introduction of paid holidays. This led further to a greater balance of work and non-work time (ibid). As well as reductions in weekly and annual hours, the twentieth century also saw a separate development which contributed to a form of work–life balance: a 'balance' based on a growing proportion of households characterised by a single (male) earner, and a wife increasingly remaining at home to rear children and perform the domestic tasks. For much of the twentieth century, a form of balance between work and non-work aspects of life was established by the division of roles within families, with one 'breadwinner' (mainly the male) responsible for income-generating activity, leaving a 'homemaker' (usually the female) responsible for domestic and childcare activities.

To sum up

Issues of work–life balance centred on long working hours during early periods of industrial development. During the twentieth century a form of balance, based on a division of household and paid work roles, became common.

By the last part of the twentieth century and the early years of the present century, the issue of work–life balance has centred primarily on the over-demanding nature and timing of some work, and the strains this placed on many people's non-work lives. Although insufficient work (unemployment) remains a key source of imbalance for some, for most who perceive an imbalance it is one of excess work and work pressure. Changes in four areas have contributed to the growing prominence of this issue of work–life balance. We shall look at each in turn.

Changes in labour market participation

Over the last half century, the most marked change in the overall pattern of economic activity in industrialised countries has been the increased participation of women in the labour market. In the UK, for example, between the early 1970s and 2011, the employment rate for women increased from 53 to 66 per cent (ONS, 2011). Among married women with dependent children, the rise has been particularly marked, narrowing the gap in employment rates between women with and without dependent children. At the end of 2010 in the UK, the employment rate of women with dependent children was 66.5 per cent, compared to 67.3 per cent for women without dependent children. Among lone parents (women and men) with dependent children, employment rates have also risen, but they remain somewhat lower (e.g. an employment rate of 57 per cent at the end of 2009) (ibid). The challenges facing lone parents in employment bring issues of work–life balance into particularly sharp relief.

This pattern of growing proportions of women who are economically active is repeated, to a greater or lesser extent, across the large majority of industrial countries (see also Chapter 2). Overall, and despite significant country variation in levels of male, and particularly female, economic activity, the picture is one of major change in the gender composition of employment over the past generation.

A consequence of these trends in female participation rates is that there has been a significant shift away from a family pattern based around a sole (generally male) 'breadwinner' and a sole (usually female) 'homemaker'. Instead in many households, a dual-earner pattern is the norm. Whatever its positive effects, such a shift has undermined a previous form of 'balance' created by one member of the household fulfilling income-generating functions, while the other focused on childcare and domestic and related tasks.

The shift away from this sharp division of paid work and domestic roles has been marked, and comparatively recent. If we take a country such as Canada, as Duxbury and Higgins (2006) report, in the late 1960s around one in three Canadian families were dual-earning; a generation later this ratio had shifted so that seven out of ten families were dual-earning. Likewise in the UK, the number of households where all people of working age are in employment grew by almost a million between 1997 and 2004.

This pattern of increased activity of women in paid employment outside the home is expected to continue. The high levels of female participation in the labour market in certain countries, such as in Scandinavia, signal the potential for significantly higher proportions of women in paid employment elsewhere, should suitable conditions prevail (ONS, 2011).

Among the large numbers of women entering paid employment with dependent children, combining the two activities of work and childcare has only been possible through working part-time. Any net increase in women's economic activity rates has largely been accounted for by a rise in part-time working. A typical dual-earner household pattern consists of a male in full-time, and a female in part-time, paid work. While there has also been an increase in men working part-time (albeit from a low base), women continue to comprise the large majority of part-time job holders. On average in OECD countries, seven out of ten part-time jobs are held by women, and a quarter of women's jobs are part-time – both these proportions are significantly exceeded in a number of countries (see also Chapter 2 for further discussion of part-time working).

In the UK, promotion of women's labour market participation after child-bearing was extended in 2003 as the government introduced New Rights for Working Parents. This gave parents of children younger than six years (or younger than 18 years in the case of disabled children) the right to request flexible working. For many, this takes the form of a request to change from full-time to part-time hours. Even prior to this new 'right to request', such a switch represented an important means of accommodating paid work and child-rearing. Ashton and colleagues (2004: 51) note that in the UK in 2002, more than two in five women (42%) returning to work after having a child changed from full-time to part-time hours. Almost a quarter (24%) continued working full-time and approaching one-third (32%) continued working part-time.

In the 2010 budget, one of a number of changes following the GFC was that the coalition government cut child tax care credits for many families, and also froze child benefit so that it did not increase at the same rate as the cost of living (Bachelor and Collinson, 2010). It is not clear yet what effects this will have on labour market participation, but it is likely to concentrate some people's minds when they are weighing up whether to go back to work, and in doing so to incur more costs for having someone else to look after their child. The 2012 budget included proposals to withdraw state support for childcare for some families, making this benefit means tested (dependent on earnings) for the first time.

Changes in patterns of work hours

The increase in women's labour market activity is probably the single most important factor stimulating interest in work–life balance. But simultaneous developments in other aspects of work and employment are also exerting an influence. Of these, perhaps the major one is the evidence that many employees are increasingly spending long hours at work and taking additional work home. Despite reductions in the basic weekly hours of many groups since the early 1980s, and the introduction or extension of maximum weekly hours legislation in Europe and elsewhere, the prevalence and growth of longer-hours working have been noted in a number of industrial countries (see also Chapter 4). Recent evidence for the UK, for example, indicates that over one in six employees usually work more than 48 hours per week, while the usual average working week (including paid and unpaid overtime) of full-time employees in the UK is 42 hours (ONS, 2010: 50). The longest average working week was reported by managers and senior officials (45 hours), followed by machine operatives (44 hours) (ibid).

So significant is the amount of hours worked in excess of basic hours that the average working time of many employees has increased over the past two decades. This has been the subject of much discussion, particularly in countries such as Australia (see, for example, Bittman and Rice, 2001; Campbell, 2002), Canada (Duxbury and Higgins, 2006) and the United States (see, for example, Schor, 1991). Particularly relevant to the present discussion is the analysis by Jacobs and Gerson (2001) in the United States. They identify that an increase in work time is particularly noticeable if *family*, rather than individual, work hours are considered.

As noted in our discussion of overtime working in Chapter 4, there are many possible reasons for the extent and growth of long-hours working. For some in low-paid jobs, it may represent the only means to earn sufficient income to achieve an acceptable standard of living. For others, it may reflect a particular attachment to work or a desire to show commitment and thereby improve job security or chances of promotion. It may also reflect a pressure in some contexts to conform to a prevailing 'long-hours culture' within work organisations (Perlow, 1999; see also Extracts 4.3 and 4.4). For others, as discussed below, it may reflect growing employer expectations and a resulting increase in workload and work pressure. In the wake of GFC, many more people feel insecure about their employment and this can lead to them working longer hours so as not to be targeted for redundancy.

In addition to working longer hours, in Chapter 4 we noted that a growing proportion of the workforce now undertake part or all of their work outside the 'traditional' 9 to 5 work day. A large-scale study of working fathers and mothers in their 30s by Ferrie and Smith (1996) reinforced this picture of a high level of unsocial hours working among families. They found that the majority of fathers worked outside normal working hours, with two-thirds working in the evenings and six out of ten at weekends (Figure 13.1). Over a third also worked during some part of the night. It was more likely for those men in professional,

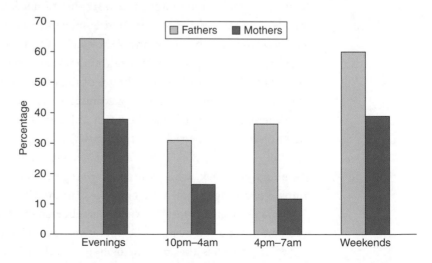

Figure 13.1   Proportions of working fathers and mothers working unsocial hours

managerial and other non-manual jobs to work in the evening, while manual workers were the ones more likely to work at night or weekends. Among women, four out of ten worked in the evening or weekend, and between one in six and one in eight at night.

For a growing proportion of employees, some work hours are worked at home (though these are not, for the most part, officially recorded as work time). Where these come on top of hours already worked 'at work', this contributes not only to longer work hours but also to a blurring of boundaries between work and non-work lives. In the Canadian study referred to above, for example, whereas one in three workers took work home in 1991, ten years later this proportion had risen to one in two (Duxbury and Higgins, 2006: 97). As we discuss below, changes in technology have significantly extended this ability of employees to continue working (or remain in contact with work) while away from the workplace.

Exercise 13.2

What do you think?

What are the main implications of the results shown in Figure 13.1 for parental roles and family life? In thinking about your answer you may want to bear in mind the comments made in Chapter 4 about the effects of night working.

Overall then, in terms of paid employment, more people work unsocial hours, or take work home with them. There has also been a growth in dual-earner families which is coupled with many people spending more hours at work. These things have fuelled debates about striking a satisfactory work–life balance.

Changes in the experience of work

As we note above, any work–life 'imbalance' may reflect not only a time-based conflict (time spent in one sphere restricting time in other spheres) but also a strain-based conflict (strain in one sphere spilling over into others). From discussions in earlier chapters, it is not only the amount of time devoted to work that is changing for many individuals and dual-earner families and giving rise to more acute work–life balance issues. Among other relevant factors has been a rise in more precarious employment – characterised by an increased use of fixed-term contracts and temporary employment in several countries – and a generally heightened sense of job insecurity, fuelled by redundancy announcements, downsizing decisions, and high levels of unemployment; and, of course, widespread insecurity following the GFC and programmes of cuts by governments at risk from levels of debt.

Job insecurity can be experienced objectively: through redundancy, a temporary contract or other forms of short-term work engagement. It can also be experienced subjectively, in the form of a perceived threat of job loss. Either kind can potentially undermine the opportunity for individuals to achieve work–life balance by restricting their ability to plan for the future, or make assumptions based on having a secure job and a predictable income. As Sennett (1998: 22) puts it, in the job-insecure world of contemporary capitalism, there is 'no long term'.

In addition, for many in employment, the problems arising from competing time demands have been heightened by increasing work pressures and strains evident within the work sphere. We examined the evidence for this in Chapter 4, particularly survey findings that report increased numbers of employees who feel under pressure at work, and especially those working with computers or experiencing major work organisation change (Green, 2004). Both of these factors are prominent aspects of life in a growing number of contemporary work organisations, as employers seek improved performance partly by increasing the productivity of their workforce.

Changes in the non-work sphere

We only have space here to outline some of the broader social and cultural developments that can be seen to be contributing to experiences of work–life imbalance. Two areas are particularly worthy of attention: changes in family structure and developments in cultural values.

Changes in family structure

Two developments in particular potentially heighten a sense of imbalance during growing female economic activity:

- a decline in extended family networks;
- an increase in family instability.

Extended family networks provide informal systems of child and elderly care, and other supportive activities. Studies in Spain and the UK have demonstrated the continuing importance of extended families (particularly the mother of the employee) for childcare (Hantrais and Ackers, 2005; Hyman, Scholarios and Baldry, 2005). However, there has been a growth in geographic mobility, in part reflecting the decline of many traditional manufacturing industries and a rise in employment opportunities elsewhere (see Chapter 2). This has led to an overall decline in close extended family networks and kinship support. In addition, as a number of commentators have pointed out, the erosion of support networks provided by extended families has been intensified by the widespread decline in the influence of the church and other community support systems. Overall this has resulted in a decline in the traditional caring capacity of communities (Esping-Andersen, 1999; Putnam, 1995, 2000).

The widespread increase in family instability has also brought particular work–life balance issues to attention. This growth in instability has been accompanied by increases in divorce and separation rates (Crompton, 2002; Esping-Andersen,

1999), and is one contributing factor to the increase in lone-parent households and single-person households. In the UK, for example, the proportion of lone-parent households with dependent children more than doubled between 1971 and 2010 (rising from 3 to 7% of all households); likewise the number of people under state pension age living alone increased from 7 to 7.5 million (29% of all households) between 2001 and 2010 (ONS, 2011).

Changes in cultural values

One background factor influencing the growth in dual-earner households and the recent growth in working hours for some is the assessment of how much income is needed to lead a satisfactory life. It is widely argued that in contemporary society there is an increasing value placed on consumption: that consumption performs a key role in shaping people's identity and satisfaction, and that expectations relating to consumption have risen (see, for example, Ransome, 2005). If this is the case, then the issue is not whether people are 'working to live' or 'living to work', but rather whether people are increasingly 'working to consume' ('working to spend'). So, the argument goes, expectations about greater consumption lead to increased levels of expenditure – and increased levels of debt – and as a result, increased pressure to earn the money to fund that pattern of consumption. This growing recognition of the relevance of consumption is summarised in the titles of two of Juliet Schor's books, published at the beginning and the end of the 1990s: work–life balance can be analysed not only in terms of *The Overworked American* (Schor, 1991) but also in terms of *The Overspent American* (Schor, 1999).

Extract 13.2

What lies behind consumption?

If pressures to consume are contributing to work–life 'imbalance', and to long work hours and work strain, or feeling rushed and pressed for time in particular, this begs the question of why we have not seen a move away from emphasis on consumption and towards creating a more relaxed and balanced life. This is exactly the question Goulding and Reed (2006: 217) ask: 'what motivates people to construct and maintain lifestyles which may result in less than optimal life satisfaction?' (see also Goulding and Reed, 2010).

One explanation for what Goulding and Reed term this 'modern society's work–life paradox' is given by Hamilton (2004), who proposes that social and economic life is driven largely by what he terms a 'deferred happiness syndrome' – a willingness to suffer in the short term (for example by long work hours and as a consequence a pressured home life) in the expectation of future happiness.

However, Jackson (2005) argues persuasively that in order to consider why people make the decisions they do – for example to engage in high levels of consumption, even though it appears to be poorly correlated with overall levels of happiness – we need to recognise that 'lifestyles in modern society ... [are] ... haunted by complexity and paradox. The materiality of our lifestyles – the stuff of everyday living – is deeply woven into the social and psychological fabric of our lives' (2005: 38).

What Jackson is saying is that to understand patterns and types of consumption, and the increased proliferation of consumer goods, we need to recognise how consumption functions at many different levels (in terms of what we might call 'lifestyle'). 'lifestyles operate partly as "social conversations": ways of communicating to ourselves and to others what sort of people we are, what kind of group we belong to…what our goals, drives and ambitions are' (Jackson, 2005: 15–16). As Jackson continues:

> This view of lifestyles relies heavily on one of the most important sociological and anthropological understandings about consumption: namely that material things embody important symbolic meanings for us…. We value goods not just for what they can do, but for what they represent to us and to others. Without this almost magical potential to speak for us in some sense, it is doubtful that plain 'stuff' could play such a key role in our lives.

What this highlights is the symbolic role that material goods play in our lives, that possessions embody more than their functional value and that most of us create our personal identity through consumption and lifestyle choices.

Jackson (2005: 20) again:

> It is precisely this promise of immense, inextinguishable personal opportunity on which the consumer society is built. Each new consumer purchase is a small piece of this continual re-invention of possibility. Each lifestyle choice opens the door to a brighter and better future. The opportunity to reinvent ourselves. The chance to realise our dreams. The basis for sustaining hope in the face of adversity. Once again, advertising executives have for decades been alive to these ways of investing mundane goods with a sense of hope. It is part of the art of marketing.

Given all the symbolic, social and psychological factors riding on consumption, and the continual, inescapable presence of advertising in all our lives, we should guard against any simplistic view that we can enter an age of post-material values (as some have argued) where greater recognition will be given to the value of a simpler, less acquisitive and more sustainable life, with positive consequences for society as a whole and for individuals, including a better sense of work–life balance. This might occur, but is likely to come about only slowly, and needs to begin with what Jackson (2005: 38) argues is 'a sophisticated engagement with the material and social basis of lifestyles…unpicking the dimensions of human motivation and desire' and understanding 'the way in which consumer lifestyles are deeply embedded in the social, psychological and cultural fabric of modern society'.

The quotes from Jackson suggest in some senses rather a romantic view of the potential benefits of consumption: that individuals can construct their ideal identity through consumption. Jackson's analysis does suggest that advocates of greater work–life balance need, as part of their argument, a deeper understanding of the role of consumption in contemporary life. But it is a problem if we focus completely on the symbolic value of consumption, because this ignores the fact that consumption is firmly set in the market-place. This emphasis on symbolic value, and 'investing mundane goods with hope', is not the kind of view of consumption that Marx would support for example.

Marx would see consumption as something which supported capitalism, and – just like the labour process under capitalism – is a source of alienation. Consumption leads to alienation from the self, and from our species (because we confuse our worth as a human being with the possessions we have), and it leads to alienation from others (because we mistake differences in ownership of goods as somehow reflecting differences between people). Marx would say that people should not be, and can not be, defined in terms of the goods or products they consume, because this depends on an exchange relationship (because these products all have a commercial value and are bought and sold in a market place).

To link consumption and identity is the kind of mistake that is associated with false consciousness – a distorted view of the world that leads people to confuse or wrongly equate things that are different. If we sign up to the idea that consumption = identity, we wrongly equate: material objects, and a sense of self or inner worth; market-value and intrinsic value; and happiness and acquisition (see Chapter 9 for discussion of alienation and false consciousness).

What do you think?

Reflect on the views about consumption expressed in Extract 13.2:

1. In your opinion, is consumption an overriding feature of people's lives today? Give some examples to support your viewpoint.
2. To what extent do you think the attitude to consumption of the average worker is responsible for distorting his/her work–life balance?
3. Does consumption, and working to support consumption, make people happy?

To sum up

Questions of the relationship between work and non-work have become more important because of changes in labour market participation (particularly the growth in the proportion of women with children engaging in paid work), developments in working time (particularly in the total work hours of households) and changing experiences of work, including greater work intensification. A fuller understanding of work–life balance needs to consider social developments outside the workplace, including changes in family and household structure, and the growing emphasis on consumption and its impact on expenditure and debt levels.

In combination, individual, community and broader social and cultural developments raise important questions about how individuals and institutions can respond to patterns of change. They also contribute to an apparently growing feeling of an inadequate balance of work and non-work lives. We turn to these patterns of response below, and then set these in a broader theoretical context. To do this, we consider how 'role theory' might contribute to identifying possible alternative strategies of response.

Responses to developing greater work–life balance

Much attention on how to resolve work–life imbalance has focused on the individual level: how individuals and households make decisions to create a better work–life balance for themselves. This is of central importance. It is also necessary to recognise that these individual responses are embedded in, interrelated with and constrained by other levels of action – at community, organisational and society levels. Only by considering each of these levels can we gain an overall picture of what an adequate response to achieving work–life balance may look like. These different levels are depicted in Figure 13.2.

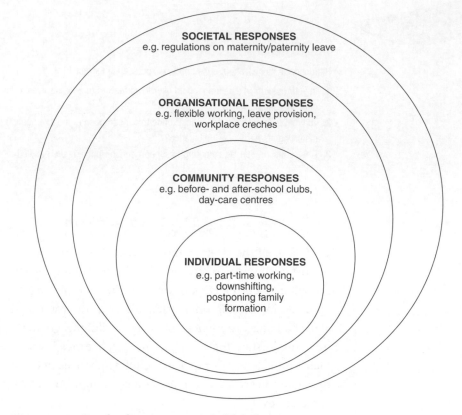

Figure 13.2   Levels of response to work–life balance pressures

Individual responses

Individual responses to balance work and non-work demands can take many forms. Five short examples follow which provide a sense of the breadth and variety of individual strategies:

- In many countries, an important work–life balance strategy in recent years has been for one member of a household (usually the female) to work part-time. This can allow couples to balance the desire for paid work and dual income with non-work responsibilities such as childcare. This may be seen as a 'modified' male breadwinner pattern with the male remaining the primary source of income generation and the female the person primarily responsible for domestic and child-rearing activities. We also noted above the considerable extent to which women in the UK move from full-time to part-time hours when they return to work after maternity leave.

- Another individual household strategy is for one or both partners to seek working arrangements that suit domestic and childcare responsibilities. These arrangements can take various forms, such as choosing jobs that offer considerable flexibility, couples working alternate work patterns (e.g. one partner working in the daytime, the other in the evening) and one parent working only during school hours and school terms. In the UK in 2009, for example, over 22 per cent of full-time employees (and 27% of part-time employees) worked some form of flexible work pattern; among part-time women workers, the most common forms of this flexible working were flexible working hours and term-time working (ONS, 2010: 51).

Another alternative is seeking work that allows some activities to be undertaken at home. Felstead, Jewson and Walters (2005a) estimated that in the UK around one in eight workers used their home to carry out some of their work. The practice has been shown to have potential work–life benefits for those involved, but there are also some potential drawbacks. To explore these, read Extract 13.3 and then try Exercise 13.4.

Extract 13.3

Homeworking and work–life balance

Susanne Tietze and her colleagues (2006) evaluated a homeworking arrangement introduced into the social services department of a UK local authority. This involved a group of professional staff who began to work from home for up to two days per week. The findings are interesting from two different perspectives: those of the homeworkers themselves and of their colleagues who were not involved in homeworking.

For the homeworkers, the outcomes were overwhelmingly positive. Being able to fit in various household and domestic tasks resulted in 'making life easier' and 'so much more convenient' (quotes from homeworkers). The homeworkers also reported much improved work performance. As one put it, 'I am flying away. I do a job in six hours which it would take me two days to do in the office.'

For the office-bound colleagues, however, the homeworking arrangement was more problematic. In part, this reflected a feeling among some of the employees remaining in the office of having more work to do, including requests to send documents by email to homeworkers who had either forgotten them or could not easily access them through the system. But more significant was a sense of injustice among the office-bound staff deriving from their exclusion from the opportunity to work partly from home. As one put it, 'I would love to work from home myself but we were told that in our jobs it wasn't feasible'; and another, 'I have a mentally disabled partner, who I care for. Sometimes it would help me to work from home.'

The organisational decision that homeworking was more suited to the work of higher-grade rather than lower-grade staff acted to further differentiate the opportunities for autonomy and variety available to higher-level staff. Thus, not only did senior staff have access to the (desired) working from home, but the lower-grade staff then had to shoulder some additional responsibility because of the greater absence of their more senior colleagues.

Source: Tietze, Musson and Scurry (2006).

Exercise 13.4

What do you think?

Consider the comments from the homeworkers in Extract 13.3 concerning the value of homeworking for fitting in other household-based tasks:

1. List up to four main benefits that homeworking could provide in terms of work–life balance.
2. The relationship between homeworking and work–life balance might not all be in a positive direction. What might be some of the problems or negative aspects of homeworking and its relationship with non-work activities?

- Individuals may also seek to create greater balance between work and non-work demands by reducing family size, and by scheduling child-bearing so this does not clash with periods of high demand at work (such as early stages of a career or when in a position requiring a large amount of travel). Reflecting this, the age of women bearing their first child has increased significantly in many industrial countries.

- Some individuals may also look for greater balance between work-related and non-work time by seeking paid work nearer their home, thereby cutting down on commuting time, and freeing up that time for other activities. One of the central benefits of working partly from home (see above) is a similar saving on time spent travelling to and from the workplace.

- A more far-reaching individual response to work–life balance is to seek to reduce income needs and thereby relieve pressure to generate income through paid work. This strategy takes different forms and attracts different labels in different countries: 'voluntary simplicity' and 'downshifting' are two such terms (Ghazi and Jones, 2004) – people opt for a simpler lifestyle to create a better balance of time between income-generating activities and other parts of their life. Goulding and Reed (2006, 2010) note the importance of personal communities (friends, close relatives and neighbours) in supporting such a strategy. This strategy, in key respects, may challenge social and cultural norms in regard to perceived family responsibilities, and more generally the prevailing norms on what constitutes a 'successful' career and life. Extract 13.2 described how the norms of acquisition and consumption are deeply embedded in contemporary society and indicates the difficulties of establishing alternative norms and values for a successful work and non-work life. We return to this issue again below.

Community-level responses

Social networks and local communities also have an important role to play in the promotion of work–life balance among their inhabitants. Local communities can play an important role through creation of care provision. These can take different forms such as youth activities and school breakfast clubs and after-school clubs, which extend the time that school premises are open to pupils. This can allow working parents to drop the children before the start of the school day and/or pick them up after the normal school time has finished. In this way, the before- and after-school clubs create a school day that more closely approximates to the adult full-time work day. Sometimes this is referred to as 'wrap-around care', which is rather a cuddly phrase for something that arguably means the needs of the child are secondary to the demands placed on parents by work.

Community provision can also importantly support work–life balance through the provision of care facilities for the elderly, such as day centres and transport facilities. Access to such provision may in turn assist carers by providing them with time to engage in some paid work during the day.

Organisational-level responses

In terms of organisational-level responses to pressures for achieving work–life balance, to date these have fallen into three main categories, often referred to as 'family-friendly' policies and practices:

- policies that provide employees with time off for child-bearing, and childcare;
- arrangements that create shorter and/or more flexible work schedules that allow work and non-work time demands to be balanced more easily (e.g. a move from full to part-time working, or flexible work hours, or term-time working, or working at or from home, or job sharing);
- workplace provisions to support parents, such as childcare facilities or subsidies (see Glass and Estes, 1997).

Of these three categories, the first is the most highly regulated in terms of minimum provision (by law workplaces have to provide maternity and parental leave; see below) while the third is generally the least available. In the UK in the late 1990s, for example, only around one in 25 workers reported access to a workplace nursery or childcare subsidy (Cully, Woodland, O'Reilly and Dix, 1999: 146). Also, access to such facilities was related to the position in the organisational hierarchy: twice the proportion of managers and senior staff (34%) reported having access to these facilities than that of other employees (17%) (Hoque and Noon, 2004: 292). The extent of employer provision of the second category – shorter and/or more flexible work schedules – varies enormously from organisation to organisation, and from country to country. Even where it is available it is often characterised by a lack of formalisation (Hyman and Summers, 2004).

In the UK, there has been a significant increase in some forms of flexible working (see Extract 13.4). Overall though, arrangements such as flexible working hours remain far less common in the UK than in some other European countries. In Germany, for example, over four out of five larger organisations (over 500 employees) operate flexible working time systems for their staff (Croucher and Singe, 2004: 153).

What studies (such as the one described in Extract 13.5) underline is that organisations need not only to have policies for work–life balance, but also an underlying culture that supports employees who utilise the flexible work options. We have reported elsewhere in this book that while organisational practices towards flexibility appear to be increasing, in other respects – such as work pressures and workload – many studies show employer expectations rising in terms of worker contribution (see Chapter 4).

WERS and work–life balance

In the UK, the 2004 Workplace Employment Relations Survey collected various information relevant to work–life balance, including information on the availability of flexible work arrangements and provision for different types of leave.

On flexible arrangements, the most common reported practices available to at least some employees were an ability to reduce hours – for example switching from full-time to part-time working (reported to exist in 70 per cent of workplaces), an ability to increase hours (57 per cent of workplaces), to change shift pattern (45 per cent of workplaces), to work flexitime (35 per cent) and to job share (in 31 per cent of workplaces).

Other practices that were less in evidence included homeworking (reported by 26 per cent of workplaces), term-time only working (20 per cent), compressed work weeks (16 per cent), annualised hours (6 per cent) and zero hours (in 5 per cent of workplaces) (Kersley et al, 2005: 28–9). Flexible practices were generally found to be more common in larger workplaces, in the public sector, in workplaces where a union was present and where more than half of the workforce was female.

Comparing findings for 1998 and 2004, responses revealed that the proportion of workplaces that indicated these forms of flexibility to be available for at least some of their employees had increased over the period, particularly in relation to switching from full-time to part-time hours, job-sharing, homeworking and term-time only working (Kersley et al, 2005: 30).

On leave arrangements to support employees with caring responsibilities, a majority of workplaces in 2004 made provision above the statutory entitlement. For example, over half (57 per cent) of workplaces provided fully paid maternity leave for some or all of the leave period, while 55 per cent provided fully paid paternity and/or discretionary leave. Almost half (49 per cent) of workplaces provided special leave for family emergencies, though just 6 per cent provided leave for carers of older adults (ibid). Such leave provisions were more common in the public than the private sector and more common in larger workplaces and where a recognised union was present.

As in the case of flexible working arrangements, the availability of leave had significantly increased between 1998 and 2004, in terms of the availability of parental leave, paid paternity/discretionary leave and special paid leave to cover family emergencies.

Source: Kersley et al (2005).

The big picture seems to be that many organisations still operate as if employees had few or no non-work responsibilities that could limit their level of commitment to the work organisation. This translates, for a substantial number, into working long hours and taking additional work home to complete. One view of this would be that it reflects a greater power of shareholders to demand improved financial performance (partly through greater employee performance). This shareholder power, and the greater power of management in the employment relationship, trumps the power of employees to establish and maintain work patterns that are less invasive of their non-work lives.

Trust based working hours

In the area of flexible working hours, Germany has long been at the forefront of developments. Flexitime (where employees have a degree of choice over the start and finish times) was first developed in Germany in the 1960s (Blyton, 1985: 127). In recent years, flexible working hours have been at the heart of the German debate over work–life balance. 'The debate in Germany about work–life balance' according to

Rainer Trinczek (2006: 113) 'typically involves arguments about flexible working hours, particularly when it comes to strategies for promoting work–life balance'.

In recent years there have been a number of initiatives in Germany involving a potentially far-reaching form of flexible hours known as 'trust-based' flexitime (*Vertrauensarbeitzeit*) which offers maximum discretion to employees over the timing of work. As Trinczek (2006: 119) explains, 'Trust-based flexitime describes a model of corporate organisation of working time in which the company renounces control of employee working hours, and it is up to staff to determine where and when their work will be done, in agreement with colleagues and superiors'. The emphasis is on the contractually agreed working time being worked by the employee in the way he or she chooses, provided agreed work is completed.

Trinczek notes the considerable spread of such systems in Germany: that somewhere between 20 and 40 per cent of all companies in Germany are using this system for at least some of their employees (more commonly for white-collar than for blue-collar workers). In the Ikea store in Regensburg, for example, sales forecasts are used to estimate several weeks in advance the number of staff required to cover the 4 am–9 pm opening hours; teams of workers then have responsibility for arranging their own shifts. Both workers and managers report the 'self-rostering' scheme as successful, both in terms of balancing work and non-work responsibilities, and staffing the store according to need (People Management, 2004: 15).

The context within which such schemes are introduced is important, however, for how the flexibility operates in practice. For example, in a recent study assessing to what extent trust-based flexitime improves the opportunity for combining work and non-work life, Trinczek (2006) reports the case of two women, both with children, and each working in the marketing departments of two different companies, one a multinational company in the software industry, the other a publishing company specialising in high quality travel literature and art books.

What Trinczek found was that the underlying working time culture in each organisation – the implicit norms and standards relating to working time – exerted an enormous impact on the way the trust-based working hours operated in practice. In the software company, for example, the working time culture emphasised the importance of 'being present in the company during an extended informal core working day [and] flexibility and spontaneity in respect of the hours worked, seen almost exclusively in terms of company needs, and a willingness "not to watch the clock"'.

In this situation, with an expectation of being reachable by customers and colleagues, and generally working longer hours than stipulated by contract, the effect was to 'place extreme limitations on the extent to which an individual can control and plan the work to be done and the hours that must be worked' (Trinczek, 2006: 127). For the individual being studied in this company, the effect was to respond by doing extra work at home and increasing her speed of work while in the office. In practice therefore the underlying working time culture of the organisation imposed substantial limitations on the extent to which the trust-based system created significant scope for greater work–life balance.

In the publishing company in contrast, the underlying culture was one which Trinczek characterises as a 'results-oriented approach' with 'a high degree of recognition of individual staff members' professional competence' and a greater trust that individuals will organise their working hours to achieve a professional level of performance. Trinczek (2006: 130) comments that this company had 'more openness to different modes of organising the work process and a clearer focus on results'.

He concludes that trust-based flexitime systems will have much more far-reaching consequences for achieving work–life balance if they are introduced where the general time culture is supportive. Thus, a trust-based system is not in itself necessarily the 'answer' to work–life imbalance; 'it is the norms and rules of work time actions as reflected in the respective work time culture that will "decide" whether these options [trust-based systems] prove to be something that employees can actually use' (ibid: 131).

Society-level responses

It is partly because of this power imbalance within organisations that governments act to regulate the employment relationship in various ways. Ideally, regulation should ensure the maintenance and development of decent terms and conditions of employment: covering work–life issues and other areas. Statutory intervention into work–life balance has developed in different ways and to differing degrees in different countries (Blunsdon and McNeil, 2006; Hantrais and Ackers, 2005). In the UK, intervention has taken such forms as extending maternity rights and introducing paternity rights (in the UK, the Employment Act 2002 introduced two weeks paternity leave for working fathers).

As we say above, this same act also gives employees a right to request flexibility in their working arrangements. The introduction of this statutory right has been reflected in a growing number of requests by workers to change their working arrangements. In the two years following the introduction of the act, one in seven employees requested a change (one in five female workers and one in ten males). The two most common changes sought were a move to part-time working and flexitime (Holt and Grainger, 2005). Elsewhere (notably in France and Scandinavia) the state's role extends significantly further in developing work–life balance, for example, by supporting childcare provisions (including statutory access to nursery care), or more extensive leave provisions to allow working adults to fulfil non-work responsibilities (Esping-Andersen, 1999; Hantrais and Ackers, 2005).

Some more insights from role theory on responses to work–life balance

In important respects, the debate about achieving better work–life balance is a debate about the social roles individuals carry out in different contexts (workplace, home, community and so on). In particular, work–life 'imbalance' can be interpreted as a problem of conflicting expectations (role conflict): where the expectations associated with one role (such as what workload is appropriate for a particular post, or how many hours someone should commit to their paid job) conflicts with expectations in another role (e.g. taking part in home life). A brief consideration of role conflict provides an alternative way of considering the responses that are already being made in pursuit of greater work–life balance. It also suggests possible areas where increased attention may be directed in the future.

According to Hall (1972), there are three main approaches or strategies for individuals to cope with role conflict:

- to adopt ways of coping with current roles;
- to change the expectations of role senders (that is, those influential in defining particular roles, such as employers or spouses);
- to change one's own attitudes to the different role expectations.

Up to now, the responses to work–life issues as outlined above appear to focus primarily on the first approach – finding better ways to cope with the different sets of role pressures. This has been through, for example, more flexible work hours, temporary leave, school clubs and other arrangements that support the combination of existing paid work activity with non-work responsibilities (such as caring for children or elderly dependants). Much of the attention of legislation, organisational policies and individual household strategies can be seen as directed towards the maintenance of work and non-work roles by a better juggling of existing role demands (like the notion of 'wrap-around care').

However, Hall's categories also help us to explore the two remaining types of response: changing the role senders', or one's own, role expectations. In terms of changing the expectations of role senders, this might entail, for example, a greater questioning of workload levels both inside and outside the workplace.

We noted earlier that work pressures are perceived to be increasing among a substantial proportion of the workforce (more people report in surveys that they are feeling rushed at work, working under pressure and so on). But is this increase in work pressure reasonable? One issue that is growing in prominence in the UK and elsewhere is whether in particular circumstances, employers may be potentially negligent for putting their employees under unreasonable pressure. An example would be where undue stress arising from the job situation potentially contravenes health and safety legislation. The broader issue here is not just what represents a reasonable workload and degree of work pressure but what constitutes a 'fair day's work', and whether for too many, work is becoming unfair.

In terms of role expectations away from paid work, as discussed in Chapter 12, for many women this is likely to reflect continuing inequality in the division of non-work responsibilities. Though evidence suggests the gender distribution of responsibilities is changing gradually, this has not kept pace with changes in women's labour force participation. At best it appears to be a lagged relationship, with delays in the renegotiation of household responsibilities following changes in employment patterns. In the meantime, many women do a 'second shift' of domestic work following completion of their work shift.

In terms of Hall's third category of response to role conflict – changing one's own attitudes to different role expectations – an important issue here relates to the perceived net gain to individuals of performing all their roles (both work and non-work) to the maximum. Let us reconsider 'downshifting' as a potential work–life balancing strategy. The idea behind downshifting is that by switching to a less time-consuming or less emotionally draining job, this will contribute to a less stressful existence and a more fulfilled life overall. One of the issues this challenges directly is the pressures that a consumer society places on people seeking to maximise their income from paid employment. Downshifting confronts this by suggesting that the greater well-being gained through reduced role pressures will outweigh any limitations from a reduced income.

In considering this third category of response, recent interest by economists in what contributes to individual and societal 'happiness' is relevant. In essence this research (based on large-scale surveys over a considerable period) indicates that as industrial societies have become more affluent, they have not proportionately increased their net amount of happiness (for a review see Layard, 2005). The proportions of people saying they are 'very happy' now appear to be no greater than they were 50 years ago, despite people being richer and in better health. Likewise, when comparing poorer and richer societies it seems that while increased average income is directly related to greater happiness among poorer countries, above a certain level of average income the relationship between income and happiness weakens. Countries with the highest incomes are not the ones reporting the highest levels of happiness (ibid).

In seeking to account for these findings, two general arguments are put forward. First, that for individuals the costs of the greater affluence – including greater anxieties and the requirement to work longer hours – offset any additional happiness that spending the extra income might be expected to generate. Second, that happiness is more related to relative, rather than absolute, income. In addition, the main sources of happiness are generally shown to be interaction with friends and family, and a stable family life. These areas may be directly restricted or undermined by over-working.

To sum up

Actions to improve work–life balance require responses from individuals and households, but these in turn are associated with other levels of response, by work organisations, communities and the state. Whilst a range of existing responses can be identified, discussions of role theory and possible role conflict highlight other areas of response that have received less attention.

Conclusion: the future of work–life balance

So what is the future for work–life balance? Predictions about the future are always problematic, but history indicates that the work–life balance issue has a future, and a significant one. We discussed earlier how work–life issues have persistently arisen at different points and in different forms throughout industrial development. In future several possible issues are likely to be influential in considering work–life balance.

First, it is likely that for several years to come, many present trends and pressures will continue. Female labour force participation rates can be expected to continue to rise, albeit at a slower rate than over the past two decades, and following GFC. This in turn will be reflected in a further growth of dual-earner households, as well as an increased involvement of lone mothers in paid work. Work–life pressures may be less if fertility rates continue to decline. Many countries have already witnessed a marked decline in fertility rates over a long period (in the UK, for example, the fertility rate halved over the course of the twentieth century; ONS, 2005: 25), and also a marked rise in the age of mothers having their first child, and in the proportion of couples with no children. Yet, the continuation of these trends in fertility rates is by no means certain. Indeed, in several developed countries – for example, Denmark, Finland, the Netherlands, and Luxemburg – the fertility rate in the early 2000s was higher than in 1980 (ibid: 26).

A second factor likely to fuel the issue of work–life balance is the continued emphasis on consumption and increasingly the consumption of leisure activities. The emphasis on consumption could lessen in the future, for example, as more people become aware of the global unsustainability of patterns of behaviour (in terms of energy use, or carbon emissions, or damaging agricultural production systems, for example). This may couple with a growth in 'post-materialist' values (Inglehart, 1997) as less emphasis is placed on material consumption (see also Chapter 3). But, some argue that for the majority, material consumption is an important source of identity and fulfilment. A Marxist analysis of consumption suggests links between consumption, false consciousness and alienation – for some of the same reasons that there is with alienation under the labour process. There are also vested interests in maintaining and expanding our consumption of an ever-widening array of goods and services. In the short term, the links between consumption, the need for income and the importance of paid work will continue to influence many people's engagement with work.

Other societal developments may also mean work–life balance is a more prominent issue in the future. First, the gradual decline in career paths for many young people, coupled with a strong desire for travel experiences (expressed in the growth in gap year and similar activities) may mean a growing rejection by the young of traditional work patterns, and a greater desire to break up periods of work with periods of travel and other non-work experiences. How widespread this trend will become is unclear, but there is likely to be greater variety in work–life arrangements for the next generation of working-age adults, compared with the present, and particularly the previous generations.

In addition, work–life balance is likely to become increasingly important for those in older age groups. The substantial increase in life expectancy and in the proportion of healthy adults in their 60s, 70s and 80s means more individuals can look forward to many years of healthy and active life beyond the current retirement ages of around 60–65. Given too the strain on pensions as a result of a growth in older claimants (and proportionately less of the population in the labour force), and the failures associated with GFC which will make many people poorer in retirement, there are evident pressures to find a different balance between work and non-work (retirement).

In principle a better balance could include, for example, a partial or gradual retirement system, with older workers adjusting to retirement by gradually reducing their work hours – and perhaps working part-time beyond the current retirement age. Partial pension schemes have been introduced in the past in countries such as Sweden (Blyton, 1984) but have generally not been sustained. Unresolved problems include occupational pension scheme restrictions and the practice of calculating pensions on the basis of earnings in the final years of employment before retiring. This acts as a major disincentive to reducing hours (and income) in the period prior to retirement.

Partial pensions or gradual retirement may make good sense for individuals with a longer life expectancy, for organisations wishing to retain skills and experience, and the state's increasing problem of funding national old age pension schemes. But experience has shown that these practices will only figure as a work–life balance option if suitable conditions are in place (such as supportive welfare arrangements and changes to the rules governing occupational pension schemes). Whether such current obstacles will be overcome remains to be seen. But the more general point holds: work–life balance is already an issue for older workers, people with young families and other groups in society, and it is likely to become more so as fixed retirement ages, lengthening life expectancies, increasingly active post-65 year olds and shortages in pension funds make present retirement arrangements less and less relevant or suitable.

A final point in this conclusion is that, whatever predictions we might make, income levels will remain critically important in understanding employee approaches to work–life balance. Balancing work and life means one thing for a professional, dual-earner household, with high income, high security regarding future income, good-quality jobs, considerable autonomy and employers that are more inclined to accommodate requests for flexibility. It means something completely different in a low-income family whose members are in low-paid and often less-secure jobs, in situations where there is less autonomy, and where employers are less likely to be sympathetic to requests for flexibility. In these different contexts, work arrangements such as part-time working are likely to have very different implications for work–life balance (Blyton and Jenkins, 2012). In a higher-income household, one member working part-time may be an optimum way of balancing household and other non-work activities with paid work. In a low-income family, one member working part-time may increase the difficulties arising from low income, and undermine any potential for part-time work to contribute positively to work–life balance (ibid; see also Warren, 2004).

Exercise 13.5

What do you think?

1. Looking into the future, do you think work–life balance issues will become more or less important in society than they are now? Why do you think this?
2. Thinking of your own future, at what points in your life do you think work–life balance will be more important to you than at other times, and why?

Work–life balance is a relevant issue for all working people, and is likely to become more so as demands for higher performance in the workplace grow. Rather than being something all of us can choose though, a danger is that work–life balance becomes just one more characteristic that separates good jobs from bad jobs. Already, as we have seen at various points in our discussion in earlier chapters, some jobs and occupations enjoy far greater access than others to relatively high income, job security, a career, interesting work, a degree of autonomy, and work that takes place in a healthy, safe and attractive working environment.

It is likely these same jobs and occupations will also be the ones offering job holders greater access to work–life balance options. This will be determined by the relative labour market power of some employee groups compared with others. Employers' desire to attract and retain certain skills means that work–life balance may be more available to some groups than others (see Blyton, 2011 for more detailed discussion). Given this, it becomes all the more important that key work–life provisions are underpinned by statutory regulation, and also that employee representatives (trade unions and staff associations) work to ensure that regulations and agreements aimed at achieving greater work–life balance are operated fairly across all employee groups.

14

Conclusion

Chapter aim

To bring together the main themes from the earlier chapters and draw some broader conclusions about the realities of work.

Key concepts

▷ change

▷ continuity

▷ informality

▷ subcultures

▷ rationality

▷ counter-rationalities

▷ complexity

Learning outcomes

After reading and thinking about the material in this chapter, you will be able to:

1. Identify the importance of both change and continuity in the nature of work.
2. Recognise the importance of subcultures that exist alongside formal management structures.
3. Understand the dual existence of management rationalities or logics, and employee counter-rationalities within the workplace.
4. Appreciate the complexity of work behaviour.

Introduction

This exploration of the realities of work has taken us through a wide range of theories, concepts and research evidence, a variety of sectors in differing economic and political contexts, a range of work settings and processes, and many experiences of working. The constant finding has been one of variety: in theories, research methods and analyses as well as results, observations and understandings. This is a valuable conclusion in its own right. It alerts us to the importance of acknowledging that different explanations are possible for the same phenomenon, because it is experienced and interpreted differently. In turn, this allows us to draw conclusions about four themes that have emerged from foregoing chapters:

▷ change and continuity;

▷ informality and subcultures;

▷ managerial rationalities and employee counter-rationalities;

▷ analytical complexity.

Change and continuity

An abiding theme in the study of work is the extent to which there have been changes from, or continuity with, the past. It has already been observed how some commentators have delineated one stage of societal development from another: for example, the theories of industrial and post-industrial society (Chapters 3 and 8) or Fordist, neo-Fordist and post-Fordist production (Chapter 6). Others have argued that the changes are in fact so great that they should be described as a new paradigm representing not only a marked economic, political, institutional, cultural and social shift, but also a quantum leap in the way we understand the world: a leap from modernist to postmodernist conceptions of the world. (For a full discussion see Harvey, 1989; Lyon, 1994; also, for an analysis linked to human resource management, see Legge, 2005: 316–55.)

We have shown in the previous chapters that there is evidence of both change *and* continuity. We drew this conclusion in the first edition of *The Realities of Work* in 1997, and the research in the intervening years has not persuaded us otherwise. Indeed there is now a growing body of empirical evidence to suggest that 'continuity' is as important as 'change' in describing contemporary work (Nolan and Wood, 2003). Through the chapters we have shown that in the workplace there have been new theories, ideas, technologies and practices to replace the old ones. But these have developed alongside patterns and work arrangements that continue to reflect important resonance with the past. Table 14.1 illustrates some of the principal areas of change and continuity that have been explored in the preceding chapters. It suggests how change in one aspect of work can produce continuity in another. Indeed, the overall extent to which work in contemporary society can be characterised as being radically different from, or fundamentally similar to, what has gone before depends largely upon which themes are being addressed:

- a focus on the features illustrated by the left-hand side of Table 14.1 would lead to the conclusion that work has undergone notable change;
- a focus on the right-hand side would suggest a pattern of continuity.

It seems to us that one of the important realities of work that has changed significantly is the growing fragmentation and uncertainty of much work experience, with an increasing proportion of jobs subject to greater job insecurity, fewer permanent contracts and more variable work arrangements. This has been exacerbated by the Global Financial Crisis. A weakening of trade union influence and only a muted political response to offset this by greater statutory protection of the employed workforce have acted to bolster the power of employers. In turn, this has allowed the latter to shift a greater share of the burden of market risk, and requirements for flexibility, onto the shoulders of employees. Thus, when faced with competing expectations of shareholders and workforce, the strength of one and the lessening power of the other have meant that management have increasingly been able to respond to market and financial pressures through

Table 14.1   Change and continuity in work

Notable CHANGE	But also CONTINUITY
New patterns of production and consumption	Persistence of the work ethic
Rise of service sector	Continued existence of routine, boring jobs
Technological change with some growth of high skilled jobs	New types of low-skill, low-discretion jobs
Increase of emotional labour	Undervaluing of social abilities as skill
More women in the labour market (feminisation)	Gendered division of labour and unfair discrimination
New forms of work (flexibility) and working time patterns	Traditional working methods and forms of control
New management initiatives for work intensification	Traditional methods of control and reliance on employee consent
Emergence of post-Fordist organisations	Taylorist/Fordist organisations remain
Recognition of institutional and less overt forms of discrimination	Unfair treatment of women and minority groups
Decline in trade union density	Desire for collective representation
Increasing importance of knowledge workers	Management techniques for appropriating 'knowledge'
Increasing globalisation and the emergence of information society	Social division between the economically advantaged and disadvantaged
Prominence of work–life issues, primarily reflecting increased participation of women in the labour market	Work–life issues, an important feature of many past campaigns for shorter work hours

redundancies, plant closures and increased work demands, rather than through longer-term market and innovation strategies (see Chapter 2).

Just as increasing employment fragmentation, insecurity and greater work pressures constitute significant changes, there are equally important continuities. Among the most notable is continued unfair discrimination within labour markets and employing organisations. This discrimination manifests itself in a number of ways, but it particularly means that some groups have greater access to higher-level, more prestigious, better-paid jobs than others. It is evident that for many in the workforce, the reality of their work experience is one of inequitable treatment compared with groups that have been more favoured in the labour market. The question of discrimination was addressed directly in Chapter 10, but at other points in the book too, the way that social arrangements have favoured some groups rather than others has been clear. Four of these points were the discussion of:

- how the notion of skill is, in important part, socially constructed (Chapter 5);
- the comparative lack of skill attributed to jobs involving emotional labour, particularly in comparison with jobs perceived as more 'rational' in character (Chapter 7);
- the ways that the work performed in households importantly influences access to, and success within, the paid employment sector (Chapter 12);
- the impact of work–life balance decisions (Chapter 13).

In each of these, the different realities for women, compared with their male counterparts, have been emphasised. Women disproportionately have suffered from an undervaluing of skills. Women are disproportionately involved in emotional labour jobs, where the content of those jobs tends to receive only limited recognition; and it continues to be women who carry a disproportionate share of responsibility for household tasks, to the detriment of the nature of their involvement in paid employment. This continuing difference in the realities of work of men and women is made more salient by the increasing feminisation of the workforce (see Chapter 2) and the increased importance being attached to striking a better balance between work and non-work lives (Chapter 13).

Exercise 14.1

What do you think?

Find an example of a theorist or commentator in any of the previous chapters who is arguing:

a. the case for change;

b. the case for continuity.

Summarise his or her arguments in a few sentences, and explain whether you find the ideas convincing.

Informality and subcultures

A common theme that emerges from various chapters is how employees cope with the realities of work by developing informal rules and a shared identity. As well as the formal individual and collective behaviours that are expected at work, there are additionally informal ways of doing things, as we saw in Chapter 9. Groups of employees develop their own, unofficial ways of working (norms) which can lead to the development of workplace subcultures. A subculture is characterised by sets of meanings that are shared by a particular group and reinforced through beliefs, values and norms. Newcomers must learn the norms of behaviour, and in so doing begin to understand the meanings and become imbued with the values and beliefs, eventually internalising them. This concept of subculture is important because it highlights the need to treat organisations as pluralist rather than unitary entities: a collection of subcultures rather than a single culture. In this sense, there may be a formal organisational culture proclaiming common values and beliefs, but behind this façade, there are likely to be different informal subcultures reflecting varying values and beliefs.

Over a period of time, strong subcultures may become embedded into the work organisation and can lead to formal collective representation (Chapter 11). It was noted in Chapter 5 the impact this has on conceptions of skill, particularly perpetuating assumptions about what constitutes men's and women's work. Similarly, subcultures may have a powerful impact (either positive or negative) on the process of discrimination at work (explored in Chapter 10) by promoting a collective understanding of fairness and unfairness in the treatment of various individuals and groups by managers. More generally, it was noted how the economic necessity of both visible work (Chapter 3) and hidden work (Chapter 12) was guided by a moral dimension, which itself often reflects dominant cultural values and beliefs.

Subcultures represent collective interests that are *different* from the formal management ideology and structures within an organisation. This arises from the pluralistic nature of all organisations. However, the types of informal, unofficial behaviours associated with coping with alienation (Chapter 9), time-discipline (Chapter 4) and stress from emotional labour (Chapter 7) are themselves often regulated by the subculture. In turn, this assists in the production of consent, thus helping to obscure the exploitative nature of the capitalist labour process. The subculture provides the mechanism for this informal regulation, so cannot really be construed as acting against profitable production; in this sense such subcultures are not usually counter-capitalism. They may perhaps be seen as counter-managerial in that they challenge aspects of control, but even then management prerogative is not opposed.

Rationalities and counter-rationalities

Often, textbooks on managing tend to paint too uniform a view of work and workers, and by extension, too uniform a view on what constitutes 'effective' management. This view, we believe, in turn reflects an over-developed sense of the omnipotence of managerial rationality pervading the workplace: that is, an assumption that the rules as defined by management are the ones strictly adhered to by the workforce. Throughout the book there are examples of the simultaneous existence of a strong workers' counter-rationality, reflecting the different interests that management and workforce bring to the workplace. Put simply, for management the *output* from work is the central issue, while for the workforce the *process* of working is an end in itself, as well as the main means of gaining income.

As discussed in Chapter 3, workers continue to go to work for more than just money in spite of an increased emphasis on consumerism and the construction of identity around consumption rather than production ('I am what I buy', rather than 'I am what I do'). Moreover, the sheer amount of time spent working means that the experience of work and the process of working remain central to the lives of the majority of people. What this reinforces is how the strategies that workers adopt contribute in various ways towards an alternative logic, or counter-rationality, and towards making work as 'humane' as possible: by easing workloads, breaking up a monotonous day, creating fun, generating interaction, building up group identities and maintaining self-esteem.

As we have also seen, these counter-rationalities often function not only for workers but also indirectly for management, and for the maintenance of capitalist wage relations. By challenging and subverting the margins of managerial rationality, workers maintain a broader consent to the core of that rationality. Rarely is there evidence of counter-rationalities going beyond fairly confined boundaries: the occasional unauthorised absence, the limited time taken up by practical jokes, the minor deviations from management's requirements over emotional labour. These do not add up to a fundamental challenge to, or rejection of, a system. They represent a way of making that system more acceptable and creating a sense that workers can exercise a measure of control over managerial definitions of work reality. Therefore, workers' counter-rationality does not typically represent a fundamental challenge to managerial authority. Workers may 'misbehave', but they do so, for the most part, within tacitly agreed and narrow limits.

This is not to say that such behaviour remains unproblematic for management. We can see how, for example, in various ways management is seeking to tighten up the utilisation of working time (see Chapter 4). But we can also see the *limited* nature of these managerial attempts to tighten up organisational regimes. Such a limitation is borne partly out of a recognition that the costs (e.g. in terms of worker morale) of suppressing all 'indulgences' are probably greater than the sum of any ensuing benefits. The limited assault on employees' counter-strategies are probably also borne out of an awareness that a complete suppression is simply not possible.

The foregoing comments diverge from a view of the workplace as a site where surveillance and compliance have reached near total levels. For the most part, such workplaces would seem to remain a small minority. Most workplaces do not operate on the basis of management seeking total and continuous conformity with detailed sets of prescribed rules governing all aspects of behaviour at work. Instead, they are more a system of negotiated order, whereby tacit agreements are established between employees and managers as to what levels of deviation from formal rules are allowed. These levels are not fixed or immutable – customs and practices are subject to modification over time – and periodically give rise to tension, as each side attempts to shift the boundary or respond to the other's attempts to shift it. But the complex requirement that capital has from wage labour – the need for consent as well as control, for active cooperation rather than merely passive compliance in translating labour power into productive labour – gives rise to a management–workforce relationship based on negotiation and a tension between the two different interest groups and the twin rationalities, rather than the uniform imposition of a dominant rationality.

Exercise 14.2

What do you think?

Drawing on the arguments and issues raised in earlier chapters:

1. Justify why is it important to take into account the perspective of the employee when trying to understand work.
2. Explain how the management of employees could be made more effective by taking closer account of employee experiences of, and attitudes towards, work.

Analytical complexity

We know life is complex, so why should it be presumed that working life is simple? Why do so many managers continue to believe in the quick fix or the latest buzzword? Why do some students seek neatly packaged answers? Why do management texts produce six-step solutions to ubiquitous problems? Why do lecturers resort to keyword acronyms to explain a multitude of varied human behaviour? It is because they are all in search of 'the simple answer', when the real answer is: there is no simple answer. Engaging with complexity is time-consuming, costly, confusing and frequently disillusioning, yet it is the only satisfactory way of exploring work.

If there are no simple solutions to complex problems, then either the complexity must be confronted or the problem redefined to simplify the challenge. Frequently academics employ the latter method, but with varying degrees of success. The process of analysing helps to understand the problem, but not necessarily to find a solution. For example, Chapter 5 revealed how different ways of 'measuring' skill were used by different researchers. All the methods had limitations, and each led to different conclusions about how the concept of skill should be understood. The solution (if it can be described as such) was to examine the complexity of the concept, and attempt to integrate all the approaches in an effort to arrive at a multifaceted 'measure' of skill, and ultimately an explanation so complex that it would be of virtually no 'practical' use in the workplace. It is this last point that alerts us to a particular problem with accepting complexity: it does not provide what the market wants. Because people (managers especially) want simple solutions and explanations, there is a pressure to produce them. Complexity is simplified, the buzzword emerges and the quick-fix solution is invented. So it is of little wonder that the realities of work invariably fail to match up with the descriptions included or implied in many management texts.

Engaging with complexity also requires a more open-minded approach to the nature of problems. If a person is looking for 'the logical solution', in the same way as, for example, Taylor (Chapter 6) believed that scientific management was the answer to all productivity problems, then the mind is closed to the equally logical possibility that there is no single solution. Indeed, the emergent picture is that the realities of work are characterised by contradiction, dilemma and paradox. For example, we discussed in Chapter 9 how the contradictions embedded in the capitalist labour process produce the dilemma of control for managers, and how, through the process of 'making out', employees paradoxically consent to their own subordination and exploitation. Throughout the analysis, the importance of contradictory theories and interpretation has surfaced, for example:

- the question of the demise or survival of the work ethic (Chapter 3);
- the theses of deskilling, upskilling or reskilling work (Chapter 6);
- the significance of emotion work (Chapter 7);

- the forms of survival strategy to cope with alienation (Chapter 9);
- the sameness and difference approaches to equal opportunities (Chapter 10);
- the 'organising' or 'service' strategy for trade union renewal (Chapter 11).

By acknowledging and confronting complexity throughout the chapters, it has been possible to demonstrate the richness and variety of the experience of work. Moreover, the pluralist approach we have taken has meant that these complex realities can be explored without the discussion flitting through a postmodern carnival or being constrained by a structuralist prison.

A final word

The different chapters have revealed the diversity of work experience. It is a diversity borne partly out of the multitude of different contexts within which work takes place, together with the very many occupations and tasks that people perform at work, and the different work schedules and contractual arrangements that employees are engaged on. However, at the same time, the diversity also derives from the different ways that people construct meaning and identity in their roles as workers: the different values they attach to work, the ways they behave and interact at work, the different strategies they employ to adjust to, and ameliorate the pressures of work, and the ways they accommodate their work and non-work lives in contemporary industrial society.

There are no signs that this diversity is set to diminish. On the contrary, the continued introduction of more varied employment contracts and work schedules, the expanding technological base of many economic sectors, the changing knowledge intensity and skill requirements of work, and the range of activities that comprise particularly the expanding service sector, all point to the continued prominence of diversity in the experience of work. Identifying and analysing this complexity will thus remain a central task in the study and understanding of the future realities of work.

Bibliography

Abbott, A. (1988) *The System of Professions*, Chicago: University of Chicago Press.

Ackroyd, S. and Thompson, P. (1999) *Organizational Misbehaviour*, London: Sage.

Adam, B. (1990) *Time and Social Theory*, Cambridge: Polity.

Adams, R. J. (1974) 'Solidarity, self- interest and the unionisation differential between Europe and North America', *Relations Industrielles*, 29 (3): 497–512.

Adib, A. and Guerrier, Y. (2003) 'The interlocking of gender with nationality, race, ethnicity and class: the narratives of women in hotel work', *Gender, Work and Organization*, 10 (4): 391–412.

Adkins, L. (1995) *Gendered Work: Sexuality, Family and the Labour Market*, Milton Keynes: Open University Press.

Aglietta, M. (1979) *A Theory of Capitalist Regulation*, London: New Left Books.

Alford, C. F. (2001) *Whistleblowers: Broken Lives and Organizational Power*, Ithaca, NY: Cornell University Press.

Ali, A. (1988) 'Scaling an Islamic work ethic', *Journal of Social Psychology*, 128 (5): 575–83.

Allen, J. and Henry, N. (1996) 'Fragments of industry and employment', in R. Crompton, D. Gallie and K. Purcell (eds), *Changing Forms of Employment*, London: Routledge: 65–82.

Amalia, M. and Nugroho, Y. (2011) 'An innovation perspective of knowledge management in a multinational subsidiary', *Journal of Knowledge Management*, 15(1): 71–87.

Angle, H. L. and Perry, J. L. (1986) 'Dual commitment and labor–management relationship climates', *Academy of Management Journal*, 29: 31–50.

Anthias, F. (1992) 'Connecting "race" and ethnic phenomena', *Sociology*, 26 (3): 421–38.

Anthias, F. and Yuval-Davis, N. (1992) *Racialized Boundaries*, London: Routledge.

Anthony, P. D. (1977) *The Ideology of Work*, London: Tavistock.

Applebaum, H. A. (1981) *Royal Blue: The Culture of Construction Workers*, New York: Holt, Rinehart and Winston.

Arber, S. and Ginn, J. (1995) 'Gender differences in the relationship between paid employment and informal care', *Work, Employment and Society*, 9 (3): 445–57.

Armstrong, P. (1988) 'Labour and monopoly capital', in R. Hyman and W. Streeck (eds), *New Technology and Industrial Relations*, Oxford: Blackwell: 143–59.

Armstrong, P. (1989) 'Management, labour process and agency', *Work, Employment and Society*, 3 (3): 307–22.

Armstrong, P. (1995) 'Accountancy and HRM', in J. Storey (ed.), *HRM: A Critical Text*, London: Routledge: 142–63.

Arrowsmith, J. and Sisson, K. (2000) 'Managing working time', in S. Bach and K. Sisson (eds), *Personnel Management*, 3rd edn, Oxford: Blackwell: 287–313.

Ashforth, B. E. and Humphrey, R. (1993) 'Emotional labour in service roles: the influence of identity', *Academy of Management Review*, 18 (1): 88–115.

Ashforth, B. E. and Humphrey, R. (1995) 'Emotion in the work place: a reappraisal', *Human Relations*, 48 (2): 97–125.

Ashforth, B. E. and Tomiuk, M. (2000) 'Emotional labour and authenticity: views from service agents', in S. Fineman (ed.), *Emotion in Organizations*, 2nd edn, London: Sage: 184–203.

Ashley, L. (2010) 'Making a difference? The use (and abuse) of diversity management at the UK's elite law firms', *Work, Employment and Society*, 24(4): 711–27.

Ashton, J., Clegg, M., Diplock, E., Richie, H. and Willison, R. (2004) *Interim Update of Key Indicators of Women's Position in Britain*, London: Department of Trade and Industry.

Attewell, P. (1990) 'What is skill?' *Work and Occupations*, 17 (4): 422–48.

Austin, E. J., Dore, T. C. P., and O'Donovan, K. M. (2008) 'Associations of personality and emotional intelligence with display rule perceptions and emotional labour', *Personality and Individual Differences*, 44: 679–88.

Baccaro, L. (2010) 'Labour and the global financial crisis', *Socio-Economic Review*, 8: 341–76.

Bacchi, C. (1990) *Same Difference: Feminism and Sexual Difference*, Sydney: Allen & Unwin.

Bach, S. and Sisson, K. (2000) 'Personnel management in perspective', in S. Bach and K. Sisson (eds).

Bachelor, L. and Collinson, P. (2010) '2010 budget: child tax credits cut and child benefit frozen', *The Guardian*, Tuesday 22 June.

Backett-Milburn, K., Airey, L., McKie, L. and Hogg, G. (2008) 'Family comes first or open all hours? How low paid women working in food retailing manage webs of obligation at home and work', *The Sociological Review*, 56 (3): 474–96.

Bacon, N. and Blyton, P. (2001) 'Exploring employee responses to "deadly combinations" of HRM initiatives', mimeo: Cardiff Business School.

Bacon, N., Blyton, P. and Dastmalchian, A. (2005) 'The significance of working time arrangements accompanying the introduction of teamworking: evidence from employees', *British Journal of Industrial Relations*, 43 (4): 681–701.

Bain, G. S. (1970) *The Growth of White Collar Unionism*, Oxford: Clarendon.

Bain, G. S. and Elsheikh, F. (1976) *Union Growth and the Business Cycle*, Oxford: Blackwell.

Bain, P., Watson, A., Mulvey, G., Taylor, P. and Gall, G. (2002) 'Taylorism, targets and the pursuit of quality by call centre management', *New Technology, Work and Employment*, 17 (3): 170–85.

Baltes, B. B., Briggs, T. E., Huff, J. W., Wright, J. A. and Neuman, G. A. (1999) 'Flexible and compressed workweek schedules: a meta-analysis of their effects on work-related criteria', *Journal of Applied Psychology*, 84 (4): 496–513.

Barham, C. and Begum, N. (2005) 'Sickness absence from work in the UK', *Labour Market Trends*, 113 (4): 149–58.

Barley, S. R. (1996) 'Technicians in the workplace: ethnographic evidence for bringing work into organization studies', *Administrative Science Quarterly*, 41 (3): 404–41.

Barney, J. (1991) 'Firm resources and sustained competitive advantage', *Journal of Management*, 17 (1): 99–120.

Barrett, L. F. and Swim, J. K. (1998) 'Appraisals of prejudice and discrimination', in J. K. Swim and C. Stangor (eds), *Prejudice: The Target's Perspective*, San Diego, Calif.: Academic Press: 11–36.

Barrett, R. (2004) 'Working at Webboyz: an analysis of control over the software development labour process', *Sociology*, 38 (4): 777–94.

Batstone, E., Gourlay, S., Levie, H. and Moore, R. (1987) *New Technology and the Process of Labour Regulation*, Oxford: Clarendon.

Baxter, J. and Western, M. (1998) 'Satisfaction with housework: examining the paradox', *Sociology*, 32 (1): 101–20.

Beauvais, L. L., Scholl, R. W. and Cooper, E. A. (1990) 'Dual commitment among unionised faculty: a longitudinal investigation', *Human Relations*, 44: 175–92.

Becker, G. (1964) *Human Capital*, New York: National Bureau of Economic Research.

Becker, H. (1963) *Outsiders: Studies in the Sociology of Deviance*, New York: Free Press.

Beechey, V. (1982) 'The sexual division of labour and the labour process: a critical assessment of Braverman', in S. Wood (ed.), *The Degradation of Work?* London: Hutchinson: 54–73.

Bell, D. (1973) *The Coming of Post-Industrial Society*, New York: Basic Books.

Bell, D. (1976) *The Cultural Contradictions of Capitalism*, London: Heinemann.

Bell, D. (1980) 'The social framework of the information society', in T. Forester (ed.), *The Microelectronics Revolution*, Oxford: Blackwell: 500–49.

Benders, J., Huijen, F. and Pekruhl, U. (2001) 'Measuring group work: findings and lesions from a European survey', *New Technology, Work and Employment*, 16 (3): 204–17.

Beneria, L. (1999) 'The enduring debate over unpaid labour', *International Labour Review*, 138 (3): 287–309.

Berg, P. (1999) 'The effects of high performance work practices on job satisfaction in the United States steel industry', *Relations Industrielles*, 54 (1): 111–35.

Berthoud, R. and Blekesaune, M. (2007) *Persistent Employment Disadvantage*, DWP Research Report 416. London: Department for Work and Pensions.

Beynon, H. (1973) *Working for Ford*, Harmondsworth: Penguin.

Bindel, J. (2004) 'Streets apart', *Guardian*, 15 May: 46–9.

Bittman, M. and Rice, J. (2001) 'The spectre of overwork: an analysis of trends between 1974 and 1997 using Australian time use diaries', *Labour and Industry*, 12: 5–26.

Blackburn, R. and Prandy, K. (1965) 'White-collar unionisation: a conceptual framework', *British Journal of Sociology*, 16: 111–22.

Blackler, F. (1995) 'Knowledge, knowledge work and organizations: an overview and interpretation', *Organization Studies*, 16 (6): 1021–46.

Blackler, F., Reed, M. and Whitaker, A. (1993) 'Editorial introduction: knowledge workers and contemporary organizations', *Journal of Management Studies*, 30 (6): 851–62.

Blackwell, L. (2003) 'Gender and ethnicity at work: occupational segregation and disadvantage in the 1991 British census', *Sociology*, 37 (4): 713–32.

Blauner, R. (1964) *Alienation and Freedom*, Chicago: University of Chicago Press.

Blunsdon, B. and McNeil, N. (2006) 'State policy and work–life integration: past, present and future approaches', in P. Blyton, B. Blunsdon, K. Reed and A. Dastmalchian (eds), *Work–Life Integration: International Perspectives on the Balancing of Multiple Roles*, Basingstoke: Palgrave Macmillan: 63–81.

Blyton, P. (1984) 'Partial retirement: some insights from the Swedish partial pension scheme', *Ageing and Society*, 4 (1): 69–83.

Blyton, P. (1985) *Changes in Working Time: An International Review*, London: Croom Helm.

Blyton, P. (1989) 'Working population and employment', in R. Bean (ed.), *International Labour Statistics*, London: Routledge: 125–43.

Blyton, P. (1994) 'Working hours', in K. Sisson (ed.), *Personnel Management*, 2nd edn, Oxford: Blackwell: 495–526.

Blyton, P. (1995) *The Development of Annual Working Hours in the United Kingdom*, Geneva: International Labour

Blyton, P. (2008) 'Working time and work-life balance', in P. Blyton, N. Bacon, J. Fiorito and E. Heery (eds) *The Sage Handbook of Industrial Relations*, London: Sage: 520–1.

Blyton, P. (2011) 'Working time, work-life balance and inequality', in P. Blyton, E. Heery and P. Turnbull (eds) *Reassessing the Employment Relationship*, Basingstoke: Palgrave Macmillan: 299–317.

Blyton, P., Blunsdon, B., Reed, K. and Dastmalchian, A. (eds) (2006) *Work–Life Integration: International Perspectives on the Balancing of Multiple Roles*, Basingstoke: Palgrave Macmillan.

Blyton, P., Blunsdon, B., Reed, K. and Dastmalchian, A. (2010) *Ways of Living: Work, Community and Lifestyle Choice*, Basingstoke: Palgrave Macmillan.

Blyton, P. and Jenkins, J. (2012) 'Life after Burberry: shifting experiences of work and non-work life following redundancy', *Work and Employment*, 26 (1): 26–41.

Blyton, P., Martinez Lucio, M., McGurk, J. and Turnbull, P. (2001) 'Globalization and trade union strategy: industrial restructuring and human resource management in the international civil aviation industry', *International Journal of Human Resource Management*, 12 (3): 445–63.

Blyton, P. Nicholson, N. and Ursell, G. (1981) 'Job status and white collar members' union activity', *Journal of Occupational Psychology*, 54 (1): 33–45.

Blyton, P. and Trinczek, R. (1995) 'Working time flexibility and annual hours', *European Industrial Relations Review*, no. 260, September: 13–14.

Blyton, P. and Turnbull, P. (1998) *The Dynamics of Employee Relations*, 2nd edn, Basingstoke: Palgrave Macmillan.

Blyton, P. and Turnbull, P. (2004) *The Dynamics of Employee Relations*, 3rd edn, Basingstoke: Palgrave Macmillan.

Boland, R. J. and Hoffman, R. (1983) 'Humor in a machine shop', in L. Pondy, P. Frost, G. Morgan and T. Dandridge (eds), *Organizational Symbolism*, Greenwich, Conn.: JAI Press: 187–98.

Boles, J. and Garbin, A. P. (1974) 'The strip club and stripper–customer patterns of interaction', *Sociology and Social Research*, 58 (1): 136–44.

Bolton, S. C. (2004) 'Conceptual confusions: emotion work as skilled work', in C. Warhurst, I. Grugulis and E. Keep (eds), *The Skills That Matter*, Basingstoke: Palgrave Macmillan: 19–37.

Bolton, S. C. (2005) *Emotion Management in the Workplace*, Basingstoke: Palgrave Macmillan.

Bolton, S. C. and Boyd, C. (2003) 'Trolley dolly or skilled emotion manager? Moving on from Hochschild's managed heart', *Work, Employment and Society*, 17 (2): 289–308.

Bolton, S. C. and Houlihan, M. (2007) 'Risky business: re-thinking the human in interactive service work', in S. Bolton and M. Houlihan (eds), *Searching for the Human in Human Resource Management*, London: Palgrave Macmillan: 245–62.

Booth, A. (1983) 'A reconsideration of trade union growth in the United Kingdom', *British Journal of Industrial Relations*, 21 (3): 379–91.

Boraas White, S. (2006) 'Volunteering in the United States, 2005', *Monthly Labor Review*, February: 65–70.

Bradley, H. (1989) *Men's Work, Women's Work*, Oxford: Blackwell.

Bradney, P. (1957) 'The joking relationship in industry', *Human Relations*, 10 (2): 179–87.

Brah, A. (1986) 'Unemployment and racism: Asian youth on the dole', in S. Allen, A. Watson, K. Purcell and S. Wood (eds), *The Experience of Unemployment*, London: Palgrave Macmillan: 61–78.

Bratton, J. (1992) *Japanization at Work*, London: Palgrave Macmillan.

Braverman, H. (1974) *Labor and Monopoly Capital*, New York: Monthly Review Press.

Brennan, J. and McGeevor, P. (1987) *Employment of Graduates from Ethnic Minorities*, London: Commission for Racial Equality.

Brewis, J. and Linstead, S. (2000a) *Sex, Work and Sex Work: Eroticizing Organization*, London: Routledge.

Brewis, J. and Linstead, S. (2000b) 'The worst thing is the screwing: consumption and the management of identity in sex work', *Gender, Work and Organization*, 7 (2): 84–97.

Broadbent, J., Dietrich, M. and Roberts, J. (1997) *The End of the Professions? The Restructuring of Professional Work*, London: Routledge.

Brown, C. and Gay, P. (1985) *Racial Discrimination: 17 Years after the Act*, London: Policy Studies Institute.

Brown, J. S. (1991) 'Research that invents the corporation', *Harvard Business Review*, January–February: 102–11.

Browning, H. L. and Singelmann, J. (1978) 'The transformation of the US labour force', *Politics and Society*, 8 (3): 481–509.

Bryson, A. (1999) ' Are unions good for industrial relations', in R. Jowell, J. Curtice, A. Park and K. Thomson (eds), *British Social Attitudes: The 16th Report*, Aldershot: Dartmouth.

Bryson, A. and Forth, J. (2010) 'The evolution of the modern worker: attitudes to work', in A. Park, J. Curtice, E. Clery and C. Bryson (eds), *British Social Attitudes: The 27th Report*, London: Sage: 103–30.

Bryson, A. and Gomez, R. (2005) ' Why have workers stopped joining trade unions? The rise in never-membership in Britain', *British Journal of Industrial Relations*, 41(1): 67–92.

Bryson, A. and McKay, S. (1997) 'What about the workers?' in R. Jowell, J. Curtice, A. Park, L. Brook, K. Thomson and C. Bryson (eds), *British Social Attitudes: The 14th Report. The End of Conservative Values?* Aldershot: Ashgate: 23–48.

Buchanan, D. A. (1986) 'Management objectives in technical change', in D. Knights and H. Willnott (eds), *Managing the Labour Process*, Aldershot: Gower: 67–84.

Buchanan, D. A. and Boddy, D. (1983) *Organisations in the Computer Age: Technological Imperatives and Strategic Choice*, Aldershot: Gower.

Bunting, M. (2004) *Willing Slaves: How the Overwork Culture Is Ruling Our Lives*, London: Harper Collins.

Burawoy, M. (1979) *Manufacturing Consent*, Chicago: University of Chicago Press.

Burawoy, M. (1985) *The Politics of Production*, London: Verso.

Burchell, B. J., Day, D., Hudson, M., Lapido, D., Mankelow, R., Nolan, J. P., Reed, H., Wichert, I. C. and Wilkinson, F. (1999) *Job Insecurity and Work Intensification: Flexibility and the Changing Boundaries of Work*, York: Joseph Rowntree Foundation.

Burris, B. H. (1993) *Technocracy at Work*, Albany: State University of New York Press.

Buyck, C. (2005) 'Wooing Europe's new breed', *Air Transport World*, 42 (9): 32–5.

Callaghan, G. and Thompson, P. (2002) 'We recruit attitude: the selection and shaping of routine call centre labour', *Journal of Management Studies*, 39 (2): 233–54.

Campbell, I. (2002) 'Extended working hours in Australia', *Labour and Industry*, 13 (1): 91–110.

Cappelli, P. (1995) 'Rethinking employment', *British Journal of Industrial Relations*, 33 (4): 563–602.

Cappelli, P. (1999) 'Career jobs are dead', *California Management Review*, 42: 146–67.

Carlzon, J. (1987) *Moments of Truth*, New York: Harper and Row.

Carruth, A. and Disney, R. (1988) 'Where have two million trade union members gone?' *Economica*, 55 (1): 1–19.

Cashmore, E. (1996) *Dictionary of Race and Ethnic Relations*, London: Routledge.

Castells, M. (1998) *The Information Age: Economy, Society and Culture* (3 vols), Oxford: Blackwell.

Castells, M. (2000) 'Materials for an exploratory theory of the network society', *British Journal of Sociology*, 51 (1): 5–24.

Cavendish, R. (1982) *Women on the Line*, London: Routledge.

Chadeau, A. (1985) 'Measuring household activities: some international comparisons', *Review of Income and Wealth*, 31 (3): 237–53.

Charles, N. (1986) 'Women and trade unions', in Feminist Review (ed.), *Waged Work*, London: Virago: 160–85.

Charles, N. and James, E. (2003) 'Gender and work orientations in conditions of job insecurity', *British Journal of Sociology*, 55 (2): 239–57.

Charlwood, A. (2002) 'Why do non-union employees want to unionise? Evidence from Britain', *British Journal of Industrial Relations*, 40 (3): 463–91.

Chartered Institute of Personnel and Development (CIPD) (2005) *Absence Management: A Survey of Policy and Practice*, London: CIPD.

Chiang, H., Han, T. and Chuang, J. (2011) 'The relationship between high-commitment HRM and knowledge-sharing behavior and its mediators', *International Journal of Manpower*, 32(5/6): 604–22.

Child, J. (1972) 'Organisation structure, environment and performance: the role of strategic choice', *Sociology*, 6 (1): 1–22.

Child, J. (1984) *Organisation: A Guide to Problems and Practice*, 2nd edn, London: Harper and Row.

Child, J. (1985) 'Managerial strategies, new technology and the labour process', in D. Knights, H. Willmott and D. Collinson (eds), *Job Redesign*, Aldershot: Gower: 107–41.

Child, J. (1997) 'Strategic choice in the analysis of action, structure, organizations and environment: retrospect and prospect', *Organization Studies*, 18 (1): 43–76.

Clarke, T. (1989) 'Imaginative flexibility in production engineering: the Volvo Uddevalla plant', paper presented to Employment Research Unit Conference, Cardiff Business School.

Clawson, D. and Fantasia, R. (1983) 'Beyond Burawoy: the dialectics of conflict and consent on the shop floor', *Theory and Society*, 12: 671–80.

Cockburn, C. (1983) *Brothers: Male Dominance and Technological Change*, London: Pluto.

Cockburn, C. (1985) *Machinery of Dominance*, London: Pluto.

Cockburn, C. (1986) 'The material of male power', in Feminist Review (ed.), *Waged Work*, London: Virago: 93–113.

Cockburn, C. (1989) 'Equal opportunities: the short and long agenda', *Industrial Relations Journal*, 20 (3): 213–25.

Cockburn, C. (1991) *In the Way of Women*, Basingstoke: Palgrave Macmillan.

Cohen, S. and Taylor, L. (1976) *Escape Attempts*, Harmondsworth: Penguin.

Colling, T. and Dickens, L. (2001) 'Gender equality and trade unions: a new basis for mobilisation', in M. Noon and E. Ogbonna (eds), *Equality, Diversity and Disadvantage in Employment*, Basingstoke: Palgrave Macmillan: 136–55.

Collins, D. (1997) 'Knowledge work or working knowledge? Ambiguity and confusion in the analysis of the "knowledge age"', *Employee Relations*, 19 (1): 38–50.

Collinson, D. L. (1988) ' "Engineering humour": masculinity, joking and conflict in shop–floor relations', *Organization Studies*, 9 (2): 181–99.

Collinson, D. L. (1992) *Managing the Shopfloor*, Berlin: de Gruyter.

Collinson, D. L. (2002) 'Managing humour', *Journal of Management Studies*, 39 (3): 269–88.

Collinson, D. L. and Knights, D. (1986) ' "Men only": theories and practices of job segregation in insurance', in D. Knights and H. Willmott (eds), *Gender and the Labour Process*, London: Sage: 140–78.

Conway, N. and Briner, R. B. (2009) 'Fifty years of psychological contract research: What do we know and what are the main challenges?' in G. P. Hodgkinson and J. K. Ford (eds), *International Review of Industrial and Organizational Psychology*, Chichester, NY: Wiley: 24: 71–130.

Cooper, C. (1996) 'Hot under the collar', *Times Higher Education Supplement*, 21 June: 12.

Corti, L. and Dex, S. (1995) 'Informal carers and employment', *Employment Gazette*, March: 101–7.

Corti, L., Laurie, H. and Dex, S. (1994) *Caring and Employment*, Employment Department Research Series no. 39, London: HMSO.

Cox, J. (1998) 'An introduction to Marx's theory of alienation', *International Socialism Journal*, 79: 41–62.

Craig, T. (2010) ' "Live to work or work to live?" The search for work-life balance in twenty-first century Japan', in P. Blyton, B. Blunsdon, K. Reed and A. Dastmalchian (eds), *Ways of Living: Work, Community and Lifestyle Choice*, Basingstoke: Palgrave Macmillan: 120–44.

Cressey, P. and MacInnes, J. (1980) 'Voting for Ford: industrial democracy and the control of labour', *Capital and Class*, 11: 5–33.

Crompton, R. (1990) 'Professions in the current context', *Work, Employment and Society*, 3 (2): 147–66.

Crompton, R. (2002) 'Employment, flexible working and the family', *British Journal of Sociology*, 53 (4): 537–58.

Crompton, R., Broackmann, M. and Lyonette, C. (2005) 'Attitudes, women's employment and the domestic division of labour: a cross-national analysis in two waves', *Work, Employment and Society*, 19 (2): 213–33.

Crompton, R. and Jones, G. (1984) *White Collar Proletariat*, London: Palgrave Macmillan.

Cross, M. (1987) 'Equality of opportunity and inequality of outcome: the MSC, ethnic minorities and training policy', in R. Jenkins and J. Solomos (eds), *Racism and Equal Opportunity Policies in the 1980s*, Cambridge: Cambridge University Press: 73–92.

Cross, M., Wrench, J. and Barnett, S. (1990) *Ethnic Minorities and the Careers Service*, Research paper no. 73, London: Department of Employment.

Croucher, R. and Singe, I. (2004) 'Co-determination and working time accounts in the German finance industry', *Industrial Relations Journal*, 35 (2): 153–68.

Crowther, S. and Garrahan, P. (1988) 'Corporate power and the local economy', *Industrial Relations Journal*, 19 (1): 51–9.

Crozier, M. (1964) *The Bureaucratic Phenomenon*, London: Tavistock.

Crusco, A. H. and Wetzel, C. G. (1984) 'The Midas touch: the effects of interpersonal touch on restaurant tipping', *Personality and Social Psychology Bulletin*, 10 (4): 512–17.

Cully, M. and Woodland, S. (1998) 'Trade union membership and recognition 1996–7', *Labour Market Trends*, 106 (7): 353–64.

Cully, M., Woodland, S., O'Reilly, A. and Dix, G. (1999) *Britain at Work*, London: Routledge.

Cunnison, S. and Stageman, J. (1995) *Feminizing the Unions*, Aldershot: Avebury.

D'Abate, C. P. (2005) 'Working hard or hardly working: a study of individuals engaging in personal business on the job', *Human Relations*, 58 (8): 1009–32.

Dale, I. and Kerr, J. (1995) 'Small and medium sized enterprises: their numbers and importance to employment', *Labour Market Trends*, December: 461–5.

Danford, A. (1998) 'Work organisation inside Japanese firms in South Wales: a break from Taylorism?' in P. Thompson and C. Warhurst (eds), *Workplaces of the Future*, Basingstoke: Palgrave Macmillan: 40–64.

Darr, A. (2004) 'The interdependence of social and technical skills in the sale of emergent technology', in C. Warhurst, I. Grugulis and E. Keep (eds), *The Skills That Matter*, Basingstoke: Palgrave Macmillan: 55–71.

Davies, H. (2010) *The Financial Crisis: Who Is to Blame?* Cambridge: Polity.

Davies, S. (1990) 'Inserting gender into Burawoy's theory of the labour process', *Work, Employment and Society*, 4 (3): 391–406.

Davis Smith, J. (1992) *Volunteering: Widening Horizons in the Third Age*, Dunfermline: Carnegie UK Trust.

De Witte, M. and Steijn, B. (2000) 'Automation, job content and underemployment', *Work, Employment and Society*, 14 (2): 245–64.

Dean, L. R. (1954) 'Union activity and dual loyalty', *Industrial and Labor Relations Review*, 12: 526–36.

Deery, S. J., Iverson, R. D. and Erwin, P. J. (1994) 'Predicting organizational and union commitment: the effect of industrial relations climate', *British Journal of Industrial Relations*, 32 (4): 581–97.

Deery, S. J., Iverson, R. D. and Walsh, J. (2002) 'Work relationships in telephone call centres: understanding emotional exhaustion and employee withdrawal', *Journal of Management Studies*, 39 (4): 471–96.

Deery, S. J. and Mahony, A. (1994) 'Temporal flexibility: management strategies and employee preferences in the retail industry', *Journal of Industrial Relations*, 36 (3): 332–52.

Delbridge, R. (1998) *Life on the Line in Contemporary Manufacturing*, Oxford: Oxford University Press.

Delbridge, R. and Turnbull, P. (1992) 'Human resource maximisation: the management of labour in just-in-time manufacturing systems', in P. Blyton and P. Turnbull (eds), *Reassessing Human Resource Management*, London: Sage: 56–73.

Delbridge, R., Turnbull, P. and Wilkinson, B. (1992) 'Pushing back the frontiers: management control and work intensification under JIT/TQM factory regimes', *New Technology, Work and Employment*, 7 (2): 97–106.

Deming, W. E. (1982) *Quality, Productivity and Competitive Position*, Cambridge, Mass.: MIT Press.

Department for Education and Employment (DfEE) (1995a) 'Changes to the coverage of the monthly count of claimant unemployment', *Labour Market Trends*, November: 398–400.

Department for Education and Employment (DfEE) (1995b) 'New developments in the pattern of claimant unemployment in the United Kingdom', *Employment Gazette*, September: 351–8.

Department of Health (1996) *Working alongside Volunteers: Promoting the Role of Volunteers in Community Care*, London: Department of Health.

Devi, S. (2000) 'Sex in the city', *Business FT Weekend Magazine*, 8 January: 14–18.

Dex, S. (1983) 'Recurrent unemployment in young black and white males', *Industrial Relations Journal*, 14 (1): 41–9.

Dibben, P. (2010) 'Trade union change, development and renewal in emerging economies: the case of Mozambique', *Work, Employment and Society*, 24 (3): 468–86.

Dickens, L. (1995) 'UK part-time employees and the law: recent and potential developments', *Gender, Work and Organization*, 2 (4): 207–15.

Ditton, J. (1977) *Part-Time Crime: An Ethnography of Fiddling and Pilferage*, London: Palgrave Macmillan.

Ditton, J. (1979) 'Baking time', *Sociological Review* 27 (1): 157–67.

Dixon, S. E. A., Meyer, K. E. and Day, M. (2010) 'Stages of organisational transformation in transition economies: a dynamic capabilities approach', *Journal of Management Studies*, 47 (3): 416–26.

Dodd, V. (2001) ' "Malicious racism" in youth prison', *Guardian*, 22 January.

Doganis, R. (1994) 'The impact of liberalization on European airline strategies and operations', *Journal of Air Transport Management*, 1 (1): 15–25.

Doherty, M. (2009) 'When the working day is through: the end of work as identity?' *Work, Employment and Society*, 23 (1): 84–101.

Dohse, K., Jurgens, U. and Malsch, T. (1985) 'From Fordism to Toyotism? The social organization of the labour process in the Japanese automobile industry', *Politics and Society*, 14 (2): 115–46.

Domagalski, T. A. (1999) 'Emotion in organizations: main currents', *Human Relations*, 52 (6): 833–52.

Doogan, K. (2001) 'Insecurity and long-term employment', *Work, Employment and Society*, 15 (3): 419–41.

Doogan, K. (2009) *New Capitalism: Transformation of Work*, Cambridge: Polity.

Douglas, M. (1975) *Implicit Meanings: Essays in Anthropology*, London: Routledge and Kegan Paul

Drucker, P. (1998) 'The future that has already happened', *The Futurist*, 32 (8): 16–18.

Dubois, P. (1979) *Sabotage in Industry*, Harmondsworth: Pelican.

Duncombe, J. and Marsden, D. (1995) ' "Workaholics" and "whingeing women": theorising intimacy and emotion work – the last frontier of gender inequality?' *Sociological Review*, 43 (1): 150–69.

Duxbury, L. and Higgins, C. (2006) 'Work–life balance in Canada: rhetoric versus reality', in P. Blyton, B. Blunsdon, K. Reed and A. Dastmalchian (eds), *Work–Life Integration: International Perspectives on the Balancing of Multiple Roles*, Basingstoke: Palgrave Macmillan: 82–112.

Easterby-Smith, M. and Lyles, M. (eds) (2003) *The Blackwell Handbook of Organizational Learning and Knowledge Management*, Oxford: Blackwell.

Edwards, P. K., Collinson, M. and Rees, C. (1998) 'The determinants of employee responses to total quality management: six case studies', *Organization Studies*, 19 (3): 449–75.

Edwards, P. K. and Scullion, H. (1982) *The Social Organisation of Industrial Conflict*, Oxford: Blackwell.

Edwards, P. K. and Whitston, C. (1991) 'Workers are working harder: effort and shop-floor relations in the 1980s', *British Journal of Industrial Relations*, 29 (4): 593–601.

Edwards, P. K. and Whitston, C. (1993) *Attending to Work: The Management of Attendance and Shopfloor Order*, Oxford: Blackwell.

Edwards, R. (1979) *Contested Terrain: The Transformation of the Workplace in the Twentieth Century*, London: Heinemann.

Ekman, P. (1973) 'Cross culture studies of facial expression', in P. Ekman (ed.), *Darwin and Facial Expression*, New York: Academic Press: 169–222.

Eldridge, J. E. T. (1971) *Sociology and Industrial Life*, Middlesex: Nelson.

Elger, T. (1990) 'Technical innovation and work reorganization in British manufacturing in the 1980s: continuity, intensification or transformation?' *Work, Employment and Society*, Special Issue, May: 67–102.

Elger, T. (1991) 'Task flexibility and the intensification of labour in UK manufacturing in the 1980s', in A. Pollert (ed.), *Farewell to Flexibility?* Oxford: Blackwell: 46–66.

Equal Opportunities Commission (1998) *Social Focus on Women and Men*, London: Office for National Statistics.

Esping-Andersen, G. (1999) *The Social Foundations of Post-Industrial Economies*, Oxford: Oxford University Press.

Essed, P. (1991) *Understanding Everyday Racism*, Newbury Park, Calif.: Sage.

European Commission (EC) (1998) *On Undeclared Work*, COM (1998) 219, Brussels: Commission of the European Communities.

European Industrial Relations Review (2004) 'Commission: report on undeclared work', *European Industrial Relations Review*, 367: 2.

Evans, S. (1990) 'Free labour and economic performance: evidence from the construction industry', *Work, Employment and Society*, 4 (2): 239–52.

Featherstone, M. (1990) *Consumer Culture and Postmodernism*, London: Sage.

Feige, E. L. (1989) 'The meaning and measurement of the underground economy', in E. L. Feige (ed.), *The Underground Economies*, Cambridge: Cambridge University Press: 175–96.

Felstead, A., Gallie, D. and Green, F. (2002) *Work Skills in Britain, 1986–2001*, London: Department for Education and Skills.

Felstead, A., Gallie, D. and Green, F. (2004) 'Job complexity and task discretion', in C. Warhurst, I. Grugulis and E. Keep (eds), *The Skills That Matter*, Basingstoke: Palgrave Macmillan: 148–69.

Felstead, A. and Jewson, N. (2000) *In Work, At Home*, London: Routledge.

Felstead, A., Jewson, N. and Walters, S. (2005a) *Changing Places of Work*, Basingstoke: Palgrave Macmillan.

Felstead, A., Jewson, N. and Walters, S. (2005b) 'The shifting locations of work: new statistical evidence on the spaces and places of employment', *Work, Employment and Society*, 19 (2): 415–31.

Felt, L. F. and Sinclair, P. R. (1992) 'Everyone does it: unpaid work in a rural peripheral region', *Work, Employment and Society*, 6 (1): 43–64.

Ferman, L. A. (1983) 'The work ethic in the world of informal work', in J. Barbash, R. J. Lampman, S. A. Levitan and G. Tyler (eds), *The Work Ethic: A Critical Analysis*, Wisconsin: Industrial Relations Research Association.

Ferrie, E. and Smith, K. (1996) *Parenting in the 1990s*, London: Family Policy Studies Centre.

Filby, M. P. (1992) ' "The figures, the personality and the bums": service work and sexuality', *Work, Employment and Society*, 6 (1): 23–42.

Financial Times (1999) 'Ford chief to meet unions over Dagenham race row', 7 October.

Fineman, S. (ed.) (1993) *Emotion in Organizations*, London: Sage.

Fineman, S. (2000) *Emotion in Organizations*, 2nd edn, London: Sage.

Firth, M. (1981) 'Racial discrimination in the British labor market', *Industrial and Labor Relations Review*, 34 (2): 265–72.

Fitzgerald, L. and Ferlie, E. (2000) 'Professionals: back to the future?' *Human Relations*, 53 (3): 713–39.

Fleming, P. (2005) 'Kindergarten cop: paternalism and resistance in a high–commitment workplace', *Journal of Management Studies*, 42 (7): 1469–89.

Fleming, P., Harley, B. and Sewell, G. (2004) 'A little knowledge is a dangerous thing: getting below the surface of the growth of "knowledge work" in Australia', *Work, Employment and Society*, 18 (4): 725–47.

Fleming, P. and Spicer, A. (2003) 'Working at a cynical distance: implications for power, subjectivity and resistance', *Organisation* 10 (1): 157–79.

Foegen, J. H. (1988) 'Hypocrisy pay', *Employee Responsibilities and Rights Journal*, 1 (1): 85–7.

Foote, N. N. (1954) 'Sex as play', *Social Problems*, 1: 159–63.

Forbes, I. and Mead, G. (1992) *Measure for Measure: A Comparative Analysis of Measures to Combat Racial Discrimination in the Member Countries of the European Community*, Research series no. 1, Sheffield: Employment Department.

Forshaw, S. and Pilgerstorfer, M. (2005) 'Illegally formed contracts of employment and equal treatment at work', *Industrial Law Journal*, 34 (2): 158–77.

Foster, D. (2007) 'Legal obligation or personal lottery? Employee experiences of disability and the negotiation of adjustments in the public sector workplace', *Work, Employment and Society*, 21 (1): 67–84.

Foster, D. and Fosh, P. (2010) 'Negotiating 'Difference': representing disabled employees in the British workplace, *British Journal of Industrial Relations*, 48 (3): 560–82.

Fox, A. (1966) *Industrial Sociology and Industrial Relations*, Research paper no 3, Royal Commission on Trade Unions and Employers' Associations, London: HMSO.

Fox, A. (1974) *Beyond Contract*, London: Faber and Faber.

Freeman, R. B. and Medoff, J. L. (1984) *What Do Unions Do?* New York: Basic Books.

Freeman, R. B. and Pelletier, J. (1990) 'The impact of industrial relations legislation on British union density', *British Journal of Industrial Relations*, 28 (2): 141–64.

Freidson, E. (1994) *Professionalism Reborn: Theory, Prophecy and Policy*, Cambridge: Polity.

Frenkel, S. J., Korczynski, M., Donoghue, L. and Shire, K. (1995) 'Re-constituting work: trends towards knowledge work and info-normative control', *Work, Employment and Society*, 9 (4): 773–96.

Frenkel, S. J., Korczynski, M., Shire, K. A. and Tam, M. (1999) *On the Front Line: Organization of Work in the Information Economy*, New York: Cornell University Press.

Friedman, A. (1977a) *Industry and Labour: Class Struggle at Work and Monopoly Capitalism*, London: Palgrave Macmillan.

Friedman, A. (1977b) 'Responsible autonomy versus direct control over the labour process', *Capital and Class*, 1 (Spring): 43–57.

Friedman, A. (1990) 'Managerial activities, techniques and technology: towards a complex theory of the labour process', in D. Knights and H. Willmott (eds), *Labour Process Theory*, London: Palgrave Macmillan: 177–208.

Friedmann, G. (1961) *The Anatomy of Work*, London: Heinemann.

Friedman, J. and Schady, N. (2009) 'How many more infants are likely to die in Africa as a result of the global financial crisis?' World Bank Policy Research Working Paper, no. 5023. August 1, 2009.

Fuchs, V. (1968) *The Service Economy*, New York: Basic Books.

Fuchs Epstein, C. and Kalleberg, A. L. (2001) 'Time and the sociology of work: issues and implications', *Work and Occupations*, 28 (1): 5–16.

Furman, F. K. (1997) *Facing the Mirror: Older Women and Beauty Shop Culture*, London: Routledge.

Fuwa, M. (2004) 'Macro-level gender inequality and the division of household labor in 22 countries', *American Sociological Review*, 69 (6): 751–67.

Gallie, D. (2005) 'Work pressures in Europe 1996–2001: trends and determinants', *British Journal of Industrial Relations*, 43 (3): 351–75.

Gallie, D., Felstead, A. and Green, F. (2004) 'Changing patterns of task discretion in Britain', *Work, Employment and Society*, 18 (2): 243–66.

Gallie, D. and White, M. (1993) *Employee Commitment and the Skills Revolution*, London: Policy Studies Institute.

Gallie, D., Zhou, Y., Felstead, A. and Green, F. (2012) 'Teamwork, skill development and employee welfare', *British Journal of Industrial Relations*, 50 (1): 23–46.

Garrahan, P. and Stewart, P. (1992) *The Nissan Enigma: Flexibility at Work in a Local Economy*, London: Mansell.

Gennard, J. and Judge G. (2005) *Employee Relations*, 4th edn, London: CIPD.

Gershuny, J. (1978) *After Industrial Society? The Emerging Self-Service Economy*, London: Palgrave Macmillan.

Gershuny, J. (1983) *Social Innovation and the Division of Labour*, Oxford: Oxford University Press.

Gershuny, J., Godwin, M. and Jones, S. (1994) 'The domestic labour revolution: a process of lagged adaptation', in M. Anderson, F. Bechhofer and J. Gershuny (eds), *The Social and Political Economy of the Household*, Oxford: Oxford University Press: 151–97.

Gershuny, J. and Miles, I. (1983) *The New Service Economy: The Transformation of Employment in Industrial Societies*, London: Pinter.

Ghazi, P. and Jones, J. (2004) *Downshifting: The Guide to Happier, Simpler Living*, 2nd edn, London: Hodder and Stoughton.

Ghosh, A. R., Ostry, J. D. and Tamirisa, N. (2009) 'Anticipating the next crisis', *Finance and Development*, 46(3): 35–7.

Glaser, B. G. and Strauss, A. L. (1967) *The Discovery of Grounded Theory: Strategies for Qualitative Research*, Chicago: Aldine.

Glass, J. L. and Estes, S. B. (1997) 'The family responsive workplace', *Annual Review of Sociology*, 23: 289–313.

Glazer, M. P. and Glazer, P. M. (1989) *The Whistleblowers*, New York: Basic Books.

Goffman, E. (1963) *Stigma*, Harmondsworth: Penguin.

Goffman, E. (1969) *The Presentation of Self in Everyday Life*, London: Allen Lane.

Goffman, E. (1971) *Relations in Public*, New York: Basic Books.

Gorz, A. (1982) *Farewell to the Working Class*, London: Pluto.

Gorz, A. (1985) *Paths to Paradise: On the Liberation from Work*, London: Pluto.

Gould, A. M. (2010) 'Working at McDonalds: some redeeming features of McJobs', *Work, Employment and Society*, 24 (4): 780–802.

Goulding, C. and Reed, K. (2006) 'Commitment, community and happiness: a theoretical framework for understanding lifestyle and work', in P. Blyton, B. Blunsdon, K. Reed and A. Dastmalchian (eds), *Work–Life Integration: International Perspectives on the Balancing of Multiple Roles*, Basingstoke: Palgrave Macmillan: 216–33.

Goulding, C. and Reed, K. (2010) 'To downshift or not to downshift? Why people make and don't make decisions to change their lives?' in P. Blyton, B. Blunsdon, K. Reed and A. Dastmalchian (eds), *Ways of Living: Work, Community and Lifestyle Choice*, Basingstoke: Palgrave Macmillan: 175–201.

Graham, L. (1995) *On the Line at Subaru–Isuzu*, Ithaca, NY: ILR/Cornell.

Grandey, A. A. (2003) 'When "the show must go on": surface acting and deep acting as determinants of emotional exhaustion and peer-rated service delivery', *Academy of Management Journal*, 46 (1): 86–96.

Grandey, A. A. and Diamond, J. A. (2010) 'Interactions with the public: Bridging job design and emotional labor perspectives', *Journal of Organizational Behavior*, 31: 338–50.

Grandey, A. A., Fisk, G. M., Mattila, A. S., Jansen, K. J. and Sideman, L. A. (2005) 'Is "service with a smile" enough? Authenticity of positive displays during service encounters', *Organizational Behavior and Human Decision Processes*, 96: 38–55.

Grant, D. (1999) 'HRM, rhetoric and the psychological contract: a case of "easier said than done"', *International Journal of Human Resource Management*, 10 (2): 327–50.

Green, F. (1992) 'Recent trends in British trade union density: how much of a compositional effect?' *British Journal of Industrial Relations*, 30 (3): 445–58.

Green, F. (2001) 'It's been a hard day's night: the concentration and intensification of work in late twentieth-century Britain', *British Journal of Industrial Relations*, 39 (1): 53–80.

Green, F. (2004) 'Why has work effort become more intense?' *Industrial Relations*, 43 (4): 709–41.

Green, F. and James, D. (2003) 'Assessing skills and autonomy: the job holder versus the line manager', *Human Resource Management Journal*, 13 (1): 63–77.

Green, F. and McIntosh, S. (2001) 'The intensification of work in Europe', *Labour Economics*, 8: 291–308.

Greenhaus, J. H. and Beutell, N. J. (1985) 'Sources of conflict between work and family roles', *Academy of Management Review*, 10: 76–88.

Grimshaw, D., Beynon, H., Rubery, J. and Ward, K. (2002) 'The restructuring of career paths in large service sector organizations: delayering, upskilling and polarisation', *Sociological Review*, 50 (1): 89–116.

Groth, M., Hennig-Thurau, T. and Walsh, G. (2009) 'Customer reactions to emotional labor: the roles of employee acting strategies and customer detection accuracy', *Academy of Management Journal*, 52 (5): 958–74.

Grugulis, I. (2007) *Skills, Training and Human Resource Development: A Critical Text*, London: Palgrave Macmillan.

Grugulis, I. and Vincent, S. (2009) 'Whose skill is it anyway? 'Soft' skills and polarization', *Work, Employment and Society*, 23(4): 597–615.

Grugulis, I., Warhurst, C. and Keep, E. (2004) 'What's happening to skill?' in C. Warhurst, I. Grugulis and E. Keep (eds), *The Skills That Matter*, Basingstoke: Palgrave Macmillan: 1–18.

Guardian (1999) 'Racist, sexist fire service panned', 17 September.

Guardian (2000) 'Hospital's macho culture goes on trial', 4 December.

Guardian (2001) 'Suicide of black worker "caused by bullying"', 9 January.

Guardian (2005) 'Neither seen nor heard', 12 November.

Guest, D. E. (1989) 'Human resource management: its implications for industrial relations and trade unions', in J. Storey (ed.), *New Perspectives on Human Resource Management*, London: Routledge: 41–55.

Guest, D. E. (1990) 'Have British workers been working harder in Thatcher's Britain? A re-consideration of the concept of effort', *British Journal of Industrial Relations*, 28 (3): 293–312.

Guest, D. E., Conway, N., Briner, R. and Dickman, M. (1996) 'The state of the psychological contract', *Issues in People Management*, no. 21, London: IPD.

Guest, D. E. and Dewe, P. (1988) 'Why do workers belong to a trade union? A social psychological study in the UK electronics industry', *British Journal of Industrial Relations*, 26 (2): 178–93.

Guest, D. E. and Dewe, P. (1991) 'Company or trade union: which wins workers allegiance? A study of commitment in the UK electronics industry', *British Journal of Industrial Relations*, 29: 81–97.

Hacket, R. D. and Bycio, P. (1996) 'An evaluation of employee absenteeism as a coping mechanism among hospital nurses', *Journal of Occupational and Organizational Psychology*, 69: 327–38.

Hakim, C. (1991) 'Grateful slaves and self-made women: fact and fantasy in women's work orientations', *European Sociological Review*, 7 (2): 101–21.

Hakim, C. (2004) *Key Issues in Women's Work*, 2nd edn, London: Glasshouse Press.

Hall, D. T. (1972) 'A model of coping with role conflict: the role behavior of college educated women', *Administrative Science Quarterly*, 17 (4): 471–86.

Hall, E. (1993) 'Smiling, deferring and flirting: doing gender by giving good service', *Work and Occupations*, 20 (4): 452–71.

Hamilton, C. (2003) *Growth Fetish*, Crows Nest, NSW, Australia: Allen and Unwin.

Hamilton, C. (2004) *Carpe Diem? The Deferred Happiness Syndrome*, Canberra: Australia Institute.

Hammer, M. and Champy, J. (1993) *Reengineering the Corporation: A Manifesto for Business Revolution*. New York: Harper Business.

Hammer, T. H., Bayazit, M. and Wazeter, D. L. (2009) 'Union leadership and member attitudes: a multi-level analysis', *Journal of Applied Psychology*, 94(2): 392–410.

Hampson, I. and Junor, A. (2005) 'Invisible work, invisible skills: interactive customer service as articulation work', *New Technology, Work and Employment*, 20 (2): 166–81.

Hampson, I. and Junor, A. (2010) 'Putting the process back in: rethinking service sector skill', *Work, Employment and Society*, 24 (3): 526–45.

Handy, C. (1984) *The Future of Work*, Oxford: Blackwell.

Hanlon, G. (1998) 'Professionalism as enterprise: service class politics and the redefinition of professionalism', *Sociology*, 32 (1): 43–63.

Hantrais, L. and Ackers, P. (2005) 'Women's choices in Europe: striking the work–life balance', *European Journal of Industrial Relations*, 11 (2): 197–212.

Harding, P. and Jenkins, R. (1989) *The Myth of the Hidden Economy*, Milton Keynes: Open University Press.

Hartmann, H. (1979) 'Capitalism, patriarchy and job segregation', in Z. Eisenstein (ed.), *Capitalist Patriarchy and the Case for Socialist Feminism*, New York: Monthly Review Press: 206–47.

Harvey, D. (1989) *The Condition of Postmodernity*, Oxford: Blackwell.

Hassard, J. (1989) 'Time and industrial sociology', in P. Blyton, J. Hassard, S. Hill and K. Starkey (eds), *Time, Work and Organization*, London: Routledge: 13–34.

Haynie, J. M., Shepherd, D. A. Patzelt, H. (2012) 'Cognitive adaptability and an entrepreneurial task: the role of metacognitive ability and feedback', *Entrepreneurship, Theory and Practice*, March, 36 (2): 237–65.

Healy, G., Heery, E., Taylor, P. and Brown, W. (eds) (2004) *The Future of Worker Representation*, Basingstoke: Palgrave Macmillan: 37–61.

Healy, G., Kirton, G. and Noon, M. (2011) 'Inequalities, intersectionality and equality and diversity initiatives', in G. Healy, G. Kirton and M. Noon (eds), *Equality, Inequalities and Diversity – Contemporary Challenges and Strategies*, Basingstoke: Palgrave Macmillan: 1–17.

Heath, A. and Cheung, S. Y. (eds) (2007) *Unequal Chances: Ethnic Minorities in Western Labour Markets*. Oxford: British Academy/Oxford University Press.

Heery, E., Delbridge, R., Salmon, J., Simms, M. and Simpson, D. (2001) 'Global labour? The transfer of the organising model to the United Kingdom', in Y. Debrah and I. Smith (eds), *Globalisation, Employment and the Workplace: Patterns of Diversity*, London: Routledge: 41–68.

Heery, E., Healy, G. and Taylor, P. (2004) 'Representation at work: themes and issues', in G. Healy, E. Heery, P. Taylor and W. Brown (eds), *The Future of Worker Representation*, Basingstoke: Palgrave Macmillan: 1–36.

Heery, E. and Noon, M. (2001) *A Dictionary of Human Resource Management*, Oxford: Oxford University Press.

Herriot, P. (1998) 'The role of the HR function in building a new proposition for staff', in P. R. Sparrow and M. Marchington (eds), *Human Resource Management – The New Agenda*, London: FT/Pitman: 106–16.

Herriot, P., Manning, W. E. G. and Kidd, J. M. (1997) 'The content of the psychological contract', *British Journal of Management*, 8: 151–62.

Hewitt, P. (1993) *About Time: The Revolution in Work and Family Life*, London: Rivers Oram.

Heyes, J. (1997) 'Annualised hours and the "knock": the organisation of working time in a chemicals plant', *Work, Employment and Society*, 11 (1): 65–81.

Hickey, R., Kuruvilla, S. and Lakhani, T. (2010) 'No panacea for success: member activism, organizing and union renewal', *British Journal of Industrial Relations*, 48 (1): 53–83.

Hicks, S. (2000) 'Trade union membership 1998–99: an analysis of data from the Certification Officer and Labour Force Survey, *Labour Market Trends*, July: 329–38.

Hicks, S. (2005) 'Trends in public sector employment', *Labour Market Trends*, 113 (12): 477–88.

Hill, R. (2000) 'New Labour Force Survey questions on working hours', *Labour Market Trends*, January: 39–47.

Hill, S. (1991) 'Why quality circles failed but Total Quality Management might succeed', *British Journal of Industrial Relations*, 29 (4): 541–68.

Hirst, A. (2002) 'Links between volunteering and employability', *Labour Market Trends*, 110 (1): 45–6.

Hirst, P. and Thompson, G. (1996) *Globalization in Question*, London: Polity.

Hochschild, A. R. (1979) 'Emotion work, feeling rules and social structure', *American Journal of Sociology*, 85 (3): 551–75.

Hochschild, A. R. (1983) *The Managed Heart: Commercialization of Human Feeling*, Berkeley: University of California Press.

Hochschild, A. R. (1989) *The Second Shift: Working Patterns and the Revolution at Home*, Berkeley: University of California Press.

Hochschild, A. R. (2003) *The Managed Heart, Twentieth Anniversary Edition*, Berkeley: University of California Press.

Hodgkins, B. (2010) 'Coalition government's deregulation drive – which employment laws could be scrapped?' *Personnel Today*, August 9, available at http://www.personneltoday.com.

Hodson, R. (1991) 'Workplace behaviors', *Work and Occupations*, 18 (3): 271–90.

Hoggett, P. (1996) 'New modes of control in the public services', *Public Administration* 74 (1): 9–36.

Holt, H. and Grainger, H. (2005) *Results of the Second Flexible Working Employee Survey*, London: DTI.

Höpfl, H. (2002) 'Playing the part: reflections on aspects of mere performance in the customer–client relationship', *Journal of Management Studies*, 39 (2): 255–67.

Hoque, K. and Noon, M. (1999) 'Racial discrimination in speculative applications: new optimism six years on?' *Human Resource Management Journal*, 9 (3): 71–82.

Hoque, K. and Noon, M. (2004) 'Equal opportunities policy and practice in Britain: evaluating the empty shell hypothesis', *Work, Employment and Society*, 18 (3): 481–506.

Horrell, S. and Rubery, J. (1991) *Employers' Working Time Policies and Women's Employment*, London: HMSO.

Horrell, S., Rubery, J. and Burchell, B. (1994) 'Gender and skills', in R. Penn, M. Rose and J. Rubery (eds), *Skill and Occupational Change*, Oxford: Oxford University Press: 189–222.

Hubbuck, J. and Carter, S. (1980) *Half a Chance? A Report on Job Discrimination against Young Blacks in Nottingham*, London: Commission for Racial Equality.

Hutton, W. (1995) *The State We're In*, London: Cape.

Hyman, J., Baldry, C., Scholarios, D. and Bunzel, D. (2003) 'Work–life balance in call centres and software development, *British Journal of Industrial Relations*, 41 (2): 215–39.

Hyman, J., Lockyer, C., Marks, A. and Scholarios, D. (2004) 'Needing a new program: why is union membership so low among software workers?' in G. Healy, E. Heery, P. Taylor and W. Brown (eds), *The Future of Worker Representation*, Basingstoke: Palgrave Macmillan: 37–61.

Hyman, J., Scholarios, D. and Baldry, C. (2005) 'Getting on or getting by? Employee flexibility and coping strategies for home and work', *Work, Employment and Society*, 19 (4): 705–25.

Hyman, J. and Summers, J. (2004) 'Lacking balance? Work–life employment practices in the modern economy', *Personnel Review*, 33 (4): 418–29.

Hyman, R. (1987) 'Strategy or structure? Capital, labour and control', *Work, Employment and Society*, 1 (1): 25–55.

Hyman, R. (1991) 'Plus ça change? The theory of production and the production of theory', in A. Pollert (ed.), *Farewell to Flexibility?* Oxford: Blackwell: 259–83.

Hyman, R. (1999) 'Imagined solidarities: can trade unions resist globalization?' in P. Leisink (ed.), *Globalization and Labour Relations*, Cheltenham: Edward Elgar.

Independent (1999) 'Systematic racism at car plant "was ignored by Ford"', 24 September.

Inglehart, R. (1997) *Modernization and Postmodernization: Cultural, Economic and Political Change in 43 Societies*, Princeton, NJ: Princeton University Press.

Ingram, A. and Sloane, P. (1984) 'The growth of shiftwork in the British food, drink and tobacco industries', *Managerial and Decision Economics*, 5 (3): 168–76.

Jackson, T. (2005) *Lifestyle Change and Market Transformation*, Briefing paper, DEFRA Market Transformation Programme, London: DEFRA.

Jacobs, J. A. and Gerson, K. (2001) 'Overworked individuals or overworked families?' *Work and Occupations*, 28 (1): 40–63.

Jacoby, S. M. (1999) 'Are career jobs heading for extinction?' *California Management Review*, 42: 123–45.

Jahoda, M. (1979) 'The impact of unemployment in the 1930s and the 1970s', *Bulletin of the British Psychological Society*, 32: 309–14.

Jahoda, M. (1982) *Employment and Unemployment*, Cambridge: Cambridge University Press.

James, N. (1989) 'Emotional labour: skill and work in the social regulation of feelings', *Sociological Review*, 37 (1): 15–42.

Jaques, E. (1956) *Measurement of Responsibility*, London: Tavistock.

Jaques, E. (1967) *Equitable Payment*, rev. edn, Harmondsworth: Penguin.

Jenkins, R. (1986) *Racism and Recruitment*, Cambridge: Cambridge University Press.

Jenkins, S., Delbridge, R. and Roberts, A. (2010) 'Emotional management in a mass customised call centre: examining skill and knowledgeability in interactive service work', *Work, Employment and Society*, 24 (3): 546–64.

Jenkins, S., Martinez Lucio, M. and Noon, M. (2002) 'Return to gender: an analysis of women's disadvantage in postal work', *Gender, Work and Organization*, 9 (1): 81–104.

Jenson, J. (1989) 'The talents of women, the skills of men', in S. Wood (ed.), *The Transformation of Work?* London: Unwin Hyman: 141–55.

Jewson, N., Mason, D., Waters, S. and Harvey, J. (1990) *Ethnic Minorities and Employment Practice: A Study of Six Employers*, Research paper no. 76, Sheffield: Employment Department.

Jones, O. (2000) 'Scientific management, culture and control: a first-hand account of Taylorism in practice', *Human Relations*, 53 (5): 631–53.

Jones, T. (1993) *Britain's Ethnic Minorities*, London: Policy Studies Institute.

Judge, T. A., Woolf, E. F. and Hurst, C. (2009) 'Is emotional labor more difficult for some than for others? A multilevel, experience-sampling study', *Personnel Psychology*, 62: 57–88.

Juran, J. M. (1979) *Quality Control Handbook*, New York: McGraw-Hill.

Juravich, T. (1985) *Chaos on the Shop Floor*, Philadelphia: Temple University Press.

Jyrkinen, M and McKie, L. (2012) 'Gender, age and ageism: experiences of women managers in Finland and Scotland', *Work, Employment and Society*, 26 (1): 61–77.

Karabanow, J. (1999) 'When caring is not enough: emotional labor and youth shelter workers', *Social Service Review*, 73 (3): 340–57.

Kazmin, A. (2004) 'Deliver them from evil', *FT Weekend Magazine*, 10 July: 14–18.

Keep, E. and Rainbird, H. (2005) 'Training', in P. Edwards (ed.), *Industrial Relations: Theory and Practice*, 2nd edn, Oxford: Blackwell: 392–419.

Kelly, J. (1982) *Scientific Management, Job Redesign and Work Performance*, London: Academic Press.

Kelly, J. (1985) 'Management's redesign of work: labour process, labour markets and product markets', in D. Knights, H. Willmott and D. Collinson (eds), *Job Redesign*, Aldershot: Gower: 30–51.

Kelly, J. (1990) 'British trade unionism 1979–89: change, continuity and contradictions', *Work, Employment and Society*, 4 (Special Issue): 29–65.

Kelly, J. (1996) 'Union militancy and social partnership', in P. Ackers, C. Smith and P. Smith (eds), *The New Workplace and Trade Unionism*, London: Routledge: 41–76.

Kelly, J. and Waddington, J. (1995) 'New prospects for British labour', *Organization*, 2 (3/4): 415–26.

Kerr, C., Dunlop, J. T., Harbison, F. H. and Myers, C. A. (1960) *Industrialism and Industrial Man*, London: Heinemann.

Kerr, W. (1954) 'Dual allegiance and emotional acceptance – recognition in industry', *Personnel Psychology*, 2: 59–66.

Kersley, B., Alpin, C., Forth, J., Bryson, A., Bewley, H., Dix, G. and Oxenbridge, S. (2005) *Inside the Workplace: First Findings from the 2004 Employment Relations Survey*, London: DTI.

Kim, H. J. (2008) 'Hotel service providers' emotional labor: The antecedents and effects on burnout', *International Journal of Hospitality Management*, 27: 151–61.

Kirton, G. (2009) 'Career plans and aspirations of recent black and minority ethnic business graduates', *Work, Employment and Society* 23 (1): 12–29.

Klandermans, P. G. (1986) 'Psychology and trade union participation: joining, acting, quitting', *Journal of Occupational Psychology*, 59: 189–204.

Kleinknecht, A. and ter Wengel, J. (1998) 'The myth of economic globalization', *Cambridge Journal of Economics*, 22 (5): 637–67.

Knights, D. and Willmott, H. (eds) (1986) *Managing the Labour Process*, Aldershot: Gower.

Knights, D. and Willmott, H. (eds) (1990) *Labour Process Theory*, London: Palgrave Macmillan.

Knights, D., Willmott, H. and Collinson, D. (eds) (1985) *Job Redesign: Critical Perspectives on the Labour Process*, Aldershot: Gower.

Kochan, T. and Osterman, P. (1994) *The Mutual Gains Enterprise*, Cambridge, Mass.: Harvard Business School Press.

Koestler, A. (1976) *The Ghost in the Machine*, London: Picador.

Konrad, A. M., Winter, S. and Gutek, B. A. (1992) 'Diversity in work group sex composition: implications for majority and minority members', *Research in the Sociology of Organizations*, 10: 115–40.

Korczynski, M. (2002) *Human Resource Management in Service Work*, Basingstoke: Palgrave Macmillan.

Korczynski, M. (2003) 'Communities of coping: collective emotional labour in service work', *Organization*, 10 (1): 55–79.

Korczynski, M. (2004) 'Back-office service work: bureaucracy challenged?' *Work, Employment and Society*, 18 (1): 97–114.

Korczynski, M. (2005) 'Skills in service work: an overview', *Human Resource Management Journal*, 15 (2): 3–14.

Korczynski, M. (2011) 'The dialectical sense of humour: routine joking in a Taylorized factory', *Organization Studies*, 32 (10): 1421–40.

Korczynski, M., Shire, K., Frenkel, S. and Tam, M. (1996) 'Front line work in the "new model service firm": Australian and Japanese comparisons', *Human Resource Management Journal*, 6 (2): 72–87.

Kreckel, R. (1980) 'Unequal opportunity structure and labour market segmentation', *Sociology*, 14 (4): 525–50.

Kumar, K. (1995) *From Post-Industrial to Post-Modern Society*, Oxford: Blackwell.

Kusterer, K. (1978) *Know How on the Job*, Boulder, Colo.: Westview Press.

Lacey, N., Wells, C. and Meure, D. (1990) *Reconstructing Criminal Law*, London: Weidenfeld and Nicolson.

Lafer, G. (2004) 'What is skill? Training for discipline in the low-wage labour market', in C. Warhurst, I. Grugulis and E. Keep (eds), *The Skills That Matter*, Basingstoke: Palgrave Macmillan: 109–27.

Lambert, S. (2008) 'Passing the buck: labor flexibility practices that transfer risk onto hourly workers', *Human Relations*, 61 (9): 1203–27.

Lashley, C. (1999) 'Empowerment through involvement: a case study of TGI Friday's restaurants', *Personnel Review*, 29 (6): 791–811.

Layard, R. (2005) *Happiness: Lessons from a New Science*, London: Allen Lane.

Lazonick, W. (1978) 'The subjection of labour to capital: the rise of the capitalist system', *Review of Radical Political Economics*, 10 (1): 1–31.

LeCroy, C. W. (2010) 'Knowledge building and social work research: a critical perspective', *Research on Social Work Practice*, 20 (3): 321–4.

Lee, G. and Wrench, J. (1987) 'Race and gender dimensions of the youth labour market: from apprenticeship to YTS', in G. Lee and R. Loveridge (eds), *The Manufacture of Disadvantage*, Milton Keynes: Open University Press: 83–99.

Lee, J.-Y., Heilmann, S. G. and Near, J. P. (2004) 'Blowing the whistle on sexual harassment: test of a model of predictors and outcomes', *Human Relations*, 57 (3): 297–322.

Legge, K. (2005) *Human Resource Management: Rhetorics and Realities*, anniversary edition, Basingstoke: Palgrave Macmillan.

Leidner, R. (1991) 'Serving hamburgers and selling insurance: gender, work and identity in interactive service jobs', *Gender and Society*, 5 (2): 154–77.

Leidner, R. (1993) *Fast Food, Fast Talk: Service Work and the Routinization of Everyday Work*, Los Angeles, CA: University of California Press.Leitch, C. M., Hill, F. M. and Harrison, R. T. (2010) 'The philosophy and practice of interpretivist research in entrepreneurship: quality, validation, and trust', *Organizational Research Methods January*, 3(1): 67–84.

Leitch, C., Hills, F. M., Harrison, R. T. (2010) 'The philosophy and practice of interpretivist research in entrepreneurship', *Organizational Research Methods*, 13 (1): 67–84.

Lessor, R. (1984) 'Social movements, the occupational arena and changes in career consciousness: the case of women flight attendants', *Journal of Occupational Behaviour*, 5: 37–51.

Lewchuck, W. and Robertson, D. (1996) 'Working conditions under lean production: a worker-based benchmarking study', in P. Stewart (ed.), *Beyond Japanese Management: The End of Modern Times?* London: Frank Cass.

Lewig, K. A. and Dollard, M. F. (2003) 'Emotional dissonance, emotional exhaustion and job satisfaction in call centre workers', *European Journal of Work and Organizational Psychology*, 12 (4): 366–92.

Lewis, A. (1995) 'The deskilling thesis revisited: on Peter Armstrong's defence of Braverman', *Sociological Review*, 43 (3): 478–500.

Lewis, D. (1997) 'Whistleblowing at work: ingredients for an effective procedure', *Human Resource Management Journal*, 7 (4): 5–11.

Liff, S. and Wajcman, J. (1996) ' "Sameness" and "difference" revisited: which way forward for equal opportunity initiatives?' *Journal of Management Studies*, 33 (1): 79–94.

Lim, V. K. G. (2002) 'The IT way of loafing on the job: cyberloafing, neutralizing and organizational justice', *Journal of Organizational Behavior*, 23: 675–94.

Linhart, R. (1981) *The Assembly Line*, London: Calder.

Linstead, S. (1985a) 'Breaking the "purity rule": industrial sabotage and the symbolic process', *Personnel Review*, 14 (3): 12–19.

Linstead, S. (1985b) 'Jokers wild: the importance of humour in the maintenance of organizational culture', *Sociological Review*, 33 (4): 741–67.

Linstead, S. (1995) 'Averting the gaze: gender and power on the perfumed picket line', *Gender, Work and Organization*, 2 (4): 190–206.

Littler, C. R. (1982) *The Development of the Labour Process in Capitalist Societies*, Aldershot: Gower.

Littler, C. R. (1985) 'Taylorism, Fordism and job design', in D. Knights, H. Willmott and D. Collinson (eds), *Job Redesign*, Aldershot: Gower: 10–29.

Littler, C. R. and Salaman, G. (1982) 'Bravermania and beyond: recent theories of the labour process', *Sociology*, 16 (2): 251–69.

Liu, Y., Prati, L. M., Perrewé, P. L., and Ferris, G. R. (2008) 'The relationship between emotional resources and emotional labor: An exploratory study', *Journal of Applied Social Psychology*, 38: 2410–39.

Lively, K. J. (2002) 'Client contact and emotional labor: upsetting the balance and evening the field', *Work and Occupations*, 29 (2): 198–225.

Livingstone, D. W. (1998) *The Education–Jobs Gap: Underemployment or Economic Democracy*, Boulder, Colo.: Westview Press.

Lloyd, C. and Payne, J. (2009) ' "Full of sound and fury, signifying nothing": interrogating new skill concepts in service work – the view from two UK call centres', *Work, Employment and Society*, 23 (4): 617–34.

Loretto, W. and White, P. (2006) 'Work, more work and retirement: older workers' perspectives', *Social Policy and Society*, 5 (4): 495–506.

Low, N., Butt, S., Ellis Paine, A. and Davis Smith, J. (2008) *Helping Out: A National Survey of Volunteering and Charitable Giving*, London: Cabinet Office.

Lundberg, H. and Karlsson, J. C. (2011) 'Under the clean surface: working as a hotel attendant', *Work, Employment and Society*, 25 (1): 141–8.

Lupton, B. (2000) 'Maintaining masculinity: men who do women's work', *British Journal of Management*, 11: S33–48.

Lynch, J. J. (1992) *The Psychology of Customer Care*, London: Palgrave Macmillan.

Lyon, D. (1986) 'From "post-industrialism" to "information society": a new social transformation?' *Sociology*, 20 (4): 577–88.

Lyon, D. (1994) *Postmodernity*, Buckingham: Open University Press.

Macan, T. H. (1994) 'Time management: test of a process model', *Journal of Applied Psychology*, 79 (3): 381–91.

Macdonald, K. M. (1995) *The Sociology of Professions*, London: Sage.

MacDonald, R. (1994) 'Fiddly jobs, undeclared working and the "something for nothing" society', *Work, Employment and Society*, 8 (4): 507–30.

MacDonald, R. (1996) 'Labours of love: voluntary working in a depressed local economy', *Journal of Social Policy*, 25 (1): 1–21.

MacDonald, R. (1997) 'Informal working, survival strategies and the idea of an "underclass"', in R. K. Brown (ed.), *The Changing Shape of Work*, Basingstoke: Palgrave Macmillan: 103–24.

Magenau, J. M., Martin, J. E. and Peterson, M. M. (1988) 'Dual and unilateral commitment among stewards and rank and file union members', *Academy of Management Journal*, 31: 359–76.

Management Today and KPMG Forensic Accounting (2000) *Business Ethics Survey*, October.

Mangham, I. L. and Overington, M. A. (1987) *Organizations as Theatre*, Chichester: Wiley.

Mann, S. (1999) 'Emotion at work: To what extent are we expressing, suppressing or faking it?' *European Journal of Work and Organizational Psychology*, 8 (3): 347–69.

Manwaring, T. and Wood, S. (1985) 'The ghost in the labour process', in D. Knights, H. Willmott and D. Collinson (eds), *Job Redesign*, Aldershot: Gower: 171–96.

Marmot, M. G. and Bell, R. (2009) 'How will the financial crisis affect health?' *British Medical Journal*, 338: b1314.

Mars, G. (1982) *Cheats at Work: An Anthropology of Workplace Crime*, London: Allen and Unwin.

Mars, G. and Nicod, M. (1984) *The World of Waiters*, Boston, Mass.: Allen and Unwin.

Marsh, C. (1991) *Hours of Work of Women and Men in Britain*, London: HMSO.

Martin, G, Staines, H. and Pate, J. (1998) 'Linking job security and career development in a new psychological contract', *Human Resource Management Journal*, 8 (3): 20–40.

Martin, J., Knopoff, K. and Beckman, C. (1998) 'An alternative to bureaucratic impersonality: bounded emotionality at The Body Shop', *Administrative Science Quarterly*, 43: 429–69.

Martinez-Inigo, D., Totterdell, P., Alcover, C. M., and Holman, D. (2007) 'Emotional labour and emotional exhaustion: Interpersonal and intrapersonal mechanisms', *Work & Stress*, 21: 30–47.

Marx, K. (1969) 'Alienated labour', in T. Burns (ed.), *Industrial Man: Selected Readings*, Harmondsworth: Penguin: 95–109.

Marx, K. (1976) *Capital*, Vol. 1, Harmondsworth: Penguin.

Mason, D. (1994) 'On the dangers of disconnecting race and racism', *Sociology*, 28 (4): 845–58.

Massey, D. (1988) 'What's happening to UK manufacturing?' in J. Allen and D. Massey (eds), *The Economy in Question*, London: Sage: 45–90.

Matthaei, J. (1982) *An Economic History of Women in America*, Brighton: Harvester.

Matusik, S. F. and Hill, C. W. L. (1998) 'The utilization of contingent work, knowledge creation and competitive advantage', *Academy of Management Review*, 23 (4): 680–97.

May, C. (2002) *The Information Society: A Sceptical View*, Cambridge: Polity.

Mayo, E. (1933) *The Human Problems of an Industrial Civilisation*, New York: Palgrave Macmillan.

McClelland, K. (1987) 'Time to work, time to live: some aspects of work and the reformation of class in Britain 1850–1880', in P. Joyce (ed.), *The Historical Meanings of Work*, Cambridge: Cambridge University Press: 180–209.

McCord, A. (2010) 'The impact of the global financial crisis on social protection in developing countries', *International Social Security Review*, 63 (2): 31–45.

McCormick, B. J. (1979) *Industrial Relations in the Coal Industry*, London: Palgrave Macmillan.

McIntosh, I. and Broderick, J. (1996) 'Neither one thing nor the other: compulsory competitive tendering and Southburg cleansing services', *Work, Employment and Society*, 10 (3): 413–30.

McKean, J. (2010) *Managing Customers through Economic Cycles*, Wiley: London.

McKee, L. and Bell, C. (1986) 'His unemployment, her problem: the domestic and marital consequences of male unemployment', in S. Allen, A. Waton, K. Purcell and S. Wood (eds), *The Experience of Unemployment*, Basingstoke: Palgrave Macmillan: 134–49.

McLoughlin, I. and Clark, J. (1994) *Technological Change at Work*, 2nd edn, Milton Keynes: Open University Press.

McRae, S. (2003) 'Constraints and choices in mothers' employment careers: a consideration of Hakim's preference theory', *British Journal of Sociology*, 54 (3): 317–38.

Means, R. and Smith, R. (1994) *Community Care: Policy and Practice*, Basingstoke: Palgrave Macmillan.

Megginson, W. L. and Netter, J. M. (2001) 'From state to market: a survey of empirical studies on privatisation', *Journal of Economic Literature*, 39 (2): 321–89.

Metcalf, D. (1989) 'Water notes dry up: the impact of the Donovan reform proposals and Thatcherism at work on labour productivity in British manufacturing industry', *British Journal of Industrial Relations*, 27 (1): 1–31.

Metcalf, D. (1991) 'British unions: dissolution or resurgence?' *Oxford Review of Economic Policy*, 7 (1): 18–32.

Meyer, S. (1981) *The Five-Dollar Day: Labor Management and Social Control in the Ford Motor Co., 1908–21*, Albany, NY: SUNY Press.

Micelli, Z. and Near, J. (1992) *Blowing the Whistle*, New York: Lexington Books.

Milberg, W. S. (1998) 'Globalization and its limits', in R. Kozul-Wright and R. Rowthorn (eds), *Transnational Corporations and the Global Economy*, Basingstoke: Palgrave Macmillan: 69–94.

Miles, R. (1993) *Racism after 'Race Relations'*, London: Routledge.

Milkman, R. (1997) *Farewell to the Factory: Auto Workers in the Late Twentieth Century*, Berkeley: University of California Press.

Miller, C. T. and Kaiser, C. R. (2001) 'A theoretical perspective on coping with stigma', *Journal of Social Issues*, 57: 73–92.

Miller, G. E. (2004) 'Frontier masculinity in the oil industry: the experience of women engineers', *Gender, Work and Organization*, 11 (1): 47–73.

Miller, T. (2010) 'My Global Financial Crisis', *Journal of Communication Inquiry*, 34 (4): 432–8.

Millward, N. (1990) 'The state of the unions', in R. Jowell, S. Witherspoon, L. Brook and B. Taylor (eds), *British Social Attitudes: The 7th Report*, Aldershot: Gower: 27–50.

Millward, N., Bryson, A. and Forth, J. (2000) *All Change at Work*, London: Routledge.

Milmo, D. (2011) 'Airlines lose economy passengers as soaring fuel bills force up ticket prices', *The Guardian*, Tuesday 7 June 2011.

Modood, T., Berthoud, R., Lakey, J., Nazroo, J., Smith, P., Virdee, S. and Beishon, S. (1997) *Ethnic Minorities in Britain: Diversity and Disadvantage*, London: Policy Studies Institute.

Modood, T., Berthoud, R. and Nazroo, J. (2002) 'Race, racism and ethnicity: a response to Ken Smith', *Sociology*, 36 (2): 419–28.

Molstad, C. (1986) 'Choosing and coping with boring work', *Urban Life*, 15 (2): 215–36.

Monnot, M. J., Wagner, S. and Beehr, T. A. (2011) 'A contingency model of union commitment and participation: meta-analysis of the antecedents of militant and nonmilitant activities', *Journal of Organizational Behavior*, 32 (8): 1127–46.

Moore, S. (2009) ' "No matter what I did I would still end up in the same position": age as a factor defining older women's experience of labour market participation', *Work, Employment and Society*, 23 (4): 655–72.

Moorhouse, H. F. (1984) 'American automobiles and workers' dreams', in K. Thompson (ed.), *Work, Employment and Unemployment*, Milton Keynes: Open University Press: 246–60.

Moorhouse, H. F. (1987) 'The "work" ethic and "leisure" activity: the hot rod in post-war America', in P. Joyce (ed.), *The Historical Meanings of Work*, Cambridge: Cambridge University Press: 237–57.

Morgan, G. (1986) *Images of Organization*, London: Sage.

Morrell, K. (2012) *Organization, Society and Politics: An Aristotelian Perspective*, London: Palgrave Macmillan.

Morris, J. A. and Feldman, D. C. (1996) 'The dimensions, antecedents and consequences of emotional labor', *Academy of Management Review*, 21 (4): 986–1010.

Morris, J. A. and Feldman, D. C. (1997) 'Managing emotions in the workplace', *Journal of Managerial Issues*, 9 (3): 257–74.

Moss, P. and Tilly, C. (1996) ' "Soft" skills and race: an investigation of black men's employment problems', *Work and Occupations*, 23: 252–76.

Mott, P. E., Mann, F. C., McLoughlin, Q. and Warwick, D. (1965) *Shiftwork: Social, Psychological, and Physical Consequences*, Ann Arbor: University of Michigan Press.

MOW International Research Team (1987) *The Meaning of Working*, London: Academic Press.

Mumby, D. and Putnam, L. (1992) 'The politics of emotion: a feminist reading of bounded rationality', *Academy of Management Review*, 17 (3): 465–86.

Mumford, L. (1934) *Technics and Civilisation*, New York: Harcourt, Brace and World.

Murray, G. and Peetz, D. (2010) *Women of the Coal Rushes*, University of New South Wales Press Ltd: UNSW.

Muzio, D., Kirkpatrick, I. and Kipping, M. (2011) 'Professions, organizations and the state: applying the sociology of the professions to the case of management consultancy', *Current Sociology*, 59 (6): 805–24.

Nanayakkara, S. (1992) *Ethics of Material Progress: The Buddhist Attitude*, Colombo: The World Fellowship of Buddhist Dhammaduta Activities Committee.

Neathey, F. (1992) 'Job assessment, job evaluation and equal value', in P. Kahn and E. Meehan (eds), *Equal Value/Comparable Worth in the UK and the USA*, Basingstoke: Palgrave Macmillan: 65–81.

New Earnings Survey (2003) *New Earnings Survey*, London: Office for National Statistics.

Newell, S., Robertson, M., Scarbrough, H. and Swan, J. (2009) *Managing Knowledge Work and Innovation*, 2nd edn, Basingstoke: Palgrave Macmillan.

Nicholson, N. (1977) 'Absence behaviour and attendance motivation: a conceptual synthesis', *Journal of Management Studies*, 14 (3): 231–52.

Nicholson, N. and Johns, G. (1985) 'The absence culture and the psychological contract: who's in control of absence?' *Academy of Management Review*, 10 (3): 397–407.

Nicholson, N., Ursell, G. and Blyton, P. (1981) *The Dynamics of White-Collar Unionism*, London: Academic Press.

Niles, F. S. (1999) 'Towards a cross-cultural understanding of work-related beliefs', *Human Relations*, 52 (7): 855–67.

Nkomo, S. (1992) 'The emperor has no clothes: rewriting "race in organizations"', *Academy of Management Review*, 17 (3): 487–513.

Nolan, P. (1989) 'Walking on water? Performance and industrial relations under Thatcher', *Industrial Relations Journal*, 20 (2): 81–92.

Nolan, P. and Wood, S. (2003) 'Mapping the future of work', *British Journal of Industrial Relations*, 41 (2): 165–74.

Nonaka, I. (1991) 'The knowledge-creating company', *Harvard Business Review*, November–December: 96–104.

Nonaka, I. and Takeuchi, H. (1995) *The Knowledge-Creating Company*, New York: Oxford University Press.

Noon, M. (1992) 'HRM: a map, model or theory', in P. Blyton and P. Turnbull (eds), *Reassessing Human Resource Management*, London: Sage: 16–32.

Noon, M. (1993) 'Racial discrimination in speculative application: evidence from the UK's top 100 firms', *Human Resource Management Journal*, 3 (4): 35–47.

Noon, M. (1994) 'From apathy to alacrity: managers and new technology in provincial newspapers', *Journal of Management Studies*, 31 (1): 19–32.

Noon, M. (2010a) 'Managing equality and diversity', in J. Beardwell and T. Claydon (eds), *Human Resource Management: A Contemporary Approach*, 6th edn, London: Pearson: 196–227.

Noon, M. (2010b) 'The shackled runner: time to rethink positive discrimination?' *Work, Employment and Society*, 24 (4): 728–39.

Noon, M. (2012) 'Simply the best? The case for using threshold selection in hiring decisions', *Human Resource Management Journal*, 22 (1): 76–88.

Noon, M., Healy, G., Forson, C. and Oikelome, F. (2012) 'The equality effects of the "hyper-formalisation" of selection', *British Journal of Management*. DoI: 10.1111/j.1467–8551.2011.00807.x

Noon, M. and Hoque, K. (2001) 'Ethnic minorities and equal treatment: the impact of gender, equal opportunities policies and trade unions', *National Institute Economic Review*, 176: 105–16.

Noon, M. and Ogbonna, E. (1998) 'Unequal provision? Ethnic minorities and employment training policy', *Journal of Education and Work*, 11 (1): 23–39.

Noon, M. and Ogbonna, E. (2001) 'Introduction: the key analytical themes', in M. Noon and E. Ogbonna (eds), *Equality, Diversity and Disadvantage in Employment*, Basingstoke: Palgrave Macmillan: 1–14.

Nyland, C. (1995) 'Taylorism and hours of work', *Journal of Management History*, 1 (2): 8–25.

O'Connell Davidson, J. (1998) *Prostitution, Power and Freedom*, Oxford: Polity.

O'Doherty, D. and Willmott, H. (2001) 'Debating labour process theory: the issue of subjectivity and the relevance of poststructuralism', *Sociology*, 35: 457–76.

O'Higgins, M. (1989) 'Assessing the underground economy in the United Kingdom', in E. L. Feige (ed.), *The Underground Economies*, Cambridge: Cambridge University Press: 175–96.

Oakland, J. S. (1989) *Total Quality Management*, Oxford: Butterworth-Heinemann.

Oakley, A. (1974) *The Sociology of Housework*, London: Martin Robertson.

Oakley, A. (1982) *Subject Woman*, London: Fontana.

Ogbonna, E. and Noon, M. (1995) 'Experiencing inequality: ethnic minorities and the employment training scheme', *Work, Employment and Society*, 9 (3): 537–58.

Ogbonna, E. and Wilkinson, B. (1990) 'Corporate strategy and corporate culture: the view from the checkout', *Personnel Review*, 19 (4): 9–15.

Oldham, G. R. and Hackman, J. R. (2010) 'Not what it was and not what it will be: the future of job design research', *Journal of Organizational Behavior*, 31(2/3): 463–79.

Oliver, M. (1996) *Understanding Disability: From Theory to Practice*, London: Palgrave Macmillan.

ONS (Office for National Statistics) (2000) *Social Trends 30*, London: The Stationery Office.

ONS (2001a) *Social Trends 31*, London: The Stationery Office.

ONS (2001b) *User Manual for the National Statistics Socio-economic Classification*, London: ONS.

ONS (2005) *Social Trends 35: 2005 edition*, London: ONS.

ONS (2006) *Social Trends 36: 2006 edition*, London: ONS.

ONS (2010) *Social Trends 40*, Newport: ONS.

ONS (2011) *Social Trends 41*, Newport: ONS.

Organisation for Economic Cooperation and Development (OECD) (1995) *OECD Employment Outlook 1995*, Paris: OECD.

OECD (1999) 'Privatisation trends', *Financial Market Trends*, no. 72: 129–45.

OECD (2000a) *OECD Economic Outlook*, no. 67, Paris: OECD.

OECD (2000b) *OECD Employment Outlook 2000*, Paris: OECD.

OECD (2000c) *OECD in Figures 2000*, Paris: OECD.

OECD (2002) 'Taking the measure of temporary employment', *OECD Employment Outlook*, Paris: OECD: 129–83

OECD (2004) *Employment Outlook*, Paris: OECD.

OECD (2005a) *Economic Outlook*, no. 77, Paris: OECD.

OECD (2005b) *Employment Outlook*, Paris: OECD.

OECD (2005c) *OECD in Figures*, 2005 edition, Paris: OECD.

OECD (2011) *Economic Outlook*, Paris: OECD.

Oswick, C. and Rosenthal, P. (2001) 'Towards a relevant theory of age discrimination in employment', in M. Noon and E. Ogbonna (eds), *Equality, Diversity and Disadvantage in Employment*, Basingstoke: Palgrave Macmillan: 156–71.

Pahl, R. (1984) *Divisions of Labour*, Oxford: Blackwell.

Pahl, R. (1988) 'Some remarks on informal work, social polarization and the social structure', *International Journal of Urban and Regional Research*, 12: 247–67.

Pai, H. H. (2004) 'Inside the grim world of the gangmasters', *Guardian*, 27 March: 1.

Palmer, B. (1975) 'Class, conception and conflict', *Review of Radical Political Economics*, 7 (2): 31–49.

Parker, D. and Kirkpatrick, C. (2005) 'Privatisation in developing countries: a review of the evidence and the policy lessons', *Journal of Development Studies*, 41 (4): 513–41.

Parkin, F. (1979) *Marxism and Class Theory: A Bourgeois Critique*, London: Tavistock.

Parry, J. (2003) 'The changing meaning of work: restructuring in the former coalmining communities of the South Wales Valley', *Work, Employment and Society*, 17 (2): 227–46.

Pass, S. (2005) *'Playing the Game': An Employee Perspective of High Performance Work Systems*, paper presented to British Universities Industrial Relations Association conference 2005.

Payne, J. (2009) 'Emotional labour and skill: a reappraisal', *Gender, Work and Organization*, 16 (3): 348–67.

Peetz, D. (1998) *Unions in a Contrary World*, Cambridge: Cambridge University Press.

Penn, R. (1982) 'Skilled manual workers in the labour process, 1856–1964', in S. Wood (ed.), *The Degradation of Work?* London: Hutchinson: 90–108.

Penn, R. (1983) 'Theories of skill and class structure', *Sociological Review*, 31 (1): 22–38.

Penn, R. (1985) *Skilled Workers in the Class Structure*, Cambridge: Cambridge University Press.

Penn, R. (1990) *Class, Power and Technology*, Cambridge: Polity.

Penn, R., Gasteen, A., Scattergood, H. and Sewel, J. (1994) 'Technical change and the division of labour in Rochdale and Aberdeen', in R. Penn, M. Rose and J. Rubery (eds), *Skill and Occupational Change*, Oxford: Oxford University Press: 130–56.

Penn, R. and Scattergood, H. (1985) 'Deskilling or enskilling? An empirical investigation of recent theories of the labour process', *British Journal of Sociology*, 36 (4): 611–30.

People Management (2004) 'Self–roster scheme is hit for IKEA', *People Management*, 28 October: 15.

Perlow, L. A. (1999) 'The time famine: toward a sociology of work time', *Administrative Science Quarterly*, 44: 57–81.

Perlow, L. A. (2001) 'Time to co-ordinate: towards an understanding of work-time standards and norms in a multicountry study of software engineers', *Work and Occupations*, 28 (1): 91–111.

Perry, N. (1998) 'Indecent exposures: theorizing whistleblowing', *Organization Studies*, 19 (2): 235–57.

Peters, T. and Austin, N. (1985) *A Passion for Excellence*, New York: Random House.

Peters, T. and Waterman, R. H. (1982) *In Search of Excellence*, New York: Harper and Row.

Phillips, A. and Taylor, B. (1986) 'Sex and skill', in Feminist Review (ed.), *Waged Work: A Reader*, London: Virago: 54–66.

Pilkington, A. (2001) 'Beyond racial dualism: racial disadvantage and ethnic diversity in the labour market', in M. Noon and E. Ogbonna (eds), *Equality, Diversity and Disadvantage in Employment*, Basingstoke: Palgrave Macmillan: 171–89.

Piore, M. J. and Sabel, C. F. (1984) *The Second Industrial Divide*, New York: Basic Books.

Polanyi, M. and Prosch, H. (1975) *Meaning*, Chicago: University of Chicago Press.

Pollard, S. (1963) 'Factory discipline and the industrial revolution', *Economic History Review*, 16: 254–71.

Pollard, S. (1965) *The Genesis of Modern Management: A Study of the Industrial Revolution in Great Britain*, Harmondsworth: Penguin.

Pollert, A. (1981) *Girls, Wives, Factory Lives*, London: Palgrave Macmillan.

Pollert, A. (ed.) (1991) *Farewell to Flexibility?* Oxford: Blackwell.

Pollitt, H. (1940) *Serving My Time: An Apprenticeship to Politics*, London: Lawrence and Wishart.

Porcellato, L., Carmichael, F., Hulme, C., Ingham, B. and Prashar, A. (2010) 'Giving older workers a voice: constraints on the employment of older people in the NorthWest of England', *Work, Employment and Society*, 24 (1): 85–103.

Prandy, K., Blackburn, R. M. and Stewart, A. (1974) 'Concepts and measures: the example of unionateness', *Sociology*, 8: 427–46.

Pringle, R. (1989) 'Bureaucracy, rationality and sexuality: the case of secretaries', in J. Hearn, D. L. Sheppard, P. Tancred-Sheriff and G. Burrell (eds), *The Sexuality of Organization*, London: Sage: 158–77.

Procter, S. and Mueller, F. (eds) (2000) *Teamworking*, Basingstoke: Palgrave Macmillan.

Prowse, P. J. and Prowse, J. M. (2006) 'Are non-union workers different to their union colleagues? Evidence from the public services', *Industrial Relations Journal*, 37(3): 222–41.

Pugliesi, K. (1999) 'The consequences of emotional labor: effects on work stress, job satisfaction and well-being', *Motivation and Emotion*, 23 (2): 125–54.

Purcell, J. (1989) 'The impact of corporate strategy on human resource management', in J. Storey (ed.), *New Perspectives on Human Resource Management*, London: Routledge: 67–91.

Purcell, J. (1995) 'Corporate strategy and its link with human resource management strategy', in J. Storey (ed.), *Human Resource Management: A Critical Text*, London: Routledge: 63–86.

Purcell, T. V. (1954) 'Dual allegiance to company and union: packinghouse workers', *Personnel Psychology*, 7: 48–58.

Putnam, R. (1995) 'Bowling alone: America's declining social capital', *Journal of Democracy*, 6: 65–78.

Putnam, R. (2000) *Bowling Alone: The Collapse and Revival of American Community*, New York: Simon and Schuster.

Radcliffe-Brown, A. R. (1952) *Structure and Function in Primitive Society*, London: Cohen and West.

Rafaeli, A. and Sutton, R. I. (1987) 'Expression of emotion as part of the work role', *Academy of Management Review*, 12 (1): 23–37.

Rafaeli, A. and Sutton, R. I. (1989) 'The expression of emotion in organizational life', in L. L. Cummings and B. M. Staw (eds), *Research in Organizational Behaviour*, Greenwich, Conn.: JAI Press: 1–42.

Ram, M. (1992) 'Coping with racism: Asian employers in the inner city', *Work, Employment and Society*, 6 (4): 601–18.

Randle, K. (1996) 'The white-coated worker: professional autonomy in a period of change', *Work, Employment and Society*, 10 (4): 737–53.

Ransome, P. (2005) *Work, Consumption and Culture*, London: Sage.

Redman, T. and Snape, E. (2005) 'Unpacking commitment: multiple loyalties and employee behaviour', *Journal of Management Studies*, 42 (2): 301–28.

Reed, M. (1996) 'Expert power and control in late modernity: an empirical review and theoretical synthesis', *Organization Studies*, 17 (4): 573–97.

Reid, D. A. (1976) 'The decline of Saint Monday', *Past and Present*, 71: 76–101.

Reynolds, G., Nicholls, P. and Alferoff, C. (2001) 'Disabled people, (re)training and employment: a qualitative exploration of exclusion', in M. Noon and E. Ogbonna (eds), *Equality, Diversity and Disadvantage in Employment*, Basingstoke: Palgrave Macmillan: 172–89.

Rhodes, E. and Braham, P. (1986) 'Equal opportunity in the context of high levels of unemployment', in R. Jenkins and J. Solomos (eds), *Racism and Equal Opportunity Policies in the 1980s*, Cambridge: Cambridge University Press: 189–209.

Riach, K. (2007) ' "Othering" older worker identity in recruitment', *Human Relations*, 60 (11): 1701–26.

Riach, K. (2009) 'Managing "difference": understanding age diversity in practice', *Human Resource Management Journal*, 19 (3): 319–35.

Richards, J. (2008) ' "Because I need somewhere to vent": the expression of conflict through workblogs', *New Technology, Work and Employment*, 23(1/2): 95–110.

Riemer, J. W. (1977) *Hard Hats: The Working World of Construction Workers*, Beverly Hills, Calif.: Sage.

Rinehart, J., Huxley, C. and Robertson, D. (1997) *Just Another Car Factory? Lean Production and Its Discontents*, Ithaca, NY: ILR Press.

Ritzer, G. (1993) *The McDonaldization of Society*, Thousand Oaks, Calif.: Pine Forge Press.

Ritzer, G. (1998) *The McDonaldization Thesis*, London: Sage.

Ritzer, G. (2011) *Globalization: The Essentials*, London: Wiley-Blackwell.

Robertson, M. and Swan, J. (2004) 'Going public: the emergence and effects of soft bureaucracy within a knowledge-intensive firm', *Organisation*, 11 (1): 123–48.

Robinson, S. D., Griffeth, R. W., Allen, D. G. and Lee, M. B. (2012) 'Comparing operationalizations of dual commitment and their relationships with turnover intentions', *The International Journal of Human Resource Management*, 23 (7): 1342–59.

Rodgers, D. (1978) *The Work Ethic in Industrial America 1850–1920*, Chicago: University of Chicago Press.

Rodrigues, S. and Collinson, D. (1995) 'Having fun? Humour as resistance in Brazil', *Organization Studies*, 16 (5): 739–68.

Roethlisberger, F. J. and Dickson, W. J. (1966) *Management and the Worker*, Cambridge, Mass.: Harvard University Press.

Ronai, C. R. and Ellis, C. (1989) 'Turn-ons for money: interactional strategies of the table dancer', *Journal of Contemporary Ethnography*, 18 (3): 271–98.

Rosa, R. R. (1995) 'Extended workshifts and excessive fatigue', *Journal of Sleep Research*, 4 (2): 51–6.

Rose, M. (1985) *Re-Working the Work Ethic*, London: Batsford.

Rose, M. (1988) *Industrial Behaviour*, 2nd edn, Harmondsworth: Penguin.

Rose, M. (1991) *The Post-Modern and the Post-Industrial*, Cambridge: Cambridge University Press.

Rose, M. (1994) 'Skill and Samuel Smiles: changing the British work ethic', in R. Penn, M. Rose and J. Rubery (eds), *Skill and Occupational Change*, Oxford: Oxford University Press: 281–335.

Rose, M. (2005) 'Do rising levels of qualification alter the work ethic, work orientation and organisational commitment for the worse? Evidence from the UK 1985–2001', *Journal of Education and Work*, 18: 133–66.

Rose, R. (1985) 'Getting by in three economies: the resources of the official, unofficial and domestic economies', in J.-E. Lane (ed.), *State and Market*, London: Sage: 103–41.

Rosen, H. (1954) 'Dual allegiance: a critique and a proposed research approach', *Personnel Psychology*, 7: 67–71.

Rosenthal, P., Hill, S. and Peccei, R. (1997) 'Checking out service: evaluating excellence, HRM and TQM in retailing', *Work, Employment and Society*, 11 (3): 481–503.

Rousseau, D. M. (1995) *Psychological Contracts in Organizations*, London: Sage.

Roy, D. (1952) 'Efficiency and "the fix": informal inter-group relations in a piecework machine shop', *American Journal of Sociology*, 57: 255–66.

Roy, D. (1953) 'Work satisfaction and social reward in quota achievement: an analysis of piecework incentive', *American Sociological Review*, 18: 507–14.

Roy, D. (1955) 'Quota restriction and goldbricking in a machine shop', *American Journal of Sociology*, 60: 427–42.

Roy, D. (1960) 'Banana time: job satisfaction and informal interaction', *Human Organization*, 18: 156–68.

Royle, T. (2000) *Working for McDonald's in Europe: The Unequal Struggle?* London: Routledge.

Royle, T. (2004) 'Employment practices of multinationals in the Spanish and German quick-food sectors: low-road convergence?' *European Journal of Industrial Relations*, 10 (1): 51–71.

Royle, T. (2005) 'The union recognition dispute at McDonald's Moscow food processing factory', *Industrial Relations Journal*, 36 (4): 318–32.

Rubery, J., Fagan, C. and Smith, M. (1995) *Changing Patterns of Work and Working Time in the European Union and the Impact on Gender Provisions*, Report for the Equal Opportunities Unit, Brussels: European Commission.

Rubery, J. and Wilkinson, F. (1979) 'Notes on the nature of the labour process in the secondary sector', *Low Pay and Labour Market Segmentation Conference Papers*, Cambridge.

Rubinstein, M. (1984) *Equal Pay for Work of Equal Value*, London: Palgrave Macmillan.

Ruiz, Y. and Walling, A. (2005) 'Home-based working using communication technologies', *Labour Market Trends*, 113 (10): 417–26.

Rupp, D. E., McCance, A. S., Spencer, S., and Sonntag, K. (2008) 'Customer (in)justice and emotional labor: The role of perspective taking, anger, and emotional regulation', *Journal of Management*, 34: 903–924.

Russell, H. (1998) 'The rewards of work', in R. Jowell, J. Curtice, A. Park, L. Brook, K. Thomson and C. Bryson (eds), *British and European Social Attitudes: The 15th Report*, Aldershot: Ashgate: 77–100.

Sabel, C. F. (1982) *Work and Politics: The Division of Labour in Industry*, Cambridge: Cambridge University Press.

Sadler, P. (1970) 'Sociological aspects of skill', *British Journal of Industrial Relations*, 8 (1): 22–31.

Saks, M. (1983) 'Removing the blinkers? A critique of recent contributions to the sociology of the professions', *Sociological Review*, 31 (1): 1–22.

Sanders, T. (2004) 'Controllable laughter: managing sex work through humour', *Work, Employment and Society*, 38 (2): 273–91.

Sargent-Cox , K., Butterworth, P. and Anstey, K. J. (2011) 'The global financial crisis and psychological health in a sample of Australian older adults: A longitudinal study', *Social Science & Medicine*, 73 (7): 1105–12.

Savery, L. K., Travaglione, A. and Firns, I. G. J. (1998) 'The links between absenteeism and commitment during downsizing', *Personnel Review*, 27 (4): 312–24.

Sayer, A. and Walker, R. (1992) *The New Social Economy: Reworking the Division of Labour*, Oxford: Blackwell.

Scarborough, H. (1999) 'Knowledge as work: conflicts in the management of knowledge workers', *Technology Analysis & Strategic Management*, 11 (1): 5–16.

Schaubroeck, J. and Jones, J. R. (2000) 'Antecedents of workplace emotional labor dimensions and moderators of their effects on physical symptoms', *Journal of Organizational Behavior*, 21: 163–83.

Schein, E. H. (1965) *Organizational Psychology*, Englewood Cliff, NJ: Prentice-Hall.

Schendler, A. (2009) *Getting Green Done: Hard Truths from the Front Lines of the Sustainability Revolution*. Perseus: Philadelphia.

Scheuer, S. (2011) 'Union membership variation in Europe: a ten-country comparative analysis', *European Journal of Industrial Relations*, 17 (1): 57–73.

Schlosser, E. (2002) *Fast Food Nation: The Dark Side of the All-American Meal*. New York: Perennial.

Schoneboom, A. (2007) 'Diary of a working boy: creative resistance among anonymous work bloggers', *Ethnography*, 8 (2): 403–23.

Schoneboom, A. (2011) 'Sleeping giants? Fired workbloggers and labour organisation', *New Technology, Work and Employment*, 26 (1): 17–28.

Schor, J. B. (1991) *The Overworked American: The Unexpected Decline of Leisure*, New York: Harper Books.

Schor, J. B. (1999) *The Overspent American*, New York: Harper Collins.

Scott, B. A. (1994) *Willing Slaves: British Workers under Human Resource Management*, Cambridge: Cambridge University Press.

Scott, B. A. and Barnes, C.M. (2011) 'A multilevel field investigation of emotional labor, affect, work withdrawal, and gender', *Academy of Management Journal*, 54 (1): 116–36.

Sennett, R. (1998) *The Corrosion of Character*, New York: Norton.

Sewell, G and Wilkinson, B. (1992a) 'Empowerment or emasculation? Shopfloor surveillance in a total quality organisation', in P. Blyton and P. Turnbull (eds), *Reassessing Human Resource Management*, London: Sage: 97–115.

Sewell, G. and Wilkinson, B. (1992b) 'Someone to watch over me: surveillance, discipline and the just-in-time labour process', *Sociology*, 26 (2): 271–90.

Seymour, D. and Sandiford, P. (2005) 'Learning emotion rules in service organizations: socialization and training in the UK public-house sector', *Work, Employment and Society*, 19 (3): 547–64.

Sharma, U. and Black, P. (2001) 'Look good, feel better: beauty therapy as emotional labour', *Sociology*, 35 (4): 913–31.

Sharpe, E. K. (2005) ' "Going above and beyond": the emotional labour of adventure guides', *Journal of Leisure* Research, 37 (1): 29–50.

Sheane, S. D. (2011) 'Putting on a good face: an examination of the emotional and aesthetic roots of presentational labour', *Economic and Industrial Democracy*, 33 (1): 145–58.

Shepherd, D. A. (2011) 'Multilevel entrepreneurship research: Opportunities for studying entrepreneurial decision making', *Journal of Management*, 37: 412–20.

Shields, M. A. and Price, S. W. (2002) 'The determinants of racial harassment at the workplace: evidence from the British nursing profession', *British Journal of Industrial Relations*, 40 (1): 1–22.

Shimonitsu, T. and Levi, L. (1992) 'Recent working life changes in Japan', *European Journal of Public Health*, 2: 76–96.

Shupe, A. and Bradley, C. (2010) *Self, Attitudes, and Emotion Work: Western Social Psychology and Eastern Zen Buddhism Confront Each Other*, New Brunswick, NJ: Transaction Publishers.

Simpson, R. (2000) 'Presenteeism and the impact of long hours on managers', in D. Winstanley and J. Woodall (eds), *Ethical Issues in Contemporary Human Resource Management*, Basingstoke: Palgrave Macmillan: 156–71.

Simpson, R. (2004) 'Masculinity at work: the experiences of men in female dominated occupations', *Work, Employment and Society*, 18 (2): 349–68.

Sliter, M., Jex, S., Wolford, K., and McInnerney, J. (2010) 'How rude! Emotional labor as a mediator between customer incivility and employee outcomes', *Journal of Occupational Health Psychology*, 15: 468–81.

Smith, C. (1989) 'Flexible specialisation, automation and mass production', *Work, Employment and Society*, 3 (2): 203–22.

Smith, D. J. (1981) *Unemployment and Racial Minorities*, London: Policy Studies Institute.

Smith, K. (2002) 'Some critical observations on the use of the concept of "ethnicity" in Modood et al, Ethnic Minorities in Britain', *Sociology*, 36 (2): 399–418.

Smith, S. and Wied-Nebbeling, S. (1986) *The Shadow Economy in Britain and Germany*, London: Anglo-German Foundation.

Snyder, M. (1987) *Public Appearances, Private Realities*, New York: Freeman.

Som, C., Hilty, L. and Köhler, A. (2009) 'The Precautionary Principle as a Framework for a Sustainable Information Society', *Journal of Business Ethics*, 85(3): 493–505.

Sorge, A., Hartman, G., Warner, M. and Nicholas, I. (1983) *Microelectronics and Manpower in Manufacturing Applications of Computer Numerical Control in Great Britain and West Germany*, Aldershot: Gower.

Sorkin, A. R. (2010) *Too Big to Fail: Inside the Battle to Save Wall Street*, Penguin: London.

Sparks, K., Cooper, C., Fried, Y. and Shirom, A. (1997) 'The effects of hours of work on health: a meta-analytic review', *Journal of Occupational and Organizational Psychology*, 70: 391–408.

Sparrow, P. (1996) 'The changing nature of psychological contracts in the UK banking sector', *Human Resource Management Journal*, 6 (4): 75–92.

Spencer, D. (2000) 'Braverman and the contribution of labour process analysis to the critique of capitalist production: twenty-five years on', *Work, Employment and Society*, 14 (2): 223–43.

Spradley, J. P. and Mann, B. J. (1975) *The Cocktail Waitress: Women's Work in a Man's World*, New York: Wiley.

Spurgeon, A. (2003) *Working Time: Its Impact of Safety and Health*, Geneva: International Labour Organization.

Steiger, T. L. (1993) 'Construction skill and skill construction', *Work, Employment and Society*, 7 (4): 535–60.

Steinberg, R. J. (1990) 'Social construction of skill', *Work and Occupations*, 17 (4): 449–82.

Strang, D. and Kim, Y.-M. (2005) 'The diffusion and domestication of managerial innovations: the spread of scientific management, quality circles and TQM between the United States and Japan', in S. Ackroyd, R. Batt, P. Thompson and P. S. Tolbert (eds), *The Oxford Handbook of Work and Organization*, Oxford: Oxford University Press: 177–99.

Sturdy, A. (1992) 'Clerical consent', in A. Sturdy, D. Knights and H. Willmott (eds), *Skill and Consent*, London: Routledge.

Suchman, L. (1996), 'Supporting articulation work', in R. Kling (ed.), *Computerisation and Controversy*, 2nd edn, San Diego: Academic Press: 407–23.

Sullivan, C. and Lewis, S. (2001) 'Home-based telework, gender and the synchronization of work and family: perspectives of teleworkers and their coresidents', *Gender, Work and Organization*, 8 (2): 123–45.

Sullivan, O. (2000) 'The division of domestic labour: twenty years of change?' *Sociology*, 34 (3): 437–56.

Tait, N. and Taylor, A. (2005) 'On-call hours to count as work for health staff', *Financial Times*, 2 December: 6.

Tancred, P. (1995) 'Women's work: a challenge to the sociology of work', *Gender, Work and Organization*, 2 (1): 11–20.

Taylor, F. W. (1911) *The Principles of Scientific Management*. New York: Harper & Brothers. (Republished by Forgotten Books, 2008 and available in full at http://books.google.co.uk/books search 'Frederick Taylor principles of scientific management').

Taylor, L. and Walton, P. (1971) 'Industrial sabotage: motives and meanings', in S. Cohen (ed.), *Images of Deviance*, Harmondsworth: Penguin: 219–45.

Taylor, P. and Bain, P. (1999) ' "An assembly line in the head": work and employee relations in the call centre', *Industrial Relations Journal*, 30 (2): 101–17.

Taylor, P. and Bain, P. (2003) ' "Subterranean worksick blues": humour as subversion in two call centres', *Organization Studies*, 24 (9): 1487–509.

Taylor, P., Hyman, J., Mulvey, G. and Bain, P. (2002) 'Work organisation, control and the experience of work in call centres', *Work, Employment and Society*, 16 (1): 133–50.

Taylor, R. (2001) *The Future of Work–Life Balance*, Swindon: ESRC.

Taylor, S. (1998) 'Emotional labour and the new workplace', in P. Thompson and C. Warhurst (eds), *Workplaces of the Future*, Basingstoke: Palgrave Macmillan: 84–103.

Taylor, S. and Tyler, M. (2000) 'Emotional labour and sexual difference in the airline industry', *Work, Employment and Society*, 14 (1): 77–95.

Teece, D. J. (2007) 'explicating dynamic capabilities: the nature and microfoundations of (sustainable) enterprise performance', *Strategic Management Journal*, 28 (13): 1319–50.

The Observer (1994) 'Baptism of fire for brigades' ethnic recruits', 10 April.

Thomas, J. J. (1992) *Informal Economic Activities*, Hemel Hempstead: Harvester Wheatsheaf.

Thomas, K. (1999) 'Introduction', in K. Thomas (ed.), *The Oxford Book of Work*, Oxford: Oxford University Press: xiii–xxiii.

Thompson, E. P. (1967) 'Time, work-discipline and industrial capitalism', *Past and Present*, 38: 56–97.

Thompson, P. (1989) *The Nature of Work*, 2nd edn, London: Palgrave Macmillan.

Thompson, P., Warhurst, C. and Callaghan, G. (2001) 'Ignorant theory and knowledgeable workers', *Journal of Management Studies*, 38 (7): 923–42.

Tidd, K. L. and Lockard, J. S. (1978) 'Monetary significance of the affiliative smile', *Bulletin of the Psychonomic Society*, 11: 344–6.

Tietze, S., Musson, G. and Scurry, T. (2006) 'Improving services, balancing lives? A multiple stakeholder perspective on the work–life balance discourse', in P. Blyton, B. Blunsdon, K. Reed and A. Dastmalchian (eds), *Work–Life Integration: International Perspectives on the Balancing of Multiple Roles*, Basingstoke: Palgrave Macmillan: 180–95.

Times (2001) 'Manual work can banish self-indulgence, say bishops', *The Times*, 16 January:13.

Tinker, T. (2002) 'Spectres of Marx and Braverman in the twilight of postmodernist labour process research', *Work, Employment and Society*, 16 (2): 251–81.

Toninelli, P. A. (ed.) (2000) *The Rise and Fall of State-Owned Enterprise in the Western World*, Cambridge: Cambridge University Press.

Townsend, K. (2005) Electronic surveillance and cohesive teams: room for resistance in an Australian call centre? *New Technology, Work and Employment*, 20 (1): 47–59.

Traxler, F., Blaschke, S. and Kittel, B. (2001) *National Labour Relations in Internationalized Markets*, Oxford: Oxford University Press.

Trinczek, R. (2006) 'Work–life balance and flexible work hours: the German experience', in P. Blyton, B. Blunsdon, K. Reed and A. Dastmalchian (eds), *Work–Life Integration: International Perspectives on the Balancing of Multiple Roles*, Basingstoke: Palgrave Macmillan: 113–34.

Turnbull, P. (1988) 'The limits to "Japanisation": just-in-time, labour relations and the UK automotive industry', *New Technology, Work and Employment*, 3 (1): 7–20.

Turner, B. A. (1971) *Exploring the Industrial Subculture*, London: Palgrave Macmillan.

Turner, R., Bostyn, A.-M. and Wight, D. (1985) 'The work ethic in a Scottish town with declining employment', in B. Roberts, R. Finnegan and D. Gallie (eds), *New Approaches to Economic Life*, Manchester: Manchester University Press: 476–89.

Turner, T. and D'Art, D. (2012) 'Public perceptions of trade unions in countries of the European Union: a causal analysis', *Labor Studies Journal*, 37 (1): 33–55.

Ursell, G. and Blyton, P. (1988) *State, Capital and Labour: Changing Patterns of Power and Dependence*, London: Palgrave Macmillan.

Van Maanen, J. and Kunda, G. (1989) ' "Real feelings": emotional expression and organizational culture', in L. L. Cummings and B. M. Staw (eds), *Research in Organizational Behaviour*, Greenwich, Conn.: JAI Press: 43–103.

Veal, A. J. (1989) 'Leisure and the future: considering the options', in F. Coalter (ed.), *Freedom and Constraint: The Paradoxes of Leisure*, London: Routledge: 264–74.

Vincent, S. (2011) 'The emotional labour process: an essay on the economy of feelings', *Human Relations*, 64 (10): 1369–92.

Visser, J. (2006) 'Union membership statistics in twenty-four countries', *Monthly Labor Review*, 129 (1): 38–49.

Volpe, J. J. (2011) 'Systemic inflammation, oligodendroglial maturation, and the encephalopathy of prematurity', *Annals of Neurology*, 70 (4): 525–9.

Waddington, J. and Kerr, A. (2009) 'Transforming a trade union? An assessment of the introduction of an organizing initiative', *British Journal of Industrial Relations*, 47 (1): 27–54.

Waddington, J. and Whitston, C. (1996) 'Empowerment versus intensification: union perspectives of change at the workplace', in P. Ackers, C. Smith and P. Smith (eds), *The New Workplace and Trade Unionism*, London: Routledge: 149–77.

Waddington, J. and Whitston, C. (1997) 'Why do people join unions in a period of membership decline?' *British Journal of Industrial Relations*, 35 (4): 515–46.

Wajcman, J. (1991) 'Patriarchy, technology and skill', *Work and Occupations*, 18 (1): 29–45.

Walby, S. (1986) *Patriarchy at Work*, Cambridge: Polity.

Walby, S. (1990) *Theorizing Patriarchy*, Oxford: Blackwell.

Walby, S. (1997) *Gender Transformations*, London: Routledge.

Wallace, C. and Pahl, R. (1986) 'Polarisation, unemployment and all forms of work', in S. Allen, A. Waton, K. Purcell and S. Wood (eds), *The Experience of Unemployment*, Basingstoke: Palgrave Macmillan: 116–33.

Wang, M., Liao, H., Zhan,Y. and Shi, J. (2011) 'Daily customer mistreatment and employee sabotage against customers: examining emotion and resource perspectives', *Academy of Management Journal*, 54 (2): 312–34.

Wareing, A. (1992) 'Working arrangements and patterns of working hours in Britain', *Employment Gazette*, November: 88–100.

Warhurst, C. and Thompson, P. (1998) 'Hands, hearts and minds: changing work and workers at the end of the century', in P. Thompson and C. Warhurst (eds), *Workplaces of the Future*, Basingstoke: Palgrave Macmillan: 1–24.

Warhurst, C. and Thompson, P. (2006) 'Mapping knowledge in work: proxies or practices?' *Work, Employment and Society*, 20 (4): 787–800.

Warr, P. (1987) *Work, Unemployment and Mental Health*, Oxford: Clarendon.

Warren, T. (2004) 'Working part-time: achieving a successful work–life balance?' *British Journal of Sociology*, 55 (1): 99–123.

Waters, M. (1995) *Globalisation*, London: Routledge.

Watson, T. J. (1986) *Management, Organisation and Employment*, London: Routledge.

Watson, T. J. (1987) *Sociology, Work and Industry*, 2nd edn, London: Routledge and Kegan Paul.

Webb, M. and Palmer, G. (1998) 'Evading surveillance and making time: an ethnographic view of the Japanese factory floor in Britain', *British Journal of Industrial Relations*, 36 (4): 611–27.

Weber, M. (1930) *The Protestant Ethic and the Spirit of Capitalism*, trans. Talcott Parsons, London: Allen & Unwin.

Weber, M. (1947) *The Theory of Social and Economic Organization*, ed. Talcott Parsons, London: Hodge.

Weber, M. (1949) *The Methodology of the Social Sciences*, Glencoe, Ill.: Free Press.

Webster, F. (1995) *Theories of the Information Society*, London: Routledge.

West, J. (2000) 'Prostitution: collectives and the politics of regulation', *Gender, Work and Organization*, 7 (2): 106–18.

Westwood, R. and Rhodes, C. (2007) *Humour, Work and Organization*, New York: Routledge.

Westwood, S. (1984) *All Day Every Day*, London: Pluto.

Wharton, A. S. (1993) 'The affective consequences of service work: managing emotions on the job', *Work and Occupations*, 20 (2): 205–32.

Wharton, A. S. (2009) 'The sociology of emotional labor', *Annual Review of Sociology*, 35: 147–65.

Wharton, A. S. and Erickson, R. (1993) 'Managing emotions on the job and at home: understanding the consequences of multiple emotional roles', *Academy of Management Review*, 18 (3): 457–86.

Wheeler, H. N. and McClendon, J. A. (1991) 'The individual decision to unionize', in G. Strauss, D. G. Gallagher and J. Fiorito (eds), *The State of the Unions*, Madison, Wis.: Industrial Relations Research Association: 47–83.

Whipp, R. (1987) 'A time to every purpose: an essay on time and work', in P. Joyce (ed.), *The Historical Meanings of Work*, Cambridge: Cambridge University Press: 210–36.

White, M. (1987) *Working Hours: Assessing the Potential for Reduction*, Geneva: International Labour Organization.

Williams, C. C. (1988) *Blue, White and Pink Collar Workers in Australia*, Sydney: Allen and Unwin.

Williams, C. C. (2003) 'Sky service: the demands of emotional labour in the airline industry', *Gender, Work and Organization*, 10 (5): 513–50.

Williams, C. C. (2004) 'Tackling undeclared work in advanced economies: towards an evidence-based public policy approach', *Policy Studies*, 25 (4): 243–58.

Williams, C. C. (2008) 'Cross-national variation in undeclared work: results from a survey of 27 European countries', *International Journal of Economic Perspectives*, 2 (2): 46–63.

Williams, C. C. (2009) 'Evaluating the prevalence of "envelope wages" in Europe', *Employee Relations*, 31 (4): 412–26.

Williams, C. C., Nadin, S. and Baric, M. (2011) 'Evaluating the participation of the self-employed in undeclared work: some evidence from a 27-nation European survey', *International Entrepreneurship and Management Journal*, 7 (3): 341–56.

Williams, C. C. and Windebank, J. (1999) 'The formalisation of work thesis: a critical evaluation', *Futures*, 31: 547–58.

Williams, C. L. (1992) 'The glass escalator: hidden advantages for men in the "female" professions', *Social Problems*, 39: 253–66.

Williams, C. L. (ed.) (1993) *Doing Women's Work: Men in Non-Traditional Occupations*, London: Sage.

Williams, K., Cutler, T., Williams, J. and Haslam, C. (1987) 'The end of mass production?' *Economy and Society*, 16 (3): 405–39.

Williams, K., Haslam, C. and Williams, J. (1992) 'Ford versus "Fordism": the beginning of mass production?' *Work, Employment and Society*, 6 (4): 517–55.

Willis, P. (1977) *Learning to Labour*, Farnborough: Saxon House.

Wilson, C. P. (1979) *Jokes: Form, Content, Use and Function*, London: Academic Press.

Wilson, D. F. (1972) *Dockers: The Impact of Industrial Change*, London: Fontana Collins.

Wilson, F. M. (2003) *Organizational Behaviour and Gender*, 2nd edn, Aldershot: Ashgate.

Winslow, C. D. and Bramer, W. L. (1994) *Future Work: Putting Knowledge to Work in the Knowledge Economy*, New York: Free Press.

Witz, A. (1992) *Professions and Patriarchy*, London: Routledge.

Wolff, R. (2011) 'Lehman Brothers: financially and morally bankrupt', *The Guardian*, Monday 12 December 2011, available at http://www.guardian.co.uk/commentisfree/cifamerica/2011/dec/12/lehman-brothers-bankrupt last accessed April 24, 2012.

Womack, J. P., Jones, D. T. and Roos, D. (1990) *The Machine That Changed the World*, New York: Rawson Macmillan.

Wood, E. A. (2000) 'Working in the fantasy factory: the attention hypothesis and the enacting of masculine power in strip clubs', *Journal of Contemporary Ethnography*, 29 (1): 5–31.

Wood, S. (ed.) (1982) *The Degradation of Work? Skill, Deskilling and the Labour Process*, London: Hutchinson.

Wood, S. (ed.) (1989) *The Transformation of Work?* London: Unwin Hyman.

Woollacott, J. (1980) 'Dirty and deviant work', in G. Esland and G. Salaman (eds), *The Politics of Work and Occupations*, Milton Keynes: Open University Press: 192–212.

World Trade Organisation (WTO) (2005) *World Trade in 2004*, New York: WTO.

World Trade Organisation (WTO) (2011) *International Trade Statistics 2011*, New York: WTO.

Worrell, D. L., Davidson, W. N. and Sharma, V. M (1991) 'Layoff announcements and stockholder wealth', *Academy of Management Journal*, 34 (3): 662–78.

Wouters, C. (1989) 'The sociology of emotions and flight attendants: Hochschild's managed heart', *Theory, Culture and Society*, 6: 95–123.

Wrench, J. (1987) 'Unequal comrades: trade unions, equal opportunities and racism', in R. Jenkins and J. Solomos (eds), *Racism and Equal Opportunity Policies in the 1980s*, Cambridge: Cambridge University Press.

Wright, T. (2011) 'Exploring the intersections of gender, sexuality and class in the transport and construction industries', in G. Healy, G. Kirton and M. Noon (eds) *Equality, Inequalities and Diversity – Contemporary Challenges and Strategies*, Basingstoke: Palgrave Macmillan: 233–51.

Yankelovich, D. (1973) 'The meaning of work', in R. Rosnow (ed.), *The Worker and the Job*, New York: Columbia University Press/Prentice Hall: 19–47.

Yousef, D. A. (2001) 'Islamic work ethic', *Personnel Review*, 30 (2): 152–69.

Zimbalist, A. (ed.) (1979) *Case Studies on the Labour Process*, New York: Monthly Review Press.

Zuboff, S. (1988) *In the Age of the Smart Machine*, Oxford: Heinemann.

Author Index

Abbott, A., 208, 211
Ackers, P., 350, 360
Ackroyd, S., 248
Adam, B., 79
Adams, R. J., 300
Adib, A., 279
Adkins, L., 325
Aglietta, M., 168
Airey, L., 103
Alferoff, C., 267, 268
Alford, C. F., 254
Ali, A., 58
Allen, D. G., 302, 303
Allen, J., 45
Amalia, M., 202
Angle, H. L., 302
Anstey, K. J., 6
Anthias, F., 270
Anthony, P. D., 57, 58
Applebaum, H. A., 127
Arber, S., 337
Armstrong, P., 150, 152, 153, 154
Arrowsmith, J., 99, 103
Ashforth, B. E., 173, 175, 185,
    193, 196
Ashley, L., 267
Ashton, J., 347
Attewell, P., 118, 121
Austin, N., 177

Baccaro, L., 7
Bacchi, C., 283
Bach, S., 27
Bachelor, L., 347
Backett-Milburn, K., 103
Bacon, N., 89, 102, 292
Bain, G. S., 294, 296
Bain, P., 143, 146, 147, 189, 191,
    198, 248, 249

Baldry, C., 343, 350
Baltes, B. B., 87, 102
Barham, C., 83
Baric, M., 323
Barley, S. R., 17
Barnes, C. M., 193, 194
Barnett, S., 272
Barney, J., 218
Barrett, L. F., 279
Barrett, R., 51
Batstone, E., 151
Baxter, J., 332
Bayazit, M., 296
Beauvais, L. L., 302
Becker, G., 114, 154
Becker, H., 325
Beckman, C., 185, 190
Beechey, V., 152, 153
Beehr, T. A., 303, 307, 312
Begum, N., 83
Bell, C., 60
Bell, D., 69, 155, 202, 218, 219
Bell, R., 6
Benders, J., 158
Beneria, L., 321
Berg, P., 88
Berthoud, R., 270, 271
Beutell, N. J., 343
Beynon, H., 145, 159
Bindel, J., 325
Bittman, M., 93, 348
Black, P., 186
Blackburn, R., 303
Blackler, F., 203, 204, 206, 208
Blackwell, L., 276
Blaschke, S., 304
Blauner, R., 89, 154, 231, 232, 233,
    234, 360
Blekesaune, M., 271

Blunsdon, B., 340, 360
Blyton, P., 26, 27, 29, 31, 33, 34, 35,
    37, 42, 89, 93, 101, 102, 103,
    105, 192, 292, 295, 296, 302,
    340, 342, 345, 358, 364, 365
Boddy, D., 151, 158
Boland, R. J., 247
Boles, J., 182
Bolton, S. C., 120, 170, 181, 183
Booth, A., 294
Boraas White, S., 334
Bostyn, A-M., 60, 67
Boyd, C., 170, 181, 183
Bradley, C., 193
Bradley, H., 130, 133
Bradney, P., 246
Brah, A., 272
Braham, P., 272
Bramer, W. L., 203
Bratton, J., 44
Braverman, H., 147, 148, 149,
    223, 237
Brennan, J., 273
Brewis, J., 325
Briggs, T. E., 87, 102
Briner, R., 72, 73
Broackmann, M., 331
Broadbent, J., 210
Broderick, J., 237
Brown, J. S., 204
Brown, W., 308
Browning, H. L., 69
Bryson, A., 46, 296, 300, 301,
    305, 306
Buchanan, D., 151, 158
Bunting, M., 72
Bunzel, D., 343
Burawoy, M., 89, 150, 152, 235, 236,
    237, 239, 240

Burchell, B. J., 45, 133
Burris, B. H., 208
Butt, S., 334
Butterworth, P., 6
Buyck, C., 30
Bycio, P., 84

Callaghan, G., 183, 189, 205
Campbell, I., 93, 348
Cappelli, P., 44, 46
Carlzon, J., 179
Carruth, A., 294
Carter, S., 273, 275
Cashmore, E., 280
Castells, M., 220, 222, 223
Cavendish, R., 145
Chadeau, A., 321
Champy, J., 156
Charles, N., 51, 131
Charlwood, A., 298, 299, 310
Chartered Institute of Personnel
    and Development., 83
Cheung, S. Y., 271
Chiang, H., 203
Child, J., 151, 285
Chuang, J., 203
Clark, J., 149, 150
Clarke, T., 135
Clawson, D., 240
Cockburn, C., 64, 112, 130, 131,
    134, 135, 283
Cohen, S., 251
Colling, T., 305
Collins, D., 205, 216
Collinson, D., 65, 131, 150, 248,
    249, 250, 251, 257, 347
Collinson, M., 216
Conway, N., 72, 73
Cooper, C., 94
Cooper, E. A., 302
Corti, L., 336, 337
Cox, J., 228
Craig, T., 340
Cressey, P., 238
Crompton, R., 62, 157, 208, 211,
    331, 350
Cross, M., 272
Croucher, R., 357
Crowther, S., 30
Crozier, M., 237
Crusco, A. H., 181
Cully, M., 297, 301, 304, 305, 306,
    307, 357
Cunnison, S., 134
Cutler, T., 146, 158

D'Abate, C. P., 244
D'Art, D., 295, 296, 306
Dale, I., 40
Danford, A., 216
Darr, A., 119
Dastmalchian, A., 102, 340
Davidson. W. N., 44
Davies, H., 2
Davies, S., 240
Davis Smith, J., 333, 334
Day, M., 202, 218
De Witte, M., 162
Dean, L. R., 302
Deery, S. J., 102, 256, 302
Delbridge, R., 145, 158, 185, 193,
    196, 216, 309
Deming, W. E., 36, 177
Department for Education and
    Employment (DfEE), 43
Department of Health., 336
Devi, S., 325
Dewe, P., 298, 299, 302, 306
Dex, S., 272, 336, 337
Dibben, P., 307
Dickens, L., 26, 305
Dickman, M., 73
Dickson, W. J., 237
Dietrich, M., 210
Disney, R., 294
Ditton, J., 89, 90, 242, 244
Dix, G., 297, 301, 304, 305, 306,
    307, 357
Dixon, S. E., 202, 218
Doganis, R., 33
Doherty, M., 75
Dohse, K., 215, 216
Dollard, M. F., 174, 185, 186,
    188, 194
Domagalski, T. A., 196
Donoghue, L., 10, 11, 206, 207
Doogan, K., 46
Douglas, M., 247
Drucker, P., 202, 217
Dubois, P., 252
Duncombe, J., 330
Dunlop, J. T., 154
Duxbury, L., 93, 346, 348, 349

Easterby-Smith, M., 202
Edwards, P. K., 83, 84, 85,
    89, 107, 252
Edwards, R., 143, 150, 152, 292
Ekman, P., 175
Eldridge, J. E. T., 233
Elger, T., 106, 107

Ellis, C., 182
Ellis Paine, A., 324
Elsheikh, F., 294
Equal Opportunities
    Commission., 99
Erickson, R., 193, 196
Erwin, P. J., 302
Esping-Andersen, G., 350, 360
Essed, P., 279
Estes, S. B., 357
European Commission., 320
Evans, S., 40

Fagan, C., 98
Fantasia, R., 240
Featherstone, M., 53
Feige, E. L., 319, 324
Feldman, D. C., 173, 194, 196
Felstead, A., 41, 115, 117, 158,
    216, 355
Felt, L. F., 318, 333
Ferlie, E., 211
Ferman, L. A., 324
Ferrie, E., 96, 348
Filby, M. P., 170, 191, 197
Financial Times., 31, 278
Fineman, S., 173
Firns, I. G. J., 86
Firth, M., 273
Fitzgerald, L., 211
Fleming, P., 205, 258
Foegen, J. H., 198
Foote, N. N., 182
Forbes, I., 270
Forshaw, S., 328
Forth, J., 46
Fosh, P., 268
Foster, D., 268
Fox, A., 66, 120, 164, 227
Freeman, R., 295, 304
Freidson, E., 208, 211
Frenkel, S., 10, 11, 119, 147,
    159, 206, 207
Friedman, A., 150, 238
Friedmann, G., 164
Friedmann, G., 6
Fuchs, V., 154, 155
Fuchs Epstein, C., 95
Furman, F. K., 186
Fuwa, M., 330

Gall, G., 143
Gallie, D., 56, 115, 117, 156,
    158, 216
Garbin, A. P., 182

Garrahan, P., 30, 215, 216
Gasteen, A., 162
Gay, P., 273
Gennard, J., 27
Gershuny, J., 27, 69, 318, 323, 324, 331, 333
Gerson, K., 93, 96, 98, 348
Ghazi, P., 356
Ghosh, A. R., 7
Ginn, J., 337
Glaser, B. G., 15
Glass, J. L., 357
Glazer, M. P., 254
Glazer, P. M., 254
Godwin, M., 331
Goffman, E., 175, 254, 325
Gomez, R., 296, 300
Gorz, A., 70
Gould, A. M., 141
Goulding, C., 351, 356
Gourlay, S., 151
Graham, L., 215
Grainger, H., 360
Grandey, A. A., 188, 189
Grant, D., 72
Green, F., 107, 115, 117, 122, 158, 216, 295, 350
Greenhaus, J. H., 343
Griffeth, R. W., 302, 303
Grimshaw, D., 159
Groth, M., 184
Grugulis, I., 115, 116, 162
Guardian, 3, 221, 251, 276, 278, 280, 281
Guerrier, Y., 279
Guest, D., 73, 107, 298, 299, 302, 306
Gutek, B. A., 283

Hacket, R. D., 84
Hackman, J. R., 231
Hakim, C., 62, 332
Hall, D. T., 360
Hall, E., 170, 178, 181, 197
Hamilton, C., 54, 351
Hammer, M., 156
Hammer, T. H., 296
Hampson, I., 119, 120, 130, 192
Han, T., 203
Handy, C., 318, 321, 333
Hanlon, G., 211
Hantrais, L., 350, 360
Harbison, F. H., 154
Harding, P., 334
Harley, B., 205

Hartman, G., 158
Hartmann, H., 134
Harvey, D., 168, 368
Harvey, J., 273, 275
Haslam, C., 146, 158
Hassard, J., 78
Haynie, 19
Healy, G., 266, 308
Heath, A., 271
Heery, E., 73, 267, 308, 309
Heilmann, S. G., 278
Hennig-Thgurau, T., 184
Henry, N., 45
Herriot, P., 72, 73
Hewitt, P., 100
Heyes, J., 85
Hickey, R., 307
Hicks, S., 29
Higgins, C., 93, 346, 348, 349
Hill, C. W. L., 218
Hill, R., 99
Hill, S., 36, 184, 268
Hilty, L., 218
Hirst, A., 335
Hirst, P., 31
Hochschild, A. R., 170, 171, 173, 176, 180, 181, 183, 184, 187, 188, 192, 193, 195, 197, 331
Hodgkins, B., 308
Hodson, R., 255
Hoffman, R., 247
Hogg, G., 103
Hoggett, P., 30
Holt, H., 360
Höpfl, H., 175
Hoque, K., 273, 275, 305, 357
Horrell, S., 104, 133
Houlihan, M., 120
Hubbuck, J., 273, 275
Huff, J. W., 87, 102
Huijen, F., 158
Humphrey, R., 173, 175, 185, 193, 196
Hurst, C., 193, 194
Hutton, W., 43
Huxley, C., 216
Hyman, J., 146, 311, 343, 350, 357
Hyman, R., 158, 238, 239, 307

Independent, 278
Inglehart, R., 54, 363
Ingram, A., 101
Iverson, R. D., 256, 302

Jackson, T., 351, 352

Jacobs, J. A., 93, 96, 98, 348
Jacoby, S. M., 46
Jahoda, M., 65, 67, 75, 342
James, D., 122
James, E., 51
James, N., 173, 174, 195, 196
Jaques, E., 120, 121
Jenkins, J., 103, 342, 364
Jenkins, R., 273, 275, 334
Jenkins, S., 185, 193, 196, 250
Jenson, J., 132
Jewson, N., 41, 273, 275, 355
Johns, G., 86
Jones, D. T., 156, 215
Jones, G., 157
Jones, J., 356
Jones, J. R., 195
Jones, O., 143
Jones, S., 331
Jones, T., 272, 275
Judge, G., 27
Judge, T. A., 193, 194
Junor, A., 119, 120, 130, 192
Juran, J. M., 36, 177
Juravich, T., 255
Jurgens, U., 215, 216
Jyrkinen, M., 268

Kaiser, C. R., 279
Kalleberg, A. L., 95
Karabanow, J., 185, 191
Karlsson, J. C., 243
Kazmin, A., 325
Keep, E., 35, 115, 116
Kelly, J., 141, 151, 294, 295, 308
Kerr, A., 297
Kerr, C., 154
Kerr, J., 40
Kerr, W., 302
Kersley, B., 99, 104, 106, 297, 358
Kidd, J. M., 72
Kim, Y-M., 36
Kipping, M., 208, 211
Kirkpatrick, C., 28
Kirkpatrick, I., 208, 211
Kirton, G., 266, 274, 275
Kittel, B., 304
Klandermans, P. G., 298
Kleinknecht, A., 31
Knights, D., 131, 149, 150
Knopoff, K., 185, 190
Kochan, T., 308
Koestler, A., 119
Köhler, A., 218
Konrad, A. M., 283

Korczynski, M., 10, 11, 21, 119, 120, 147, 157, 159, 183, 185, 188, 191, 206, 207, 245, 247, 248, 249
Kreckel, R., 123
Kumar, K., 205, 219
Kunda, G., 173, 180, 189, 191
Kuruvilla, S., 307
Kusterer, K., 119

Lacey, N., 325
Lafer, G., 116
Lakhani, T., 307
Lambert, S., 103
Lashley, C., 178
Laurie, H., 337
Layard, R., 362
Lazonick, W., 81
Le Croy, C. W., 203
Lee, G., 272
Lee, J.-Y., 278
Lee, M. B., 302, 303
Legge, K., 66, 368
Leidner, R., 141, 180, 196
Lessor, R., 197
Levi, L., 95
Levie, H., 151
Lewchuck, W., 215
Lewig, K. A., 174, 185, 186, 188, 194
Lewis, A., 154
Lewis, D., 254
Lewis, S., 41
Liff, S., 63, 282, 283
Lim, V. K. G., 241
Linhart, R., 145
Linstead, S., 175, 178, 197, 198, 199, 249, 252, 325
Littler, C. R., 141, 143, 146, 150, 164
Lively, K. J., 174
Livingstone, D. W., 115
Lloyd, C., 116, 120
Lockard, J. S., 181
Lockyer, C., 311
Loretto, W., 268
Low, N., 334
Lundberg, H., 243
Lupton, B., 284
Lyles, M., 202
Lynch, J. J., 176, 178
Lyon, D., 219, 368
Lyonette, C., 331

Macan, T. H., 87
Macdonald, K. M., 211

MacDonald, R., 322, 326, 327, 335
MacInnes, J., 238
Magenau, J. M., 302
Mahony, A., 102
Malsch, T., 215, 216
Management Today, 244
Mangham, I. L., 175
Mann, B. J., 132, 181, 246, 247
Mann, F. C., 101
Mann, S., 173, 174, 194
Manning, W. E. G., 72
Manwaring, T., 119
Marks, A., 311
Marmot, M. G., 6
Mars, G., 90, 181, 242, 243, 244
Marsden, D., 330
Marsh, C., 104
Martin, G., 73
Martin, J., 185, 190
Martin, J. E., 302
Martinez Lucio, M., 26, 250
Marx, K., 80, 106, 227, 228, 230
Mason, D., 270, 273, 275
Massey, D., 41
Mathewson, S. B., 255
Matthaei, J., 130
Matusik, S. F., 218
May, C., 230
Mayo, E., 237
McClelland, K., 83
McClendon, J. A., 298, 300
McCord, A., 6
McCormick, B. J., 84
McGeevor, P., 273
McGurk, J., 26
McIntosh, I., 237
McIntosh, S., 107
McKay, S., 301, 306
McKee, L., 60
McKie, L., 103, 268
McLoughlin, I., 149, 150
McLoughlin, Q., 101
McNeil, N., 360
McRae, S., 62
Mead, G., 270
Means, R., 336
Medoff, J. L., 304
Megginson, W. L., 28
Metcalf, D., 111, 107, 296, 304
Meure, D., 325
Meyer, K. E., 202, 218
Meyer, S., 145
Micelli, Z., 254
Milberg, W. S., 25
Miles, I., 69

Miles, R., 270
Milkman, R., 161
Miller, C. T., 279
Miller, G. E., 284
Miller, T., 7
Millward, N., 297, 299, 300, 301
Milmo, D., 33
Modood, T., 270, 271, 272, 275, 281
Molstad, C., 255
Monnot, M. J., 303, 307, 312
Moore, R., 151
Moore, S., 266
Moorhouse, H. F., 63, 65, 74
Morgan, G., 140
Morrell, K., 229
Morris, J. A., 173, 194, 196
Moss, P., 115
Mott, P. E., 101
MOW International Research Team, 55, 61, 63
Mueller, F., 106, 159
Mulvey, G., 143, 146
Mumby, D., 195
Mumford, L., 78
Murray, G., 2
Musson, G., 355
Muzio, D., 208, 211
Myers, C. A., 154

Nadin, S., 323
Nanayakkara, S., 59
Nazroo, J., 270
Near, J., 254, 278
Neathey, F., 133
Netter, J. M., 28
Neuman, G. A., 87, 102
Newell, S., 202
Nicholas, I., 158
Nicholls, P., 267, 268
Nicholson, N., 83, 86, 302
Nicod, M., 181
Niles, F. S., 59
Nkomo, S., 271
Nolan, P., 107, 368
Nonaka, I., 202, 211, 212, 218
Noon, M., 73, 151, 239, 250, 266, 267, 268, 272, 273, 275, 282, 288, 305, 357
Nyland, C., 143

O'Connell Davidson, J., 325
O'Doherty, D., 149
O'Higgins, M., 322
O'Reilly, A., 297, 301, 304, 305, 306, 307, 357

Oakland, J. S., 36
Oakley, A., 135
OECD (Organisation for Economic Cooperation and Development), 25, 26, 30, 41, 42
Ogbonna, E., 170, 180, 190, 268, 272
Oldham, G. R., 231
Oliver, M., 268
ONS (Office for National Statistics), 12, 37, 39, 43, 93, 94, 95, 103, 104, 334, 346, 347, 351
Osterman, P., 308
Ostry, J. D., 7
Oswick, C., 268
Overington, M. A., 175

Pahl, R., 67, 135, 323, 326, 327
Pai, H. H., 328
Palmer, B., 143
Palmer, G., 90, 91, 217
Parker, D., 28
Parkin, F., 123
Parry, J., 65
Pass, S., 257
Pate, J., 73
Patzelt, H., 19
Payne, J., 116, 120, 196, 197
Peccei, R., 184, 268
Peetz, D., 2, 297, 299, 300
Pekruhl, U., 158
Pelletier, J., 295
Penn, R., 127, 153, 162
People Management, 359
Perlow, L. A., 94, 95, 96, 348
Perry, J. L., 302
Perry, N., 254
Peters, T., 177
Peterson, M. M., 302
Phillips, A., 132, 133, 134
Pilgerstorfer, M., 328
Pilkington, A., 271
Piore, M. J., 53, 155
Polanyi, M., 119
Pollard, S., 81, 82
Pollert, A., 131, 145, 158
Pollitt, H., 83
Porcellato, L., 268
Prandy, K., 303
Price, S. W., 276, 277
Pringle, R., 196
Procter, S., 106, 159
Prosch, H., 119
Prowse, J. M., 297
Prowse, P. J., 297
Pugliesi, K., 173, 194

Purcell, J., 151
Purcell, T. V., 302
Putnam, L., 195
Putnam, R., 350

Radcliffe-Brown, A. R., 245
Rafaeli, A., 173, 180, 181
Rainbird, H., 35
Ram, M., 275
Randle, K., 211
Ransome, P., 53, 351
Redman, T., 302
Reed, K., 340, 351, 356
Reed, M., 207, 208
Rees, C., 216
Reid, D. A., 81
Reynolds, G., 267, 268
Rhodes, C., 254
Rhodes, E., 272
Riach, K., 268
Rice, J., 93, 348
Richards, J., 259
Riemer, J. W., 127
Rinehart, J., 216
Ritzer, G., 32, 140, 143
Roberts, J., 210
Robertson, D., 202, 215, 216
Robertson, M., 202
Robinson, S. D., 302, 303
Rodgers, D., 58
Rodrigues, S., 248
Roethlisberger, F. J., 237
Ronai, C. R., 182
Roos, D., 156, 215
Rosa, R. R., 96
Rose, M., 53, 63, 74, 141, 150, 219
Rose, R., 318, 321, 324
Rosen, H., 302
Rosenthal, P., 184, 268
Rousseau, D. M., 72
Roy, D., 92, 236, 250
Royle, T., 141, 311
Rubery, J., 98, 132, 133, 159
Rubinstein, M., 26
Ruiz, Y., 41
Russell, H., 54

Sabel, C. F., 53, 155
Sadler, P., 123
Saks, M., 211
Salaman, G., 150, 151
Salmon, J., 309
Sanders, T., 247, 325
Sandiford, P., 180
Sargent-Cox, K., 6

Savery, L. K., 86
Sayer, A., 41
Scarborough, H., 202, 209
Scattergood, H., 162
Schady, N., 6
Schaubroeck, J., 195
Schein, E. H., 143
Schendler, A., 2
Scheuer, S., 296, 304
Schlosser, E., 141
Scholarios, D., 311, 343, 350
Scholl, R. W., 302
Schoneboom, A., 259
Schor, J., 93, 348, 351
Scott, A., 90
Scott, B. A., 193, 194
Scullion, H., 83, 84, 85, 252
Scurry, T., 355
Sennett, R., 46, 350
Sewel, J., 162
Sewell, G., 158, 205, 216
Seymour, D., 180
Sharma, U., 186
Sharma, V. M., 44
Sharpe, E. K., 186, 187, 190
Sheane, S. D., 186
Shepherd, D. A., 19
Shields, M. A., 276, 277
Shimonitsu, T., 95
Shire, K. A., 10, 11, 119, 147, 159, 206, 207
Shupe, A., 193
Simms, M., 309
Simpson, D., 309
Simpson, R., 94, 95, 284
Sinclair, P. R., 318, 333
Singe, I., 357
Singelmann, J., 69
Sisson, K., 27, 99, 103
Sloane, P., 101
Smith, C., 158
Smith, D. J., 272
Smith, K., 96, 270, 348
Smith, M., 98
Smith, R., 336
Smith, S., 318, 319, 320, 324
Snape, E., 302
Snyder, M., 171, 175
Som, C., 218
Sorge, A., 158
Sorkin, A. R., 7
Sparks, K., 96
Sparrow, P., 72
Spencer, D., 153
Spicer, A., 258

Spradley, J. P., 132, 181, 246, 247
Spurgeon, A., 96, 101, 102
Stageman, J., 134
Staines, H., 73
Steiger, T. L., 127, 128
Steijn, B., 162
Steinberg, R. J., 133
Stewart, A., 303
Stewart, P., 215, 216
Strang, D., 36
Strauss, A. L., 15
Sturdy, A., 157
Suchman, L., 129, 130
Sullivan, C., 41, 330, 331
Summers, J., 357
Sutton, R. I., 173, 180, 181
Swan, J., 202
Swim, J. K., 279

Tait, N., 27
Takeuchi, H., 218
Tam, M., 119, 147, 159, 207
Tamirisa, N., 7
Tancred, P., 21
Taylor, A., 27
Taylor, B., 132, 133, 134
Taylor, F. W., 80, 142
Taylor, L., 251, 252, 253, 254, 263, 265, 267
Taylor, P., 143, 146, 147, 189, 191, 198, 248, 249, 308
Taylor, R., 343
Taylor, S., 193, 185, 189, 191, 196, 197
Teece, D., 202
ter Wengel, J., 31
Thomas, J. J., 319, 322, 324
Thomas, K., 9
Thompson, E. P., 81
Thompson, G., 31
Thompson, P., 149, 183, 189, 205, 206, 308
Tidd, K. L., 181
Tietze, S., 355
Tilly, C., 115
Times, 59
Tinker, T., 149, 153, 154
Tomiuk, M., 185
Toninelli, P. A., 28
Townsend, K., 241

Travaglione, A., 86
Traxler, F., 304
Trinczek, R., 88, 102, 340, 359
Turnbull, P., 26, 27, 29, 34, 35, 42, 158, 192, 216, 295, 296
Turner, B. A., 124
Turner, R., 60, 67
Turner, T., 295, 296, 306
Tyler, M., 183, 189, 191, 196, 197

Ursell, G., 302

Van Maanen, J., 173, 180, 189, 191
Veal, A. J., 71
Vincent, S., 162, 191
Visser, J., 296, 304, 308
Volpe, J. J., 125

Waddington, J., 294, 297, 299, 310
Wagner, S., 303, 307, 312
Wajcman, J., 63, 135, 282, 283
Walby, S., 62, 130, 134
Walker, R., 41
Wallace, C., 67
Walling, A., 41
Walsh, G., 184
Walsh, J., 256
Walters, S., 41, 355
Walton, P., 252, 253, 254
Ward, K., 159
Wareing, A., 104
Warhurst, C., 115, 116, 183, 189, 205, 206
Warner, M., 158
Warr, P., 60, 342
Warren, T., 342, 364
Warwick, D., 101
Waterman, R. H., 177
Waters, S., 273, 275
Watson, A., 143
Watson, T. J., 150, 233
Wazeter, D. L., 296
Webb, M., 90, 91, 217
Weber, M., 17, 57, 123, 124
Webster, F., 69, 218, 219
Wells, C., 325
West, J., 325
Western, M., 332
Westwood, R., 245
Westwood, S., 145, 248, 251, 257

Wetzel, C. G., 181
Wharton, A., 184, 193, 195, 196, 198
Wheeler, H. N., 298, 300
Whipp, R., 82
Whitaker, A., 208
White, M., 56, 89, 105
White, P., 268
Whitston, C., 83, 84, 89, 107, 297, 299, 310
Wied-Nebbeling, S., 318, 319, 320, 324
Wight, D., 60, 67
Wilkinson, B., 158, 170, 180, 190, 216
Wilkinson, F., 132
Williams, C., 180, 185, 186, 320, 323
Williams, C. L., 283, 284
Williams, J., 146, 158
Williams, K., 145, 146, 158
Willis, P., 65
Willmott, H., 149, 150
Wilson, C. P., 247
Wilson, D. F., 84, 85
Wilson, F., 21
Windebank, J., 323
Winslow, C. D., 203
Winter, S., 283
Witz, A., 211
Wolff, R., 3, 4, 6
Womack, J. P., 156, 215
Wood, E. A., 178, 182, 190, 197
Wood, S., 119, 145, 150, 158, 368
Woodland, S., 297, 301, 304, 305, 306, 307, 357
Woolf, E. F., 193, 194
Woollacott, J., 325
World Trade Organisation., 32
Worrell, D. L., 44
Wouters, C., 193
Wrench, J., 272, 305
Wright, J. A., 87, 102
Wright, T., 283

Yankelovich, D., 60
Yousef, D. A., 59
Yuval-Davis, N., 270

Zhou, Y., 216
Zimbalist, A., 150
Zuboff, S., 158, 163

Subject Index

absence, 83–7
    organised, 85–6
    time discipline, 81–3
alienation
    and Blauner, 231–4
    in emotion work, 192–3
    and Marx, 227–31
    non-alienating conditions, 228, 230
    survival strategies, 235–6
ante-Fordism, 166–7
Aristotle, 229
assembly line, 144–7
aviation industry, 26

boredom at work *see* monotony
boundary spanning roles, 179
Braverman, H.
    critics, 150–3
    thesis of deskilling, 147–50

call centres, 146–7, 160, 183–4, 185,
    188–9, 191–2, 241, 258
carers (domestic), 336–7
cash-in-hand pay, 326–8
change and continuity, 20–1, 368–70
classification of work, 10–12, 16–18
collectivism, 290–4
commitment
    dual, 126
    to organisation, 239
    to trade union, 302–3
    to work, 55–7, 71–2
competitive environment
    intensification, 33–5
    knowledge, 202, 211–12, 214–18,
        220–3
    production technologies, 33,
        35, 214–17
    quality, 36
    strategies, 33–4, 220–3
    see also globalisation

competitive tendering, 29
concealed work, 317, 324–8
    measurement problems, 320–1
consent, 237–40, 259–61
consumption, 52–3, 351–3, 362
    changing patterns, 52–4, 60–9,
        71–2, 176–7
    mass, 146
continuous improvement, 215–17
control
    of absence, 86
    and consent, 152, 238–41,
        371–2, 373
    of knowledge, 214–18, 223–4
    and management objectives,
        150–2, 371–2
control strategies
    close supervision, 238
    division of labour, 141–3, 148–9
    responsible autonomy, 150, 237–40
    surveillance, 142–3, 160, 189–90
    see also resistance
counteractions, 8
    see also counter-rationalities
counter-rationalities, 292, 371–2
credentialism, 115–17
culture *see* workplace culture
customer care, 21, 64, 177–9
customer-oriented bureaucracy, 157
cynicism at work, 258

data types, 18–19
definitions of work, 8–10
deregulation, 25–6, 27–9
deviant work, 318, 324–6
discretion *see* skill
discrimination
    definition, 264
    process of, 285–7
    in recruitment and selection,
        264, 273–5

in training schemes, 272
in work, 275–82
disposability of labour, 239
domestic work, 318, 329–33
    responsibility for, 62–3, 132–3,
        134, 330–3
    valuation of, 320–1
downshifting, 54, 354, 356, 361–3
dramaturgical perspective, 175–6
dual commitment, 126, 302–3

economy
    competition, 31–5, 176
    structure, 68–9, 176, 220–3
education-jobs gap, 114–15
embedded knowledge, 128, 204,
    206–7, 207–8, 212, 217
embodied knowledge, 203, 204,
    206–7, 207–8
embrained knowledge, 203,
    206–7, 207–8
emotion work
    adventure guides, 186–7
    in airlines, 170–1, 175–6, 181–4,
        185–7, 188, 192–3, 195, 197, 198
    and alienation, 192–3
    in banks, 172, 195
    and coping strategies, 190–2
    definitions, 173–6
    gender implications, 195–8
    as a performance, 175–6
    and recruitment, 179–80
    in restaurants, 178, 180, 181
    and skill, 195–7, 199
    in strip clubs, 182
    in supermarkets, 180, 184–5, 189
    and surveillance, 189–90
    in telesales, 183, 189, 191
    and training, 179–80, 183
emotional dissonance, 186, 188,
    192–3

empirical perspective, 19–20
employability, 73
employment
 deregulation, 28–9
 Fair Wages Resolutions, 29–30
 flexibility, 28–9
 harmonisation of rights, 27
 job insecurity, 45–6
employment structure
 gender differences, 38–9,
  62–3, 332–3
 location, 41
 manufacturing and services, 37–8
 part-time, 38–9, 53, 62–3,
  98–9, 100
 self-employment, 40
 size of organisations, 40–1
 temporary work, 45
empowerment, 150, 178, 185,
  232, 239
 see also control and consent;
  responsible automony under
  control strategies
encoded knowledge, 204, 207–8
encultured knowledge, 204,
  207–8, 217
entrepreneurial professional, 207–9
equal pay legislation, 27
equality
 difference and sameness, 269–76,
  282, 283–5
 glass ceiling/escalator, 284
 information age, 221–2
 see also discrimination; gender
  issues
escape, 256–9
 mental withdrawal, 191, 257–9
 physical withdrawal, 83–4
 problems of interpretation, 259–62
 see also absence
ethnicity, 269–71
estrangement, 193, 228, 230,
  232, 233
expert work, 207
extrinsic reward, 52–4

fairness, 265, 282–3, 285–7
 see also equality
'false consciousness', 230, 231,
  352–3, 363
feminisation, 21, 132–3, 369, 370
fiddling, 241–4
 problems of interpretation, 259–62
 time fiddles, 90–1
 toleration by management, 243–4
 typology, 241–2

flexibility
 functional, 105
 numerical, 95–104
flexible specialisation, 155–6
forced labour, 227–9
Fordism, 145–7, 166–8, 368

gender issues
 carers, 336–7
 criticism of Braverman, 152–3
 criticism of Burawoy, 240
 domestic work, 135, 329–33
 emotion work, 195–9
 employment, 38–9, 62–3,
  332–3, 337
 feminisation, 21, 132–3, 369, 370
 job evaluation, 133
 joking, 246–7, 250
 masculinity, 60, 64–5, 130–2, 250
 part-time work, 38–9
 skill, 129–36
 stereotypes, 130–3, 195–8
 trade unions, 133–4
 work centrality, 61–4, 132
 working hours, 97–104
 see also discrimination;
  equality
global financial crisis (GFC), 2–7,
  301, 332, 347, 348, 349
 consequences, 5–7, 347, 348, 363
 and hidden work, 322, 324
 and work-life balance, 347, 348,
  349, 363
globalisation, 25–7, 31–5, 159–60,
  162–3, 221–2

harassment, 250–1, 276–9
health
 emotion work, 192–5
 working hours, 96, 101
 see also stress
hidden work
 definitions, 316–18
 measurement problems, 318–22
 trends, 322–3
 see also concealed and
  unrecognised work
holidays, 81
hours of work see time: duration
human capital theory, 113–16, 154
human resource management,
  66, 313
humour see joking

ideal types, 8–18
illegal activities, 243, 315, 324–8

informal economy see hidden work
informal regulation, 235–7, 370–1
 see also joking; fiddling; sabotage;
  absence
information age, 220–3
information society, 218–19
insecurity see job insecurity
institutional discrimination, 279–82
instrumentality, 68–9, 86–7, 142–3,
  181, 209, 232, 295, 298–300
intellective skills, 163–4, 206–7
intensification see work
 intensification
international comparisons
 part-time working, 38–9
 unemployment, 42–4
 work ethic, 54–7, 57–9
 working hours, 95–101
intrinsic reward, 52–4
 see also work ethic; work values
inward investment, 30–1

job evaluation, 113, 118, 133
job insecurity, 45–6
joking, 245–52
 as informal regulation, 246–7
 and monotony, 250–1
 problems of interpretation, 259–62
 and workplace culture, 246–7,
  249–50
just-in-time (JIT) production,
  35–6, 105

kaizen see continuous improvement
knowledge
 capture, 213–17
 and competitive advantage, 202
 creation, 211–13
 explicit, 212, 213
 expropriation, 213–18, 223–4
 spiral, 212–13
 tacit, 212–13, 215
 types, 203–4, 206–7
 work, definitions, 203–4,
  criticisms, 205–6
 workers, 206–210
knowledge-creating company,
  211–12, 218

labour market see employment;
  unemployment
labour process
 contradictions in, 238–40
 labour power, 148, 227–30
 theory, 147–9, 216, 227–31
leisure, 9, 53, 70–1, 330, 363

liberal/independent
   professionals, 207–9

'making out', 235–7, 240–1,
   260–1, 373
   gender implications, 240
   problems of interpretation, 259–62
   see also fiddling time
management
   counter-rationalities, 371–2
   objectives, 142–3, 150–2, 157–8,
      238–40
   prerogative, 66, 227–9
   see also control
manufacturing *see* economy;
   production
masculinity at work, 60–1, 64–5,
   130–2
McDonaldisation, 143
Meaning of Working (MOW)
   survey, 55, 61–2
minimum wage, 28, 52
models, 16
   see also theories
monotony in work, 22, 78, 87, 91–2,
   142, 159, 160, 250–1
morality of work, 57–9, 68–9, 74, 75,
   81, 84, 243, 268
multinational corporations, 32–3
mystery shoppers, 189

nation-state, 26, 27
neo-Fordism, 167–8, 368
network society, 220–2
non-declared work, 318, 326–8

objectification, 228
objectivity-subjectivity, 20
   and alienation, 227–35
   and discrimination, 282, 287
   and skill, 118, 136–7
   and time, 78, 79, 80, 108–9
occupational classes, 10–11
occupational closure, 128, 208–10,
   211, 283–4
   see also social closure
occupational language, 124–5
offshoring, 159–60
organisational professionals, 208
organisational size, 40–1

paradigms, 166–8, 368
perspectives on work, 19–21
plurality
   in discrimination, 288
   findings, 368–9

of interests, 150–1, 291–4
   perspectives, 19–21
   subcultures, 370–1
political environment, 25–31
post-Fordism, 24, 167, 368–9
post-industrial society, 68–9, 154,
   202, 218–20
post-materialism, 54, 70–2,
   352, 363
presenteeism, 94–5
privatisation, 25–6, 28
production
   batch, 155, 158
   JIT, 35–6, 105
   mass, 20, 145–6, 155, 158
professionals, 207–9
professions, 210–11, 291
prostitution, 247, 315, 324–5
psychological contract, 72–4
public sector, 29–30

qualifications, 115
qualitative and quantitative methods,
   18–19
quality, 36
   see also customer care; just-in-time
      production

race, 269–71
racism at work, 275–82
recruitment and selection
   and discrimination, 264, 273–5
   for emotion work, 179–80, 181–3
redundancy, 44–5
resistance, 152, 259–62
   see also fiddling; sabotage *and*
      absence

sabotage, 252–6
   problems of interpretation,
      259–62
   unintentional, 254–5
   virtuous, 253–4
   see also resistance
scientific management *see*
   Taylorism
selection *see* recruitment
self-estrangement, 192–3, 228, 230,
   232–3
service sector *see* economy
sex workers, 182, 318, 324–5
sexuality at work, 190–1, 207–8
shadow economy *see* hidden work
skill
   analytical perspectives, 111–13
   automating and informating, 163–4

compensatory theory, 162–3
complexity, 117–20, 122
conceptual framework, 164–8
deskilling, 147–54, 166–8
discretion, 120–3, 140, 142, 148,
   149, 150, 155–6, 164–5, 167
gender implications, 129–36
gender stereotypes, 130–3, 195–9
in the job, 112–13, 117–22
and knowledge, 206–7, 214–15
in the person, 112–13, 113–17
polarisation, 161–2
range, 164–5
in the setting, 112–13, 123–9
social, 118–19
social construction, 123–9
soft, 115–16
symbolism, 127–8
tacit, 118–19, 203–4,
   211–13, 215–16
upskilling, 154–61, 166–8, 218–19
work attitudes, 115
small firms, 40–1
social change in economic life
   initiative (SCELI), 53
social closure, 123, 124–9
   and professions, 208, 210–11
social construction
   gender, 129–36
   skill, 123–9
social dumping, 27
socio-economic class, 12
solidarity, 298–9
standardisation, 140–1, 145–7
steel industry, 88–9, 102
stereotypes, 266–9
   age, 268
   disability, 268
   ethnicity, 267–8
   gender, 130–3, 185–8
strategic choice, 151, 285–6
stress
   emotion work, 186, 193–5
subjectivity *see* objectivity
supranational alliances, 26–7

tax dodging, 318, 326–8
Taylorism, 141–3
teamworking, 88–9, 106–7, 158–9
technology
   appropriation by men,
      127–8, 134–6
   automating and
      informating, 163–4
   and deskilling, 148–9
   and upskilling, 154–6

teleworking, 41, 167, 355
theories, 13–16
    and common sense, 14–15
    deductive and inductive, 15
    and perspectives, 19–21
    purpose, 15–16
    testing, 13–14
time
    and capitalism, 81–2
    duration, 79, 93–9
    flexitime, 103–4
    historical importance, 78, 81–2
    intensification, 105–8
    international comparisons, 96, 97
    making and fiddling time,
        83–6, 89–91
    organisation, 79, 100–4
    overtime, 95–7, 99–100
    part-time, 98–9, 341
    porosity, 106
    presenteeism, 94–5
    seasonal hours, 102–3
    shiftwork, 88–9, 101
    structures, 100–4
    task flexibility, 105–6
    time and motion, 80
    time discipline, 80, 81–2
    trust-based working hours, 258–9
    utilisation, 79, 105–8
    zero hours, 99
    see also absence;
        work-life balance
total quality management (TQM)
    see quality
trade liberalisation, 25–6, 28–9
trade unions
    attitudes to, 304–7
    closed shop, 126
    and ethnic minorities, 305
    future prospects, 307–11
    and gender, 133–4
    and job dissatisfaction, 295,
        298–300

membership, 294–300, 304–7
    organising model, 308–9
    partnerships, 308–9
    reasons for joining, 291–301
    recognition, 295, 296
    skilled status, 126, 133–4
    strategies, 308–11
training
    and discrimination, 272
    and skill, 113–17
typologies, 16–18

unemployment, 42–4, 60–1, 65–6,
    326–7
    see also redundancy
unitarism, 66
unrecognised work, 317, 318,
    329–37
    measurement problems, 320–1
    see also domestic work and
        voluntary work

valorisation, 148, 151
victimisation see harassment
voluntary work, 66, 318, 333–7

wages
    Fair Wages Resolutions, 29–30
    low pay, 33–4, 52
welfare system, 52, 323
    benefit fraud, 326–7
    see also unemployment
whistle-blowing, 253–4
work
    analysis, 19–22, 373–4
    classifications, 10–12, 16–18
    definitions, 8–10
    perspectives, 19–21
work attitudes
    physical versus mental work, 64–5
    reasons for working, 51
    and unemployment, 60–1, 66–7
    unpaid work, 66–7

see also emotion work;
        hidden work
work blogging, 259
work ethic
    cultural comparisons, 57–9
    demise, 68–72
    diversity, 74
    historical roots, 57–8
work intensification, 105–8, 215–17
    see also time: utilisation
work-life balance, 339–65
    behaviour-based conflict, 343–4
    and cultural values, 351–2
    definitions, 342–4
    and family structure, 350–1
    future of, 362–5
    and labour market
        participation, 345–7
    responses to, 353–62
    and role theory, 360–2
    strain-based conflict, 343–4
    time-based conflict, 343–4
    and work hours, 345,
        347–9, 357–9
    see also downshifting, employment,
        flexibility, and teleworking
work values
    centrality of work, 61–4, 71–2
    conscientiousness, 64–6, 71–2
    disciplined compliance, 66–7
    international comparisons, 54–5,
        56, 61, 68
    obligation to work, 60–1, 71–2
    overwork, 71–2
    and psychological contract, 72–6
    right to work, 61
    see also presenteeism
workaholic, 94–5
workplace culture, 246–7
    and joking, 247–9, 249–50
    and racism, 251, 259–62
    sub-cultures, 85–6, 124–5,
        257–8, 370–1